Houghton Mifflin Harcourt

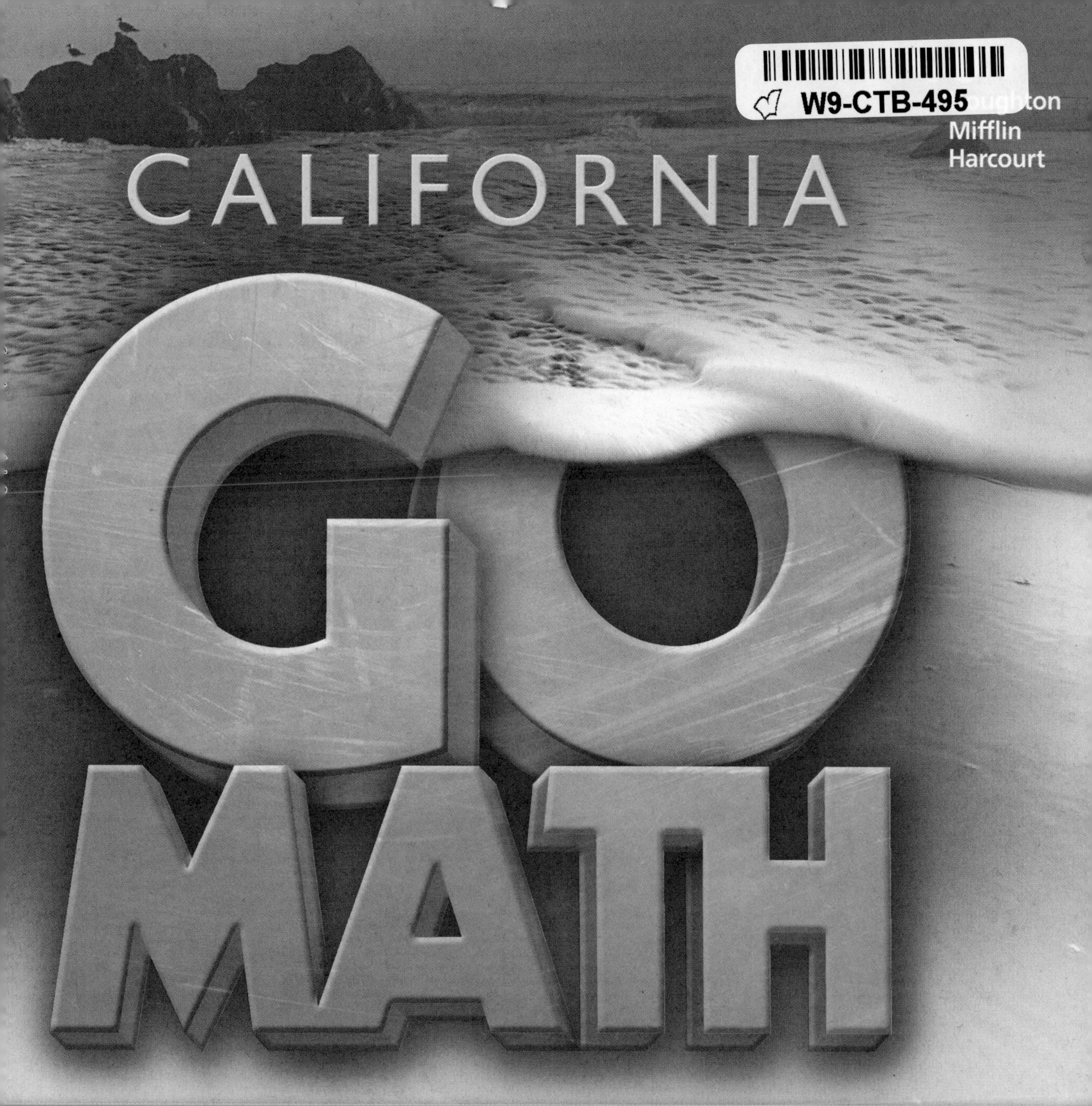

CALIFORNIA GO MATH

Middle School Grade 6

Hunter Zeid P5

Edward B. Burger
Juli K. Dixon
Timothy D. Kanold
Matthew R. Larson
Steven J. Leinwand
Martha E. Sandoval-Martinez

Printed in the U.S.A.

ISBN 978-0-544-20700-4

15 0877 25 24 23 22 21

4500841540 E F G

Authors

Edward B. Burger, Ph.D., is the President of Southwestern University, a former Francis Christopher Oakley Third Century Professor of Mathematics at Williams College, and a former vice provost at Baylor University. He has authored or coauthored more than sixty-five articles, books, and video series; delivered over five hundred addresses and workshops throughout the world; and made more than fifty radio and television appearances. He is a Fellow of the American Mathematical Society as well as having earned many national honors, including the Robert Foster Cherry Award for Great Teaching in 2010. In 2012, Microsoft Education named him a "Global Hero in Education."

Juli K. Dixon, Ph.D., is a Professor of Mathematics Education at the University of Central Florida. She has taught mathematics in urban schools at the elementary, middle, secondary, and post-secondary levels. She is an active researcher and speaker with numerous publications and conference presentations. Key areas of focus are deepening teachers' content knowledge and communicating and justifying mathematical ideas. She is a past chair of the NCTM Student Explorations in Mathematics Editorial Panel and member of the Board of Directors for the Association of Mathematics Teacher Educators.

Timothy D. Kanold, Ph.D., is an award-winning international educator, author, and consultant. He is a former superintendent and director of mathematics and science at Adlai E. Stevenson High School District 125 in Lincolnshire, Illinois. He is a past president of the National Council of Supervisors of Mathematics (NCSM) and the Council for the Presidential Awardees of Mathematics (CPAM). He has served on several writing and leadership commissions for NCTM during the past decade. He presents motivational professional development seminars with a focus on developing professional learning communities (PLC's) to improve the teaching, assessing, and learning of students. He has recently authored nationally recognized articles, books, and textbooks for mathematics education and school leadership, including *What Every Principal Needs to Know about the Teaching and Learning of Mathematics*.

Matthew R. Larson, Ph.D., is the K-12 mathematics curriculum specialist for the Lincoln Public Schools and served on the Board of Directors for the National Council of Teachers of Mathematics from 2010-2013. He is a past chair of NCTM's Research Committee and was a member of NCTM's Task Force on Linking Research and Practice. He is the author of several books on implementing the Common Core Standards for Mathematics. He has taught mathematics at the secondary and college levels and held an appointment as an honorary visiting associate professor at Teachers College, Columbia University.

Steven J. Leinwand is a Principal Research Analyst at the American Institutes for Research (AIR) in Washington, D.C., and has over 30 years in leadership positions in mathematics education. He is past president of the National Council of Supervisors of Mathematics and served on the NCTM Board of Directors. He is the author of numerous articles, books, and textbooks and has made countless presentations with topics including student achievement, reasoning, effective assessment, and successful implementation of standards.

Martha E. Sandoval-Martinez is a mathematics instructor at El Camino College in Torrance, California. She was previously a Math Specialist at the University of California at Davis and former instructor at Santa Ana College, Marymount College, and California State University, Long Beach. In her current and former positions, she has worked extensively to improve fundamental pre-algebra and algebra skills in students who have historically struggled with mathematics.

California Consulting Reviewers

Elizabeth Jiménez, CEO
GEMAS Consulting
Pomona, CA

Erin Bostick Mason, MA.Ed.
Adjunct Faculty
Dept. of Language, Literature and Culture
College of Education, California State University
San Bernardino, CA

Jill Kerper Mora, Ed.D.
Associate Professor Emerita
School of Teacher Education
San Diego State University
San Diego, CA

California Advisory Board

Ashley A. Downing
Eagle Peak Middle School
Ukiah Unified School District
Redwood Valley, CA

Robert Kaplinsky
Teacher Specialist, Mathematics
Downey Unified School District
Downey, CA

Peggy M. Mendez
Charles Wagner Elementary School
Placentia, CA

Melissa Samson
Kraemer Middle School
Placentia, CA

Lori With
BMS Math Teacher
Benicia Middle School
Benicia, CA

UNIT 1 CALIFORNIA

Numbers

MODULE 1 Integers

CA CC

MODULE 2 Factors and Multiples

CA CC

MODULE 3 Rational Numbers

CA CC

UNIT 2

CALIFORNIA

Number Operations

MODULE 4 Operations with Fractions

CA CC

MODULE 5

Operations with Decimals

CA CC

UNIT 3 CALIFORNIA

Proportionality: Ratios and Rates

MODULE 6 Representing Ratios and Rates

CA CC

MODULE 7 Applying Ratios and Rates

CA CC

MODULE 8

Percents

CA CC

UNIT 4 Equivalent Expressions

MODULE 9 Generating Equivalent Numerical Expressions

MODULE 10 Generating Equivalent Algebraic Expressions

UNIT 5

Equations and Inequalities

MODULE 11 Equations and Relationships

MODULE 12 Relationships in Two Variables

UNIT 6 CALIFORNIA

Relationships in Geometry

MODULE 13 Area and Polygons

MODULE 14 Distance and Area in the Coordinate Plane

MODULE 15

Surface Area and Volume of Solids

CA CC

UNIT 7
CALIFORNIA

Measurement and Data

MODULE 16 Displaying, Analyzing, and Summarizing Data

CA CC

California Common Core Standards for Mathematics

Correlations for *HMH California Go Math* Grade 6

Standard	Descriptor	Taught	Reinforced
6.RP RATIOS AND PROPORTIONAL RELATIONSHIPS			
Understand ratio concepts and use ratio reasoning to solve problems.			
6.RP.1	Understand the concept of a ratio and use ratio language to describe a ratio relationship between two quantities.	SE: 149–150, 152	SE: 153–154, 167–168, 197–198
6.RP.2	Understand the concept of a unit rate $\frac{a}{b}$ associated with a ratio *a:b* with $b \neq 0$, and use rate language in the context of a ratio relationship.	SE: 155–156, 158	SE: 159–160, 167–168
6.RP.3	Use ratio and rate reasoning to solve real-world and mathematical problems, e.g., by reasoning about tables of equivalent ratios, tape diagrams, double number line diagrams, or equations.	SE: 151–152, 157–158, 162–164, 173, 176, 179, 182, 185–188, 195–196, 211–214, 217, 220, 222; *See also parts a–d that follow.*	SE: 153–154, 159–160, 165–166, 167–168, 177–178, 183–184, 189–190, 197–198, 199–200, 215–216, 223–224, 225–226; *See also parts a–d that follow.*
6.RP.3a	Make tables of equivalent ratios relating quantities with whole-number measurements, find missing values in the tables, and plot the pairs of values on the coordinate plane. Use tables to compare ratios.	SE: 151, 161, 164, 173–176	SE: 153–154, 165–166, 177–178
6.RP.3b	Solve unit rate problems including those involving unit pricing and constant speed.	SE: 155, 157–158, 175, 180–182, 195–196	SE: 159–160, 167–168, 177–178, 183–184, 197–198
6.RP.3c	Find a percent of a quantity as a rate per 100 (e.g., 30% of a quantity means $\frac{30}{100}$ times the quantity); solve problems involving finding the whole, given a part and the percent.	SE: 205–208, 218, 221–222	SE: 209–210, 223–224, 225–226
6.RP.3d	Use ratio reasoning to convert measurement units; manipulate and transform units appropriately when multiplying or dividing quantities.	SE: 185–188, 193–196	SE: 189–190, 197–198, 199–200

tandard	Descriptor	Taught	Reinforced
.NS THE NUMBER SYSTEM			
pply and extend previous understandings of multiplication and division to divide fractions by fractions.			
.NS.1	Interpret and compute quotients of fractions, and solve word problems involving division of fractions by fractions, e.g., by using visual fraction models and equations to represent the problem.	SE: 85–88, 91–94, 97–98	SE: 89–90, 95–96, 99–100, 101–102
ompute fluently with multi-digit numbers and find common factors and multiples.			
.NS.2	Fluently divide multi-digit numbers using the standard algorithm.	SE: 107–110	SE: 111–112, 135–136
.NS.3	Fluently add, subtract, multiply, and divide multi-digit decimals using the standard algorithm for each operation.	SE: 113–116, 119–122, 125–128, 131–132	SE: 117–118, 123–124, 129–130, 133–134, 135–136
.NS.4	Find the greatest common factor of two whole numbers less than or equal to 100 and the least common multiple of two whole numbers less than or equal to 12. Use the distributive property to express a sum of two whole numbers 1–100 with a common factor as a multiple of a sum of two whole numbers with no common factor.	SE: 31–34, 37–38, 79–82	SE: 35–36, 39–40, 41–42, 83–84, 102
pply and extend previous understandings of numbers to the system of rational numbers.			
.NS.5	Understand that positive and negative numbers are used together to describe quantities having opposite directions or values (e.g., temperature above/below zero, elevation above/below sea level, credits/debits, positive/negative electric charge); use positive and negative numbers to represent quantities in real-world contexts, explaining the meaning of 0 in each situation.	SE: 7	SE: 11–12, 25–26, 65
.NS.6	Understand a rational number as a point on the number line. Extend number line diagrams and coordinate axes familiar from previous grades to represent points on the line and in the plane with negative number coordinates.	SE: 7, 10, 47–50, 53, 56, 334, 336; *See also parts a–c that follow.*	SE: 12, 17, 25–26, 51–52, 58, 65–66, 337–338, 359–360; *See also parts a–c.*
6.NS.6a	Recognize opposite signs of numbers as indicating locations on opposite sides of 0 on the number line; recognize that the opposite of the opposite of a number is the number itself, e.g., $-(-3) = 3$, and that 0 is its own opposite.	SE: 8–10, 54, 56	SE: 11–12, 25–26, 57–58, 66
6.NS.6b	Understand signs of numbers in ordered pairs as indicating locations in quadrants of the coordinate plane; recognize that when two ordered pairs differ only by signs, the locations of the points are related by reflections across one or both axes.	SE: 333, 336, 403–404, 406	SE: 337–338, 359–360, 407–408, 415–416

Standard	Descriptor	Taught	Reinforced
6.NS.6c	Find and position integers and other rational numbers on a horizontal or vertical number line diagram; find and position pairs of integers and other rational numbers on a coordinate plane.	SE: 9–10, 53–54, 56, 333–334, 336	SE: 17, 25–26, 58, 65–66, 337–338, 359–360
6.NS.7	Understand ordering and absolute value of rational numbers.	SE: 13–14, 16, 19, 22, 55–56, 60, 62; *See also parts a–d below.*	SE: 17–18, 23–24, 25–26, 57–58, 63–64, 65–66; *See also parts a–d below.*
6.NS.7a	Interpret statements of inequality as statements about the relative position of two numbers on a number line diagram.	SE: 13, 15–16, 59–62	SE: 17–18, 64
6.NS.7b	Write, interpret, and explain statements of order for rational numbers in real-world contexts.	SE: 15–16, 61–62	SE: 17–18, 26, 63–64, 65–66
6.NS.7c	Understand the absolute value of a rational number as its distance from 0 on the number line; interpret absolute value as magnitude for a positive or negative quantity in a real-world situation.	SE: 19–22, 55–56	SE: 23–24, 25–26, 57–58
6.NS.7d	Distinguish comparisons of absolute value from statements about order.	SE: 21–22	SE: 23–24, 25–26
6.NS.8	Solve real-world and mathematical problems by graphing points in all four quadrants of the coordinate plane. Include use of coordinates and absolute value to find distances between points with the same first coordinate or the same second coordinate.	SE: 335–336, 405–406	SE: 337–338, 407–408, 415–416

Standard	Descriptor	Taught	Reinforced
6.EE EXPRESSIONS AND EQUATIONS			
Apply and extend previous understandings of arithmetic to algebraic expressions.			
6.EE.1	Write and evaluate numerical expressions involving whole-number exponents.	SE: 239–242, 245–248, 251–254	SE: 243–244, 249–250, 255–256, 257–258
6.EE.2	Write, read, and evaluate expressions in which letters stand for numbers.	SE: *See parts a–c below.*	SE: *See parts a–c below.*
6.EE.2a	Write expressions that record operations with numbers and with letters standing for numbers.	SE: 263–265, 267	SE: 268–270, 285–286
6.EE.2b	Identify parts of an expression using mathematical terms (sum, term, product, factor, quotient, coefficient); view one or more parts of an expression as a single entity.	SE: 263, 267, 281–282	SE: 268, 270, 283–284
6.EE.2c	Evaluate expressions at specific values of their variables. Include expressions that arise from formulas used in real-world problems. Perform arithmetic operations, including those involving whole-number exponents, in the conventional order when there are no parentheses to specify a particular order (Order of Operations).	SE: 271–274	SE: 275–276, 285–286
6.EE.3	Apply the properties of operations to generate equivalent expressions.	SE: 278–282	SE: 283–284, 285–286
6.EE.4	Identify when two expressions are equivalent (i.e., when the two expressions name the same number regardless of which value is substituted into them).	SE: 265, 267, 277, 282	SE: 268–269, 283–284, 285–286
Reason about and solve one-variable equations and inequalities.			
6.EE.5	Understand solving an equation or inequality as a process of answering a question: which values from a specified set, if any, make the equation or inequality true? Use substitution to determine whether a given number in a specified set makes an equation or inequality true.	SE: 299, 302, 306–307, 310, 314–315, 318, 321–322, 324	SE: 304, 311, 319–320, 324–326, 345–346
6.EE.6	Use variables to represent numbers and write expressions when solving a real-world or mathematical problem; understand that a variable can represent an unknown number, or, depending on the purpose at hand, any number in a specified set.	SE: 266–267, 300, 302, 305, 308, 310, 313, 318, 323–324	SE: 268–270, 303–304, 311–312, 319–320, 325–326, 345–346

Standard	Descriptor	Taught	Reinforced
6.EE.7	Solve real-world and mathematical problems by writing and solving equations of the form $x + p = q$ and $px = q$ for cases in which p, q and x are all non-negative rational numbers.	SE: 301–302, 305, 308–310, 316–318, 385–386, 388, 433–434	SE: 303–304, 311–312, 319–320, 390, 435–436
6.EE.8	Write an inequality of the form $x > c$ or $x < c$ to represent a constraint or condition in a real-world or mathematical problem. Recognize that inequalities of the form $x > c$ or $x < c$ have infinitely many solutions; represent solutions of such inequalities on number line diagrams.	SE: 321, 323–324	SE: 325–326, 327–328
Represent and analyze quantitative relationships between dependent and independent variables.			
6.EE.9	Use variables to represent two quantities in a real-world problem that change in relationship to one another; write an equation to express one quantity, thought of as the dependent variable, in terms of the other quantity, thought of as the independent variable. Analyze the relationship between the dependent and independent variables using graphs and tables, and relate these to the equation.	SE: 339–344, 347–350, 353–356	SE: 345–346, 351–352, 357–358, 359–360

tandard	Descriptor	Taught	Reinforced
.G GEOMETRY			
olve real-world and mathematical problems involving area, surface area, and volume.			
.G.1	Find the area of right triangles, other triangles, special quadrilaterals, and polygons by composing into rectangles or decomposing into triangles and other shapes; apply these techniques in the context of solving real-world and mathematical problems.	SE: 373–376, 379–382, 385–388, 391–394	SE: 377–378, 383–384, 389–390, 395–396, 397–398
.G.2	Find the volume of a right rectangular prism with fractional edge lengths by packing it with unit cubes of the appropriate unit fraction edge lengths, and show that the volume is the same as would be found by multiplying the edge lengths of the prism. Apply the formulas $V = l\,w\,h$ and $V = b\,h$ to find volumes of right rectangular prisms with fractional edge lengths in the context of solving real-world and mathematical problems.	SE: 427–430, 433–434	SE: 431–432, 435–436, 437–438
.G.3	Draw polygons in the coordinate plane given coordinates for the vertices; use coordinates to find the length of a side joining points with the same first coordinate or the same second coordinate. Apply these techniques in the context of solving real-world and mathematical problems.	SE: 409–412	SE: 413–414, 415–416
6.G.4	Represent three-dimensional figures using nets made up of rectangles and triangles, and use the nets to find the surface area of these figures. Apply these techniques in the context of solving real-world and mathematical problems.	SE: 421–424	SE: 425–426, 437–438

Standard	Descriptor	Taught	Reinforced
6.SP STATISTICS AND PROBABILITY			
Develop understanding of statistical variability.			
6.SP.1	Recognize a statistical question as one that anticipates variability in the data related to the question and accounts for it in the answers.	SE: 471, 475	SE: 476–477
6.SP.2	Understand that a set of data collected to answer a statistical question has a distribution which can be described by its center, spread, and overall shape.	SE: 473, 475	SE: 475–478
6.SP.3	Recognize that a measure of center for a numerical data set summarizes all of its values with a single number, while a measure of variation describes how its values vary with a single number.	SE: 451, 454	SE: 455–456
Summarize and describe distributions.			
6.SP.4	Display numerical data in plots on a number line, including dot plots, histograms, and box plots.	SE: 465, 468, 472, 475, 479–480, 482	SE: 469–470, 476–478, 483–484, 485
6.SP.5a	Summarize numerical data sets in relation to their context, such as by: Reporting the number of observations.	SE: 449, 452, 477–480	SE: 453–454, 481–482
6.SP.5b	Summarize numerical data sets in relation to their context, such as by: Describing the nature of the attribute under investigation, including how it was measured and its units of measurement.	SE: 452, 454, 479, 481–482	SE: 455–456, 483–484
6.SP.5c	Summarize numerical data sets in relation to their context, such as by: Giving quantitative measures of center (median and/or mean) and variability (interquartile range and/or mean absolute deviation), as well as describing any overall pattern and any striking deviations from the overall pattern with reference to the context in which the data were gathered.	SE: 451–454, 457–461, 466–468, 474–475, 479, 481–482	SE: 455–456, 462–464, 469–470, 476–478, 483–484, 485–486
6.SP.5d	Summarize numerical data sets in relation to their context, such as by: Relating the choice of measures of center and variability to the shape of the data distribution and the context in which the data were gathered.	SE: 453, 474–475, 479, 481–482	SE: 455–456, 477–478, 483–484

Standard	Descriptor	Citations
MP MATHEMATICAL PRACTICES STANDARDS		*The mathematical practices standards are integrated throughout the book. See, for example, the citations below.*
MP.1	**Make sense of problems and persevere in solving them.**	**36, 97–98, 190, 270, 304, 378, 456**
MP.2	**Reason abstractly and quantitatively.**	**64, 90, 195, 256, 322, 384, 464**
MP.3	**Construct viable arguments and critique the reasoning of others.**	**24, 112, 210, 250, 320, 408, 470**
MP.4	**Model with mathematics.**	**17, 100, 217–218, 251, 326, 387, 470**
MP.5	**Use appropriate tools strategically.**	**8, 91,185, 278, 305, 373, 460**
MP.6	**Attend to precision.**	**13, 93, 216, 244, 338, 426, 454**
MP.7	**Look for and make use of structure.**	**18, 118, 216, 265–266, 313, 432, 473**
MP.8	**Look for and express regularity in repeated reasoning.**	**19, 125, 239, 244, 312, 380, 464**

Succeeding with HMH California Go Math

Actively participate in your learning with your write-in Student Edition. Explore concepts, take notes, answer questions, and complete your homework right in your textbook!

LESSON 7.3 **Converting Within Measurement Systems**

CA CC 6.RP.3d Use ratio reasoning to convert measurement units; manipulate and transform units appropriately when multiplying or dividing quantities.

ESSENTIAL QUESTION How do you convert units within a measurement system?

EXPLORE ACTIVITY Real World CA CC 6.RP.3d

Using a Model to Convert Units

The two most common systems of measurement are the cust... the metric system. You can use a model to convert from one ... within the same measurement system.

STEP 1 Use the model to complete each statement below.

1 yard = 3 feet

2 yards = _______ feet

3 yards = _______ feet

4 yards = _______ feet

STEP 2 Rewrite your answers in Step 1 as ratios.

$\frac{\square \text{ feet}}{2 \text{ yards}} = \frac{\square \text{ feet}}{1 \text{ yard}}$ $\frac{\square \text{ feet}}{3 \text{ yards}} = \frac{\square \text{ feet}}{1 \text{ yard}}$ $\frac{\square \text{ feet}}{4 \text{ yards}} = \frac{\square \text{ feet}}{1 \text{ yard}}$

The ratio of feet to yards in any measurement is $\frac{3}{1}$. So, any ratio forming a proportion with $\frac{3}{1}$ can represent a ratio of feet to yards.

$\frac{3}{1} = \frac{12}{4}$, so 12 feet = _______ yards.

$\frac{3}{1} = \frac{54}{18}$, so _______ feet = 18 yards.

Reflect

1. Communicate Mathematical Ideas How could you draw a model to show the relationship between feet and inches?

Lesson 7.3 185

EXPLORE ACTIVITY Real World

Explore Activities help you develop a deeper understanding of math concepts.

ESSENTIAL QUESTION

Essential Questions ensure that you know exactly what you are learning.

Representing Rates with Tables and Graphs

You can use tables and graphs to represent real-world problems involving equivalent rates.

Math On the Spot my.hrw.com

EXAMPLE 1 Real World CA CC 6.RP.3a, 6.RP.3b

An express train travels from Webster to Washington, D.C., at a constant speed and makes the trip in 2 hours.

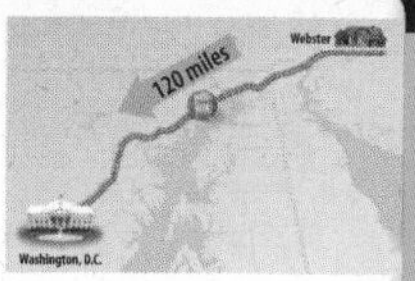

Animated Math my.hrw.com

A Make a table to show the distance the train travels in various amounts of time.

STEP 1 Write a ratio of distance to time to find the rate.

$\frac{\text{distance}}{\text{time}} = \frac{120 \text{ miles}}{2 \text{ hours}} = \frac{60 \text{ miles}}{1 \text{ hour}} = 60$ miles per hour

STEP 2 Use the unit rate to make a table.

Time (h)	1	2	3	4	5
Distance (mi)	60	120	180	240	300

B Graph the information from the table.

Write ordered pairs with time as the x-coordinate and distance as the y-coordinate.

(1, 60), (2, 120), (3, 180), (4, 240), (5, 300)

Graph the ordered pairs. Fractions and decimals can represent times and distances, so connect the points.

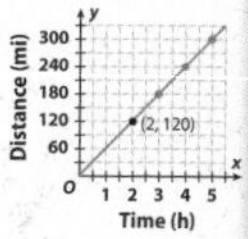

C Use the graph to find how long the train takes to travel 90 miles.

The point (1.5, 90) is on the graph, so the train takes 1.5 hours.

YOUR TURN

3. A shower uses 12 gallons of water in 3 minutes. Complete the table and the graph. Suppose the shower used 32 gallons of water. How long did it take?

Time (min)	2	3	4		6
Water used (gal)				20	

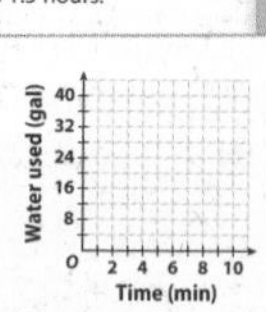

Personal Math Trainer Online Practice and Help my.hrw.com

Lesson 7.1 175

YOUR TURN

Your Turn exercises check your understanding of new concepts.

Math On the Spot

my.hrw.com

Scan QR codes with your smart phone to watch Math On the Spot tutorial videos for every example in the book!

Unit Project

Apply new skills and concepts to solve real-world problems in Unit Projects and Math in Careers Activities.

Unit Project CA CC 6.NS.4

Euclid's Method

The Greek mathematician Euclid lived more than 2,000 years ago. He created a method for finding the greatest common factor of two numbers. Euclid's method for finding the GCF of 156 and 60 is shown below. No description of the steps is given, but the colors of the numbers should help you understand the method.

MATH IN CAREERS ACTIVITY

Climatologist Each year a tree is alive, it adds called a tree ring, between its core and its bark. the measurements taken by a climatologist of th rings of a particular tree for different years. List of increasing ring width. Which year was the ho know? Which year was the coldest? How do you

70 Unit 1

Reading Start-Up

Get vocabulary, language, and note-taking support throughout the book.

Reading Start-Up

Visualize Vocabulary

Use the ✓ words to complete the web. You may put more than one word in each box.

−15, −45, −60 | 25, 71, 102 | Integers | −20 and 20 | 9

Vocabulary

Review Words
- absolute value (valor absoluto)
- decimal (decimal)
- dividend (dividendo)
- divisor (divisor)
- fraction (fracción)
- integers (enteros)
- ✓ negative numbers (números negativos)

Understand Vocabulary

Fill in each blank with the correct term from the preview words.

1. A ______________ is any number that can be written as a ratio of two integers.
2. A ______________ is used to show the relationships between groups.

Active Reading

Tri-Fold Before beginning the module, create a tri-fold to help you learn the concepts and

Module 3 45

Assessment Readiness

Prepare for new high-stakes tests with SBAC aligned practice items and Performance Tasks.

UNIT 7 MIXED REVIEW
Assessment Readiness

Personal Math Trainer — Online Practice and Help — my.hrw.com

1. Consider the dot plot. The dot plot shows the number of participants in each age group in a science fair.

11 12 13 14 15 16 17

Select Yes or No.

A. The range of the data is 6. ○ Yes ○ No
B. The mode of the ages is 13. ○ Yes ○ No
C. The median age is 15. ○ Yes ○ No

2. Choose True or False for each statement.

A. The prime factorization of 120 is $2 \times 3 \times 5$. ○ True ○ False
B. The greatest common factor of 36 and 84 is 12. ○ True ○ False
C. The least common multiple of 36 and 84 is 3,024. ○ True ○ False

3. Sarita records the distance in miles she runs each day for 5 days:

5 4 5.5 4.5 5.5.

What is the mean distance Sarita ran? Explain your answer.

4. The data set shows the ages of the workers at Mr. Ito's office.

26	30	45	43	26
14	28	33	56	29

What is the mean absolute deviation? Describe how you found it.

Performance Tasks

★★6. Kinesha collected data about the heights of stud

a. What measures of center and variation are mos
b. Which of the data displays that you learned about in this unit could Kinesha use to display the data?
c. Which data display could be used to show the measures of center and variation you named in part **a**?

★★★7. The number of goals for the 13 players on a soccer team are

4, 9, 0, 1, 1, 2, 0, 0, 2, 8, 8, 3, 1.

a. Find the median, lower quartile, and upper quartile.
b. Find the range and the interquartile range of the data.
c. Identify any outliers.
d. Find the mean and mode of the data. Which of the median, mean, and mode is the best to use when describing the data? Explain your reasoning.

GO DIGITAL
my.hrw.com

Enhance Your Learning!

The eStudent Edition provides additional multimedia resources to enhance your learning. You can write in answers, take notes, watch videos, explore concepts with virtual manipulatives, and get homework help!

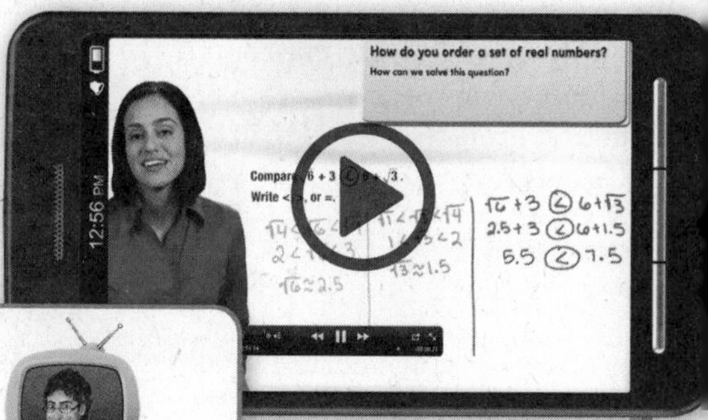

Math On the Spot

my.hrw.com

Math On the Spot video tutorials provide step-by-step instruction of the math concepts covered in each example.

my.hrw.com

Real-World Videos show you how specific math topics can be used in all kinds of situations.

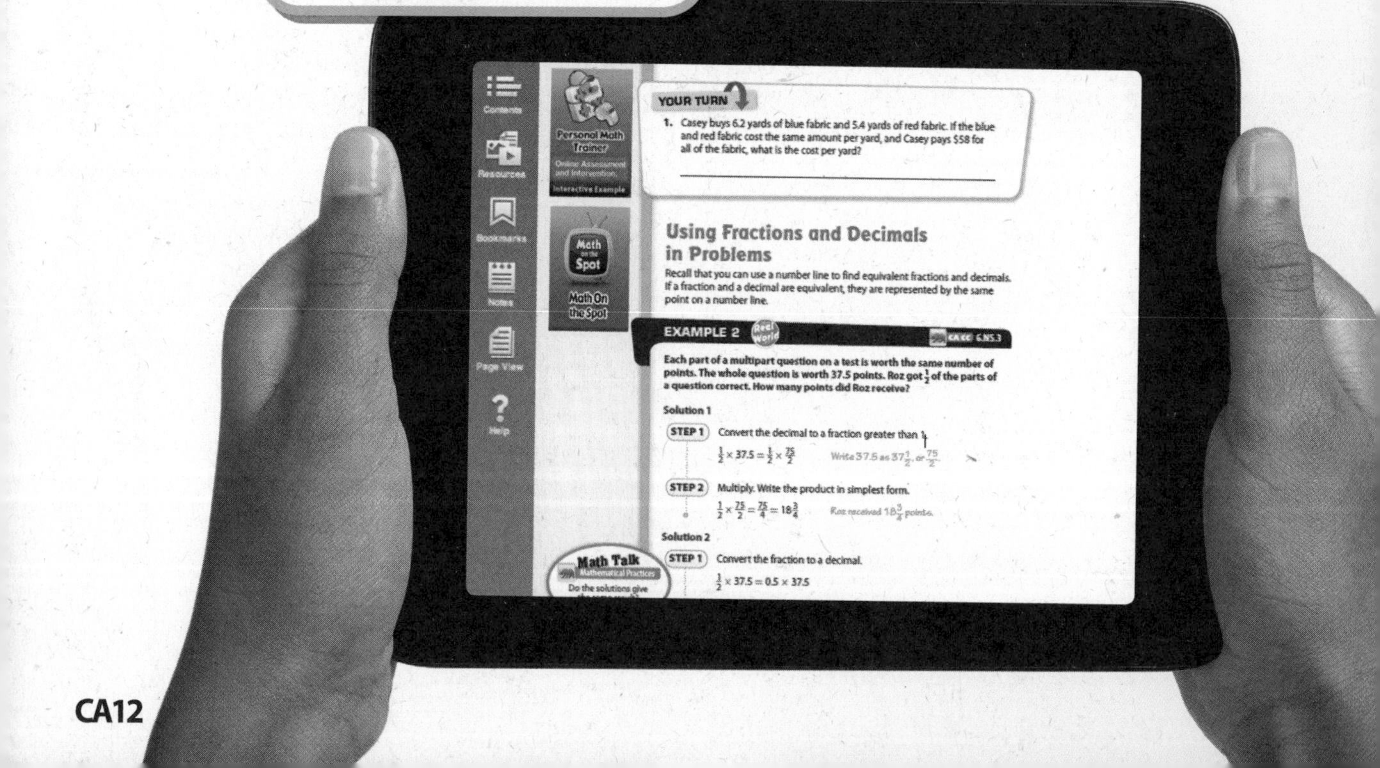

Personal Math Trainer lets you practice, take quizzes and tests, and get homework help with instant feedback!

Personal Math Trainer provides a variety of learning aids that develop and improve your understanding of math concepts, including videos, guided examples, and step-by-step solutions.

Personal Math Trainer

Online Practice and Help

my.hrw.com

Animated Math

my.hrw.com

Animated Math activities and virtual manipulatives let you interactively explore and practice key math concepts and skills.

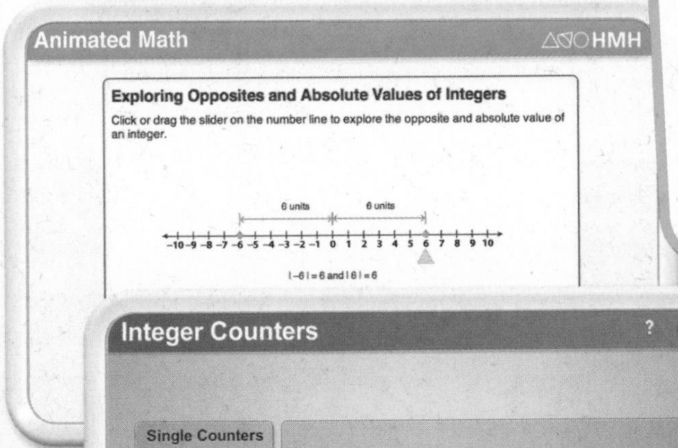

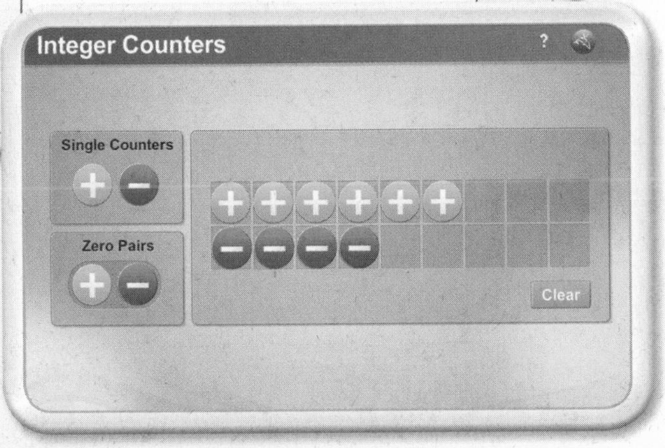

Standards for Mathematical Practice

CALIFORNIA

The topics described in the Standards for Mathematical Content will vary from year to year. However, the *way* in which you learn, study, and think about mathematics will not. The Standards for Mathematical Practice describe skills that you will use in all of your math courses. These pages show some features of your book that will help you gain these skills and use them to master this year's topics.

MP.1 Make sense of problems and persevere in solving them.

Mathematically proficient students start by explaining to themselves the meaning of a problem… They analyze givens, constraints, relationships, and goals. They make conjectures about the form… of the solution and plan a solution pathway…

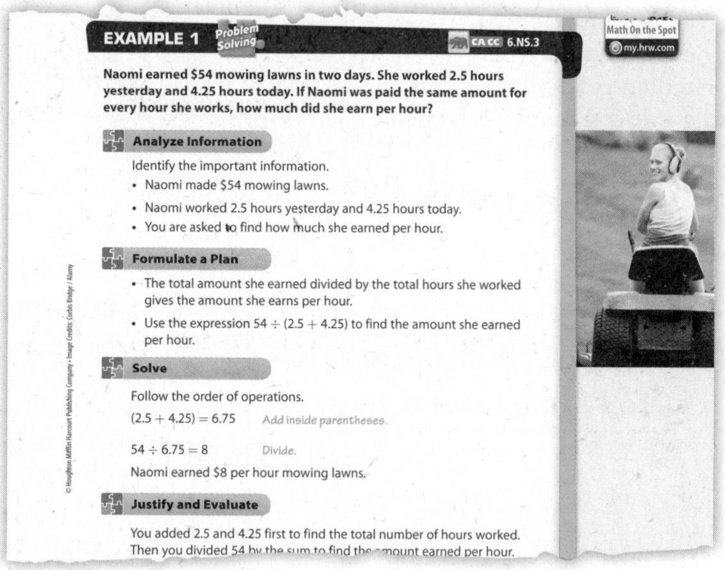

EXAMPLE 1 Problem Solving CA CC 6.NS.3

Math On the Spot my.hrw.com

Naomi earned $54 mowing lawns in two days. She worked 2.5 hours yesterday and 4.25 hours today. If Naomi was paid the same amount for every hour she works, how much did she earn per hour?

Analyze Information

Identify the important information.

- Naomi made $54 mowing lawns.
- Naomi worked 2.5 hours yesterday and 4.25 hours today.
- You are asked to find how much she earned per hour.

Formulate a Plan

- The total amount she earned divided by the total hours she worked gives the amount she earns per hour.
- Use the expression $54 \div (2.5 + 4.25)$ to find the amount she earned per hour.

Solve

Follow the order of operations.

$(2.5 + 4.25) = 6.75$ Add inside parentheses.

$54 \div 6.75 = 8$ Divide.

Naomi earned $8 per hour mowing lawns.

Justify and Evaluate

You added 2.5 and 4.25 first to find the total number of hours worked. Then you divided 54 by the sum to find the amount earned per hour.

Problem-solving examples and exercises lead students through problem solving steps.

MP.2 Reason abstractly and quantitatively.

Mathematically proficient students… bring two complementary abilities to bear on problems…: the ability to decontextualize—to abstract a given situation and represent it symbolically… and the ability to contextualize, to pause… in order to probe into the referents for the symbols involved.

Focus on Higher Order Thinking exercises in every lesson and a **Project** in every unit require you to use logical reasoning, represent situations symbolically, use mathematical models to solve problems, and state your answers in terms of a problem context.

MP.3 Construct viable arguments and critique the reasoning of others.

Mathematically proficient students… justify their conclusions, [and]… distinguish correct… reasoning from that which is flawed.

Reflect

1. **Critique Reasoning** Jo says she can find the percent equivaler multiplying the percent equivalent of $\frac{1}{4}$ by 3. How can you use bar model to support this claim?

ESSENTIAL QUESTION CHECK-IN

Essential Question Check-in and **Reflect** in every lesson ask you to evaluate statements, explain relationships, apply mathematical principles, make conjectures, construct arguments, and justify your reasoning.

MP.4 Model with mathematics.

Mathematically proficient students can apply… mathematics… to… problems… in everyday life, society, and the workplace.

EXAMPLE 2 Real World

EXAMPLE 2 Real World CA CC 6.RP.3, 6.RP.3a

My Notes

You make 5 cups of punch by mixing 3 cups of cranberry juice with 2 cups of apple juice. How much cranberry juice and how much apple juice do you need to make four times the original recipe?

Method 1 Use a table.

STEP 1 Make a table comparing the numbers of cups of cranberry juice and apple juice needed to make two times, three times, four times, and five times the original recipe.

Multiply both terms of the original ratio by the same number to find an equivalent ratio.

		3 × 2	3 × 3	3 × 4
Cranberry Juice	3	6	9	12
Apple Juice	2	4	6	8

Real-world examples and **mathematical modeling** apply mathematics to other disciplines and real-world contexts such as science and business.

MP.5 Use appropriate tools strategically.

Mathematically proficient students consider the available tools when solving a… problem… [and] are… able to use technological tools to explore and deepen their understanding…

EXPLORE ACTIVITY Real World CA CC 6.NS.1

Modeling Mixed Number Division

Antoine is making sushi rolls. He has $2\frac{1}{2}$ cups of rice and will use $\frac{1}{4}$ cup of rice for each sushi roll. How many sushi rolls can he make?

A To find the number of sushi rolls that can be made, you need to determine how many fourths are in $2\frac{1}{2}$. Use fraction pieces to represent $2\frac{1}{2}$ on the model below.

1				1				$\frac{1}{2}$	
$\frac{1}{4}$	$\frac{1}{4}$	$\frac{1}{4}$	$\frac{1}{4}$	$\frac{1}{4}$	$\frac{1}{4}$	$\frac{1}{4}$	$\frac{1}{4}$	$\frac{1}{4}$	$\frac{1}{4}$

B How many fourths are in $2\frac{1}{2}$? ______________

Antoine has enough rice to make ______________ sushi rolls.

Reflect

1. Communicate Mathematical Ideas Which mathematical operation

Exploration Activities in lessons use concrete and technological tools, such as manipulatives or graphing calculators, to explore mathematical concepts.

MP.6 Attend to precision.

Mathematically proficient students… communicate precisely… with others and in their own reasoning… [They] give carefully formulated explanations…

31. Communicate Mathematical Ideas Write an example of an that cannot be simplified, and explain how you know that it simplified.

Key Vocabulary

rate *(tasa)*
A ratio that compares two quantities measured in different units.

Precision refers not only to the correctness of calculations but also to the proper use of mathematical language and symbols. **Communicate Mathematical Ideas** exercises and **Key Vocabulary** highlighted for each module and unit help you learn and use the language of math to communicate mathematics precisely.

MP.7 Look for and make use of structure.

Mathematically proficient students… look closely to discern a pattern or structure… They can also step back for an overview and shift perspectives.

Bacteria reproduce by dividing, a process that can be observed in a microscope. Some scientists observe the hourly growth of bacteria and record their observations in a table.

Time (h)	Total bacteria
0	1
1	2
2	$2 \times 2 =$ □
3	$2 \times 2 \times 2 =$ □
4	$2 \times 2 \times 2 \times 2 =$ □

After 2 hours, there are $2 \times 2 = ?$ bacteria.

A Complete the table. What pattern(s) do you see in the Total bacteria column?

____

Throughout the lessons, you will observe regularity in mathematical structures in order to make generalizations and make connections between related problems. For example, you can use what you known about multiplication to understand how to use exponents.

MP.8 Look for and express regularity in repeated reasoning.

Mathematically proficient students… look both for general methods and for shortcuts… [and] maintain oversight of the process, while attending to the details.

46. Look for a Pattern Find the values of the powers in the follo pattern: $10^1, 10^2, 10^3, 10^4$…. Describe the pattern, and use it 10^6 without using multiplication.

25. Justify Reasoning Determine whether $3x + 12 + x$ is $4(3 + x)$. Use properties of operations to justify your an

Reflect

8. Make a Conjecture Use the pattern in the table to make a c about how you can use multiplication to divide one fraction

You will look for repeated calculations and mathematical patterns in examples and exercises. Recognizing patterns can help you make generalizations and obtain a better understanding of the underlying mathematics.

CALIFORNIA

GRADE 5 PART 1

Review Test

Personal Math Trainer

Online Practice and Help

my.hrw.com

1. Al used the expression $8 + 25 \times 2 - 45$ to find how many CDs he has. How many CDs does he have?

____

2. Jamie baked 24 biscuits. Her sister Mia ate 3 biscuits, and her brother David ate 2 biscuits. Which expression can Jamie use to find how many biscuits are left? Select Yes or No.

A. $24 + (3 + 2)$

○ Yes ○ No

B. $24 - (3 + 2)$

○ Yes ○ No

C. $(24 - 3) + 2$

○ Yes ○ No

D. $24 - 3 - 2$

○ Yes ○ No

3. What is the unknown number in sequence 2 in the chart?

Sequence Number	1	2	3	5	7
Sequence 1	3	6	9	15	21
Sequence 2	15	30	45	75	?

____

4. Patel hopes to be one of the first fans to get into the stadium for the baseball game because the first 30,000 fans will receive a baseball cap. Write 30,000 as a whole number multiplied by a power of ten.

____

5. The Davis family pays $200,000 for a new house. They make a down payment that is $\frac{1}{10}$ of the price of the house. How much is the down payment?

____

6. Jackie found a rock that has a mass of 78.852 grams. What is the mass of the rock rounded to the nearest tenth?

____

7. A company manufactures 295 toy cars each day. How many toy cars does the company manufacture in 34 days?

____

8. There are 6 buses transporting students to a baseball game, with 32 students on each bus. Each row at the baseball stadium seats 8 students. If the students fill up all of the rows, how many rows of seats will the students need altogether?

____

9. The portions of a house that need to be heated can be modeled by one rectangular prism with a length of 45 feet, a width of 20 feet, and a height of 18 feet, and a second rectangular prism with a base area of 350 square feet and a height of 9 feet. What is the total volume?

____

10. Marci mailed 9 letters at the post office. Each letter weighed 3.5 ounces. What was the total weight of the letters?

____

11. Denise, Keith, and Tim live in the same neighborhood. Denise lives 0.3 mile from Keith. The distance that Tim and Keith live from each other is 0.2 times as great as the distance between Denise and Keith. How far from each other do Tim and Keith live?

____

12. Madison needs to buy enough meat to make 1,000 hamburgers for the company picnic. Each hamburger will weigh 0.25 pound. How many pounds of hamburger meat should Madison buy?

____

13. Rayna wrote 260,980 as $(2 \times 100{,}000) + (6 \times 10{,}000) + (9 \times 1{,}000) + (8 \times 100)$. What error did Rayna make? Write the correct expanded form.

____

____

____

____

____

____

14. The highest scores at a gymnastics meet were 9.675, 9.25, 9.325, and 9.5. Write the scores in order from least to greatest.

____

15. Ann and Joe's father donated $3 for every lap they swam in a swim-a-thon. Ann swam 21 laps, and Joe swam 15 laps. Use the Distributive Property to find the amount of money their father donated.

____

____

____

____

16. A grain of sand has a diameter of 0.049 millimeter. Write 0.049 in words.

____

Performance Task

17. Jennifer has $12 to spend on lunch and the roller rink. Admission to the roller rink is $5.75. Jennifer estimates that she can buy a large drink and a turkey sandwich and still have enough money to get into the rink. Do you agree? Support your answer.

Sandwiches	Drinks
Tuna $3.95	Small $1.29
Turkey $4.85	Medium $1.59
Grilled Cheese $3.25	Large $1.79

____

____

____

____

____

____

CALIFORNIA

GRADE 5 PART 2

Review Test

Personal Math Trainer

my.hrw.com

Online Practice and Help

1. Charles bought $\frac{7}{8}$ foot of electrical wire and $\frac{5}{6}$ foot of copper wire for his science project. What is the least common denominator of the fractions?

____

2. Tom jogged $\frac{3}{5}$ mile on Monday and $\frac{2}{6}$ mile on Tuesday. How much farther did Tom jog on Monday than on Tuesday?

____

3. Three fences on a ranch measure $\frac{15}{16}$ mile, $\frac{7}{8}$ mile, and $\frac{7}{16}$ mile. Give an estimate of the total length of all three fences? Explain your answer.

____

____

4. Lawrence bought $\frac{2}{3}$ pound of roast beef. He used $\frac{3}{4}$ of it to make a sandwich. How much roast beef did Lawrence use for his sandwich? You may use a model to help you solve the problem.

____

5. Sarah built a table using 6 pieces of wood that were each $3\frac{3}{4}$ inches wide. How wide was the table?

____

6. Vanessa made 6 sandwiches for a party and cut them all into fourths. How many $\frac{1}{4}$-sandwich pieces did she have?

____

7. Dr. Watson combines 400 mL of detergent, 800 mL of alcohol, and 1,500 mL of water. How many liters of solution does he have?

____

8. Give the most descriptive name for the figure.

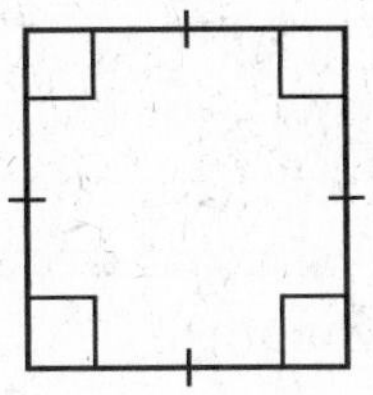

____

9. Find the volume of the rectangular prism.

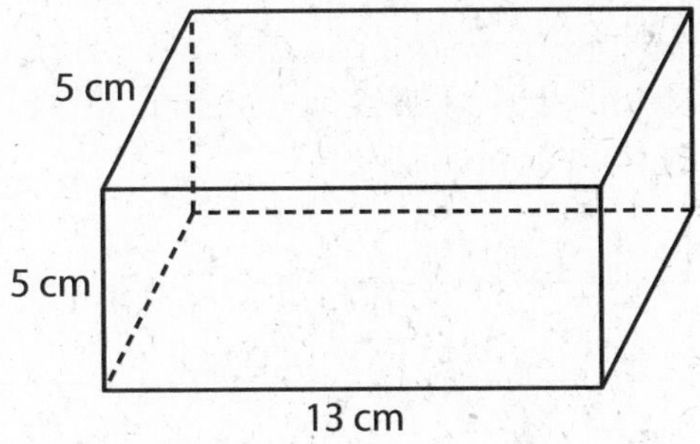

____

10. What ordered pair describes the location of Point A?

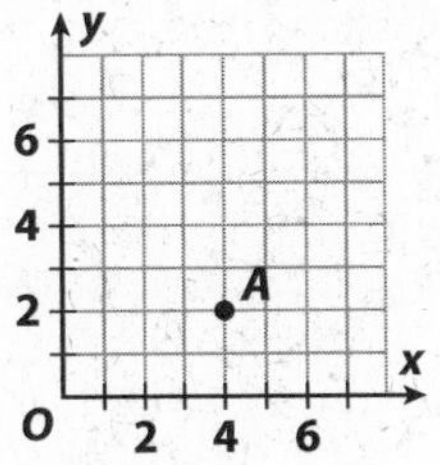

____

11. What ordered pair describes the location of Point A?

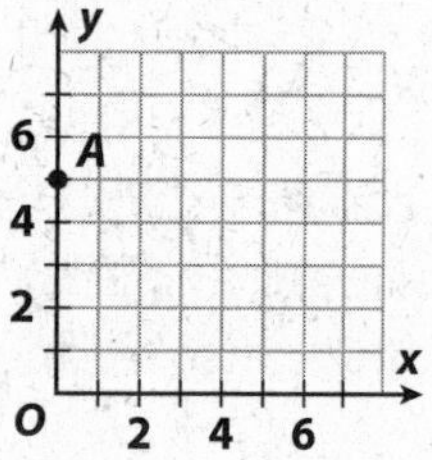

12. When Bruce started bowling, he won $\frac{1}{4}$ of the games he played. Within six months, he was winning $\frac{7}{16}$ of his games. If he improves at the same rate, what fraction of his games should he expect to win after another six months?

13. Gina wants to ship 3 books that weigh $2\frac{7}{16}$ pounds, $1\frac{7}{8}$ pounds and $\frac{1}{2}$ pound. The maximum weight she can ship is 6 pounds. Estimate to see if Gina can ship all 3 books. Explain your answer.

14. How much trail mix will each person get if 5 people share $\frac{1}{2}$ pound of trail mix?

15. Write a story to represent the division problem $6 \div \frac{1}{3}$.

16. What is the volume in cubic centimeters of the solid?

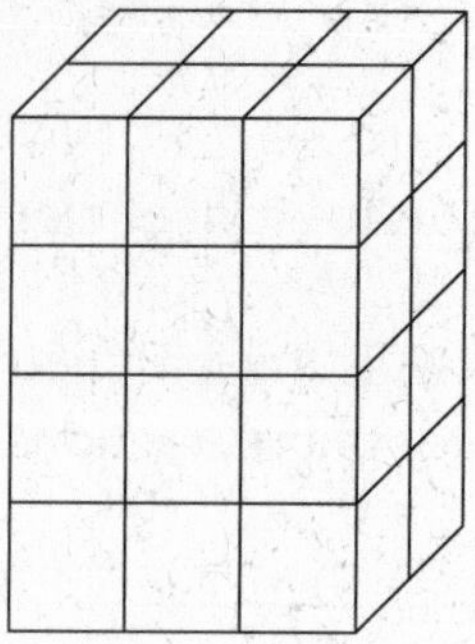

Performance Task

17. Shia measured the thickness of some buttons. She graphed the results in a line plot.

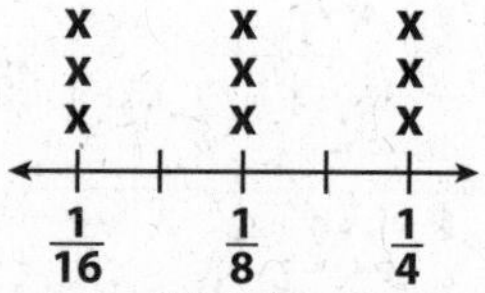

Button thicknesses (in.)

Part A: Suppose Shia makes a stack of all the buttons. How tall will the stack be?

Part B: Suppose Shia wants the stack to be 2 inches high. How many buttons that are $\frac{1}{16}$ inch thick must be added to the stack of buttons?

CALIFORNIA

GRADE 6 PART 1

Benchmark Test

Personal Math Trainer
Online Practice and Help
my.hrw.com

1. Suppose you have developed a scale that indicates the brightness of sunlight. Each category in the table is 9 times brighter than the category above it. For example, a day that is dazzling is 9 times brighter than a day that is radiant. How many times brighter is a dazzling day than an illuminated day?

Sunlight Intensity	
Category	**Brightness**
Dim	2
Illuminated	3
Radiant	4
Dazzling	5

____

2. Which group of numbers is in order from least to greatest? Select Yes or No.

A. 2.58, $2\frac{5}{8}$, 2.6, $2\frac{2}{3}$ ○ Yes ○ No

B. $2\frac{2}{3}$, $2\frac{5}{8}$, 2.68, 2.78 ○ Yes ○ No

C. $2\frac{5}{8}$, $2\frac{2}{3}$, 2.68, 2.78 ○ Yes ○ No

D. 2.58, 2.6, $2\frac{5}{8}$, $2\frac{2}{3}$ ○ Yes ○ No

3. Which temperature is coldest: −13 °F, 20 °F, −20 °F, or 13 °F?

____

4. Patricia paid $385 for 5 nights at a hotel. Find the unit rate.

____

5. The fuel for a chain saw is a mix of oil and gasoline. The label says to mix 6 ounces of oil with 16 gallons of gasoline. How much oil would you use if you had 32 gallons of gasoline?

____

6. Lee is putting together fruit baskets for gifts. He has 18 apples, 24 pears, and 30 oranges. What is the greatest number of fruit baskets he can make if he uses all the fruit and each basket is the same?

____

7. It takes light about 134 milliseconds to travel the distance around Earth's Equator. How many seconds is this?

____

8. From the beginning of cross-country season to the end, Tisha reduced her time by 17%, Anchara reduced hers by $\frac{1}{6}$, Juanita reduced hers by $\frac{4}{25}$, and Julia reduced hers from 16:00 to 13:30. Who reduced her time by the greatest percent?

____

9. A stack of blocks is 15.2 inches tall. If there are 10 blocks stacked one on top of the other, how tall is each block?

____

10. The ratio of students in Jaíme's class who have a dog or cat at home to those who don't is 12 : 8. What percent of the class do NOT have a dog or cat at home?

____

11. Ninety percent of a school's students, or 540 students, attended a school assembly. How many students are there at the school?

____

12. Find the quotient $9\frac{3}{5} \div \frac{8}{15}$.

____

13. Find the product 4.51×3.4.

____

14. Jorge is building a table out of boards that are 3.75 inches wide. He wants the table to be at least 36 inches wide. What is the least number of boards he can use?

____

15. Nikita is making spaghetti sauce and pizzas for a large party. Her spaghetti sauce recipe calls for $1\frac{3}{4}$ cups of tomato paste, and her pizza recipe uses $\frac{2}{3}$ cup of tomato paste per pizza. She will triple her spaghetti sauce recipe and make 6 pizzas. Write and evaluate an expression for how many $\frac{3}{4}$ cup cans of tomato paste she will need in all.

____

____

16. Explain how you can use multiplication to find the quotient $\frac{3}{4} \div \frac{3}{16}$. Then evaluate the expression.

____

____

17. A chef has 6 cups of berries and will use $\frac{2}{3}$ cup of berries for each serving of fruit salad. How many servings can be made?

____

Performance Task

18. School A has 480 students and 16 classrooms. School B has 192 students and 12 classrooms.

Part A: What is the ratio of students to classrooms at School A?

Part B: What is the ratio of students to classrooms at School B?

Part C: How many students would have to transfer from School A to School B for the ratios of students to classrooms at both schools to be the same? Explain your reasoning.

____

____

____

____

____

____

____

____

____

____

____

GRADE 6 PART 2

Benchmark Test

1. Kahlil is recording a beat for a song that he is working on. He wants the length of the beat to be more than 10 seconds long. His friend tells him the beat needs to be 5 seconds longer than that to match the lyrics he has written.

Write an inequality to represent the beat's length. Give three possible beat lengths that satisfy the inequality.

____

2. Write an expression for the missing value in the table.

Tom's Age	Kim's Age
10	13
11	14
12	15
a	?

____

3. What is the area of the polygon?

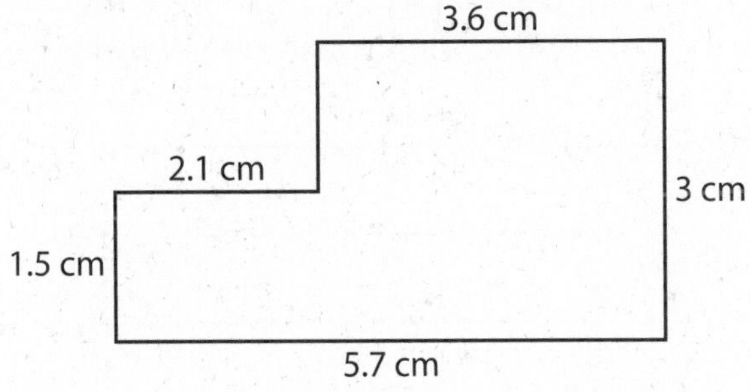

____

4. A plant's height is 1.4 times its age. Write an equation for this situation, where *h* is the plant's height and *y* is the plant's age.

____

5. A rectangular box is $8\frac{1}{2}$ inches long, $5\frac{1}{4}$ inches wide, and 4 inches high. What is its volume?

____

6. Write the phrase as an algebraic expression.

4 times the sum of a number and 20

____

7. Wilson bought gift cards for some lawyers and their assistants. Each lawyer got a gift card worth ℓ dollars. Each assistant got a gift card worth *a* dollars. There are 14 lawyers. Each lawyer has 3 assistants. The expression for the total cost of the gift cards is $14\ell + 42a$. Use the Distributive Property to write an expression that is equivalent to the given expression.

____

8. At the beginning of the year, Jason had \$120 in his savings account. Each month, he added \$15 to his account. Write an expression for the amount of money in Jason's savings account each month. Then use the expression to find the amount of money in his account at the end of the year.

Month	January	February	March	*m*
Amount	\$135	\$150	\$165	\$?

____

9. Which question is a statistical question? Select Yes or No.

A. What are the ages of schools in the school district?

○ Yes ○ No

B. How old is the middle school building?

○ Yes ○ No

C. How many classrooms are there in the elementary school building?

○ Yes ○ No

D. How many daily class periods are there in U.S. high schools?

○ Yes ○ No

10. Find the interquartile range for the data set: 10, 3, 8, 6, 9, 12, 13.

____

11. Mike was in charge of collecting contributions for the Food Bank. He received contributions of \$80, \$70, \$60, \$40, and \$80. Find the mean and the median of the contributions.

____

12. One side of trapezoid is 10 inches. The side parallel to this is twice as long as this side. The height is half as long as the given side length. Find the area of the trapezoid.

____

13. Find the perimeter of the rectangle with vertices at $R(-2, 3)$, $S(4, 3)$, $T(4, -1)$ and $U(-2, -1)$.

____

14. Brian is ordering tickets online for a concert. The price of each ticket for the concert is t dollars. For online orders, there is an additional charge of \$11 per ticket, and a service charge of \$14 for the entire order. The cost for 7 tickets can be represented by the expression $7(t + 11) + 14$.

Write two expressions equivalent to the cost expression. Then, find the total cost of Brian's online order if the price of each ticket for this concert is \$33.

____

Performance Task

15. Jillian wants to find the surface area of a pyramid. The base is a square with with sides that are 4 inches long. The other faces are isosceles triangles. The ratio of the height of each triangle to its base is 3 : 2.

Part A: Give the base length and the height of each triangular face.
Part B: Find the combined area of the triangular faces.
Part C: Find the surface area of the pyramid.

____

____

____

____

____

UNIT 1

Numbers

MODULE 1

Integers

CA CC 6.NS.5, 6.NS.6, 6.NS.6a, 6.NS.6c, 6.NS.7, 6.NS.7a, 6.NS.7b, 6.NS.7c, 6.NS.7d

MODULE 2

Factors and Multiples

CA CC 6.NS.4

MODULE 3

Rational Numbers

CA CC 6.NS.6, 6.NS.6a, 6.NS.6c, 6.NS.7, 6.NS.7a, 6.NS.7b, 6.NS.7c

ATH IN CAREERS

Climatologist A climatologist is a scientist who studies long-term trends in climate conditions. These scientists collect, evaluate, and interpret data and use mathematical models to study the dynamics of weather patterns and to understand and predict Earth's climate.

If you are interested in a career in climatology, you should study these mathematical subjects:

- Algebra
- Trigonometry
- Probability and Statistics
- Calculus

Research other careers that require the analysis of data and use of mathematical models.

ACTIVITY At the end of the unit, check out how **climatologists** use math.

Unit Project Preview

Euclid's Method

To complete the Unit Project at the end of this unit, you will determine a method for finding the greatest common factor of two numbers by studying an example of the method in use. You will describe and demonstrate the method and research the mathematician who invented the method. To successfully complete the Unit Project you'll need to master these skills:

- Find the greatest common factor of two numbers.
- Divide whole numbers.

1. What is a factor of a whole number?

____

____

2. 1, 2, 4, 5, 10, and 20 are all factors of both 40 and 60. What is the greatest number that is a factor of both 40 and 60? Explain your reasoning.

____

____

Tracking Your Learning Progression

This unit addresses important California Common Core Standards in the Critical Areas of finding common factors and multiples and understanding rational numbers.

Domain 6.NS The Number System

Cluster Compute fluently with multi-digit numbers and find common factors and multiples.

The unit also supports additional standards.

Domain 6.NS The Number System

Cluster Apply and extend previous understandings of numbers to the system of rational numbers.

Integers

MODULE 1

CALIFORNIA

ESSENTIAL QUESTION

How can you use integers to solve real-world problems?

Real-World Video

my.hrw.com

Integers can be used to describe the value of many things in the real world. The height of a mountain in feet may be a very great integer while the temperature in degrees Celsius at the top of that mountain may be a negative integer.

GO DIGITAL
my.hrw.com

my.hrw.com
Go digital with your write-in student edition, accessible on any device.

Math On the Spot
Scan with your smart phone to jump directly to the online edition, video tutor, and more.

Animated Math
Interactively explore key concepts to see how math works.

Personal Math Trainer
Get immediate feedback and help as you work through practice sets.

Are YOU Ready?

Complete these exercises to review skills you will need for this module.

Personal Math Trainer
my.hrw.com
Online Practice and Help

Compare Whole Numbers

EXAMPLE

3,564 ● 3,528	Compare digits in the thousands place: $3 = 3$
3,564 ● 3,528	Compare digits in the hundreds place: $5 = 5$
3,564 (>) 3,528	Compare digits in the tens place: $6 > 2$

Compare. Write $<$, $>$, or $=$.

1. 471 ◯ 468 **2.** 5,005 ◯ 5,050 **3.** 398 ◯ 389

4. 10,973 ◯ 10,999 **5.** 8,471 ◯ 9,001 **6.** 108 ◯ 95

Order Whole Numbers

EXAMPLE

356, 348, 59, 416	Compare digits. Find the greatest number.
356, 348, 59, 416	Find the next greatest number.
356, 348, 59, 416	Find the next greatest number.
356, 348, 59, 416	Find the least number.
$416 > 356 > 348 > 59$	Order the numbers.

Order the numbers from greatest to least.

7. 156; 87; 177; 99

____

8. 591; 589; 603; 600

____

9. 2,650; 2,605; 3,056; 2,088

____

10. 1,037; 995; 10,415; 1,029

____

Locate Numbers on a Number Line

EXAMPLE

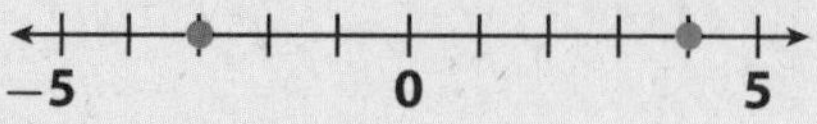

Graph +4 by starting at 0 and counting 4 units to the right.
Graph –3 by starting at 0 and counting 3 units to the left.

Graph each number on the number line.

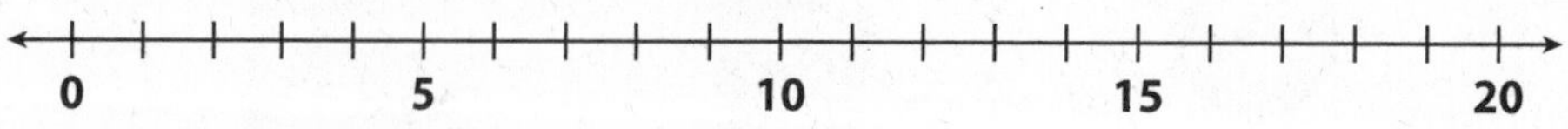

11. 12 **12.** 20 **13.** 2 **14.** 9

Reading Start-Up

Visualize Vocabulary

Use the ✔ words to complete the chart. Write the correct vocabulary word next to the symbol.

Symbol	
$<$	
$>$	
$=$	
$+$	
$-$	

Vocabulary

Review Words

✔ equal *(igual)*
✔ greater than *(más que)*
✔ less than *(menos que)*
✔ negative sign *(signo negativo)*
number line *(recta numérica)*
✔ plus sign *(signo más)*
symbol *(símbolo)*
whole number *(número entero)*

Preview Words

absolute value *(valor absoluto)*
inequality *(desigualdad)*
integers *(enteros)*
negative numbers *(números negativos)*
opposites *(opuestos)*
positive numbers *(números positivos)*

Understand Vocabulary

Complete the sentences using the preview words.

1. An ______________ is a statement that two quantities are not equal.

2. The set of all whole numbers and their opposites are ______________.

3. Numbers greater than 0 are ______________________. Numbers less than 0 are ______________________.

Active Reading

Key-Term Fold Before beginning the module, create a key-term fold to help you learn the vocabulary in this module. Write the highlighted vocabulary words on one side of the flap. Write the definition for each word on the other side of the flap. Use the key-term fold to quiz yourself on the definitions in this module.

GETTING READY FOR

Integers

Understanding the standards and the vocabulary terms in the standards will help you know exactly what you are expected to learn in this module.

CA CC 6.NS.6a

Recognize opposite signs of numbers as indicating locations on opposite sides of 0 on the number line; recognize that the opposite of the opposite of a number is the number itself, e.g., $-(-3) = 3$, and that 0 is its own opposite.

Key Vocabulary

integers *(enteros)*
The set of all whole numbers and their opposites.

opposites *(opuestos)*
Two numbers that are equal distance from zero on a number line.

What It Means to You

You will learn that opposites are the same distance from 0 on a number line but in different directions.

EXAMPLE 6.NS.6A

Use the number line to determine the opposites.

$-(5) = -5$ *The opposite of 5 is −5.*

$-(-5) = 5$ *The opposite of −5 is 5.*

$-(0) = 0$ *The opposite of 0 is 0.*

CA CC 6.NS.7

Understand ordering and absolute value of rational numbers.

Key Vocabulary

absolute value *(valor absoluto)*
A number's distance from 0 on the number line.

rational number *(número racional)*
Any number that can be expressed as a ratio of two integers.

Visit **my.hrw.com** to see all **CA Common Core Standards** explained.

my.hrw.com

What It Means to You

You can use a number line to order rational numbers.

EXAMPLE 6.NS.7

At a golf tournament, David scored +6, Celia scored −16, and Xavier scored −4. One of these three players was the winner of the tournament. Who won the tournament?

The winner will be the player with the lowest score. Draw a number line and graph each player's score.

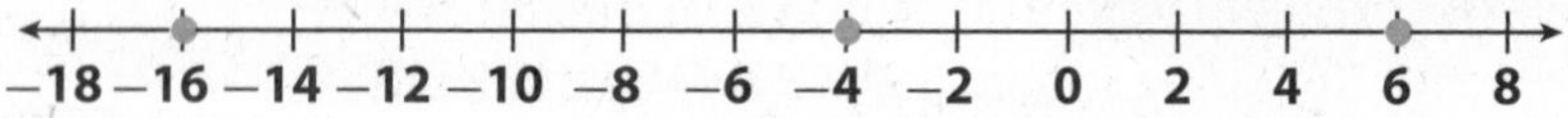

Celia's score, −16, is the farthest to the left, so it is the lowest score. Celia won the tournament.

LESSON **1.1**

Identifying Integers and Their Opposites

CA CC 6.NS.5

Understand that positive and negative numbers are used together to describe quantities having opposite directions or values; use positive and negative numbers to represent quantities in real-world contexts, explaining the meaning of 0 in each situation. *Also 6.NS.6, 6.NS.6a, 6.NS.6c*

ESSENTIAL QUESTION

How do you identify an integer and its opposite?

EXPLORE ACTIVITY 1 Real World

CA CC 6.NS.5, 6.NS.6

Positive and Negative Numbers

Positive numbers are numbers greater than 0. Positive numbers can be written with or without a plus sign; for example, 3 is the same as +3. **Negative numbers** are numbers less than 0. Negative numbers must always be written with a negative sign.

The number 0 is neither positive nor negative.

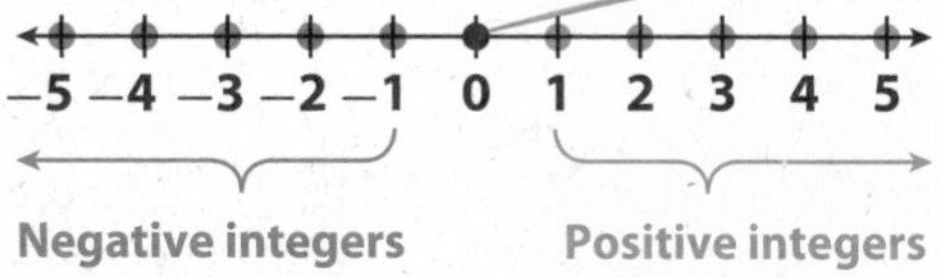

The elevation of a location describes its height above or below sea level, which has elevation 0. Elevations below sea level are represented by negative numbers, and elevations above sea level are represented by positive numbers.

A The table shows the elevations of several locations in a state park. Graph the locations on the number line according to their elevations.

Location	Little Butte *A*	Cradle Creek *B*	Dinosaur Valley *C*	Mesa Ridge *D*	Juniper Trail *E*
Elevation (ft)	5	–5	–9	8	–3

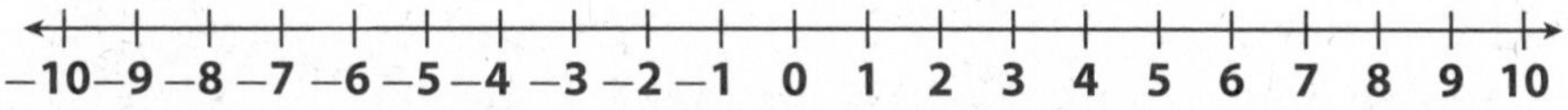

B What point on the number line represents sea level? ________________

C Which location is closest to sea level? How do you know?

____

D Which two locations are the same distance from sea level? Are these locations above or below sea level?

____

E Which location has the lowest elevation? How do you know?

____

EXPLORE ACTIVITY 1 *(cont'd)*

Reflect

1. **Analyze Relationships** Morning Glory Stream is 7 feet below sea level. What number represents the elevation of Morning Glory Stream?

____

2. **Multiple Representations** Explain how to graph the elevation of Morning Glory Stream on a number line.

____

EXPLORE ACTIVITY 2

CA CC 6.NS.6a

Opposites

Two numbers are **opposites** if, on a number line, they are the same distance from 0 but on different sides of 0. For example, 5 and −5 are opposites. 0 is its own opposite.

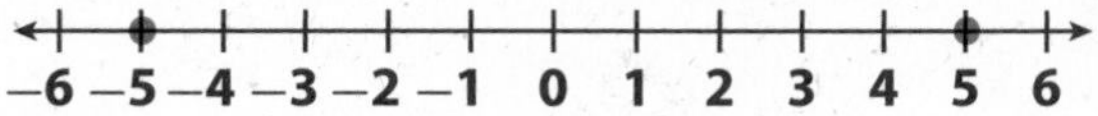

Integers are the set of all whole numbers and their opposites.

Remember, the set of whole numbers is 0, 1, 2, 3, 4, 5, 6, ...

On graph paper, use a ruler or straightedge to draw a number line. Label the number line with each integer from −10 to 10. Fold your number line in half so that the crease goes through 0. Numbers that line up after folding the number line are opposites.

A Use your number line to find the opposites of 7, −6, 1, and 9. _______________

B How does your number line show that 0 is its own opposite?

____

C What is the opposite of the opposite of 3? _______________

Reflect

3. **Justify Reasoning** Explain how your number line shows that 8 and −8 are opposites.

____

4. **Multiple Representations** Explain how to use your number line to find the opposite of the opposite of −6.

____

____

____

Integers and Opposites on a Number Line

Positive and negative numbers can be used to represent real-world quantities. For example, 3 can represent a temperature that is 3 °F above 0. −3 can represent a temperature that is 3 °F below 0. Both 3 and −3 are 3 units from 0.

Math On the Spot
my.hrw.com

EXAMPLE 1 Real World

CA CC 6.NS.6a, 6.NS.6c

Sandy kept track of the weekly low temperature in her town for several weeks. The table shows the low temperature in °F for each week.

Week	Week 1	Week 2	Week 3	Week 4
Temperature (°F)	−1	3	−4	2

A Graph the temperature from Week 3 and its opposite on a number line. What do the numbers represent?

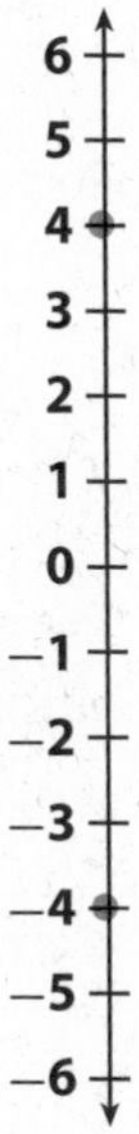

STEP 1 Graph the value from Week 3 on the number line.

The value from Week 3 is −4.
Graph a point 4 units below 0.

STEP 2 Graph the opposite of −4.

Graph a point 4 units above 0.

The opposite of −4 is 4.

−4 represents a temperature that is 4 °F below 0 and 4 represents a temperature that is 4 °F above 0.

B The value for Week 5 is the opposite of the opposite of the value from Week 1. What was the low temperature in Week 5?

STEP 1 Graph the value from Week 1 on the number line.

The value from Week 1 is −1.

STEP 2 Graph the opposite of −1.

The opposite of −1 is 1.

STEP 3 Graph the opposite of 1.

The opposite of 1 is −1.

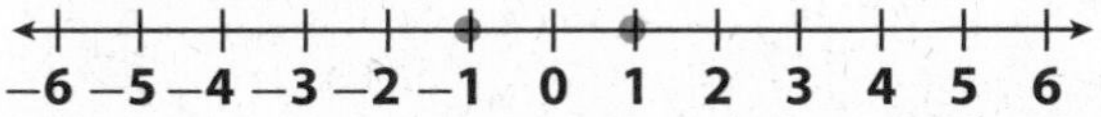

The opposite of the opposite of −1 is −1.
The low temperature in Week 5 was −1 °F.

Reflect

5. **Analyze Relationships** Explain how you can find the opposite of the opposite of any number without using a number line.

My Notes

Personal Math Trainer

Online Practice and Help

my.hrw.com

YOUR TURN

Graph the opposite of the number shown on each number line.

6. 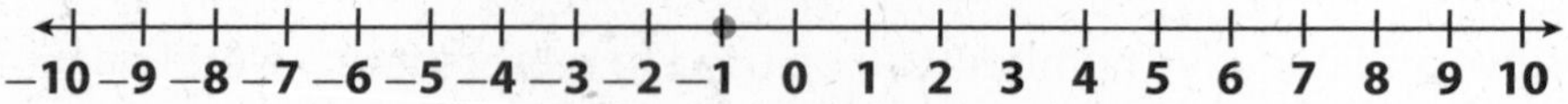

7. 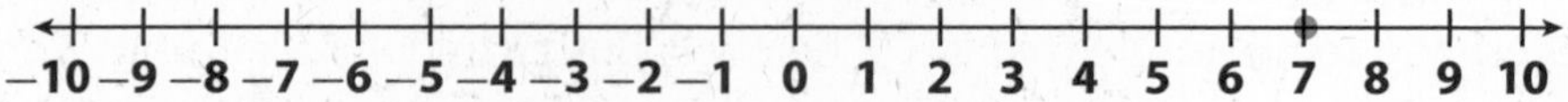

Write the opposite of each number.

8. 10 ____________ **9.** –5 ____________ **10.** 0 ____________

11. What is the opposite of the opposite of 4? ____________

Math Talk
Mathematical Practices

Explain how you could use a number line to find the opposite of –8.

Guided Practice

1. Graph and label the following points on the number line. (Explore Activity 1)

a. –2 **b.** 9 **c.** –8 **d.** –9 **e.** 5 **f.** 8

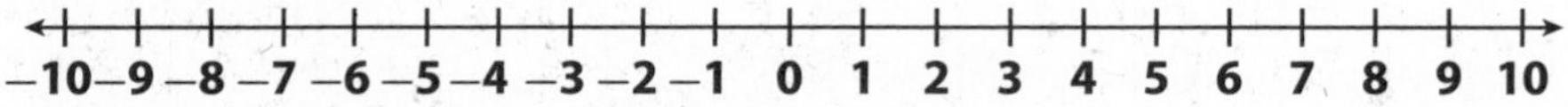

Graph the opposite of the number shown on each number line.
(Explore Activity 2 and Example 1)

2. 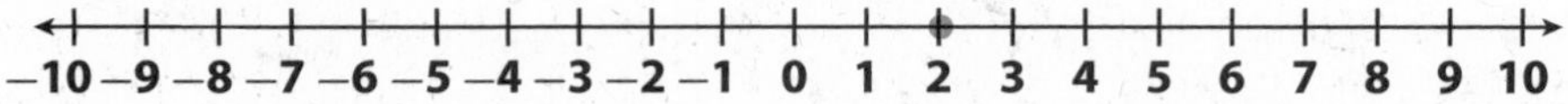

3. 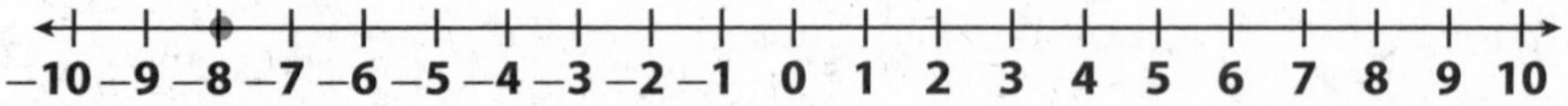

4. 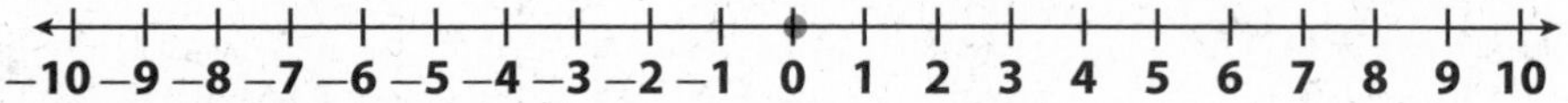

Write the opposite of each number. (Explore Activity 2 and Example 1)

5. 4 ____________ **6.** –11 ____________ **7.** 3 ____________

8. –3 ____________ **9.** 0 ____________ **10.** 22 ____________

ESSENTIAL QUESTION CHECK-IN

11. The amount of money in Geraldo's savings account went from $450 to $420. Explain how to use a negative integer to describe the change.

____

____

Name ______________ Class ______________ Date ______________

1.1 Independent Practice

CA CC 6.NS.5, 6.NS.6, 6.NS.6a, 6.NS.6c

Personal Math Trainer
Online Practice and Help
my.hrw.com

12. **Chemistry** Atoms normally have an electric charge of 0. Certain conditions, such as static, can cause atoms to have a positive or a negative charge. Atoms with a positive or negative charge are called *ions*.

Ion	A	B	C	D	E
Charge	−3	+1	−2	+3	−1

a. Which ions have a negative charge? ______________

b. Which ions have charges that are opposites? ______________

c. Which ion's charge is not the opposite of another ion's charge? ______________

Name the integer that meets the given description.

13. the opposite of −17 ______________

14. 4 units left of 0 ______________

15. the opposite of the opposite of 2 ______________

16. 15 units right of 0 ______________

17. 12 units right of 0 ______________

18. the opposite of −19 ______________

19. **Analyze Relationships** A trainer studying dog diets weighs each dog weekly. Changes in weights from last week are shown in the chart.

Dog	Lady	Coco	Zeus	Bandit	Sparky	Rocky
Weight Change (in pounds)	−2	6	2	5	0	−5

a. Did Coco lose or gain weight since last week? ______________

b. Which dog's weight change is the opposite of Zeus's? ______________

c. Which dogs have lost weight since last week? ______________

d. Which dog's weight remained the same? How do you know?

____

e. A dog named Lucky had a weight change that was the opposite of Coco's.

What was Lucky's weight change? ______________

f. The trainer's goal was to have Lucky gain weight. Was the goal met? Explain.

____

Find the distance between the given number and its opposite on a number line.

20. 6 ________________

21. −2 ________________

22. 0 ________________

23. −7 ________________

24. **What If?** Three contestants are competing on a trivia game show. The table shows their scores before the final question.

Contestant	Score Befc Final Quest
Timothy	−25
Shawna	18
Kaylynn	−14

a. How many points must Shawna earn for her score to be the opposite of Timothy's score before the final question? ________________

b. Which person's score is closest to 0? ________________

c. Who do you think is winning the game before the final question? Explain.

____

H.O.T. FOCUS ON HIGHER ORDER THINKING

Work Area

25. **Communicate Mathematical Ideas** Which number is farther from 0 on a number line: −9 or 6? Explain your reasoning.

____

____

26. **Analyze Relationships** A number is *k* units to the left of 0 on the number line. Describe the location of its opposite.

____

____

27. **Critique Reasoning** Roberto says that the opposite of a certain integer is −5. Cindy concludes that the opposite of an integer is always negative. Explain Cindy's error.

____

____

____

28. **Multiple Representations** Explain how to use a number line to find the opposites of the integers 3 units away from −7.

____

____

____

LESSON
1.2 Comparing and Ordering Integers

CA CC **6.NS.7b**

Write, interpret, and explain statements of order for rational numbers in real-world contexts. *Also 6.NS.7, 6.NS.7a*

ESSENTIAL QUESTION

How do you compare and order integers?

EXPLORE ACTIVITY Real World CA CC **6.NS.7, 6.NS.7a**

Comparing Positive and Negative Integers

The Westfield soccer league ranks its teams using a number called the "win/loss combined record." A team with more wins than losses will have a positive combined record, and a team with fewer wins than losses will have a negative combined record. The table shows the total win/loss combined record for each team at the end of the season.

Team	Sharks *A*	Jaguars *B*	Badgers *C*	Tigers *D*	Cougars *E*	Hawks *F*	Wolves *G*
Win/Loss Combined Record	0	4	−4	−6	2	−2	6

A Graph the win/loss combined record for each team on the number line.

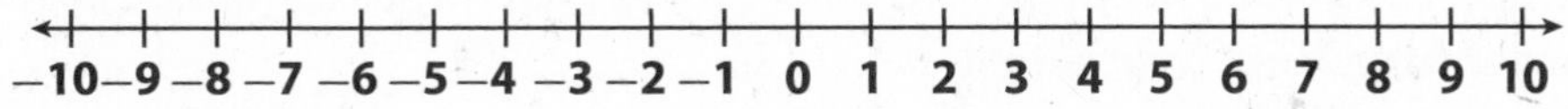

B Which team had the best record in the league? How do you know?

____

C Which team had the worst record? How do you know?

____

Reflect

1. **Analyze Relationships** Explain what the data tell you about the win/loss records of the teams in the league.

____

____

____

____

Math On the Spot
my.hrw.com

Ordering Positive and Negative Integers

When you read a horizontal number line from left to right, the numbers are in order from least to greatest.

EXAMPLE 1 Real World

CA CC 6.NS.7

Fred recorded the following golf scores during his first week at a golf academy. Negative numbers represent scores below *par*, a standard score. In golf, a lower score beats a higher score.

Day	Mon	Tues	Wed	Thurs	Fri	Sat	Sun
Score	4	−2	3	−5	−1	0	−3

Graph Fred's scores on the number line, and then list the numbers in order from least to greatest.

STEP 1 Graph the scores on the number line.

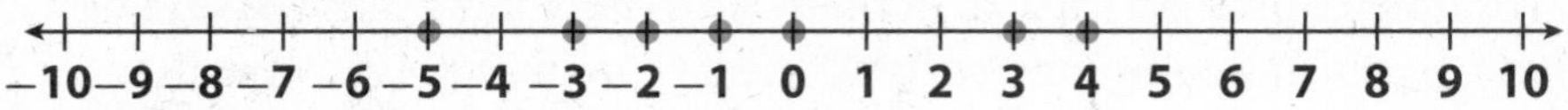

STEP 2 Read from left to right to list the scores in order from least to greatest.

The scores listed from least to greatest are −5, −3, −2, −1, 0, 3, 4.

Math Talk
Mathematical Practices

What day did Fred have his best golf score? How do you know?

YOUR TURN

Graph the values in each table on a number line. Then list the numbers in order from least to greatest.

2.

Change in Stock Price ($)					
−5	4	0	−3	−6	2

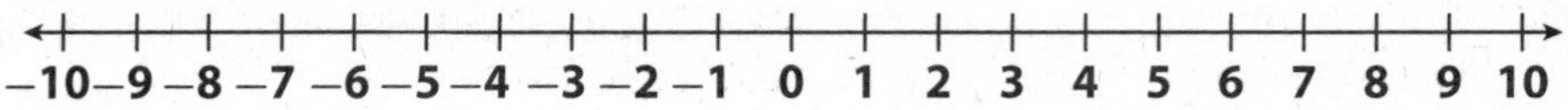

____

3.

Elevation (meters)							
9	−1	−6	2	−10	0	5	8

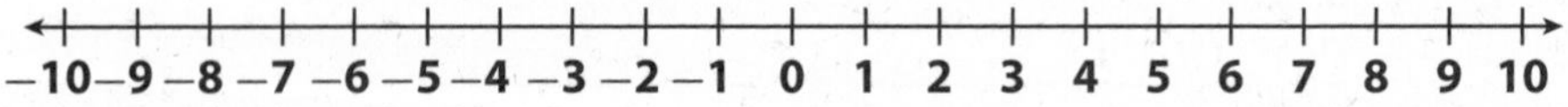

____

Personal Math Trainer
Online Practice and Help
my.hrw.com

Writing Inequalities

An **inequality** is a statement that two quantities are not equal. The symbols < and > are used to write inequalities.

- The symbol > means "is greater than."
- The symbol < means "is less than."

You can use a number line to help write an inequality.

Math On the Spot
my.hrw.com

EXAMPLE 2 Real World

CA CC 6.NS.7a, 6.NS.7b

A In 2010, Sacramento, California, received 23 inches in annual precipitation. In 2011, the city received 17 inches in annual precipitation. In which year was there more precipitation?

Graph 23 and 17 on the number line.

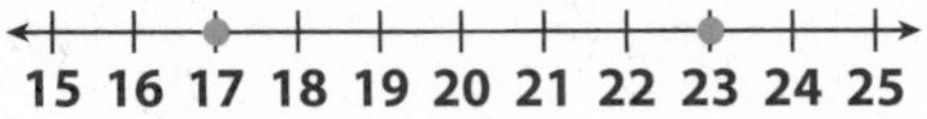

- 23 is to the *right* of 17 on the number line.

  This means that 23 is **greater than** 17.

  Write the inequality as 23 > 17.

- 17 is to the *left* of 23 on the number line.

  This means that 17 is **less than** 23.

  Write the inequality as 17 < 23.

  There was more precipitation in 2010.

B Write two inequalities to compare −6 and 7.
−6 < 7; 7 > −6

C Write two inequalities to compare −9 and −4.
−4 > −9; −9 < −4

Math Talk
Mathematical Practices

Is there a greatest integer? Is there a greatest negative integer? Explain.

YOUR TURN

Compare. Write > or <. Use the number line to help you.

4. −10 ○ −2 **5.** −6 ○ 6 **6.** −7 ○ −8

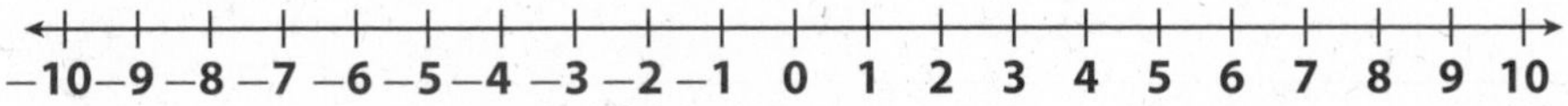

7. Write two inequalities to compare −2 and −18. ______________

8. Write two inequalities to compare 39 and −39. ______________

Personal Math Trainer
Online Practice and Help
my.hrw.com

Guided Practice

1a. Graph the temperature for each city on the number line. (Explore Activity)

City	A	B	C	D	E
Temperature (°F)	−9	10	−2	0	4

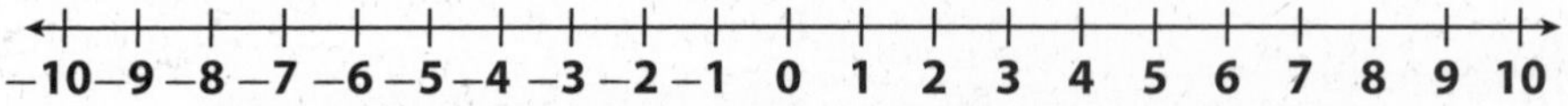

b. Which city was coldest? Which city was warmest? ______________

List the numbers in order from least to greatest. (Example 1)

2. 4, −6, 0, 8, −9, 1, −3

____

3. −65, 34, 7, −13, 55, 62, −7

____

4. Write two inequalities to compare −17 and −22. ______________________________

Compare. Write $<$ or $>$. (Example 2)

5. −9 ◯ 2

6. −1 ◯ −3

7. −8 ◯ −4

8. −2 ◯ −6

9. Compare the temperatures for the following cities. Write $<$ or $>$. (Example 2)

City	Alexandria	Redwood Falls	Grand Marais	Winona	International Falls
Average Temperature in March (°C)	−3	0	−2	2	−4

a. Alexandria and Winona ______________________________

b. Redwood Falls and International Falls ______________________________

ESSENTIAL QUESTION CHECK-IN

10. Give a real-world example of how integers are used. Explain what 0, negative integers, and positive integers mean in the situation. Describe how you might compare two such integers.

____

____

____

____

Name ______ Class ______ Date ______

1.2 Independent Practice

CA CC 6.NS.7, 6.NS.7a, 6.NS.7b

Personal Math Trainer
my.hrw.com
Online Practice and Help

11. **Multiple Representations** A hockey league tracks the plus-minus records for each player. A plus-minus record is the difference in even strength goals for and against the team when a player is on the ice. The following table lists the plus-minus values for several hockey players.

Player	A. Jones	B. Sutter	E. Simpson	L. Mays	R. Tomas	S. Klatt
Plus-minus	−8	4	9	−3	−4	3

a. Graph the values on the number line.

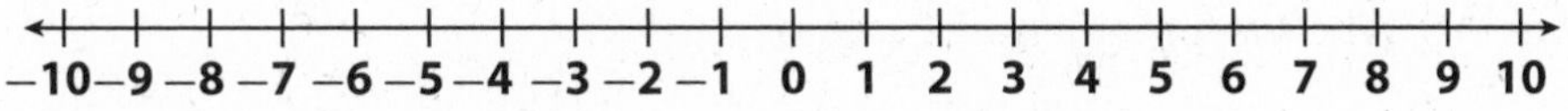

b. Which player has the best plus-minus record? ______

Astronomy **The table lists the average surface temperature of some planets. Write an inequality to compare the temperatures of each pair of planets.**

Planet	**Average Surface Temperature (°C)**
Mercury	167
Uranus	−197
Neptune	−200
Earth	15
Mars	−65
Jupiter	−110

12. Uranus and Jupiter ______

13. Mercury and Mars ______

14. Arrange the planets in order of average surface temperature from greatest to least. ______

______

15. **Represent Real-World Problems** For a stock market project, five students each pretended to invest money in a different stock. They tracked gains and losses in the value of their stock for one week. In the following table, a gain is represented by a positive number and a loss is represented by a negative number.

Students	Andre	Bria	Carla	Daniel	Ethan
Gains and Losses ($)	7	−2	−5	2	4

Graph the students' results on the number line. Then list them in order from least to greatest.

a. Graph the values on the number line.

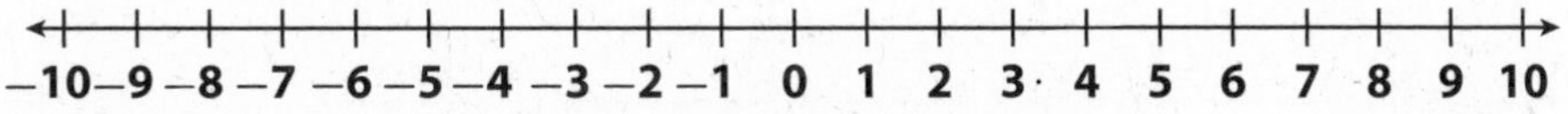

b. The results listed from least to greatest are ______.

Geography **The table lists the lowest elevation for several countries. A negative number means the elevation is below sea level, and a positive number means the elevation is above sea level. Compare the lowest elevation for each pair of countries. Write $<$ or $>$.**

Country	Lowest Elevation (feet)
Argentina	−344
Australia	−49
Czech Republic	377
Hungary	249
United States	−281

16. Argentina and the United States ________________

17. Czech Republic and Hungary ________________

18. Hungary and Argentina ________________

19. Which country in the table has the lowest elevation? ________________

20. **Problem Solving** Golf scores represent the number of strokes above or below par. A negative score means that you hit a number below par while a positive score means that you hit a number above par. The winner in golf has the lowest score. During a round of golf, Angela's score was −5 and Lisa's score was −8. Who won the game? Explain.

____

H.O.T. FOCUS ON HIGHER ORDER THINKING

Work Area

21. **Critique Reasoning** Jorge wrote the inequality $-12°F < -3°F$ to compare the temperatures at 9 A.M. and 9 P.M. It was colder at 9 P.M. than at 9 A.M. What was the temperature at 9 A.M.? Explain.

____

22. **Analyze Relationships** There are three numbers a, b, and c, where $a > b$ and $b > c$. Describe the positions of the numbers on a number line.

____

____

____

____

23. **Look for a Pattern** Order −3, 5, 16, and −10 from least to greatest. Then order the same numbers from closest to zero to farthest from zero. Describe how your lists are similar. Would this be true if the numbers were −3, 5, −16 and −10?

____

____

____

____

____

LESSON

1.3 Absolute Value

CA CC 6.NS.7c

Understand the absolute value of a rational number as its distance from 0 on the number line; interpret absolute value as magnitude for a positive or negative quantity in a real-world situation. *Also 6.NS.7, 6.NS.7d*

ESSENTIAL QUESTION

How do you find and use absolute value?

EXPLORE ACTIVITY 1 CA CC 6.NS.7, 6.NS.7c

Finding Absolute Value

The **absolute value** of a number is the number's distance from 0 on a number line. For example, the absolute value of −3 is 3 because −3 is 3 units from 0. The absolute value of −3 is written |−3|.

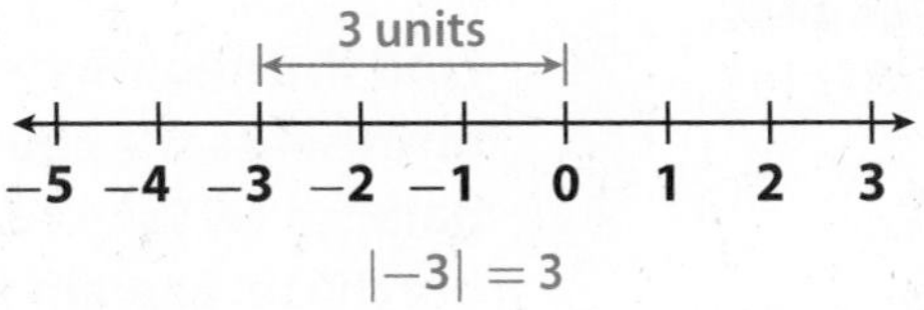

Because absolute value represents a distance, it is always nonnegative.

Graph the following numbers on the number line. Then use your number line to find each absolute value.

−7 5 7 −2 4 −4

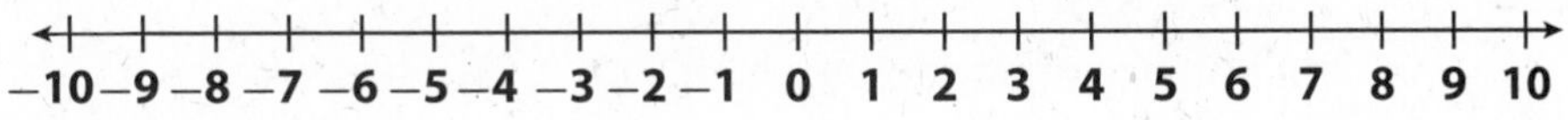

A |−7| = ____ **B** |5| = ____ **C** |7| = ____

D |−2| = ____ **E** |4| = ____ **F** |−4| = ____

Reflect

1. **Analyze Relationships** Which pairs of numbers have the same absolute value? How are these numbers related?

____

____

2. **Justify Reasoning** Negative numbers are less than positive numbers. Does this mean that the absolute value of a negative number must be less than the absolute value of a positive number? Explain.

____

____

____

____

Math On the Spot
my.hrw.com

Animated Math
my.hrw.com

Absolute Value in a Real-World Situation

In real-world situations, you may choose to describe values using either negative numbers or the absolute values of those numbers, depending on the wording you are using. For example, if you have a balance of −$35 dollars in an account, you may also choose to represent that as a debt of $35.

EXAMPLE 1 Real World

CA CC 6.NS.7c

Jake uses his online music store gift card to buy an album of songs by his favorite band.

Find the negative number that represents the change in the balance on Jake's card after his purchase. Explain how absolute value would be used to express that number in this situation.

STEP 1 Find the negative integer that represents the change in the balance.

−$10 *The balance decreased by $10, so use a negative number.*

The balance changed by −$10.

STEP 2 Use the number line to find the absolute value of −$10.

−10 is 10 units from 0 on the number line.

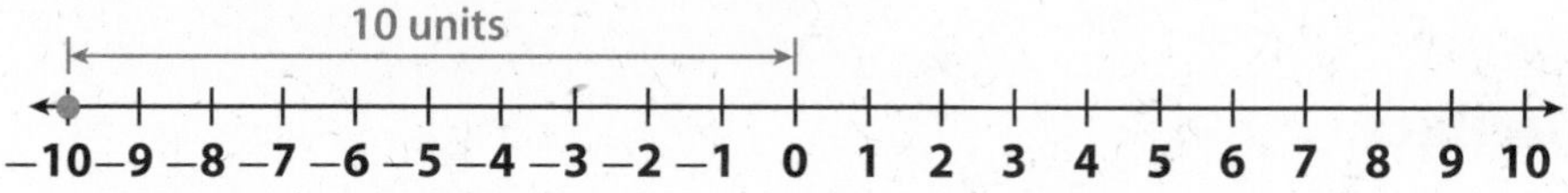

The absolute value of −$10 is $10, or $|-10| = 10$.

STEP 3 Use the absolute value to describe the change in Jake's balance.

The balance on Jake's card decreased by $10.

Math Talk
Mathematical Practices

Use absolute value to describe a change in weight of −4 pounds.

Reflect

3. **Communicate Mathematical Ideas** Must the absolute value of a number always be positive?

____

____

____

YOUR TURN

4. The temperature at night reached $-13\,°F$. Write an equivalent statement about the temperature using the absolute value of the number.

____

Find each absolute value.

5. $|-12|$ __________ **6.** $|91|$ __________ **7.** $|-55|$ __________

8. $|0|$ __________ **9.** $|88|$ __________ **10.** $|1|$ __________

Personal Math Trainer
Online Practice and Help
my.hrw.com

EXPLORE ACTIVITY 2 Real World

CA CC 6.NS.7c, 6.NS.7d

Comparing Absolute Values

Maria, Susan, George, and Antonio are playing a game on their smartphones. In order to stay in the game, a player has to achieve a positive number of energy points. The points needed are shown.

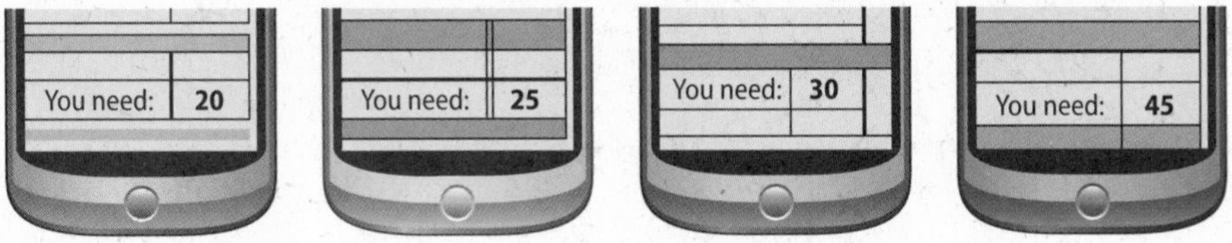

__________ __________ __________ __________

Answer the following questions. When you have finished, you will have enough clues to match each smartphone with the correct person.

When a player needs a positive number of points, it means that the player's point total is negative.

A Maria's point total is less than -30. Does Maria need more than 30 points or fewer than 30 points to stay in the game? __________

B Susan's point total is greater than -25. Does Susan need more than 25 points or fewer than 25 points? __________

C George's point total is 5 less than Susan's point total. Does George need more points than Susan or fewer than Susan? __________

D Antonio needs 15 fewer points than Maria needs. Is Antonio's point total greater than or less than Maria's point total? __________

E Write each person's name underneath his or her smartphone.

EXPLORE ACTIVITY 2 *(cont'd)*

Reflect

11. Analyze Relationships Use absolute value to describe the relationship between a point total and the number of points needed.

____

Guided Practice

1. Vocabulary If a number is ______________, then the number is less than its absolute value. (Explore Activity 1)

2. If Ryan pays his car insurance for the year in full, he will get a credit of $28. If he chooses to pay a monthly premium, he will pay a $10 late fee for any month that the payment is late. (Explore Activity 1, Example 1)

a. Which of these values could be represented with a negative number? Explain.

____

____

b. Use the number line to find the absolute value of your answer from part a. ______________

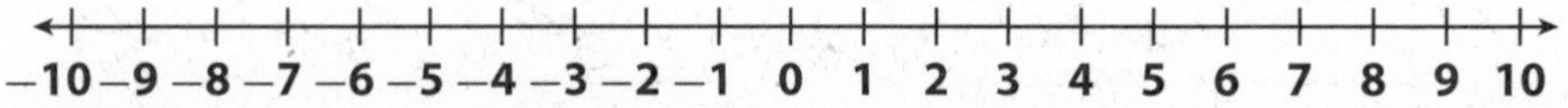

3. Leo, Gabrielle, Sinea, and Tomas are playing a video game. Their scores are described in the table below. (Explore Activity 2)

Name	Leo	Gabrielle	Sinea
Score	less than −100 points	20 more points than Leo	50 points less than Leo

a. Leo wants to earn enough points to have a positive score. Does he need to earn more than 100 points or less than 100 points? ______________

b. Gabrielle wants to earn enough points to not have a negative score. Does she need to earn more points than Leo or fewer points than Leo? ______________

c. Sinea wants to earn enough points to have a higher score than Leo. Does she need to earn more than 50 points or fewer than 50 points? ______________

ESSENTIAL QUESTION CHECK-IN

4. When is the absolute value of a number equal to the number?

____

Name ________________ Class ________________ Date ________________

1.3 Independent Practice

CA CC 6.NS.7, 6.NS.7c, 6.NS.7d

Personal Math Trainer
Online Practice and Help
my.hrw.com

5. **Financial Literacy** Jacob earned $80 babysitting and deposited the money into his savings account. The next week he took $85 out of his savings account to buy video games. Use integers to describe the weekly changes in Jacob's savings account balance.

____

____

6. **Financial Literacy** Sara's savings account balance changed by −$34 one week and by −$67 the next week. Which amount represents the greater change? ________________

7. **Analyze Relationships** Bertrand collects movie posters. The number of movie posters in his collection changes each month as he buys and sells posters. The table shows how many posters he bought or sold in the given months.

Month	January	February	March	April
Posters	Sold 20	Bought 12	Bought 22	Sold 28

   a. Which months have changes that can be represented by positive numbers? Which months have changes that can be represented by negative numbers? Explain.

   ____

   ____

   ____

   ____

   b. According to the table, in which month did the size of Bertrand's poster collection change the most? Use absolute value to explain your answer.

   ____

   ____

   ____

8. **Earth Science** Death Valley has an elevation of −282 feet relative to sea level. Explain how to use absolute value to describe the elevation of Death Valley as a positive integer.

____

____

9. **Communicate Mathematical Ideas** Lisa and Alice are playing a game. Each player either receives or has to pay play money based on the result of the spin. The table lists how much a player receives or pays for various spins.

Red	Pay \$5
Blue	Receive \$4
Yellow	Pay \$1
Green	Receive \$3
Orange	Pay \$2

   a. Express each amount in the table as a positive or a negative number.

   ____

   b. Describe the change to Lisa's amount of money when the spinner lands on red.

   ____

   ____

10. **Financial Literacy** Sam and Freda both paid their credit card bills in full. Each person made returns that resulted in credits to their accounts. Sam's new balance is −\$36, and Freda's is −\$42. Which person has more money credited to his or her card? ______________________________

11. **Financial Literacy** Emily spent \$55 from her savings on a new dress. Explain how to describe the change in Emily's savings balance in two different ways.

____

____

____

H.O.T. FOCUS ON HIGHER ORDER THINKING

Work Area

12. **Make a Conjecture** Can two different numbers have the same absolute value? If yes, give an example. If no, explain why not.

____

13. **Communicate Mathematical Ideas** Does $-|-4| = |-(-4)|$? Justify your answer.

____

14. **Critique Reasoning** Angelique says that finding the absolute value of a number is the same as finding the opposite of the number. For example, $|-5| = 5$. Explain her error.

____

____

____

____

MODULE QUIZ

Ready to Go On?

Personal Math Trainer
Online Practice and Help
my.hrw.com

1.1 Identifying Integers and Their Opposites

1. The table shows the elevations in feet of several locations around a coastal town. Graph and label the locations on the number line according to their elevations.

Location	Post Office *A*	Library *B*	Town Hall *C*	Laundromat *D*	Pet Store *E*
Elevation (feet)	8	−3	−9	3	1

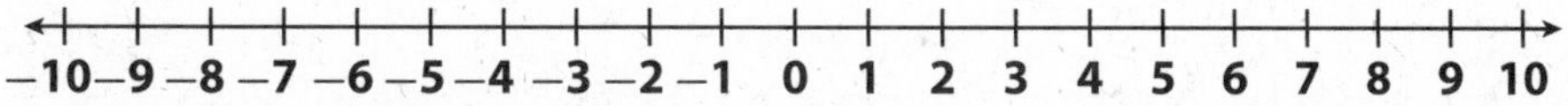

Write the opposite of each number.

2. −22 ____________

3. 0 ____________

1.2 Comparing and Ordering Integers

List the numbers in order from least to greatest.

4. −2, 8, −15, −5, 3, 1 ____________

Compare. Write < or >.

5. −3 ◯ −15

6. 9 ◯ −10

1.3 Absolute Value

Graph each number on the number line. Then use your number line to find the absolute value of each number.

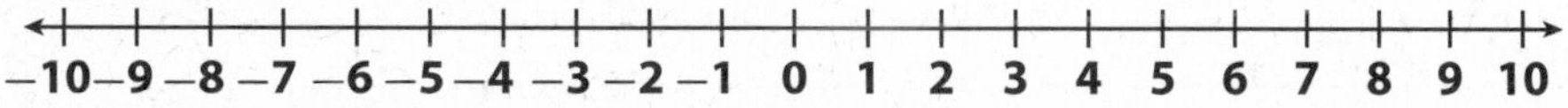

7. 2 ____________

8. −8 ____________

9. −5 ____________

ESSENTIAL QUESTION

10. How can you use absolute value to represent a negative number in a real-world situation?

____

____

MODULE 1
MIXED REVIEW

Assessment Readiness

Personal Math Trainer
Online Practice and Help
my.hrw.com

1. Diego graphs several points on the number line.

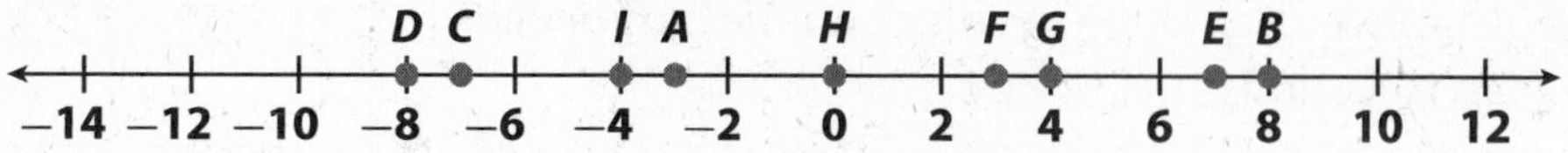

Select Yes or No if the pair of points are opposites.

A. A and G ○ Yes ○ No
B. G and I ○ Yes ○ No
C. B and D ○ Yes ○ No

2. How would you use a number line to put temperatures in order from greatest to least?

Choose True or False for each statement.

A. Graph the integers, and then read them from left to right. ○ True ○ False
B. Graph the absolute values of the integers, and then read them from right to left. ○ True ○ False
C. Graph the integers, and then read them from right to left. ○ True ○ False

3. The table shows the elevations of the lowest points in six countries. Tell how to use a number line to find the country with the lowest point and the country with the highest low point, then name them. Grant says that $-133 > 154$, so Egypt is farther from sea level than China is. Explain his error.

Country	China	Egypt	Azerbaijan	Serbia	Israel	Laos
Lowest Elevation (m)	−154	−133	−28	35	−408	70

4. One rectangular prism has a base area of 120 square feet, and a height of 12 feet. A second has dimensions 84 inches, 6 feet, and 16 feet. Is the volume of the second more than or less than half that of the first? Explain.

Factors and Multiples

MODULE 2

CALIFORNIA

ESSENTIAL QUESTION

How can you use greatest common factors and least common multiples to solve real-world problems?

LESSON 2.1

Greatest Common Factor

CA CC 6.NS.4

LESSON 2.2

Least Common Multiple

CA CC 6.NS.4

Real-World Video

my.hrw.com

Organizers of banquets and other special events plan many things, including menus, seating arrangements, table decorations, and party favors. Factors and multiples can be helpful in this work.

GO DIGITAL

my.hrw.com

my.hrw.com

Go digital with your write-in student edition, accessible on any device.

Math On the Spot

Scan with your smart phone to jump directly to the online edition, video tutor, and more.

Animated Math

Interactively explore key concepts to see how math works.

Personal Math Trainer

Get immediate feedback and help as you work through practice sets.

Are YOU Ready?

Complete these exercises to review skills you will need for this module.

Personal Math Trainer
Online Practice and Help
my.hrw.com

Multiples

EXAMPLE $5 \times 1 = 5$ $5 \times 2 = 10$ $5 \times 3 = 15$ $5 \times 4 = 20$ $5 \times 5 = 25$

To find the first five multiples of 5, multiply 5 by 1, 2, 3, 4, and 5.

List the first five multiples of the number.

1. 7 ________ **2.** 11 ________ **3.** 15 ________

Factors

EXAMPLE
$1 \times 12 = 12$
$2 \times 6 = 12$
$3 \times 4 = 12$
The factors of 12 are 1, 2, 3, 4, 6, 12.

To find the factors of 12, use multiplication facts of 12. Continue until pairs of factors repeat.

Write all the factors of the number.

4. 24 ________ **5.** 36 ________

6. 45 ________ **7.** 32 ________

Multiplication Properties (Distributive)

EXAMPLE
$$\begin{aligned} 7 \times 14 &= 7 \times (10 + 4) \\ &= (7 \times 10) + (7 \times 4) \\ &= 70 + 28 \\ &= 98 \end{aligned}$$

To multiply a number by a sum, multiply the number by each addend and add the products.

Use the Distributive Property to find the product.

8.
$$\begin{aligned} 8 \times 15 &= 8 \times (\square + \square) \\ &= (\square \times \square) + (\square \times \square) \\ &= \square + \square \\ &= \square \end{aligned}$$

9.
$$\begin{aligned} 6 \times 17 &= 6 \times (\square + \square) \\ &= (\square \times \square) + (\square \times \square) \\ &= \square + \square \\ &= \square \end{aligned}$$

Reading Start-Up

Visualize Vocabulary

Use the ✔ words to complete the graphic.

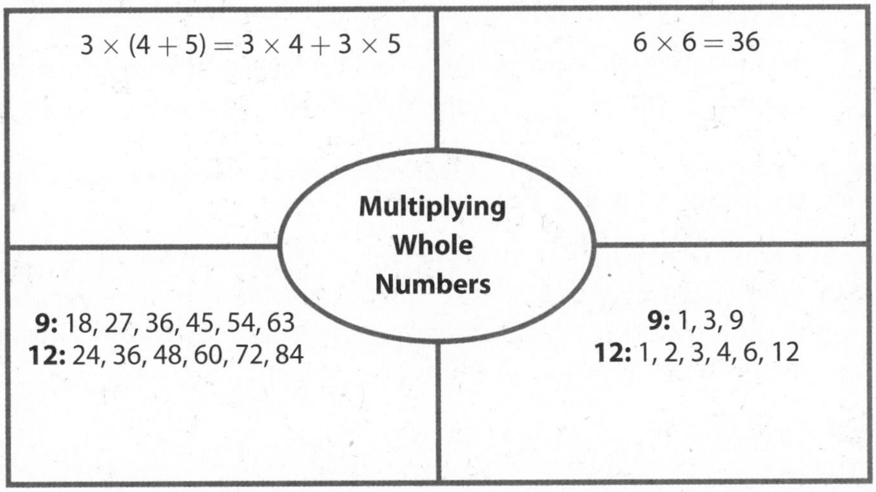

Vocabulary

Review Words

✔ area *(área)*
✔ Distributive Property *(Propiedad distributiva)*
✔ factor *(factor)*
✔ multiple *(múltiplo)*
✔ product *(producto)*

Preview Words

greatest common factor (GCF) *(máximo común divisor (MCD))*
least common multiple (LCM) *(mínimo común múltiplo (m.c.m.))*

Understand Vocabulary

Complete the sentences below using the preview words.

1. Of all the whole numbers that divide evenly into two or more numbers, the one with the highest value is called the ______________________________.

2. Of all the common products of two numbers, the one with the lowest value is called the ______________________________.

Active Reading

Two-Panel Flip Chart Create a two-panel flip chart to help you understand the concepts in this module. Label one flap "Greatest Common Factor." Label the other flap "Least Common Multiple." As you study each lesson, write important ideas under the appropriate flap.

CALIFORNIA

GETTING READY FOR

Factors and Multiples

Understanding the standards and the vocabulary terms in the standards will help you know exactly what you are expected to learn in this module.

CA CC 6.NS.4

Find the **greatest common factor** of two whole numbers less than or equal to 100 and the least common multiple of two whole numbers less than or equal to 12. Use the Distributive Property to express a sum of two whole numbers 1–100 with a common factor as a multiple of a sum of two whole numbers with no common factor.

Key Vocabulary

greatest common factor (GCF)
(máximo común divisor (MCD))
The largest common factor of two or more given numbers.

What It Means to You

You will determine the greatest common factor of two numbers and solve real-world problems involving the greatest common factor.

EXAMPLE 6.NS.4

There are 12 boys and 18 girls in Ms. Ruiz's science class. Each lab group must have the same number of boys and the same number of girls. What is the greatest number of groups Ms. Ruiz can make if every student must be in a group?

Factors of 12: 1, 2, 3, 4, 6, 12

Factors of 18: 1, 2, 3, 6, 9, 18

The GCF of 12 and 18 is 6. The greatest number of groups Ms. Ruiz can make is 6.

CA CC 6.NS.4

Find the greatest common factor of two whole numbers less than or equal to 100 and the **least common multiple** of two whole numbers less than or equal to 12.

Key Vocabulary

least common multiple (LCM)
(mínimo común múltiplo (m.c.m.))
The smallest number, other than zero, that is a multiple of two or more given numbers.

What It Means to You

You will determine the least common multiple of two numbers and solve real-world problems involving the least common multiple.

EXAMPLE 6.NS.4

Lydia's family will provide juice boxes and granola bars for 24 players. Juice comes in packs of 6, and granola bars in packs of 8. What is the least number of packs of each needed so that every player has a drink and a granola bar and there are none left over?

Multiples of 6: 6, 12, 18, 24, 30, ...

Multiples of 8: 8, 16, 24, 32, ...

The LCM of 6 and 8 is 24. Lydia's family should buy $24 \div 6 = 4$ packs of juice and $24 \div 8 = 3$ packs of granola bars.

Visit **my.hrw.com** to see all **CA Common Core Standards** explained.

my.hrw.com

LESSON 2.1 Greatest Common Factor

CA CC 6.NS.4

Find the greatest common factor of two whole numbers less than or equal to 100 and the least common multiple of two whole numbers less than or equal to 12. Use the distributive property to express a sum of two whole numbers 1–100 with a common factor as a multiple of a sum of two whole numbers with no common factor.

ESSENTIAL QUESTION

How can you find and use the greatest common factor of two whole numbers?

EXPLORE ACTIVITY 1 Real World

CA CC 6.NS.4

Understanding Common Factors

The **greatest common factor (GCF)** of two numbers is the greatest factor shared by those numbers.

A florist makes bouquets from 18 roses and 30 tulips. All the bouquets include both roses and tulips. All bouquets are identical, and all the flowers are used. You can make tables to see the possible ways the florists can make the bouquets.

A Complete the tables to show the possible ways to divide each type of flower among the bouquets.

What are the possible ways the florist can make bouquets of roses?

Number of Bouquets	1	2	3	6	9	18
Number of Roses in Each Bouquet	18	9				

What are the possible ways the florist can make bouquets of tulips?

Number of Bouquets	1	2	3	5	6	10	15	30
Number of Tulips in Each Bouquet	30							

B Can the florist make five bouquets using all the flowers? Explain.

____

C What are the common factors of 18 and 30? What do they represent?

____

D What is the GCF of 18 and 30? ______________________

Reflect

1. **What If?** Suppose the florist has 18 roses and 36 tulips. What is the GCF of the numbers of roses and tulips? Explain.

____

Math On the Spot
my.hrw.com

My Notes

Finding the Greatest Common Factor

One way to find the GCF of two numbers is to list all of their factors. Then you can identify common factors and the GCF.

EXAMPLE 1 Real World

CA CC 6.NS.4

A baker has 24 sesame bagels and 36 plain bagels to put into boxes. Each box must have the same number of each type of bagel. What is the greatest number of boxes that the baker can make using all of the bagels? How many sesame bagels and how many plain bagels will be in each box?

STEP 1 List the factors of 24 and 36. Then circle the common factors.

The baker can divide 24 sesame bagels into groups of 1, 2, 3, 4, 6, 8, 12, or 24.

Factors of 24:	(1)	(2)	(3)	(4)	(6)	8	(12)	24	
Factors of 36:	(1)	(2)	(3)	(4)	(6)	9	(12)	18	36

STEP 2 Find the GCF of 24 and 36.

The GCF is 12. So, the greatest number of boxes that the baker can make is 12. There will be 2 sesame bagels in each box, because $24 \div 12 = 2$. There will be 3 plain bagels, because $36 \div 12 = 3$.

Reflect

2. **Critical Thinking** What is the GCF of two prime numbers? Give an example.

____

YOUR TURN

Find the GCF of each pair of numbers.

3. 14 and 35 ___________ **4.** 20 and 28 ___________

5. The sixth-grade class is competing in the school field day. There are 32 girls and 40 boys who want to participate. Each team must have the same number of girls and the same number of boys. What is the greatest number of teams that can be formed? How many boys and how many girls will be on each team?

____

Personal Math Trainer
Online Practice and Help
my.hrw.com

EXPLORE ACTIVITY 2 CA CC 6.NS.4

Using the Distributive Property

You can use the Distributive Property to rewrite a sum of two or more numbers as a product of their GCF and a sum of numbers with no common factor other than 1. To understand how, you can use grid paper to draw area models of 45 and 60. Here are all the possible area models of 45.

Animated Math
my.hrw.com

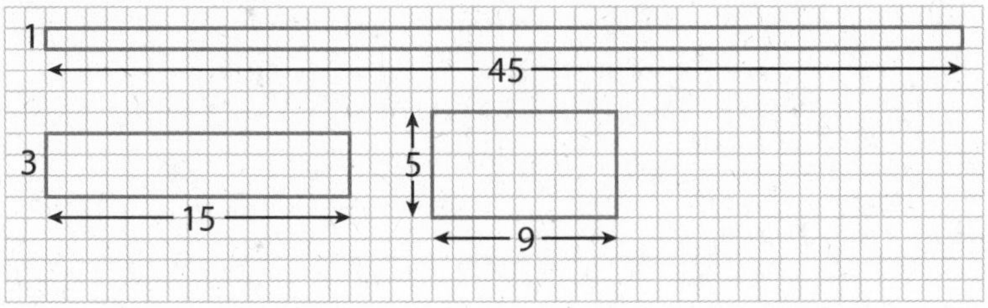

A What do the side lengths of the area models (1, 3, 5, 9, 15, and 45) represent? ______________________

B On your own grid paper, show all of the possible area models of 60.

____

C What side lengths do the area models of 45 and 60 have in common? What do the side lengths represent?

____

D What is the greatest common side length? What does it represent?

____

E Write 45 as a product of the GCF and another number. ____________

Write 60 as a product of the GCF and another number. ____________

F Use your answers above to rewrite $45 + 60$.

$45 + 60 = 15 \times \_\_\_\_ + 15 \times \_\_\_\_$

Use the Distributive Property and your answer above to write $45 + 60$ as a product of the GCF and a sum of two numbers.

$15 \times \_\_\_\_ + 15 \times \_\_\_\_ = 15 \times (\_\_\_\_ + \_\_\_\_) = 15 \times 7$

Math Talk
Mathematical Practices

How can you check to see if your product is correct?

Reflect

Write the sum of the numbers as the product of their GCF and another sum.

6. $27 + 18$ ______________________

7. $120 + 36$ ______________________

8. $9 + 35$ ______________________

Guided Practice

1. Lee is sewing vests using 16 green buttons and 24 blue buttons. All the vests are identical, and all have both green and blue buttons. What are the possible numbers of vests Lee can make? What is the greatest number of vests Lee can make? (Explore Activity 1, Example 1)

List the factors of 16 and 24. Then circle the common factors.

Factors of 16:								
Factors of 24:								

What are the common factors of 16 and 24? ______________

What are the possible numbers of vests Lee can make? ______________

What is the GCF of 16 and 24? ______________

What is the greatest number of vests Lee can make? ______________

Write the sum of numbers as a product of their GCF and another sum.
(Explore Activity 2)

2. $36 + 45$

What is the GCF of 36 and 45? ______________

Write each number as a product of the GCF and another number.
Then use the Distributive Property to rewrite the sum.

$(\square \times \square) + (\square \times \square) = (\square) \times (\square + \square)$

3. $75 + 90$

What is the GCF of 75 and 90? ______________

Write each number as a product of the GCF and another number.
Then use the Distributive Property to rewrite the sum.

$(\square \times \square) + (\square \times \square) = (\square) \times (\square + \square)$

? ESSENTIAL QUESTION CHECK-IN

4. Suppose you write a sum of numbers as a product of their GCF and another sum. What is the GCF of the numbers in the other sum? Explain.

____

Name ______________________ Class ______________ Date ______________

2.1 Independent Practice

CA CC 6.NS.4

Personal Math Trainer
my.hrw.com
Online Practice and Help

List the factors of each number.

5. 12 ______________

6. 50 ______________

7. 39 ______________

8. 64 ______________

Find the GCF of each pair of numbers.

9. 40 and 48 ______________

10. 30 and 45 ______________

11. 10 and 45 ______________

12. 25 and 90 ______________

13. 21 and 40 ______________

14. 28 and 70 ______________

15. 60 and 72 ______________

16. 45 and 81 ______________

17. 28 and 32 ______________

18. 55 and 77 ______________

19. Carlos is arranging books on shelves. He has 32 novels and 24 autobiographies. Each shelf will have the same numbers of novels and autobiographies. If Carlos must place all of the books on shelves, what are the possible numbers of shelves Carlos will use?

____

20. The middle school band has 56 members. The high school band has 96 members. The bands are going to march one after the other in a parade. The director wants to arrange the bands into the same number of columns. What is the greatest number of columns in which the two bands can be arranged if each column has the same number of marchers? How many marchers will be in each column?

____

21. For football tryouts at a local school, 12 coaches and 42 players will split into groups. Each group will have the same numbers of coaches and players. What is the greatest number of groups that can be formed? How many coaches and players will be in each of these groups?

____

22. Lola is placing appetizers on plates. She has 63 spring rolls and 84 cheese cubes. She wants to include both appetizers on each plate. Each plate must have the same numbers of spring rolls and cheese cubes. What is the greatest number of plates she can make using all of the appetizers? How many of each type of appetizer will be on each of these plates?

____

Write the sum of the numbers as the product of their GCF and another sum.

23. 56 + 64 ______________________

24. 48 + 14 ______________________

25. 30 + 54 ______________________

26. 24 + 40 ______________________

27. 55 + 66 ______________________

28. 49 + 63 ______________________

29. 40 + 25 ______________________

30. 63 + 15 ______________________

31. Explain why the greatest common factor of two numbers is sometimes 1.

____

____

____

H.O.T. FOCUS ON HIGHER ORDER THINKING

Work Area

32. Communicate Mathematical Ideas Tasha believes that she can rewrite the difference 120 − 36 as a product of the GCF of the two numbers and another difference. Is she correct? Explain your answer.

____

____

____

33. Persevere in Problem Solving Explain how to find the greatest common factor of three numbers.

____

____

____

____

____

34. Critique Reasoning Xiao's teacher asked him to rewrite the sum 60 + 90 as the product of the GCF of the two numbers and a sum. Xiao wrote 3(20 + 30). What mistake did Xiao make? How should he have written the sum?

____

____

____

____

LESSON 2.2

Least Common Multiple

CA CC 6.NS.4

Find the greatest common factor of two whole numbers less than or equal to 100 and the least common multiple of two whole numbers less than or equal to 12. Use the distributive property to express a sum of two whole numbers 1–100 with a common factor as a multiple of a sum of two whole numbers with no common factor.

ESSENTIAL QUESTION

How do you find and use the least common multiple of two numbers?

EXPLORE ACTIVITY Real World

CA CC 6.NS.4

Finding the Least Common Multiple

A multiple of a number is the product of the number and another number. For example, 9 is a multiple of the number 3. The **least common multiple (LCM)** of two or more numbers is the least number, other than zero, that is a multiple of all the numbers.

Ned is training for a biathlon. He will swim every sixth day and bicycle every eighth day. On what days will he both swim and bicycle?

A In the chart below, shade each day that Ned will swim. Circle each day Ned will bicycle.

1	2	3	4	5	6	7	8	9	10
11	12	13	14	15	16	17	18	19	20
21	22	23	24	25	26	27	28	29	30
31	32	33	34	35	36	37	38	39	40
41	42	43	44	45	46	47	48	49	50
51	52	53	54	55	56	57	58	59	60
61	62	63	64	65	66	67	68	69	70
71	72	73	74	75	76	77	78	79	80
81	82	83	84	85	86	87	88	89	90
91	92	93	94	95	96	97	98	99	100

B On what days will Ned both swim and bicycle? ____________

The numbers of the days that Ned will swim and bicycle are common multiples of 6 and 8.

Reflect

1. **Communicate Mathematical Ideas** What does the LCM represent in this situation?

____

Math On the Spot
my.hrw.com

Applying the LCM

You can use the LCM of two whole numbers to solve problems.

EXAMPLE 1 Real World

CA CC 6.NS.4

A store is holding a promotion. Every third customer receives a free key chain, and every fourth customer receives a free magnet. Which customer will be the first to receive both a key chain and a magnet?

STEP 1 List the multiples of 3 and 4. Then circle the common multiples.

Multiples of 3:	3	6	9	12	15	18	21	24	27
Multiples of 4:	4	8	12	16	20	24	28	32	36

STEP 2 Find the LCM of 3 and 4.

The LCM is 12.

The first customer to get both a key chain and a magnet is the 12th customer.

Math Talk
Mathematical Practices
What steps do you take to list multiples of a number?

YOUR TURN

2. Find the LCM of 4 and 9 by listing the multiples. __________

Multiples of 4: __________

Multiples of 9: __________

Personal Math Trainer
Online Practice and Help
my.hrw.com

Guided Practice

1. After every ninth visit to a restaurant you receive a free beverage. After every twelfth visit you receive a free appetizer. If you visit the restaurant 100 times, on which visits will you receive a free beverage and a free appetizer? At which visit will you first receive a free beverage and a free appetizer? (Explore Activity 1, Example 1)

____

ESSENTIAL QUESTION CHECK-IN

2. Do two whole numbers always have a least common multiple? Explain.

____

____

Name ______________________ Class ______________ Date ______________

2.2 Independent Practice

CA CC 6.NS.4

Personal Math Trainer
Online Practice and Help
my.hrw.com

Find the LCM of each pair of numbers.

3. 8 and 56 ______________

4. 25 and 50 ______________

5. 12 and 30 ______________

6. 6 and 10 ______________

7. 16 and 24 ______________

8. 14 and 21 ______________

9. 9 and 15 ______________

10. 5 and 11 ______________

11. During February, Kevin will water his ivy every third day, and water his cactus every fifth day.

a. On which date will Kevin first water both plants together?

____

b. Will Kevin water both plants together again in February? Explain.

____

____

12. **Vocabulary** Given any two numbers, which is greater, the LCM of the numbers or the GCF of the numbers? Why?

____

____

____

Use the subway train schedule.

13. The red line and the blue line trains just arrived at the station. When will they next arrive at the station at the same time?

In ________ minutes

14. The blue line and the yellow line trains just arrived at the station. When will they next arrive at the station at the same time?

In ________ minutes

15. All three trains just arrived at the station. When will they next all arrive at the station at the same time?

In ________ minutes

Train Schedule	
Train	**Arrives Every...**
Red line	8 minutes
Blue line	10 minutes
Yellow line	12 minutes

16. You buy a lily and an African violet on the same day. You are instructed to water the lily every fourth day and water the violet every seventh day after taking them home. What is the first day on which you will water both plants on the same day? How can you use this answer to determine each of the next days you will water both plants on the same day?

____

____

____

H.O.T. FOCUS ON HIGHER ORDER THINKING

Work Area

17. What is the LCM of two numbers if one number is a multiple of the other? Give an example.

____

____

18. What is the LCM of two numbers that have no common factors greater than 1? Give an example.

____

____

19. **Draw Conclusions** The least common multiple of two numbers is 60, and one of the numbers is 7 less than the other number. What are the numbers? Justify your answer.

____

____

____

____

20. **Communicate Mathematical Ideas** Describe how to find the least common multiple of three numbers. Give an example.

____

____

____

____

____

____

MODULE QUIZ

Ready to Go On?

Personal Math Trainer
Online Practice and Help
my.hrw.com

2.1 Greatest Common Factor

Find the GCF of each pair of numbers.

1. 20 and 32 ________

2. 24 and 56 ________

3. 36 and 90 ________

4. 45 and 75 ________

5. 28 girls and 32 boys volunteer to plant trees at a school. The principal divides the girls and boys into groups that have girls and boys in each group. What is the greatest number of groups the principal can make? ________

Write the sum of the numbers as the product of their GCF and another sum.

6. $32 + 20$ ________

7. $18 + 27$ ________

2.2 Least Common Multiple

Find the LCM of each pair of numbers.

8. 6 and 12 ________

9. 6 and 10 ________

10. 8 and 9 ________

11. 9 and 12 ________

12. Juanita runs every third day and swims every fifth day. If Juanita runs and swims today, in how many days will she run and swim again on the same day? ________

ESSENTIAL QUESTION

13. What types of problems can be solved using the greatest common factor? What types of problems can be solved using the least common multiple?

____

____

____

____

CALIFORNIA

MODULE 2
MIXED REVIEW

Assessment Readiness

Personal Math Trainer

my.hrw.com

Online Practice and Help

1. A sporting goods store gave a free T-shirt to every 8th customer and a free water bottle to every 10th customer for a promotional event.

Select Yes or No if the customer would receive both a free T-shirt and a free water bottle.

A. the 20th customer ○ Yes ○ No
B. the 40th customer ○ Yes ○ No
C. the 160th customer ○ Yes ○ No

2. Laura found the greatest common factor of several pairs of numbers.

Choose True or False for each statement.

A. The greatest common factor of 24 and 18 is 6. ○ True ○ False
B. The greatest common factor of 24 and 48 is 48. ○ True ○ False
C. The greatest common factor of 96 and 56 is 4. ○ True ○ False

3. A diver plans to visit three reefs in the Pacific Ocean. Reef A has an elevation of -27 meters, and Reef B has an elevation of -31 meters. Martina says Reef A is deeper than Reef B because $-27 > -31$. Is Martina correct? Explain your reasoning.

4. Tia is buying paper cups and plates. Cups come in packages of 12, and plates come in packages of 10. She wants to buy the same number of cups and plates, but she wants to buy the least number of packages possible. How much should Tia expect to pay if each package of cups costs \$3 and each package of plates costs \$5? Explain.

Rational Numbers

MODULE 3
CALIFORNIA

ESSENTIAL QUESTION

How can you use rational numbers to solve real-world problems?

Real-World Video

In sports like baseball, coaches, analysts, and fans keep track of players' statistics such as batting averages, earned run averages, and runs batted in. These values are reported using rational numbers.

my.hrw.com

GO DIGITAL
my.hrw.com

my.hrw.com
Go digital with your write-in student edition, accessible on any device.

Math On the Spot
Scan with your smart phone to jump directly to the online edition, video tutor, and more.

Animated Math
Interactively explore key concepts to see how math works.

Personal Math Trainer
Get immediate feedback and help as you work through practice sets.

Are YOU Ready?

Complete these exercises to review skills you will need for this module.

Personal Math Trainer
Online Practice and Help
my.hrw.com

Write an Improper Fraction as a Mixed Number

EXAMPLE

$\frac{11}{3} = \frac{3}{3} + \frac{3}{3} + \frac{3}{3} + \frac{2}{3}$ — *Write as a sum using names for one plus a proper fraction.*

$= 1 + 1 + 1 + \frac{2}{3}$ — *Write each name for one as one.*

$= 3 + \frac{2}{3}$ — *Add the ones.*

$= 3\frac{2}{3}$ — *Write the mixed number.*

Write each improper fraction as a mixed number.

1. $\frac{7}{2}$ ________ **2.** $\frac{12}{5}$ ________ **3.** $\frac{11}{7}$ ________ **4.** $\frac{15}{4}$ ________

Write a Mixed Number as an Improper Fraction

EXAMPLE

$3\frac{3}{4} = 1 + 1 + 1 + \frac{3}{4}$ — *Write the whole number as a sum of ones.*

$= \frac{4}{4} + \frac{4}{4} + \frac{4}{4} + \frac{3}{4}$ — *Use the denominator of the fraction to write equivalent fractions for the ones.*

$= \frac{15}{4}$ — *Add the numerators.*

Write each mixed number as an improper fraction.

5. $2\frac{1}{2}$ ________ **6.** $4\frac{3}{5}$ ________ **7.** $3\frac{4}{9}$ ________ **8.** $2\frac{5}{7}$ ________

Compare and Order Decimals

EXAMPLE Order from least to greatest: 7.32, 5.14, 5.16.

7.32 is greatest.

$5.14 < 5.16$

The order is 5.14, 5.16, 7.32.

Use place value to compare numbers, starting with ones, then tenths, then hundredths.

Compare the decimals.

9. 8.86 ______ 8.65 **10.** 0.732 ______ 0.75 **11.** 0.22 ______ 0.022

12. Order 0.98, 0.27, and 0.34 from greatest to least. ________________

Reading Start-Up

Visualize Vocabulary

Use the ✔ words to complete the web. You may put more than one word in each box.

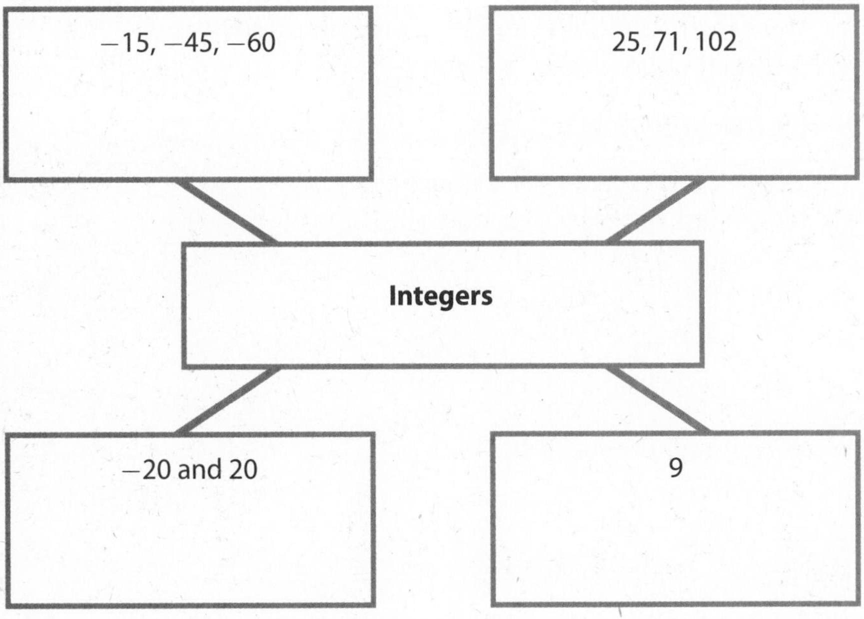

Vocabulary

Review Words

absolute value *(valor absoluto)*
decimal *(decimal)*
dividend *(dividendo)*
divisor *(divisor)*
fraction *(fracción)*
integers *(enteros)*
✔ negative numbers *(números negativos)*
✔ opposites *(opuestos)*
✔ positive numbers *(números positivos)*
✔ whole number *(número entero)*

Preview Words

rational number *(número racional)*
Venn diagram *(diagrama de Venn)*

Understand Vocabulary

Fill in each blank with the correct term from the preview words.

1. A ______________________ is any number that can be written as a ratio of two integers.

2. A ______________________ is used to show the relationships between groups.

Active Reading

Tri-Fold Before beginning the module, create a tri-fold to help you learn the concepts and vocabulary in this module. Fold the paper into three sections. Label the columns "What I Know," "What I Need to Know," and "What I Learned." Complete the first two columns before you read. After studying the module, complete the third column.

GETTING READY FOR

Rational Numbers

Understanding the standards and the vocabulary terms in the standards will help you know exactly what you are expected to learn in this module.

CA CC 6.NS.7b

Write, interpret, and explain statements of order for rational numbers in real-world contexts.

Key Vocabulary

rational number
(número racional)
Any number that can be expressed as a ratio of two integers.

What It Means to You

You can order rational numbers to understand relationships between values in the real world.

EXAMPLE 6.NS.7B

The fraction of crude oil produced in the United States by four states in 2011 is shown.

CA	$\frac{1}{100}$	TX	$\frac{9}{50}$
ND	$\frac{3}{50}$	AL	$\frac{3}{25}$

Which state produced the least oil?

$CA = \frac{1}{100}$ $\qquad TX = \frac{9}{50} = \frac{18}{100}$

$ND = \frac{3}{50} = \frac{6}{100}$ $\qquad AL = \frac{3}{25} = \frac{12}{100}$

California (CA) produced the least crude oil in 2011.

CA CC 6.NS.7c

Understand the absolute value of a rational number as its distance from 0 on the number line; interpret absolute value as magnitude for a positive or negative quantity in a real-world situation.

Key Vocabulary

absolute value *(valor absoluto)*
A number's distance from 0 on the number line.

What It Means to You

You can use absolute value to describe a number's distance from 0 on a number line and compare quantities in real-world situations.

EXAMPLE 6.NS.7C

Use the number line to determine the absolute values of -4.5°F and -7.5°F and to compare the temperatures.

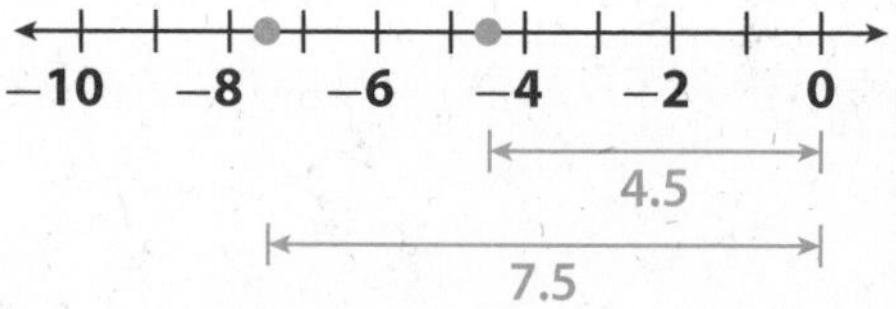

$|-4.5| = 4.5$ *The absolute value of −4.5 is 4.5.*

$|-7.5| = 7.5$ *The absolute value of −7.5 is 7.5.*

-7.5 is farther to the left of 0 than -4.5, so $-7.5 < -4.5$ and -7.5°F is colder than -4.5°F.

Visit **my.hrw.com** to see all **CA Common Core Standards** explained.

my.hrw.com

LESSON 3.1
Classifying Rational Numbers

CA CC 6.NS.6

Understand a rational number as a point on the number line. Extend number line diagrams and coordinate axes familiar from previous grades to represent points on the line and in the plane with negative number coordinates.

ESSENTIAL QUESTION

How can you classify rational numbers?

EXPLORE ACTIVITY Real World

CA CC Prep for 6.NS.6

Representing Division as a Fraction

Alicia and her friends Brittany, Kenji, and Ellis are taking a pottery class. The four friends have to share 3 blocks of clay. How much clay will each of them receive if they divide the 3 blocks evenly?

A The top faces of the 3 blocks of clay can be represented by squares. Use the model to show the part of each block that each friend will receive. Explain your method.

____

____

B Each piece of one square is equal to what fraction of a block of clay?

____

C Explain how to arrange the pieces to model the amount of clay each person gets. Sketch the model.

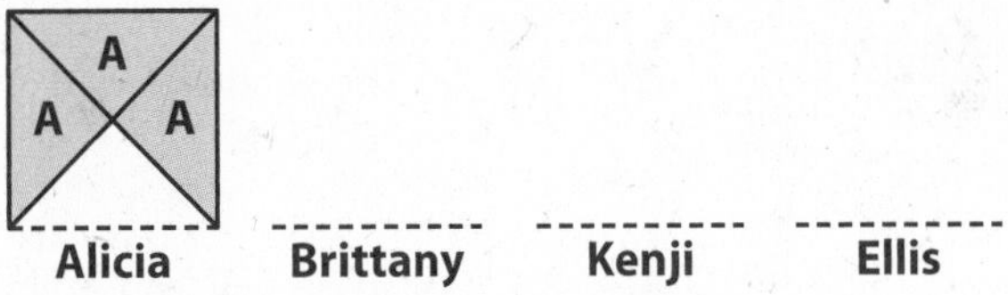

____

D What fraction of a square does each person's pieces cover? Explain.

____

____

E How much clay will each person receive?

____

F **Multiple Representations** How does this situation represent division?

____

____

EXPLORE ACTIVITY *(cont'd)*

Reflect

1. **Communicate Mathematical Ideas** $3 \div 4$ can be written $\frac{3}{4}$. How are the dividend and divisor of a division expression related to the parts of a fraction?

____

____

2. **Analyze Relationships** How could you represent the division as a fraction if 5 people shared 2 blocks? if 6 people shared 5 blocks?

____

Math On the Spot
my.hrw.com

Rational Numbers

A **rational number** is any number that can be written as $\frac{a}{b}$, where a and b are integers and $b \neq 0$.

Math Talk
Mathematical Practices

What division is represented by the fraction $\frac{34}{1}$?

EXAMPLE 1

CA CC 6.NS.6

Write each rational number as $\frac{a}{b}$.

A $3\frac{2}{5}$ — *Convert the mixed number to a fraction greater than 1.* — $3\frac{2}{5} = \frac{17}{5}$

B 0.6 — *The decimal is six tenths. Write as a fraction.* — $0.6 = \frac{6}{10}$

C 34 — *Write the whole number as a fraction with a denominator of 1.* — $34 = \frac{34}{1}$

D −7 — *Write the integer as a fraction with a denominator of 1.* — $-7 = \frac{-7}{1}$

Personal Math Trainer
Online Practice and Help
my.hrw.com

YOUR TURN

Write each rational number as $\frac{a}{b}$.

3. −15 ________________

4. 0.31 ________________

5. $4\frac{5}{9}$ ________________

6. 62 ________________

Classifying Rational Numbers

A **Venn diagram** is a visual representation used to show the relationships between groups. The Venn diagram below shows how rational numbers, integers, and whole numbers are related.

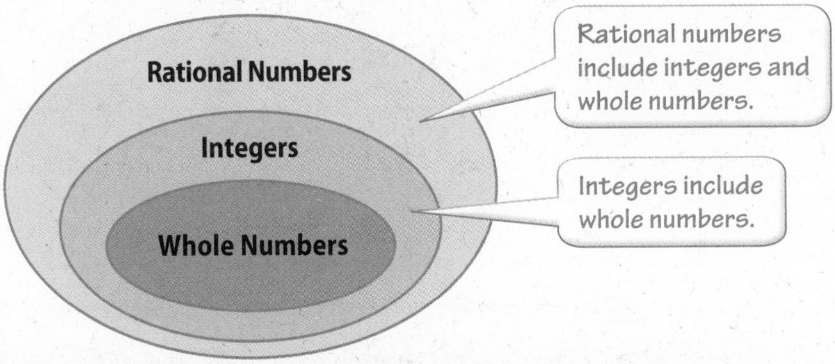

Math On the Spot
my.hrw.com

EXAMPLE 2

CA CC 6.NS.6

Place each number in the Venn diagram. Then classify each number by indicating in which set or sets each number belongs.

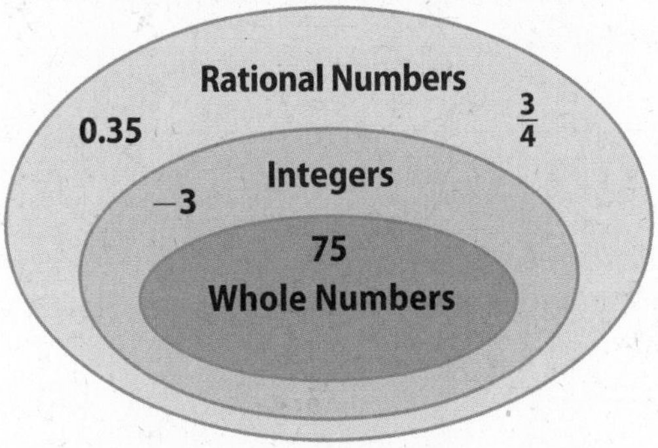

A 75 — The number 75 belongs in the sets of whole numbers, integers, and rational numbers.

B −3 — The number −3 belongs in the sets of integers and rational numbers.

C $\frac{3}{4}$ — The number $\frac{3}{4}$ belongs in the set of rational numbers.

D 0.35 — The number 0.35 belongs in the set of rational numbers.

Reflect

7. Analyze Relationships Describe how the Venn diagram models the relationship between rational numbers, integers, and whole numbers.

____

____

____

____

My Notes

Personal Math Trainer

Online Practice and Help

my.hrw.com

YOUR TURN

Place each number in the Venn diagram. Then classify each number by indicating in which set or sets it belongs.

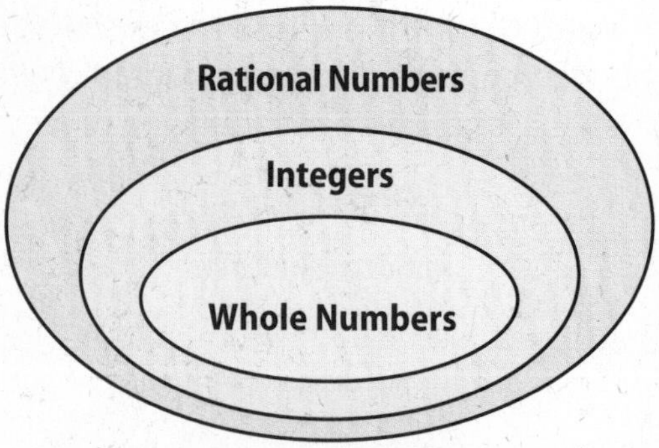

8. 14.1 ______________________

9. $7\frac{1}{5}$ ______________________

10. −8 ______________________

11. 101 ______________________________________

Guided Practice

1. Sarah and four friends are decorating picture frames with ribbon. They have 4 rolls of ribbon to share evenly. (Explore Activity 1)

a. How does this situation represent division?

____

b. How much ribbon does each person receive? ______________

Write each rational number in the form $\frac{a}{b}$, where a and b are integers. (Example 1)

2. 0.7 __________ **3.** −29 __________ **4.** $8\frac{1}{3}$ __________

Place each number in the Venn diagram. Then classify each number by indicating in which set or sets each number belongs. (Example 2)

5. −15 ______________________

6. $5\frac{10}{11}$ ______________________

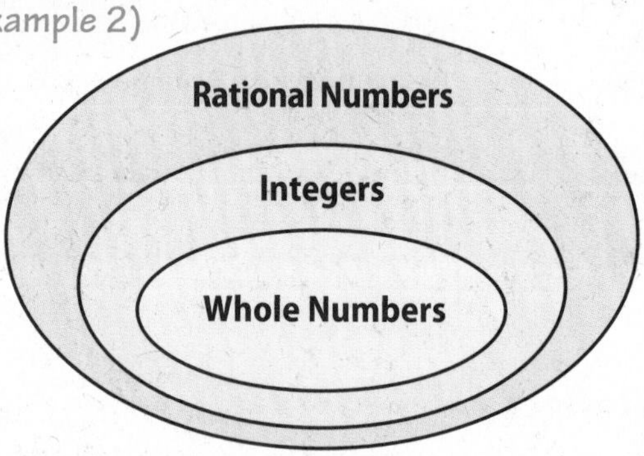

ESSENTIAL QUESTION CHECK-IN

7. How is a rational number that is not an integer different from a rational number that is an integer?

____

____

____

Name ____________________ Class ____________ Date ____________

3.1 Independent Practice

CA CC 6.NS.6

Personal Math Trainer
my.hrw.com
Online Practice and Help

List two numbers that fit each description. Then write the numbers in the appropriate location on the Venn diagram.

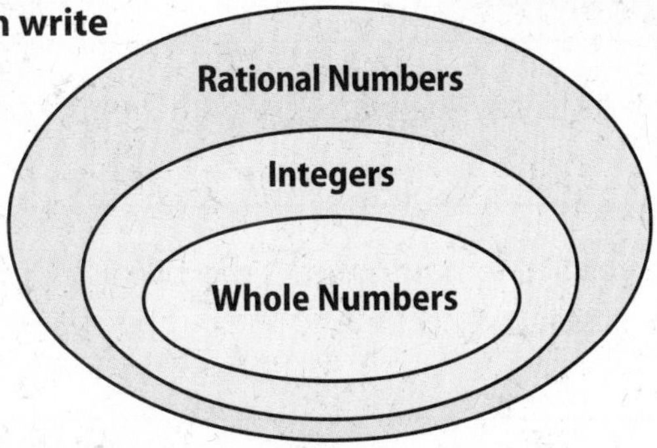

8. Integers that are not whole numbers

____

9. Rational numbers that are not integers

____

10. **Multistep** A nature club is having its weekly hike. The table shows how many pieces of fruit and bottles of water each member of the club brought to share.

Member	Pieces of Fruit	Bottles of Water
Baxter	3	5
Hendrick	2	2
Mary	4	3
Kendra	5	7

a. If the hikers want to share the fruit evenly, how many pieces should each person receive?

____

b. Which hikers received more fruit than they brought on the hike?

____

c. The hikers want to share their water evenly so that each member has the same amount. How much water does each hiker receive?

____

11. Sherman has 3 cats and 2 dogs. He wants to buy a toy for each of his pets. Sherman has $22 to spend on pet toys. How much can he spend on each pet? Write your answer as a fraction and as an amount in dollars and cents.

____

12. A group of 5 friends are sharing 2 pounds of trail mix. Write a division problem and a fraction to represent this situation.

____

13. **Vocabulary** A ________ diagram can represent set relationships visually.

Financial Literacy For 14–16, use the table. The table shows Jason's utility bills for one month. Write a fraction to represent the division in each situation. Then classify each result by indicating the set or sets to which it belongs.

March Bills	
Water	\$35
Gas	\$14
Electric	\$108

14. Jason and his 3 roommates share the cost of the electric bill evenly.

____

15. Jason plans to pay the water bill with 2 equal payments.

____

16. Jason owes \$15 for last month's gas bill also. The total amount of the two gas bills is split evenly among the 4 roommates.

____

17. Lynn has a watering can that holds 16 cups of water, and she fills it half full. Then she waters her 15 plants so that each plant gets the same amount of water. How many cups of water will each plant get?

____

H.O.T. FOCUS ON HIGHER ORDER THINKING

Work Area

18. Critique Reasoning DaMarcus says the number $\frac{24}{6}$ belongs only to the set of rational numbers. Explain his error.

____

____

____

____

19. Analyze Relationships Explain how the Venn diagrams in this lesson show that all integers and all whole numbers are rational numbers.

____

____

____

____

20. Critical Thinking Is it possible for a number to be a rational number that is not an integer but is a whole number? Explain.

____

____

LESSON 3.2

Identifying Opposites and Absolute Value of Rational Numbers

CA CC 6.NS.6c

Find and position integers and other rational numbers on a horizontal or vertical number line diagram; find and position pairs of integers and other rational numbers on a coordinate plane. *Also 6.NS.6, 6.NS.6a, 6.NS.7, 6.NS.7c*

ESSENTIAL QUESTION

How do you identify opposites and absolute value of rational numbers?

EXPLORE ACTIVITY Real World

CA CC 6.NS.6, 6.NS.6c

Positive and Negative Rational Numbers

All rational numbers can be represented as points on a number line. Positive rational numbers are greater than 0. They are located to the right of 0 on a number line. Negative rational numbers are less than 0. They are located to the left of 0 on a number line.

Water levels with respect to sea level, which has elevation 0, may be measured at beach tidal basins. Water levels below sea level are represented by negative numbers.

A The table shows the water level at a tidal basin at different times during a day. Graph the level for each time on the number line.

Time	4 A.M. *A*	8 A.M. *B*	Noon *C*	4 P.M. *D*	8 P.M. *E*
Level (ft)	3.5	2.5	−0.5	−2.5	0.5

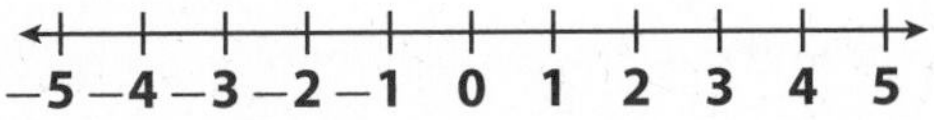

B How did you know where to graph −0.5? ______________________

C At what time or times is the level closest to sea level? How do you know?

____

D Which point is located halfway between −3 and −2? ______________

E Which point is the same distance from 0 as *D*? ______________

Reflect

1. **Communicate Mathematical Ideas** How would you graph −2.25? Would it be left or right of point *D*?

____

Rational Numbers and Opposites on a Number Line

Math On the Spot
my.hrw.com

You can find the opposites of rational numbers that are not integers the same way you found the opposites of integers. Two rational numbers are opposites if they are the same distance from 0 but on different sides of 0.

$2\frac{3}{4}$ and $-2\frac{3}{4}$ are opposites.

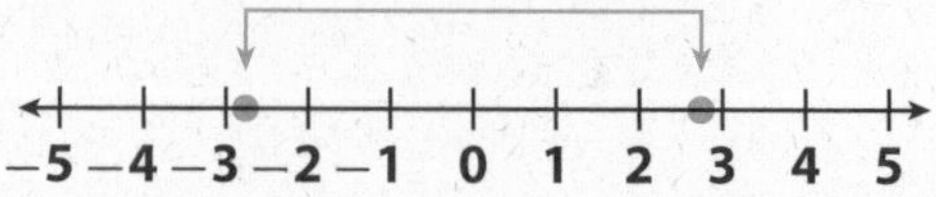

EXAMPLE 1 Real World

CA CC 6.NS.6a, 6.NS.6c

Until June 24, 1997, the New York Stock Exchange priced the value of a share of stock in eighths, such as $\$27\frac{1}{8}$ or at $\$41\frac{3}{4}$. The change in value of a share of stock from day to day was also represented in eighths as a positive or negative number.

The table shows the change in value of a stock over two days. Graph the change in stock value for Wednesday and its opposite on a number line.

Day	Tuesday	Wednesday
Change in value ($)	$1\frac{5}{8}$	$-4\frac{1}{4}$

STEP 1 Graph the change in stock value for Wednesday on the number line.

The change in value for Wednesday is $-4\frac{1}{4}$.

Graph a point $4\frac{1}{4}$ units below 0.

STEP 2 Graph the opposite of $-4\frac{1}{4}$.

The opposite of $-4\frac{1}{4}$ is the same distance from 0 but on the other side of 0.

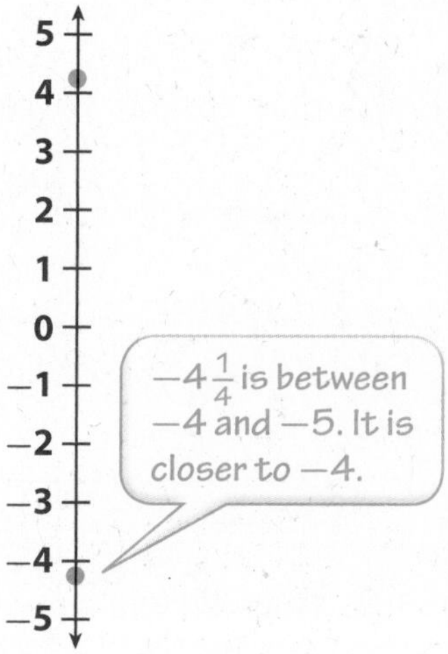

The opposite of $-4\frac{1}{4}$ is $4\frac{1}{4}$.

The opposite of the change in stock value for Wednesday is $4\frac{1}{4}$.

YOUR TURN

Personal Math Trainer
Online Practice and Help
my.hrw.com

2. What are the opposites of 7, –3.5, 2.25, and $9\frac{1}{3}$?

Absolute Values of Rational Numbers

You can find the absolute value of a rational number that is not an integer the same way you found the absolute value of an integer. The absolute value of a rational number is the number's distance from 0 on the number line.

Math On the Spot
my.hrw.com

EXAMPLE 2 Real World

CA CC 6.NS.7, 6.NS.7c

The table shows the average low temperatures in January in one location during a five-year span. Find the absolute value of the average January low temperature in 2009.

Year	2008	2009	2010	2011	2012
Temperature (°C)	−3.2	−5.4	−0.8	3.8	−2

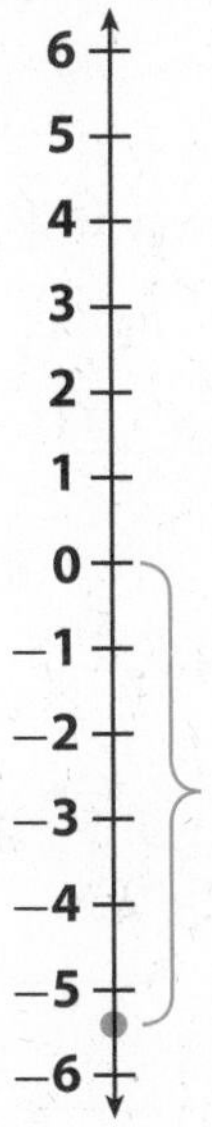

STEP 1 Graph the 2009 average January low temperature.

The 2009 average January low is −5.4 °C.
Graph a point 5.4 units below 0.

STEP 2 Find the absolute value of −5.4.

−5.4 is 5.4 units from 0.

$|-5.4| = 5.4$

My Notes

Reflect

3. **Communicate Mathematical Ideas** What is the absolute value of the average January low temperature in 2011? How do you know?

____

____

Math Talk
Mathematical Practices
How do you know where to graph −5.4?

YOUR TURN

Graph each number on the number line. Then use your number line to find each absolute value.

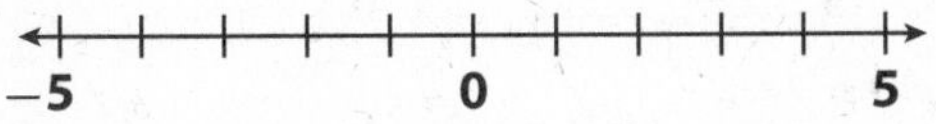

4. -4.5; $|-4.5| =$ ____________

5. $1\frac{1}{2}$; $\left|1\frac{1}{2}\right| =$ ____________

6. 4; $|4| =$ ____________

7. $-3\frac{1}{4}$; $\left|-3\frac{1}{4}\right| =$ ____________

Personal Math Trainer
Online Practice and Help
my.hrw.com

Guided Practice

Graph each number and its opposite on a number line. (Explore Activity and Example 1)

1. -2.8

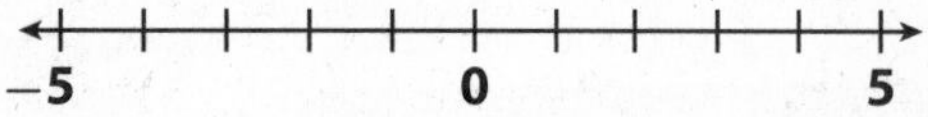

2. 4.3

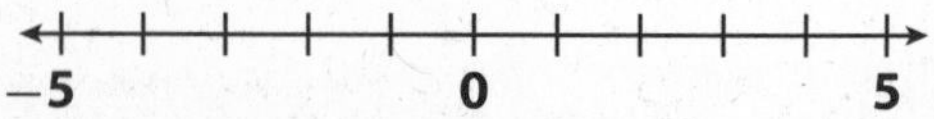

3. $-3\frac{4}{5}$

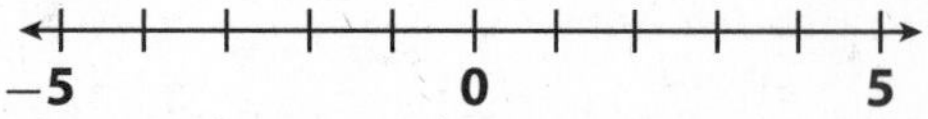

4. $1\frac{1}{3}$

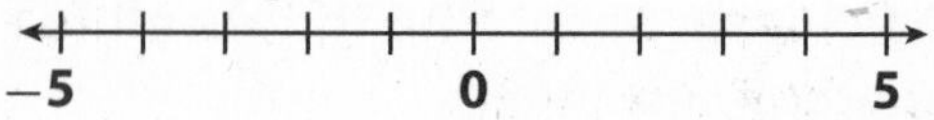

Find the opposite of each number. (Example 1)

5. 3.78 ________________

6. $-7\frac{5}{12}$ ________________

7. 0 ________________

8. 4.2 ________________

9. 12.1 ________________

10. 2.6 ________________

11. Vocabulary Explain why 2.15 and -2.15 are opposites. (Example 1)

____

____

Find the absolute value of each number. (Example 2)

12. 5.23 ________________

13. $-4\frac{2}{11}$ ________________

14. 0 ________________

15. $-6\frac{3}{5}$ ________________

16. -2.12 ________________

17. 8.2 ________________

ESSENTIAL QUESTION CHECK-IN

18. Use absolute value to write a definition of the opposite of a nonzero rational number. Give an example.

____

____

____

____

____

____

Name ______________________ Class ______________________ Date ______________________

3.2 Independent Practice

CA CC 6.NS.6, 6.NS.6a, 6.NS.6c, 6.NS.7, 6.NS.7c

Personal Math Trainer

Online Practice and Help

my.hrw.com

19. Financial Literacy A store's balance sheet represents the amounts customers owe as negative numbers and credits to customers as positive numbers.

Customer	Girardi	Lewis	Stein	Yuan	Wenner
Balance ($)	−85.23	20.44	−116.33	13.50	−9.85

a. Write the opposite of each customer's balance.

____

____

b. Mr. Yuan wants to use his credit to pay off the full amount that another customer owes. Which customer's balance does Mr. Yuan have enough money to pay off? ______________________

c. Which customer's balance would be farthest from 0 on a number line? Explain.

____

____

20. Multistep Trina went scuba diving and reached an elevation of −85.6 meters, which is below sea level. Jessie went hang-gliding and reached an altitude of 87.9 meters, which is above sea level.

a. Who is closer to the surface of the ocean? Explain.

____

b. Trina wants to hang-glide at the same number of meters above sea level as she scuba-dived below sea level. Will she fly higher than Jessie did? Explain.

____

____

21. Critical Thinking Carlos finds the absolute value of −5.3, and then finds the opposite of his answer. Jason finds the opposite of −5.3, and then finds the absolute value of his answer. Whose final value is greater? Explain.

____

____

____

22. Explain the Error Two students are playing a math game. The object of the game is to make the least possible number by arranging given digits inside absolute value bars on a card. In the first round, each player will use the digits 3, 5, and 7.

| − 7 5 . 3 |

a. One student arranges the numbers on the card as shown. What was this student's mistake?

b. What is the least possible number the card can show? ____________

H.O.T. FOCUS ON HIGHER ORDER THINKING

Work Area

23. Analyze Relationships If you plot the point −8.85 on a number line, would you place it to the left or right of −8.8? Explain.

24. Make a Conjecture If the absolute value of a negative number is 2.78, what is the distance on the number line between the number and its absolute value? Explain your answer.

25. Multiple Representations The deepest point in the Indian Ocean is the Java Trench, which is 25,344 feet below sea level. Elevations below sea level are represented by negative numbers.

a. Write the elevation of the Java Trench. ____________

b. A mile is 5,280 feet. Between which two integers is the elevation in miles? ____________

c. Graph the elevation of the Java Trench in miles.

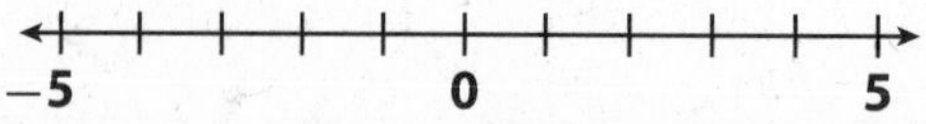

26. Draw Conclusions A number and its absolute value are equal. If you subtract 2 from the number, the new number and its absolute value are not equal. What do you know about the number? What is a possible number that satisfies these conditions?

LESSON 3.3

Comparing and Ordering Rational Numbers

CA CC 6.NS.7a

Interpret statements of inequality as statements about the relative position of two numbers on a number line diagram. *Also 6.NS.7, 6.NS.7b*

ESSENTIAL QUESTION

How do you compare and order rational numbers?

EXPLORE ACTIVITY CA CC Prep for 6.NS.7a

Equivalent Fractions and Decimals

Fractions and decimals that represent the same value are *equivalent*. The number line shows some equivalent fractions and decimals from 0 to 1.

A Complete the number line by writing the missing decimals or fractions.

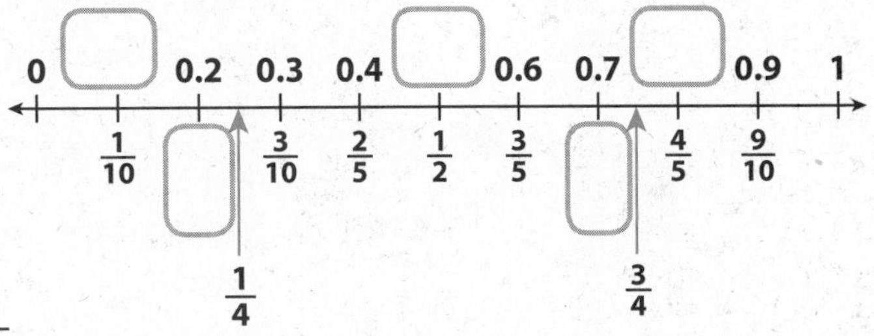

B Use the number line to find a fraction that is equivalent to 0.25. Explain.

____

____

C Explain how to find a decimal equivalent to $1\frac{7}{10}$.

____

____

D Use the number line to complete each statement.

0.2 = ______ ______ $= \frac{3}{10}$ 0.75 = ______ 1.25 = ______

Reflect

1. **Communicate Mathematical Ideas** How does a number line represent equivalent fractions and decimals?

____

____

2. Name a decimal between 0.4 and 0.5.

____

Math On the Spot
my.hrw.com

Ordering Fractions and Decimals

You can order fractions and decimals by rewriting the fractions as equivalent decimals or by rewriting the decimals as equivalent fractions.

EXAMPLE 1

CA CC 6.NS.7, 6.NS.7a

Animated Math
my.hrw.com

A Order 0.2, $\frac{3}{4}$, 0.8, $\frac{1}{2}$, $\frac{1}{4}$, and 0.4 from least to greatest.

STEP 1 Write the fractions as equivalent decimals.

$\frac{1}{4} = 0.25$ $\frac{1}{2} = 0.5$ $\frac{3}{4} = 0.75$

STEP 2 Use the number line to write the decimals in order.

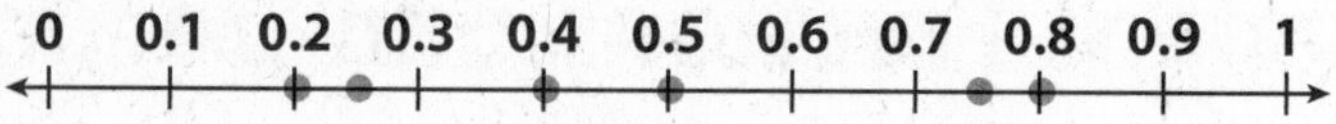

$0.2 < 0.25 < 0.4 < 0.5 < 0.75 < 0.8$

The numbers from least to greatest are 0.2, $\frac{1}{4}$, 0.4, $\frac{1}{2}$, $\frac{3}{4}$, 0.8.

B Order $\frac{1}{12}$, $\frac{2}{3}$, and 0.35 from least to greatest.

STEP 1 Write the decimal as an equivalent fraction.

$$0.35 = \frac{35}{100} = \frac{7}{20}$$

60 is a multiple of the denominators of all three fractions.

STEP 2 Find equivalent fractions with 60 as the common denominator.

$$\frac{1 \times 5}{12 \times 5} = \frac{5}{60} \qquad \frac{2 \times 20}{3 \times 20} = \frac{40}{60} \qquad \frac{7 \times 3}{20 \times 3} = \frac{21}{60}$$

STEP 3 Order fractions with common denominators by comparing the numerators.

$$5 < 21 < 40$$

The fractions in order from least to greatest are $\frac{5}{60}$, $\frac{21}{60}$, $\frac{40}{60}$.

The numbers in order from least to greatest are $\frac{1}{12}$, 0.35, and $\frac{2}{3}$.

Personal Math Trainer
Online Practice and Help
my.hrw.com

YOUR TURN

Order the fractions and decimals from least to greatest.

3. 0.85, $\frac{3}{5}$, 0.15, $\frac{7}{10}$ ________

Comparing and Ordering Rational Numbers

You can use a number line to compare and order positive and negative rational numbers.

Math On the Spot
my.hrw.com

EXAMPLE 2 Real World

CA CC 6.NS.7a, 6.NS.7b

Five friends completed a triathlon that included a 3-mile run, a 12-mile bike ride, and a $\frac{1}{2}$-mile swim. To compare their running times they created a table that shows the difference between each person's time and the average time, with negative numbers representing times less than the average.

Runner	John	Sue	Anna	Mike	Tom
Time above or below average (minutes)	$\frac{1}{2}$	1.4	$-1\frac{1}{4}$	−2.0	1.95

Use a number line to order the numbers from greatest to least.

STEP 1 Write the fractions as equivalent decimals.

$\frac{1}{2} = 0.5 \quad -1\frac{1}{4} = -1.25$

STEP 2 Use the number line to write the decimals in order.

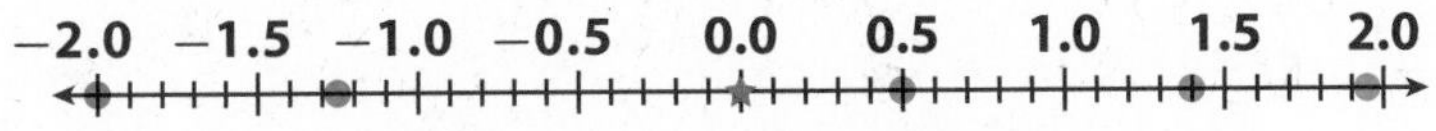

★Difference from Average Time

The numbers in order from greatest to least are 1.95, 1.4, $\frac{1}{2}$, $-1\frac{1}{4}$, −2.0.

Math Talk
Mathematical Practices
Who was the fastest runner? Explain.

Reflect

4. **Communicate Mathematical Ideas** Explain how you can use the number line to compare the rational numbers for Anna and Mike.

____

____

YOUR TURN

5. To compare their bike times, the friends created a table that shows the difference between each person's time and the average bike time. Order the bike times from least to greatest.

Biker	John	Sue	Anna	Mike	Tom
Time above or below average (minutes)	−1.8	1	$1\frac{2}{5}$	$1\frac{9}{10}$	−1.25

____

Personal Math Trainer
Online Practice and Help
my.hrw.com

Guided Practice

Find the equivalent fraction or decimal for each number. (Explore Activity 1)

1. $0.6 =$ ______ **2.** $\frac{1}{4} =$ ______ **3.** $0.9 =$ ______

4. $0.1 =$ ______ **5.** $\frac{3}{10} =$ ______ **6.** $1.4 =$ ______

7. $\frac{4}{5} =$ ______ **8.** $0.4 =$ ______ **9.** $\frac{6}{8} =$ ______

Use the number line to order the rational numbers from least to greatest. (Example 1)

10. $0.75, \frac{1}{2}, 0.4,$ and $\frac{1}{5}$

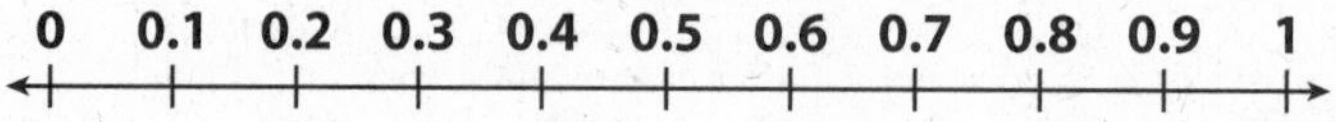

______

11. The table shows the lengths of fish caught by three friends at the lake last weekend. Write the lengths in order from greatest to least. (Example 1)

Lengths of Fish (cm)		
Emma	**Anne**	**Emily**
12.7	$12\frac{3}{5}$	$12\frac{3}{4}$

______

List the rational numbers in order from least to greatest. (Example 1, Example 2)

12. $2.3, 2\frac{4}{5}, 2.6$

13. $0.5, \frac{3}{16}, 0.75, \frac{5}{48}$

14. $0.5, \frac{1}{5}, 0.35, \frac{12}{25}, \frac{4}{5}$

15. $\frac{3}{4}, -\frac{7}{10}, -\frac{3}{4}, \frac{8}{10}$

16. $-\frac{3}{8}, \frac{5}{16}, -0.65, \frac{2}{4}$

17. $-2.3, -2\frac{4}{5}, -2.6$

18. $-0.6, -\frac{5}{8}, -\frac{7}{12}$ -0.72

19. $1.45, 1\frac{1}{2}, 1\frac{1}{3}, 1.2$

20. $-0.3, 0.5, 0.55, -0.35$

ESSENTIAL QUESTION CHECK-IN

21. Identify a temperature colder than –7.2 °F. Write an inequality that relates the temperatures. Describe their positions on a horizontal number line.

______

Name ______________________ Class ______________ Date ______________

3.3 Independent Practice

CA CC 6.NS.7, 6.NS.7a, 6.NS.7b

Personal Math Trainer
Online Practice and Help
my.hrw.com

22. Rosa and Albert receive the same amount of allowance each week. The table shows what part of their allowance they each spent on video games and pizza one week.

	Video games	Pizza
Rosa	0.4	$\frac{2}{5}$
Albert	$\frac{1}{2}$	0.25

a. Who spent more of their allowance on video games? Write an inequality to compare the portion spent on video games.

____

b. Who spent more of their allowance on pizza? Write an inequality to compare the portion spent on pizza.

____

c. **Draw Conclusions** Who spent the greater part of their total allowance? How do you know?

____

____

23. A group of friends is collecting aluminum for a recycling drive. Each person who donates at least 4.25 pounds of aluminum receives a free movie coupon. The weight of each person's donation is shown in the table.

	Brenda	Claire	Jim	Micah	Peter
Weight (lb)	4.3	5.5	$6\frac{1}{6}$	$\frac{15}{4}$	$4\frac{3}{8}$

a. Order the weights of the donations from greatest to least.

____

b. Which of the friends will receive a free movie coupon? Which will not?

____

c. **What If?** Would the person with the smallest donation win a movie coupon if he or she had collected $\frac{1}{2}$ pound more of aluminum? Explain.

____

____

____

24. The table shows how the birth weights of five kittens compare to the average birth weight of a kitten. A negative number represents a weight that is below the average.

Kitten	A	B	C	D	E
Weight above or below average (ounces)	-0.75	$1\frac{7}{8}$	3.1	$-1\frac{1}{8}$	$2\frac{1}{2}$

a. Order the numbers in the table from least to greatest.

____

b. Which kitten weighed the least? ______________________________

c. **Critical Thinking** Which kitten's birth weight differed the most from the average?

____

H.O.T. FOCUS ON HIGHER ORDER THINKING

Work Area

25. **Communicate Mathematical Ideas** Explain how you would order from least to greatest three numbers that include a positive number, a negative number, and zero.

____

____

____

26. **Analyze Relationships** Luke and Lena's parents allow them to borrow against their allowances. The inequality $-\$11.50 < -\$10.75$ compares the current balances they have with their parents. Luke has a greater debt with his parents than Lena has. How much does Luke owe his parents? Explain.

____

____

27. **Communicate Mathematical Ideas** If you know the order from least to greatest of 5 negative rational numbers, how can you use that information to order the absolute values of those numbers from least to greatest? Explain.

____

____

____

____

____

MODULE QUIZ

Ready to Go On?

Personal Math Trainer
Online Practice and Help
my.hrw.com

3.1 Classifying Rational Numbers

1. Five friends divide three bags of apples equally between them. Write the division represented in this situation as a fraction. ____________

Write each rational number in the form $\frac{a}{b}$, where a and b are integers.

2. $5\frac{1}{6}$ ____________ **3.** -12 ____________

Determine if each number is a whole number, integer, or rational number. Include all sets to which each number belongs.

4. -12 ____________

5. $\frac{7}{8}$ ____________

3.2 Identifying Opposites and Absolute Value of Rational Numbers

6. Graph -3, $1\frac{3}{4}$, -0.5, and 3 on the number line.

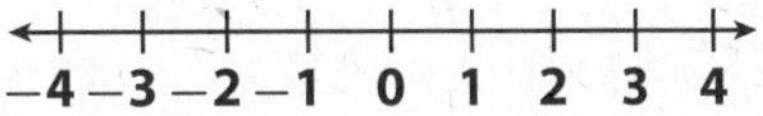

7. Find the opposites of $\frac{1}{3}$ and $-\frac{7}{12}$. ____________

8. Find the absolute values of 9.8 and $-\frac{10}{3}$. ____________

3.3 Comparing and Ordering Rational Numbers

9. Over the last week, the daily low temperatures in degrees Fahrenheit have been -4, 6.2, $18\frac{1}{2}$, -5.9, 21, $-\frac{1}{4}$, and 1.75. List these numbers in order from greatest to least.

____

ESSENTIAL QUESTION

10. How can you order rational numbers from least to greatest?

____

____

CALIFORNIA

MODULE 3
MIXED REVIEW

Assessment Readiness

Personal Math Trainer
Online Practice and Help
my.hrw.com

1. Ms. Fortes asked her class to place sets of rational numbers in order.

Select Yes or No if the numbers are in order from least to greatest.

A. $-\frac{1}{5}, -\frac{2}{3}, 2, 0.4$ ○ Yes ○ No
B. $-\frac{1}{3}, -0.25, 0.2, 1$ ○ Yes ○ No
C. $-0.5, |-1|, 1.5, 5.0$ ○ Yes ○ No

2. The following statements are about rational numbers.

Choose True or False for each statement.

A. The opposite of a rational number is always negative. ○ True ○ False
B. The opposite of the opposite of a rational number is always the number itself. ○ True ○ False
C. The absolute value of a number is sometimes equal to the number itself. ○ True ○ False

3. Kaia rewrote the sum $96 + 12$ as $12(8 + 1)$. She used the same method to rewrite the sum $95 + 15$ as $5(19 + 3)$. Describe her method and tell whether she can use it to rewrite the sum $38 + 11$. Explain.

4. The temperature at which water freezes is 0 °C, but water with salt has a lower freezing temperature. Liz measured the temperature of several samples of water with salt. Explain how Liz can use a number line to tell which sample is coldest and which is warmest. Which sample's temperature is closest to the freezing temperature for water?

Sample	A	B	C	D
Temperature (°C)	1.2	−1.1	−0.1	0.5

UNIT 1
Study Guide Review

MODULE 1 Integers

Key Vocabulary
absolute value *(valor absoluto)*
inequality *(desigualdad)*
integers *(enteros)*
negative numbers *(números negativos)*
opposites *(opuestos)*
positive numbers *(números positivos)*

ESSENTIAL QUESTION

How can you use integers to solve real-world problems?

EXAMPLE 1

James recorded the temperature at noon in Fairbanks, Alaska, over a week in January.

Day	Mon	Tues	Wed	Thurs	Fri
Temperature	3	2	7	−3	−1

Graph the temperatures on the number line, and then list the numbers in order from least to greatest.

Graph the temperatures on the number line.

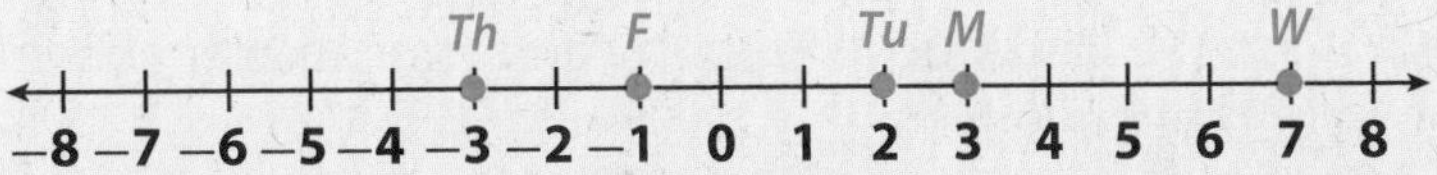

Read from left to right to list the temperatures in order from least to greatest.

The temperatures listed from least to greatest are −3, −1, 2, 3, 7.

EXAMPLE 2

Graph −4, 0, 2, and −1 on the number line. Then use the number line to find each absolute value.

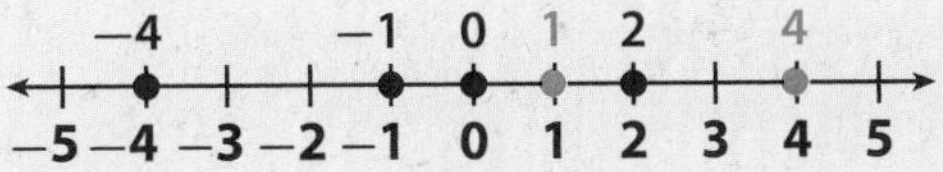

A number and its opposite are the same distance from 0 on the number line. The absolute value of a negative number is its opposite.

$|-4| = 4$ $\quad |0| = 0$ $\quad |2| = 2$ $\quad |-1| = 1$

EXERCISES

1. Graph 7, −2, 5, 1, and −1 on the number line. (Lesson 1.1)

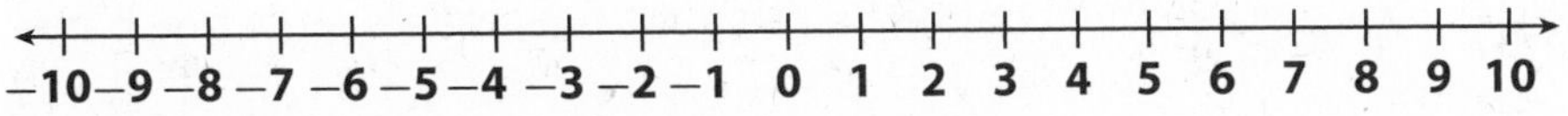

List the numbers from least to greatest. (Lesson 1.2)

2. 4, 0, −2, 3 ______________

3. −3, −5, 2, −2 ______________

Compare using < or >. (Lesson 1.2)

4. 4 ◯ 1 **5.** −2 ◯ 2 **6.** −3 ◯ −5 **7.** −7 ◯ 2

Find the opposite and absolute value of each number. (Lessons 1.1, 1.3)

8. 6 ______________

9. −2 ______________

MODULE 2

Factors and Multiples

Key Vocabulary

greatest common factor (GCF) *(máximo común divisor (MCD))*

least common multiple (LCM) *(mínimo común múltiplo (mcm))*

ESSENTIAL QUESTION

How do you find and use the greatest common factor of two whole numbers? How do you find and use the least common multiple of two numbers?

EXAMPLE 1

Use the Distributive Property to rewrite 32 + 24 as a product of their greatest common factor and another number.

A. List the factors of 24 and 32. Circle the common factors.

24: (1) (2) 3 (4) 6 (8) 12 24

32: (1) (2) (4) (8) 16 32

B. Rewrite each number as a product of the GCF and another number.

24: 8×3 **32:** 8×4

C. Use the Distributive Property and your answer above to rewrite 32 + 24 using the GCF and another number.

$32 + 24 = 8 \times 3 + 8 \times 4$

$32 + 24 = 8 \times (3 + 4)$

$32 + 24 = 8 \times 7$

EXAMPLE 2

On Saturday, every 8th customer at Adam's Bagels will get a free coffee. Every 12th customer will get a free bagel. Which customer will be the first to get a free coffee and a free bagel?

A. List the multiples of 8 and 12. Circle the common multiples.

8: 8 16 (24) 32 40 (48)

12: 12 (24) 36 (48)

B. Find the LCM of 8 and 12.

The LCM is 24. The 24th customer will be the first to get a free coffee and a free bagel.

EXERCISES

1. Find the GCF of 49 and 63 (Lesson 2.1) ________

Rewrite each sum as a product of the GCF of the addends and another number. (Lesson 2.1)

2. $15 + 45 =$ ________ **3.** $9 + 27 =$ ________

4. Find the LCM of 9 and 6 (Lesson 2.2) ________

MODULE 3 # Rational Numbers

Key Vocabulary

rational number *(número racional)*

Venn diagram *(diagrama de Venn)*

ESSENTIAL QUESTION

How can you use rational numbers to solve real-world problems?

EXAMPLE 1

Use the Venn diagram to determine in which set or sets each number belongs.

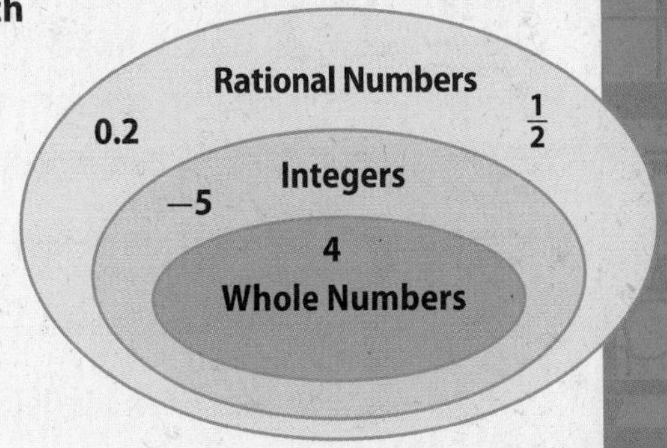

A. $\frac{1}{2}$ belongs in the set of rational numbers.

B. -5 belongs in the sets of integers and rational numbers.

C. 4 belongs in the sets of whole numbers, integers, and rational numbers.

D. 0.2 belongs in the set of rational numbers.

EXAMPLE 2

Order $\frac{2}{5}$, 0.2, and $\frac{4}{15}$ from greatest to least.

Write the decimal as an equivalent fraction. $0.2 = \frac{2}{10} = \frac{1}{5}$

Find equivalent fractions with 15 as the common denominator. $\frac{2 \times 3}{5 \times 3} = \frac{6}{15}$ $\frac{1 \times 3}{5 \times 3} = \frac{3}{15}$ $\frac{4}{15} = \frac{4}{15}$

Order fractions with common denominators by comparing the numerators. $6 > 4 > 3$ $\frac{6}{15} > \frac{4}{15} > \frac{3}{15}$

The numbers in order from greatest to least are, $\frac{2}{5}$, $\frac{4}{15}$, and 0.2.

EXERCISES

Classify each number by indicating in which set or sets it belongs. (Lesson 3.1)

1. 8 ______

2. 0.25 ______

Find the absolute value of each rational number. (Lesson 3.2)

3. $|3.7|$ ______ **4.** $\left|-\frac{2}{3}\right|$ ______

Graph each set of numbers on the number line and order the numbers from greatest to least. (Lesson 3.1, 3.3)

5. $-0.5, -1, -\frac{1}{4}, 0$

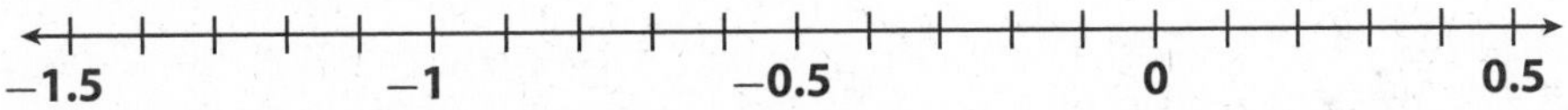

______

Unit Project

CA CC 6.NS.4

Euclid's Method

The Greek mathematician Euclid lived more than 2,000 years ago. He created a method for finding the greatest common factor of two numbers. Euclid's method for finding the GCF of 156 and 60 is shown below. No description of the steps is given, but the colors of the numbers should help you understand the method.

- 156 ÷ **60** = 2, with a remainder of **36**.
- **60** ÷ **36** = 1, with a remainder of **24**.
- **36** ÷ **24** = 1, with a remainder of **12**.
- **24** ÷ **12** = 2, with a remainder of 0.

The last divisor is 12, so the GCF of 156 and 60 is 12.

For this project, create a presentation that includes

(1) a description of how to use Euclid's method to find the GCF of two numbers;

(2) a demonstration showing how to use the method to find the GCF of 546 and 238; and

(3) a brief report explaining why Euclid is called the "Father of Geometry."
Use the space below to write down any questions you have or important information from your teacher.

MATH IN CAREERS | **ACTIVITY**

Climatologist Each year a tree is alive, it adds a layer of growth, called a tree ring, between its core and its bark. The table shows the measurements taken by a climatologist of the width of tree rings of a particular tree for different years. List the years in order of increasing ring width. Which year was the hottest? How do you know? Which year was the coldest? How do you know?

Year	Width of ring (in mm)
1900	$\frac{14}{25}$
1910	$\frac{29}{50}$
1920	$\frac{53}{100}$
1930	$\frac{13}{20}$
1940	$\frac{3}{5}$

CALIFORNIA

UNIT 1
MIXED REVIEW

Assessment Readiness

Personal Math Trainer
Online Practice and Help
my.hrw.com

1. Select Yes or No to indicate whether the expressions are equal.

A. 65 and 6(10 + 5) ○ Yes ○ No

B. |3 − 8| and |3 + 8| ○ Yes ○ No

C. 14 and the opposite of −14 ○ Yes ○ No

2. The number line shows several points.

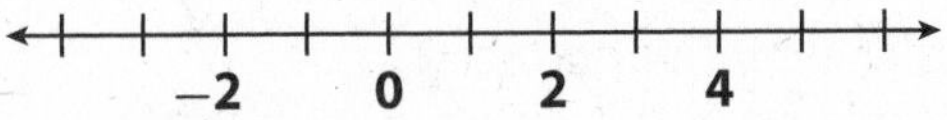

Choose True or False for each statement.

A. *C* is the opposite of *D*. ○ True ○ False

B. $A < B$ ○ True ○ False

C. *E* is between 4 and 5. ○ True ○ False

3. Melanie made 72 peanut butter cookies and 60 oatmeal cookies. She wants to make identical groups of cookies for her friends. Each group will be as large as possible, and she will use all of the cookies. How many cookies will each friend receive? Explain.

4. Dirk has a bank account for which he makes regular deposits and withdrawals. The numbers 134, 96, −40, −60, 119, and −100 represent last month's transactions. Order these numbers from least to greatest. Explain how you know which transactions represent withdrawals.

Performance Tasks

★**5.** A geometry class has a pizza party. There are 14 students that will have pizza. Each pizza has 8 slices. The teacher wants to buy the least number of pizzas so that there are the same number of slices for each student. How many pizzas should be purchased? Explain.

★★**6.** Tom, Mary, Hector, and Sue get the scores 2, −4, 3, and −2 playing a game. They forget their individual scores but do remember the following facts:

Tom's score was the opposite of Mary's.

Tom's score was greater than only Sue's score.

Determine each player's score. Describe your reasoning.

★★★**7.** The official run time of a movie is 140 minutes. Your friend who has seen the movie says, "It's about 2.3 hours."

a. Write the official run time in hours as a fraction and as a decimal.

b. Did your friend overestimate or underestimate the length of the movie? Illustrate your answer using two different comparisons. Which method did you prefer?

UNIT 2

Number Operations

MODULE 4

Operations with Fractions

CA CC 6.NS.1, 6.NS.4

MODULE 5

Operations with Decimals

CA CC 6.NS.2, 6.NS.3

MATH IN CAREERS

Chef The role of a chef is diverse and can include planning menus, overseeing food preparation, training staff, and ordering and purchasing food items. Chefs use mathematics when scaling recipes as well as in budgeting and financial planning.

If you are interested in a career as a chef, you should study these mathematical subjects:

- Basic Math
- Business Math

Research other careers that require the use of scaling quantities, and financial planning.

ACTIVITY At the end of the unit, check out how **chefs** use math.

Unit Project Preview

A Fine Kettle of Fish

To complete the Unit Project at the end of this unit, you will decide on the species and numbers of tropical fish you will buy to stock an aquarium. To do this, you must calculate the total length of the fish for which your aquarium can provide a safe and healthy home. To successfully complete the Unit Project you'll need to master these skills:

- Operate with fractions and mixed numbers.
- Operate with decimals.
- Convert between fractions and decimals.

1. Give some examples of how fractions might be used in this project.

____

2. Give some examples of how decimals might be used in this project.

____

3. The recommended total length of all the fish in one aquarium is 20 inches. Which would be a better choice, five 4-inch fish or one 20-inch fish? Why?

____

____

____

Tracking Your Learning Progression

This unit addresses important California Common Core Standards in the Critical Area of fraction and decimal operations.

Domain 6.NS The Number System

Cluster Apply and extend previous understandings of multiplication and division to divide fractions.

The unit also supports additional standards.

Domain 6.NS The Number System

Cluster Compute fluently with multi-digit numbers and find common factors and multiples.

Operations with Fractions

MODULE 4

CALIFORNIA

ESSENTIAL QUESTION

How can you use operations with fractions to solve real-world problems?

Real-World Video

my.hrw.com

To find your average rate of speed, divide the distance you traveled by the time you traveled. If you ride in a taxi and drive $\frac{1}{2}$ mile in $\frac{1}{4}$ hour, your rate was 2 mi/h which may mean you were in heavy traffic.

GO DIGITAL

my.hrw.com

my.hrw.com

Go digital with your write-in student edition, accessible on any device.

Math On the Spot

Scan with your smart phone to jump directly to the online edition, video tutor, and more.

Animated Math

Interactively explore key concepts to see how math works.

Personal Math Trainer

Get immediate feedback and help as you work through practice sets.

Are YOU Ready?

Complete these exercises to review skills you will need for this module.

Personal Math Trainer
Online Practice and Help
my.hrw.com

Write an Improper Fraction as a Mixed Number

EXAMPLE	$\frac{13}{5} = \frac{5}{5} + \frac{5}{5} + \frac{3}{5}$	Write as a sum using names for one plus a proper fraction.
	$= 1 + 1 + \frac{3}{5}$	Write each name for one as one.
	$= 2 + \frac{3}{5}$	Add the ones.
	$= 2\frac{3}{5}$	Write the mixed number.

Write each improper fraction as a mixed number.

1. $\frac{9}{4}$ ________ **2.** $\frac{8}{3}$ ________ **3.** $\frac{23}{6}$ ________ **4.** $\frac{11}{2}$ ________

5. $\frac{17}{5}$ ________ **6.** $\frac{15}{8}$ ________ **7.** $\frac{33}{10}$ ________ **8.** $\frac{29}{12}$ ________

Multiplication Facts

EXAMPLE $7 \times 6 = \blacksquare$

Use a related fact you know.
$6 \times 6 = 36$
Think: $7 \times 6 = (6 \times 6) + 6$
$= 36 + 6$
$= 42$

$7 \times 6 = 42$

Multiply.

9. 6×5 ______ **10.** 8×9 ______ **11.** 10×11 ______ **12.** 7×8 ______

13. 9×7 ______ **14.** 8×6 ______ **15.** 9×11 ______ **16.** 11×12 ______

Division Facts

EXAMPLE $63 \div 7 = \blacksquare$

Think: 7 times what number equals 63?
$7 \times 9 = 63$

$63 \div 7 = 9$ So, $63 \div 7 = 9$.

Divide.

17. $35 \div 7$ ______ **18.** $56 \div 8$ ______ **19.** $28 \div 7$ ______ **20.** $48 \div 8$ ______

21. $36 \div 4$ ______ **22.** $45 \div 9$ ______ **23.** $72 \div 8$ ______ **24.** $40 \div 5$ ______

Reading Start-Up

Visualize Vocabulary

Use the ✔ words to complete the triangle. Write the review word that fits the description in each section of the triangle.

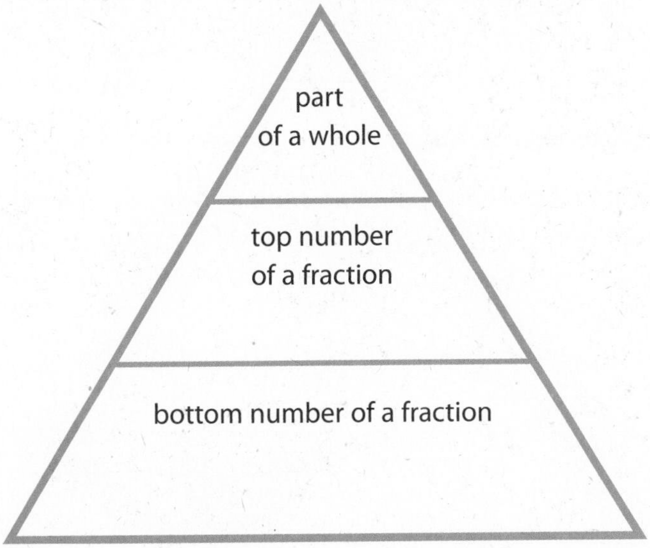

Vocabulary

Review Words

area *(área)*
✔ denominator *(denominador)*
✔ fraction *(fracción)*
greatest common factor (GCF) *(máximo común divisor (MCD))*
least common multiple (LCM) *(mínimo común múltiplo (m.c.m.))*
length *(longitud)*
✔ numerator *(numerador)*
product *(producto)*
width *(ancho)*

Preview Words

mixed number *(número mixto)*
order of operations *(orden de las operaciones)*
reciprocals *(recíprocos)*

Understand Vocabulary

In each grouping, select the choice that is described by the given vocabulary word.

1. reciprocals — Ⓐ 1:15 — Ⓑ $\frac{3}{4} \div \frac{1}{6}$ — Ⓒ $\frac{3}{5}$ and $\frac{5}{3}$

2. mixed number — Ⓐ $\frac{1}{3} - \frac{1}{5}$ — Ⓑ $3\frac{1}{2}$ — Ⓒ -5

3. order of operations — Ⓐ $5 - 3 + 2 = 0$ — Ⓑ $5 - 3 + 2 = 4$ — Ⓒ $5 - 3 + 2 = 6$

Active Reading

Layered Book Before beginning the module, create a layered book to help you learn the concepts in this module. Label each flap with lesson titles. As you study each lesson, write important ideas, such as vocabulary and processes, under the appropriate flap. Refer to your finished layered book as you work on exercises from this module.

GETTING READY FOR

Operations with Fractions

Understanding the standards and the vocabulary terms in the standards will help you know exactly what you are expected to learn in this module.

CA CC 6.NS.1

Interpret and compute quotients of fractions, and solve word problems involving division of fractions by fractions, e.g., by using visual fraction models and equations to represent the problem.

Key Vocabulary

quotient *(cociente)*
The result when one number is divided by another.

fraction *(fracción)*
A number in the form $\frac{a}{b}$, where $b \neq 0$.

What It Means to You

You will learn how to divide two fractions. You will also understand the relationship between multiplication and division.

EXAMPLE 6.NS.1

Zachary is making vegetable soup. The recipe makes $6\frac{3}{4}$ cups of soup. How many $1\frac{1}{2}$-cup servings will the recipe make?

$$6\frac{3}{4} \div 1\frac{1}{2}$$
$$= \frac{27}{4} \div \frac{3}{2}$$
$$= \frac{27}{4} \cdot \frac{2}{3}$$
$$= \frac{9}{2}$$
$$= 4\frac{1}{2}$$

The recipe will make $4\frac{1}{2}$ servings.

CA CC 6.NS.4

Find the greatest common factor of two whole numbers less than or equal to 100 and the least common multiple of two whole numbers less than or equal to 12. Use the distributive property to express a sum of two whole numbers 1–100 with a common factor as a multiple of a sum of two whole numbers with no common factor.

What It Means to You

You can use greatest common factors and least common multiples to simplify answers when you calculate with fractions.

EXAMPLE 6.NS.4

Add. Write the answer in simplest form.

$\frac{1}{3} + \frac{1}{6} = \frac{2}{6} + \frac{1}{6}$ Use the LCM of 3 and 6 as a common denominator.

$= \frac{2+1}{6}$ Add the numerators.

$= \frac{3}{6}$

$= \frac{3 \div 3}{6 \div 3}$ Simplify by dividing by the GCF. The GCF of 3 and 6 is 3.

$= \frac{1}{2}$ Write the answer in simplest form.

Visit **my.hrw.com** to see all **CA Common Core Standards** explained.

my.hrw.com

LESSON

4.1 Applying GCF and LCM to Fraction Operations

CA CC 6.NS.4

Find the greatest common factor of two whole numbers less than or equal to 100 and the least common multiple of two whole numbers less than or equal to 12. Use the distributive property to express a sum of two whole numbers 1–100 with a common factor as a multiple of a sum of two whole numbers with no common factor.

ESSENTIAL QUESTION

How do you use the GCF and LCM when adding, subtracting, and multiplying fractions?

Multiplying Fractions

To multiply two fractions you first multiply the numerators and then multiply the denominators.

$$\frac{\text{numerator} \times \text{numerator}}{\text{denominator} \times \text{denominator}} = \frac{\text{numerator}}{\text{denominator}}$$

The resulting product may need to be written in simplest form. To write a fraction in simplest form, you can divide both the numerator and the denominator by their greatest common factor.

Example 1 shows two methods for making sure that the product of two fractions is in simplest form.

Math On the Spot

my.hrw.com

EXAMPLE 1

CA CC 6.NS.4

Multiply. Write the product in simplest form.

A $\frac{1}{3} \times \frac{3}{5}$

$\frac{1}{3} \times \frac{3}{5} = \frac{1 \times 3}{3 \times 5}$ Write the problem as a single fraction.

$= \frac{3}{15}$ Multiply numerators. Multiply denominators.

$= \frac{3 \div 3}{15 \div 3}$ Simplify by dividing by the GCF. The GCF of 3 and 15 is 3.

$= \frac{1}{5}$ Write the answer in simplest form.

B $\frac{6}{7} \times \frac{2}{3}$

6 in the numerator and 3 in the denominator have a common factor other than one. Divide by the GCF 3.

$\frac{6}{7} \times \frac{2}{3} = \frac{6 \times 2}{7 \times 3}$ Write the problem as a single fraction.

$= \frac{{}^{2}\cancel{6} \times 2}{7 \times \cancel{3}_{1}}$ Simplify before multiplying using the GCF.

$= \frac{2 \times 2}{7 \times 1}$ Multiply numerators. Multiply denominators.

$= \frac{4}{7}$

Math Talk
Mathematical Practices

Compare the methods in the Example. How do you know if you can use the method in **B**?

Personal Math Trainer

Online Practice and Help

my.hrw.com

YOUR TURN

Multiply. Write each product in simplest form.

1. $\frac{1}{6} \times \frac{3}{5}$ ______

2. $\frac{3}{4} \times \frac{7}{9}$ ______

3. $\frac{3}{7} \times \frac{2}{3}$ ______

4. $\frac{4}{5} \times \frac{2}{7}$ ______

5. $\frac{7}{10} \times \frac{8}{21}$ ______

6. $\frac{6}{7} \times \frac{1}{6}$ ______

Math On the Spot

my.hrw.com

Multiplying Fractions and Whole Numbers

To multiply a fraction by a whole number, you can rewrite the whole number as a fraction and multiply the two fractions. Remember to use the GCF to write the product in simplest form.

EXAMPLE 2 Real World

CA CC 6.NS.4

A class has 18 students. The teacher asks how many students in the class have pets and finds $\frac{5}{9}$ of the students have pets. How many students have pets?

STEP 1 Estimate the product. Multiply the whole number by the nearest benchmark fraction.

$\frac{5}{9}$ is close to $\frac{1}{2}$, so multiply $\frac{1}{2}$ times 18.

$\frac{1}{2} \times 18 = 9$

STEP 2 Multiply. Write the product in simplest form.

$\frac{5}{9} \times 18$

You can write $\frac{5}{9}$ times 18 three ways.

$\frac{5}{9} \times 18 \quad \frac{5}{9} \cdot 18 \quad \frac{5}{9}(18)$

$\frac{5}{9} \times 18 = \frac{5}{9} \times \frac{18}{1}$ — Rewrite 18 as a fraction.

$= \frac{5 \times \cancel{18}^{2}}{{}_{1}\cancel{9} \times 1}$ — Simplify before multiplying using the GCF.

$= \frac{5 \times 2}{1 \times 1}$ — Multiply numerators. Multiply denominators.

$= \frac{10}{1} = 10$ — Simplify by writing as a whole number.

10 students have pets.

Math Talk Mathematical Practices

How can you check to see if the answer is correct?

Reflect

7. **Analyze Relationships** Is the product of a fraction less than 1 and a whole number greater than or less than the whole number? Explain.

____

____

YOUR TURN

Multiply. Write each product in simplest form.

8. $\frac{5}{8} \times 24$ ________

9. $\frac{3}{5} \times 20$ ________

10. $\frac{1}{3} \times 8$ ________

11. $\frac{1}{4} \times 14$ ________

12. $3\frac{7}{10} \times 7$ ________

13. $2\frac{3}{10} \times 10$ ________

Personal Math Trainer
Online Practice and Help
my.hrw.com

Adding and Subtracting Fractions

You have learned that to add or subtract two fractions, you can rewrite the fractions so they have the same denominator. You can use the least common multiple of the denominators of the fractions to rewrite the fractions.

Math On the Spot
my.hrw.com

EXAMPLE 3

CA CC 6.NS.4

Add $\frac{8}{15} + \frac{1}{6}$. Write the sum in simplest form.

STEP 1 Rewrite the fractions as equivalent fractions. Use the LCM of the denominators.

$\frac{8}{15} \rightarrow \frac{8 \times 2}{15 \times 2} \rightarrow \frac{16}{30}$ The LCM of 15 and 6 is 30.

$\frac{1}{6} \rightarrow \frac{1 \times 5}{6 \times 5} \rightarrow \frac{5}{30}$

STEP 2 Add the numerators of the equivalent fractions. Then simplify.

$\frac{16}{30} + \frac{5}{30} = \frac{21}{30}$

$= \frac{21 \div 3}{30 \div 3}$ Simplify by dividing by the GCF. The GCF of 21 and 30 is 3.

$= \frac{7}{10}$

Math Talk
Mathematical Practices
Can you use another common multiple of the denominators in Example 3 to find the sum? Explain.

Reflect

14. Can you also use the LCM of the denominators of the fractions to rewrite the difference $\frac{8}{15} - \frac{1}{6}$? What is the difference?

____

Personal Math Trainer
Online Practice and Help
my.hrw.com

YOUR TURN

Add or subtract. Write each sum or difference in simplest form.

15. $\frac{5}{14} + \frac{1}{6}$ ______

16. $\frac{5}{12} - \frac{3}{20}$ ______

17. $\frac{5}{12} - \frac{3}{8}$ ______

18. $1\frac{3}{10} + \frac{1}{4}$ ______

19. $\frac{2}{3} + 6\frac{1}{5}$ ______

20. $3\frac{1}{6} - \frac{1}{7}$ ______

Guided Practice

Multiply. Write each product in simplest form. (Example 1)

1. $\frac{1}{2} \times \frac{5}{8}$ ______

2. $\frac{3}{5} \times \frac{5}{9}$ ______

3. $\frac{3}{8} \times \frac{2}{5}$ ______

4. $2\frac{3}{8} \times 16$ ______

5. $1\frac{4}{5} \times \frac{5}{12}$ ______

6. $1\frac{2}{10} \times 5$ ______

Find each amount. (Example 2)

7. $\frac{1}{4}$ of 12 bottles of water = ______ bottles

8. $\frac{2}{3}$ of 24 bananas = ______ bananas

9. $\frac{3}{5}$ of \$40 restaurant bill = \$ ______

10. $\frac{5}{6}$ of 18 pencils = ______ pencils

Add or subtract. Write each sum or difference in simplest form.

11. $\frac{3}{8} + \frac{5}{24}$ ______

12. $\frac{1}{20} + \frac{5}{12}$ ______

13. $\frac{9}{20} - \frac{1}{4}$ ______

14. $\frac{9}{10} - \frac{3}{14}$ ______

15. $3\frac{3}{8} + \frac{5}{12}$ ______

16. $5\frac{7}{10} - \frac{5}{18}$ ______

ESSENTIAL QUESTION CHECK-IN

17. How can using the GCF and LCM help you when you add, subtract, and multiply fractions?

______

______

______

______

Name ____________ Class ____________ Date ____________

4.1 Independent Practice

CA CC 6.NS.4

Personal Math Trainer

my.hrw.com

Online Practice and Help

Solve. Write each answer in simplest form.

18. Erin buys a bag of peanuts that weighs $\frac{3}{4}$ of a pound. Later that week, the bag is $\frac{2}{3}$ full. How much does the bag of peanuts weigh now? Show your work.

19. **Multistep** Marianne buys 16 bags of potting soil that comes in $\frac{5}{8}$-pound bags.

a. How many pounds of potting soil does Marianne buy?

b. If Marianne's father calls and says he needs 13 pounds of potting soil, how many additional bags should she buy?

20. **Music** Two fifths of the instruments in the marching band are brass, one third are percussion, and the rest are woodwinds.

a. What fraction of the band is woodwinds?

b. One half of the woodwinds are clarinets. What fraction of the band is clarinets?

c. One eighth of the brass instruments are tubas. If there are 240 instruments in the band, how many are tubas?

21. Marcial found a recipe for fruit salad that he wanted to try to make for his birthday party. He decided to triple the recipe.

Fruit Salad

$3\frac{1}{2}$ cups thinly sliced rhubarb

15 seedless grapes, halved

$\frac{1}{2}$ orange, sectioned

10 fresh strawberries, halved

$\frac{3}{5}$ apple, cored and diced

$\frac{2}{3}$ peach, sliced

1 plum, pitted and sliced

$\frac{1}{4}$ cup fresh blueberries

a. What are the new amounts for the oranges, apples, blueberries, and peaches?

b. **Communicate Mathematical Ideas** The amount of rhubarb in the original recipe is $3\frac{1}{2}$ cups. Using what you know of whole numbers and what you know of fractions, explain how you could triple that mixed number.

22. One container holds $1\frac{7}{8}$ quarts of water and a second container holds $5\frac{3}{4}$ quarts of water. How many more quarts of water does the second container hold than the first container? ____________

23. Each of 15 students will give a $1\frac{1}{2}$-minute speech in English class.

a. How long will it take to give the speeches? ____________

b. Suppose the teacher begins recording on a digital camera with an hour available. Show that there is enough time to record everyone if she gives a 15-minute introduction at the beginning of class and every student takes a minute to get ready.

____

____

____

____

c. How much time is left on the digital camera? ____________

H.O.T. FOCUS ON HIGHER ORDER THINKING

24. **Represent Real-World Problems** Kate wants to buy a new bicycle from a sporting-goods store. The bicycle she wants normally sells for \$360. The store has a sale in which all bicycles cost $\frac{5}{6}$ of the regular price. What is the sale price of the bicycle? ____________

25. **Error Analysis** To find the product $\frac{3}{7} \times \frac{4}{9}$, Cameron found the GCF of 3 and 9. He then multiplied the fractions $\frac{1}{7}$ and $\frac{4}{9}$ to find the product $\frac{4}{63}$. What was Cameron's error?

____

____

____

____

Work Area

26. **Justify Reasoning** To multiply a whole number by a fraction, you can first write the whole number as a fraction with a denominator of 1. Explain why following this step does not change the product.

____

____

____

____

LESSON
4.2 Dividing Fractions

CA CC 6.NS.1

Interpret and compute quotients of fractions, and solve word problems involving division of fractions by fractions, e.g., by using visual fraction models and equations to represent the problem.

ESSENTIAL QUESTION

How do you divide fractions?

EXPLORE ACTIVITY 1 Real World

CA CC 6.NS.1

Modeling Fraction Division

For some real-world problems, you may need to divide a fraction by a fraction. For others, you may need to divide a fraction by a whole number.

A **You have $\frac{3}{4}$ cup of salsa for making burritos. Each burrito requires $\frac{1}{8}$ cup of salsa. How many burritos can you make?**

To find the number of burritos that can be made, you need to determine how many $\frac{1}{8}$-cup servings are in $\frac{3}{4}$ cup. In the diagram, $\frac{3}{4}$ of a whole is divided into quarters and into eighths. How many

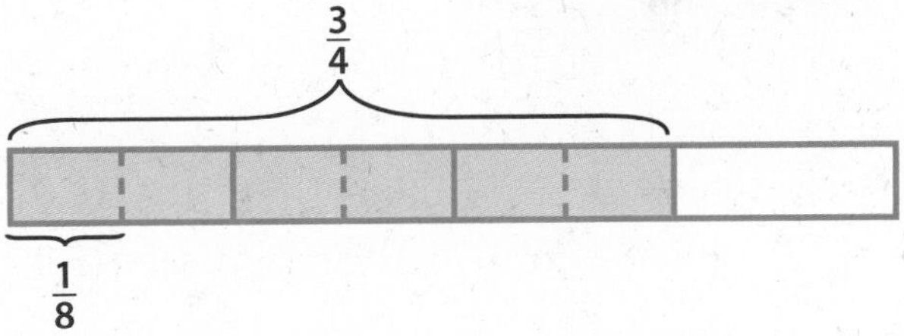

eighths are there in $\frac{3}{4}$? ______

You have enough salsa to make ______ burritos.

B **Five people share $\frac{1}{2}$ pound of cheese equally. How much cheese does each person receive?**

To find how much cheese each person receives, you can divide $\frac{1}{2}$ pound into 5 equal parts. Use the diagram to determine what fraction of a whole pound each person receives.

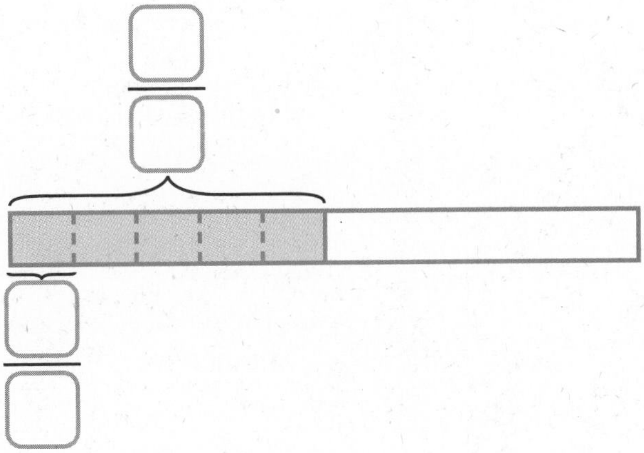

Each person receives ______ pound.

Reflect

1. Write the division shown by the models in **A** and **B**.

____

Math On the Spot
my.hrw.com

Reciprocals

Another way to divide fractions is to use *reciprocals*. Two numbers whose product is 1 are **reciprocals**.

$\frac{3}{4} \times \frac{4}{3} = \frac{12}{12} = 1$ $\frac{3}{4}$ and $\frac{4}{3}$ are reciprocals.

To find the reciprocal of a fraction, switch the numerator and denominator.

$$\frac{\text{numerator}}{\text{denominator}} \cdot \frac{\text{denominator}}{\text{numerator}} = 1$$

EXAMPLE 1

CA CC Prep for 6.NS.1

Find the reciprocal of each number.

A $\frac{2}{9} \rightarrow \frac{9}{2}$ Switch the numerator and denominator.

The reciprocal of $\frac{2}{9}$ is $\frac{9}{2}$.

B $\frac{1}{8} \rightarrow \frac{8}{1}$ Switch the numerator and denominator.

The reciprocal of $\frac{1}{8}$ is $\frac{8}{1}$, or 8.

C 5

$5 = \frac{5}{1}$ Rewrite as a fraction.

$\frac{5}{1} \rightarrow \frac{1}{5}$ Switch the numerator and the denominator.

The reciprocal of 5 is $\frac{1}{5}$.

Math Talk
Mathematical Practices
How can you check that the reciprocal in **A** is correct?

Reflect

2. Is any number its own reciprocal? If so, what number(s)? Justify your answer.

____

3. **Communicate Mathematical Ideas** Does every number have a reciprocal? Explain.

____

____

4. The reciprocal of a whole number is a fraction with ________ in the numerator.

YOUR TURN

Find the reciprocal of each number.

5. $\frac{7}{8}$ ____________ **6.** 9 ____________ **7.** $\frac{1}{11}$ ____________

Personal Math Trainer
Online Practice and Help
my.hrw.com

EXPLORE ACTIVITY 2 CA CC 6.NS.1

Using Reciprocals to Divide

A The diagram below models the division problem $5 \div \frac{5}{8}$.

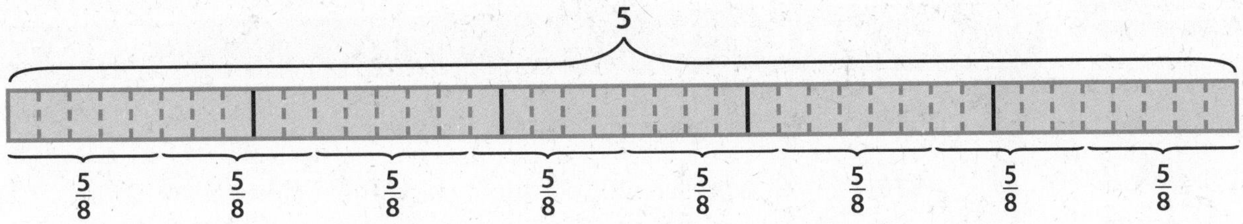

Each unit is divided into eighths. How many sections representing $\frac{5}{8}$ are

there in 5? ________ sections

$5 \div \frac{5}{8} =$ ________

B Use the diagrams to complete the division problems.

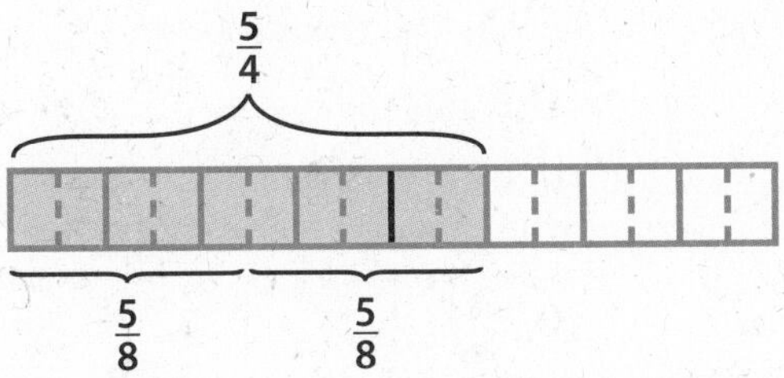

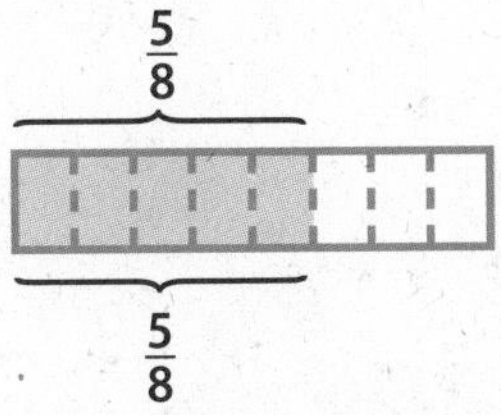

$\frac{5}{4} \div \frac{5}{8} =$ ________

$\frac{5}{8} \div \frac{5}{8} =$ ________

C Complete the table. What do you notice about the quotient and product in each row? What do you notice about the divisor in column 1 and the multiplier in column 2?

____

____

____

Quotient	Product
$5 \div \frac{5}{8} =$	$5 \times \frac{8}{5} =$
$\frac{5}{4} \div \frac{5}{8} =$	$\frac{5}{4} \times \frac{8}{5} =$
$\frac{5}{8} \div \frac{5}{8} =$	$\frac{5}{8} \times \frac{8}{5} =$

Reflect

8. **Make a Conjecture** Use the pattern in the table to make a conjecture about how you can use multiplication to divide a number by a fraction.

____

9. Sketch a model on a separate piece of paper that you could use to solve the division problem $\frac{6}{7} \div \frac{2}{7}$. How can you use the pattern you see in the table in **C** to solve this division problem?

____

____

Math On the Spot
my.hrw.com

Using Reciprocals to Divide Fractions

Dividing by a fraction is equivalent to multiplying by its reciprocal.

$\frac{1}{5} \div \frac{1}{4} = \frac{4}{5}$ $\frac{1}{5} \times \frac{4}{1} = \frac{4}{5}$

EXAMPLE 2

CA CC 6.NS.1

Animated Math
my.hrw.com

Divide $\frac{5}{9} \div \frac{2}{3}$. Write the quotient in simplest form.

STEP 1 Rewrite as multiplication, using the reciprocal of the divisor.

$\frac{5}{9} \div \frac{2}{3} = \frac{5}{9} \times \frac{3}{2}$ The reciprocal of $\frac{2}{3}$ is $\frac{3}{2}$.

STEP 2 Multiply and simplify.

$\frac{5}{9} \times \frac{3}{2} = \frac{15}{18}$ Multiply the numerators. Multiply the denominators.

$= \frac{5}{6}$ Write the answer in simplest form.

$\frac{15 \div 3}{18 \div 3} = \frac{5}{6}$

$\frac{5}{9} \div \frac{2}{3} = \frac{5}{6}$

Personal Math Trainer
Online Practice and Help
my.hrw.com

YOUR TURN

Divide.

10. $\frac{9}{10} \div \frac{2}{5} =$ ______ **11.** $\frac{9}{10} \div \frac{3}{5} =$ ______

Guided Practice

Find the reciprocal of each fraction. (Example 1)

1. $\frac{2}{5}$ ______ **2.** 9 ______ **3.** $\frac{10}{3}$ ______

Divide. (Explore 1, Explore 2, and Example 2)

4. $\frac{4}{3} \div \frac{5}{3} =$ ______ **5.** $\frac{3}{10} \div \frac{4}{5} =$ ______ **6.** $\frac{1}{2} \div \frac{2}{5} =$ ______

ESSENTIAL QUESTION CHECK-IN

7. Explain how to divide a number by a fraction.

______

Name ______________________ Class ______________________ Date ______________________

4.2 Independent Practice

CA CC 6.NS.1

Personal Math Trainer
Online Practice and Help
my.hrw.com

8. $8 \div \frac{2}{3} =$ ______

9. $7 \div \frac{3}{4} =$ ______

10. $\frac{4}{15} \div \frac{2}{5} =$ ______

11. $\frac{5}{8} \div \frac{7}{8} =$ ______

12. $\frac{7}{16} \div \frac{3}{8} =$ ______

13. $\frac{4}{5} \div \frac{7}{10} =$ ______

14. Alison has $\frac{1}{2}$ cup of yogurt for making fruit parfaits. Each parfait requires $\frac{1}{8}$ cup of yogurt. How many parfaits can she make?

______

15. How many tenths are there in $\frac{4}{5}$?

______

16. **Biology** Suppose one honeybee makes $\frac{1}{12}$ teaspoon of honey during its lifetime. How many honeybees are needed to make $\frac{1}{2}$ teaspoon of honey?

______

17. A team of runners is needed to run a $\frac{1}{4}$-mile relay race. If each runner must run $\frac{1}{16}$ mile, how many runners will be needed?

______

18. A pitcher contains $\frac{2}{3}$ quart of water. If an equal amount of water is poured into each of 6 glasses, how much water will each glass contain?

______

19. Jackson wants to divide a $\frac{3}{4}$-pound box of trail mix into small bags. Each of the bags will hold $\frac{1}{12}$ pound of trail mix. How many bags of trail mix can Jackson fill?

______

20. You make a salad to share with friends. Your sister eats $\frac{1}{3}$ of it before they arrive.

a. You want to divide the leftover salad evenly among six friends. What expression describes the situation? Explain.

______

b. What fraction of the original salad does each friend receive?

______

21. Six people share $\frac{3}{5}$ pound of peanuts equally. What fraction of a pound of peanuts does each person receive?

______

22. Liam has $\frac{9}{10}$ gallon of paint for painting the birdhouses he sells at the craft fair. Each birdhouse requires $\frac{1}{20}$ gallon of paint. How many birdhouses can Liam paint? Show your work.

____

H.O.T. FOCUS ON HIGHER ORDER THINKING

Work Area

23. Interpret the Answer The length of a ribbon is $\frac{3}{4}$ meter. Sun Yi needs pieces measuring $\frac{1}{3}$ meter for an art project. What is the greatest number of pieces measuring $\frac{1}{3}$ meter that can be cut from the ribbon? How much ribbon will be left after Sun Yi cuts the ribbon? Explain your reasoning.

____

____

____

24. Represent Real-World Problems Write and solve a real-world problem that can be solved using the expression $\frac{3}{4} \div \frac{1}{6}$.

____

____

____

25. Justify Reasoning When Kaitlin divided a fraction by $\frac{1}{2}$, the result was a mixed number. Was the original fraction less than or greater than $\frac{1}{2}$? Explain your reasoning.

____

____

26. Communicate Mathematical Ideas The reciprocal of a fraction less than 1 is always a fraction greater than 1. Why is this?

____

____

____

27. Make a Prediction Susan divides the fraction $\frac{5}{8}$ by $\frac{1}{16}$. Her friend Robyn divides $\frac{5}{8}$ by $\frac{1}{32}$. Predict which person will get the greater quotient. Explain and check your prediction.

____

____

____

LESSON 4.3

Dividing Mixed Numbers

CA CC 6.NS.1

Interpret and compute quotients of fractions, and solve word problems involving division of fractions by fractions.

ESSENTIAL QUESTION

How do you divide mixed numbers?

EXPLORE ACTIVITY Real World

CA CC 6.NS.1

Modeling Mixed Number Division

Antoine is making sushi rolls. He has $2\frac{1}{2}$ cups of rice and will use $\frac{1}{4}$ cup of rice for each sushi roll. How many sushi rolls can he make?

A To find the number of sushi rolls that can be made, you need to determine how many fourths are in $2\frac{1}{2}$. Use fraction pieces to represent $2\frac{1}{2}$ on the model below.

1				1				$\frac{1}{2}$	
$\frac{1}{4}$	$\frac{1}{4}$	$\frac{1}{4}$	$\frac{1}{4}$	$\frac{1}{4}$	$\frac{1}{4}$	$\frac{1}{4}$	$\frac{1}{4}$	$\frac{1}{4}$	$\frac{1}{4}$

B How many fourths are in $2\frac{1}{2}$? ______________

Antoine has enough rice to make ______________ sushi rolls.

Reflect

1. **Communicate Mathematical Ideas** Which mathematical operation could you use to find the number of sushi rolls that Antoine can make? Explain.

____

____

2. **Multiple Representations** Write the division shown by the model.

____

3. **What If?** Suppose Antoine instead uses $\frac{1}{8}$ cup of rice for each sushi roll. How would his model change? How many rolls can he make? Explain.

____

____

____

Math On the Spot
my.hrw.com

Using Reciprocals to Divide Mixed Numbers

Dividing by a fraction is equivalent to multiplying by its reciprocal. You can use this fact to divide mixed numbers. First rewrite the mixed numbers as fractions greater than 1. Then multiply the dividend by the reciprocal of the divisor.

EXAMPLE 1 Real World

CA CC 6.NS.1

One serving of Harold's favorite cereal contains $1\frac{2}{5}$ ounces. How many servings are in a $17\frac{1}{2}$-ounce box?

My Notes

STEP 1 Write a division statement to represent the situation.

$17\frac{1}{2} \div 1\frac{2}{5}$

You need to find how many groups of $1\frac{2}{5}$ are in $17\frac{1}{2}$.

STEP 2 Rewrite the mixed numbers as fractions greater than 1.

$17\frac{1}{2} \div 1\frac{2}{5} = \frac{35}{2} \div \frac{7}{5}$

STEP 3 Rewrite the problem as multiplication using the reciprocal of the divisor.

$\frac{35}{2} \div \frac{7}{5} = \frac{35}{2} \times \frac{5}{7}$ *The reciprocal of $\frac{7}{5}$ is $\frac{5}{7}$.*

STEP 4 Multiply.

$\frac{35}{2} \times \frac{5}{7} = \frac{\cancel{35}^{5}}{2} \times \frac{5}{\cancel{7}_{1}}$ *Simplify first using the GCF.*

$= \frac{5 \times 5}{2 \times 1}$ *Multiply numerators. Multiply denominators.*

$= \frac{25}{2}$, or $12\frac{1}{2}$ *Write the result as a mixed number.*

There are $12\frac{1}{2}$ servings of cereal in the box.

Reflect

4. **Analyze Relationships** Explain how can you check the answer.

5. **What If?** Harold serves himself $1\frac{1}{2}$-ounces servings of cereal each morning. How many servings does he get from a box of his favorite cereal? Show your work.

YOUR TURN

6. Sheila has $10\frac{1}{2}$ pounds of potato salad. She wants to divide the potato salad into containers, each of which holds $1\frac{1}{4}$ pounds. How many containers does she need? Explain.

____

Personal Math Trainer
Online Practice and Help
my.hrw.com

Solving Problems Involving Area

Recall that to find the area of a rectangle, you multiply length $\times$ width. If you know the area and only one dimension, you can divide the area by the known dimension to find the other dimension.

Math On the Spot
my.hrw.com

EXAMPLE 2 Real World

CA CC 6.NS.1

The area of a rectangular sandbox is $56\frac{2}{3}$ square feet. The length of the sandbox is $8\frac{1}{2}$ feet. What is the width?

STEP 1 Write the situation as a division problem.

$$56\frac{2}{3} \div 8\frac{1}{2}$$

STEP 2 Rewrite the mixed numbers as fractions greater than 1.

$$56\frac{2}{3} \div 8\frac{1}{2} = \frac{170}{3} \div \frac{17}{2}$$

STEP 3 Rewrite the problem as multiplication using the reciprocal of the divisor.

$$\frac{170}{3} \div \frac{17}{2} = \frac{170}{3} \times \frac{2}{17}$$

$$= \frac{\overset{10}{\cancel{170}} \times 2}{3 \times \underset{1}{\cancel{17}}}$$ Multiply numerators. Multiply denominators.

$$= \frac{20}{3}, \text{ or } 6\frac{2}{3}$$ Simplify and write as a mixed number.

The width of the sandbox is $6\frac{2}{3}$ feet.

Math Talk
Mathematical Practices
Explain how to find the length of a rectangle when you know the area and the width.

Reflect

7. **Check for Reasonableness** How can you determine if your answer is reasonable?

____

____

____

____

Personal Math Trainer

Online Practice and Help

my.hrw.com

YOUR TURN

8. The area of a rectangular patio is $12\frac{3}{8}$ square meters. The width of the patio is $2\frac{3}{4}$ meters. What is the length? ________

9. The area of a rectangular rug is $14\frac{1}{12}$ square yards. The length of the rug is $4\frac{1}{3}$ yards. What is the width? ________

Guided Practice

Divide. Write each answer in simplest form. (Explore Activity and Example 1)

1. $4\frac{1}{4} \div \frac{3}{4}$

$\frac{\square}{4} \div \frac{3}{4} =$

$\frac{\square}{4} \times \frac{\square}{\square} =$

____

2. $1\frac{1}{2} \div 2\frac{1}{4}$

$\frac{\square}{2} \div \frac{\square}{4} =$

$\frac{\square}{2} \times \frac{\square}{\square} =$

____

3. $4 \div 1\frac{1}{8} =$ ________

4. $3\frac{1}{5} \div 1\frac{1}{7} =$ ________

5. $8\frac{1}{3} \div 2\frac{1}{2} =$ ________

6. $15\frac{1}{3} \div 3\frac{5}{6} =$ ________

Write each situation as a division problem. Then solve. (Example 2)

7. A sandbox has an area of 26 square feet, and the length is $5\frac{1}{2}$ feet. What is the width of the sandbox? ________

8. Mr. Webster is buying carpet for an exercise room in his basement. The room will have an area of 230 square feet. The width of the room is $12\frac{1}{2}$ feet. What is the length? ________

ESSENTIAL QUESTION CHECK-IN

9. How is dividing mixed numbers like dividing fractions?

____

____

Name ____________________ Class ____________ Date ____________

4.3 Independent Practice

CA CC 6.NS.1

Personal Math Trainer
Online Practice and Help
my.hrw.com

10. Jeremy has $4\frac{1}{2}$ cups of iced tea. He wants to divide the tea into $\frac{3}{4}$-cup servings. Use the model to find the number of servings he can make.

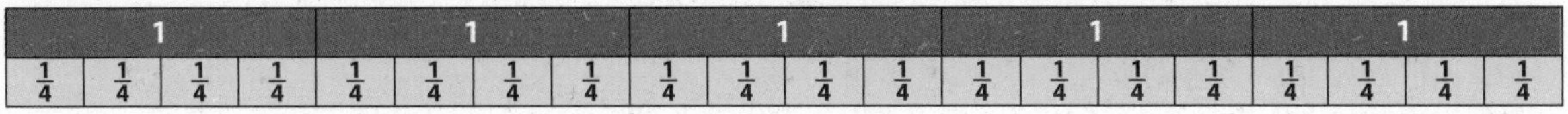

____

11. A ribbon is $3\frac{2}{3}$ yards long. Mae needs to cut the ribbon into pieces that are $\frac{2}{3}$ yard long. Use the model to find the number of pieces that are $\frac{2}{3}$ yard long that she can cut. Use the model to find the number of such pieces she can cut. How much ribbon will be left after she cuts these pieces?

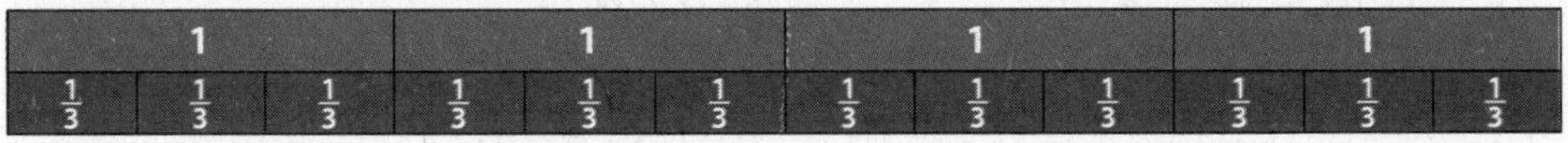

____

12. Dao has $2\frac{3}{8}$ pounds of hamburger meat. He is making $\frac{1}{4}$-pound hamburgers. Does Dao have enough meat to make 10 hamburgers? Explain.

____

13. **Multistep** Zoey made $5\frac{1}{2}$ cups of trail mix for a camping trip. She wants to divide the trail mix into $\frac{3}{4}$-cup servings.

a. Ten people are going on the camping trip. Can Zoey make enough $\frac{3}{4}$-cup servings so that each person on the trip has one serving?

____

b. What size would the servings need to be for everyone to have a serving? Explain.

____

c. If Zoey decides to use the $\frac{3}{4}$-cup servings, how much more trail mix will she need? Explain.

____

____

14. The area of a rectangular picture frame is $30\frac{1}{3}$ square inches. The length of the frame is $6\frac{1}{2}$ inches. Find the width of the frame.

____

15. The area of a rectangular mirror is $11\frac{11}{16}$ square feet. The width of the mirror is $2\frac{3}{4}$ feet. If there is a 5 foot tall space on the wall to hang the mirror, will it fit? Explain.

____

16. Ramon has a rope that is $25\frac{1}{2}$ feet long. He wants to cut it into 6 pieces that are equal in length. How long will each piece be?

____

17. Eleanor and Max used two rectangular wooden boards to make a set for the school play. One board was 6 feet long, and the other was $5\frac{1}{2}$ feet long. The two boards had equal widths. The total area of the set was $60\frac{3}{8}$ square feet. What was the width?

____

H.O.T. FOCUS ON HIGHER ORDER THINKING

Work Area

18. **Draw Conclusions** Micah divided $11\frac{2}{3}$ by $2\frac{5}{6}$ and got $4\frac{2}{17}$ for an answer. Does his answer seem reasonable? Explain your thinking. Then check Micah's answer.

____

____

____

____

____

19. **Explain the Error** To divide $14\frac{2}{3} \div 2\frac{3}{4}$, Erik multiplied $14\frac{2}{3} \times \frac{4}{3}$. Explain Erik's error.

____

____

____

20. **Analyze Relationships** Explain how you can find the missing number in $3\frac{4}{5} \div \blacksquare = 2\frac{5}{7}$. Then find the missing number.

____

____

____

LESSON 4.4

Solving Multistep Problems with Fractions and Mixed Numbers

CA CC 6.NS.1

Interpret and compute quotients of fractions, and solve word problems involving division of fractions by fractions, e.g., by using visual fraction models and equations to represent the problem.

ESSENTIAL QUESTION

How can you solve word problems involving more than one fraction operation?

Solving Problems with Rational Numbers

Math On the Spot
my.hrw.com

Sometimes more than one operation will be needed to solve a multistep problem. You can use parentheses to group different operations. Recall that according to the **order of operations,** you perform operations in parentheses first.

EXAMPLE 1 Problem Solving

CA CC 6.NS.1

Jon is cooking enough lentils for lentil barley soup and lentil salad. The lentil barley soup recipe calls for $\frac{3}{4}$ cup of dried lentils. The lentil salad recipe calls for $1\frac{1}{2}$ cups of dried lentils. Jon has a $\frac{1}{8}$-cup scoop. How many scoops of dried lentils will Jon need to have enough for the soup and the salad?

Analyze Information

Identify the important information.

- Jon needs $\frac{3}{4}$ cup of dried lentils for soup and $1\frac{1}{2}$ cups for salad.
- Jon has a $\frac{1}{8}$-cup scoop.
- You need to find the total number of many scoops of lentils he needs.

Formulate a Plan

You can use the expression $\left(\frac{3}{4} + 1\frac{1}{2}\right) \div \frac{1}{8}$ to find the number of scoops of dried lentils Jon will need for the soup and the salad.

Solve

Follow the order of operations. Perform the operations in parentheses first.

First add to find the total amount of dried lentils Jon will need.

$$\frac{3}{4} + 1\frac{1}{2} = \frac{3}{4} + \frac{3}{2}$$

$$= \frac{3}{4} + \frac{6}{4}$$

$$= \frac{9}{4}$$

$$= 2\frac{1}{4}$$

John needs $2\frac{1}{4}$ cups of lentils.

Jon needs $2\frac{1}{4}$ cups of dried lentils for both the soup and the salad.

To find how many $\frac{1}{8}$-cup scoops he needs, divide the total amount of dried lentils into groups of $\frac{1}{8}$.

$$2\frac{1}{4} \div \frac{1}{8} = \frac{9}{4} \div \frac{1}{8}$$

$$= \frac{9}{4} \times \frac{8}{1}$$

Simplify before multiplying using the GCF.

$$= \frac{9 \times \cancel{8}^{2}}{\cancel{4}_{1} \times 1}$$

$$= \frac{18}{1} = 18$$

Jon will need 18 scoops of dried lentils to have enough for both the lentil barley soup and the lentil salad.

Math Talk
Mathematical Practices

What if Jon had a $\frac{1}{4}$-cup scoop instead of a $\frac{1}{8}$-cup scoop? How many scoops would he need? Explain.

Justify and Evaluate

You added $\frac{3}{4}$ and $1\frac{1}{2}$ first to find the total number of cups of lentils. Then you divided the sum by $\frac{1}{8}$ to find the number of $\frac{1}{8}$-cup scoops.

Personal Math Trainer
Online Practice and Help
my.hrw.com

YOUR TURN

1. Before making some soup, a chef mixes $\frac{1}{2}$ cup of cream with $\frac{3}{4}$ cup of milk. If the scientist uses $\frac{1}{8}$ cup of the combined liquids to make one batch of soup, how many batches of soup can be made? ______

Guided Practice

1. An art student uses a roll of wallpaper to decorate two gift boxes. The student will use $1\frac{1}{3}$ yards of paper for one box and $\frac{5}{6}$ yard of paper for the other box. The paper must be cut into pieces that are $\frac{1}{6}$ yard long. How many pieces will the student cut to use for the gift boxes? (Example 1) ______

ESSENTIAL QUESTION CHECK-IN

2. Describe a real-world problem that you could solve using more than one fraction operation. Show how to solve your problem.

______

______

______

______

Name ________________ Class ________________ Date ________________

4.4 Independent Practice

CA CC 6.NS.1.1

Personal Math Trainer

my.hrw.com

Online Practice and Help

3. Karl participated in a two-day charity walk. His parents donated money for each mile he walked. Karl walked $3\frac{1}{4}$ miles on the first day and $5\frac{1}{2}$ miles on the second day. His parents donated \$175. How much money did his parents pay for each mile?

____

4. An art teacher has $1\frac{1}{2}$ pounds of red clay and $\frac{3}{4}$ pound of yellow clay. The teacher mixes the red clay and yellow clay together. Each student in the class needs $\frac{1}{8}$ pound of the clay mixture to finish the assigned art project for the class. How many students can get enough clay to finish the project?

____

5. A hairstylist schedules $\frac{1}{4}$ hour to trim a customer's hair and $\frac{1}{6}$ hour to style the customer's hair. The hairstylist plans to work $3\frac{1}{3}$ hours each day for 5 days each week. How many appointments can the hairstylist schedule each week if each customer must be trimmed and styled?

____

6. A picture framer has a board $10\frac{1}{12}$ feet long. The framer notices that $2\frac{3}{8}$ feet of the board is scratched and cannot be used. The rest of the board will be used to make small picture frames. Each picture frame needs $1\frac{2}{3}$ feet of the board. At most, how many complete picture frames can be made?

____

7. Jim's lawn is a rectangle that is $15\frac{5}{6}$ yards long and $10\frac{2}{5}$ yards wide. Jim buys sod in pieces that are $1\frac{1}{3}$ yards long and $1\frac{1}{3}$ yards wide. How many pieces of sod will Jim need to buy to cover his lawn with sod?

____

8. Eva wants to make two pieces of pottery. She needs $\frac{3}{5}$ pound of clay for one piece and $\frac{7}{10}$ pound of clay for the other piece. She has three bags of clay that weigh $\frac{4}{5}$ pound each. How many bags of clay will Eva need to make both pieces of pottery? How many pounds of clay will she have left over?

____

9. Mark wants to paint a mural. He has $1\frac{1}{3}$ gallons of yellow paint, $1\frac{1}{4}$ gallons of green paint, and $\frac{7}{8}$ gallon of blue paint. Mark plans to use $\frac{3}{4}$ gallon of each color. How many gallons of paint will he have left after painting the mural?

____

10. Trina works after school and on weekends. She always works three days each week. This week she worked $2\frac{3}{4}$ hours on Monday, $3\frac{3}{5}$ hours on Friday, and $5\frac{1}{2}$ hours on Saturday. Next week she plans to work the same number of hours as this week, but will work for the same number of hours each day. How many hours will she work on each day?

____

Work Area

H.O.T. FOCUS ON HIGHER ORDER THINKING

11. Represent Real-World Problems Describe a real-world problem that can be solved using the expression $29 \div \left(\frac{3}{8} + \frac{5}{6}\right)$. Find the answer in the context of the situation.

____

____

____

____

____

12. Justify Reasoning Indira and Jean begin their hike at 10 a.m. one morning. They plan to hike from the $2\frac{2}{5}$-mile marker to the $8\frac{1}{10}$-mile marker along the trail. They plan to hike at an average speed of 3 miles per hour. Will they reach the $8\frac{1}{10}$-mile marker by noon? Explain your reasoning.

____

____

____

____

____

13. Multiple Representations You are measuring walnuts for banana-walnut oatmeal and a spinach and walnut salad. You need $\frac{3}{8}$ cup of walnuts for the oatmeal and $\frac{3}{4}$ cup of walnuts for the salad. You have a $\frac{1}{4}$-cup scoop. Describe two different ways to find how many scoops of walnuts you will need.

____

____

____

____

____

MODULE QUIZ

Ready to Go On?

Personal Math Trainer
Online Practice and Help
my.hrw.com

4.1 Applying GCF and LCM to Fraction Operations

Solve.

1. $\frac{4}{5} \times \frac{3}{4}$ ________

2. $\frac{5}{7} \times \frac{9}{10}$ ________

3. $\frac{3}{8} + 2\frac{1}{2}$ ________

4. $1\frac{3}{5} - \frac{5}{6}$ ________

4.2 Dividing Fractions

Divide.

5. $\frac{1}{3} \div \frac{7}{9}$ ________

6. $\frac{1}{3} \div \frac{5}{8}$ ________

7. Luci cuts a board that is $\frac{3}{4}$ yard long into pieces that are $\frac{3}{8}$ yard long. How many pieces does she cut? ________

4.3 Dividing Mixed Numbers

Divide.

8. $3\frac{1}{3} \div \frac{2}{3}$ ________

9. $1\frac{7}{8} \div 2\frac{2}{5}$ ________

10. $4\frac{1}{4} \div 4\frac{1}{2}$ ________

11. $8\frac{1}{3} \div 4\frac{2}{7}$ ________

4.4 Solving Multistep Problems with Fractions and Mixed Numbers

12. Jamal hiked on two trails. The first trail was $5\frac{1}{3}$ miles long, and the second trail was $1\frac{3}{4}$ times as long as the first trail. How many miles did Jamal hike? ________

ESSENTIAL QUESTION

13. Describe a real-world situation that is modeled by dividing two fractions or mixed numbers.

____

____

____

____

CALIFORNIA

MODULE 4
MIXED REVIEW

Assessment Readiness

Personal Math Trainer

Online Practice and Help

my.hrw.com

1. Consider each equation. Is the equation true?

Select Yes or No for equations A–C.

A. $\frac{2}{3} + \frac{3}{8} = \frac{5}{24}$ ○ Yes ○ No

B. $3\frac{3}{4} - 2\frac{2}{5} = 1\frac{7}{20}$ ○ Yes ○ No

C. $8\frac{5}{9} + 6\frac{7}{12} = 15\frac{5}{36}$ ○ Yes ○ No

2. Party leftovers of $1\frac{3}{4}$ pounds of cheese, $1\frac{2}{3}$ pounds of crackers, and $\frac{3}{4}$ gallon of juice will be divided equally into containers.

Choose True or False for each statement.

A. If each juice container holds $\frac{1}{8}$ gallon of juice, then you need 6 juice containers. ○ True ○ False

B. If each cracker bag can contain $\frac{5}{6}$ pound of crackers, then you need 4 bags. ○ True ○ False

C. If there are 7 containers for cheese, then each container has $\frac{1}{4}$ pound of cheese. ○ True ○ False

3. A rectangular stone in a piece of costume jewelry has a width of $\frac{4}{5}$ inch and an area of $\frac{7}{10}$ square inch. Is a silver wire with a length of $3\frac{1}{2}$ inches long enough to outline the stone? Explain how you solved this problem.

4. Dan weighed his dogs Spot and Rover in March and in April, and recorded the weight change for each dog. He recorded a change of $2\frac{1}{2}$ pounds for Spot and $-2\frac{3}{4}$ pounds for Rover. He says Spot's weight changed by a greater amount because $2\frac{1}{2} > -2\frac{3}{4}$. Do you agree? Explain.

Operations with Decimals

MODULE 5

CALIFORNIA

ESSENTIAL QUESTION

How can you use operations with decimals to solve real-world problems?

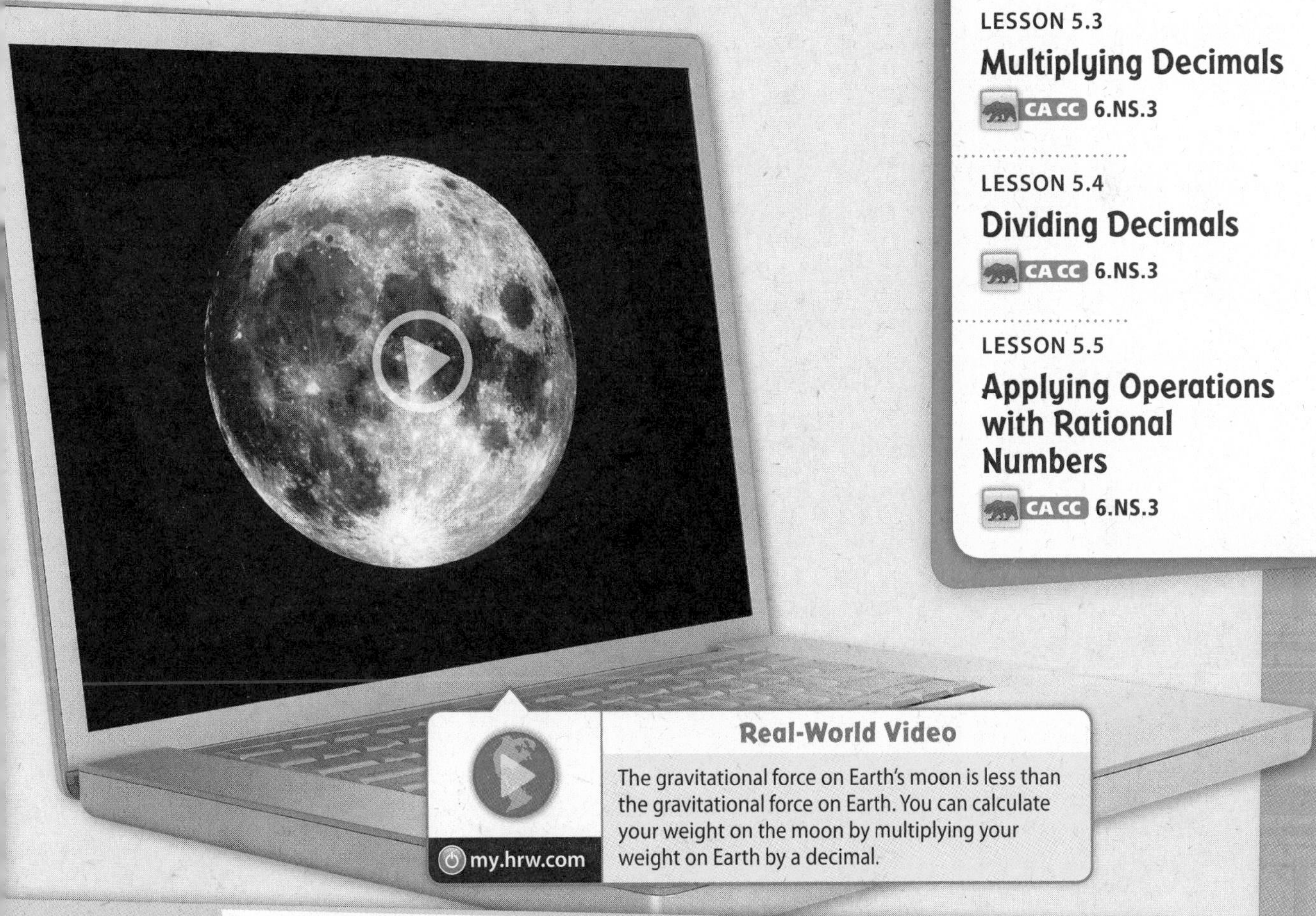

my.hrw.com

Real-World Video

The gravitational force on Earth's moon is less than the gravitational force on Earth. You can calculate your weight on the moon by multiplying your weight on Earth by a decimal.

GO DIGITAL
my.hrw.com

my.hrw.com
Go digital with your write-in student edition, accessible on any device.

Math On the Spot
Scan with your smart phone to jump directly to the online edition, video tutor, and more.

Animated Math
Interactively explore key concepts to see how math works.

Personal Math Trainer
Get immediate feedback and help as you work through practice sets.

Are YOU Ready?

Complete these exercises to review skills you will need for this module.

Personal Math Trainer
my.hrw.com
Online Practice and Help

Represent Decimals

EXAMPLE

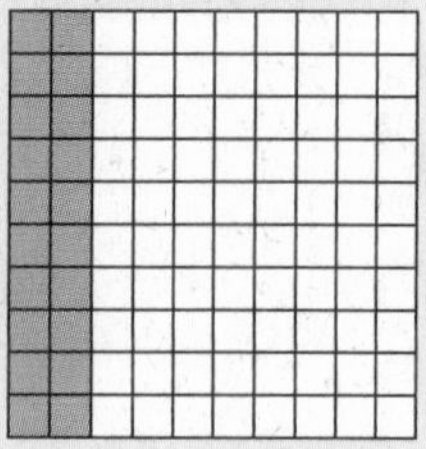

Think: 1 square = 1 of 100 equal parts
$= \frac{1}{100}$, or 0.01
10 squares = 10 of 100 equal parts
$= \frac{1}{10}$, or 0.1
So, 20 squares represent 2×0.1, or 0.2.

Write the decimal represented by the shaded square.

1.

______

2.

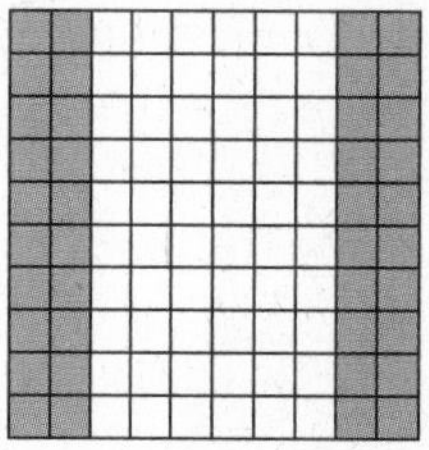

______

3.

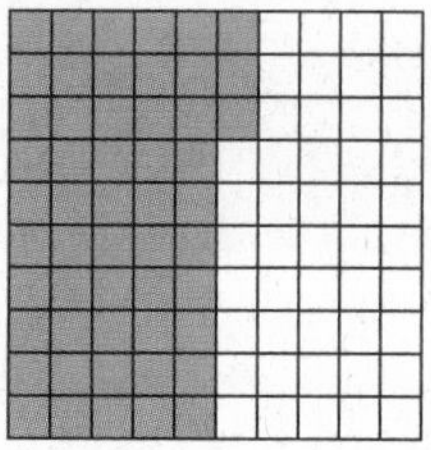

______

4.

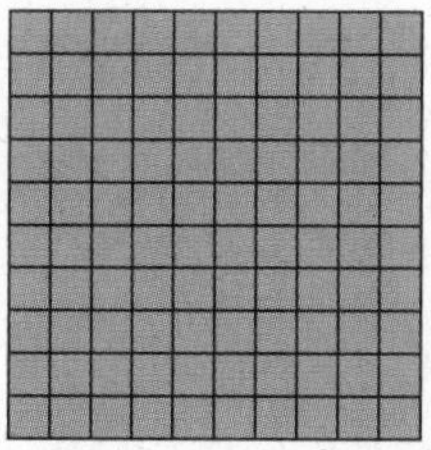

______

Multiply Decimals by Powers of 10

EXAMPLE 6.574×100 — Count the zeros in 100: 2 zeros.

$6.574 \times 100 = 657.4$ — Move the decimal point 2 places to the right.

Find the product.

5. 0.49×10 ______ **6.** $25.34 \times 1{,}000$ ______ **7.** 87×100 ______

Words for Operations

EXAMPLE Write a numerical expression for the product of 5 and 9. — Think: *Product* means "to multiply."
5×9 — Write 5 times 9.

Write a numerical expression for the word expression.

8. 20 decreased by 8 ______ **9.** the quotient of 14 and 7 ______

10. the difference between 72 and 16 ______ **11.** the sum of 19 and 3 ______

Reading Start-Up

Visualize Vocabulary

Use the ✔ words to complete the chart. You may put more than one word in each section.

Dividing Numbers

÷	$450 \div 9 = 50$
$\frac{450}{9}$	Not division

Understand Vocabulary

Match the term on the left to the definition on the right.

1. divide — **A.** The bottom number in a fraction.

2. denominator — **B.** The top number in a fraction.

3. quotient — **C.** To split into equal groups.

4. numerator — **D.** The answer in a division problem.

Vocabulary

Review Words

- decimal *(decimal)*
- ✔ denominator *(denominador)*
- divide *(dividir)*
- ✔ dividend *(dividendo)*
- ✔ divisor *(divisor)*
- ✔ fraction bar *(barra de fracciones)*
- ✔ multiply *(multiplicar)*
- ✔ numerator *(numerador)*
- ✔ operation *(operación)*
- ✔ product *(producto)*
- ✔ quotient *(cociente)*
- ✔ rational number *(número racional)*
- ✔ symbol *(símbolo)*
- whole number *(número entero)*

Active Reading

Booklet Before beginning the module, create a booklet to help you learn the concepts in this module. Write the main idea of each lesson on its own page of the booklet. As you study each lesson, record examples that illustrate the main idea and make note of important details. Refer to your finished booklet as you work on assignments and study for tests.

GETTING READY FOR

Operations with Decimals

Understanding the standards and the vocabulary terms in the standards will help you know exactly what you are expected to learn in this module.

CA CC 6.NS.2

Fluently divide multi-digit numbers using the standard algorithm.

Key Vocabulary

quotient *(cociente)*
The result when one number is divided by another.

What It Means to You

You will use your prior knowledge of division of whole numbers to perform division with decimals.

EXAMPLE 6.NS.2

Eugenia and her friends bought frozen yogurt for 45 cents per ounce. Their total was $11.25. How many ounces did they buy?

Divide 11.25 by 0.45.

$$\begin{array}{r} 25 \\ 0.45\overline{)11.25} \\ \underline{90} \\ 225 \\ \underline{225} \\ 0 \end{array}$$

They bought 25 ounces of frozen yogurt.

CA CC 6.NS.3

Fluently add, subtract, multiply, and divide multi-digit decimals using the standard algorithm for each operation.

Key Vocabulary

algorithm *(algoritmo)*
A set of rules or a procedure for solving a mathematical problem in a finite number of steps.

What It Means to You

You will use your prior knowledge of operations with whole numbers to perform operations with decimals.

EXAMPLE 6.NS.3

Estimate and find the exact answer.

A. 3.25×4.8

$3 \times 5 = 15$

$$\begin{array}{r} 3.25 \\ \underline{\times 4.8} \\ 2600 \\ \underline{13000} \\ 15.600 \end{array}$$

B. $132.5 - 18.9$

$133 - 19 = 114$

$$\begin{array}{r} 132.5 \\ \underline{-18.9} \\ 113.6 \end{array}$$

Visit my.hrw.com to see all CA Common Core Standards explained.

my.hrw.com

LESSON 5.1

Dividing Whole Numbers

CA CC 6.NS.2

Fluently divide multi-digit numbers using the standard algorithm.

ESSENTIAL QUESTION

How do you divide multi-digit whole numbers?

EXPLORE ACTIVITY Real World

CA CC 6.NS.2

Estimating Quotients

You can use estimation to predict the quotient of multi-digit whole numbers.

dividend ÷ divisor = quotient $\text{divisor}\overline{\smash{)}\text{dividend}}$ with quotient above

A local zoo had a total of 98,464 visitors last year. The zoo was open every day except for three holidays. On average, about how many visitors did the zoo have each day?

A To estimate the average number of visitors per day, you can divide the total number of visitors by the number of days. To estimate the quotient, first estimate the dividend by rounding the number of visitors to the nearest ten thousand.

98,464 rounded to the nearest ten thousand is ________.

B There were 365 days last year. How many days was the petting zoo open? ________

C Estimate the divisor by rounding the number of days that the zoo was open to the nearest hundred.

________ rounded to the nearest hundred is ________.

D Estimate the quotient. ________ ÷ ________ = ________

The average number of visitors per day last year was about ________.

Reflect

1. How can you check that your quotient is correct?

____

____

2. **Critical Thinking** Do you think that your estimate is greater than or less than the actual answer? Explain.

____

Math On the Spot

my.hrw.com

Using Long Division

The exact average number of visitors per day at the zoo in the Explore Activity is the quotient of 98,464 and 362. You can use long division to find this quotient.

EXAMPLE 1 Real World

CA CC 6.NS.2

A local zoo had a total of 98,464 visitors last year. The zoo was open every day except three holidays. On average, how many visitors did the zoo have each day?

Math Talk Mathematical Practices

How does the estimate from the Explore Activity compare to the actual average number of visitors per day?

STEP 1 362 is greater than 9 and 98, so divide 984 by 362. Place the first digit in the quotient in the hundreds place. Multiply 2 by 362 and place the product under 984. Subtract.

$$\begin{array}{r} 2 \\ 362\overline{)\,98{,}464} \\ -72\,4 \\ \hline 260 \end{array}$$

STEP 2 Bring down the tens digit. Divide 2,606 by 362. Multiply 7 by 362 and place the product under 2,606. Subtract.

$$\begin{array}{r} 27 \\ 362\overline{)\,98{,}464} \\ -72\,4 \\ \hline 26\,06 \\ -25\,34 \\ \hline 72 \end{array}$$

STEP 3 Bring down the ones digit. Divide the ones.

$$\begin{array}{r} 272 \\ 362\overline{)\,98{,}464} \\ -72\,4 \\ \hline 26\,06 \\ -25\,34 \\ \hline 724 \\ -724 \\ \hline 0 \end{array}$$

The average number of visitors per day last year was 272.

Personal Math Trainer

Online Practice and Help

my.hrw.com

YOUR TURN

Find each quotient.

3. 34,989 ÷ 321 ______________

4. 73,375 ÷ 125 ______________

Dividing with a Remainder

Suppose you and your friend want to divide 9 polished rocks between you so that you each get the same number of polished rocks. You will each get 4 rocks with 1 rock left over. You can say that the quotient $9 \div 2$ has a remainder of 1.

Sometimes a remainder is written as a fraction of the divisor. For example, you can write $9 \div 2 = 4\frac{1}{2}$.

Math On the Spot
my.hrw.com

EXAMPLE 2 Real World

CA CC 6.NS.2

My Notes

Callie has 1,850 books. She must pack them into boxes to ship to a bookstore. Each box holds 12 books. How many boxes will she need to pack all of the books?

Divide 1,850 by 12.

```
      154 R2
12)1,850
   -12
     65
    -60
     50
    -48
      2
```

The quotient is 154, remainder 2. You can write 154 R2. You can also write the quotient as $154\frac{2}{12}$, or $154\frac{1}{6}$.

Callie will need 155 boxes to pack all of the books.

Reflect

5. **Interpret the Answer** What does the remainder mean in this situation?

____

____

YOUR TURN

Divide.

6. 5,796 ÷ 25 __________

7. $67\overline{)3{,}098}$ __________

8. A museum gift shop manager wants to put 1,578 polished rocks into small bags to sell as souvenirs. If the shop manager wants to put 15 rocks in each bag, how many complete bags can be filled? How many rocks will be left over? __________

Personal Math Trainer
Online Practice and Help
my.hrw.com

Guided Practice

1. Estimate: 31,969 ÷ 488 (Explore Activity)

Round the numbers and then divide.

31,969 ÷ 488 = ________ ÷ ________ = ________

Divide. (Example 1, Example 2)

2. 3,072 ÷ 32 = ________

```
      9□
32 )3, 0 7 2
  −□□□
     1 9 2
   −□□□
        □
```

3. 4,539 ÷ 51 = ________

```
      □□
51 )4, 5 3 9
  −□□□
     4 5 9
   −□□□
        □
```

4. 9,317 ÷ 95 = ________

```
      □□
95 )9, 3 1 7
  −□□□
    □□□
   −□□□
        □
```

5. 2,226 ÷ 53 = ________

6. Divide 4,514 by 74. ________

7. 3,493 ÷ 37 = ________

8. 2,001 ÷ 83 = ________

9. 39,751 ÷ 313 = ________

10. 35,506 ÷ 438 = ________

11. During a food drive, a local middle school collected 8,982 canned food items. Each of the 28 classrooms that participated in the drive donated about the same number of items. Estimate the number of items each classroom donated. (Explore Activity) ________

12. A theater has 1,120 seats in 35 equal rows. How many seats are in each row? (Example 1) ________

13. There are 1,012 souvenir paperweights that need to be packed in boxes. Each box will hold 12 paperweights. How many boxes will be needed? (Example 2) ________

? ESSENTIAL QUESTION CHECK-IN

14. What steps do you take to divide multi-digit whole numbers?

____

____

____

____

____

Name ____________ Class ____________ Date ____________

5.1 Independent Practice

CA CC 6.NS.2

Personal Math Trainer
Online Practice and Help
my.hrw.com

Divide.

15. 44,756 ÷ 167 = ____________

16. 87,628 ÷ 931 = ____________

17. 66,253 ÷ 317 = ____________

18. 76,255 ÷ 309 = ____________

19. 50,779 ÷ 590 = ____________

20. 97,156 ÷ 107 = ____________

21. 216,016 ÷ 368 = ____________

22. 107,609 ÷ 72 = ____________

23. Emilio plants 8,450 trees. He plants 125 in each row, with an extra row for any leftover trees. How many full rows are there? How many trees are in the extra row? What fraction of the number of trees in a full row is the number of trees in the extra row?

____

24. Camilla has 8,160 silver beads and 2,880 black beads to make necklaces. Each necklace will contain 85 silver beads and 30 black beads. How many necklaces can she make? ____________

25. During a promotional weekend, a state fair gives a free admission to every 175th person who enters the fair. On Saturday, there were 6,742 people attending the fair. On Sunday, there were 5,487 people attending the fair. How many people received a free admission over the two days?

____

26. Last year a school raised $19,950 by selling $15 tickets to a carnival fundraiser. This year the school will charge $20 per ticket. If the school sells the same number of tickets as it did last year, how much money will be raised?

____

27. Given that 9,554 ÷ 562 = 17, how can you find the quotient 95,540 ÷ 562?

____

____

28. **Earth Science** The diameter of the Moon is about 3,476 kilometers. The distance from Earth to the Moon is about 384,400 kilometers. About how many moons could be lined up in a row between Earth and the Moon? Round to the nearest whole number.

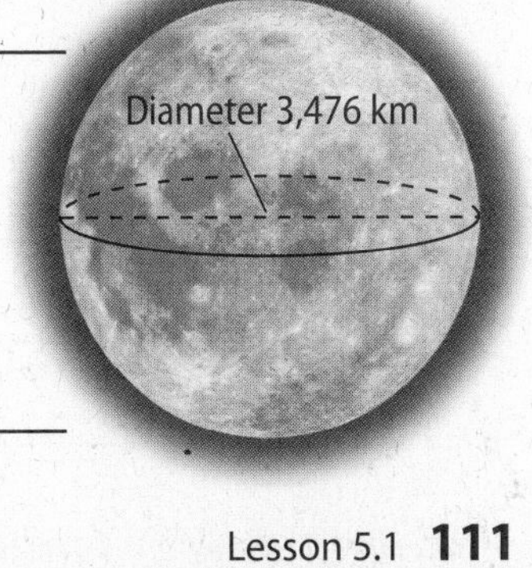

____

29. **Vocabulary** Explain how you could check the answer to a division question in which there is a remainder.

30. Yolanda is buying a car with a base price of \$16,750. She must also pay the options, fees, and taxes shown. The car dealership will give her 48 months to pay off the entire amount. Yolanda can only afford to pay \$395 each month. Will she be able to buy the car? Explain.

Jackson Auto Dealer

4-door sedan	
base price	\$16,750
options	\$ 500
fees	\$ 370
taxes	\$ 1,425

H.O.T. FOCUS ON HIGHER ORDER THINKING

Work Area

31. **Check for Reasonableness** Is 40 a reasonable estimate of a quotient for $78{,}114 \div 192$? Explain your reasoning.

32. **Critique Reasoning** Harrison predicted that the actual quotient for $57{,}872 \div 305$ will be less than the estimate $60{,}000 \div 300 = 200$. Is Harrison correct? Explain how Harrison arrived at his prediction (without dividing the actual numbers).

33. **Make a Prediction** In preparation for a storm, the town council buys 13,750 pounds of sand to fill sandbags. Volunteers are trying to decide whether to fill bags that can hold 25 pounds of sand or bags that can hold 50 pounds of sand. Will they have more or fewer sandbags if they fill the 25-pound bags? How many more or fewer? Explain your reasoning.

LESSON **5.2** # Adding and Subtracting Decimals

CA CC 6.NS.3

Fluently add, subtract, multiply, and divide multi-digit decimals using the standard algorithm for each operation.

ESSENTIAL QUESTION

How do you add and subtract decimals?

EXPLORE ACTIVITY Real World — CA CC 6.NS.3

Modeling Decimal Addition

You have probably used decimal grids to model decimals. For example, the decimal 0.25, or $\frac{25}{100}$, can be modeled by shading 25 squares in a 10×10 grid. You can also use decimal grids to add decimal values.

A chemist combines 0.17 mL of water and 0.49 mL of hydrogen peroxide in a beaker. How much total liquid is in the beaker?

A How many grid squares should you shade to represent 0.17 mL of water? Why?

____

B How many grid squares should you shade to represent 0.49 mL of hydrogen peroxide?

____

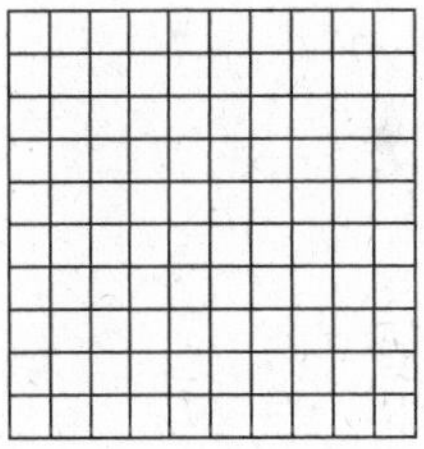

C Use the grid at the right to model the addition. Use one color for 0.17 mL of water and another color for 0.49 mL of hydrogen peroxide.

D How much total liquid is in the beaker? $0.17 + 0.49 =$ _________ mL

Reflect

Multiple Representations **Show how to shade each grid to represent the sum. Then find the sum.**

1. $0.24 + 0.71 =$ _________

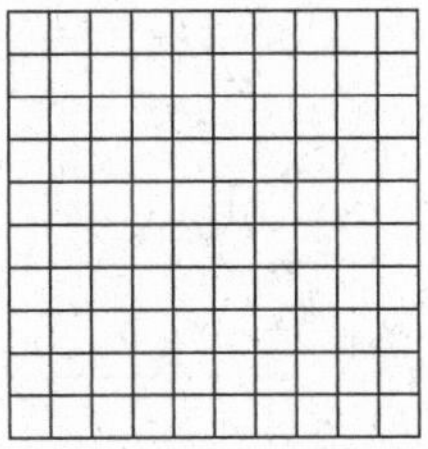

2. $0.08 + 0.65 =$ _________

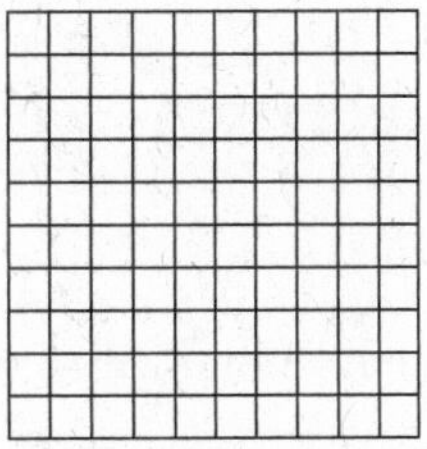

Math On the Spot
my.hrw.com

Adding Decimals

Adding decimals is similar to adding whole numbers. First align the numbers by place value. Start adding at the right and regroup when necessary. Bring down the decimal point into your answer.

EXAMPLE 1 Real World

CA CC 6.NS.3

Susan rode her bicycle 3.12 miles on Monday and 4.7 miles on Tuesday. How many miles did she ride in all?

STEP 1 Align the decimal points.

STEP 2 Add zeros as placeholders when necessary.

	3	.	1	2
+	4	.	7	0
	7	.	8	2

STEP 3 Add from right to left.

Susan rode 7.82 miles in all.

STEP 4 Use estimation to check that the answer is reasonable. Round each decimal to the nearest whole number.

$$\begin{array}{r} 3.12 \\ +\,4.70 \\ \hline 7.82 \end{array} \longrightarrow \begin{array}{r} 3 \\ +\,5 \\ \hline 8 \end{array}$$

Since 8 is close to 7.82, the answer is reasonable.

Reflect

3. Why can you rewrite 4.7 as 4.70?

____

____

4. Why is it important to align the decimal points when adding?

____

____

Personal Math Trainer
Online Practice and Help
my.hrw.com

YOUR TURN

Add.

5. $0.42 + 0.27 =$ ____________

6. $0.61 + 0.329 =$ ____________

7. $3.25 + 4.6 =$ ____________

8. $17.27 + 3.88 =$ ____________

Subtracting Decimals

The procedure for subtracting decimals is similar to the procedure for adding decimals.

Math On the Spot
my.hrw.com

EXAMPLE 2 Real World

CA CC 6.NS.3

A Mia is 160.2 centimeters tall. Rosa is 165.1 centimeters tall. How much taller is Rosa than Mia?

STEP 1 Align the decimal points.

STEP 2 Add zeros as placeholders when necessary.

STEP 3 Subtract from right to left, regrouping when necessary.

	1	6	4 ~~5~~	.	1 ~~1~~
−	1	6	0	.	2
			4	.	9

Rosa is 4.9 centimeters taller than Mia.

To check that your answer is reasonable, you can estimate. Round each decimal to the nearest whole number.

$$\begin{array}{r} 165.1 \\ -\ 160.2 \\ \hline 4.9 \end{array} \longrightarrow \begin{array}{r} 165 \\ -\ 160 \\ \hline 5 \end{array}$$

Since 5 is close to 4.9, the answer is reasonable.

B Matthew throws a discus 58.7 meters. Zachary throws the discus 56.12 meters. How much farther did Matthew throw the discus?

STEP 1 Align the decimal points.

STEP 2 Add zeros as placeholders when necessary.

STEP 3 Subtract from right to left, regrouping when necessary.

	5	8	.	6 ~~7~~	10 ~~0~~
−	5	6	.	1	2
		2	.	5	8

Matthew threw the discus 2.58 meters farther than Zachary.

To check that your answer is reasonable, you can estimate. Round each decimal to the nearest whole number.

$$\begin{array}{r} 58.7 \\ -\ 56.12 \\ \hline 2.58 \end{array} \longrightarrow \begin{array}{r} 59 \\ -\ 56 \\ \hline 3 \end{array}$$

Since 3 is close to 2.58, the answer is reasonable.

My Notes

Math Talk
Mathematical Practices
How can you check a subtraction problem?

Guided Practice

Shade the grid to find each sum. (Explore Activity)

1. 0.72 + 0.19 = ________

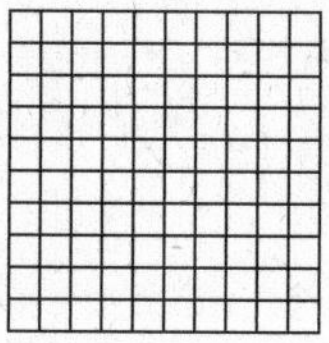

2. 0.38 + 0.4 = ________

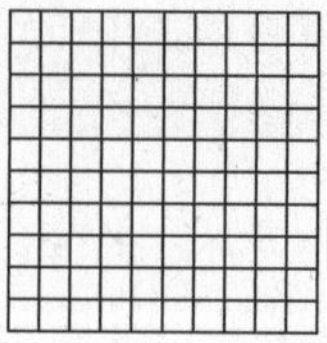

Add. Check that your answer is reasonable. (Example 1)

3. 54.87 → 55
+ 7.48 → + 7
☐ ☐

4. 2.19 → ☐
+ 34.92 → + ☐
☐ ☐

5. 0.215 → ☐
+ 3.74 → + ☐
☐ ☐

Subtract. Check that your answer is reasonable. (Example 2)

6. 9.73 → 10
− 7.16 → − 7
☐ ☐

7. 18.419 → ☐
− 6.47 → − ☐
☐ ☐

8. 5.006 → ☐
− 3.2 → − ☐
☐ ☐

Add or subtract. (Example 1, Example 2)

9. 17.2 + 12.9 = ________

10. 28.341 + 37.5 = ________

11. 25.36 − 2.004 = ________

12. 15.52 − 8.17 = ________

13. 25.68 + 12 = ________

14. 150.25 − 78 = ________

15. Perry connects a blue garden hose and a green garden hose to make one long hose. The blue hose is 16.5 feet. The green hose is 14.75 feet. How long is the combined hose? (Example 1)

____

16. Keisha has $20.08 in her purse. She buys a book for $8.72. How much does she have left? (Example 2)

____

ESSENTIAL QUESTION CHECK-IN

17. How is adding and subtracting decimals similar to adding and subtracting whole numbers?

____

____

Name ______________________ Class ______________ Date ______________

5.2 Independent Practice

CA CC 6.NS.3

Personal Math Trainer
Online Practice and Help
my.hrw.com

Add or subtract.

18. 28.6 − 0.975 = ____________

19. 5.6 − 0.105 = ____________

20. 7.03 + 33.006 = ____________

21. 57.42 + 4 + 1.602 = ____________

22. 2.25 + 65.47 + 2.333 = ____________

23. 18.419 − 6.47 = ____________

24. 83 − 12.76 = ____________

25. 102.01 − 95.602 = ____________

26. **Multiple Representations** Ursula wrote the sum 5.815 + 6.021 as a sum of two mixed numbers.

a. What sum did she write? ____________

b. Compare the sum of the mixed numbers to the sum of the decimals. ____________

Use the café menu to answer 27–29.

Café Menu	
Garden Salad	$2.29
Fruit Salad	$2.89
Veggie Burger	$4.75
Toasted Cheese Sandwich	$4.59
Bottle of Water	$1.39
Lemonade	$1.29

27. Stephen and Jahmya are having lunch. Stephen buys a garden salad, a veggie burger, and lemonade. Jahmya buys a fruit salad, a toasted cheese sandwich, and a bottle of water. Whose lunch cost more? How much more?

____

28. Jahmya wants to leave $1.75 as a tip for her server. She has a $20 bill. How much change should she receive after paying for her food and leaving a tip?

____

29. **What If?** In addition to his meal, Stephen orders a fruit salad for take-out, and wants to leave $2.25 as a tip for his server. He has a $10 bill and a $5 bill. How much change should he receive after paying for his lunch, the fruit salad, and the tip?

____

30. A carpenter who is installing cabinets uses thin pieces of material called shims to fill gaps. The carpenter uses four shims to fill a gap that is 1.2 centimeters wide. Three of the shims are 0.75 centimeter, 0.125 centimeter, and 0.09 centimeter wide. What is the width of the fourth shim?

____

31. A CD of classical guitar music contains 5 songs. The length of each song is shown in the table.

Track 1	Track 2	Track 3	Track 4	Track 5
6.5 minutes	8 minutes	3.93 minutes	4.1 minutes	5.05 minutes

a. Between each song is a 0.05-minute break. How long does it take to listen to the CD from the beginning of the first song to the end of the last song? ______________

b. **What If?** Juan wants to buy the CD from an Internet music site. He downloads the CD onto a disc that can hold up to 60 minutes of music. How many more minutes of music can he still buy after downloading the CD? ______________

H.O.T. FOCUS ON HIGHER ORDER THINKING

Work Area

32. **Analyze Relationships** Use the decimals 2.47, 9.57, and 7.1 to write two different addition facts and two different subtraction facts.

____

____

33. **Communicate Mathematical Ideas** The Commutative Property of Addition states that you can change the order of addends in a sum. The Associative Property of Addition states that you can change the grouping of addends in a sum. Use an example to show how the Commutative Property of Addition and the Associative Property of Addition apply to adding decimals.

____

____

____

____

____

34. **Critique Reasoning** Indira predicts that the actual difference of $19 - 7.82$ will be greater than the estimate of $19 - 8 = 11$. Is Indira correct? Explain how Indira might have arrived at that prediction without subtracting the actual numbers.

____

____

____

LESSON

5.3 Multiplying Decimals

CA CC 6.NS.3

Fluently add, subtract, multiply, and divide multi-digit decimals using the standard algorithm for each operation.

ESSENTIAL QUESTION

How do you multiply decimals?

EXPLORE ACTIVITY CA CC 6.NS.3

Modeling Decimal Multiplication

Use decimal grids or area models to find each product.

A **0.3 × 0.5**

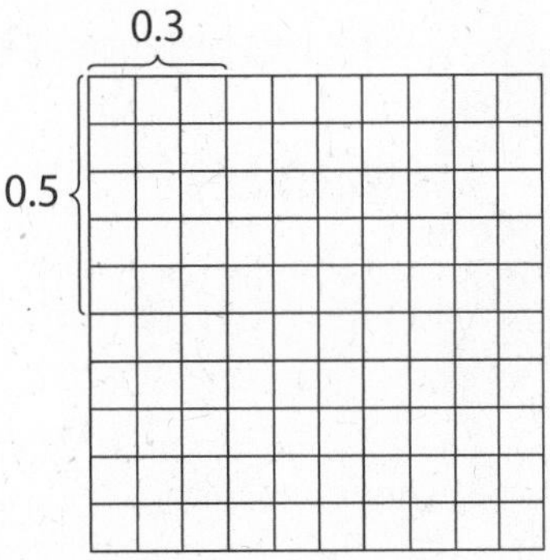

0.3 × 0.5 represents 0.3 of 0.5. Shade 5 *rows* of the decimal grid to represent 0.5.

Shade 0.3 of each 0.1 that is already shaded

to represent 0.3 of ________.

________ square(s) are double-shaded.

This represents ________ hundredth(s), or 0.15.

0.3 × 0.5 = ________

B **3.2 × 2.1**

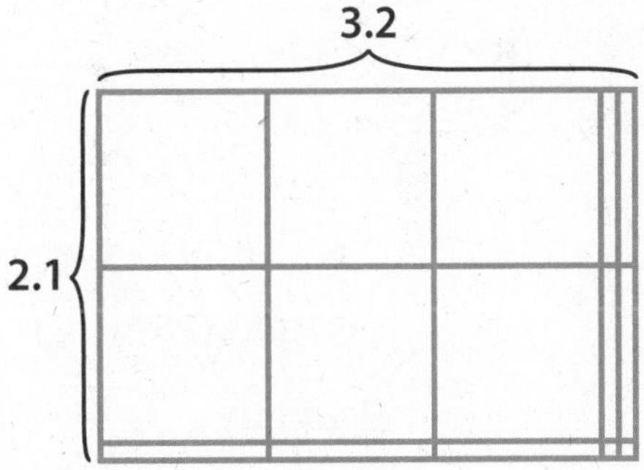

Use an area model. In the model, the large squares represent wholes, the small rectangles along the right and lower edges represent tenths, and the small squares at the lower right represent hundredths. The model is 3 and 2 tenths units long, and 2 and 1 tenth units wide.

The area of the model is

________ whole(s) + ________ tenth(s) + ________ hundredth(s) square units.

3.2 × 2.1 = ________

Reflect

1. **Analyze Relationships** How are the products 3.2 × 2.1 and 32 × 21 alike? How are they different?

____

____

Math On the Spot
my.hrw.com

Multiplying Decimals

To multiply decimals, first multiply as you would with whole numbers. Then place the decimal point in the product. The number of decimal places in the product equals the sum of the number of decimal places in the factors.

EXAMPLE 1 Real World

CA CC 6.NS.3

Delia bought 3.8 pounds of peppers. The peppers cost $1.99 per pound. What was the total cost of Delia's peppers?

1.99	←	2 decimal places
× 3.8	← +	1 decimal place
1592		
+ 5970		
7.562	←	3 decimal places

The peppers cost $7.56. — Round the answer to hundr... to show a dollar amount.

Reflect

2. **Communicate Mathematical Ideas** How can you use estimation to check that you have placed the decimal point correctly in your product?

____

____

____

____

____

Math Talk
Mathematical Practices

How is the number of decimal places in the product 0.7×0.3 related to the denominator of $\frac{7}{10} \times \frac{3}{10}$?

YOUR TURN

Multiply.

3.

12.6	← ☐	decimal place(s)
× 15.3	← + ☐	decimal place(s)
378		
☐		
+ ☐		
☐	← ☐	decimal place(s)

4.

9.76	← ☐	decimal place(s)
× 0.46	← + ☐	decimal place(s)
☐		
+ ☐		
☐	← ☐	decimal place(s)

Personal Math Trainer
Online Practice and Help
my.hrw.com

Estimating to Check Reasonableness

In Example 1, you used estimation to check whether the decimal point was placed correctly in the product. You can also use estimation to check that your answer is reasonable.

Math On the Spot
my.hrw.com

Animated Math
my.hrw.com

EXAMPLE 2 Real World

CA CC 6.NS.3

Blades of grass grow 3.75 inches per month. If the grass continues to grow at this rate, how much will the grass grow in 6.25 months?

$$\begin{array}{rl} 3.75 & \leftarrow \text{ 2 decimal places} \\ \times\ 6.25 & \leftarrow +\text{ 2 decimal places} \\ \hline 1875 & \\ 7500 & \\ +\ 225000 & \\ \hline 23.4375 & \leftarrow \text{ 4 decimal places} \end{array}$$

The grass will grow 23.4375 inches in 6.25 months.

Estimate to check whether your answer is reasonable.

Round 3.75 to the nearest whole number. ______

Round 6.25 to the nearest whole number. ______

Multiply the whole numbers. ______ × ______ = 24

The answer is reasonable because 24 is close to 23.4375.

YOUR TURN

Multiply.

5. $\begin{array}{r} 7.14 \\ \times\ 6.78 \\ \hline 5712 \\ \square \\ +\ \square \\ \hline \square \end{array}$

6. $\begin{array}{r} 11.49 \\ \times\ 8.27 \\ \hline \square \\ \square \\ +\ \square \\ \hline \square \end{array}$

7. Rico bicycles at an average speed of 15.5 miles per hour.

What distance will Rico bicycle in 2.4 hours? __________ miles

8. Use estimation to show that your answer to **7** is reasonable.

____

Personal Math Trainer
Online Practice and Help
my.hrw.com

Guided Practice

1. Use the grid to multiply 0.4 × 0.7. (Explore Activity)

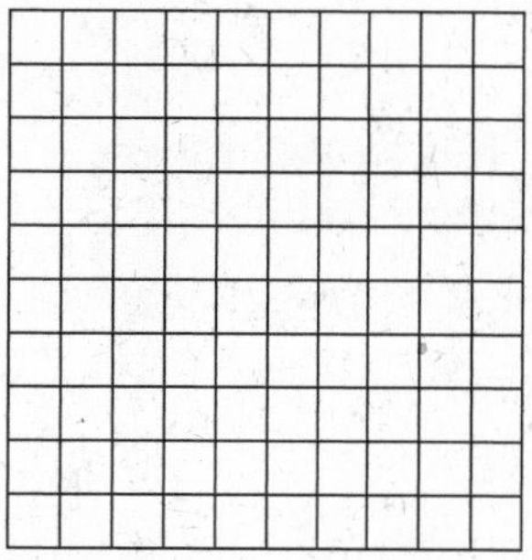

0.4 × 0.7 = ________________

2. Draw an area model to multiply 1.1 × 2.4. (Explore Activity)

1.1 × 2.4 = ________________

Multiply. (Example 1 and Example 2)

3. 0.18 × 0.06 = ________________

4. 35.15 × 3.7 = ________________

5. 0.96 × 0.12 = ________________

6. 62.19 × 32.5 = ________________

7. 3.4 × 4.37 = ________________

8. 3.762 × 0.66 = ________________

9. Chan Hee bought 3.4 pounds of cheese that cost $6.95 per pound.

How much did he spend on cheese? $________________

10. Adita earns $9.40 per hour working at an animal shelter.

How much money will she earn for 18.5 hours of work? $________________

Catherine tracked her gas purchases for one month.

Week	Gallons	Cost per gallon ($)
1	10.4	2.65
2	11.5	2.54
3	9.72	2.75
4	10.6	2.70

11. How much did Catherine spend on gas in week 2?

$________________

12. How much more did she spend in week 4 than in week 1? $________________

ESSENTIAL QUESTION CHECK-IN

13. How can you check the answer to a decimal multiplication problem?

____

____

Name ____________________ Class ____________________ Date ____________________

5.3 Independent Practice

CA CC 6.NS.3

Personal Math Trainer

my.hrw.com

Online Practice and Help

Make a reasonable estimate for each situation.

14. A gallon of water weighs 8.354 pounds. Simon uses 11.81 gallons of water while taking a shower. About how many pounds of water did Simon use? ____________________

15. A snail moves at a speed of 2.394 inches per minute. If the snail keeps moving at this rate, about how many inches will it travel in 7.489 minutes? ____________________

16. Tricia's garden is 9.87 meters long and 1.09 meters wide. What is the area of her garden? ____________________

Kaylynn and Amanda both work at the same store. The table shows how much each person earns, and the number of hours each person works in a week.

	Wage	Hours worked per week
Kaylynn	\$8.75 per hour	37.5
Amanda	\$10.25 per hour	30.5

17. Estimate how much Kaylynn earns in a week. ____________________

18. Estimate how much Amanda earns in a week. ____________________

19. Calculate the exact difference between Kaylynn and Amanda's weekly salaries. ____________________

20. Victoria's printer can print 8.804 pages in one minute. How many pages will it print in 0.903 minute? ____________________

A taxi charges a flat fee of \$4.00 plus \$2.25 per mile. Use this information for 21–22.

21. How much will it cost to travel 8.7 miles? ____________________

22. **Multistep** How much will the taxi driver earn if he takes one passenger 4.8 miles and another passenger 7.3 miles? Explain your process.

____

____

Kay goes for several bike rides one week. The table shows her speed and the number of hours spent per ride.

	Speed (in miles per hour)	Hours Spent on Bike
Monday	8.2	4.25
Tuesday	9.6	3.1
Wednesday	11.1	2.8
Thursday	10.75	1.9
Friday	8.8	3.75

23. How many miles did Kay bike on Thursday? ______________

24. On which day did Kay bike a whole number of miles? ______________

25. What is the difference in miles between Kay's longest bike ride and her shortest bike ride? ______________

26. **Check for Reasonableness** Kay estimates that Wednesday's ride was about 3 miles longer than Tuesday's ride. Is her estimate reasonable? Explain.

____

____

____

____

H.O.T. FOCUS ON HIGHER ORDER THINKING

Work Area

27. **Explain the Error** To estimate the product 3.48×7.33, Marisa multiplied 4×8 to get 32. Explain how she can make a closer estimate.

____

____

28. **Represent Real-World Problems** A jeweler buys gold jewelry and resells the gold to a refinery. The jeweler buys gold for $1,235.55 per ounce, and then resells it for $1,376.44 per ounce. How much profit does the jeweler make from buying and reselling 73.5 ounces of gold?

____

29. **Problem Solving** To find the weight of the gold in a 22 karat gold object, multiply the object's weight by 0.917. To find the weight of the gold in a 14 karat gold object, multiply the object's weight by 0.583. A 22 karat statue and a 14 karat gold statue both weigh 73.5 ounces. Which one contains more gold? How much more gold does it contain?

____

LESSON

5.4 Dividing Decimals

CA CC 6.NS.3

Fluently add, subtract, multiply, and divide multi-digit decimals using the standard algorithm for each operation.

ESSENTIAL QUESTION

How do you divide decimals?

EXPLORE ACTIVITY CA CC 6.NS.3

Modeling Decimal Division

Use decimal grids to find each quotient.

A **6.39 ÷ 3**

Shade grids to model 6.39. Separate the model into 3 equal groups.

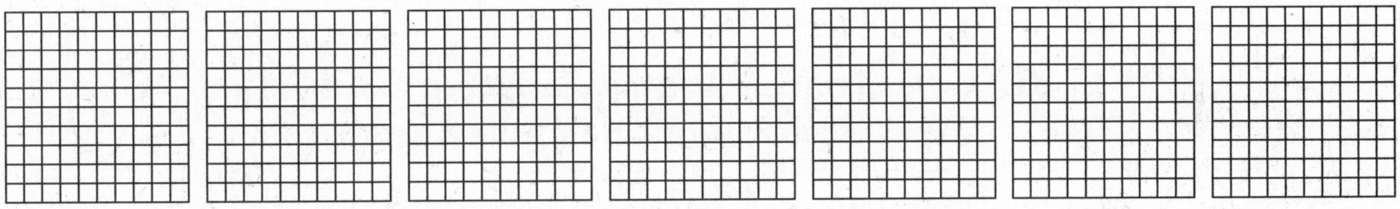

How many are in each group? ______________________

6.39 ÷ 3 = ______________________

B **6.39 ÷ 2.13**

Shade grids to model 6.39. Separate the model into groups of 2.13.

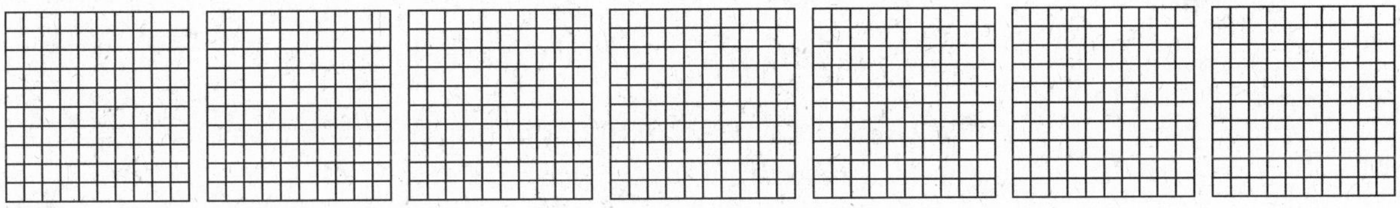

How many groups do you have? ______________________

6.39 ÷ 2.13 = ______________________

Reflect

1. **Multiple Representations** When using models to divide decimals, when might you want to use grids divided into tenths instead of hundredths?

____

____

Math On the Spot
my.hrw.com

Dividing by Whole Numbers

When you divide by a whole number and get a decimal quotient, the placement of the decimal point in the quotient is determined by the placement of the decimal in the dividend.

EXAMPLE 1 Real World

CA CC 6.NS.3

My Notes

A **Marco paid $39 for 8 tubes of oil paint. About how much did each tube cost?**

Divide using long division.

Since 39 is not evenly divisble by 8, place a decimal point in the quotient. Add zeros to the right of the decimal point as needed.

Round to the nearest hundredth to find the dollar amount.

Each tube cost about $4.88.

```
    4.875
8)39.000
 -32
   70
  -64
    60
   -56
     40
    -40
      0
```

B **A school track is 9.76 meters wide. It is divided into 8 lanes of equal width. How wide is each lane?**

Divide using long division as with whole numbers.

Place a decimal point in the quotient directly above the decimal point in the dividend.

Each lane is 1.22 meters wide.

```
   1.22
8)9.76
 -8
  17
 -16
   16
  -16
    0
```

C **Aerobics classes cost $153.86 for 14 sessions. What is the fee for one session?**

Divide using long division as with whole numbers.

Place a decimal point in the quotient directly above the decimal point in the dividend.

The fee for one aerobics class is $10.99.

```
     10.99
14)153.86
  -14
    13
    -0
    138
   -126
     126
    -126
       0
```

Math Talk
Mathematical Practices

How can you check to see that the answer is correct?

YOUR TURN

2. Inez spent $19 on a package of 8 bandanas. About how much did each bandana cost? ____________

Divide.

3. $5\overline{)9.75}$ ____________

4. $7\overline{)6.44}$ ____________

5. $87.6 \div 3 =$ ____________

6. $99.82 \div 14 =$ ____________

Personal Math Trainer
Online Practice and Help
my.hrw.com

Dividing by a Decimal

When you multiply both the dividend and the divisor of a quotient like $8 \div 4$ by the same power of 10, the quotient does not change.

$$\frac{8}{4} = \frac{8 \times 10}{4 \times 10} = \frac{80}{40} = 2 \qquad \frac{8}{4} = \frac{8 \times 100}{4 \times 100} = \frac{800}{400} = 2$$

To divide a number by a decimal, first change the divisor to a whole number by multiplying it by a power of 10. Then multiply the dividend by the same power of 10.

$$\frac{8.2}{4.1} = \frac{8.2 \times 10}{4.1 \times 10} = \frac{82}{41} = 2$$

Multiply both the dividend and the divisor by 10.

Math On the Spot
my.hrw.com

EXAMPLE 2 Real World

CA CC 6.NS.3

A Every smoothie sold contains 0.5 cup of raspberries. How many smoothies can be sold using 3.25 cups of raspberries?

STEP 1 The divisor has one decimal place, so multiply both the dividend and the divisor by 10 so that the divisor is a whole number.

$0.5\overline{)3.25}$ $\qquad$ $0.5\overline{)3.25}$

$0.5 \times 10 = 5$

$3.25 \times 10 = 32.5$

STEP 2 Divide.

$$\begin{array}{r} 6.5 \\ 5\overline{)32.5} \\ -30 \\ \hline 2\,5 \\ -2\,5 \\ \hline 0 \end{array}$$

6 smoothies can be sold.

B Anthony spent $11.52 for some pens that were on sale for $0.72 each. How many pens did Anthony buy?

STEP 1 The divisor has two decimal places, so multiply both the dividend and the divisor by 100 so that the divisor is a whole number.

$0.72\overline{)11.52}$ $\qquad$ $0.72\overline{)11.52}$

$0.72 \times 100 = 72$

$11.52 \times 100 = 1152$

STEP 2 Divide.

$$\begin{array}{r} 16 \\ 72\overline{)1152} \\ -72 \\ \hline 432 \\ -432 \\ \hline 0 \end{array}$$

Anthony bought 16 pens.

Math Talk
Mathematical Practices

The number of smoothies sold is not equal to the quotient. Why?

YOUR TURN

Divide.

7. $4.25 \div 0.5$ ________ $\qquad$ **8.** $15.12 \div 0.84$ ________

Personal Math Trainer
Online Practice and Help
my.hrw.com

Guided Practice

Divide. (Explore Activity, Examples 1 and 2)

1. $4\overline{)29}$ ______

2. $8\overline{)49}$ ______

3. $2\overline{)6.8}$ ______

4. $0.96\overline{)0.144}$ ______

5. $38.5 \div 0.5 =$ ______

6. $6.45 \div 3 =$ ______

7. $5.6372 \div 0.17 =$ ______

8. $8.19 \div 4.2 =$ ______

9. $66.5 \div 3.5 =$ ______

10. $0.234 \div 0.78 =$ ______

11. $78.74 \div 12.7 =$ ______

12. $36.45 \div 0.09 =$ ______

13. $90 \div 0.36 =$ ______

14. $18.88 \div 1.6 =$ ______

15. Corrine has 10 pounds of trail mix to divide into 8 bags. How many pounds of trail mix will go in each bag? ______

16. Michael paid $11.48 for sliced cheese at the deli counter. The cheese cost $3.28 per pound. How much cheese did Michael buy? ______

17. A four-person relay team completed a race in 73 seconds. On average, what was each runner's time? ______

18. Elizabeth has a piece of ribbon that is 4.5 meters long. She wants to cut it into pieces that are 0.25 meter long. How many pieces of ribbon will she have? ______

19. Lisa paid $43.95 for 16.1 gallons of gasoline. What was the cost per gallon, rounded to the nearest hundredth? ______

20. One inch is equivalent to 2.54 centimeters. How many inches are there in 50.8 centimeters? ______

ESSENTIAL QUESTION CHECK-IN

21. When you divide a decimal by a decimal why do you multiply the dividend and the divisor by a power of 10?

______

______

______

Name ______________________ Class ______________ Date ______________

5.4 Independent Practice

CA CC 6.NS.3

Personal Math Trainer

my.hrw.com

Online Practice and Help

The owner of a souvenir shop wants to order some custom-printed mugs and T-shirts.

Custom Printing Costs				
Quantity	25	50	75	100
Mugs	$107.25	$195.51	$261.75	$329.00
T-shirts	$237.50	$441.00	$637.50	$829.00

22. What is the price per mug for 25 coffee mugs? ______________

23. Find the price per T-shirt for 75 T-shirts. ______________

A movie rental website charges $5.00 per month for membership and $1.25 per movie.

24. How many movies did Andrew rent this month if this month's bill

was $16.25? ______________

25. Marissa has $18.50 this month to spend on movie rentals.

a. How many movies can she view this month? ______________

b. **Critique Reasoning** Marisa thinks she can afford 11 movies in one month. What mistake could she be making?

____

____

Victoria went shopping for ingredients to make a stew. The table shows the weight and the cost of each of the ingredients that she bought.

Ingredient	Weight (in pounds)	Cost
Potatoes	6.3	$7.56
Carrots	8.5	$15.30
Beef	4	$9.56
Bell peppers	2.50	$1.25

26. What is the price for one pound of bell peppers? ______________

27. Which ingredient costs the most per pound? ______________

28. **What If?** If carrots were $0.50 less per pound, how much would Victoria

have paid for 8.5 pounds of carrots? ______________

29. Brenda is planning her birthday party. She wants to have 10.92 liters of punch, 6.5 gallons of frozen yogurt, 3.9 pounds of cheese, and 25 guests at the birthday party.

a. Brenda and each guest drink the same amount of punch. How many liters of punch will each person drink? ____________________

b. Brenda and each guest eat the same amount of frozen yogurt. How many gallons of frozen yogurt will each person eat? ____________

c. Brenda and each guest eat the same amount of cheese. How many pounds of cheese will each person eat? ____________________

To make costumes for a play, Cassidy needs yellow and white fabric that she will cut into strips. The table shows how many yards of each fabric she needs, and how much she will pay for those yards.

Fabric	Yards	Cost
Yellow	12.8	$86.40
White	9.5	$45.60

30. Which fabric color costs more per yard? ____________________

31. Cassidy wants to cut the yellow fabric into strips that are 0.3 yards wide. How many strips of yellow fabric can Cassidy make? ____________

Work Area

H.O.T. FOCUS ON HIGHER ORDER THINKING

32. **Problem Solving** Eight friends purchase various supplies for a camping trip and agree to share the total cost equally. They spend $85.43 on food, $32.75 on water, and $239.66 on other items. How much does each person owe? ____________________

33. **Analyze Relationships** Constance is saving money to buy a new bicycle that costs $195.75. She already has $40 saved and plans to save $8 each week. How many weeks will it take her to save enough money to purchase the bicycle? ____________________

34. **Represent Real-World Problems** A grocery store sells twelve bottles of water for $13.80. A convenience store sells ten bottles of water for $11.80. Which store has the better buy? Explain.

____

____

LESSON 5.5

Applying Operations with Rational Numbers

CA CC 6.NS.3

Fluently add, subtract, multiply, and divide multi-digit decimals using the standard algorithm for each operation.

ESSENTIAL QUESTION

How can you solve problems involving multiplication and division of fractions and decimals?

Interpreting a Word Problem

When you solve a word problem involving rational numbers, you often need to think about the problem to decide which operations to use.

Math On the Spot
my.hrw.com

EXAMPLE 1 Problem Solving CA CC 6.NS.3

Naomi earned $54 mowing lawns in two days. She worked 2.5 hours yesterday and 4.25 hours today. If Naomi was paid the same amount for every hour she works, how much did she earn per hour?

Analyze Information

Identify the important information.

- Naomi made $54 mowing lawns.
- Naomi worked 2.5 hours yesterday and 4.25 hours today.
- You are asked to find how much she earned per hour.

Formulate a Plan

- The total amount she earned divided by the total hours she worked gives the amount she earns per hour.
- Use the expression $54 \div (2.5 + 4.25)$ to find the amount she earned per hour.

Solve

Follow the order of operations.

$(2.5 + 4.25) = 6.75$ Add inside parentheses.

$54 \div 6.75 = 8$ Divide.

Naomi earned $8 per hour mowing lawns.

Justify and Evaluate

You added 2.5 and 4.25 first to find the total number of hours worked. Then you divided 54 by the sum to find the amount earned per hour.

Personal Math Trainer
Online Practice and Help
my.hrw.com

YOUR TURN

1. Casey buys 6.2 yards of blue fabric and 5.4 yards of red fabric. If the blue and red fabric cost the same amount per yard, and Casey pays $58 for all of the fabric, what is the cost per yard?

____

Math On the Spot
my.hrw.com

Using Fractions and Decimals in Problems

Recall that you can use a number line to find equivalent fractions and decimals. If a fraction and a decimal are equivalent, they are represented by the same point on a number line.

EXAMPLE 2 Real World — CA CC 6.NS.3

Each part of a multipart question on a test is worth the same number of points. The whole question is worth 37.5 points. Roz got $\frac{1}{2}$ of the parts of a question correct. How many points did Roz receive?

Solution 1

STEP 1 Convert the decimal to a fraction greater than 1.

$\frac{1}{2} \times 37.5 = \frac{1}{2} \times \frac{75}{2}$ — *Write 37.5 as $37\frac{1}{2}$, or $\frac{75}{2}$.*

STEP 2 Multiply. Write the product in simplest form.

$\frac{1}{2} \times \frac{75}{2} = \frac{75}{4} = 18\frac{3}{4}$ — *Roz received $18\frac{3}{4}$ points.*

Solution 2

STEP 1 Convert the fraction to a decimal.

$\frac{1}{2} \times 37.5 = 0.5 \times 37.5$

STEP 2 Multiply.

$0.5 \times 37.5 = 18.75$ — *Roz received 18.75 points.*

Math Talk
Mathematical Practices
Do the solutions give the same result? Explain.

Personal Math Trainer
Online Practice and Help
my.hrw.com

YOUR TURN

2. The bill for a pizza was $14.50. Charles paid for $\frac{3}{5}$ of the bill. Show two ways to find how much he paid.

____

Guided Practice

1. Bob and Cheryl are taking a road trip that is 188.3 miles. Bob drove $\frac{5}{7}$ of the total distance. How many miles did Bob drive? (Example 1) __________

2. The winner of a raffle will receive $\frac{3}{4}$ of the \$530.40 raised from raffle ticket sales. How much money will the winner get? (Example 2) __________

5.5 Independent Practice

CA CC 6.NS.3

Personal Math Trainer
Online Practice and Help
my.hrw.com

3. Chanasia has 8.75 gallons of paint. She wants to use $\frac{2}{5}$ of the paint to paint her living room. How many gallons of paint will Chanasia use?

____

4. Harold bought 3 pounds of red apples and 4.2 pounds of green apples from a grocery store where both kinds of apples are \$1.75 a pound. How much did Harold spend on apples?

____

Samuel and Jason sell cans to a recycling center that pays \$0.40 per pound of cans. The table shows the number of pounds of cans that they sold for several days.

Day	Samuel's cans (pounds)	Jason's cans (pounds)
Monday	16.2	11.5
Tuesday	11.8	10.7
Wednesday	12.5	7.1

5. Samuel wants to use his earnings from Monday and Tuesday to buy some batteries that cost \$5.60 each. How many batteries can Samuel buy? Show your work.

____

6. Jason wants to use his earnings from Monday and Tuesday for online movie rentals. The movies cost \$2.96 each to rent. How many movies can Jason rent? Show your work.

____

7. **Multistep** Samuel and Jason spend $\frac{3}{4}$ of their combined earnings from Wednesday to buy a gift. How much do they spend? Is there enough left over from Wednesday's earnings to buy a card that costs \$3.25? Explain.

____

____

8. **Multiple Representations** Give an example of a problem that could be solved using the expression $9.5 \times (8 + 12.5)$. Solve your problem.

____

____

____

____

Tony and Alice are trying to reduce the amount of television they watch. For every hour they watch television, they have to put $2.50 into savings. The table shows how many hours of television Tony and Alice have watched in the past two months.

	Hours watched in February	Hours watched in March
Tony	35.4	18.2
Alice	21.8	26.6

9. Tony wants to use his savings at the end of March to buy video games. The games cost $35.75 each. How many games can Tony buy?

____

10. Alice wants to use her savings at the end of the two months to buy concert tickets. If the tickets cost $17.50 each, how many can she buy?

____

H.O.T. FOCUS ON HIGHER ORDER THINKING

Work Area

11. **Represent Real-World Problems** A caterer prepares three times as many pizzas as she usually prepares for a large party. The caterer usually prepares 5 pizzas. The caterer also estimates that each party guest will eat $\frac{1}{3}$ of a pizza. Write an expression that represents this situation. How many party guests will the pizzas serve?

____

Nadia charges $7.50 an hour for babysitting. She babysits 18.5 hours the first week of the month and 20 hours the second week of the month.

12. **Explain the Error** To find her total earnings for those two weeks, Nadia writes $7.5 \times 18.5 + 20 = \$158.75$. Explain her error. Show the correct solution.

____

____

____

13. **What If?** Suppose Nadia raises her rate by $0.75 an hour. How many hours would she need to work to earn the same amount of money she made in the first two weeks of the month? Explain.

____

MODULE QUIZ

Ready to Go On?

Personal Math Trainer

Online Practice and Help

my.hrw.com

5.1 Dividing Whole Numbers

1. Landon is building new bookshelves for his bookstore's new mystery section. Each shelf can hold 34 books. There are 1,265 mystery books. How many shelves will he need to build? ________________

5.2 Adding and Subtracting Decimals

2. On Saturday Keisha ran 3.218 kilometers. On Sunday she ran 2.41 kilometers. How much farther did she run on Saturday than on Sunday? ________________

5.3 Multiplying Decimals

3. Marta walked at 3.9 miles per hour for 0.72 hours. How far did she walk? ________________

Multiply.

4. 0.07×1.22 ________________

5. 4.7×2.65 ________________

5.4 Dividing Decimals

Divide.

6. $64 \div 0.4$ ________________

7. $4.7398 \div 0.26$ ________________

8. $26.73 \div 9$ ________________

9. $4 \div 3.2$ ________________

5.5 Applying Multiplication and Division of Rational Numbers

10. Doors for the small cabinets are 11.5 inches long. Doors for the large cabinets are 2.3 times as long as the doors for the small cabinets. How many large doors can be cut from a board that is $10\frac{1}{2}$ feet long? ________________

ESSENTIAL QUESTION

11. Describe a real-world situation that could be modeled by dividing two rational numbers.

____

____

CALIFORNIA

MODULE 5

MIXED REVIEW

Assessment Readiness

Personal Math Trainer

Online Practice and Help

my.hrw.com

1. Consider each equation. Is the equation true?

Select Yes or No for equations A–C.

A. $9{,}217 \div 84 = 109$ R1 ○ Yes ○ No

B. $51{,}828 \div 427 = 121$ R161 ○ Yes ○ No

C. $102.6 \div 0.216 = 475$ ○ Yes ○ No

2. Choose True or False for each statement.

A. To subtract decimals, you should first align the numbers at the decimal points. ○ True ○ False

B. To solve a problem that involves multiplication of both decimals and fractions, you can write the numbers in the same form before you multiply. ○ True ○ False

C. When decimals are divided, the number of decimal places in the quotient must be the same as the number in the divisor. ○ True ○ False

3. During a promotional event, a sporting goods store gave a free T-shirt to every 8th customer and a free water bottle to every 10th customer. Which customer was the first to get a free T-shirt and a free water bottle? If the store had 100 water bottles and 100 T-shirts to give away, how many people got both a free T-shirt and a water bottle? Explain how you know.

4. Keri walks her dog every morning. The length of the walk is 0.55 kilometer on each weekday. On each weekend day, the walk is 1.4 times as long as a walk on a weekday. How many kilometers does Keri walk in one week? Explain your solution.

UNIT 2

Study Guide Review

MODULE 4 Operations with Fractions

Key Vocabulary
reciprocals *(recíprocos)*

ESSENTIAL QUESTION

How can you use operations with fractions to solve real-world problems?

EXAMPLE 1

Add.

$\frac{7}{9}+\frac{5}{12}$ The LCM of 9 and 12 is 36.

$\frac{7\times 4}{9\times 4}+\frac{5\times 3}{12\times 3}$ Use the LCM to make fractions with common denominators.

$\frac{28}{36}+\frac{15}{36}=\frac{43}{36}$ Simplify.

$\frac{43}{36}=1\frac{7}{36}$

Subtract.

$\frac{9}{10}-\frac{5}{6}$ The LCM of 10 and 6 is 30.

$\frac{9\times 3}{10\times 3}-\frac{5\times 5}{6\times 5}$ Use the LCM to make fractions with common denominators.

$\frac{27}{30}-\frac{25}{30}=\frac{2}{30}$ Simplify.

$\frac{2}{30}=\frac{1}{15}$

EXAMPLE 2

Multiply.

A. $\frac{4}{5}\times\frac{1}{8}$

$\frac{4\times 1}{5\times 8}=\frac{4}{40}$ Multiply numerators. Multiply denominators.

$\frac{4\div 4}{40\div 4}=\frac{1}{10}$ Simplify by dividing by the GCF.

B. $2\frac{1}{4}\times\frac{1}{5}$

$\frac{9}{4}\times\frac{1}{5}$ Rewrite the mixed number as a fraction greater than 1.

$\frac{9\times 1}{4\times 5}=\frac{9}{20}$ Multiply numerators. Multiply denominators.

EXAMPLE 3

Divide.

A. $\frac{2}{7}\div\frac{1}{2}$

$\frac{2}{7}\times\frac{2}{1}$ Rewrite the problem as multiplication using the reciprocal of the second fraction.

$\frac{2\times 2}{7\times 1}=\frac{4}{7}$ Multiply numerators. Multiply denominators.

B. $2\frac{1}{3}\div 1\frac{3}{4}$

$\frac{7}{3}\div\frac{7}{4}$ Write both mixed numbers as improper fractions.

$\frac{{}^{1}\cancel{7}\times 4}{3\times \cancel{7}_{1}}=\frac{4}{3}$ Multiply by the reciprocal of the second fraction.

$1\frac{1}{3}$ Simplify: $\frac{4}{3}=1\frac{1}{3}$

EXERCISES

Add. Write the answer in simplest form. (Lesson 4.1)

1. $\frac{3}{8}+\frac{4}{5}$ ________ **2.** $1\frac{9}{10}+\frac{3}{4}$ ________ **3.** $\frac{2}{8}+\frac{6}{12}$ ________

Subtract. Write the answer in simplest form. (Lesson 4.1)

4. $1\frac{3}{7}-\frac{4}{5}$ ________ **5.** $\frac{7}{8}-\frac{5}{12}$ ________ **6.** $3\frac{5}{10}-\frac{4}{8}$ ________

Multiply. Write the answer in simplest form. (Lesson 4.1)

7. $\frac{1}{7} \times \frac{4}{5}$ ______

8. $\frac{5}{6} \times \frac{2}{3}$ ______

9. $\frac{3}{7} \times \frac{14}{15}$ ______

10. $1\frac{1}{3} \times \frac{5}{8}$ ______

11. $1\frac{2}{9} \times 1\frac{1}{2}$ ______

12. $2\frac{1}{7} \times 3\frac{2}{3}$ ______

Divide. Write the answer in simplest form. (Lessons 4.2, 4.3)

13. $\frac{3}{7} \div \frac{2}{3}$ ______

14. $\frac{1}{8} \div \frac{3}{4}$ ______

15. $1\frac{1}{5} \div \frac{1}{4}$ ______

16. On his twelfth birthday, Ben was $4\frac{3}{4}$ feet tall. On his thirteenth birthday, Ben was $5\frac{3}{8}$ feet tall. How much did Ben grow between his twelfth and thirteenth birthdays? (Lesson 4.1)

______

17. Ron had 20 apples. He used $\frac{2}{5}$ of the apples to make pies. How many apples did Ron use for pies? (Lesson 4.4)

______

18. The area of a rectangular garden is $38\frac{1}{4}$ square meters. The width of the garden is $4\frac{1}{2}$ meters. Find the length of the garden. (Lesson 4.4)

______

MODULE 5 Operations with Decimals

Key Vocabulary

order of operations *(orden de las operaciones)*

ESSENTIAL QUESTION

How can you use operations with decimals to solve real-world problems?

EXAMPLE 1

To prepare for a race, Lloyd ran every day for two weeks. He ran a total of 67,592 meters. Lloyd ran the same distance every day. He took a two-day rest and then started running again. The first day after his rest, he ran the same distance plus 1,607.87 meters more. How far did Lloyd run that day?

Step 1 Divide to see how far Lloyd ran every day during the two weeks.

$$14\overline{)67{,}592} = 4{,}828$$

Lloyd ran 4,828 meters a day.

Step 2 Add 1,607.87 to 4,828 to find out how far Lloyd ran the first day after his rest.

$$\begin{array}{r} 1{,}607.87 \\ +\ 4{,}828.00 \\ \hline 6{,}435.87 \end{array}$$

Lloyd ran 6,435.87 meters that day.

EXAMPLE 2

Rebecca bought 2.5 pounds of red apples. The apples cost $0.98 per pound. What was the total cost of Rebecca's apples?

$$\begin{array}{r l}
2.5 & \leftarrow \quad 1 \text{ decimal place} \\
\times\ .98 & \leftarrow +2 \text{ decimal places} \\
\hline
200 & \\
+\ 2250 & \\
\hline
2.450 & \leftarrow \quad 3 \text{ decimal places}
\end{array}$$

The apples cost $2.45.

EXAMPLE 3

Rashid spent $37.29 on gas for his car. Gas was $3.39 per gallon. How many gallons did Rashid purchase?

Step 1 The divisor has two decimal places, so multiply both the dividend and the divisor by 100 so that the divisor is a whole number:

$3.39\overline{)37.29}$ $\qquad$ $339\overline{)3729}$

Step 2 Divide:

$$\begin{array}{r}
11 \\
339\overline{)3729} \\
-339 \\
\hline
339 \\
-339 \\
\hline
0
\end{array}$$

Rashid purchased 11 gallons of gas.

EXERCISES

Add. (Lesson 5.2)

1. 12.24 + 3.9 ________ **2.** 0.986 + 0.342 ________ **3.** 2.479 + 0.31 ________

Subtract. (Lesson 5.2)

4. 6.19 − 3.05 ________ **5.** 7.285 − 0.975 ________ **6.** 14.31 − 13.41 ________

Multiply. (Lesson 5.3)

7. $\begin{array}{r}12\\ \times 0.4\\ \hline\end{array}$ ________ **8.** $\begin{array}{r}0.15\\ \times\ 9.1\\ \hline\end{array}$ ________ **9.** $\begin{array}{r}3.12\\ \times 0.25\\ \hline\end{array}$ ________

Divide. (Lessons 5.1, 5.4)

10. 78,974 ÷ 21 ________ **11.** 19,975 ÷ 25 ________ **12.** 67,396 ÷ 123 ________

13. $5\overline{)64.5}$ ________ **14.** $0.6\overline{)25.2}$ ________ **15.** $2.1\overline{)36.75}$ ________

16. A pound of rice crackers costs $2.88. Matthew purchased $\frac{1}{4}$ pound of crackers. How much did he pay for the crackers? (Lesson 5.5) ________

Unit Project

CA CC 6.NS.1, 6.NS.2, 6.NS.3, 6.NS.4

A Fine Kettle of Fish

You have purchased an aquarium tank that is $3\frac{1}{4}$ ft long, $1\frac{1}{3}$ ft wide, and $1\frac{3}{4}$ ft tall. You plan to stock it with tropical fish. Create a presentation describing the type and number of fish you select for your aquarium. Follow these guidelines to make your decisions:

- The volume of the tank, in cubic feet, is the length times the width times the height.
- Use the rule 1 cubic foot = 7.48 gallons to find the amount of water in your tank.
- Use the rule 1 inch of fish per 2.25 gallons of water to find the total length of the fish you can safely have in your tank.
- Your aquarium must have at least 8 fish and at least 3 different species.

You can visit a store or search online for the lengths, prices, and appearances of different species of tropical fish. Your presentation should include the number and lengths of the fish you have decided to buy and the total cost of them all. Use the space below to write down any questions you have or important information from your teacher.

MATH IN CAREERS ACTIVITY

Chef Chef Alonso is creating a recipe called Spicy Italian Chicken with the following ingredients: $\frac{3}{4}$ pound chicken, $2\frac{1}{2}$ cups tomato sauce, 1 teaspoon oregano, and $\frac{1}{2}$ teaspoon of his special hot sauce. What is the number Chef Alonso should multiply the amount of chicken by so that the recipe will make 2 full servings, each with $\frac{1}{2}$ pound of chicken? Find the amount of all the ingredients in the new recipe.

CALIFORNIA

UNIT 2
MIXED REVIEW

Assessment Readiness

Personal Math Trainer
my.hrw.com
Online Practice and Help

1. The price of regular gas at Fuel Up Gas Station is $3.39 per gallon. Based on the amount of gas each person bought and the total amount he or she paid, could the following people have gone to Fuel Up and purchased regular gas?

   Select Yes or No.

   A. Kasey paid $50.85 for 15 gallons. ○ Yes ○ No
   B. Kelvin paid $41.40 for 12 gallons. ○ Yes ○ No
   C. Kate paid $46.90 for 14 gallons. ○ Yes ○ No

2. Choose True or False.

   A. $2\frac{1}{7} \times 3\frac{2}{3} = 6\frac{1}{7}$ ○ True ○ False
   B. $1\frac{1}{5} \div \frac{1}{4} = 4\frac{4}{5}$ ○ True ○ False
   C. $1\frac{1}{3} \times \frac{5}{8} = \frac{5}{6}$ ○ True ○ False
   D. $3\frac{4}{5} \div 1\frac{1}{2} = 5\frac{7}{10}$ ○ True ○ False

3. Luis made some trail mix. He mixed $4\frac{2}{3}$ cups of popcorn, $1\frac{1}{4}$ cups of peanuts, $1\frac{1}{3}$ cups of raisins, and $\frac{3}{4}$ cup of sunflower seeds. He gave 5 of his friends an equal amount of trail mix each. How much did each friend get? Explain the steps you take to solve the problem.

4. Landon drove 103.5 miles on Tuesday, 320.75 miles on Wednesday, and 186.30 miles on Thursday for work. His company pays $0.07 for each mile he drives. He expects to be paid more than $40.00. Is he correct? Explain.

Performance Tasks

★**5.** Chef Alonso is creating a recipe with the following ingredients: 1 pound chicken, $3\frac{1}{3}$ cups tomato sauce, $1\frac{1}{3}$ teaspoons oregano, and $\frac{2}{3}$ teaspoon of his special hot sauce. The chef only has three measuring spoons: 1 teaspoon, $\frac{1}{2}$ teaspoon, and $\frac{1}{4}$ teaspoon. Can he measure the amounts of hot sauce and oregano exactly? Explain your answer.

★★**6.** Caterers of a party make a punch with 12.75 liters of grapefruit juice, 8.32 liters of sparkling water, and 14.25 liters of orange juice. The cups for serving the punch come in two sizes, 0.5 liter and 0.8 liter. There are 50 of the 0.5-liter cups and 10 of the 0.8-liter cups. If each cup is used only once, do they have enough cups to serve all of the punch?

★★★**7.** The city zoo had an equal number of visitors on Saturday and Sunday. In all, 32,096 people visited the zoo that weekend.

a. How many visited each day?

b. On Saturday, $\frac{1}{8}$ of the people were senior citizens, $\frac{1}{8}$ were infants, $\frac{1}{4}$ were children, and $\frac{1}{2}$ were adults. How many of each group visited the zoo on Saturday? Show your work.

c. On Sunday, $\frac{1}{16}$ of the people were senior citizens, $\frac{3}{16}$ were infants, $\frac{3}{8}$ were children, and $\frac{3}{8}$ were adults. How many of each group visited the zoo on Sunday? Show your work.

d. The chart shows how much each type of ticket costs. How much money did the zoo make on the weekend? Show your work.

Type of Ticket	Cost
Infants	Free
Children over 2	$4.50
Adults	$7.25
Senior Citizens	$5.75

UNIT 3

Proportionality: Ratios and Rates

MODULE 6
Representing Ratios and Rates
CA CC 6.RP.1, 6.RP.2, 6.RP.3

MODULE 7
Applying Ratios and Rates
CA CC 6.RP.3, 6.RP.3a, 6.RP.3d

MODULE 8
Percents
CA CC 6.RP.3, 6.RP.3c

MATH IN CAREERS

Residential Builder A residential builder, also called a homebuilder, specializes in the construction of residences that range from single-family custom homes to buildings that contain multiple housing units, such as apartments and condominiums. Residential builders use math in numerous ways, such as blueprint reading, measuring and scaling, using ratios and rates to calculate the amounts of different building materials needed, and estimating costs for jobs.

If you are interested in a career as a residential builder, you should study these mathematical subjects:

- Algebra
- Geometry
- Business Math
- Technical Math

Research other careers that require using ratios and rates, and measuring and scaling.

ACTIVITY At the end of the unit, check out how **residential builders** use math.

Unit Project Preview

How Big Is Big?

The Unit Project at the end of this unit will give you an opportunity to make sense of a very large real-world number. Using measurement conversions and what you will learn about rates and proportions, you will look for ways to make the enormous earnings of a famous person easier to understand. To successfully complete the Unit Project you'll need to master these skills:

- Identify proportional relationships.
- Use rates and proportions to solve problems.
- Convert between measurement systems.

1. Give some examples of rates and the units used to measure them.

____

____

2. If you know how much money someone earns per hour, how can you determine:

a. the amount the person makes per minute?

____

b. the amount the person earns per day?

____

Tracking Your Learning Progression

This unit addresses important California Common Core Standards in the Critical Areas of developing understanding of and ability to apply ratio concepts.

Domain **6.RP** Ratios and Proportional Relationships

Cluster Understand ratio concepts and use ratio reasoning to solve problems.

Representing Ratios and Rates

MODULE 6

CALIFORNIA

ESSENTIAL QUESTION

How can you use ratios and rates to solve real-world problems?

Real-World Video

my.hrw.com

Scientists studying sand structures determined that the perfect sand and water mixture is equal to 1 bucket of water for every 100 buckets of sand. This recipe can be written as the ratio $\frac{1}{100}$.

GO DIGITAL

my.hrw.com

my.hrw.com

Go digital with your write-in student edition, accessible on any device.

Math On the Spot

Scan with your smart phone to jump directly to the online edition, video tutor, and more.

Animated Math

Interactively explore key concepts to see how math works.

Personal Math Trainer

Get immediate feedback and help as you work through practice sets.

Are YOU Ready?

Complete these exercises to review skills you will need for this module.

Personal Math Trainer

Online Practice and Help

my.hrw.com

Simplify Fractions

EXAMPLE Simplify $\frac{15}{24}$.

15: 1, (3), 5, 15

24: 1, 2, (3), 4, 6, 8, 12, 24

$\frac{15 \div 3}{24 \div 3} = \frac{5}{8}$

List all the factors of the numerator and denominator.

Circle the greatest common factor (GCF).

Divide the numerator and denominator by the GCF.

Write each fraction in simplest form.

1. $\frac{6}{9}$ ______ **2.** $\frac{4}{10}$ ______ **3.** $\frac{15}{20}$ ______ **4.** $\frac{20}{24}$ ______

5. $\frac{16}{56}$ ______ **6.** $\frac{45}{72}$ ______ **7.** $\frac{18}{60}$ ______ **8.** $\frac{32}{72}$ ______

Write Equivalent Fractions

EXAMPLE

$\frac{6}{8} = \frac{6 \times 2}{8 \times 2}$

$= \frac{12}{16}$

Multiply the numerator and denominator by the same number to find an equivalent fraction.

$\frac{6}{8} = \frac{6 \div 2}{8 \div 2}$

$= \frac{3}{4}$

Divide the numerator and denominator by the same number to find an equivalent fraction.

Write the equivalent fraction.

9. $\frac{12}{15} = \frac{\square}{5}$ **10.** $\frac{5}{6} = \frac{\square}{30}$ **11.** $\frac{16}{24} = \frac{4}{\square}$ **12.** $\frac{3}{9} = \frac{21}{\square}$

13. $\frac{15}{40} = \frac{\square}{8}$ **14.** $\frac{18}{30} = \frac{\square}{10}$ **15.** $\frac{48}{64} = \frac{12}{\square}$ **16.** $\frac{2}{7} = \frac{18}{\square}$

Reading Start-Up

Visualize Vocabulary

Use the ✔ words to complete the chart. Choose the review words that describe multiplication and division.

Understanding Multiplication and Division		
Symbol	**Operation**	**Term for the answer**
$\times$		
$\div$		

Understand Vocabulary

Match the term on the left to the definition on the right.

1. rate
2. ratio
3. unit rate
4. equivalent ratios

A. Rate in which the second quantity is one unit.

B. Comparison of two quantities by division.

C. Ratios that name the same comparison.

D. Ratio of two quantities that have different units.

Vocabulary

Review Words

colon *(dos puntos)*
denominator *(denominador)*
✔ divide *(dividir)*
fraction bar *(barra de fracciones)*
✔ multiply *(multiplicar)*
numerator *(numerador)*
✔ product *(producto)*
quantity *(cantidad)*
✔ quotient *(cociente)*
term *(término)*

Preview Words

equivalent ratios *(razones equivalentes)*
rate *(tasa)*
ratio *(razón)*
unit rate *(tasa unitaria)*

Active Reading

Two-Panel Flip Chart Create a two-panel flip chart, to help you understand the concepts in this module. Label one flap "Ratios" and the other flap "Rates." As you study each lesson, write important ideas under the appropriate flap. Include information about unit rates and any sample equations that will help you remember the concepts when you look back at your notes.

GETTING READY FOR

Representing Ratios and Rates

Understanding the standards and the vocabulary terms in the standards will help you know exactly what you are expected to learn in this module.

CA CC 6.RP.3

Use ratio and rate reasoning to solve real-world and mathematical problems, e.g., by reasoning about tables of equivalent ratios, tape diagrams, double number line diagrams, or equations.

Key Vocabulary

ratio *(razón)*
A comparison of two quantities by division.

rate *(tasa)*
A ratio that compares two quantities measured in different units.

equivalent ratios *(razones equivalentes)*
Ratios that name the same comparison.

What It Means to You

You will use equivalent ratios to solve real-world problems involving ratios and rates.

EXAMPLE 6.RP.3

A group of 10 friends is in line to see a movie. The table shows how much different groups will pay in all. Predict how much the group of 10 will pay.

Number in group	3	5	6	12
Amount paid ($)	15	25	30	60

The ratios are all the same.

$\frac{3}{15} = \frac{1}{5}$ $\quad \frac{6}{30} = \frac{1}{5}$ $\quad \frac{5}{25} = \frac{1}{5}$ $\quad \frac{12}{60} = \frac{1}{5}$

Find the denominator that gives a ratio equivalent to $\frac{1}{5}$ for a group of 10.

$\frac{10}{?} = \frac{1}{5} \rightarrow \frac{10 \div 10}{50 \div 10} = \frac{1}{5} \rightarrow \frac{10}{50} = \frac{1}{5}$

A group of 10 will pay $50.

CA CC 6.RP.3b

Solve unit rate problems including those involving unit pricing and constant speed.

Key Vocabulary

unit rate *(tasa unitaria)*
A rate in which the second quantity in the comparison is one unit.

What It Means to You

You will solve problems involving unit rates by division.

EXAMPLE 6.RP.3b

A 2-liter bottle of spring water costs $2.02. A 3-liter bottle of the same water costs $2.79. Which is the better deal?

2-liter bottle

$\frac{\$2.02}{2 \text{ liters}}$

$\frac{\$2.02 \div 2}{2 \text{ liters} \div 2}$

$\frac{\$1.01}{1 \text{ liter}}$

3-liter bottle

$\frac{\$2.79}{3 \text{ liters}}$

$\frac{\$2.79 \div 3}{3 \text{ liters} \div 3}$

$\frac{\$0.93}{1 \text{ liter}}$

The 3-liter bottle is the better deal.

Visit **my.hrw.com** to see all **CA Common Core Standards** explained.

my.hrw.com

LESSON
6.1 Ratios

CA CC 6.RP.1

Understand the concept of a ratio and use ratio language to describe a relationship between two quantities. *Also 6.RP.3, 6.RP.3a*

ESSENTIAL QUESTION

How do you use ratios to compare two quantities?

EXPLORE ACTIVITY Real World — CA CC 6.RP.1

Exploring Ratios

A **ratio** is a comparison of two quantities. It shows how many times as great one quantity is than another.

For example, the ratio of star-shaped beads to moon-shaped beads in a bracelet is 3 to 1. This means that for every 3 star beads, there is 1 moon bead.

A Write the ratio of moon beads to star beads. ____________

B Write the ratio of moon beads to all the beads. ____________

C If the bracelet has 2 moon beads, how many star beads does it have? ____________

D If the bracelet has 9 star beads, how many moon beads does it have? How do you know?

____

____

____

Reflect

1. **Make a Prediction** Write a rule that you can use to find the number of star beads in a bracelet when you know the number of moon beads. Then write a rule that you can use to find the number of moon beads when you know the number of star beads.

____

____

____

2. **Make a Prediction** Write a rule that you can use to find the total number of beads in a bracelet when you know the number of moon beads.

____

Math On the Spot
my.hrw.com

Writing Ratios

The numbers in a ratio are called *terms*. Suppose that in a pet store there are 5 dogs for every 3 cats. The ratio of dogs to cats is 5 to 3. The terms of the ratio are 5 and 3. The ratio can also be written as follows.

5 dogs to 3 cats 5 to 3 5:3 $\frac{5}{3}$

A ratio can compare a part to a part, a part to the whole, or the whole to a part.

EXAMPLE 1 Real World

CA CC 6.RP.1

A Write the ratio of comedies to dramas in three different ways.

part to part

8:3 $\frac{8}{3}$ 8 comedies to 3 dramas

Sam's Video Collection	
Comedies	8
Dramas	3
Cartoons	2
Science Fiction	1

B Write the ratio of dramas to total videos in three different ways.

part to whole

3:14 $\frac{3}{14}$ 3 dramas to 14 total videos

The total number of videos is $8 + 3 + 2 + 1 = 14$.

Math Talk
Mathematical Practices
What is the ratio of videos that are dramas to videos that are not dramas? Is this a part to part or part to whole ratio?

Reflect

3. **Interpret the Answer** Write and interpret the ratio of cartoons to dramas.

____

____

4. **Analyze Relationships** The ratio of floor seats to balcony seats in a theater is 20:1. Does this theater have more floor seats or more balcony seats? How do you know?

____

YOUR TURN

Write each ratio in three different ways.

5. bagel chips to peanuts ______________

6. total party mix to pretzels ______________

7. cheese crackers to peanuts ______________

Party Mix
Makes 8 cups
3 cups pretzels
3 cups bagel chips
1 cup cheese crackers
1 cup peanuts

Personal Math Trainer
Online Practice and Help
my.hrw.com

Equivalent Ratios

Equivalent ratios are ratios that name the same comparison. You can find equivalent ratios by using a multiplication table or by multiplying or dividing both terms of a ratio by the same number. So, equivalent ratios have a multiplicative relationship.

$$\frac{2}{7} \xrightarrow{\times 2} \frac{4}{14} \qquad \frac{8}{24} \xrightarrow{\div 4} \frac{2}{6}$$

Math On the Spot
my.hrw.com

A ratio with terms that have no common factors is said to be in simplest form.

EXAMPLE 2 Real World

CA CC 6.RP.3, 6.RP.3a

You make 5 cups of punch by mixing 3 cups of cranberry juice with 2 cups of apple juice. How much cranberry juice and how much apple juice do you need to make four times the original recipe?

Method 1 Use a table.

STEP 1 Make a table comparing the numbers of cups of cranberry juice and apple juice needed to make two times, three times, four times, and five times the original recipe.

Multiply both terms of the original ratio by the same number to find an equivalent ratio.

		3×2	3×3	3×4
Cranberry Juice	3	6	9	12
Apple Juice	2	4	6	8
		2×2	2×3	2×4

STEP 2 The last column of the table shows the numbers of cups of the two juices you need for four times the original recipe.

You need 12 cups of cranberry juice and 8 cups of apple juice.

Method 2 Multiply both terms of the ratio by the same number.

STEP 1 Write the original ratio in fraction form.

$$\frac{3}{2}$$

STEP 2 Multiply the numerator and denominator by the same number.

To make four times the original recipe, multiply by 4.

$$\frac{3}{2} \xrightarrow{\times 4} \frac{12}{8}$$

To make four times the original recipe, you will need 12 cups of cranberry juice and 8 cups of apple juice.

My Notes

Math Talk
Mathematical Practices

The ratio of apple juice to grape juice in a recipe is 8 cups to 10 cups. What is this ratio in simplest form? Explain.

YOUR TURN

Personal Math Trainer
Online Practice and Help
my.hrw.com

Write three ratios equivalent to the given ratio.

8. $\frac{8}{10}$ ____________________ **9.** $\frac{5}{2}$ ____________________

Guided Practice

The number of dogs compared to the number of cats in an apartment complex is represented by the model shown. (Explore Activity)

1. Write a ratio that compares the number of dogs to the number of cats. ____________

2. Complete the statement: In the apartment complex, there are ________ cats per dog.

3. If there are 15 cats in the apartment complex, how many dogs are there?

15 ÷ ________ **=** ________ **dogs**

4. How many cats are there if there are 5 dogs in the apartment complex?

5 × ________ **=** ________ **cats**

The contents of Dana's box of muffins are shown. Write each ratio in three different ways. (Example 1)

Dana's Dozen Muffins
5 corn
4 bran
2 banana nut
1 blueberry

5. banana nut muffins to corn muffins ____________________

6. corn muffins to total muffins ____________________

Vocabulary **Write three ratios equivalent to the given ratio. Include the simplest form if it is not already given. Circle the simplest form.** (Example 2)

7. $\frac{10}{12}$ ____________ **8.** $\frac{14}{2}$ ____________ **9.** $\frac{4}{7}$ ____________

ESSENTIAL QUESTION CHECK-IN

10. Use an example to describe the multiplicative relationship between two equivalent ratios.

____

____

Name ______________________ Class ______________ Date ______________

6.1 Independent Practice

CA CC 6.RP.1, 6.RP.3, 6.RP.3a

Personal Math Trainer
Online Practice and Help
my.hrw.com

Interpret each ratio and write three equivalent ratios.

11. The ratio of cups of water to cups of milk in a recipe is 1 to 3.

____

12. The ratio of peppers to tomatoes in a garden is $\frac{20}{15}$.

____

13. In each bouquet of flowers, there are 4 roses and 6 white carnations. Complete the table to find how many roses and carnations there are in 4 bouquets of flowers.

Roses	4			
Carnations	6			

____

14. Ed is using the recipe shown to make fruit salad. He wants to use 30 diced strawberries in his fruit salad. How many bananas, apples, and pears should Ed use in his fruit salad?

____

Fruit Salad Recipe
4 bananas, diced
3 apples, diced
6 pears, diced
10 strawberries, diced

15. **Critique Reasoning** Arsenia has 120 movie posters and 100 band posters. She plans to sell 24 movie posters. She says that if she also sells 24 of the band posters, the ratio of movie posters to band posters in her collection will remain the same. Is that true? Why or why not?

____

____

____

16. Bob needs to mix 2 cups of orange juice concentrate with 3.5 cups of water to make orange juice. Bob has 6 cups of concentrate. How much orange juice can he make? ______________

17. **Multistep** The ratio of North American butterflies to South American butterflies at a butterfly park is 5 : 3. The ratio of South American butterflies to European butterflies is 3 : 2. There are 30 North American butterflies at the butterfly park.

a. How many South American butterflies are there? ______________

b. How many European butterflies are there? ______________

18. Sinea and Ren are going to the carnival next week. The table shows the amount that each person spent on snacks, games, and souvenirs the last time they went to the carnival.

	Snacks	Games	Souvenirs
Sinea	\$5	\$8	\$12
Ren	\$10	\$8	\$20

a. Write the ratio of the amount Sinea spent on games to the amount she spent on souvenirs. Using this ratio, if she spends \$24 on games, how much will she spend on souvenirs?

____

b. Write the ratio of the amount Ren spent on souvenirs to the amount he spent on snacks. Using this ratio, if he spends \$12 on snacks, how much will he spend on souvenirs?

____

c. Use the ratio comparisons indicated by the data in the table. If Sinea spends \$15 on snacks next week, how much will Ren spend on snacks? How much will he spend on souvenirs? Explain.

____

____

____

H.O.T. FOCUS ON HIGHER ORDER THINKING

Work Area

19. **Multiple Representations** The diagram compares the ratio of girls in the chorus to boys in the chorus. What is the ratio of girls to boys? If there are 50 students in the chorus, how many are girls and how many are boys?

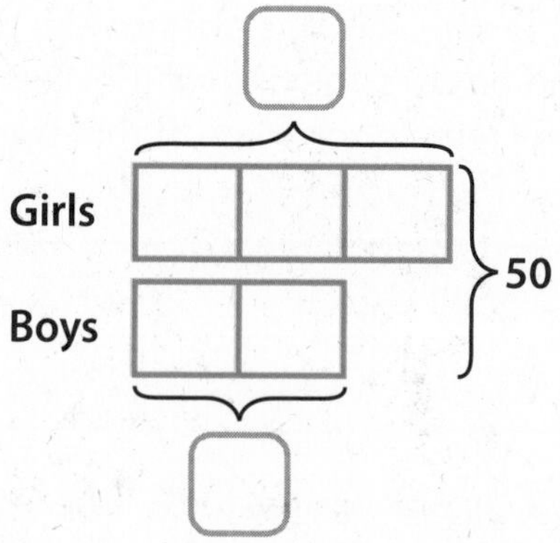

____

20. **Analyze Relationships** How is the process of finding equivalent ratios like the process of finding equivalent fractions?

____

____

21. **Explain the Error** Tina says that 6:8 is equivalent to 36:64. What did Tina do wrong?

____

LESSON

6.2 Rates

CA CC 6.RP.2

Understand the concept of a unit rate a/b associated with a ratio $a:b$ with $b \neq 0$, and use rate language in the context of a ratio relationship. *Also 6.RP.3, 6.RP.3b*

ESSENTIAL QUESTION

How do you use rates to compare quantities?

EXPLORE ACTIVITY Real World

CA CC 6.RP.2, 6.RP.3b

Using Rates to Compare Prices

A **rate** is a comparison of two quantities that have different units.

Chris drove 107 miles in two hours. This can be expressed as $\frac{107 \text{ miles}}{2 \text{ hours}}$. Notice that the units are different: miles and hours.

Shana is at the grocery store comparing two brands of juice. Brand A costs $3.84 for a 16-ounce bottle. Brand B costs $4.50 for a 25-ounce bottle.

To compare the costs, Shana must compare prices for equal amounts of juice. How can she do this?

A Complete the tables.

Brand A (each row divided by 2 to get the next, in both columns: ÷ 2)

Ounces	Price ($)
16	3.84
8	1.92
4	
2	
1	

Brand B (each row divided by 5 to get the next, in both columns: ÷ 5)

Ounces	Price ($)
25	4.50
5	
1	

B Brand A costs $ ________________ per ounce.

Brand B costs $ ________________ per ounce.

C Which brand is the better buy? Why? ________________

Reflect

1. **Analyze Relationships** Describe another method to compare the costs.

____

____

Calculating Unit Rates

A **unit rate** is a rate in which the second quantity is one unit. When the first quantity in a unit rate is an amount of money, the unit rate is sometimes called a *unit price* or *unit cost*.

Math On the Spot
my.hrw.com

EXAMPLE 1 Real World

CA CC 6.RP.2

A Gerald signs up for the classes shown. What is the cost per class?

Use the information in the problem to write a rate: $\frac{\$90}{6 \text{ classes}}$

To find the unit rate, divide both quantities in the rate by the same number so that the second quantity is 1.

$$\frac{\$90}{6 \text{ classes}} = \frac{\$15}{1 \text{ class}} \quad (\div 6)$$

Gerald's yoga classes cost $15 per class.

B The cost of 2 cartons of milk is $5.50. What is the unit price?

$$\frac{\$5.50}{2 \text{ cartons}} = \frac{\$2.75}{1 \text{ carton}} \quad (\div 2)$$

The unit price is $2.75 per carton of milk.

C A cruise ship travels 20 miles in 50 minutes. How far does the ship travel per minute?

$$\frac{20 \text{ miles}}{50 \text{ minutes}} = \frac{0.4 \text{ mile}}{1 \text{ minute}} \quad (\div 50)$$

The ship travels 0.4 mile per minute.

Math Talk
Mathematical Practices
Interpret the unit rate in part **C** using a fraction.

Reflect

2. **Critical Thinking** How can you write any rate as a unit rate?

____

3. **Multiple Representations** Explain how you could use a diagram like the one shown below to find the unit rate in **A**. Then complete the diagram to find the unit rate.

____

____

____

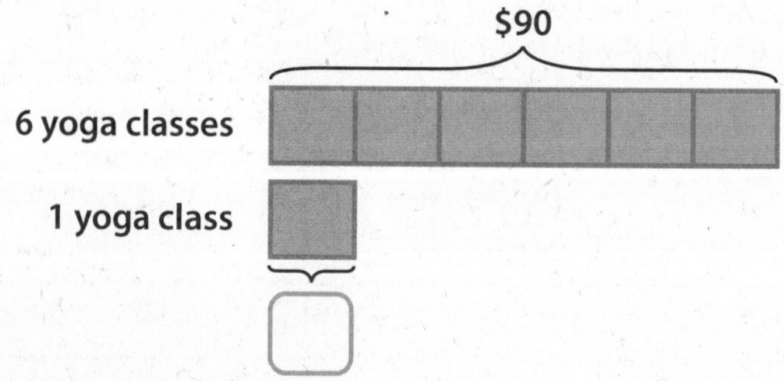

YOUR TURN

4. There are 156 players on 13 teams. How many players are on each team? ________ players

Personal Math Trainer
Online Practice and Help
my.hrw.com

Problem Solving with Unit Rates

You can solve rate problems by using a unit rate or by using equivalent rates.

Math On the Spot
my.hrw.com

EXAMPLE 2 Real World

CA CC 6.RP.3, 6.RP.3b

At a summer camp, the campers are divided into groups. Each group has 16 campers and 2 cabins. How many cabins are needed for 112 campers?

Method 1 First write the given rate as a unit rate.

$$\frac{16 \text{ campers}}{2 \text{ cabins}} \overset{\div 2}{=} \frac{8 \text{ campers}}{1 \text{ cabin}}$$

There are 8 campers per cabin.

Then divide the number of campers by the unit rate.

112 campers ÷ 8 campers per cabin = 14 cabins

Method 2 Use equivalent rates.

$$\frac{16 \text{ campers}}{2 \text{ cabins}} \overset{\times 7}{=} \frac{112 \text{ campers}}{\blacksquare \text{ cabins}}$$

Ask: 16 times what factor equals 112?

$$\frac{16 \text{ campers}}{2 \text{ cabins}} \overset{\times 7}{=} \frac{112 \text{ campers}}{14 \text{ cabins}}$$

Multiply the denominator by this factor.

The camp needs 14 cabins.

Animated Math
my.hrw.com

Check Use a diagram to check that the unit rate is 8 campers to 1 cabin.

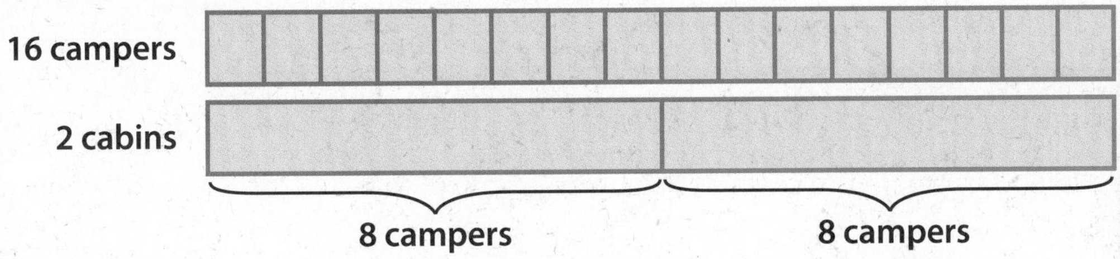

Then use the unit rate to check the answer.

Because 8 × 14 = 112, the answer is correct. That is, 14 cabins are needed.

Personal Math Trainer
Online Practice and Help
my.hrw.com

YOUR TURN

5. Petra jogs 3 miles in 27 minutes. Find the unit rate in minutes per mile. How long would it take her to jog 5 miles? Show your work.

____

____

Guided Practice

Mason's favorite brand of peanut butter is available in two sizes. Each size and its price are shown in the table. Use the table for 1 and 2. (Explore Activity)

1. What is the unit rate for each size of peanut butter?

Regular: $ ____________ per ounce

Family size: $ ____________ per ounce

	Size (oz)	Price ($)
Regular	16	3.36
Family size	40	7.60

2. Which size is the better buy? ____________

3. Martin charges $10 for every 5 bags of leaves he rakes. Last weekend, he raked 24 bags of leaves. Complete the diagram and the equivalent rates to find how much he earned. (Examples 1 and 2)

$\frac{\square}{1 \text{ bag}} = \frac{\square}{24 \text{ bags}}$

$10

5 bags of leaves

1 bag of leaves

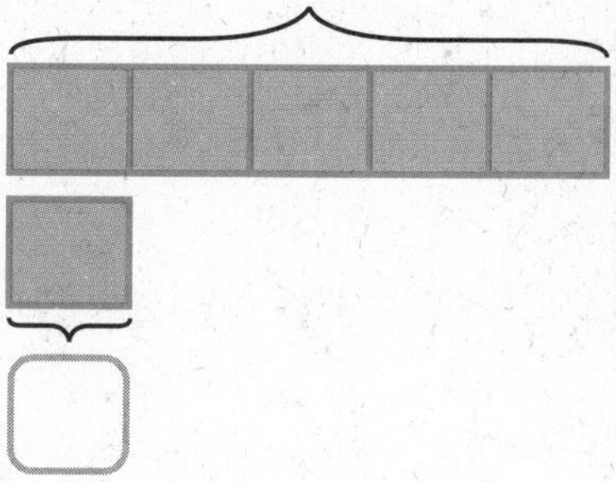

Find the unit rate. (Example 1)

4. Lisa walks 48 blocks in 3 hours. ____________ blocks per hour

5. Gordon types 1,800 words in 25 minutes. ____________ words per minute

6. A particular frozen yogurt has 75 calories in 2 ounces. How many calories are in 8 ounces of the yogurt? (Example 2) ____________

7. The cost of 10 oranges is $1. What is the cost of 5 dozen oranges? (Example 2) ____________

ESSENTIAL QUESTION CHECK-IN

8. How can you use a rate to compare the costs of two boxes of cereal that are different sizes?

____

____

Name ____________________ Class ____________________ Date ____________________

6.2 Independent Practice

CA CC 6.RP.2, 6.RP.3, 6.RP.3b

Personal Math Trainer
my.hrw.com
Online Practice and Help

Taryn and Alastair both mow lawns. Each charges a flat fee to mow a lawn. The table shows the number of lawns mowed in the past week, the time spent mowing lawns, and the money earned.

	Number of Lawns Mowed	Time Spent Mowing Lawns (in hours)	Money Earned
Taryn	9	7.5	$112.50
Alastair	7	5	$122.50

9. How much does Taryn charge to mow a lawn? ____________________

10. How much does Alastair charge to mow a lawn? ____________________

11. Who earns more per hour, Taryn or Alastair? ____________________

12. **What If?** If Taryn and Alastair want to earn an additional $735 each, how many additional hours will each spend mowing lawns? Assume each mows at the rate shown in the table and charges by the hour. Explain.

____

____

____

13. **Multistep** Tomas makes balloon sculptures at a circus. In 180 minutes, he uses 252 balloons to make 36 identical balloon sculptures.

a. How many minutes does it take to make one balloon sculpture? How many balloons are used in one sculpture? ____________________

b. What is Tomas's unit rate for balloons used per minute? ____________________

c. Complete the diagram to find out how many balloons he will use in 10 minutes. ____________________

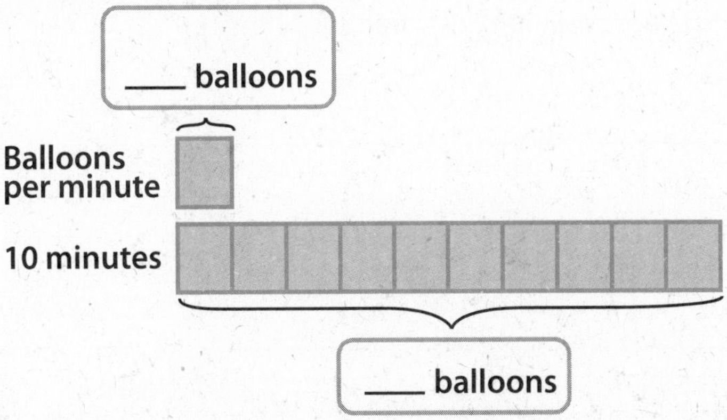

14. Abby can buy an 8-pound bag of dog food for $7.40 or a 4-pound bag of the same dog food for $5.38. Which is the better buy? ______

15. A bakery offers a sale price of $3.50 for 4 muffins. What is the price per dozen? ______

16. Mrs. Jacobsen wants to order toy instruments to give as prizes to her music students. The table shows the prices for various order sizes.

	25 items	50 items	80 items
Whistles	$21.25	$36.00	$60.00
Kazoos	$10.00	$18.50	$27.20

a. What is the difference between the highest unit price for whistles and the lowest unit price for whistles? ______

b. What is the highest unit price per kazoo? ______

c. **Persevere in Problem Solving** To get the lowest unit price, which item and how many of that item would Mrs. Jacobsen have to order? ______

H.O.T. FOCUS ON HIGHER ORDER THINKING

Work Area

17. **Draw Conclusions** There are 2.54 centimeters in 1 inch. How many centimeters are there in 1 foot? in 1 yard? Explain your reasoning.

______

______

______

18. **Critique Reasoning** A 2-pound box of spaghetti costs $2.50. Philip says that the unit cost is $\frac{2}{2.50} = \$0.80$ per pound. Explain his error.

______

______

______

19. **Look for a Pattern** A grocery store sells three different quantities of sugar. A 1-pound bag costs $1.10, a 2-pound bag costs $1.98, and a 3-pound bag costs $2.64. Describe how the unit cost changes as the quantity of sugar increases.

______

______

______

______

LESSON 6.3

Using Ratios and Rates to Solve Problems

CA CC 6.RP.3

Use ratio and rate reasoning to solve real-world and mathematical problems, e.g., by reasoning about tables of equivalent ratios, tape diagrams, double number line diagrams, or equations. *Also 6.RP.3a*

ESSENTIAL QUESTION

How can you use ratios and rates to make comparisons and predictions?

EXPLORE ACTIVITY 1 Real World CA CC 6.RP.3a

Using Tables to Compare Ratios

Anna's recipe for lemonade calls for 2 cups of lemonade concentrate and 3 cups of water. Bailey's recipe calls for 3 cups of lemonade concentrate and 5 cups of water.

A In Anna's recipe, the ratio of concentrate to water is ______________.
Use equivalent ratios to complete the table.

		2×2	$2 \times \square$	$2 \times \square$	$2 \times \square$
Concentrate (c)	2	4			
Water (c)	3		9	12	15
		3×2	3×3	3×4	3×5

B In Bailey's recipe, the ratio of concentrate to water is ______________.
Use equivalent ratios to complete the table.

		3×2	3×3	3×4	$3 \times \square$
Concentrate (c)	3	6	9	12	
Water (c)	5				25
		5×2	5×3	$5 \times \square$	$5 \times \square$

C Find two columns, one in each table, in which the amount of water is the same. Circle these two columns.

D Whose recipe makes stronger lemonade? How do you know?

____

____

E Compare the ratios: $\frac{10}{15} \bigcirc \frac{9}{15}$ $\quad \frac{2}{3} \bigcirc \frac{3}{5}$

EXPLORE ACTIVITY 1 *(cont'd)*

Reflect

1. **Analyze Relationships** Suppose each person pours herself one cup of the lemonade she made. How much concentrate is in each person's cup? How do you know?

______

______

______

Math On the Spot
my.hrw.com

Comparing Ratios

You can use equivalent ratios to solve real-world problems.

EXAMPLE 1 Real World

CA CC 6.RP.3

A fruit and nut bar recipe calls for 4 cups of chopped nuts and 6 cups of dried fruit. Tonya increased the recipe. She used 6 cups of chopped nuts and 9 cups of dried fruit. Did Tonya use the correct ratio of nuts to fruit?

STEP 1 Find the ratio of nuts to fruit in the recipe.

$\frac{4}{6}$ *4 cups of nuts to 6 cups of fruit*

STEP 2 Find the ratio of nuts to fruit that Tonya used.

$\frac{6}{9}$ *6 cups of nuts to 9 cups of fruit*

18 is a multiple of 6 and 9, so find equivalent ratios with 18 in the second term.

STEP 3 Find equivalent ratios that have the same second term.

$\frac{4}{6} = \frac{12}{18}$ (×3) $\qquad \frac{6}{9} = \frac{12}{18}$ (×2)

$$\frac{12}{18} = \frac{12}{18}$$

The ratios $\frac{4}{6}$ and $\frac{6}{9}$ are equivalent. So, Tonya used the same ratio of nuts to fruit that was given in the recipe.

Math Talk
Mathematical Practices
Explain how you compare two ratios to check if they are equivalent.

YOUR TURN

2. In the science club, there are 2 sixth-graders for every 3 seventh-graders. At this year's science fair, there were 7 projects by sixth-graders for every 12 projects by seventh-graders. Is the ratio of sixth-graders to seventh-graders in the science club equivalent to the ratio of science fair projects by sixth-graders to projects by seventh-graders? Explain.

______

Personal Math Trainer
Online Practice and Help
my.hrw.com

EXPLORE ACTIVITY 2 Real World   CA CC 6.RP.3

Using Rates to Make Predictions

Janet drives from Clarkson to Humbolt in 2 hours. Suppose Janet drives for 10 hours. If she maintains the same driving rate, can she drive more than 600 miles? Justify your answer.

A double number line is useful because the regular intervals represent equivalent rates that compare different quantities. The one shown compares the number of miles driven to the time driven for different amounts of time.

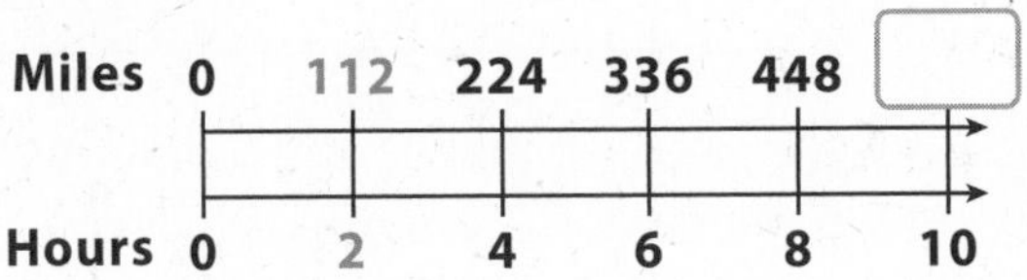

A Use the double number line to identify Janet's rate for two hours.

____

____

B Describe the relationship between Janet's rate for two hours and the other rates shown on the double number line.

____

____

C Complete the number line.

D If Janet maintains the same driving rate, can she drive more than 600 miles in 10 hours? Explain.

____

Reflect

3. In 15 minutes, Lena can finish 2 math problems. At that rate, how many math problems can she finish in 75 minutes? Use a double number line to find the answer.

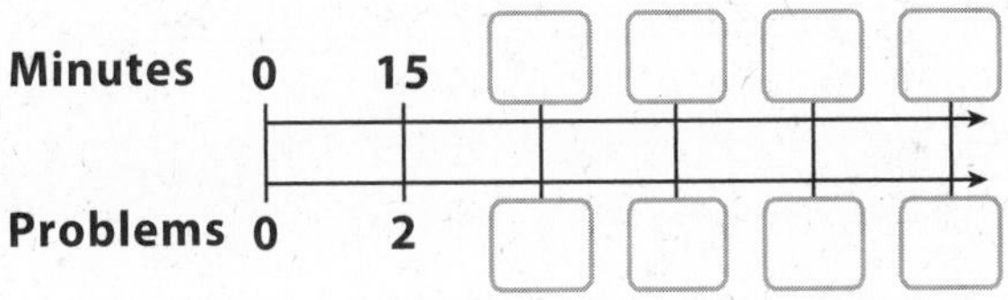

____

4. How could you use a unit rate to answer part **D**?

____

Guided Practice

1. Celeste is making fruit baskets for a local hospital. The directions say to use 5 apples for every 6 oranges. Celeste is filling her baskets with 2 apples for every 3 oranges. (Explore Activity 1)

a. Complete the tables to find equivalent ratios. Circle two columns, one in each table, in which the number of oranges is the same.

Apples	5			
Oranges	6			

Apples	2			
Oranges	3			

b. Compare the ratios. Is Celeste using the correct ratio of apples to oranges? Explain.

2. Neha used 4 bananas and 5 oranges in her fruit salad. Daniel used 7 bananas and 9 oranges. Did Neha and Daniel use the same ratio of bananas to oranges? If not, who used the greater ratio of bananas to oranges? Explain. (Example 1)

3. Tim is a first grader and reads 28 words per minute. Assuming he maintains the same rate, use the double number line to decide if he can read 150 words in 5 minutes. (Explore Activity 2)

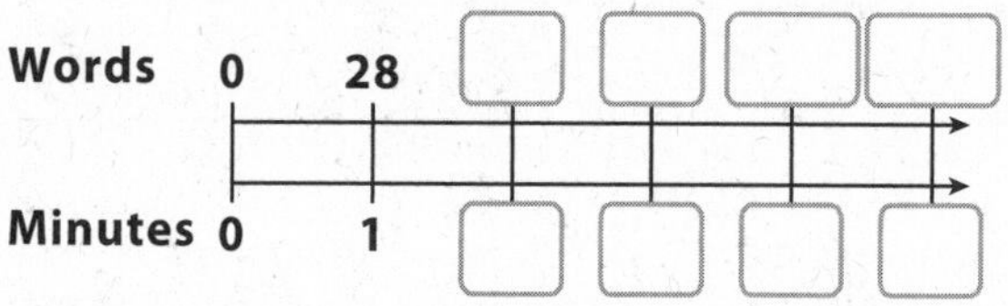

4. A cafeteria sells 30 drinks every 15 minutes. Predict whether, at that rate, the cafeteria will sell at least 90 drinks every hour. (Explore Activity 2)

ESSENTIAL QUESTION CHECK-IN

5. What must you assume when you use a rate to make a prediction?

Name ______________________ Class ______________ Date ______________

6.3 Independent Practice

CA CC 6.RP.3, 6.RP.3a

Personal Math Trainer
Online Practice and Help
my.hrw.com

6. Gina's art teacher mixes 9 pints of yellow paint with 6 pints of blue paint to create green paint. Gina mixes 4 pints of yellow paint with 3 pints of blue paint. Did Gina use the same ratio of yellow paint to blue paint that her teacher used? Explain.

____

____

7. The Suarez family paid $23.25 for 3 movie tickets. At that rate, could the family use a $100 gift certificate to buy 12 tickets? ______________

8. A store sells snacks by weight. A six ounce bag of mixed nuts costs $3.60. Will a two ounce bag of nuts cost more than or less than $1.25? ______________

9. Sue's car used 12 gallons of gas on a 300 mile trip. Jen's car used 5 gallons of gas on a 140 mile trip. Whose car got more miles per gallon? ______________

10. **Multistep** The table shows two cell phone plans that offer free minutes for each given number of paid minutes used. Pablo has Plan A and Sam has Plan B.

	Cell Phone Plans	
	Plan A	**Plan B**
Free minutes	2	8
Paid minutes	10	25

a. What is Pablo's ratio of free to paid minutes?

____

b. What is Sam's ratio of free to paid minutes?

____

c. Does Pablo's cell phone plan offer the same ratio of free to paid minutes as Sam's? Explain.

____

____

11. **Consumer Math** A store has apples on sale at $3.00 for 2 pounds.

a. How many pounds of apples can you buy for $9? Explain.

____

b. Suppose each of the apples weighs about 5 ounces. Can you buy 24 apples for $9? Explain.

____

____

12. **Science** One California fan palm tree grew 85 inches in 5 years. A queen palm tree grew 96 inches in 8 years. Which tree grew faster? Explain.

____

____

____

13. Theo drove 228 miles in 4 hours. Lex drove 186 miles in 3 hours. At those rates, could either man drive 112 miles in 2 hours? Explain.

____

14. One fabric costs $15.00 for two yards. Another costs $37.50 for 5 yards. Do these fabrics have the same unit cost? Explain.

____

H.O.T. FOCUS ON HIGHER ORDER THINKING

Work Area

15. **Problem Solving** Complete each ratio table.

	12	18	24
4.5			18

80.8	40.4		10.1
	512	256	

16. **Represent Real-World Problems** Write a real-world problem that compares the ratios 5 to 9 and 12 to 15.

____

____

____

17. **Analyze Relationships** Explain how you can be sure that all the rates you have written on a double number line are correct.

____

____

18. **Draw Conclusions** Paul can choose to be paid $50 for a job, or he can be paid $12.50 per hour. Under what circumstances should he choose the hourly wage? Explain.

____

____

____

MODULE QUIZ

Ready to Go On?

Personal Math Trainer

Online Practice and Help

my.hrw.com

6.1 Ratios

Use the table to find each ratio.

Color of socks	white	black	blue	brown
Number of socks	8	6	4	5

1. white socks to brown socks ________

2. blue socks to nonblue socks ________

3. black socks to all of the socks ________

4. Find two ratios equivalent to the ratio in Exercise 1.

____

6.2 Rates

Find each rate.

5. Earl runs 75 meters in 30 seconds. How many meters does Earl run per second? ________

6. The cost of 3 scarves is $26.25. What is the unit price? ________

6.3 Using Ratios and Rates to Solve Problems

7. Danny charges $35 for 3 hours of swimming lessons. Martin charges $24 for 2 hours of swimming lessons. Who offers a better deal? ________

8. There are 32 female performers in a dance recital. The ratio of men to women is 3 : 8. How many men are in the dance recital? ________

ESSENTIAL QUESTION

9. How can you use ratios and rates to solve problems?

____

____

____

____

CALIFORNIA

MODULE 6
MIXED REVIEW

Assessment Readiness

Personal Math Trainer
my.hrw.com
Online Practice and Help

1. Consider each set of ratios. Are all of the ratios equivalent?

Select Yes or No for the sets of ratios in A–C.

A. $\frac{2}{3}, \frac{6}{9}, \frac{18}{24}$ ○ Yes ○ No

B. $\frac{4}{20}, \frac{5}{25}, \frac{6}{30}$ ○ Yes ○ No

C. 12 : 20, 30 : 50, 75 : 125 ○ Yes ○ No

2. Sheila can ride her bicycle 6,000 meters in 15 minutes. Cal can ride his bicycle 3,400 meters in 8 minutes.

Choose True or False for each statement.

A. Sheila can ride her bicycle 800 meters in 2 minutes. ○ True ○ False

B. Cal can ride his bicycle 750 meters in 1 minute. ○ True ○ False

C. Cal rides at a slower speed than Sheila. ○ True ○ False

3. A total of 64 musicians entered a music contest, and $\frac{5}{8}$ of these musicians are guitarists. Some of the guitarists play jazz solos, and the rest play classical solos. The ratio of the number of guitarists playing jazz solos to the total number of guitarists in the contest is 1: 4. How many guitarists play classical solos in the contest? Explain your reasoning.

4. Mikaela is competing in a race in which she both runs and rides a bicycle. She runs 4.5 kilometers in 0.5 hour and rides her bicycle 18.75 kilometers in 0.75 hour. If she runs for 1 hour and bikes for 1 hour at the same rates as she does in the race, how far will she travel? Explain your reasoning.

Applying Ratios and Rates

MODULE 7

CALIFORNIA

ESSENTIAL QUESTION

How can you use ratios and rates to solve real-world problems?

LESSON 7.1

Ratios, Rates, Tables, and Graphs

CA CC 6.RP.3, 6.RP.3a, 6.RP.3b

LESSON 7.2

Applying Ratio and Rate Reasoning

CA CC 6.RP.3, 6.RP.3b

LESSON 7.3

Converting Within Measurement Systems

CA CC 6.RP.3d

LESSON 7.4

Converting Between Measurement Systems

CA CC 6.RP.3, 6.RP.3b, 6.RP.3d

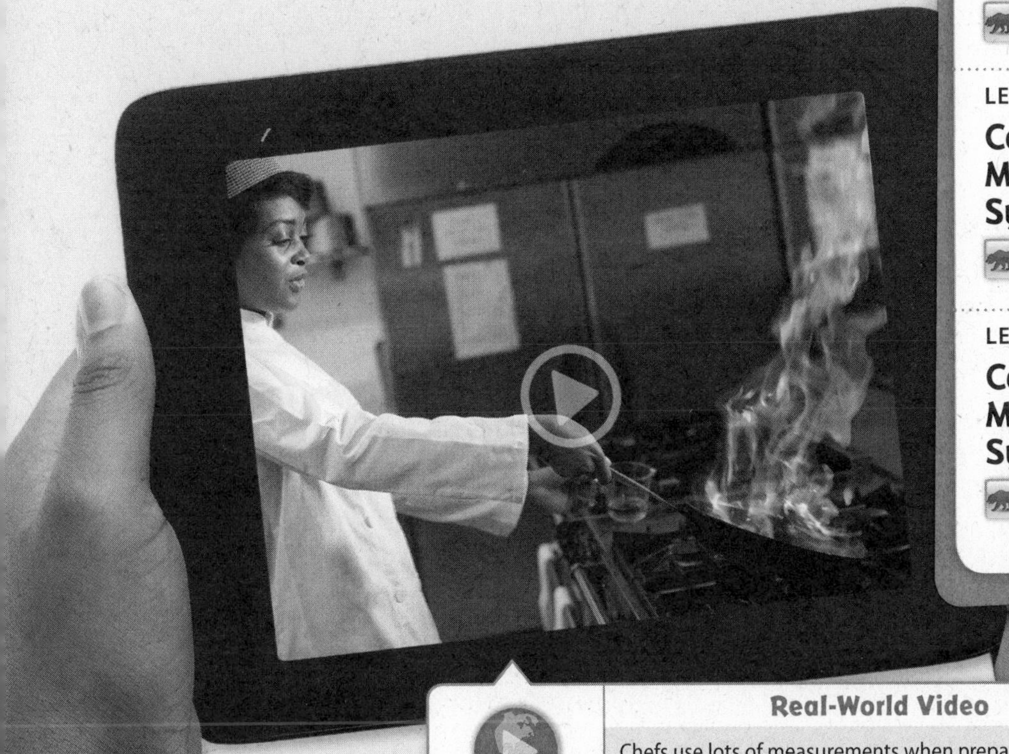

Real-World Video

my.hrw.com

Chefs use lots of measurements when preparing meals. If a chef needs more or less of a dish, he can use ratios to scale the recipe up or down. Using proportional reasoning, the chef keeps the ratios of all ingredients constant.

GO DIGITAL
my.hrw.com

my.hrw.com

Go digital with your write-in student edition, accessible on any device.

Math On the Spot

Scan with your smart phone to jump directly to the online edition, video tutor, and more.

Animated Math

Interactively explore key concepts to see how math works.

Personal Math Trainer

Get immediate feedback and help as you work through practice sets.

Are YOU Ready?

Complete these exercises to review skills you will need for this module.

Personal Math Trainer
Online Practice and Help
my.hrw.com

Graph Ordered Pairs (First Quadrant)

EXAMPLE

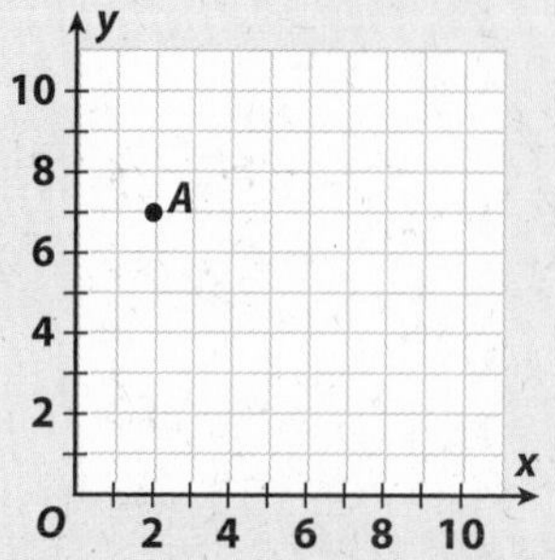

To graph $A(2, 7)$, start at the origin.
Move 2 units right.
Then move 7 units up.
Graph point $A(2, 7)$.

Graph each ordered pair on the coordinate plane above.

1. $B(9, 6)$ **2.** $C(0, 2)$ **3.** $D(6, 10)$ **4.** $E(3, 4)$

Write Equivalent Fractions

EXAMPLE

$\frac{14}{21} = \frac{14 \times 2}{21 \times 2} = \frac{28}{42}$ Multiply the numerator and denominator by the same number to find an equivalent fraction.

$\frac{14}{21} = \frac{14 \div 7}{21 \div 7} = \frac{2}{3}$ Divide the numerator and denominator by the same number to find an equivalent fraction.

Write the equivalent fraction.

5. $\frac{6}{8} = \frac{\square}{32}$ **6.** $\frac{4}{6} = \frac{\square}{12}$ **7.** $\frac{1}{8} = \frac{\square}{56}$ **8.** $\frac{9}{12} = \frac{\square}{4}$

9. $\frac{5}{9} = \frac{25}{\square}$ **10.** $\frac{5}{6} = \frac{20}{\square}$ **11.** $\frac{36}{45} = \frac{12}{\square}$ **12.** $\frac{20}{36} = \frac{10}{\square}$

Multiples

EXAMPLE List the first five multiples of 4.

$4 \times 1 = 4$
$4 \times 2 = 8$
$4 \times 3 = 12$
$4 \times 4 = 16$
$4 \times 5 = 20$

Multiply 4 by the numbers 1, 2, 3, 4, and 5.

List the first five multiples of each number.

13. 3 __________ 14. 7 __________ 15. 8 __________

Reading Start-Up

Visualize Vocabulary

Use the ✔ words to complete the graphic.

Comparing Unit Rates

Single item

Ratio of two quantities that have different units

Numbers that follow a rule

Rate in which the second quantity is one unit

Vocabulary

Review Words

equivalent ratios *(razones equivalentes)*
factor *(factor)*
graph *(gráfica)*
✔ pattern *(patrón)*
point *(punto)*
✔ rate *(tasa)*
ratio *(razón)*
✔ unit *(unidad)*
✔ unit rate *(tasa unitaria)*

Preview Words

conversion factor *(factor de conversión)*
proportion *(proporción)*
scale *(escala)*
scale drawing *(dibujo a escala)*

Understand Vocabulary

Complete the sentences using the preview words.

1. A ______________________ is a rate that compares two equivalent measurements.

2. In a scale drawing, the ______________ describes how the dimensions in the actual object compare to the dimensions in the drawing.

Active Reading

Tri-Fold Before beginning the module, create a tri-fold to help you learn the concepts and vocabulary in this module. Fold the paper into three sections. Label one column "Rates and Ratios," the second column "Proportions," and the third column "Converting Measurements." Complete the tri-fold with important vocabulary, examples, and notes as you read the module.

CALIFORNIA

GETTING READY FOR

Applying Ratios and Rates

Understanding the standards and the vocabulary terms in the standards will help you know exactly what you are expected to learn in this module.

CA CC 6.RP.3

Use ratio and rate reasoning to solve real-world and mathematical problems, e.g., by reasoning about tables of equivalent ratios, tape diagrams, double number line diagrams, or equations.

Key Vocabulary

ratio *(razón)*
A comparison of two quantities by division.

rate *(tasa)*
A ratio that compares two quantities measured in different units.

What It Means to You

You will use ratios and rates to solve real-world problems such as those involving proportions.

EXAMPLE 6.RP.3

The distance from Austin to Dallas is about 200 miles. How far apart will these cities appear on a map with the scale of $\frac{1\text{ in.}}{50\text{ mi}}$?

$$\frac{1\text{ inch}}{50\text{ miles}} = \frac{\blacksquare\text{ inches}}{200\text{ miles}}$$ *Write the scale as a unit rate.*

$$\frac{1\text{ inch} \times 4}{50\text{ miles} \times 4} = \frac{\blacksquare\text{ inches}}{200\text{ miles}}$$ *200 is a common denominator.*

$$\blacksquare = 4$$

Austin and Dallas are 4 inches apart on the map.

CA CC 6.RP.3d

Use ratio reasoning to convert measurement units; manipulate and transform units appropriately when multiplying or dividing quantities.

Key Vocabulary

unit rate *(tasa unitaria)*
A rate in which the second quantity in the comparison is one unit.

What It Means to You

You will use unit rates to convert measurement units.

EXAMPLE 6.RP.3d

The Washington Monument is about 185 yards tall. This height is almost equal to the length of two football fields. About how many feet is this?

$$185\text{ yd} \cdot \frac{3\text{ ft}}{1\text{ yd}}$$

$$= \frac{185\text{ yd}}{1} \cdot \frac{3\text{ ft}}{1\text{ yd}}$$

$$= 555\text{ ft}$$

The Washington Monument is about 555 feet tall.

Visit **my.hrw.com** to see all **CA Common Core Standards** explained.

my.hrw.com

LESSON **7.1**

Ratios, Rates, Tables, and Graphs

CA CC **6.RP.3a**

Make tables of equivalent ratios relating quantities with whole number measurements, find missing values in the tables, and plot the pairs of values on the coordinate plane. Use tables to compare ratios. *Also 6.RP.3, 6.RP.3b*

ESSENTIAL QUESTION

How can you represent real-world problems involving ratios and rates with tables and graphs?

EXPLORE ACTIVITY 1 Real World

CA CC **6.RP.3, 6.RP.3a**

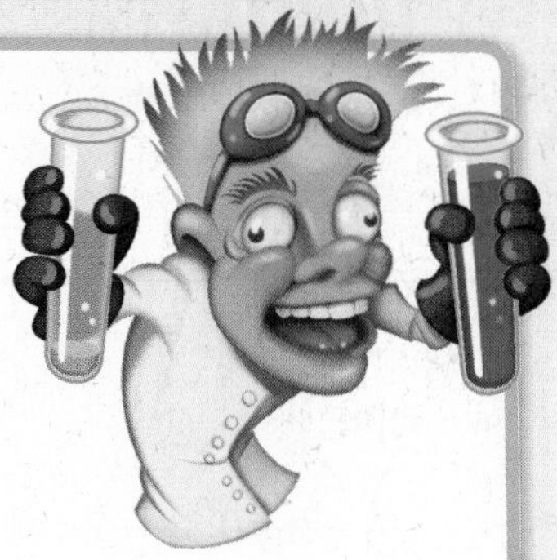

Finding Ratios from Tables

Students in Mr. Webster's science classes are doing an experiment that requires 250 milliliters of distilled water for every 5 milliliters of ammonia. The table shows the amount of distilled water needed for various amounts of ammonia.

Ammonia (mL)	2	3	3.5		5
Distilled water (mL)	100			200	250

A Use the numbers in the first column of the table to write a ratio of distilled water to ammonia. ________

B How much distilled water is used for 1 milliliter of ammonia? ________

Use your answer to write another ratio of distilled water to ammonia.

____

C The ratios in **A** and **B** are **equivalent/not equivalent.**

D How can you use your answer to **B** to find the amount of distilled water to add to a given amount of ammonia?

____

____

Math Talk
Mathematical Practices
How is the amount of distilled water in each mixture related to the amount of ammonia?

E Complete the table. What are the equivalent ratios shown in the table?

$$\frac{100}{2} = \frac{\square}{3} = \frac{\square}{3.5} = \frac{200}{\square} = \frac{250}{5}$$

Reflect

1. **Look for a Pattern** For every 1 milliliter of ammonia, there are ________ milliliters of distilled water. So for 6 milliliters of ammonia, ________ milliliters of distilled water must be added.

EXPLORE ACTIVITY 2 Real World CA CC 6.RP.3a

Graphing with Ratios

A Copy the table from Explore Activity 1 that shows the amounts of ammonia and distilled water.

Ammonia (mL)	2	3	3.5		5
Distilled water (mL)	100			200	250

B Write the information in the table as ordered pairs. Use the amounts of ammonia as the *x*-coordinates and the amounts of distilled water as the *y*-coordinates.

(2, _____) (3, _____), (3.5, _____), (_____, 200), (5, 250)

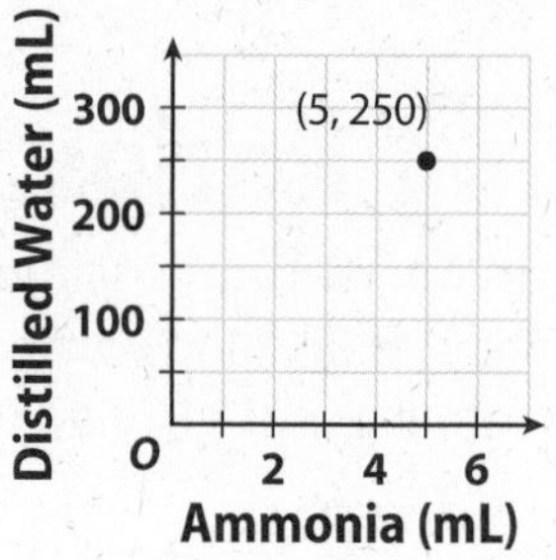

Graph the ordered pairs. Because fractions and decimals can represent amounts of chemicals, connect the points.

Describe your graph. ____________________

C For each ordered pair that you graphed, write the ratio of the *y*-coordinate to the *x*-coordinate. ____________________

D The ratio of distilled water to ammonia is $\frac{\square}{1}$. How are the ratios in **C** related to this ratio? ____________________

E The point (2.5, 125) is on the graph but not in the table. The ratio of the *y*-coordinate to the *x*-coordinate is ______. How is this ratio related to the ratios in **C** and **D**? ____________________

2.5 milliliters of ammonia requires ______ milliliters of distilled water.

F **Conjecture** What do you think is true for every point on the graph?

____

____

Reflect

2. **Communicate Mathematical Ideas** How can you use the graph to find the amount of distilled water to use for 4.5 milliliters of ammonia?

____

____

____

Representing Rates with Tables and Graphs

You can use tables and graphs to represent real-world problems involving equivalent rates.

Math On the Spot
my.hrw.com

EXAMPLE 1 Real World

CA CC 6.RP.3a, 6.RP.3b

An express train travels from Webster to Washington, D.C., at a constant speed and makes the trip in 2 hours.

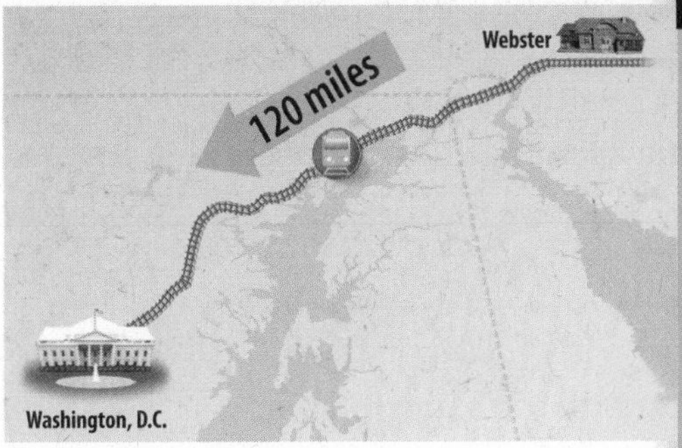

A Make a table to show the distance the train travels in various amounts of time.

STEP 1 Write a ratio of distance to time to find the rate.

$$\frac{\text{distance}}{\text{time}} = \frac{120 \text{ miles}}{2 \text{ hours}} = \frac{60 \text{ miles}}{1 \text{ hour}} = 60 \text{ miles per hour}$$

STEP 2 Use the unit rate to make a table.

Time (h)	1	2	3	4	5
Distance (mi)	60	120	180	240	300

B Graph the information from the table.

Write ordered pairs with time as the *x*-coordinate and distance as the *y*-coordinate.

(1, 60), (2, 120), (3, 180), (4, 240), (5, 300)

Graph the ordered pairs. Fractions and decimals can represent times and distances, so connect the points.

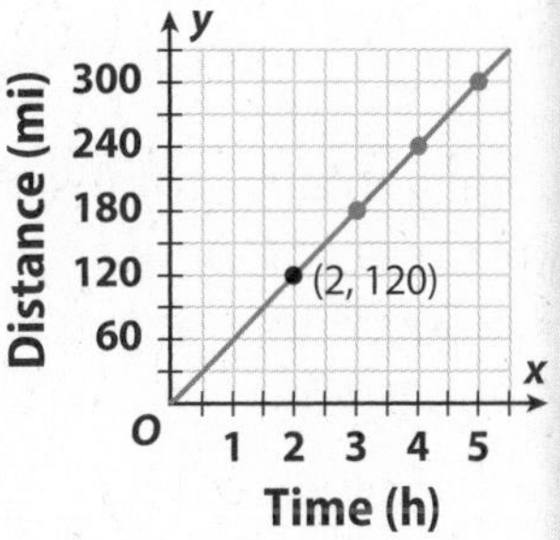

C Use the graph to find how long the train takes to travel 90 miles.

The point (1.5, 90) is on the graph, so the train takes 1.5 hours.

Animated Math
my.hrw.com

YOUR TURN

3. A shower uses 12 gallons of water in 3 minutes. Complete the table and the graph. Suppose the shower used 32 gallons of water. How long did it take?

Time (min)	2	3	4		6
Water used (gal)				20	

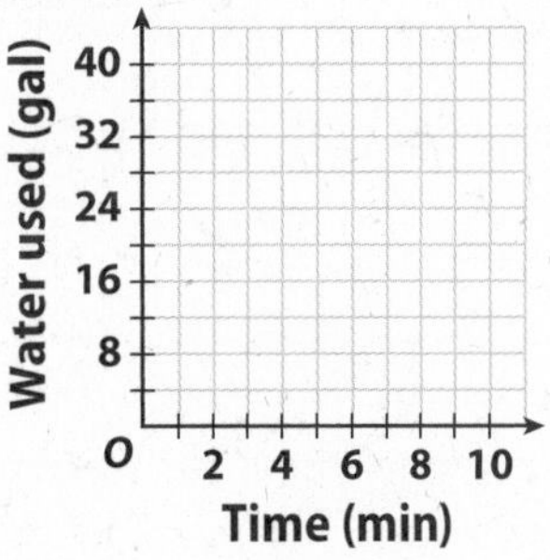

Personal Math Trainer
Online Practice and Help
my.hrw.com

Guided Practice

1. **Science** The ratio of oxygen atoms to sulfur atoms in sulfur dioxide is always the same. The table shows the numbers of atoms in different quantities of sulfur dioxide. Complete the table. (Explore Activity 1)

Sulfur atoms	6	9	21	
Oxygen atoms	12			54

What are the equivalent ratios shown in the table?

____

2. Use the table in Exercise 1 to graph the relationship between sulfur atoms and oxygen atoms. Because numbers of atoms must be whole numbers, do not connect the points. (Explore Activity 2)

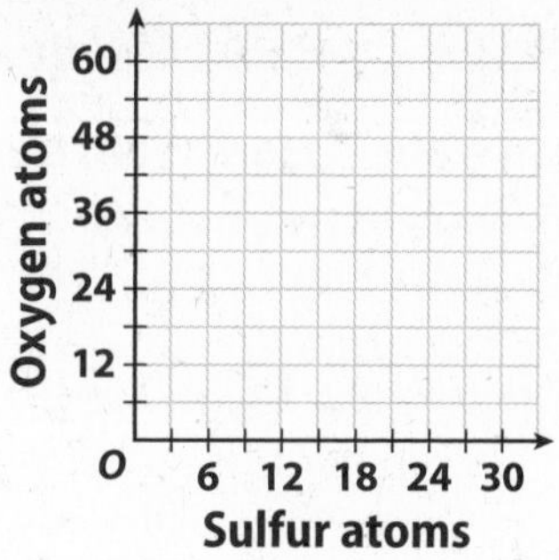

3. Stickers are made with the same ratio of length to width. A sticker 2 inches wide has a length of 4 inches. Complete the table. (Explore Activity 1)

Width (in.)	2	4	7	
Length (in.)	4			16

What are the equivalent ratios shown in the table?

____

4. Graph the relationship between the width and the length of the stickers in Exercise 3. (Explore Activity 2)

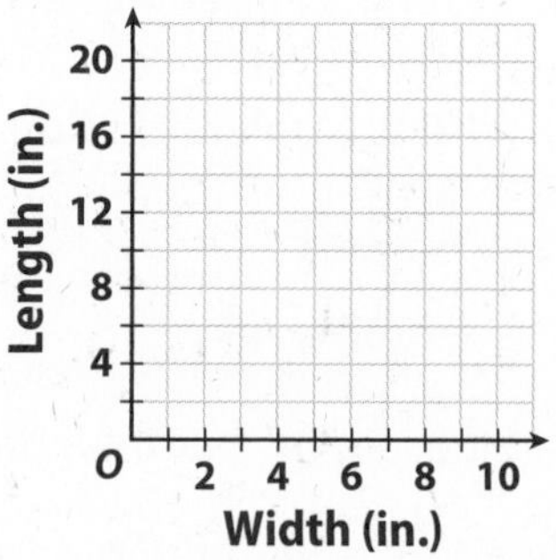

5. Five boxes of candles contain a total of 60 candles. Each box holds the same number of candles. Complete the table and the graph. Suppose you have 84 candles. How many boxes is that? (Example 1)

Boxes	5	8	
Candles	60		120

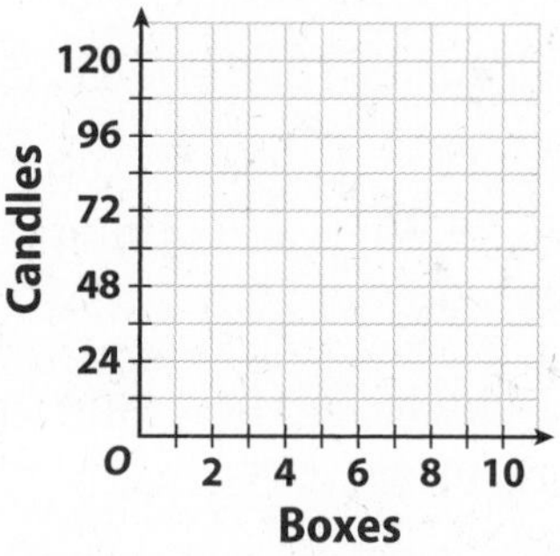

ESSENTIAL QUESTION CHECK-IN

6. How do you represent real-world problems involving ratios or rates visually?

____

____

____

Name ______________________ Class ______________ Date ____________

7.1 Independent Practice

CA CC 6.RP.3, 6.RP.3a, 6.RP.3b

Personal Math Trainer
Online Practice and Help
my.hrw.com

The table shows information about the number of sweatshirts sold and the money collected at a fundraiser for school athletic programs. Use the table for Exercises 7–12.

Sweatshirts sold	3	5	8		12
Money collected ($)	60			180	

7. Find the rate of money collected per sweatshirt sold. Show your work.

____

____

8. Use the unit rate to complete the table.

9. Explain how to graph information from the table.

____

____

____

____

10. Write the information in the table as ordered pairs. Graph the relationship from the table.

____

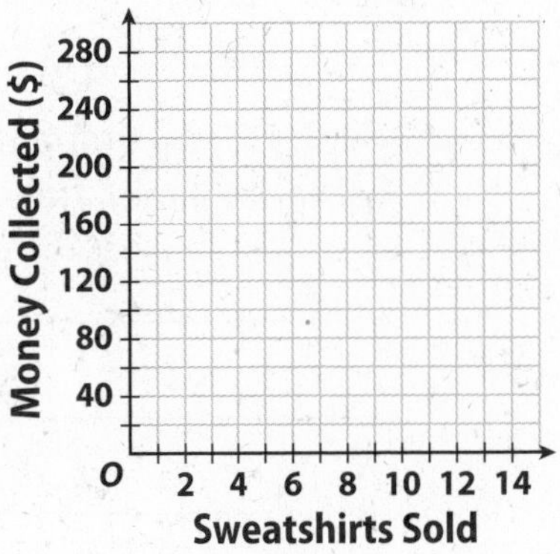

11. **What If?** How much money would be collected if 24 sweatshirts were sold? Show your work.

____

____

____

12. **Analyze Relationships** Does the point (5.5, 110) make sense in this context? Explain.

____

____

____

13. **Communicate Mathematical Ideas** The table shows the distance Mindy drove on one day of her vacation. Find the distance Mindy would have gone if she had driven for one more hour at the same rate. Explain how you solved the problem.

Time (h)	1	2	3	4	5
Distance (mi)	55	110	165	220	275

____

Use the graph for Exercises 14–15.

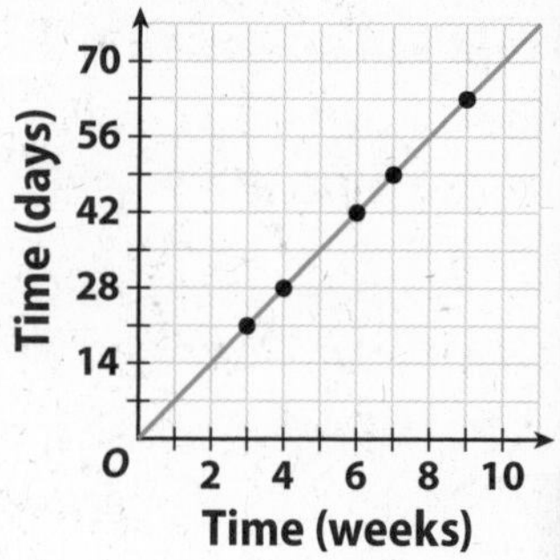

14. What number of weeks corresponds to 56 days? Explain your reasoning.

____

15. **Represent Real-World Problems** What is a real-life relationship that can be described by the graph?

____

____

H.O.T. FOCUS ON HIGHER ORDER THINKING

Work Area

16. **Make a Conjecture** Complete the table. Then find the rates $\frac{\text{distance}}{\text{time}}$ and $\frac{\text{time}}{\text{distance}}$.

Time (min)	1	2	5	
Distance (m)			25	100

$\frac{\text{distance}}{\text{time}} =$ ______

$\frac{\text{time}}{\text{distance}} =$ ______

a. Are the $\frac{\text{time}}{\text{distance}}$ rates equivalent? Explain.

____

b. Suppose you graph the points (time, distance) and your friend graphs (distance, time). How would your graphs be different?

____

____

____

17. **Communicate Mathematical Ideas** To graph a rate or ratio from a table, how do you determine the scales to use on each axis?

____

____

____

LESSON 7.2

Applying Ratio and Rate Reasoning

CA CC 6.RP.3

Use ratio and rate reasoning to solve real-world and mathematical problems, e.g., by reasoning about tables of equivalent ratios, tape diagrams, double number line diagrams, or equations. *Also 6.RP.3b*

ESSENTIAL QUESTION

How can you solve problems with proportions?

Using Ratio Reasoning

A **proportion** is an equation that states that two ratios or rates are equivalent.

$\frac{1}{3}$ and $\frac{2}{6}$ are equivalent ratios. $\frac{1}{3} = \frac{2}{6}$ is a proportion.

Math On the Spot
my.hrw.com

EXAMPLE 1 Real World CA CC 6.RP.3

Sheldon and Leonard are partners in a business. Sheldon makes \$2 in profits for every \$5 that Leonard makes. If together they make a profit of \$28 on the first item they sell, how much profit does Sheldon make?

STEP 1 Write a proportion.

Notice that if the ratio of Sheldon's profit to Leonard's is \$2 to \$5, the ratio of Sheldon's profit to the total profit is \$2 to \$7.

Sheldon's profit is unknown.

$$\frac{\text{Sheldon's profit}}{\text{Total profit}} \rightarrow \frac{\$2}{\$7} = \frac{\blacksquare}{\$28} \leftarrow \frac{\text{Sheldon's profit}}{\text{Total profit}}$$

STEP 2 Use ratio reasoning to find the unknown value.

$$\frac{\$2}{\$7} \overset{\times 4}{=} \frac{\$8}{\$28}$$

Because \$7 × 4 = \$28, multiply \$2 by 4.

If they make a total profit of \$28, then Sheldon makes a profit of \$8.

Math Talk
Mathematical Practices

For every dollar that Leonard makes, how much does Sheldon make? Explain.

YOUR TURN

1. The members of the PTA are ordering pizza for a meeting. They plan to order 2 cheese pizzas for every 3 pepperoni pizzas they order. How many cheese pizzas will they order if they order a total of 25 pizzas?

____

Personal Math Trainer
Online Practice and Help
my.hrw.com

Math On the Spot
my.hrw.com

Using Rates to Solve Proportions

You can also use equivalent rates to solve real-world problems involving proportions.

EXAMPLE 2 Real World

CA CC 6.RP.3b

The distance Ali runs in 40 minutes is shown on the pedometer. At this rate, how far can he run in 60 minutes?

STEP 1 Write a proportion.

$$\frac{\text{time}}{\text{distance}} \rightarrow \frac{40 \text{ minutes}}{3 \text{ miles}} = \frac{60 \text{ minutes}}{\blacksquare \text{ miles}} \leftarrow \frac{\text{time}}{\text{distance}}$$

60 is not a multiple of 40. So, there is no whole number by which you can multiply 3 miles to find ■ miles. You can use division to find a multiplier.

STEP 2 Find a multiplier.

To find a number by which you can multiply 40 to get 60, divide 60 by 40.

$$60 \div 40 = 1\frac{20}{40}$$

$$= 1\frac{1}{2} \text{ or } \frac{3}{2}$$

STEP 3 Find an equivalent rate.

$$\frac{40 \text{ minutes}}{3 \text{ miles}} \overset{\times \frac{3}{2}}{=} \frac{60 \text{ minutes}}{\frac{9}{2} \text{ miles}} \qquad 3 \times \frac{3}{2} = \frac{9}{2}$$

At this rate, Ali can run $\frac{9}{2}$ miles, or $4\frac{1}{2}$ miles, in 60 minutes.

YOUR TURN

2. Ms. Reynolds has a system of 10 sprinklers that water her entire lawn. The sprinklers run one at a time, and each runs for the same amount of time. The first 4 sprinklers run for a total of 50 minutes. How long does it take to water her entire lawn?

____

Personal Math Trainer
Online Practice and Help
my.hrw.com

Using Proportional Relationships to Find Distance on a Map

Math On the Spot
my.hrw.com

A **scale drawing** is a drawing of a real object that is proportionally smaller or larger than the real object. A **scale** is a ratio between two sets of measurements. It shows how a dimension in a scale drawing is related to the actual object.

A map is a scale drawing. The measurements on a map are in proportion to the actual distances. If 1 inch on a map equals an actual distance of 2 miles, the scale is 1 inch = 2 miles. You can write a scale as a rate to solve problems.

EXAMPLE 3 Real World

CA CC 6.RP.3b

The distance between two schools on Lehigh Avenue is shown on the map. What is the actual distance between the schools?

Scale: 1 inch = 2 miles

STEP 1 Write a proportion using the scale as a unit rate.

$$\frac{\text{actual distance}}{\text{map distance}} \rightarrow \frac{2 \text{ miles}}{1 \text{ inch}} = \frac{\blacksquare \text{ miles}}{3 \text{ inches}}$$

STEP 2 Use the proportion to find the distance.

$$\frac{2 \text{ miles}}{1 \text{ inch}} \overset{\times 3}{=} \frac{6 \text{ miles}}{3 \text{ inches}}$$

Because $1 \times 3 = 3$, multiply 2 by 3.

The actual distance between the two schools is 6 miles.

YOUR TURN

3. The distance between Sandville and Lewiston is shown on the map. What is the actual distance between the towns? ________

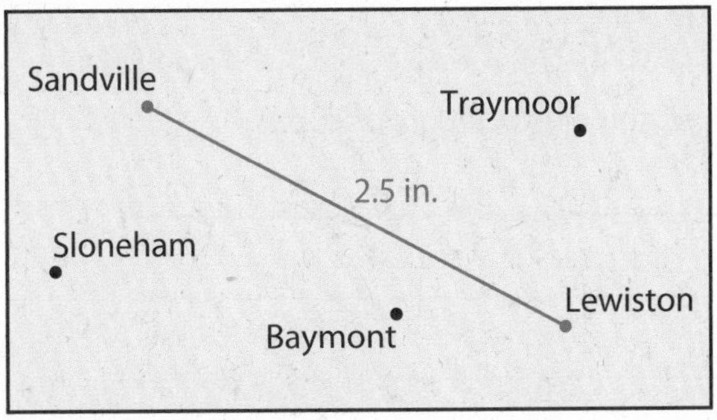

Scale: 1 inch = 20 miles

Personal Math Trainer
Online Practice and Help
my.hrw.com

Guided Practice

Find the unknown value in each proportion. (Example 1)

1. $\frac{3}{5} = \frac{\blacksquare}{30}$

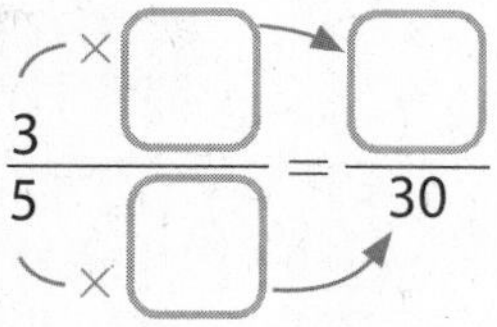

2. $\frac{4}{10} = \frac{\blacksquare}{5}$

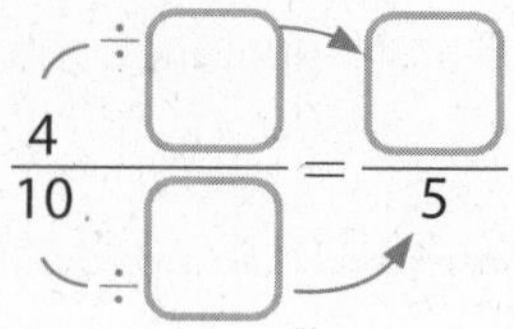

In Exercises 3–6, solve using ratio or rate reasoning.
(Examples 1 and 2)

3. Leila and Jo are two of the partners in a business. Leila makes \$3 in profits for every \$4 that Jo makes. If their total profit on the first item sold is \$105, how much profit does Leila make? ________

4. Hendrick wants to enlarge a photo that is 4 inches wide and 6 inches tall. The enlarged photo keeps the same ratio. How tall is the enlarged photo if it is 1 foot wide? ________

5. A person on a moving sidewalk travels 24 feet in 7 seconds. The moving sidewalk has a length of 180 feet. How long will it take to move from one end of the sidewalk to the other?

____

6. Contestants in a dance marathon rest for the same amount of time every hour. A couple rests for 27 minutes in 6 hours. How long does the couple rest in 8 hours?

____

7. What is the actual distance between Gendet and Montrose? (Example 3)

____

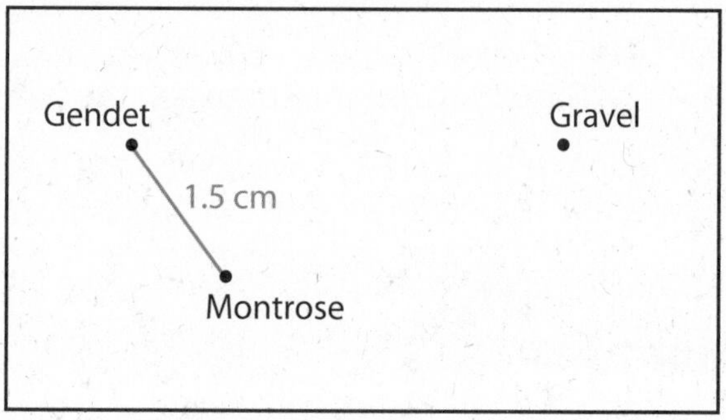

Scale: 1 centimeter = 16 kilometers

ESSENTIAL QUESTION CHECK-IN

8. Describe a real-world problem you could solve using a proportion.

____

____

____

Name ________________________ Class ____________ Date ____________

7.2 Independent Practice

CA CC 6.RP.3, 6.RP.3b

Personal Math Trainer
Online Practice and Help
my.hrw.com

9. The scale of the map is missing. The actual distance from Liberty to West Quall is 72 miles, and it is 6 inches on the map.

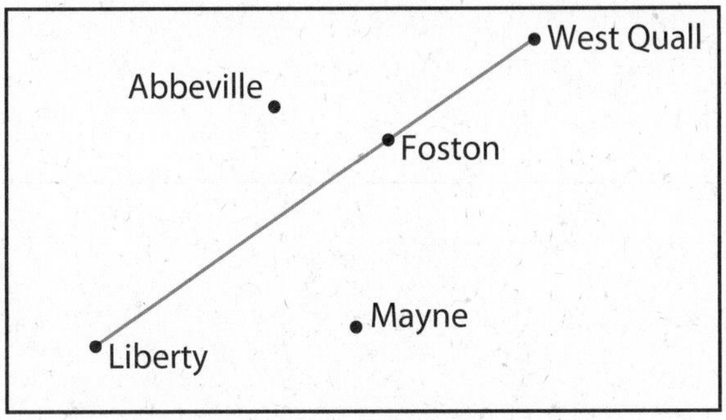

a. What is the scale of the map?

____

b. Foston is between Liberty and West Quall and is 4 inches from Liberty on the map. How far is Foston from West Quall?

____

10. A punch recipe says to mix 4 cups pineapple juice, 8 cups orange juice, and 12 cups seltzer in order to make 18 servings of punch.

a. How many cups of each ingredient do you need to make 108 cups of punch?

________ cups pineapple juice

________ cups orange juice

________ cups seltzer

b. How many servings can be made from 108 cups of punch? ____________

c. For every cup of seltzer you use, how much orange juice do you use?

____

11. On an airplane, there are two seats on the left side in each row and three seats on the right side. There are 150 seats altogether.

a. How many seats are on the left side of the plane? ____________

b. How many seats are on the right side? ____________

12. Carrie and Krystal are taking a road trip from Greenville to North Valley. Each person has her own map, and the scales on the maps are different.

a. On Carrie's map, Greenville and North Valley are 4.5 inches apart. The scale on her map is 1 inch = 20 miles. How far is Greenville from North Valley?

____

b. The scale on Krystal's map is 1 inch = 18 miles. How far apart are Greenville and North Valley on Krystal's map?

____

13. **Multistep** A machine can produce 27 inches of ribbon every 3 minutes. How many feet of ribbon can the machine make in one hour? Explain.

____

____

____

____

____

Marta, Loribeth, and Ira all have bicycles. The table shows the number of miles of each rider's last bike ride, as well as the time it took each rider to complete the ride.

	Time Spent on Last Bike Ride (in minutes)	Distance of Last Ride (in miles)
Marta	80	8
Loribeth	60	9
Ira	75	15

14. What was Marta's unit rate, in miles per minute? ______________

15. Whose speed was the fastest on their last bike ride? ______________

16. If all three riders travel for 3.5 hours at the same speed as their last ride, how many total miles will the 3 riders travel altogether? Explain.

17. **Critique Reasoning** Jason watched a caterpillar move 10 feet in 2 minutes. Jason says that the caterpillar's unit rate is $\frac{1}{5}$ foot per minute. Is Jason correct? Explain.

H.O.T. FOCUS ON HIGHER ORDER THINKING

Work Area

18. **Analyze Relationships** If the number in the numerator of a unit rate is 1, what does this indicate about the equivalent unit rates? Give an example.

19. **Multiple Representations** A boat travels at a constant speed. After 20 minutes, the boat has traveled 2.5 miles. The boat travels a total of 10 miles to a bridge.

a. Graph the relationship between the distance the boat travels and the time it takes.

b. How long does it take the boat to reach the bridge? Explain.

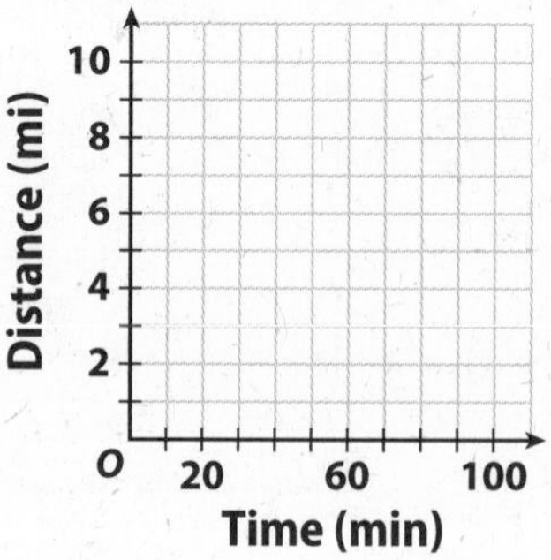

LESSON 7.3

Converting Within Measurement Systems

CA CC 6.RP.3d

Use ratio reasoning to convert measurement units; manipulate and transform units appropriately when multiplying or dividing quantities.

ESSENTIAL QUESTION

How do you convert units within a measurement system?

EXPLORE ACTIVITY Real World CA CC 6.RP.3d

Using a Model to Convert Units

The two most common systems of measurement are the customary system and the metric system. You can use a model to convert from one unit to another within the same measurement system.

STEP 1 Use the model to complete each statement below.

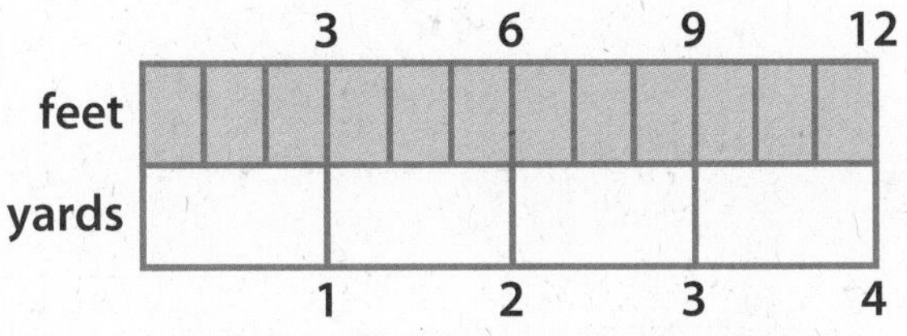

1 yard = 3 feet

2 yards = ________ feet

3 yards = ________ feet

4 yards = ________ feet

STEP 2 Rewrite your answers in Step 1 as ratios.

$\frac{\square \text{ feet}}{2 \text{ yards}} = \frac{\square \text{ feet}}{1 \text{ yard}}$ $\frac{\square \text{ feet}}{3 \text{ yards}} = \frac{\square \text{ feet}}{1 \text{ yard}}$ $\frac{\square \text{ feet}}{4 \text{ yards}} = \frac{\square \text{ feet}}{1 \text{ yard}}$

The ratio of feet to yards in any measurement is $\frac{3}{1}$. So, any ratio forming a proportion with $\frac{3}{1}$ can represent a ratio of feet to yards.

$\frac{3}{1} = \frac{12}{4}$, so 12 feet = ________ yards.

$\frac{3}{1} = \frac{54}{18}$, so ________ feet = 18 yards.

Reflect

1. **Communicate Mathematical Ideas** How could you draw a model to show the relationship between feet and inches?

____

____

____

Math On the Spot
my.hrw.com

Converting Units Using Ratios and Proportions

You can use ratios and proportions to convert both customary and metric units. Use the table below to convert from one unit to another within the same measurement system.

Customary Measurements		
Length	**Weight**	**Capacity**
1 foot = 12 inches 1 yard = 3 feet 1 mile = 1,760 yards	1 pound = 16 ounces 1 ton = 2,000 pounds	1 cup = 8 fluid ounces 1 pint = 2 cups 1 quart = 2 pints 1 gallon = 4 quarts
Metric Measurements		
Length	**Mass**	**Capacity**
1 kilometer = 1,000 meters 1 meter = 100 centimeters 1 centimeter = 10 millimeters	1 kilogram = 1,000 grams 1 gram = 1,000 milligrams	1 liter = 1,000 milliliters

Each relationship in the table can be described by two equivalent ratios. For example, because 1 quart = 2 pints, you can write the equivalent ratios $\frac{\text{1 quart}}{\text{2 pints}}$ and $\frac{\text{2 pints}}{\text{1 quart}}$.

My Notes

EXAMPLE 1 Real World

CA CC 6.RP.3d

A An average human brain weighs 3 pounds. What is this weight in ounces?

Use a proportion to convert 3 pounds to ounces.

STEP 1 Identify the ratio that compares the units involved.

The units pounds and ounces are customary units of weight. Find the relationship of those units in the Weight section of the Customary Measurements table.

1 pound = 16 ounces

STEP 2 Write a proportion.

$$\frac{\text{1 pound}}{\text{16 ounces}} = \frac{\text{3 pounds}}{\blacksquare\text{ ounces}}$$

Write the ratio $\frac{\text{1 pound}}{\text{16 ounces}}$.

$$\frac{\text{1 pound}}{\text{16 ounces}} \overset{\times 3}{=} \frac{\text{3 pounds}}{\text{48 ounces}}$$

Because $1 \times 3 = 3$, multiply 16 by 3.

A weight of 3 pounds is equal to 48 ounces.

Math Talk
Mathematical Practices
How would you solve Example 1 using the ratio $\frac{\text{16 ounces}}{\text{1 pound}}$?

B A moderate amount of daily sodium consumption is 2,000 milligrams. What is this mass in grams?

Use a proportion to convert 2,000 milligrams to grams.

STEP 1 Identify the ratio that compares the units involved.

The units, milligrams and grams, are metric units of mass. Find the relationship of those units in the Mass section of the Metric Measurements table: 1 gram = 1,000 milligrams.

STEP 2 Write a proportion.

$$\frac{1{,}000 \text{ milligrams}}{1 \text{ gram}} = \frac{2{,}000 \text{ milligrams}}{\blacksquare \text{ gram}}$$

Write the ratio $\frac{1{,}000 \text{ milligrams}}{1 \text{ gram}}$.

$$\frac{1{,}000 \text{ milligrams}}{1 \text{ gram}} \overset{\times 2}{=} \frac{2{,}000 \text{ milligrams}}{2 \text{ grams}}$$

Because $1{,}000 \times 2 = 2{,}000$, multiply 1 by 2.

A mass of 2,000 milligrams is equal to 2 grams.

Reflect

2. **Analyze Relationships** Suppose you wanted to convert 27 feet to yards. Would the number of yards be less than or greater than 27? How do you know?

____

3. **Communicate Mathematical Ideas** In **B**, what other ratio based on the table could you use? What would your proportion be?

____

YOUR TURN

Use ratios and proportions to solve.

4. The height of a doorway is 6 feet. What is the height of the doorway in inches? _______

5. A recipe calls for 40 fluid ounces of milk. What is the amount of milk called for in cups? _______

6. Josie's water bottle has a capacity of 2 liters. What is the capacity of her water bottle in milliliters? _______

7. A piece of ribbon is 350 centimeters long. What is the length of the piece of ribbon in meters? _______

Personal Math Trainer
Online Practice and Help
my.hrw.com

Math On the Spot

my.hrw.com

Converting Units by Using Conversion Factors

Another way to convert measurements is by multiplying by a conversion factor. A **conversion factor** is a ratio comparing two equivalent measurements.

EXAMPLE 2 Real World

CA CC 6.RP.3d

A Elena wants to buy 2 gallons of milk but can only find quart containers for sale. How many quarts does she need?

STEP 1 You want to convert gallons to quarts.

The appropriate conversion factor is $\frac{4 \text{ quarts}}{1 \text{ gallon}}$ because when you multiply 2 gallons by that conversion factor, you can divide out the common unit gallons. The resulting unit is quarts.

STEP 2 Multiply the given measurement by the conversion factor.

$$2\ \cancel{\text{gallons}} \times \frac{4 \text{ quarts}}{1\ \cancel{\text{gallon}}} = \frac{2 \times 4}{1} \text{ quarts}$$

Divide out the common unit.

$$= 8 \text{ quarts}$$

Elena needs 8 quarts of milk.

Math Talk
Mathematical Practices

Why can you multiply a measurement by a conversion factor without changing the measurement?

B A container of a powdered fruit drink mix has a mass of 1.25 kilograms. What is that mass in milligrams?

STEP 1 You want to convert kilograms to milligrams.

There is no equation in the table that relates kilograms and milligrams directly. However, you can convert kilograms to grams first. Then you can convert grams to milligrams.

STEP 2 Multiply the given measurement by the conversion factor.

$$1.25\ \cancel{\text{kg}} \times \frac{1{,}000 \text{ g}}{1\ \cancel{\text{kg}}} = 1.25 \times 1{,}000 \text{ g} = 1{,}250 \text{ g}$$

$$1{,}250\ \cancel{\text{g}} \times \frac{1{,}000 \text{ mg}}{1\ \cancel{\text{g}}} = 1{,}250 \times 1{,}000 \text{ mg} = 1{,}250{,}000 \text{ mg}$$

You can also do both conversions at the same time.

$$1.25\ \cancel{\text{kg}} \times \frac{1{,}000\ \cancel{\text{g}}}{1\ \cancel{\text{kg}}} \times \frac{1{,}000 \text{ mg}}{1\ \cancel{\text{g}}} = 1.25 \times 1{,}000 \times 1{,}000 \text{ mg}$$

$$= 1{,}250{,}000 \text{ mg}$$

A mass of 1.25 kilograms is equal to 1,250,000 milligrams.

YOUR TURN

8. An oak tree is planted when it is 250 centimeters tall. What is the height of the oak tree in meters?

____

9. A pitcher contains $1\frac{3}{4}$ quarts of milk. How many fluid ounces of milk does the pitcher contain?

____

Personal Math Trainer
Online Practice and Help
my.hrw.com

Guided Practice

Use the model below to complete each statement. (Explore Activity 1)

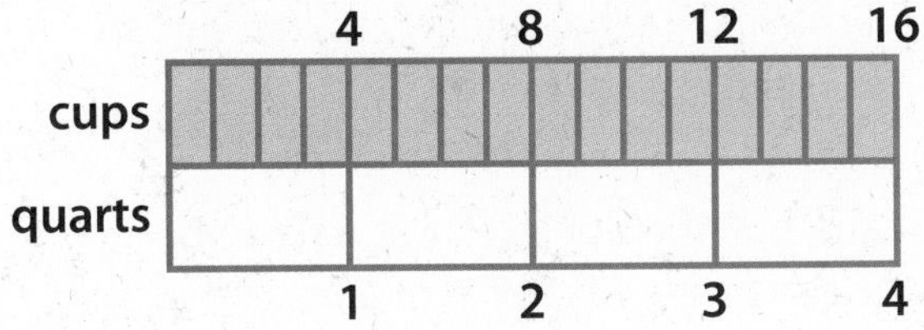

1. $\frac{4}{1} = \frac{12}{3}$, so 12 cups = ______________ quarts

2. $\frac{4}{1} = \frac{48}{12}$, so ______________ cups = 12 quarts

Use ratios and proportions to solve. (Example 1)

3. Mary Catherine makes 2 gallons of punch. How many cups of punch does she make?

____

4. The mass of a moon rock is 3.5 kilograms. What is the mass of the moon rock in grams?

____

Use a conversion factor to solve. (Example 2)

5. A serving of chickpeas contains 1,750 milligrams of potassium. How many grams of potassium is that?

____

6. On a hike, Jason found a California king snake that was 42 inches long. How many feet is that?

____

ESSENTIAL QUESTION CHECK-IN

7. How do you convert units within a measurement system?

____

____

Name ________________ Class ________________ Date ________________

7.3 Independent Practice

CA CC 6.RP.3d

Personal Math Trainer
Online Practice and Help
my.hrw.com

8. What is a conversion factor that you can use to convert gallons to pints? How did you find it?

____

____

9. Three friends each have some ribbon. Carol has 42 inches of ribbon, Tino has 2.5 feet of ribbon, and Baxter has 1.5 yards of ribbon. Express the total length of ribbon the three friends have in inches, in feet, and in yards.

__________ inches = __________ feet = __________ yards

10. Suzanna wants to measure a board, but she doesn't have a ruler to measure with. However, she does have several copies of a book that she knows is 17 centimeters tall.

a. Suzanna lays the books end to end and finds that the board is the same length as 21 books. How many centimeters long is the board?

____

b. Suzanna needs a board that is at least 3.5 meters long. Is the board long enough? Explain.

____

Sheldon needs to buy 8 gallons of coleslaw for a family reunion. The table shows the prices for different sizes of two brands of coleslaw. Use the table for Exercises 11 and 12.

	Price of small size	Price of large size
Brand A	$2.50 for 1 pint	$4.50 for 1 quart
Brand B	$4.25 for 1 quart	$9.50 for 1 gallon

11. Which size container of Brand A coleslaw is the better deal for Sheldon? Explain.

____

____

12. **Multistep** Which size and brand of coleslaw is the best deal?

____

13. In Beijing in 2008, the women's 3,000 meter steeplechase became an Olympic event. What is this distance in kilometers?

____

14. How would you convert 5 feet 6 inches to inches?

____

____

15. A quarter horse often excels at running races of $\frac{1}{4}$ mile or less. How many feet is that?

____

The California condor is the largest land bird in North America. One of the smallest is the bee hummingbird.

16. A bird's wingspan is the distance from the tip of one wing to the tip of the other. A California condor can have a wingspan of $9\frac{1}{2}$ feet. A bee hummingbird can have a wingspan of $2\frac{1}{2}$ inches. How much longer is the California condor's wingspan than the bee hummingbird's?

____

17. A California condor can have a mass of 13 kilograms. A bee hummingbird can have a mass of 1.6 grams. How many times as great as the bee hummingbird's mass is the California condor's mass?

____

18. Three friends recorded the distance from each of their homes to the park using different units. The distances are shown in the table.

Name	Distance from Home to the Park
Clark	$1\frac{3}{4}$ miles
Julio	2,640 yards
Jim	17,160 feet

a. Who lives closest to the park? Who lives farthest from the park?

____

b. **Critique Reasoning** Clark says he lives less than half as far from the park as Jim does. Is Clark right? Explain.

____

____

____

H.O.T. FOCUS ON HIGHER ORDER THINKING

Work Area

19. **Analyze Relationships** Sophie bought a water fountain for her cat. The fountain holds 50 fluid ounces of water. To fill it, Sophie uses a jar that holds 1 pint. How many times must she fill the jar to fill the fountain completely? Will she have water left in the jar? How much? Explain.

____

____

____

20. **Persevere in Problem Solving** A football field has the dimensions shown.

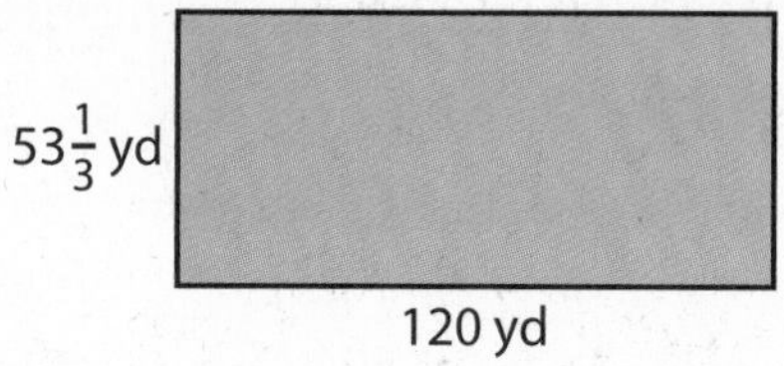

a. What are the dimensions of a football field in feet?

____

b. A chalk line is placed around the perimeter of the football field. What is the length of this line in feet?

____

c. About how many laps around the perimeter of the field would equal 1 mile? Explain.

____

____

____

21. **Look for a Pattern** What is the result if you multiply a number of cups by $\frac{8 \text{ fluid ounces}}{1 \text{ cup}}$ and then multiply the result by $\frac{1 \text{ cup}}{8 \text{ fluid ounces}}$? Give an example.

____

____

22. **Make a Conjecture** 1 hour = 3,600 seconds and 1 mile = 5,280 feet. Make a conjecture about how you could convert a speed of 15 miles per hour to feet per second. Then convert.

____

____

____

____

LESSON 7.4

Converting Between Measurement Systems

CA CC 6.RP.3d

Use ratio reasoning to convert measurement units; manipulate and transform units appropriately when multiplying or dividing quantities. *Also 6.RP.3, 6.RP.3b*

ESSENTIAL QUESTION

How can you use ratios to convert measurements?

EXPLORE ACTIVITY Real World

CA CC 6.RP.3d

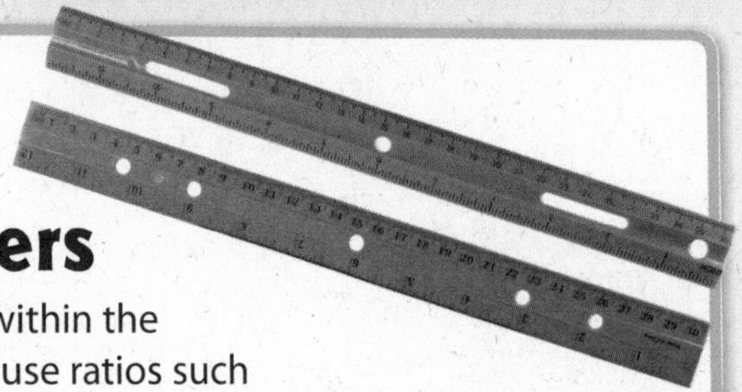

Converting Inches to Centimeters

You have used ratio reasoning to convert measurement units within the customary system and within the metric system. Now you will use ratios such as 1 inch to 2.54 centimeters to convert between systems.

The length of a sheet of paper is 11 inches. What is this length in centimeters?

A You can use a bar diagram to solve this problem. Each part represents 1 inch.

1 inch = ________ centimeter(s)

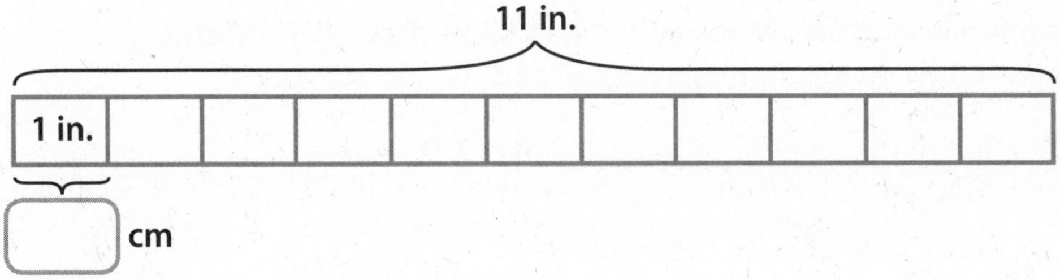

B How does the diagram help you solve the problem?

____

C 11 inches = ________ centimeters

Reflect

1. Another way to solve this problem is to write a proportion and find equivalent ratios. How is this method similar to using the diagram?

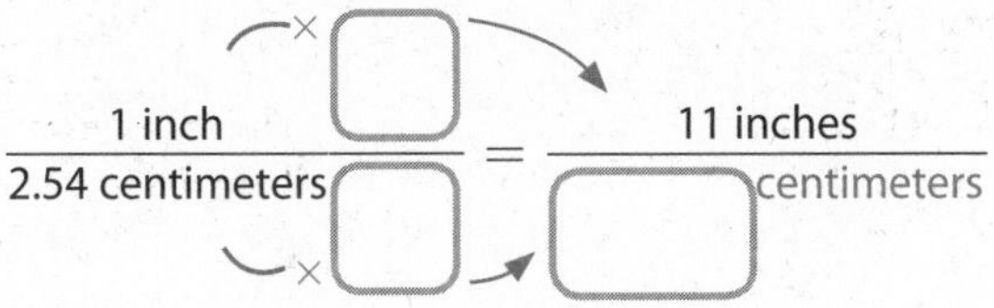

____

____

Using Conversion Factors

The table shows equivalencies between the customary and metric systems. You can use these equivalencies to find conversion factors for converting a measurement in one system to a measurement in the other system.

Customary to Metric Conversion		
Length	**Weight/Mass**	**Capacity**
1 inch = 2.54 centimeters 1 foot ≈ 0.305 meter 1 yard ≈ 0.914 meter 1 mile ≈ 1.61 kilometers	1 ounce ≈ 28.3 grams 1 pound ≈ 0.454 kilogram	1 fluid ounce ≈ 29.6 millilite 1 quart ≈ 0.946 liter 1 gallon ≈ 3.79 liters

Metric to Customary Conversion		
Length	**Weight/Mass**	**Capacity**
1 centimeter ≈ 0.39 inch 1 meter ≈ 3.28 feet 1 meter ≈ 1.09 yards 1 kilometer ≈ 0.621 mile	1 gram ≈ 0.035 ounce 1 kilogram ≈ 2.20 pounds	1 milliliter ≈ 0.034 fluid ounc 1 liter ≈ 1.06 quarts 1 liter ≈ 0.264 gallon

Most conversions are approximate, as indicated by the symbol ≈.

Math On the Spot
my.hrw.com

EXAMPLE 1 Real World

CA CC 6.RP.3d

While working out, Alima adds 11.35 kilograms to the machine. About how many pounds does she add?

STEP 1 Find the conversion factor for converting kilograms to pounds.

1 kilogram ≈ 2.20 pounds

Write the conversion factor as a ratio: $\frac{\text{2.20 pounds}}{\text{1 kilogram}}$

STEP 2 Convert the given measurement.

$11.35 \text{ kilograms} \times \frac{\text{2.20 pounds}}{\text{1 kilogram}} \approx \blacksquare \text{ pounds}$

$11.35 \text{ \cancel{kilograms}} \times \frac{\text{2.20 pounds}}{\text{1 \cancel{kilogram}}} \approx 24.97 \text{ pounds}$

Alima adds about 25 pounds.

Personal Math Trainer
Online Practice and Help
my.hrw.com

YOUR TURN

2. 6 quarts ≈ ________ liters

3. 14 feet ≈ ________ meters

4. 255.6 grams ≈ ________ ounces

5. 7 liters ≈ ________ quarts

Converting Measurements to Solve Problems

When you solve problems that involve multiplying or dividing measurements, you need to be careful to convert the units correctly.

Math On the Spot
my.hrw.com

EXAMPLE 2 Real World

CA CC 6.RP.3, 6.RP.3b, 6.RP.3d

Bob's driveway is 45 feet long by 18 feet wide. He plans to pave the entire driveway. The asphalt paving costs \$24 per square meter. What will be the total cost of the paving?

STEP 1 First find the dimensions of the driveway in meters.

Convert each measurement to meters.
Use 1 foot $\approx$ 0.305 meter.

Length: $45 \text{ feet} \times \frac{0.305 \text{ meter}}{1 \text{ foot}} \approx 13.725$ meters

Width: $18 \text{ feet} \times \frac{0.305 \text{ meter}}{1 \text{ foot}} \approx 5.49$ meters

The length and width are approximate because the conversion between feet and meters is approximate.

STEP 2 Next find the area in square meters.

area = length $\times$ width

$\approx 13.725 \times 5.49$

≈ 75.35025 square meters

STEP 3 Now find the total cost of the paving.

square meters $\times$ cost per square meter = total cost

$75.35025 \times \$24 \approx \$1{,}808.41$

Math Talk
Mathematical Practices
About how many square feet are there in a square meter? Explain.

Reflect

6. **Error Analysis** Yolanda found the area of Bob's driveway in square meters as shown. Explain why Yolanda's answer is incorrect.

Area = $45 \times 18 = 810$ square feet

$810 \text{ square feet} \times \frac{0.305 \text{ meter}}{1 \text{ foot}} \approx 247.05$ square meters

My Notes

Personal Math Trainer

Online Practice and Help

my.hrw.com

YOUR TURN

7. A flower bed is 2 meters wide and 3 meters long. What is the area of the flower bed in square feet? Round your answer to the nearest hundredth.

_________ square feet

Guided Practice

Complete each diagram to solve the problem. (Explore Activity)

1. Kate ran 5 miles. How far did she run in kilometers?

5 miles ≈ ____________ kilometers

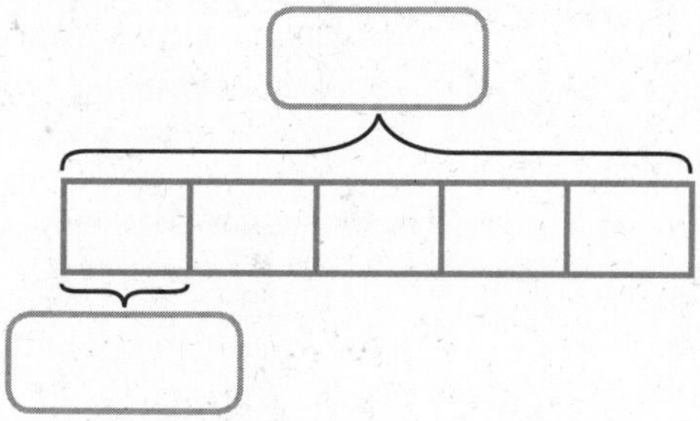

2. Alex filled a 5-gallon jug with water. How many liters of water are in the container?

5 gallons ≈ ____________ liters

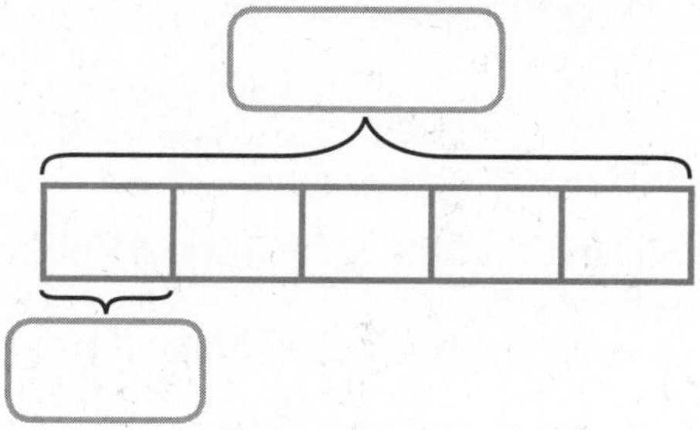

Use a conversion factor to convert each measurement. (Examples 1 and 2)

3. A ruler is 12 inches long. What is the length of this ruler in centimeters?

____________ centimeters

4. A kitten weighs 4 pounds. What is the approximate mass of the kitten in kilograms?

____________ kilograms

Convert each measurement. (Examples 1 and 2)

5. 20 yards ≈ __________ meters

6. 12 ounces ≈ __________ grams

7. 5 quarts ≈ __________ liters

8. 400 meters ≈ __________ yards

9. 10 liters ≈ __________ gallons

10. 137.25 meters ≈ __________ feet

11. 165 centimeters ≈ __________ inches

12. 10,000 kilometers ≈ __________ miles

ESSENTIAL QUESTION CHECK-IN

13. Show two methods you can use to convert 60 inches to centimeters.

____

____

Name ______________________ Class ______________ Date ______________

7.4 Independent Practice

CA CC 6.RP.3, 6.RP.3b, 6.RP.3d

Personal Math Trainer
Online Practice and Help
my.hrw.com

Tell which measure is greater.

14. Six feet or two meters ______________

15. One inch or one centimeter ______________

16. One yard or one meter ______________

17. One mile or one kilometer ______________

18. One ounce or one gram ______________

19. One quart or one liter ______________

20. 10 pounds or 10 kilograms ______________

21. Four liters or one gallon ______________

22. Two miles or three kilometers ______________

23. What is the limit in kilograms?

____

24. What is the limit in miles per hour?

____

25. Which container holds more, a half-gallon milk jug or a 2-liter juice bottle?

____

26. The label on a can of lemonade gives the volume as 12 fl oz, or 355 mL. Verify that these two measurements are nearly equivalent.

____

27. The mass of a textbook is 1.25 kilograms. About how many pounds is this?

____

28. **Critique Reasoning** Michael estimated his mass as 8 kilograms. Is his estimate reasonable? Justify your answer.

____

29. Your mother bought a three-liter bottle of water. When she got home, she discovered a small leak in the bottom and asked you to find a container to transfer the water into. All you could find were two half-gallon jugs.

a. Will your containers hold all of the water?

____

____

____

b. **What If?** Suppose an entire liter of water leaked out in the car. In that case, would you be able to fit all of the remaining water into one of the half-gallon jugs?

____

____

____

____

30. The track team ran a mile and a quarter during its practice. How many kilometers did the team run? ____________

31. A countertop is 16 feet long and 3 feet wide.

a. What is the area of the countertop in square meters? ____________

b. Tile costs $28 per square meter. How much will it cost to cover the countertop with new tile? ____________

32. At a school picnic, your teacher asks you to mark a field every ten yards so students can play football. The teacher accidentally gave you a meter stick instead of a yard stick. How far apart in meters should you mark the lines if you still want them to be in the right places?

____

33. You weigh a gallon of 2% milk in science class and learn that it is approximately 8.4 pounds. You pass the milk to the next group, and then realize that your teacher wanted an answer in kilograms. Explain how you can adjust your answer without making another measurement. Then give the mass in kilograms.

____

H.O.T. FOCUS ON HIGHER ORDER THINKING

Work Area

34. **Analyze Relationships** Annalisa, Keiko, and Stefan want to compare their heights. Annalisa is 64 inches tall. Stefan tells her, "I'm about 7.5 centimeters taller than you." Keiko knows she is 1.5 inches shorter than Stefan. Give the heights of all three people in both inches and centimeters to the nearest half unit.

____

____

____

____

35. **Communicate Mathematical Ideas** Mikhael wants to install flooring in his fitness room. The flooring costs $20 per square yard. Explain how to find the price per square meter.

____

____

____

____

MODULE QUIZ

Ready to Go On?

Personal Math Trainer

Online Practice and Help

my.hrw.com

7.1 Ratios, Rates, Tables, and Graphs

1. Charlie runs laps around a track. The table shows how long it takes him to run different numbers of laps. How long would it take Charlie to run 5 laps?

Number of Laps	2	4	6	8	10
Time (min)	10	20	30	40	50

____

7.2 Applying Ratio and Rate Reasoning

2. Emily is entering a bicycle race for charity. Her mother pledges $0.40 for every 0.25 mile she bikes. If Emily bikes 15 miles, how much will her mother donate? _______________

3. Rob is saving to buy a new MP3 player. For every $15 he earns babysitting, he saves $6. On Saturday, Rob earned $75 babysitting.

How much money did he save? _______________

7.3 Converting Within Measurement Systems

Convert each measurement.

4. 18 meters = ______ centimeters

5. 5 pounds = ______ ounces

6. 6 quarts = ______ fluid ounces

7. 9 liters = ______ milliliters

7.4 Converting Between Measurement Systems

Convert each measurement.

8. 5 inches = ______ centimeters

9. 198.9 grams ≈ ________ ounces

10. 8 gallons ≈ ______ liters

11. 12 feet ≈ ______ meters

ESSENTIAL QUESTION

12. Write a real-world problem that could be solved using a proportion.

____

____

____

CALIFORNIA

MODULE 7
MIXED REVIEW

Assessment Readiness

my.hrw.com Personal Math Trainer Online Practice and Help

1. Consider each table. Is the unit rate equal to 5 gallons per minute?

Select Yes or No for the tables in A–C.

A.

Time (min)	6	8	16	22
Water (gal)	15	20	40	55

○ Yes ○ No

B.

TIme (min)	5	10	15	20
Water (gal)	15	30	45	60

○ Yes ○ No

C.

TIme (min)	7	14	15	20
Water (gal)	35	70	75	100

○ Yes ○ No

2. The graph below represents the distance Manuel jogs over several hours.

Choose True or False for each statement.

A. If Manuel continues at the same rate, the point (3, 18) will be on the graph. ○ True ○ False

B. Manuel jogs 6 miles in 1.25 hours. ○ True ○ False

C. Manuel jogs $4\frac{1}{2}$ miles in $\frac{3}{4}$ hour. ○ True ○ False

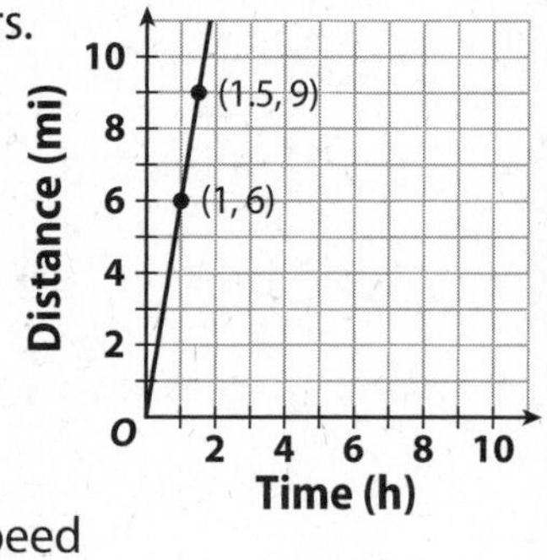

3. Jonah's and his aunt's houses are 8,750 meters apart. Jonah's walking speed is 5 kilometers per hour. How long will it take him to walk from his house to his aunt's house? Explain your thinking.

4. The unlabeled graph shows the relationship between two customary units of measure. Identify a pair of units that can be represented by the graph. Explain your reasoning.

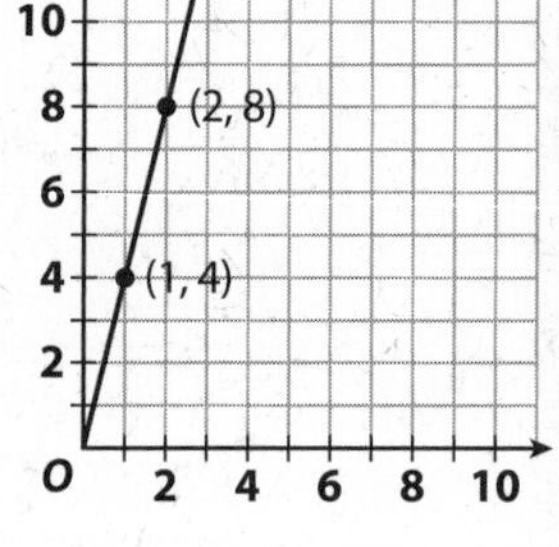

Percents

MODULE **8**

CALIFORNIA

ESSENTIAL QUESTION

How can you use percents to solve real-world problems?

Real-World Video

my.hrw.com

When you eat at a restaurant, your bill will include sales tax for most items. It is customary to add a tip for your server in many restaurants. Both taxes and tips are calculated as a percent of the bill.

GO DIGITAL

my.hrw.com

my.hrw.com

Go digital with your write-in student edition, accessible on any device.

Math On the Spot

Scan with your smart phone to jump directly to the online edition, video tutor, and more.

Animated Math

Interactively explore key concepts to see how math works.

Personal Math Trainer

Get immediate feedback and help as you work through practice sets.

Are YOU Ready?

Complete these exercises to review skills you will need for this module.

Personal Math Trainer
Online Practice and Help
my.hrw.com

Write Equivalent Fractions

EXAMPLE $\frac{9}{12} = \frac{9 \times 4}{12 \times 4} = \frac{36}{48}$ Multiply the numerator and denominator by the same number to find an equivalent fraction.

$\frac{9}{12} = \frac{9 \div 3}{12 \div 3} = \frac{3}{4}$ Divide the numerator and denominator by the same number to find an equivalent fraction.

Write the equivalent fraction.

1. $\frac{9}{18} = \frac{\square}{6}$ **2.** $\frac{4}{6} = \frac{\square}{18}$ **3.** $\frac{25}{30} = \frac{5}{\square}$ **4.** $\frac{12}{15} = \frac{36}{\square}$

5. $\frac{15}{24} = \frac{\square}{8}$ **6.** $\frac{24}{32} = \frac{\square}{8}$ **7.** $\frac{50}{60} = \frac{10}{\square}$ **8.** $\frac{5}{9} = \frac{20}{\square}$

Multiply Fractions

EXAMPLE $\frac{5}{12} \times \frac{3}{10} = \frac{\overset{1}{\cancel{5}}}{\underset{4}{\cancel{12}}} \times \frac{\overset{1}{\cancel{3}}}{\underset{2}{\cancel{10}}}$ Divide by the common factors.

$= \frac{1}{8}$ Simplify.

Multiply. Write each product in simplest form.

9. $\frac{3}{8} \times \frac{4}{11} =$ ________ **10.** $\frac{8}{15} \times \frac{5}{6} =$ ________ **11.** $\frac{7}{12} \times \frac{3}{14} =$ ________

12. $\frac{9}{20} \times \frac{4}{5} =$ ________ **13.** $\frac{7}{10} \times \frac{20}{21} =$ ________ **14.** $\frac{8}{18} \times \frac{9}{20} =$ ________

Decimal Operations (Multiplication)

EXAMPLE

$$\begin{array}{r} 1.6 \\ \times 0.3 \\ \hline 0.48 \end{array}$$

Multiply as you would with whole numbers.
Count the total number of decimal places in the factors.
Place the decimal point that number of places in the product.

Multiply.

15. 20×0.25 ________ **16.** 0.3×16.99 ________ **17.** 0.2×75 ________

18. 5.5×1.1 ________ **19.** 11.99×0.8 ________ **20.** 7.25×0.5 ________

21. 4×0.75 ________ **22.** 0.15×12.50 ________ **23.** 6.5×0.7 ________

Reading Start-Up

Visualize Vocabulary

Use the ✔ words to complete the graphic. You may put more than one word in each box.

0.25

$\frac{3}{4}$, 3:4

Reviewing Fractions and Decimals

$\frac{2}{3} = \frac{6}{9}$

$\frac{4}{8} \rightarrow \frac{1}{2}$

Vocabulary

Review Words

✔ [redacted]cimal *(decimal)*
✔[redacted]uivalent fractions *(fracciones equivalentes)*
denominator *(denominador)*
✔ fraction *(fracción)*
mixed number *(número mixto)*
numerator *(numerador)*
✔ ratio *(razón)*
✔ simplest form *(mínima expresión)*

Preview Words

equivalent decimals *(decimales equivalentes)*
model *(modelo)*
percent *(porcentaje)*
proportional reasoning *(razonamiento proporcional)*

Understand Vocabulary

Match the term on the left to the correct expression on the right.

1. percent — **A.** A ratio that compares a number to 100.

2. model — **B.** Decimals that name the same amount.

3. equivalent decimals — **C.** Something that represents another thing.

Active Reading

Pyramid Before beginning the module, create a pyramid to help you organize what you learn. Label one side "Decimals," one side "Fractions," and the other side "Percents." As you study the module, write important vocabulary and other notes on the appropriate side.

GETTING READY FOR

Percents

Understanding the standards and the vocabulary terms in the standards will help you know exactly what you are expected to learn in this module.

CA CC 6.RP.3c

Find a percent of a quantity as a rate per 100 (e.g., 30% of a quantity means $\frac{30}{100}$ times the quantity); solve problems involving finding the whole, given a part and the percent.

Key Vocabulary

Percent *(porcentaje)*
A ratio comparing a number to 100.

What It Means to You

You will learn to write numbers in various forms, including fractions, decimals, and percents.

EXAMPLE 6.RP.3c

Little brown bats flap their wings about $\frac{3}{4}$ as fast as pipistrelle bats do. How fast does the little brown bat flap its wings as a percent of the pipistrelle bat's wing flap rate?

$\frac{3}{4} = 3 \div 4 = 0.75$ Divide the numerator by the denominator.

$0.75 = 75\%$ Move the decimal point 2 places to the right.

CA CC 6.RP.3c

Find a percent of a quantity as a rate per 100 (e.g., 30% of a quantity means $\frac{30}{100}$ times the quantity); solve problems involving finding the whole, given a part and the percent.

What It Means to You

You will solve problems involving percent.

EXAMPLE 6.RP.3c

About 67% of a person's total (100%) body weight is water. If Cameron weights 90 pounds, about how much of his weight is water?

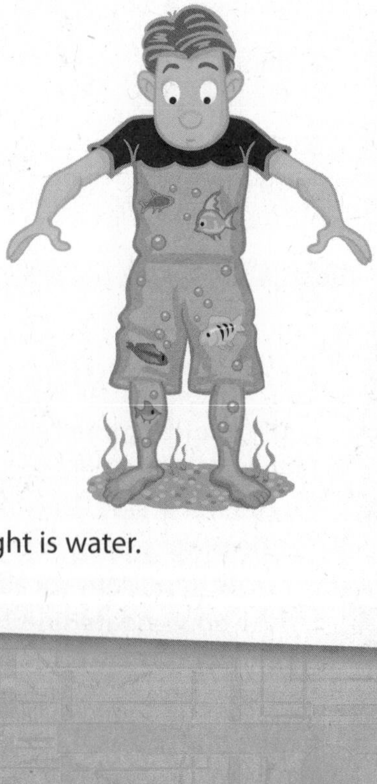

67% of 90

$\frac{67}{100} \cdot 90$

$= \frac{67}{100} \cdot \frac{90}{1}$

$= 60.3$

About 60.3 pounds of Cameron's weight is water.

Visit **my.hrw.com** to see all **CA Common Core Standards** explained.

my.hrw.com

LESSON

8.1 Understanding Percent

CA CC 6.RP.3c

Find a percent of a quantity as a rate per 100 (e.g., 30% of a quantity means 30/100 times the quantity); solve problems involving finding the whole, given a part and the percent.

ESSENTIAL QUESTION

How can you write a ratio as a percent?

EXPLORE ACTIVITY 1 Real World CA CC 6.RP.3c

Using a Grid to Model Percents

A **percent** is a ratio that compares a number to 100. The symbol % is used to show a percent.

17% is equivalent to the following.

- $\frac{17}{100}$
- 17 to 100
- 17 : 100

The free-throw ratios for three basketball players are shown.

Player 1: $\frac{17}{25}$ Player 2: $\frac{33}{50}$ Player 3: $\frac{14}{20}$

A Rewrite each ratio as a number compared to 100. Then shade the grid to represent the free-throw ratio.

Player 1: $\frac{17}{25} = \frac{\square}{100}$ Player 2: $\frac{33}{50} = \frac{\square}{100}$ Player 3: $\frac{14}{20} = \frac{\square}{100}$

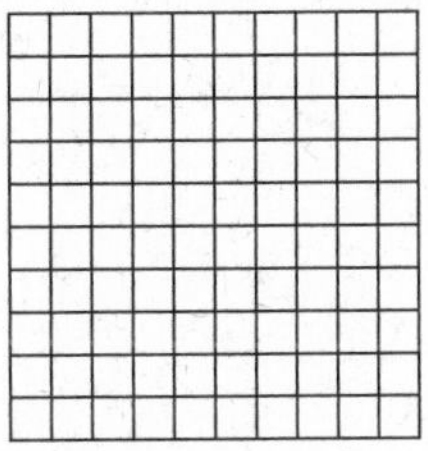
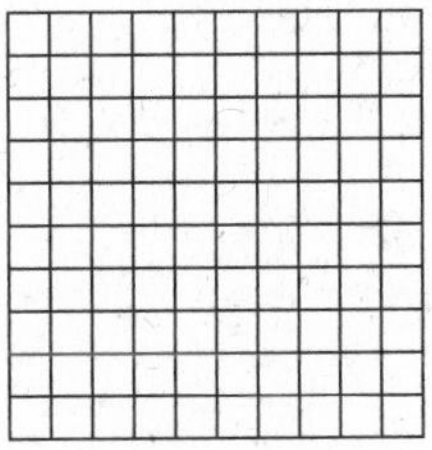
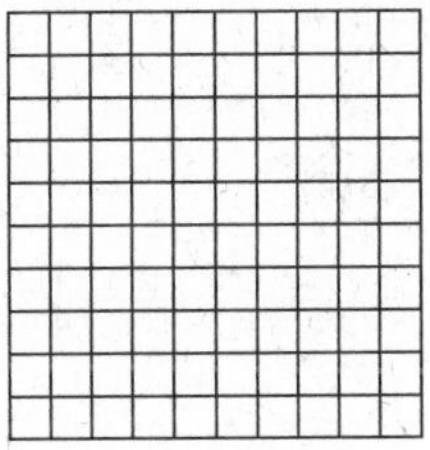

B Which player has the greatest free-throw ratio? ____________________

How is this shown on the grids? ____________________

C Use a percent to describe each player's free-throw ratio. Write the percents in order from least to greatest.

____

D How did you determine how many squares to shade on each grid?

____

____

EXPLORE ACTIVITY 2 CA CC 6.RP.3c

Connecting Fractions and Percents

You can use a percent bar model to model a ratio expressed as a fraction and to find an equivalent percent.

A Use a percent bar model to find an equivalent percent for $\frac{1}{4}$.

Draw a model to represent 100 and divide it into fourths. Shade $\frac{1}{4}$.

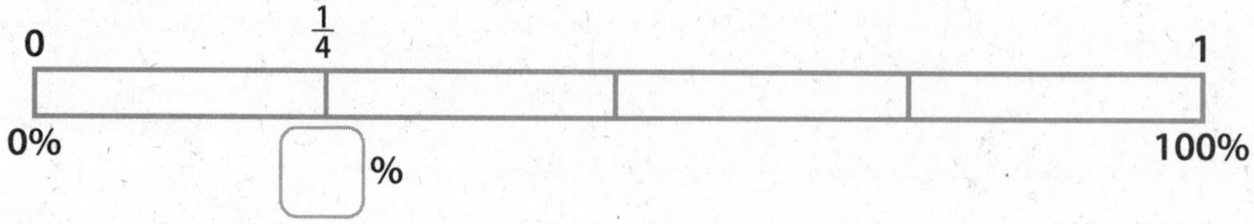

$\frac{1}{4}$ of 100 = 25, so $\frac{1}{4}$ of 100% = ______________________.

Tell which operation you can use to find $\frac{1}{4}$ of 100.

Then find $\frac{1}{4}$ of 100%. ______________________

B Use a percent bar model to find an equivalent percent for $\frac{1}{3}$.

Draw a model and divide it into thirds. Shade $\frac{1}{3}$.

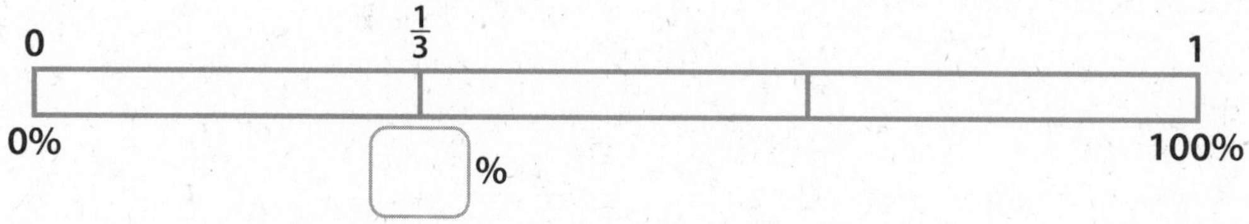

$\frac{1}{3}$ of 100 = $33\frac{1}{3}$, so $\frac{1}{3}$ of 100% = ______________________%.

Tell which operation you can use to find $\frac{1}{3}$ of 100.

Then find $\frac{1}{3}$ of 100%. ______________________

Reflect

1. **Critique Reasoning** Jo says she can find the percent equivalent of $\frac{3}{4}$ by multiplying the percent equivalent of $\frac{1}{4}$ by 3. How can you use a percent bar model to support this claim?

____

____

____

Using Benchmarks and Proportional Reasoning

You can use certain *benchmark* percents to write other percents and to estimate fractions.

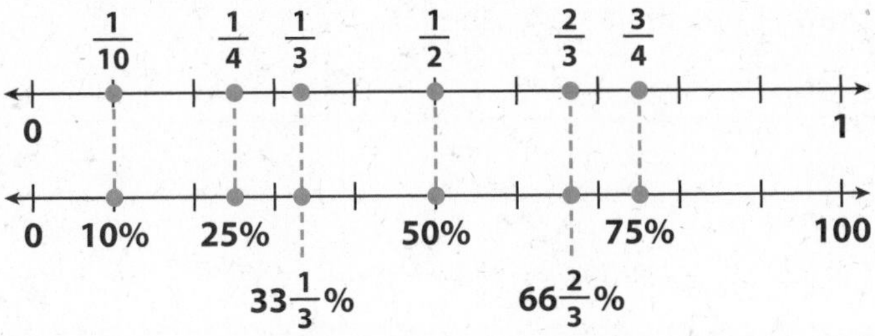

Math On the Spot
my.hrw.com

EXAMPLE 1 Real World

CA CC 6.RP.3c

A Find an equivalent percent for $\frac{3}{10}$.

STEP 1 Write $\frac{3}{10}$ as a multiple of a benchmark fraction.

$\frac{3}{10} = 3 \cdot \frac{1}{10}$ Think: $\frac{3}{10} = \frac{1}{10} + \frac{1}{10} + \frac{1}{10}$

STEP 2 Find an equivalent percent for $\frac{1}{10}$.

$\frac{1}{10} = 10\%$ *Use the number lines to find the equivalent percent for $\frac{1}{10}$.*

STEP 3 Multiply.

$\frac{3}{10} = 3 \cdot \frac{1}{10} = 3 \cdot 10\% = 30\%$

B 76% of the students at a middle school bring their own lunch. About what fraction of the students bring their own lunch?

STEP 1 Note that 76% is close to the benchmark 75%.

STEP 2 Find a fraction equivalent for 75%:

$75\% = \frac{3}{4}$

About $\frac{3}{4}$ of the students bring their own lunch.

Math Talk
Mathematical Practices

Explain how you could use equivalent ratios to write $\frac{3}{10}$ as a percent.

Personal Math Trainer

Online Practice and Help

my.hrw.com

YOUR TURN

Use a benchmark to find an equivalent percent for each fraction.

2. $\frac{9}{10}$ ____________________ **3.** $\frac{2}{5}$ ____________________

4. 64% of the animals at an animal shelter are dogs. About what fraction of the animals at the shelter are dogs?

____

Guided Practice

1. Shade the grid to represent the ratio $\frac{9}{25}$. Then find a percent equivalent to the given ratio. (Explore Activity 1)

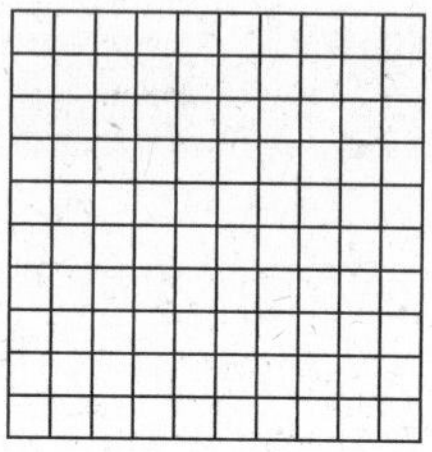

$$\frac{9 \times \square}{25 \times \square} = \frac{\square}{100} = \text{\_\_\_\_\_\_\_\_\_\_}$$

2. Use the percent bar model to find the missing percent. (Explore Activity 2)

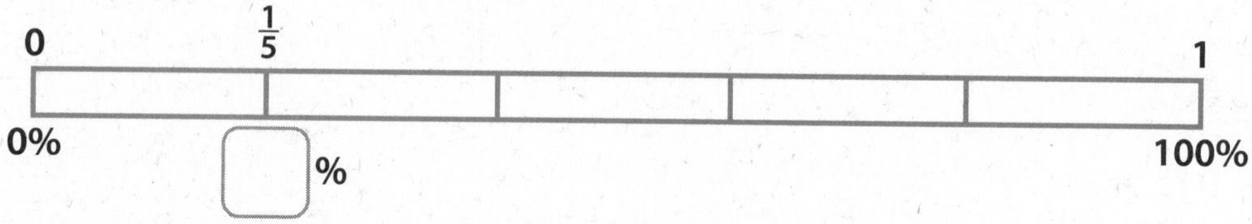

Identify a benchmark you can use to find an equivalent percent for each ratio. Then find the equivalent percent. (Example 1)

3. $\frac{6}{10}$ Benchmark: $\frac{1}{\square}$

____

4. $\frac{2}{4}$ Benchmark: $\frac{\square}{4}$

____

5. $\frac{4}{5}$ Benchmark: $\frac{\square}{5}$

____

6. 41% of the students at an art college want to be graphic designers. About what fraction of the students want to be graphic designers? (Example 1)

____

ESSENTIAL QUESTION CHECK-IN

7. How do you write a ratio as a percent?

____

____

Name _______________ Class _______________ Date _______________

8.1 Independent Practice

CA CC 6.RP.3c

Personal Math Trainer
Online Practice and Help
my.hrw.com

Shade the grid to represent the ratio. Then find the missing number.

8. $\frac{23}{50} = \frac{\square}{100}$

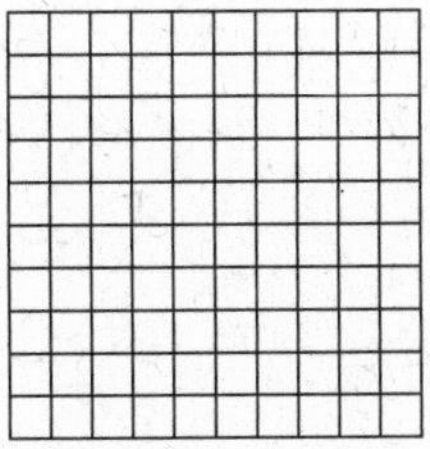

9. $\frac{11}{20} = \frac{\square}{100}$

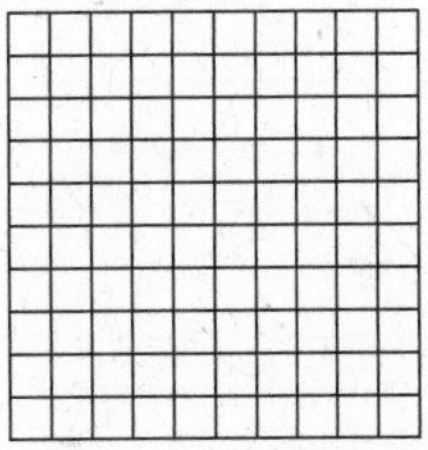

10. Mark wants to use a grid like the ones in Exercises 1 and 2 to model the percent equivalent of the fraction $\frac{2}{3}$. How many grid squares should he shade? What percent would his model show?

____

11. The ratios of saves for a baseball pitcher to the number of save opportunities are given for three relief pitchers: $\frac{9}{10}, \frac{4}{5}, \frac{17}{20}$. Write each ratio as a percent. Order the percents from least to greatest.

____

Circle the greater quantity.

12. $\frac{1}{3}$ of a box of Corn Krinkles

50% of a box of Corn Krinkles

13. 30% of your minutes are used up.

$\frac{1}{4}$ of your minutes are used up.

14. **Multiple Representations** Explain how you could write 35% as the sum of two benchmark percents or as a multiple of a percent.

____

15. Use the percent bar model to find the missing percent.

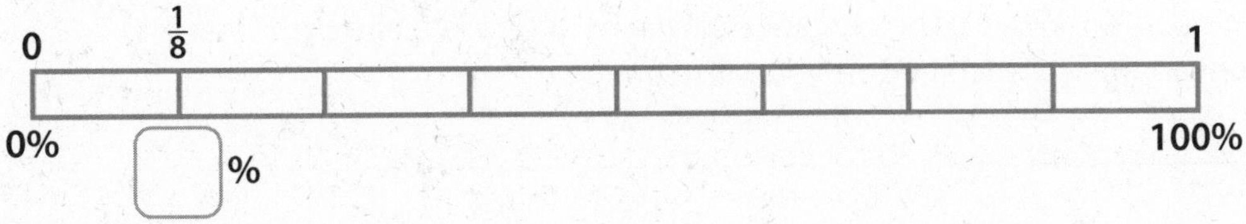

16. Multistep Carl buys songs and downloads them to his computer. The bar graph shows the numbers of each type of song he downloaded last year.

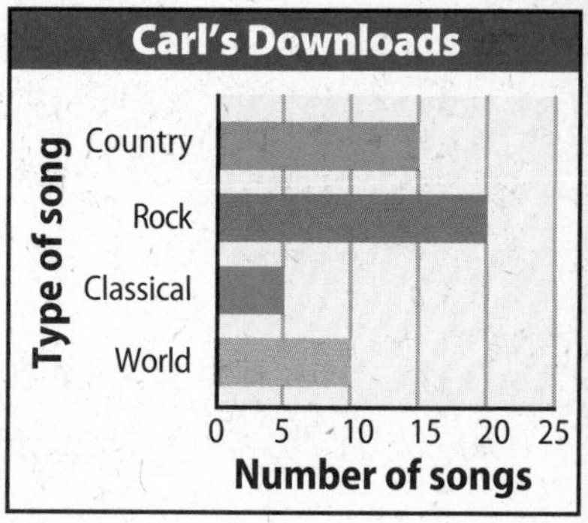

a. What is the total number of songs Carl downloaded last year?

____

b. What fraction of the songs were country? Find the fraction for each type of song. Write each fraction in simplest form and give its percent equivalent.

____

____

____

H.O.T. FOCUS ON HIGHER ORDER THINKING

Work Area

17. Critique Reasoning Marcus bought a booklet of tickets to use at the amusement park. He used 50% of the tickets on rides, $\frac{1}{3}$ of the tickets on video games, and the rest of the tickets in the batting cage. Marcus says he used 10% of the tickets in the batting cage. Do you agree? Explain.

____

____

____

____

18. Look for a Pattern Complete the table.

Fraction	$\frac{1}{5}$	$\frac{2}{5}$	$\frac{3}{5}$	$\frac{4}{5}$	$\frac{5}{5}$	$\frac{6}{5}$
Percent	20%					

a. Analyze Relationships What is true when the numerator and denominator of the fraction are equal? What is true when the numerator is greater than the denominator?

____

____

b. Justify Reasoning What is the percent equivalent of $\frac{3}{2}$? Use a pattern like the one in the table to support your answer.

____

____

LESSON 8.2

Percents, Fractions, and Decimals

CA CC 6.RP.3

Use ratio and rate reasoning to solve real-world and mathematical problems, e.g., by reasoning about tables of equivalent ratios, tape diagrams, double number line diagrams, or equations.

ESSENTIAL QUESTION

How can you write equivalent percents, fractions, and decimals?

Writing Percents as Decimals and Fractions

You can write a percent as an equivalent fraction or as an equivalent decimal. Equivalent percents, decimals, and fractions all represent equal parts of the same whole.

Math On the Spot
my.hrw.com

EXAMPLE 1 Real World

CA CC 6.RP.3

Lorenzo spends 35% of his budget on rent for his apartment. Write this percent as a fraction and as a decimal.

STEP 1 Write the percent as a fraction.

$35\% = \frac{35}{100}$ *Percent means per 100.*

STEP 2 Write the fraction in simplest form.

$\frac{35}{100} = \frac{35 \div 5}{100 \div 5} = \frac{7}{20}$

STEP 3 Write the percent as a decimal.

$35\% = \frac{35}{100}$ *Write the fraction equivalent of 35%.*

$= 0.35$ *Write the decimal equivalent of $\frac{35}{100}$.*

So, 35% written as a fraction is $\frac{7}{20}$ and written as a decimal is 0.35.

Math Talk
Mathematical Practices

Is 35% more than half or less than half? How do you know? To what benchmark fraction is 35% close?

YOUR TURN

Write each percent as a fraction and as a decimal.

1. 15% ________________ **2.** 48% ________________

3. 80% ________________ **4.** 75% ________________

5. 36% ________________ **6.** 40% ________________

Personal Math Trainer
Online Practice and Help
my.hrw.com

EXPLORE ACTIVITY CA CC 6.RP.3

Modeling Decimal, Fraction, and Percent Equivalencies

Using models can help you understand how decimals, fractions, and percents are related.

A Model 0.78 by shading a 10-by-10 grid.

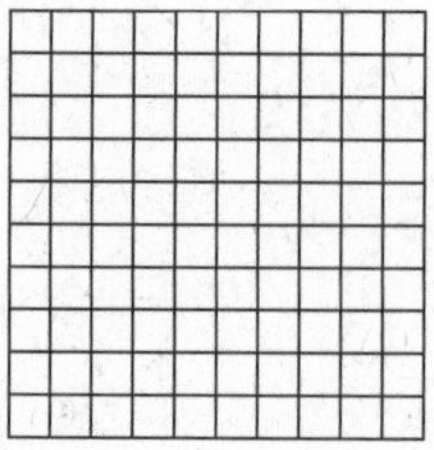

$0.78 = \frac{\square}{100}$,

________ out of a hundred, or ________%.

B Model 1.42 by shading 10-by-10 grids.

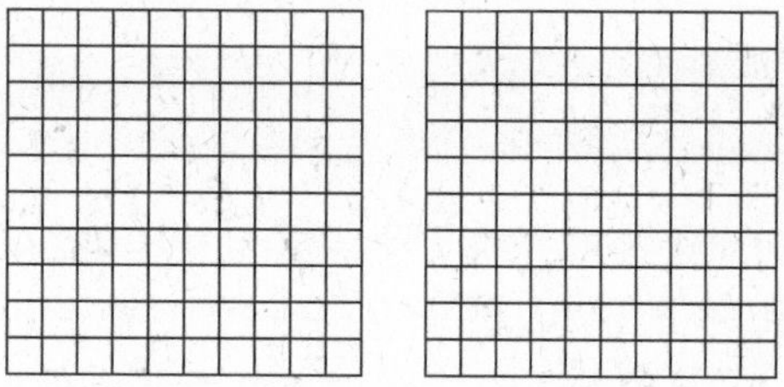

$1.42 = \frac{\square}{100} + \frac{\square}{100} = \frac{\square}{100} = 1\frac{\square}{100}$.

1.42 = 100% + ________% = ________%

C Model 125% by shading 10-by-10 grids.

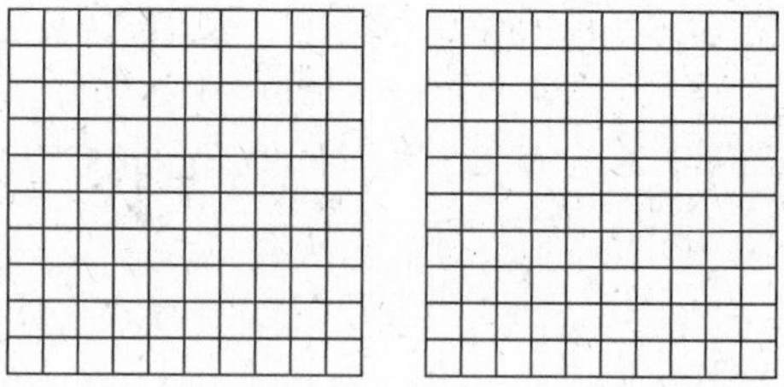

The model shows 100% + ________% = 125%.

125% = the decimal ________.

$125\% = \frac{\square}{100} + \frac{\square}{100} = \frac{\square}{100} = 1\frac{\square}{100} = 1\frac{\square}{\square}$.

Reflect

7. **Multiple Representations** What decimal, fraction, and percent equivalencies are shown in each model? Explain.

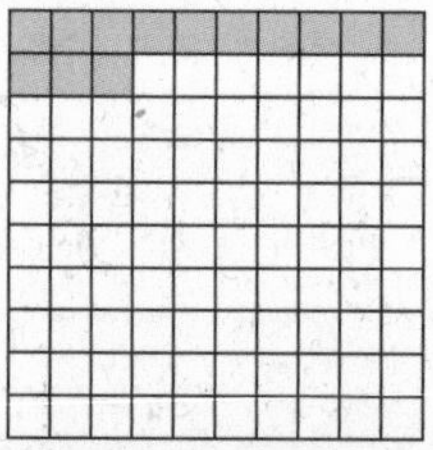

a. ____

____

____

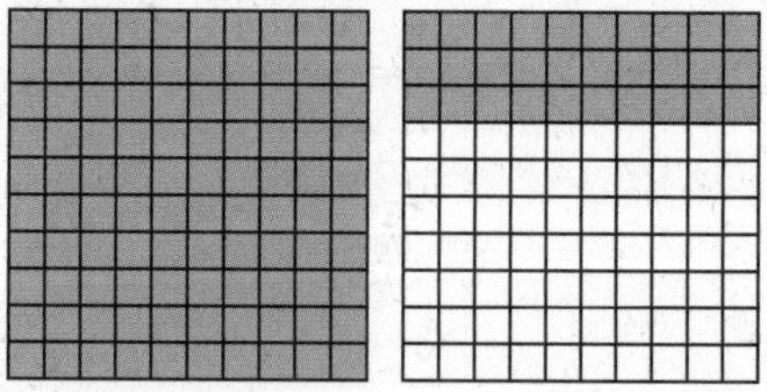

b. ____

____

Writing Fractions as Decimals and Percents

You can write some fractions as percents by writing an equivalent fraction with a denominator of 100. This method is useful when the fraction has a denominator that is a factor or a multiple of 100. If a fraction does not have a denominator that is a factor or multiple of 100, you can use long division.

Math On the Spot
my.hrw.com

EXAMPLE 2 Real World

CA CC 6.RP.3

A 96 out of 200 animals treated by a veterinarian are horses. Write $\frac{96}{200}$ as a decimal and as a percent.

Notice that the denominator is a multiple of 100.

STEP 1 Write an equivalent fraction with a denominator of 100.

$\frac{96}{200} = \frac{48}{100}$ *Divide both the numerator and denominator by 2.*

STEP 2 Write the decimal equivalent.

$\frac{48}{100} = 0.48$

STEP 3 Write the percent equivalent.

$\frac{48}{100} = 48\%$ *Percent means per 100.*

Notice that the denominator is not a factor or multiple of 100.

B $\frac{1}{8}$ of the animals treated by the veterinarian are dogs. Write $\frac{1}{8}$ as a decimal and as a percent.

STEP 1 Use long division to divide the numerator by the denominator.

$$\frac{1}{8} = 8\overline{)1.000} = 0.125$$

$$\begin{array}{r} 0.125 \\ 8\overline{)1.000} \\ -8 \\ \hline 20 \\ -16 \\ \hline 40 \\ -40 \\ \hline 0 \end{array}$$

Add a decimal point and zeros to the right of the numerator as needed.

The decimal equivalent of $\frac{1}{8}$ is 0.125.

STEP 2 Write the decimal as a percent.

$0.125 = \frac{125}{1{,}000}$ *Write the fraction equivalent of the decimal.*

$\frac{125}{1{,}000} = \frac{12.5}{100}$ (÷ 10 numerator and denominator) *Write an equivalent fraction with a denominator of 100.*

$\frac{12.5}{100} = 12.5\%$ *Write as a percent.*

The percent equivalent of $\frac{1}{8}$ is 12.5%.

Personal Math Trainer
Online Practice and Help
my.hrw.com

YOUR TURN

Write each fraction as a decimal and as a percent.

8. $\frac{9}{25}$ ______________

9. $\frac{7}{8}$ ______________

Guided Practice

1. Helene spends 12% of her budget on transportation expenses. Write this percent as a fraction and as a decimal. (Example 1)

____

Model the decimal. Then write percent and fraction equivalents.
(Explore Activity)

2. 0.53

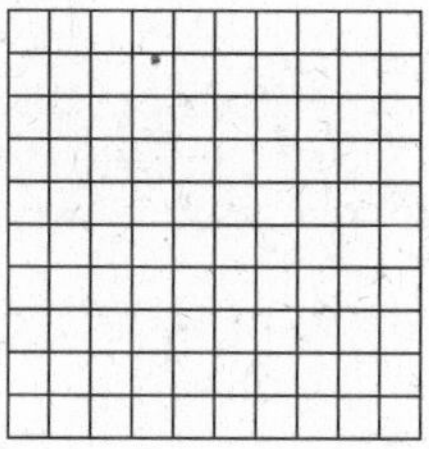

____

3. 1.07

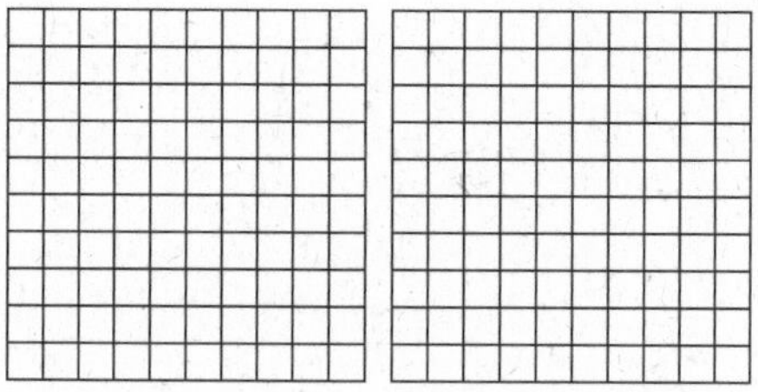

____

Write each fraction as a decimal and as a percent. (Example 2)

4. $\frac{7}{20}$ of the packages ______________

5. $\frac{3}{8}$ of a pie ______________

ESSENTIAL QUESTION CHECK-IN

6. How does the definition of *percent* help you write fraction and decimal equivalents?

____

____

____

____

____

Name ______________________ Class ______________ Date ______________

8.2 Independent Practice

CA CC 6.RP.3

Personal Math Trainer
my.hrw.com
Online Practice and Help

Write each percent as a fraction and as a decimal.

7. 72% full
____

8. 25% successes
____

9. 500% increase
____

10. 5% tax
____

11. 37% profit
____

12. 165% improvement
____

Write each fraction as a decimal and as a percent.

13. $\frac{5}{8}$ of an inch
____

14. $\frac{258}{300}$ of the contestants
____

15. $\frac{350}{100}$ of the revenue
____

16. The poster shows how many of its games the football team has won so far. Express this information as a fraction, a percent, and as a decimal.

____

17. Use the information on Justine's test paper to express the part of the 80 test questions she got correct as a fraction, percent, and decimal.

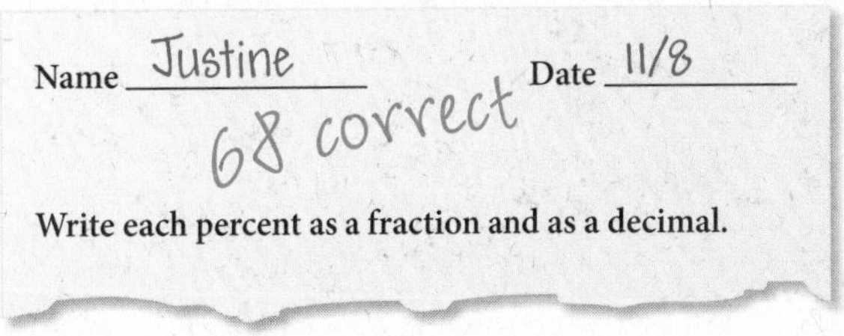

____

Each diagram is made of smaller, identical pieces. Tell how many pieces you would shade to model the given percent.

18. 75% _______________

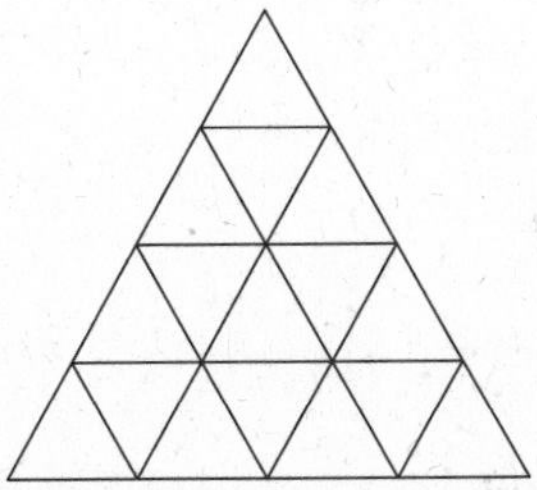

19. 25% _______________

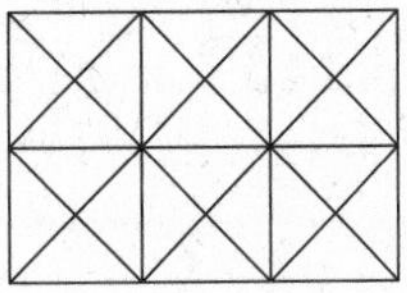

20. **Multiple Representations** At Brian's Bookstore, 0.3 of the shelves hold mysteries, 25% of the shelves hold travel books, and $\frac{7}{20}$ of the shelves hold children's books. Which type of book covers the most shelf space in the store? Explain how you arrived at your answer.

____

____

H.O.T. FOCUS ON HIGHER ORDER THINKING

Work Area

21. **Critical Thinking** A newspaper article reports the results of an election between two candidates. The article says that Smith received 60% of the votes and that Murphy received $\frac{1}{3}$ of the votes. A reader writes in to complain that the article cannot be accurate. What reason might the reader have to say this?

____

____

____

22. **Represent Real-World Problems** Evan budgets $2,000 a month to spend on certain living expenses for his family. Complete the table to express the portion spent on each cost as a percent, fraction, and decimal.

	Food: $500	Rent: $1,200	Transportation: $300
Fraction			
Percent			
Decimal			

23. **Communicate Mathematical Ideas** Find the sum of each row in the table. Explain why these sums make sense.

____

____

____

24. **Explain the Error** Your friend says that 14.5% is equivalent to the decimal 14.5. Explain why your friend is incorrect by comparing the fractional equivalents of 14.5% and 14.5.

____

____

LESSON
8.3 Solving Percent Problems

CA CC 6.RP.3c

Find a percent of a quantity as a rate per 100 (e.g., 30% of a quantity means $\frac{30}{100}$ times the quantity); solve problems involving finding the whole, given a part and the percent. *Also 6.RP.3*

ESSENTIAL QUESTION

How do you use percents to solve problems?

EXPLORE ACTIVITY Real World CA CC 6.RP.3

Modeling a Percent Problem

You can use a model to solve a percent problem.

A sports store received a shipment of 400 baseball gloves. 30% were left-handed. How many left-handed gloves were in the shipment?

A Use the diagram to solve this problem.

30% means 30 out of _______.

There were _______ left-handed gloves for every 100 baseball gloves.

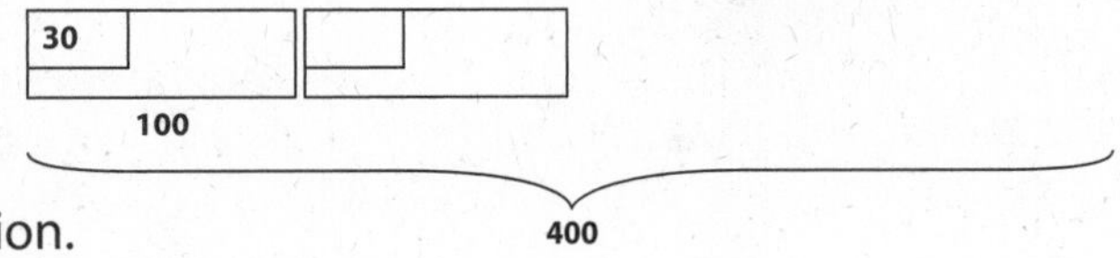

Complete the diagram to model this situation.

B Describe how the diagram models the shipment of gloves.

____

____

____

C Explain how you can use the diagram to find the total number of left-handed gloves in the shipment.

____

D Use a bar model to solve this problem. The bar represents 100%, or the entire shipment of 400 gloves. The bar is divided into 10 equal parts. Complete the labels along the bottom of the bar.

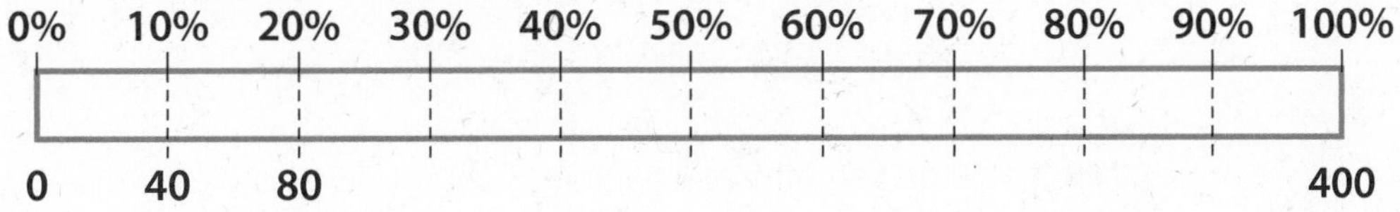

EXPLORE ACTIVITY *(cont'd)*

Reflect

1. **Justify Reasoning** How did you determine the labels along the bottom of the bar model in Step D?

____

____

2. **Communicate Mathematical Ideas** How can you use the bar model to find the number of left-handed gloves?

____

Math On the Spot
my.hrw.com

Finding a Percent of a Number

A percent is equivalent to the ratio of a part to a whole. To find a percent of a number, you can write a ratio to represent the percent, and find an equivalent ratio that compares the part to the whole.

The word "of" indicates multiplication.

To find 30% of 400, you can use:

Proportional Reasoning

$$\frac{30}{100} = \frac{?}{400} \begin{matrix} \leftarrow \text{part} \\ \leftarrow \text{whole} \end{matrix} \quad (\times 4)$$

$$= \frac{120}{400}$$

Multiplication

$$30\% \text{ of } 400 = \frac{30}{100} \text{ of } 400$$

$$= \frac{30}{100} \times 400$$

$$= 120$$

EXAMPLE 1

CA CC 6.RP.3c

A Use proportional reasoning to find 28% of 25.

STEP 1 Write a proportion comparing the percent to the ratio of part to whole.

$$\frac{?}{25} = \frac{28}{100}$$

Notice that 25 is a factor of 100.

STEP 2 Find the multiplication factor.

$$\begin{matrix} \text{part} \rightarrow \\ \text{whole} \rightarrow \end{matrix} \frac{?}{25} = \frac{28}{100} \quad (\times 4)$$

Since $25 \cdot 4 = 100$, find what number times 4 equals 28.

STEP 3 Find the numerator.

$$\frac{7}{25} = \frac{28}{100}$$

Since $4 \cdot 7 = 28$, 28% of 25 = 7.

28% of 25 is 7.

Math Talk
Mathematical Practices

Could you also use the proportion $\frac{28}{100} = \frac{?}{25}$ to find 28% of 25? Explain.

B Multiply by a fraction to find 35% of 60.

STEP 1 Write the percent as a fraction.

$35\% \text{ of } 60 = \frac{35}{100} \text{ of } 60$

STEP 2 Multiply.

$\frac{35}{100} \text{ of } 60 = \frac{35}{100} \cdot 60$

$= \frac{2{,}100}{100}$

$= 21$ Simplify.

35% of 60 is 21.

C Multiply by a decimal to find 5% of 180.

STEP 1 Write the percent as a decimal.

$5\% = \frac{5}{100} = 0.05$

STEP 2 Multiply.

$180 \cdot 0.05 = 9$

5% of 180 is 9.

Animated Math

my.hrw.com

Reflect

3. **Analyze Relationships** In **B**, the percent is 35%. What is the part and what is the whole?

____

____

4. **Communicate Mathematical Ideas** Explain how to use proportional reasoning to find 35% of 600.

____

____

____

____

____

YOUR TURN

Find the percent of each number.

5. 38% of 50 ______ **6.** 27% of 300 ______ **7.** 60% of 75 ______

Personal Math Trainer

Online Practice and Help

my.hrw.com

Math On the Spot
my.hrw.com

Finding a Percent Given a Part and a Whole

You can use proportional reasoning to solve problems in which you need to find a percent.

EXAMPLE 2 Real World

CA CC 6.RP.3

The school principal spent $2,000 to buy some new computer equipment. Of this money, $120 was used to buy some new keyboards. What percent of the money was spent on keyboards?

STEP 1 Since you want to know the part of the money spent on keyboards, compare the part to the whole.

part → whole → $\frac{\$120}{\$2{,}000}$

STEP 2 Write a proportion comparing the percent to the ratio of part to whole.

part → whole → $\frac{?}{100} = \frac{120}{2{,}000}$ ← part ← whole

STEP 3 Find the multiplication factor.

$\frac{?}{100} = \frac{120}{2{,}000}$ (×20 on top and bottom)

Since $100 \cdot 20 = 2{,}000$, find what number times 20 equals 120.

STEP 4 Find the numerator.

$\frac{6}{100} = \frac{120}{2{,}000}$

Since $20 \cdot 6 = 120$, the percent is 6%.

The principal spent 6% of the money on keyboards.

Reflect

8. **Communicate Mathematical Ideas** Write 57% as a ratio. Which part of the ratio represents the part and which part represents the whole? Explain.

____

____

____

Personal Math Trainer
Online Practice and Help
my.hrw.com

YOUR TURN

9. Out of the 25 students in Mrs. Green's class, 19 have a pet. What percent of the students in Mrs. Green's class have a pet? _______________

Finding a Whole Given a Part and a Percent

You can use proportional reasoning to solve problems in which you know a part and a percent and need to find the whole.

Math On the Spot
my.hrw.com

EXAMPLE 3 Real World

CA CC 6.RP.3c

Twelve of the students in the school choir like to sing solos. These 12 students make up 24% of the choir. How many students are in the choir?

STEP 1 Since you want to know the total number of students in the choir, compare the part to the whole.

part → / whole → $\frac{12}{?}$

STEP 2 Write a proportion comparing the percent to the ratio of part to whole.

part → / whole → $\frac{12}{?} = \frac{24}{100}$ ← part / ← whole

You know that 12 students represent 24%.

STEP 3 Find the multiplication factor.

$\frac{12}{?} = \frac{24}{100}$ (×2 on top, ×2 on bottom)

Since $12 \cdot 2 = 24$, find what number times 2 is equal to 100.

STEP 4 Find the denominator.

$\frac{12}{50} = \frac{24}{100}$

Since $50 \cdot 2 = 100$, the denominator is 50.

There are 50 students in the choir.

Math Talk
Mathematical Practices

Suppose 10 more students join the choir. None of them are soloists. What percent are soloists now?

Reflect

10. **Check for Reasonableness** In Example 3, 24% is close to 25%. How could you use this fact to check that 50 is a reasonable number for the total number of students in the choir?

____

____

____

____

YOUR TURN

11. 6 is 30% of ________.

12. 15% of ________ is 75.

Personal Math Trainer
Online Practice and Help
my.hrw.com

Guided Practice

1. A store has 300 televisions on order, and 80% are high definition. How many televisions on order are high definition? Use the bar model and complete the bottom of the bar. (Explore Activity)

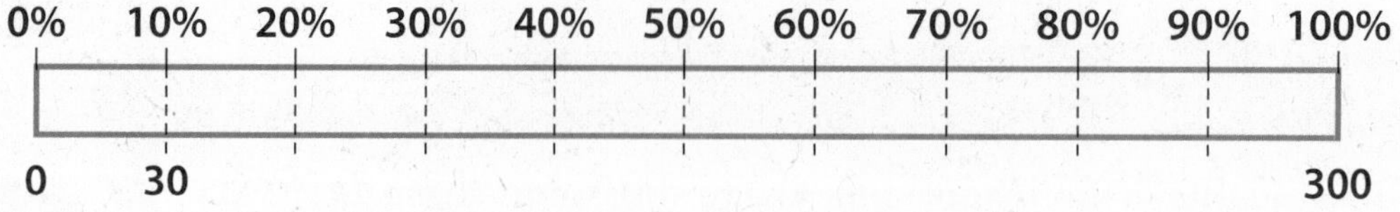

____

2. Use proportional reasoning to find 65% of 200. (Example 1)

part → $\frac{\square}{100} = \frac{?}{\square}$ ← part
whole → ← whole

65% of 200 is ________________.

3. Use multiplication to find 5% of 180. (Example 1)

$\frac{5}{100}$ of $180 = \frac{5}{100} \, \square \, 180$

$= \frac{\square}{100} = \square$

5% of 180 is ________________.

4. Alana spent \$21 of her \$300 paycheck on a gift. What percent of her paycheck was spent on the gift? (Example 2)

part → $\frac{?}{\square} = \frac{\$\square}{\$\square}$ ← part
whole → ← whole

Alana spent ________________ of her paycheck on the gift.

5. At Pizza Pi, 9% of the pizzas made last week had broccoli on them. If 27 pizzas had broccoli, how many pizzas in all were made last week? (Example 3)

part → $\frac{\square}{100} = \frac{27}{?}$ ← part
whole → ← whole

There were ________________ pizzas made last week.

ESSENTIAL QUESTION CHECK-IN

6. How can you use proportional reasoning to solve problems involving percent?

____

____

____

____

Name ____________________ Class ____________ Date ____________

8.3 Independent Practice

CA CC 6.RP.3, 6.RP.3c

Personal Math Trainer
Online Practice and Help
my.hrw.com

Find the percent of each number.

7. 64% of 75 tiles ________

8. 20% of 70 plants ________

9. 32% of 25 pages ________

10. 85% of 40 e-mails ________

11. 72% of 350 friends ________

12. 5% of 220 files ________

Complete each sentence.

13. 4 students is ________ % of 20 students.

14. 2 doctors is ________ % of 25 doctors.

15. ________ % of 50 shirts is 35 shirts.

16. ________ % of 200 miles is 150 miles.

17. 4% of ________ days is 56 days.

18. 60 minutes is 20% of ________ minutes.

19. 80% of ________ games is 32 games.

20. 360 kilometers is 24% of ________ kilometers.

21. 75% of ________ peaches is 15 peaches.

22. 9 stores is 3% of ________ stores.

23. At a shelter, 15% of the dogs are puppies. There are 60 dogs at the shelter.

How many are puppies? ________

24. Carl has 200 songs on his MP3 player. Of these songs, 24 are country songs. What percent of

Carl's songs are country songs? ________

25. **Consumer Math** The sales tax in the town where Amanda lives is 7%. Amanda paid $35 in sales tax on a new stereo. What was

the price of the stereo? ________

26. **Financial Literacy** Ashton is saving money to buy a new bike. He needs $120 but has only saved 60% so far. How much more money

does he need to buy the scooter? ________

27. **Consumer Math** Monica paid sales tax of $1.50 when she bought a new bike helmet. If the sales tax rate was 5%, how much did the store charge

for the helmet before tax? ________

28. Use the circle graph to determine how many hours per day Becky spends on each activity.

School: ________ hours

Eating: ________ hours

Sleep: ________ hours

Homework: ________ hours

Free time: ________ hours

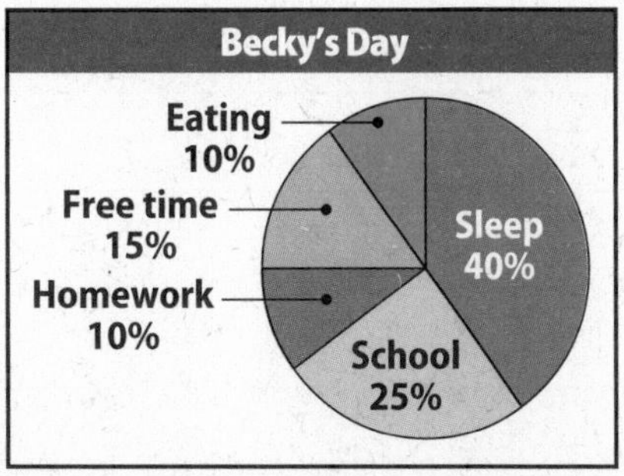

H.O.T. FOCUS ON HIGHER ORDER THINKING

Work Area

29. **Multistep** Marc ordered a rug. He gave a deposit of 30% of the cost and will pay the rest when the rug is delivered. If the deposit was $75, how much more does Marc owe? Explain how you found your answer.

____

____

____

____

____

30. **Earth Science** Your weight on different planets is affected by gravity. An object that weighs 150 pounds on Earth weighs only 56.55 pounds on Mars. The same object weighs only 24.9 pounds on the Moon.

a. What percent of an object's Earth weight is its weight on Mars and on the Moon?

____

b. Suppose *x* represents an object's weight on Earth. Write two expressions: one that you can use to find the object's weight on Mars and another that you can use to write the object's weight on the Moon.

____

c. The space suit Neil Armstrong wore when he stepped on the Moon for the first time weighed about 180 pounds on Earth. How much did it weigh on the Moon?

____

d. **What If?** If you could travel to Jupiter, your weight would be 236.4% of your Earth weight. How much would Neil Armstrong's space suit weigh on Jupiter?

____

31. **Explain the Error** Your friend used the proportion $\frac{25}{100} = \frac{50}{?}$ to find 25% of 50 and says that the answer is 200. Explain why your friend is incorrect and find the correct answer.

____

____

____

____

MODULE QUIZ

Ready to Go On?

Personal Math Trainer
Online Practice and Help
my.hrw.com

8.1 Understanding Percent

Shade the grid and write the equivalent percent for each fraction.

1. $\frac{19}{50}$ ____________

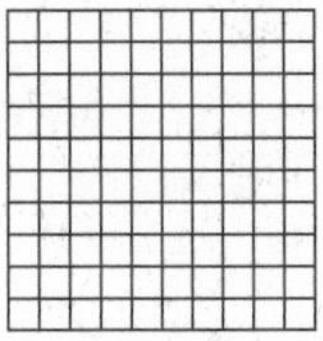

2. $\frac{13}{20}$ ____________

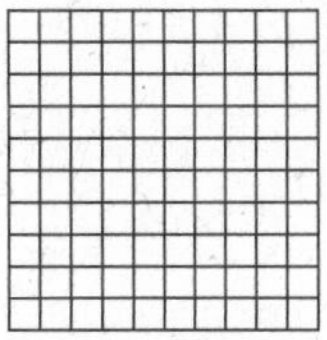

8.2 Percents, Fractions, and Decimals

Write each number in two equivalent forms.

3. $\frac{3}{5}$ ____________

4. 62.5% ____________

5. 0.24 ____________

6. $\frac{31}{50}$ ____________

7. Selma spent $\frac{7}{10}$ of her allowance on a new backpack. What percent of her allowance did she spend? __________

8.3 Solving Percent Problems

Complete each sentence.

8. 12 is 30% of ________.

9. 45% of 20 is ________.

10. 18 is ________ % of 30.

11. 56 is 80% of ________.

12. A pack of cinnamon-scented pencils sells for \$4.00. What is the sales tax rate if the total cost of the pencils is \$4.32? __________

ESSENTIAL QUESTION

13. How can you solve problems involving percents?

____

____

____

____

CALIFORNIA

MODULE 8
MIXED REVIEW
Assessment Readiness

Personal Math Trainer
Online Practice and Help
my.hrw.com

1. The grid represents the percent of students at a school who typically walk to school.

Select Yes or No if the given value is equivalent to the percent represented by the grid.

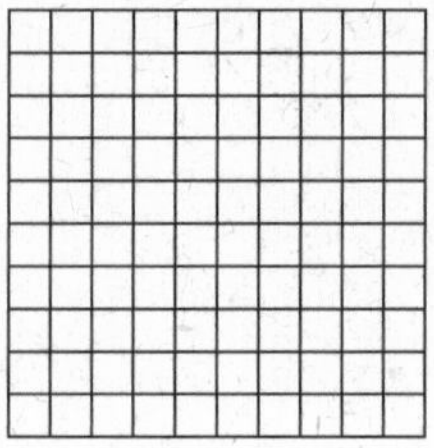

A. 0.42 ◯ Yes ◯ No

B. $\frac{43}{100}$ ◯ Yes ◯ No

C. $\frac{21}{50}$ ◯ Yes ◯ No

2. 55% of the 400 students at a school went to the game.

Choose True or False for each statement.

A. 55 students went to the game. ◯ True ◯ False

B. 180 students did **not** go to the game. ◯ True ◯ False

C. More than half the students went to the game. ◯ True ◯ False

3. Jen buys sesame bagels and plain bagels. If the ratio of sesame to plain is 1 : 3 and Jen bought 2 dozen bagels, what percent of the bagels are plain? How many bagels are plain? Suppose each plain bagel has 0.53 gram of salt, and each sesame bagel has 0.65 gram. Use a percent to compare the amount of salt in a plain bagel to that in a sesame bagel.

4. Andy buys a computer that costs $575. The sales tax is 5%. Describe a method he could use to estimate the sales tax. Will the estimated tax be greater than or less than the actual tax? Explain.

UNIT 3

Study Guide Review

MODULE 6 Representing Ratios and Rates

Key Vocabulary

equivalent ratios *(razones equivalentes)*

rate *(tasa)*

ratio *(razón)*

unit rate *(tasa unitaria)*

ESSENTIAL QUESTION

How can you use ratios and rates to solve real-world problems?

EXAMPLE 1

Tina pays \$45.50 for 13 boxes of wheat crackers. What is the unit price?

$\frac{\$45.50}{13 \text{ boxes}} = \frac{\$3.50}{1 \text{ box}}$ The unit price is \$3.50 per box of crackers.

EXAMPLE 2

A trail mix recipe calls for 3 cups of raisins and 4 cups of peanuts. Mitt made trail mix for a party and used 5 cups of raisins and 6 cups of peanuts. Did Mitt use the correct ratio of raisins to peanuts?

$\frac{3 \text{ cups of raisins}}{4 \text{ cups of peanuts}}$ Ratio for recipe $\frac{5 \text{ cups of raisins}}{6 \text{ cups of peanuts}}$ Ratio Mitt used

$\frac{3}{4} = \frac{9}{12}$ (×3) $\frac{5}{6} = \frac{10}{12}$ (×2)

$\frac{9}{12} < \frac{10}{12}$, so Mitt did not use the correct ratio of raisins to peanuts.

EXERCISES

Write three equivalent ratios for each ratio. (Lesson 6.1)

1. $\frac{18}{6}$ ____________ **2.** $\frac{5}{45}$ ____________ **3.** $\frac{3}{5}$ ____________

4. To make a dark orange color, Ron mixes 3 ounces of red paint with 2 ounces of yellow paint. Write the ratio of red paint to yellow paint three ways. (Lesson 6.1) ____________

5. A box of a dozen fruit tarts costs \$15.00. What is the cost of one fruit tart? (Lesson 6.2) ____________

Compare the ratios. (Lesson 6.3)

6. $\frac{2}{5}$ ◯ $\frac{3}{4}$ **7.** $\frac{9}{2}$ ◯ $\frac{10}{7}$ **8.** $\frac{2}{11}$ ◯ $\frac{3}{12}$ **9.** $\frac{6}{7}$ ◯ $\frac{8}{9}$

MODULE 7

Applying Ratios and Rates

ESSENTIAL QUESTION

How can you use ratios and rates to solve real-world problems?

Key Vocabulary

conversion factor *(factor de conversión)*
proportion *(proporción)*
scale *(escala)*
scale drawing *(dibujo a escala)*

EXAMPLE 1

A. Jessica earns the same amount for each dog she walks. She earns \$15 for walking 3 dogs. Find the unit rate and make a table. Then graph the relationship between the number of dogs Jessica walks and her earnings.

Number of dogs	1	2	3	4	5
Earnings (\$)	5	10	15	20	25

$\frac{\text{earnings}}{\text{dogs}} = \frac{\$15}{3 \text{ dogs}} = \frac{\$5}{1 \text{ dog}} = \$5$ per dog

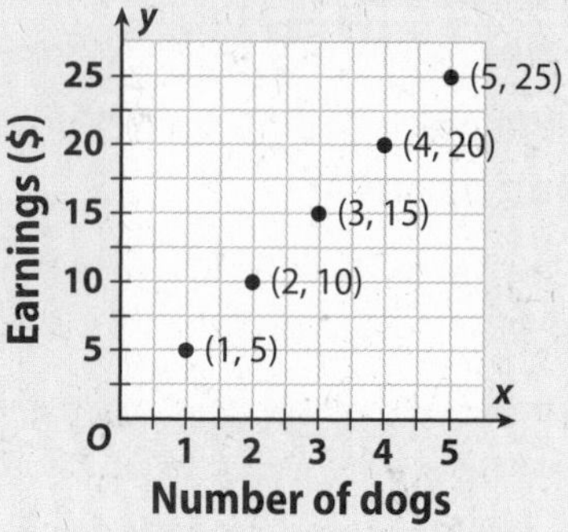

B. A veterinarian tells Lee that his dog should have a 35-centimeter collar. What is this measurement in inches?

Use the conversion factor 1 centimeter $\approx$ 0.39 inch, written as the rate $\frac{0.39 \text{ in.}}{1 \text{ cm}}$

$35 \text{ cm} \times \frac{0.39 \text{ in.}}{1 \text{ cm}} \approx 13.65 \text{ in.}$

The collar should be about 13.65 inches.

EXERCISES

1. Gavin's class is selling bracelets to raise money for charity. He sold 4 bracelets and raised \$16. Find the unit rate and make a table. Graph the relationship between the number of bracelets he sells and the amount he raises. (Lesson 7.1)

Bracelets sold	1	2	3	4	5
Amount raised (\$)				16	

Unit rate = \$4 per bracelet

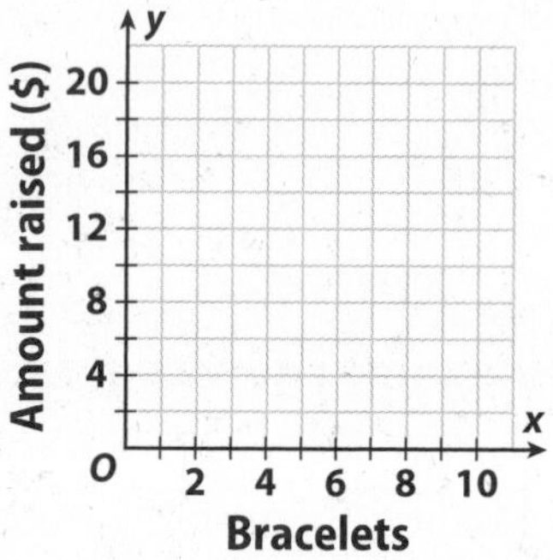

2. Isobel and Marnie volunteer at a daycare center. Isobel works 3 hours for every 2 hours Marnie works. If the two girls together work 20 hours one month, how many hours does Isobel work?

(Lesson 7.2) ____________________

3. A small dog weighs 5 pounds. How many ounces is that?

(Lesson 7.3) ____________________

4. The average adult has about 5 quarts of blood. How many liters is that? (Lesson 7.4) ____________________

MODULE 8 Percents

ESSENTIAL QUESTION

How can you use percents to solve real-world problems?

EXAMPLE 1

Find an equivalent percent for $\frac{7}{10}$.

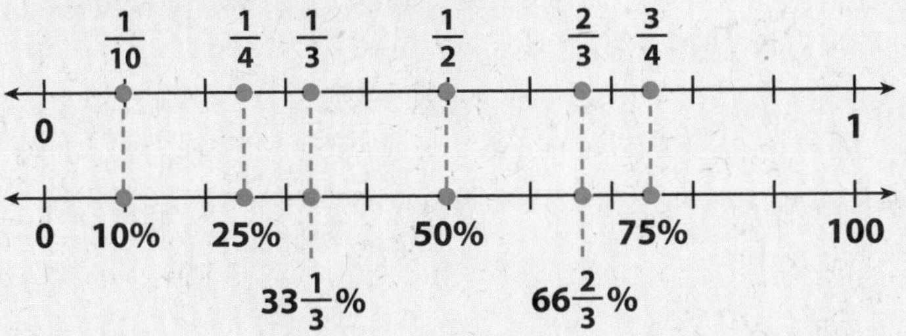

$\frac{7}{10} = 7 \times \frac{1}{10}$ $\quad$ $\frac{7}{10} = 7 \times 10\%$ $\quad$ $\frac{7}{10} = 70\%$

Find an equivalent percent for $\frac{1}{5}$.

$\frac{1}{5}$ of $100 = 20$, so $\frac{1}{5}$ of $100\% = 20\%$

$\frac{1}{5} = 20\%$

EXAMPLE 2

Thirteen of the 50 states in the United States do not touch the ocean. Write $\frac{13}{50}$ as a decimal and a percent.

$\frac{13}{50} = \frac{26}{100}$ $\quad$ $\frac{26}{100} = 0.26$ $\quad$ $0.26 = 26\%$ $\quad$ $\frac{13}{50} = 0.26 = 26\%$

EXERCISES

Write each fraction as a decimal and a percent. (Lessons 8.1, 8.2)

1. $\frac{3}{4}$ ____________
2. $\frac{7}{20}$ ____________
3. $\frac{8}{5}$ ____________

Complete each statement. (Lessons 8.1, 8.2)

4. 25% of 200 is ________.
5. 16 is ________ of 20.
6. 21 is 70% of ________.

7. 42 of the 150 employees at Carlo's Car Repair wear contact lenses. What percent of the employees wear contact lenses? (Lesson 8.3) ____________

8. Last week at Best Bargain, 75% of the computers sold were laptops. If 340 computers were sold there last week, how many laptops were sold? (Lesson 8.3) ____________

Unit Project

CA CC 6.RP.3, 6.RP.3a, 6.RP.3d

How Big Is Big?

Many celebrities and professional athletes make huge amounts of money each year. Is it possible to understand how big those numbers are? Choose a celebrity or athlete. Find out how much money that person earned last year. Then create a presentation that answers these questions:

- How much did the person make per hour? Assume the person worked 40 hours per week for 52 weeks.
- If the person's earnings were converted to dollar bills, how many miles would the bills stretch if they were laid end-to-end?
- How many days would it take to spend the earnings at the rate of $1 per second?

In addition to those questions, write and answer two similar questions of your own. Your questions should be aimed at converting the person's earnings into terms that are easier to understand. Use the space below to write down any questions you have or important information from your teacher.

MATH IN CAREERS ACTIVITY

Residential Builder Kaylee, a residential builder, is deciding on a painting bid for an 825-square-foot room in a custom-designed home she is building. A gallon of paint costs $38.50, and its label says it covers about 350 square feet. The paint is only available in one-gallon cans. One contractor's bid is based on the cost of the paint per square foot. The second contractor's bid is based on the amount of paint he must buy. The labor cost of both contractors is the same. What is the difference between the two bids?

CALIFORNIA

UNIT 3
MIXED REVIEW

Assessment Readiness

Personal Math Trainer
my.hrw.com
Online Practice and Help

1. The Office Store sells printer paper. Last week, the store sold 324 packs of white paper, which was 40% of the paper it sold for the whole week. The store also sold 81 packs of blue paper, 243 packs of yellow paper, and 162 packs of pink paper. The store manager needs to determine the percentages of the other paper sold.

Select Yes or No to indicate whether the statement agrees with the information in the above problem.

A. 15% of the paper sold was blue. ◯ Yes ◯ No

B. 30% of the paper sold was yellow. ◯ Yes ◯ No

C. 20% of the paper sold was pink. ◯ Yes ◯ No

2. Choose True or False.

A. There is 0.15 centimeter in 15 meters. ◯ True ◯ False

B. Eight pounds is equal to 128 ounces. ◯ True ◯ False

C. There are 108 inches in 9 yards. ◯ True ◯ False

D. 16 kilometers is equal to 16,000 meters. ◯ True ◯ False

3. Barbara can walk 3,200 meters in 24 minutes. Mavis can walk 11,808 feet in 24 minutes. Who walks at a faster rate of speed? Explain the steps you take to solve the problem. Use 1 m $\approx$ 3.28 ft or 1 ft $\approx$ 0.305 ft.

4. The table shows the number of windows and the number of panes of glass in the windows. Jim predicts that for 15 windows there are 75 panes. Is Jim correct? Use the ratio of windows to panes to explain if Jim's prediction is correct or incorrect.

Windows	2	3	4	5
Panes	12	18	24	30

Performance Tasks

★**5.** A recipe calls for 6 cups of water and 4 cups of flour.

a. If the recipe is increased to use 6 cups of flour, how much water should be used? Explain.

b. If the recipe is decreased to 2 cups of water, how much flour should be used? Explain.

★★**6.** Ivan saves 20% of his monthly paycheck for music equipment. He earned $335 last month.

a. How much did he save for music equipment? Explain.

b. If he uses $20.10 of what he earned to buy sheet music, what percent of his earnings is this amount? Explain.

★★★**7.** Davette wants to buy flannel sheets. She reads that a mass of at least 190 grams per square meter is considered high quality.

a. Davette finds a sheet that has a mass of 920 grams per 5 square meters. Does this sheet satisfy the requirement for high-quality sheets? If not, what should the mass be for 5 square meters? Explain.

b. Davette finds three more options for flannel sheets:

Option 1: 1,101 g of flannel in 6 square meters, $45.00

Option 2: 1,248 g of flannel in 6.5 square meters, $42.25

Option 3: 1,300 g of flannel in 6.4 square meters, $52.00

She would like to buy the sheet that meets the requirement for high quality and has the lowest price per square meter. Which option should she buy? Justify your answer.

UNIT 4

Equivalent Expressions

MODULE 9

Generating Equivalent Numerical Expressions

CA CC 6.EE.1

MODULE 10

Generating Equivalent Algebraic Expressions

CA CC 6.EE.2a, 6.EE.2b, 6.EE.2c, 6.EE.3, 6.EE.4, 6.EE.6

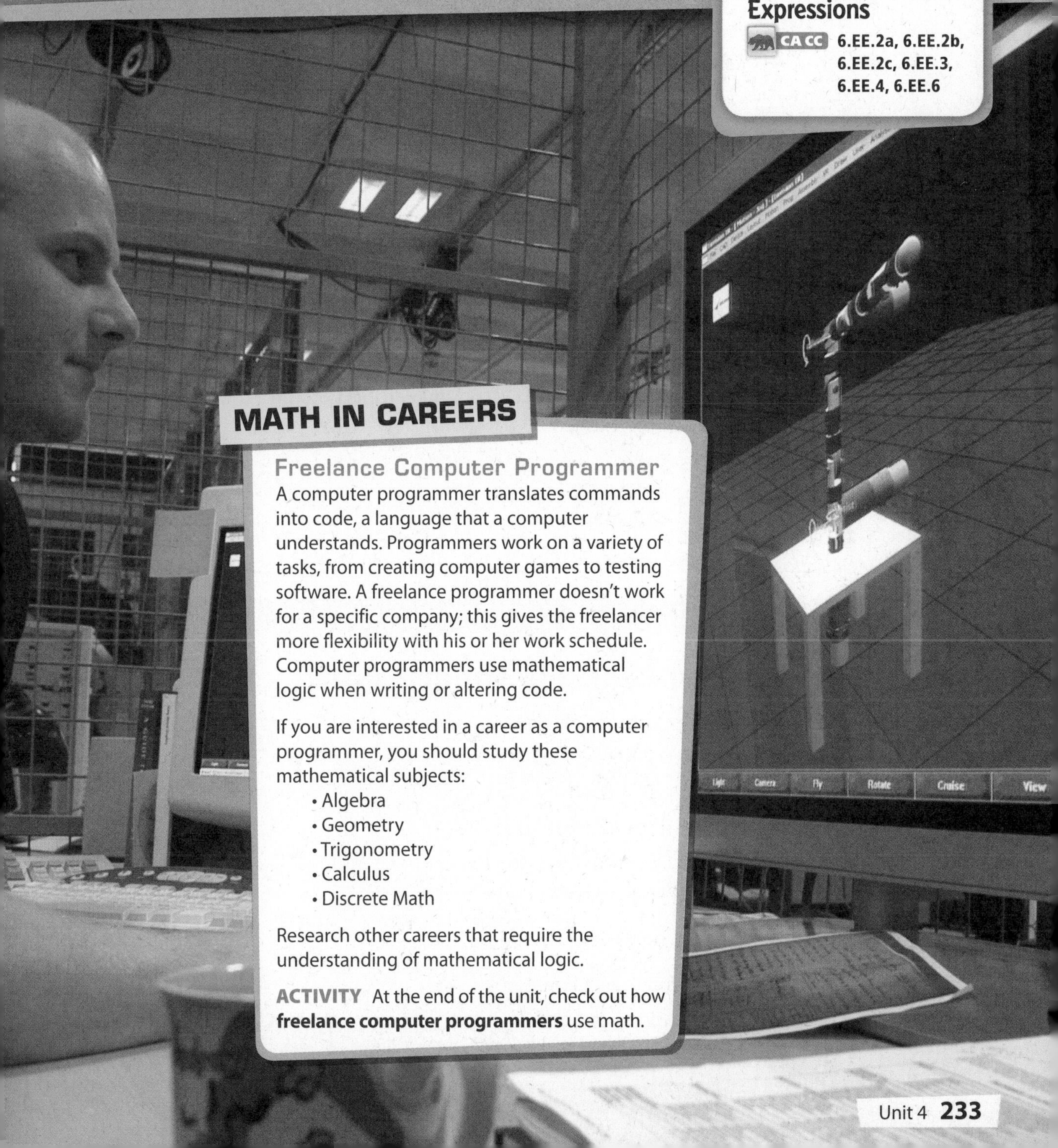

MATH IN CAREERS

Freelance Computer Programmer

A computer programmer translates commands into code, a language that a computer understands. Programmers work on a variety of tasks, from creating computer games to testing software. A freelance programmer doesn't work for a specific company; this gives the freelancer more flexibility with his or her work schedule. Computer programmers use mathematical logic when writing or altering code.

If you are interested in a career as a computer programmer, you should study these mathematical subjects:

- Algebra
- Geometry
- Trigonometry
- Calculus
- Discrete Math

Research other careers that require the understanding of mathematical logic.

ACTIVITY At the end of the unit, check out how **freelance computer programmers** use math.

Unit Project Preview

The Power of 2

The Unit Project at the end of this unit will give you an opportunity to see how quickly multiples of 2 increase in magnitude. You will multiply 2 by itself 20 times, and for each product look for a real-world representation of that product. To successfully complete the Unit Project you'll need to master these skills:

- Understand exponents.
- Calculate powers of integers.

1. Consider a number greater than 2. Which do you think is larger, the sum if you add a number to itself 10 times, or the product if you multiply the number by itself 10 times? Explain.

____

____

____

2. Jonathan said he could use the Distributive Property to find the product below. Was he right? Explain.

$$5 \times (5 \times 5) = (5 \times 5) \times (5 \times 5) = 25 \times 25 = 625$$

____

____

Tracking Your Learning Progression

This unit addresses important California Common Core Standards in the Critical Areas of understanding algebraic expressions and solving equations and inequalities.

Domain 6.EE Expressions and Equations

Cluster Apply and extend previous understandings of arithmetic to algebraic expressions.

The unit also supports additional standards.

Domain 6.EE Expressions and Equations

Cluster Reason about and solve one-variable equations and inequalities.

Generating Equivalent Numerical Expressions

MODULE 9

CALIFORNIA

ESSENTIAL QUESTION

How can you generate equivalent numerical expressions and use them to solve real-world problems?

Real-World Video

my.hrw.com

Assume that you post a video on the internet. Two of your friends view it, then two friends of each of those view it, and so on. The number of views is growing exponentially. Sometimes we say the video went viral.

GO DIGITAL
my.hrw.com

my.hrw.com
Go digital with your write-in student edition, accessible on any device.

Math On the Spot
Scan with your smart phone to jump directly to the online edition, video tutor, and more.

Animated Math
Interactively explore key concepts to see how math works.

Personal Math Trainer
Get immediate feedback and help as you work through practice sets.

Are YOU Ready?

Complete these exercises to review skills you will need for this module.

Personal Math Trainer
Online Practice and Help
my.hrw.com

Whole Number Operations

EXAMPLE 270×83

$$\begin{array}{r l}
270 & \\
\times\ 83 & \\
\hline
810 & \leftarrow\ 3 \times 270 \\
+21{,}600 & \leftarrow\ 80 \times 270 \\
\hline
22{,}410 & \leftarrow\ (3 \times 270) + (80 \times 270)
\end{array}$$

Find the product.

1. 992×16 ________

2. 578×27 ________

3. 839×65 ________

4. 367×23 ________

Use Repeated Multiplication

EXAMPLE $5 \times 5 \times 5 \times 5$ — *Multiply the first two factors.*

$25 \times 5 \times 5$ — *Multiply the result by the next factor.*

125×5 — *Multiply that result by the next factor.*

625 — *Continue until there are no more factors to multiply.*

Find the product.

5. $7 \times 7 \times 7$ ________

6. $3 \times 3 \times 3 \times 3$ ________

7. $6 \times 6 \times 6 \times 6 \times 6$ ________

8. $2 \times 2 \times 2 \times 2 \times 2 \times 2$ ________

Division Facts

EXAMPLE $54 \div 9 = \blacksquare$ Think: *9 times what number equals 54?* $9 \times 6 = 54$

$54 \div 9 = 6$ *So, $54 \div 9 = 6$.*

Divide.

9. $20 \div 4$ ________

10. $21 \div 7$ ________

11. $42 \div 7$ ________

12. $56 \div 8$ ________

Reading Start-Up

Visualize Vocabulary

Use the ✔ words to complete the graphic. You may put more than one word in each box.

Reviewing Factorization

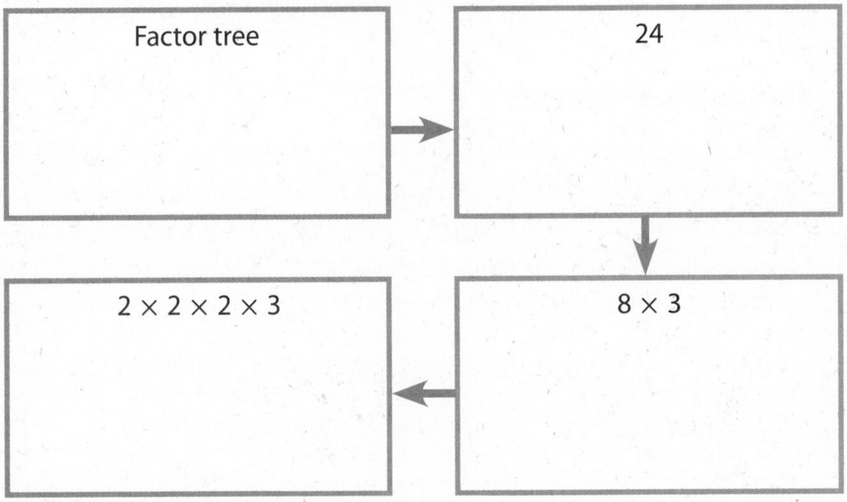

Vocabulary

Review Words

✔ factor *(factor)*

factor tree *(árbol de factores)*

✔ integers *(entero)*

✔ numerical expression *(expresión numérica)*

✔ operations *(operaciones)*

✔ prime factorization *(factorización prima)*

repeated multiplication *(multiplicación repetida)*

simplified expression *(expresión simplificada)*

Preview Words

base *(base)*

exponent *(exponente)*

order of operations *(orden de las operaciones)*

power *(potencia)*

Understand Vocabulary

Complete the sentences using the preview words.

1. A number that is formed by repeated multiplication by the same factor is a ____________________.

2. A rule for simplifying expressions is ______________________________.

3. The ________________ is a number that is multiplied. The number that indicates how many times this number is used as a factor is the ________________.

Active Reading

Three-Panel Flip Chart Before beginning the module, create a three-panel flip chart to help you organize what you learn. Label each flap with one of the lesson titles from this module. As you study each lesson, write important ideas like vocabulary, properties, and formulas under the appropriate flap.

GETTING READY FOR

Generating Equivalent Numerical Expressions

Understanding the standards and the vocabulary terms in the standards will help you know exactly what you are expected to learn in this module.

CA CC 6.EE.1

Write and evaluate numerical expressions involving whole-number exponents.

Key Vocabulary

exponent *(exponente)*
The number that indicates how many times the base is used as a factor.

order of operations *(orden de las operaciones)* A rule for evaluating expressions: first perform the operations in parentheses, then compute powers and roots, then perform all multiplication and division from left to right, and then perform all addition and subtraction from left to right.

What It Means to You

You will simplify numerical expressions using the order of operations.

EXAMPLE 6.EE.1

Ellen is playing a video game in which she captures frogs. There were 3 frogs onscreen, but the number of frogs doubled every minute when she went to get a snack. She returned after 4 minutes and captured 7 frogs. Write an expression for the number of frogs remaining. Simplify the expression.

3×2	number of frogs after 1 minute
$3 \times 2 \times 2$	number of frogs after 2 minutes
$3 \times 2 \times 2 \times 2$	number of frogs after 3 minutes
$3 \times 2 \times 2 \times 2 \times 2$	number of frogs after 4 minutes

Since 3 and 2 are prime numbers, $3 \times 2 \times 2 \times 2 \times 2$ is the prime factorization of the number of frogs remaining.

$3 \times 2 \times 2 \times 2 \times 2$ can be written with exponents as 3×2^4.

The expression $3 \times 2^4 - 7$ is the number of frogs remaining after Ellen captured the 7 frogs.

Use the order of operations to simplify $3 \times 2^4 - 7$.

$3 \times 2^4 - 7 = 3 \times 16 - 7$

$= 48 - 7$

$= 41$

41 frogs remain.

Visit **my.hrw.com** to see all **CA Common Core Standards** explained.

my.hrw.com

LESSON

9.1 Exponents

CA CC 6.EE.1

Write and evaluate numerical expressions involving whole-number exponents.

ESSENTIAL QUESTION

How do you use exponents to represent numbers?

EXPLORE ACTIVITY Real World CA CC 6.EE.1

Identifying Repeated Multiplication

Bacteria reproduce by dividing, a process that can be observed in a microscope. Some scientists observe the hourly growth of bacteria and record their observations in a table.

Time (h)	Total bacteria
0	1
1	2
2	$2 \times 2 = \square$
3	$2 \times 2 \times 2 = \square$
4	$2 \times 2 \times 2 \times 2 = \square$

After 2 hours, there are $2 \times 2 = ?$ bacteria.

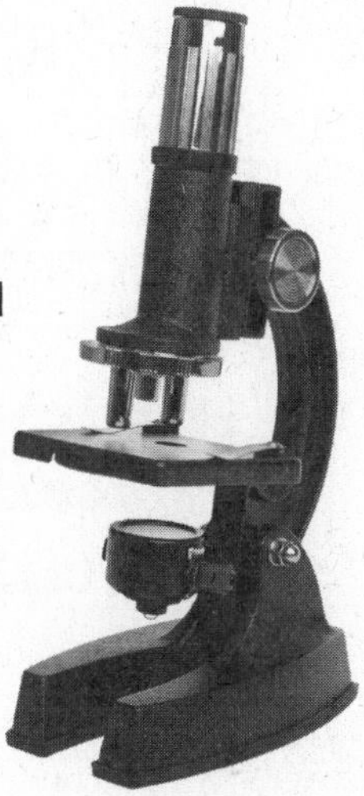

A Complete the table. What pattern(s) do you see in the Total bacteria column?

____

____

B Complete each statement.

At 2 hours, the total is equal to the product of two 2s.

At 3 hours, the total is equal to the product of ________________ 2s.

At 4 hours, the total is equal to the product of ________________ 2s.

Reflect

1. **Communicate Mathematical Ideas** How is the time, in hours, related to the number of times 2 is used as a factor? Show how to find the number of bacteria at 10 hours.

____

____

Math On the Spot
my.hrw.com

Using Exponents

A number that is formed by repeated multiplication of the same factor is called a **power**. You can use an *exponent* and a *base* to write a power. For example, 7^3 means the product of three 7s:

$$7^3 = 7 \times 7 \times 7$$

The **base** is the number that is multiplied.

The **exponent** tells how many times the base appears in the expression.

Power	How to read the power
6^2	6 squared, 6 to the power of 2, 6 raised to the 2nd power
7^3	7 cubed, 7 to the power of 3, 7 raised to the 3rd power
9^4	9 to the power of 4, 9 raised to 4th power

EXAMPLE 1

CA CC 6.EE.1

Use an exponent to write each expression.

A $3 \times 3 \times 3 \times 3 \times 3$

Find the base, or the number being multiplied. The base is 3.

Find the exponent by counting the number of 3s being multiplied. The exponent is 5.

$$\underbrace{3 \times 3 \times 3 \times 3 \times 3}_{\text{5 factors of 3}} = 3^5$$

B $\frac{4}{5} \times \frac{4}{5} \times \frac{4}{5} \times \frac{4}{5}$

Find the base, or the number being multiplied. The base is $\frac{4}{5}$.

Find the exponent by counting the number of times $\frac{4}{5}$ appears in the expression. The exponent is 4.

$$\underbrace{\frac{4}{5} \times \frac{4}{5} \times \frac{4}{5} \times \frac{4}{5}}_{\text{4 factors of } \frac{4}{5}} = \left(\frac{4}{5}\right)^4$$

Math Talk
Mathematical Practices

In the Explore Activity, how can you use an exponent to show the total bacteria at 10 hours?

YOUR TURN

Use exponents to write each expression.

2. $4 \times 4 \times 4$ ______

3. 6 ______

4. $\frac{1}{8} \times \frac{1}{8}$ ______

5. $5 \times 5 \times 5 \times 5 \times 5 \times 5$ ______

Personal Math Trainer
Online Practice and Help
my.hrw.com

Finding the Value of a Power

To find the value of a power, remember that the exponent indicates how many times to use the base as a factor.

Math On the Spot
my.hrw.com

Property of Zero as an Exponent

The value of any nonzero number raised to the power of 0 is 1.

Example: $5^0 = 1$

EXAMPLE 2

CA CC 6.EE.1

Find the value of each power.

A 10^4

Identify the base and the exponent.
The base is 10, and the exponent is 4.

Evaluate: $10^4 = 10 \times 10 \times 10 \times 10 = 10{,}000$

B 0.4^3

Identify the base and the exponent.
The base is 0.4, and the exponent is 3.

Evaluate: $0.4^3 = 0.4 \times 0.4 \times 0.4 = 0.064$

C $\left(\frac{3}{5}\right)^0$

Identify the base and the exponent.
The base is $\frac{3}{5}$, and the exponent is 0.

Evaluate.

$\left(\frac{3}{5}\right)^0 = 1$ Any number raised to the power of 0 is 1.

D $\left(\frac{2}{3}\right)^2$

Identify the base and the exponent.
The base is $\frac{2}{3}$, and the exponent is 2.

Evaluate.

$\left(\frac{2}{3}\right)^2 = \left(\frac{2}{3}\right) \times \left(\frac{2}{3}\right) = \frac{4}{9}$

Math Talk
Mathematical Practices

Is the value of 2^3 the same as the value of 3^2? Explain.

YOUR TURN

Find the value of each power.

6. 3^4 ______ **7.** 1^9 ______ **8.** $\left(\frac{2}{5}\right)^3$ ______ **9.** 12^2 ______

Personal Math Trainer
Online Practice and Help
my.hrw.com

Guided Practice

1. Complete the table. (Explore Activity 1)

Exponential form	Product	Simplified product
5^1	5	5
5^2	5×5	
5^3		125
	$5 \times 5 \times 5 \times 5$	
5^5		

Use an exponent to write each expression. (Example 1)

2. $\underbrace{6 \times 6 \times 6}$ ______

__ factors of 6

3. $10 \times 10 \times 10 \times 10 \times 10 \times 10 \times 10$ ______

4. $\frac{3}{4} \times \frac{3}{4} \times \frac{3}{4} \times \frac{3}{4} \times \frac{3}{4}$ ______

5. $\frac{7}{9} \times \frac{7}{9} \times \frac{7}{9} \times \frac{7}{9} \times \frac{7}{9} \times \frac{7}{9} \times \frac{7}{9} \times \frac{7}{9}$ ______

Find the value of each power. (Example 2)

6. 8^3 ______

7. 7^4 ______

8. 10^3 ______

9. $\left(\frac{1}{4}\right)^2$ ______

10. $\left(\frac{1}{3}\right)^3$ ______

11. $\left(\frac{6}{7}\right)^2$ ______

12. 0.8^2 ______

13. 0.5^3 ______

14. 1.1^2 ______

15. 8^0 ______

16. 12^1 ______

17. $\left(\frac{1}{2}\right)^0$ ______

18. $(13)^2$ ______

19. $\left(\frac{2}{5}\right)^2$ ______

20. 0.9^2 ______

ESSENTIAL QUESTION CHECK-IN

21. How do you use an exponent to represent a number such as 16?

______

______

______

______

______

Name ______________________ Class ______________________ Date ______________________

9.1 Independent Practice

CA CC 6.EE.1

Personal Math Trainer
my.hrw.com
Online Practice and Help

Write the missing exponent.

22. $100 = 10^{\square}$

23. $8 = 2^{\square}$

24. $25 = 5^{\square}$

25. $27 = 3^{\square}$

26. $\frac{1}{169} = \left(\frac{1}{13}\right)^{\square}$

27. $14 = 14^{\square}$

28. $32 = 2^{\square}$

29. $\frac{64}{81} = \left(\frac{8}{9}\right)^{\square}$

Write the missing base.

30. $1{,}000 = \square^3$

31. $256 = \square^4$

32. $16 = \square^4$

33. $9 = \square^2$

34. $\frac{1}{9} = \left(\square\right)^2$

35. $64 = \square^2$

36. $\frac{9}{16} = \left(\square\right)^2$

37. $729 = \square^3$

For Exercises 38–42, write the answer with and without using an exponent.

38. Hadley's softball team has a phone tree in case a game is canceled. The coach calls 3 players. Then each of those players calls 3 players, and so on. How many players will be notified during the third round of calls?

____

39. Tim is reading a book. On Monday he reads 3 pages. On each day after that, he reads 3 times the number of pages that he read on the previous day. How many pages does he read on Thursday?

____

40. The square tile shown has a side length of 10.5 inches. What power can you write to represent the area of the tile? Find the area of the tile.

____

41. Antonia is saving for a video game. On the first day, she saves two dollars in her piggy bank. Each day after that, she doubles the number of dollars she saved on the previous day. How many dollars does she save on the sixth day?

____

42. A certain colony of bacteria triples in length every 10 minutes. Its length is now 1 millimeter. How long will it be in 40 minutes?

____

43. What power can you write to represent the volume of the cube shown? Write the power as an expression with a base and an exponent, and then find the volume of the cube.

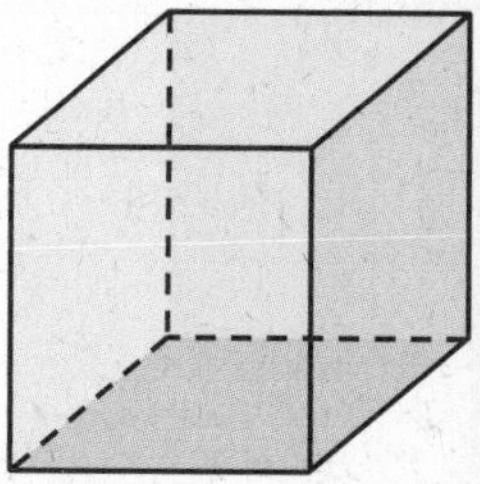

44. Write a power represented with a positive base and a positive exponent whose value is less than the base.

H.O.T. FOCUS ON HIGHER ORDER THINKING

Work Area

45. Communicate Mathematical Ideas What is the value of 1 raised to the power of any exponent? What is the value of 0 raised to the power of any nonzero exponent? Explain.

46. Look for a Pattern Find the values of the powers in the following pattern: 10^1, 10^2, 10^3, 10^4.... Describe the pattern, and use it to evaluate 10^6 without using multiplication.

47. Critical Thinking Some numbers can be written as powers of different bases. For example, $81 = 9^2$ and $81 = 3^4$. Write the number 64 using three different bases.

48. Justify Reasoning Oman said that it is impossible to raise a number to the power of 2 and get a value less than the original number. Do you agree with Oman? Justify your reasoning.

LESSON

9.2 Prime Factorization

CA CC 6.EE.1

Write and evaluate numerical expressions involving whole-number exponents

ESSENTIAL QUESTION

How do you write the prime factorization of a number?

Finding Factors of a Number

Whole numbers that are multiplied to find a product are called factors of that product. A number is divisible by its factors. For example, 4 and 2 are factors of 8 because $4 \times 2 = 8$, and 8 is divisible by 4 and by 2.

Math On the Spot

my.hrw.com

EXAMPLE 1 Real World

CA CC Prep for 6.EE.1

Ana wants to build a rectangular garden with an area of 24 square feet. What are the possible whole number lengths and widths of the garden?

STEP 1 Recall that area = length × width. For Ana's garden, $24\ ft^2 = \text{length} \times \text{width}$.

STEP 2 List the factors of 24 in pairs. List each pair only once.

$24 = 1 \times 24$
$24 = 2 \times 12$
$24 = 3 \times 8$
$24 = 4 \times 6$

$4 \times 6 = 6 \times 4$, so you only list 4×6.

You can also use a diagram to show the factor pairs.

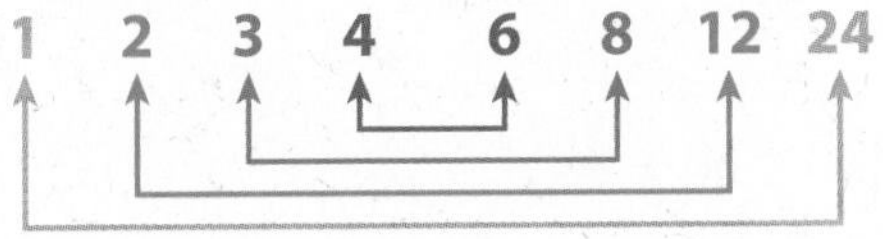

The factors of 24 are 1, 2, 3, 4, 6, 8, 12, 24.

STEP 3 The possible lengths and widths are:

Length (ft)	24	12	8	6
Width (ft)	1	2	3	4

Math Talk
Mathematical Practices

Give an example of a whole number that has exactly two factors. What type of number has exactly two factors?

YOUR TURN

List all the factors of each number.

1. 21 ______

2. 37 ______

3. 42 ______

4. 30 ______

Personal Math Trainer

Online Practice and Help

my.hrw.com

EXPLORE ACTIVITY 1 CA CC 6.EE.1

Finding the Prime Factorization of a Number

Animated Math
my.hrw.com

The prime factorization of a number is the number written as the product of its prime factors. For example, the prime factors of 12 are 3, 2, and 2.

There are several different ways to write the prime factorization of 12. Some examples are shown below. The symbol · means "times."

$2 \times 2 \times 3$ $\qquad$ $2 \cdot 2 \cdot 3$ $\qquad$ $2^2 \cdot 3$

Use exponents to show repeated factors.

Use a factor tree to find the prime factorization of 240.

A List the factor pairs of 240.

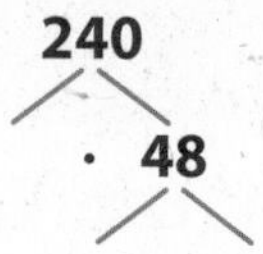

B Choose any factor pair to begin the tree. If a number in this pair is prime, circle it. If a number in the pair can be written as a product of two factors, draw additional branches and write the factors.

C Continue adding branches until the factors at the ends of the branches are prime numbers.

D Write the prime factorization of 240.

Then write the prime factorization using exponents.

Reflect

5. **What If?** What will the factor tree for 240 look like if you start the tree with a different factor pair? Check your prediction by creating another factor tree for 240 that starts with a different factor pair.

EXPLORE ACTIVITY 2 CA CC 6.EE.1

Using a Ladder Diagram

A ladder diagram is another way to find the prime factorization of a number.

Use a ladder diagram to find the prime factorization of 132.

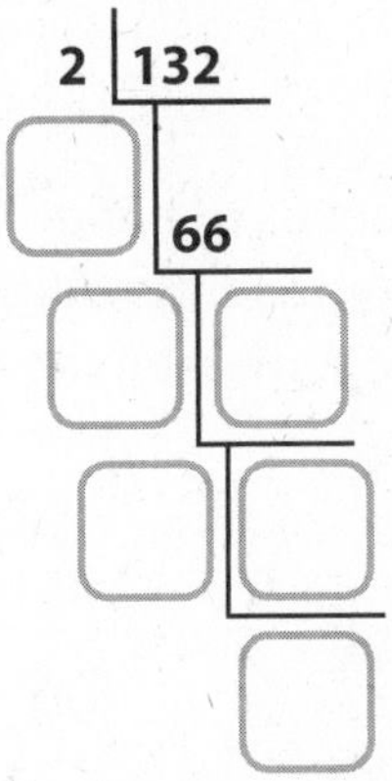

A Write 132 in the top "step" of the ladder. Choose a prime factor of 132 to write next to the step with 132. Choose 2. Divide 132 by 2 and write the quotient 66 in the next step of the ladder.

B Now choose a prime factor of 66. Write the prime factor next to the step with 66. Divide 66 by that prime factor and write the quotient in the next step of the ladder.

C Keep choosing prime factors, dividing, and adding to the ladder until you get a quotient of 1.

D What are the prime factors of 132? How can you tell from the ladder diagram?

____

____

E Write the prime factorization of 132 using exponents.

____

Reflect

6. Complete a factor tree and a ladder diagram to find the prime factorization of 54.

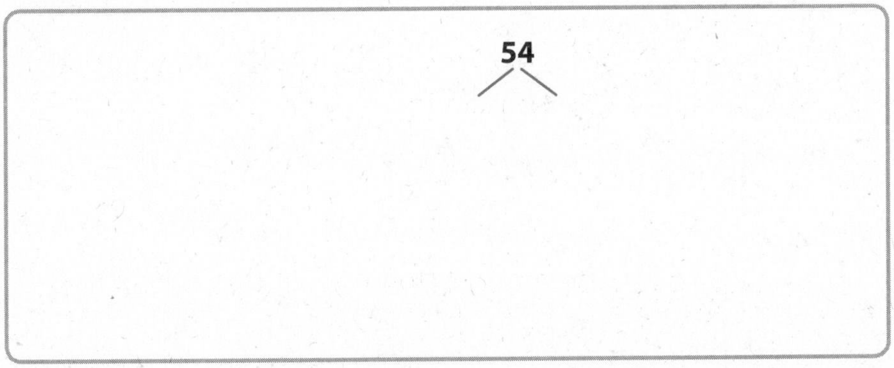

7. **Communicate Mathematical Ideas** If one person uses a ladder diagram and another uses a factor tree to write a prime factorization, will they get the same result? Explain.

____

____

Guided Practice

Use a diagram to list the factor pairs of each number. (Example 1)

1. 18

2. 52

______________________ ______________________

3. Karl needs to build a stage that has an area of 72 square feet. The length of the stage should be longer than the width. What are the possible whole number measurements for the length and width of the stage? (Example 1)

Complete the table with possible measurements of the stage.

Length	72					
Width		2				

Use a factor tree to find the prime factorization of each number. (Explore Activity 1)

4. 402

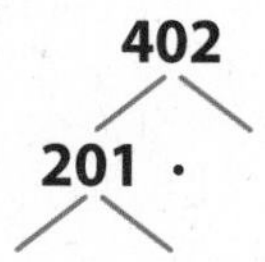

5. 36

______________________ ______________________

Use a ladder diagram to find the prime factorization of each number. (Explore Activity 2)

6. 32

7. 27

______________________ ______________________

ESSENTIAL QUESTION CHECK-IN

8. Tell how you know when you have found the prime factorization of a number.

____

____

Name ________________ Class ________________ Date ________________

9.2 Independent Practice

CA CC 6.EE.1

Personal Math Trainer

Online Practice and Help

my.hrw.com

9. **Multiple Representations** Use the grid to draw three different rectangles so that each has an area of 12 square units and they all have different widths. What are the dimensions of the rectangles?

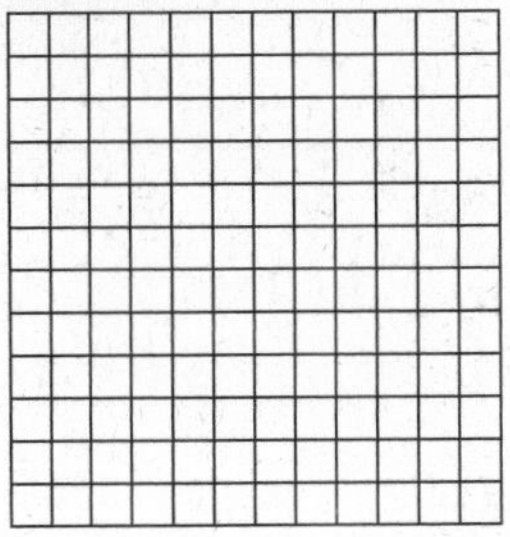

10. Brandon has 32 stamps. He wants to display the stamps in rows, with the same number of stamps in each row. How many different ways can he display the stamps? Explain.

11. **Communicate Mathematical Ideas** How is finding the factors of a number different from finding the prime factorization of a number?

Find the prime factorization of each number.

12. 891 ________________

13. 504 ________________

14. 23 ________________

15. 230 ________________

16. The number 2 is chosen to begin a ladder diagram to find the prime factorization of 66. What other numbers could have been used to start the ladder diagram for 66? How does starting with a different number change the diagram?

17. **Critical Thinking** List five numbers that have 3, 5, and 7 as prime factors.

18. In a game, you draw a card with three consecutive numbers on it. You can choose one of the numbers and find the sum of its prime factors. Then you can move that many spaces on a game board. You draw a card with the numbers 25, 26, 27. Which number should you choose if you want to move as many spaces as possible? Explain.

____

____

____

____

19. **Explain the Error** When asked to write the prime factorization of the number 27, a student wrote $9 \cdot 3$. Explain the error and write the correct answer.

____

H.O.T. FOCUS ON HIGHER ORDER THINKING

Work Area

20. **Communicate Mathematical Ideas** Explain why it is possible to draw more than two different rectangles with an area of 36 square units, but it is not possible to draw more than two different rectangles with an area of 15 square units. The sides of the rectangles are whole numbers.

____

____

____

21. **Critique Reasoning** Alice wants to find all the prime factors of the number you get when you multiply $17 \cdot 11 \cdot 13 \cdot 7$. She thinks she has to use a calculator to perform all the multiplications and then find the prime factorization of the resulting number. Do you agree? Why or why not?

____

____

____

22. **Look for a Pattern** Ryan wrote the prime factorizations shown below. If he continues this pattern, what prime factorization will he show for the number one million? What prime factorization will he show for one billion?

$10 = 5 \cdot 2$

$100 = 5^2 \cdot 2^2$

$1{,}000 = 5^3 \cdot 2^3 = 1{,}000$

____

LESSON
9.3 Order of Operations

CA CC 6.EE.1

Write and evaluate numerical expressions involving whole-number exponents.

ESSENTIAL QUESTION

How do you use the order of operations to evaluate expressions with exponents?

EXPLORE ACTIVITY Real World CA CC 6.EE.1

Exploring the Order of Operations

Order of Operations

1. Perform operations in parentheses.
2. Find the value of numbers with exponents.
3. Multiply or divide from left to right.
4. Add or subtract from left to right.

Amy and three friends launch a new website. Each of the four friends e-mails the web address to three new friends. These new friends forward the web address to three more friends. If no one receives the e-mail more than once, how many people will receive the web address in the second wave of e-mails?

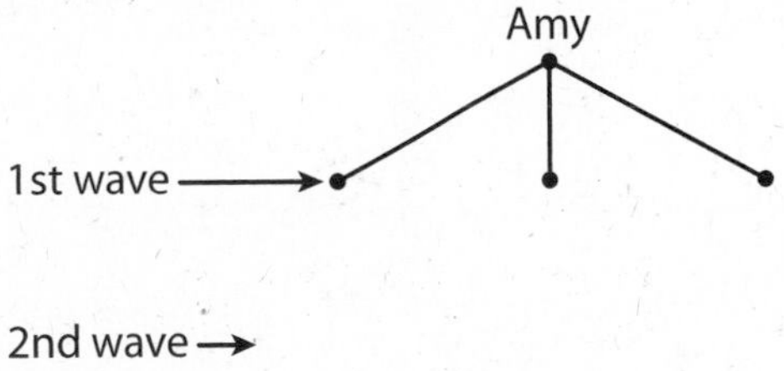

A Use a diagram to model the situation for Amy. Each dot represents one e-mail. Complete the diagram to show the second wave.

B Complete the table to show how many e-mails are sent in each wave of Amy's diagram.

Wave	Number of e-mails	Power of 3
1st		
2nd		

C Amy is just one of four friends initiating the first wave of e-mails. Write an expression for the total number of e-mails sent in the 2nd wave.

number of people × number of e-mails in 2nd wave written as a power

□ × □

D Identify the computation that should be done first to simplify the expression in **C**. Then simplify the expression.

Multiply 4 and 3 / Find the value of 3^2

The value of the expression is 4 × ________ = ________.

EXPLORE ACTIVITY *(cont'd)*

Reflect

1. In **B**, why does it makes sense to write the numbers of e-mails as powers? What is the pattern for the number of e-mails in each wave for Amy?

____

____

____

Math On the Spot
my.hrw.com

Evaluating Numerical Expressions

A numerical expression is an expression involving numbers and operations. You can use the order of operations to evaluate numerical expressions.

EXAMPLE 1

CA CC 6.EE.1

Evaluate each expression.

A $5 + 18 \div 3^2$

$5 + 18 \div 3^2 = 5 + 18 \div 9$	Evaluate 3^2.
$= 5 + 2$	Divide.
$= 7$	Add.

B $21 + \frac{3^2}{3}$

$21 + \frac{3^2}{3} = 21 + \frac{9}{3}$	Evaluate 3^2.
$= 21 + 3$	Divide.
$= 24$	Add.

Math Talk
Mathematical Practices

How do you know you must divide in **B**?

C $6 \times 2^3 \div 3 + 1$

$6 \times 2^3 \div 3 + 1 = 6 \times 8 \div 3 + 1$	Evaluate 2^3.
$= 48 \div 3 + 1$	Multiply.
$= 16 + 1$	Divide.
$= 17$	Add.

YOUR TURN

Evaluate each expression using the order of operations.

2. $7 + 15 \times 9^2 =$ ____________ **3.** $220 - 450 \div 3^2 =$ ____________

Personal Math Trainer
Online Practice and Help
my.hrw.com

Using Exponents with Parentheses

Remember to perform operations inside parentheses first when you evaluate expressions.

Math On the Spot
my.hrw.com

EXAMPLE 2

CA CC 6.EE.1

Evaluate each expression using the order of operations.

A $4 \times (9 \div 3)^2$

$4 \times (9 \div 3)^2 = 4 \times 3^2$	Perform operations inside parentheses.
$= 4 \times 9$	Evaluate 3^2.
$= 36$	Multiply.

B $5^3 + (12 - 2)^2$

$5^3 + (12 - 2)^2 = 5^3 + 10^2$	Perform operations inside parentheses.
$= 125 + 100$	Evaluate powers.
$= 225$	Add.

C $8 + \frac{(12 - 8)^2}{2}$

$8 + \frac{(12 - 8)^2}{2} = 8 + \frac{4^2}{2}$	Perform operations inside parentheses.
$= 8 + \frac{16}{2}$	Evaluate 4^2.
$= 8 + 8$	Divide.
$= 16$	Add.

My Notes

Reflect

4. **Critique Reasoning** John wants to evaluate the expression $(5 + 3)^2$. As a first step, he writes $5^2 + 3^2$. Will he get the correct value for the expression? If not, what should he do to evaluate the expression?

____

____

____

YOUR TURN

Evaluate each expression using the order of operations.

5. $5 \times (20 \div 4)^2 =$ ______________________________

6. $8^2 - (5 + 2)^2 =$ ______________________________

7. $7 - \frac{(63 \div 9)^2}{7} =$ ______________________________

Personal Math Trainer
Online Practice and Help
my.hrw.com

Guided Practice

1. In a video game, a guppy that escapes a net turns into three goldfish. Each goldfish can turn into two betta fish. Each betta fish can turn into two angelfish. Complete the diagram and write the number of fish at each stage. Write and evaluate an expression for the number of angelfish that can be formed from one guppy. (Explore Activity)

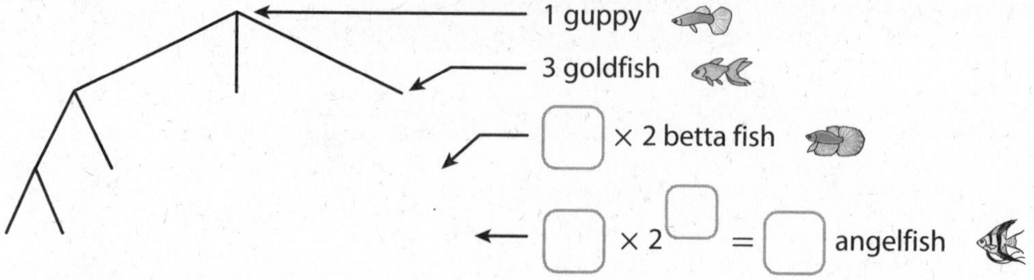

____

Complete to evaluate each expression. (Examples 1 and 2)

2. $89 - 4^2 \times 4 + 12 = 89 - \underline{\qquad} \times 4 + 12$

$= 89 - \underline{\qquad} + 12$

$= \underline{\qquad} + 12$

$= \underline{\qquad}$

3. $6 \times (36 \div 12)^2 + 8 = 6 \times (\underline{\qquad})^2 + 8$

$= 6 \times \underline{\qquad} + 8$

$= \underline{\qquad} + 8$

$= \underline{\qquad}$

4. $12 \times \left(\frac{(4+2)^2}{4}\right) - 7 = 12 \times \left(\frac{(\square)^2}{4}\right) - 7$

$= 12 \times \left(\frac{\square}{4}\right) - 7$

$= 12 \times \underline{\qquad} - 7$

$= \underline{\qquad} - 7$

$= \underline{\qquad}$

5. $320 \div \left(\frac{(11-9)^3}{2}\right) \times 8 = 320 \div \left(\frac{(\square)^3}{2}\right) \times 8$

$= 320 \div \left(\frac{\square}{2}\right) \times 8$

$= 320 \div \underline{\qquad} \times 8$

$= \underline{\qquad} \times 8$

$= \underline{\qquad}$

ESSENTIAL QUESTION CHECK-IN

6. How do you use the order of operations to evaluate expressions with exponents?

____

____

____

Name________________________ Class________________ Date________________

9.3 Independent Practice

CA CC 6.EE.1

Personal Math Trainer
my.hrw.com
Online Practice and Help

Evaluate each expression using the order of operations.

7. $5 \times 2 + 3^2$ ____________

8. $15 - 7 \times 2 + 2^3$ ____________

9. $(11 - 8)^3 - 2 \times 6$ ____________

10. $6 + 3(13 - 2) - 5^2$ ____________

11. $12 + \frac{9^2}{3}$ ____________

12. $\frac{8 + 6^2}{11} + 7 \times 2$ ____________

13. **Explain the Error** Jay evaluated the expression $3 \times (3 + 12 \div 3) - 4$. For his first step, he added $3 + 12$ to get 15. What was Jay's error? Find the correct answer.

____

____

14. **Multistep** A clothing store has the sign shown in the shop window. Pani sees the sign and wants to buy 3 shirts and 2 pairs of jeans. The cost of each shirt before the discount is \$12, and the cost of each pair of jeans is \$19 before the discount.

a. Write and evaluate an expression to find the amount Pani pays if a \$3 discount is applied to her total.

____

b. Pani says she should get a \$3 discount on the price of each shirt and a \$3 discount on the price of each pair of jeans. Write and evaluate an expression to find the amount she would pay if this is true.

____

c. **Analyze Relationships** Why are the amounts Pani pays in **a** and **b** different?

____

____

d. If you were the shop owner, how would you change the sign? Explain.

____

____

____

____

15. Ellen is playing a video game in which she captures butterflies. There are 3 butterflies onscreen, but the number of butterflies doubles every minute. After 4 minutes, she was able to capture 7 of the butterflies.

a. **Look for a Pattern** Write an expression for the number of butterflies after 4 minutes. Use a power of 2 in your answer.

____

b. Write an expression for the number of butterflies remaining after Ellen captured the 7 butterflies. Evaluate the expression.

____

16. Show how to write and evaluate an expression to represent and solve this problem: Jeff and his friend each text four classmates about a concert. Each classmate then texts four students from another school about the concert. If no one receives the message more than once, how many students from the other school receive a text about the concert?

____

H.O.T. FOCUS ON HIGHER ORDER THINKING

Work Area

17. **Geometry** The figure shown is a rectangle. The green shape in the figure is a square. The blue and white shapes are rectangles, and the area of the blue rectangle is 24 square inches.

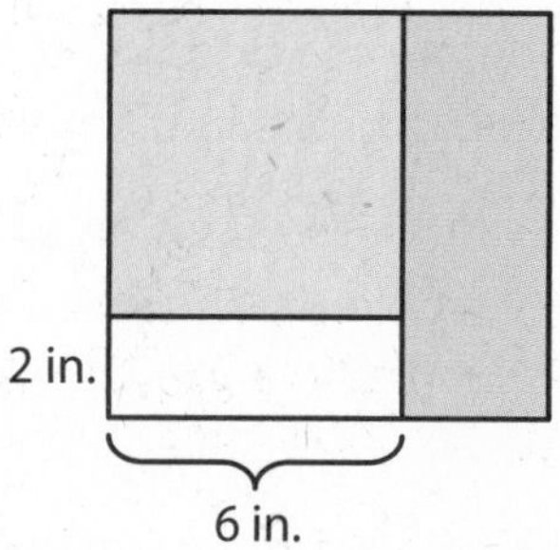

a. Write an expression for the area of the entire figure that includes an exponent. Then find the area.

____

b. Find the dimensions of the entire figure.

____

18. **Explain the Error** Rob and Lila try to simplify $18 \times 4^2 + (9 - 3)^2$. Rob evaluates the expression and gets 360. Lila evaluates it and gets 324. Which student is correct? What error did the other student make?

____

____

____

19. **Persevere in Problem Solving** Use parentheses to make this statement true: $8 \times 4 - 2 \times 3 + 8 \div 2 = 25$

____

MODULE QUIZ

Ready to Go On?

Personal Math Trainer
Online Practice and Help
my.hrw.com

9.1 Exponents

Find the value of each power.

1. 7^3 ________ **2.** 9^2 ________ **3.** $\left(\frac{7}{9}\right)^2$ ________ **4.** $\left(\frac{1}{2}\right)^6$ ________

5. $\left(\frac{2}{3}\right)^3$ ________ **6.** $\left(\frac{1}{3}\right)^4$ ________ **7.** 12^0 ________ **8.** 1.4^2 ________

9.2 Prime Factorization

Find the factors of each number.

9. 96 ________________

10. 120 ________________

Find the prime factorization of each number.

11. 58 ________________ **12.** 212 ________________

13. 2,800 ________________ **14.** 900 ________________

9.3 Order of Operations

Evaluate each expression using the order of operations.

15. $(21 - 3) \div 3^2$ ________________ **16.** $7^2 \times (6 \div 3)$ ________________

17. $17 + 15 \div 3 - 2^4$ ________________ **18.** $(8 + 56) \div 4 - 3^2$ ________________

19. The nature park has a pride of 7 adult lions and 4 cubs. The adults eat 6 pounds of meat each day and the cubs eat 3 pounds. Evaluate $7 \times 6 + 4 \times 3$ to find the amount of meat consumed each day by the lions. ________________

ESSENTIAL QUESTION

20. How do you use numerical expressions to solve real-world problems?

____

____

____

____

CALIFORNIA

MODULE 9
MIXED REVIEW

Assessment Readiness

Personal Math Trainer
my.hrw.com
Online Practice and Help

1. Consider each expression.

Select Yes or No in A–E to tell whether the value of the expression is less than the base of the expression.

A. 2^3 ○ Yes ○ No

B. $\left(\frac{5}{6}\right)^3$ ○ Yes ○ No

C. 3^1 ○ Yes ○ No

D. $\left(\frac{5}{2}\right)^3$ ○ Yes ○ No

E. 1^3 ○ Yes ○ No

2. Choose True or False for A–D.

A. The expression $3.6 \times 3.6 \times 3.6 \times 3.6$ is equivalent to the expression 3.6×4. ○ True ○ False

B. The prime factorization of 80 is $2^4 \cdot 5$. ○ True ○ False

C. The number 23 has only two factors. ○ True ○ False

D. 100 is equal to 10^{10}. ○ True ○ False

3. Andrew says that the value of expression A is more than 3 times the value of expression B. Do you agree? Why or why not?

Expression A: $1 + (5 + 5)^2$ Expression B: $1 + 5 + 5^2$

4. Joe wants to carpet a 12 foot by 18 foot rectangular living room and a square bedroom. One side length of the square bedroom is 12 feet. Carpet costs $3.50 per square foot. What percent of the total amount Joe will pay will be spent on carpeting the bedroom? Show your work.

Generating Equivalent Algebraic Expressions

MODULE 10

CALIFORNIA

ESSENTIAL QUESTION

How can you generate equivalent algebraic expressions and use them to solve real-world problems?

LESSON 10.1

Modeling and Writing Expressions

CA CC 6.EE.2a, 6.EE.2b, 6.EE.4, 6.EE.6

LESSON 10.2

Evaluating Expressions

CA CC 6.EE.2c

LESSON 10.3

Generating Equivalent Expressions

CA CC 6.EE.2b, 6.EE.3, 6.EE.4

Real-World Video

my.hrw.com

Carpenters use formulas to calculate a project's materials supply. Sometimes formulas can be written in different forms. The perimeter of a rectangle can be written as $P = 2(l + w)$ or $P = 2l + 2w$.

GO DIGITAL
my.hrw.com

my.hrw.com
Go digital with your write-in student edition, accessible on any device.

Math On the Spot
Scan with your smart phone to jump directly to the online edition, video tutor, and more.

Animated Math
Interactively explore key concepts to see how math works.

Personal Math Trainer
Get immediate feedback and help as you work through practice sets.

Are YOU Ready?

Complete these exercises to review skills you will need for this module.

Personal Math Trainer
Online Practice and Help
my.hrw.com

Use of Parentheses

EXAMPLE $(6 + 4) \times (3 + 8 + 1) = 10 \times 12$ — *Do the operations inside parentheses first.*

$= 120$ — *Multiply.*

Evaluate.

1. $11 + (20 - 13)$ ______

2. $(10 - 7) - (14 - 12)$ ______

3. $(4 + 17) - (16 - 9)$ ______

4. $(23 - 15) - (18 - 13)$ ______

5. $8 \times (4 + 5 + 7)$ ______

6. $(2 + 3) \times (11 - 5)$ ______

Words for Operations

EXAMPLE Write a numerical expression for the quotient of 20 and 5. — *Think: Quotient means to divide.*

$20 \div 5$ — *Write 20 divided by 5.*

Write a numerical expression for the word expression.

7. the difference between 42 and 19 ______

8. the product of 7 and 12 ______

9. 30 more than 20 ______

10. 100 decreased by 77 ______

Evaluate Expressions

EXAMPLE Evaluate $2(5) - 3^2$.

$2(5) - 3^2 = 2(5) - 9$ — *Evaluate exponents.*

$= 10 - 9$ — *Multiply.*

$= 1$ — *Subtract.*

Evaluate the expression.

11. $3(8) - 15$ ______

12. $4(12) + 11$ ______

13. $3(7) - 4(2)$ ______

14. $4(2 + 3) - 12$ ______

15. $9(14 - 5) - 42$ ______

16. $7(8) - 5(8)$ ______

Reading Start-Up

Visualize Vocabulary

Use the review words to complete the graphic. You may put more than one word in each oval.

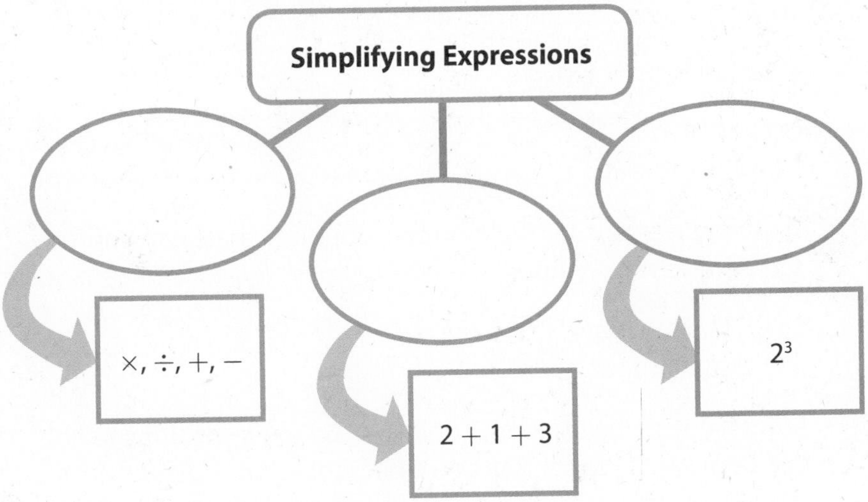

Understand Vocabulary

Complete the sentences using the preview words.

1. An expression that contains at least one variable is an

______________________________ .

2. A part of an expression that is added or subtracted is a ____________ .

3. A ______________ is a specific number whose value does not change.

Vocabulary

Review Words

- base *(base)*
- exponent *(exponente)*
- numerical expression *(expresión numérica)*
- operations *(operaciones)*
- order of operations *(orden de las operaciones)*

Preview Words

- algebraic expression *(expresión algebraica)*
- coefficient *(coeficiente)*
- constant *(constante)*
- equivalent expression *(expresión equivalente)*
- evaluating *(evaluar)*
- like terms *(términos semejantes)*
- term *(término, en una expresión)*
- variable *(variable)*

Active Reading

Key-Term Fold Before beginning the module, create a key-term fold to help you learn the vocabulary in this module. Write the highlighted vocabulary words on one side of the flap. Write the definition for each word on the other side of the flap. Use the key-term fold to quiz yourself on the definitions used in this module.

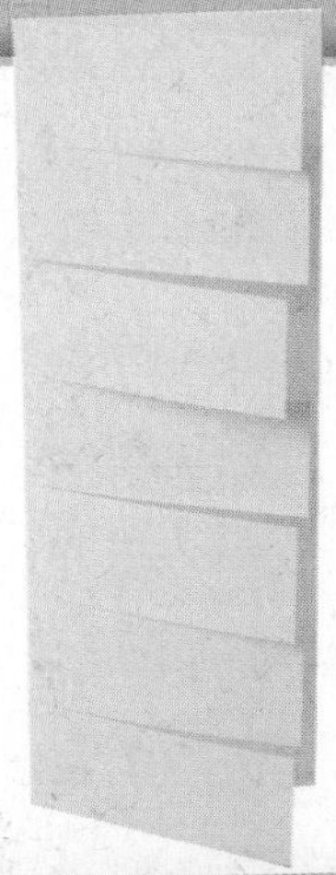

GETTING READY FOR

Generating Equivalent Algebraic Expressions

Understanding the standards and the vocabulary terms in the standards will help you know exactly what you are expected to learn in this module.

CA CC 6.EE.2

Write, read, and evaluate expressions in which letters stand for numbers.

Key Vocabulary

expression *(expresión)*
A mathematical phrase that contains operations, numbers, and/or variables.

What It Means to You

You will use models to compare expressions.

EXAMPLE 6.EE.2

On a math quiz, Tina scored 3 points more than Yolanda. Juan scored 2 points more than Yolanda and earned 2 points as extra credit.

Write expressions for the numbers of points that Juan and Tina scored. Use y to represent the number of points that Yolanda scored.

Tina's points: $y + 3$
Juan's points: $y + 2 + 2$

Suppose Yolanda scored 82 points. Use the expressions to find the number of points Tina and Juan scored.

Tina's points: $y + 3 = 82 + 3 = 85$ points
Juan's points: $y + 2 + 2 = 82 + 2 + 2 = 86$ points

CA CC 6.EE.3

Apply the properties of operations to generate equivalent expressions.

Key Vocabulary

equivalent expressions
(expresión equivalente)
Expressions that have the same value for all values of the variables.

What It Means to You

You will use the properties of operations to find an equivalent expression.

EXAMPLE 6.EE.3

William earns \$13 an hour working at a movie theater. He worked h hours in concessions and three times as many hours at the ticket counter. Write and simplify an expression for the amount of money William earned.

\$13 · hours at concessions + \$13 · hours at ticket counter

$13h + 13(3h)$

$13h + 39h$ Multiply $13 \cdot 3h$.

$h(13 + 39)$ Distributive Property

$52h$ Simplify.

Visit my.hrw.com to see all CA Common Core Standards explained.

my.hrw.com

LESSON 10.1

Modeling and Writing Expressions

CA CC 6.EE.2a

Write expressions that record operations with numbers and with letters standing for numbers. *Also 6.EE.2b, 6.EE.4, 6.EE.6*

ESSENTIAL QUESTION

How can you model and write algebraic expressions?

Writing Algebraic Expressions

An **algebraic expression** is an expression that contains one or more variables and may also contain operation symbols, such as + or −.

Math On the Spot my.hrw.com

A **variable** is a letter or symbol used to represent an unknown or unspecified number. The value of a variable may change.

A **constant** is a specific number whose value does not change.

150 is a constant and y is a variable.

Algebraic Expressions	x	$w + n$	$150 + y$

In algebraic expressions, multiplication and division are usually written without the symbols × and ÷.

- Write $3 \times n$ as $3n$, $3 \cdot n$, or $n \cdot 3$.
- Write $3 \div n$ as $\frac{3}{n}$.

Some different ways to describe expressions with words are shown below.

Operation	Addition	Subtraction	Multiplication	Division
Words	• added to • plus • sum • more than	• subtracted from • minus • difference • less than	• times • multiplied by • product • groups of	• divided by • divided into • quotient

EXAMPLE 1

CA CC 6.EE.2a, 6.EE.2b

A **Write each phrase as an algebraic expression.**

Phrase: The sum of 7 and x

The operation is addition.

Expression: $7 + x$

Phrase: The quotient of z and 3

The operation is division.

Expression: $\frac{z}{3}$

B **Write a phrase for each expression.**

Expression: $11x$ *The operation is multiplication.*

Phrase: The product of 11 and x

Expression: $8 - y$ *The operation is subtraction.*

Phrase: y less than 8

Personal Math Trainer

Online Practice and Help

my.hrw.com

YOUR TURN

Write each phrase as an algebraic expression.

1. n times 7 ______ **2.** 4 minus y ______ **3.** 13 added to x ______

Write a phrase for each expression.

4. $\frac{x}{12}$ ____________________

5. $10y$ ____________________

6. $c + 3$ ____________________

Math On the Spot

my.hrw.com

Modeling Algebraic Expressions

Algebraic expressions can also be represented with models. A rectangular bar can represent a variable, and a square bar can represent a unit.

EXAMPLE 2

CA CC 6.EE.2a

Use a bar model to represent each expression.

A $7 + x$ *Combine 7 and x.*

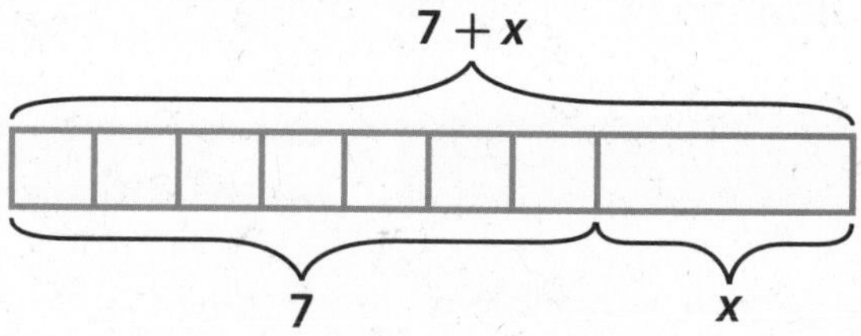

B $\frac{z}{3}$ *Divide z into 3 equal parts.*

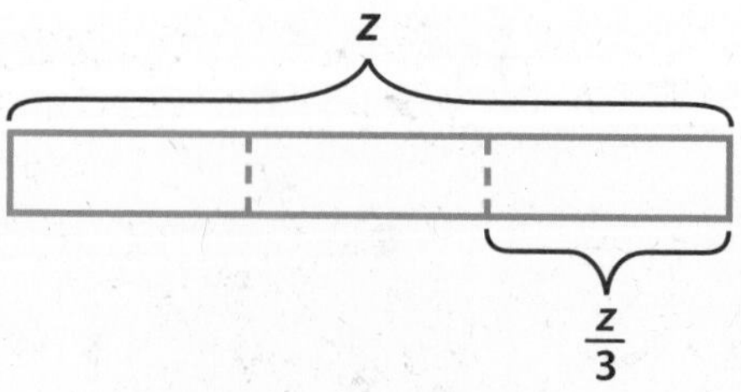

YOUR TURN

Draw a bar model to represent each expression.

7. $t - 2$

8. $4y$

Personal Math Trainer
Online Practice and Help
my.hrw.com

Comparing Expressions Using Models

Algebraic expressions are *equivalent* if they are equal for all values of the variable. For example, $x + 2$ and $x + 1 + 1$ are equivalent.

Math On the Spot
my.hrw.com

EXAMPLE 3 Real World

CA CC 6.EE.4

My Notes

Katriana and Andrew started the day with the same amount of money. Katriana spent 5 dollars on lunch. Andrew spent 3 dollars on lunch and 2 dollars on a snack after school. Do Katriana and Andrew have the same amount of money left?

STEP 1 Write an algebraic expression to represent the money Katriana has left. Represent the expression with a model.

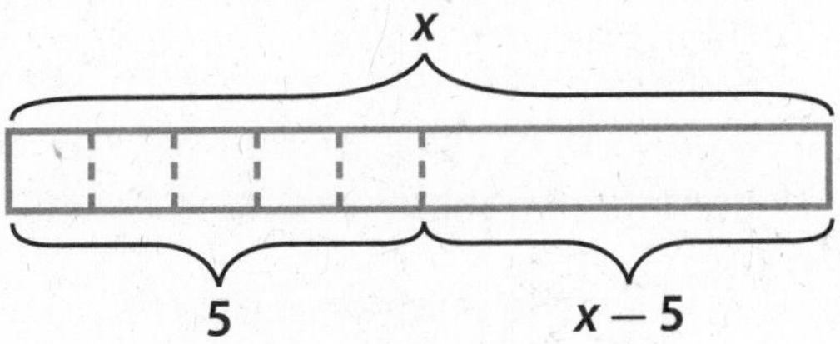

$x - 5$

The variable represents the amount of money both Katriana and Andrew have at the beginning of the day.

STEP 2 Write an algebraic expression to represent the money Andrew has left. Represent the expression with a model.

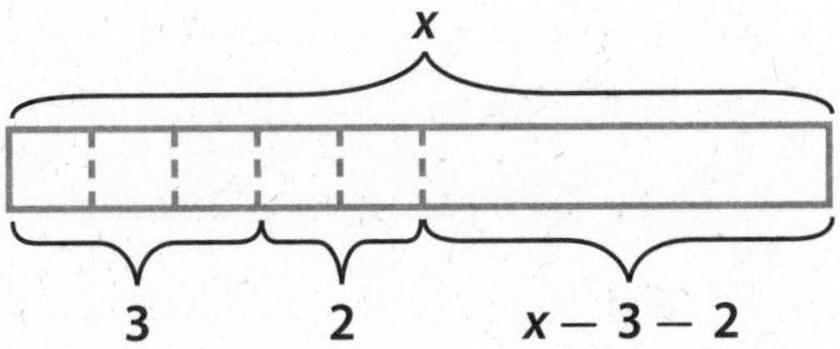

$x - 3 - 2$

STEP 3 Compare the models.

The models are equivalent, so the expressions are equivalent.

Andrew and Katriana have the same amount of money left.

Personal Math Trainer
Online Practice and Help
my.hrw.com

YOUR TURN

9. On a math quiz, Tina scored 3 points more than Julia. Juan scored 2 points more than Julia and earned 2 points in extra credit. Write an expression and draw a bar model to represent Tina's score and Juan's score. Did Tina and Juan make the same grade on the quiz? Explain.

____

Math On the Spot
my.hrw.com

Modeling Real-World Situations

You can use expressions to represent real-world situations.

EXAMPLE 4 Real World — CA CC 6.EE.2.6

A Tickets to the water park cost $53 per person. Write an expression to show the total cost of tickets for a group of people.

A group of is a clue to multiply. The ticket price of $53 is a constant. The number of people who need tickets is a variable.

Use x for the number of people.

The algebraic expression for the total cost of tickets is $53x$.

B Genise has some savings. After babysitting, she adds $75 to her savings. How much money has Genise saved?

Adds is a clue to use addition. The $75 Genise added to her savings is a constant. The amount of money Genise had saved before is unknown, so use a variable.

Use y for Genise's savings before she adds the babysitting money.

The algebraic expression for Genise's total savings is $y + 75$.

Math Talk
Mathematical Practices
How do you know what operation to use to find the amount each niece receives?

YOUR TURN

10. Helen divides up some money to give equally to her four nieces. If d represents the total amount, write an expression to represent how much money each niece receives. ____________

Guided Practice

Write each phrase as an algebraic expression. (Example 1)

1. 3 less than y ____________

2. The product of 2 and p ____________

Write a phrase for each algebraic expression. (Example 1)

3. $y + 12$ ____________

4. $\frac{p}{10}$ ____________

5. Draw a bar model to represent the expression $m \div 4$. (Example 2)

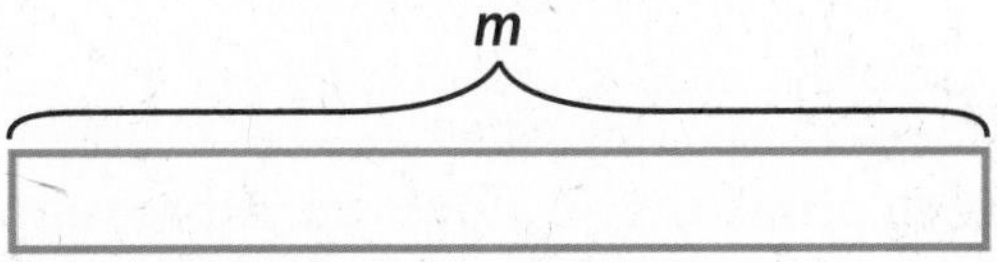

At 6 p.m., the temperature in Redding, CA, *t*, is the same as the temperature in Fresno, CA. By 9 p.m., the temperature in Redding has dropped 2 degrees and in Fresno it has dropped 4 degrees. By 11 p.m., the temperature in Redding has dropped another 3 degrees. (Example 3)

6. Represent each city's temperature at 11 p.m. with an algebraic expression and a bar model.

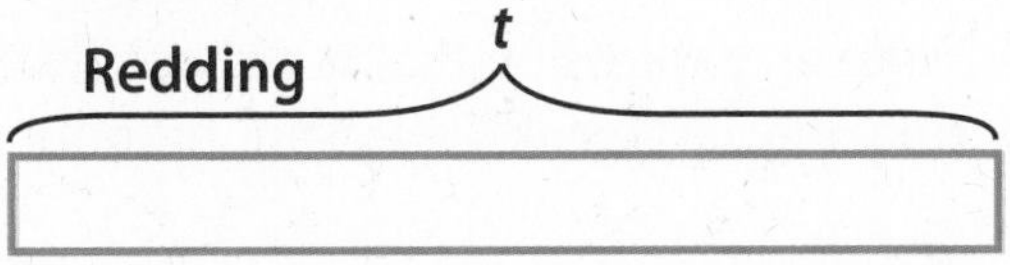

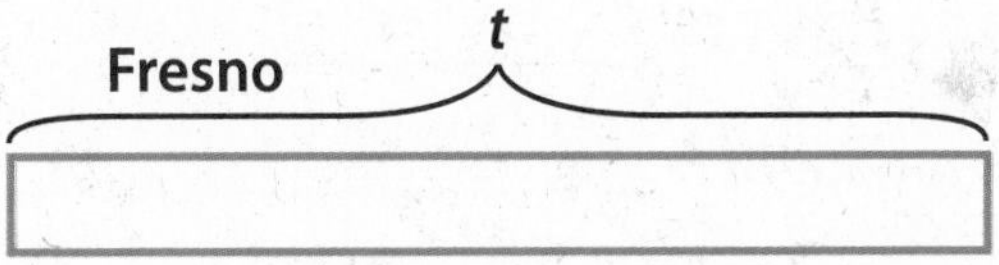

____________ ____________

7. Are the expressions that represent the temperatures in the two cities equivalent? Justify your answer.

____

____

8. Noelle bought some boxes of water bottles for a picnic. Each box contained 24 bottles of water. If c is the number of boxes, write an expression to show how many bottles of water Noelle bought. (Example 4)

____

ESSENTIAL QUESTION CHECK-IN

9. Give an example of a real-world situation that could be represented by an algebraic expression.

____

____

____

Name ______ Class ______ Date ______

10.1 Independent Practice

CA CC 6.EE.2a, 6.EE.2b, 6.EE.4, 6.EE.2.6

Personal Math Trainer
Online Practice and Help
my.hrw.com

10. Write an algebraic expression with the constant 7 and the variable *y*.

______

Write each phrase as an algebraic expression.

11. *n* divided by 8 ______

12. *p* multiplied by 4 ______

13. *b* plus 14 ______

14. 90 times *x* ______

15. *a* take away 16 ______

16. *k* less than 24 ______

17. 3 groups of *w* ______

18. the sum of 1 and *q* ______

19. the quotient of 13 and *z* ______

20. *c* added to 45 ______

21. 8 less than *w* ______

Write a phrase in words for each algebraic expression.

22. $m + 83$ ______

23. $42s$ ______

24. $\frac{9}{d}$ ______

25. $t - 29$ ______

26. $2 + g$ ______

27. $11x$ ______

28. $\frac{h}{12}$ ______

29. $5 - k$ ______

Sarah and Noah work at a bookstore and get paid the same hourly wage. The table shows their work schedule for last week.

Bookstore Work Schedule (hours)			
	Monday	Tuesday	Wednesday
Sarah	5	3	
Noah			8

30. Write an expression that represents Sarah's total pay last week. Represent her hourly wage with *w*. ______

31. Write an expression that represents Noah's total pay last week. Represent his hourly wage with *w*. ______

32. Are the expressions equivalent? Did Sarah and Noah earn the same amount last week? Use models to justify your answer.

______

33. Mia buys 3 gallons of gas that costs *d* dollars per gallon. Bob buys *g* gallons of gas that costs $3 per gallon.

a. Write an expression for the amount Mia pays for gas. ______

b. Write an expression for the amount Bob pays for gas. ______

c. What do the numeral and the variable represent in each expression?

______

______

______

______

34. The student council is asking people to donate money for the new park outside the school. Everyone who makes the suggested donation amount will be given a bracelet. If everyone donates the suggested amount, and *b* bracelets are given away, what algebraic expression represents the total amount collected in donations?

____

35. Mr. Delgado has some young orange trees. He wants to plant them in 46 rows. If *t* is the total number of orange trees, write an algebraic expression to represent how many trees he can plant in each row.

____

36. There are 15 violinists in the orchestra this year. Next year, two violinists will leave and some new violinists will join the orchestra. If *v* is the number of violinists who will join the orchestra, write an expression to represent the number of violinists in the orchestra next year.

____

37. Jill, Meg, and Beth are sisters. Jill is 2 years younger than Meg. Beth is half as old as Meg. Use the same variable to write three algebraic expressions based on this situation. Tell what the variable represents and what each expression represents.

____

____

38. **Multistep** Will, Hector, and Lydia volunteered at the animal shelter in March and April. The table shows the number of hours Will and Hector volunteered in March. Let *x* represent the number of hours Lydia volunteered in March.

March Volunteering	
Will	3 hours
Hector	5 hours

a. Will's volunteer hours in April were equal to his March volunteer hours plus Lydia's March volunteer hours. Write an expression to represent Will's volunteer hours in April. _______________

b. Hector's volunteer hours in April were equal to 2 hours less than his March volunteer hours plus Lydia's March volunteer hours. Write an expression to represent Hector's volunteer hours in April. _______________

c. Did Will and Hector volunteer the same number of hours in April?

Explain. _______________

39. The town of Rayburn received 6 more inches of snow than the town of Greenville. Let *g* represent the amount of snow in Greenville. Write an algebraic expression to represent the amount of snow in Rayburn. _______________

40. Abby baked 48 dinner rolls and divided them evenly into bags. Let b represent the number of bags. Write an algebraic expression to represent the number of dinner rolls in each bag. ____________

41. Eli is driving at a speed of 55 miles per hour. Let h represent the number of hours that Eli drives at this speed. Write an algebraic expression to represent the number of miles that Eli travels during this time. ____________

H.O.T. FOCUS ON HIGHER ORDER THINKING

42. **Multistep** Bob's Bagels offers two breakfast options, as shown.

a. Let x represent the number of customers who order coffee and a bagel. How much money will Bob's Bagels make from these orders? ____________________

b. Let y represent the number of customers who order tea and a breakfast sandwich. How much money will Bob's Bagels make from these orders? ____________________

c. Write an algebraic expression for the total amount Bob's Bagels will make from all coffee and bagel orders and from all tea and breakfast sandwich orders. ____________

43. **Represent Real-World Problems** The number of shoes in a closet is s.

a. How many pairs of shoes are in the closet? Explain.

____

b. **What If?** Suppose you add a pair of shoes to the closet. How many pairs are in the closet? ____________________

44. **Problem Solving** Write an expression that has three terms, two different variables, and one constant. ____________________

45. **Represent Real-World Problems** Describe a situation that can be modeled by the expression $x - 8$.

____

____

46. **Critique Reasoning** Ricardo says that the expression $y + 4$ is equivalent to the expression $1y + 4$. Is he correct? Explain.

____

____

____

Work Area

LESSON 10.2

Evaluating Expressions

CA CC 6.EE.2c

Evaluate expressions at specific values of their variables. Include expressions that arise from formulas used in real-world problems. Perform arithmetic operations, including those involving whole-number exponents, in the conventional order when there are no parentheses to specify a particular order (Order of Operations).

ESSENTIAL QUESTION

How can you use the order of operations to evaluate algebraic expressions?

Evaluating Algebraic Expressions

Recall that an algebraic expression contains one or more variables. You can substitute a number for each variable and then find the value of the expression. This process is called **evaluating** the expression. For example, to evaluate $2m$ for $m = 5$, you would substitute 5 for m.

$2m = 2(5) = 10$ — Parentheses are another way to show multiplication. $2(5) = 2 \times 5 = 2 \cdot 5 = 10$

Math On the Spot

my.hrw.com

EXAMPLE 1

CA CC 6.EE.2c

Evaluate each expression for the given value of the variable.

A $x - 9; x = 15$

$15 - 9$ — Substitute 15 for x.

6 — Subtract.

When $x = 15$, $x - 9 = 6$.

B $\frac{16}{n}; n = 8$

$\frac{16}{8}$ — Substitute 8 for n.

2 — Divide.

When $n = 8$, $\frac{16}{n} = 2$.

C $0.5y; y = 1.4$

$0.5(1.4)$ — Substitute 1.4 for y.

0.7 — Multiply.

When $y = 1.4$, $0.5y = 0.7$.

D $6k; k = \frac{1}{3}$

$6\left(\frac{1}{3}\right)$ — Substitute $\frac{1}{3}$ for k.

2 — Multiply.

When $k = \frac{1}{3}$, $6k = 2$.

My Notes

Personal Math Trainer
Online Practice and Help
my.hrw.com

Math On the Spot
my.hrw.com

YOUR TURN

Evaluate each expression for the given value of the variable.

1. $4x; x = 8$ _____ **2.** $6.5 - n; n = 1.8$ _____ **3.** $\frac{m}{6}; m = 18$ _____

Using the Order of Operations

Algebraic expressions may have more than one operation or more than one variable. To evaluate these expressions, substitute the given value for each variable and then use the order of operations.

EXAMPLE 2

CA CC 6.EE.2c

Evaluate each expression for the given value of the variable.

A $4(x - 4); x = 7$

$4(7 - 4)$	Substitute 7 for *x*.
$4(3)$	Subtract inside the parentheses.
12	Multiply.

When $x = 7, 4(x - 4) = 12$.

B $4x - 4; x = 7$

$4(7) - 4$	Substitute 7 for *x*.
$28 - 4$	Multiply.
24	Subtract.

When $x = 7, 4x - 4 = 24$.

C $w - x + y; w = 6, x = 5, y = 3$

$6 - 5 + 3$	Substitute 6 for *w*, 5 for *x*, and 3 for *y*.
$1 + 3$	Subtract.
4	Add.

When $w = 6, x = 5, y = 3, w - x + y = 4$.

D $x^2 - x; x = 9$

$9^2 - 9$	Substitute 9 for each *x*.
$81 - 9$	Evaluate exponents.
72	Subtract.

When $x = 9, x^2 - x = 72$.

Math Talk
Mathematical Practices

Is $w - x + y$ equivalent to $w - y + x$? Explain any difference in the order the math operations are performed.

YOUR TURN

Evaluate each expression for $n = 5$.

4. $3(n + 1)$ ______ **5.** $4(n - 4) + 14$ ______ **6.** $6n + n^2$ ______

Evaluate each expression for $a = 3$, $b = 4$, and $c = 6$.

7. $ab - c$ ______ **8.** $bc + 5a$ ______ **9.** $a^3 - (b + c)$ ______

Personal Math Trainer
Online Practice and Help
my.hrw.com

Evaluating Real-World Expressions

You can evaluate algebraic expressions to solve real-world problems.

Math On the Spot
my.hrw.com

EXAMPLE 3 Real World

CA CC 6.EE.2c

A scientist measures the air temperature in Death Valley, California, and records 50 °C. The expression $1.8c + 32$ gives the temperature in degrees Fahrenheit for a given temperature in degrees Celsius c. Find the temperature in degrees Fahrenheit that is equivalent to 50 °C.

STEP 1 Find the value of c.

$c = 50$ °C

STEP 2 Substitute the value into the expression.

$1.8c + 32$

$1.8(50) + 32$ Substitute 50 for c.

$90 + 32$ Multiply.

122 Add.

122 °F is equivalent to 50 °C.

YOUR TURN

10. The expression $6x^2$ gives the surface area of a cube, and the expression x^3 gives the volume of a cube, where x is the length of one side of the cube. Find the surface area and the volume of a cube with a side length of 2 meters.

$S =$ ____________ m^2; $V =$ ____________ m^3

11. The expression $60m$ gives the number of seconds in m minutes. How many seconds are there in 7 minutes?

____________ seconds

Personal Math Trainer
Online Practice and Help
my.hrw.com

Guided Practice

Evaluate each expression for the given value(s) of the variable(s). (Examples 1 and 2)

1. $x - 7; x = 23$ ____________

2. $3a - b; a = 4, b = 6$ ____________

3. $\frac{1}{2}w + 2; w = \frac{1}{9}$ ____________

4. $5(6.2 + z); z = 3.8$ ____________

5. $\frac{8}{t} + t^2; t = 4$ ____________

6. $5m - m^2; m = 3$ ____________

7. The table shows the prices for games in Bella's soccer league. Her parents and grandmother attended a soccer game. How much did they spend if they all went together in one car? (Example 3)

Soccer Game Prices	
Student tickets	\$6
Nonstudent tickets	\$12
Parking	\$5

a. Write an expression that represents the cost of one carful of nonstudent soccer fans. Use *x* as the number of people who rode in the car and attended the game.

__________ is an expression that represents the cost of one carful of nonstudent soccer fans.

b. Since there are three attendees, evaluate the expression $12x + 5$ for $x = 3$.

$12(\_\_\_) + 5 = \_\_\_\_ + 5 = \_\_\_\_$

The family spent ______ to attend the game.

8. Stan wants to add trim around the edge of a rectangular tablecloth that is 7 feet long and 5 feet wide. The perimeter of the tablecloth is twice the length plus twice the width. How much trim does Stan need to buy? (Example 3)

a. Write an expression that represents the perimeter of the rectangular tablecloth. Let *l* represent the length of the tablecloth and *w* represent its width. The expression would be ____________.

b. Evaluate your expression for $l = 7$ and $w = 5$.

$2(\_\_\_\_) + 2(\_\_\_\_) = 14 + \_\_\_\_ = \_\_\_\_$

Stan needs to buy __________ of trim.

ESSENTIAL QUESTION CHECK-IN

9. How do you know the correct order in which to evaluate algebraic expressions?

____

____

Name ________________ Class ________________ Date ________________

10.2 Independent Practice

Personal Math Trainer
Online Practice and Help
my.hrw.com

CA CC 6.EE.2c

10. The table shows ticket prices at the Movie 16 theater. Let *a* represent the number of adult tickets, *c* the number of children's tickets, and *s* the number of senior citizen tickets.

Movie 16 Ticket Prices	
Adults	\$8.75
Children	\$6.50
Seniors	\$6.50

a. Write an expression for the total cost of the three types of tickets.

____

____

b. The Andrews family bought 2 adult tickets, 3 children's tickets, and 1 senior ticket. Evaluate your expression in **a** to find the total cost of the tickets.

____

____

c. The Spencer family bought 4 adult tickets and 2 children's tickets. Did the Spencer family spend the same amount as the Andrews family? Explain.

____

____

11. The area of a square is given by x^2, where x is the length of one side. Mary's original garden was in the shape of a square. She has decided to double the area of her garden. Write an expression that represents the area of Mary's new garden. Evaluate the expression if the side length of Mary's original garden was 8 feet.

____

12. Ramon has \$2,340 in his savings account. Write an expression for the amount in his account after he deposits *d* dollars and withdraws *w* dollars. If he deposits \$100 and then withdraws half as much as he deposited, how much is in his account?

____

13. **Look for a Pattern** Evaluate the expression $6x - x^2$ for $x = 0, 1, 2, 3, 4, 5,$ and 6. Use your results to fill in the table. Describe any pattern that you see.

x	0	1	2	3	4	5	6
$6x - x^2$							

____

____

____

____

____

____

14. The kinetic energy (in joules) of a moving object can be calculated from the expression $\frac{1}{2}mv^2$, where m is the mass of the object in kilograms and v is its speed in meters per second. Find the kinetic energy of a 0.145 kg baseball that is thrown at a speed of 40 meters per second.

$E =$ ______ joules

15. The area of a triangular sail is given by the expression $\frac{1}{2}bh$, where b is the length of the base and h is the height. What is the area of a triangular sail in a model sailboat when $b = 12$ inches and $h = 7$ inches?

$A =$ ______ in.^{2}

16. The volume of a pyramid with a square base is given by the expression $\frac{1}{3}s^2h$, where s is the length of a side of the base and h is the height. The length of a side of the square base of a particular pyramid is 24 feet. The height of the pyramid is 30 feet. Find the volume of the pyramid.

____

H.O.T. FOCUS ON HIGHER ORDER THINKING

Work Area

17. Draw Conclusions Consider the expressions $3x(x - 2) + 2$ and $2x^2 + 3x - 12$.

a. Evaluate each expression for $x = 2$ and for $x = 7$. Based on your results, do you know whether the two expressions are equivalent? Explain.

____

b. Evaluate each expression for $x = 5$. Based on your results, do you know whether the two expressions are equivalent? Explain.

____

18. Critique Reasoning Marjorie evaluated the expression $3x + 2$ for $x = 5$ as shown:

$$3x + 2 = 35 + 2 = 37$$

What was Marjorie's mistake? What is the correct value of $3x + 2$ for $x = 5$?

____

LESSON 10.3

Generating Equivalent Expressions

CA CC 6.EE.3

Apply the properties of operations to generate equivalent expressions. *Also 6.EE.2b, 6.EE.4*

ESSENTIAL QUESTION

How can you identify and write equivalent expressions?

EXPLORE ACTIVITY 1 CA CC 6.EE.4

Identifying Equivalent Expressions

One way to test whether two expressions might be equivalent is to evaluate them for the same value of the variable.

Match the expressions in List A with their equivalent expressions in List B.

List A	List B
$5x + 65$	$5x + 1$
$5(x + 1)$	$5x + 5$
$1 + 5x$	$5(13 + x)$

A Evaluate each of the expressions in the lists for $x = 3$.

List A	List B
$5(3) + 65 =$ ☐	$5(3) + 1 =$ ☐
$5(3 + 1) =$ ☐	$5(3) + 5 =$ ☐
$1 + 5(3) =$ ☐	$5(13 + 3) =$ ☐

B Which pair(s) of expressions have the same value for $x = 3$?

____

____

C How could you further test whether the expressions in each pair are equivalent?

____

D Do you think the expressions in each pair are equivalent? Why or why not?

____

____

EXPLORE ACTIVITY 1 *(cont'd)*

Reflect

1. **Error Analysis** Lisa evaluated the expressions $2x$ and x^2 for $x = 2$ and found that both expressions were equal to 4. Lisa concluded that $2x$ and x^2 are equivalent expressions. How could you show Lisa that she is incorrect?

____

____

EXPLORE ACTIVITY 2 CA CC 6.EE.3

Modeling Equivalent Expressions

You can also use models to determine if two expressions are equivalent. *Algebra tiles* are one way to model expressions.

Algebra Tiles

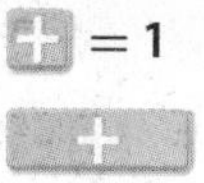

Determine if the expression $3(x + 2)$ is equivalent to $3x + 6$.

A Model each expression using algebra tiles.

$3(x + 2)$

$3x + 6$

B The model for $3(x + 2)$ has ________ x tiles and ________ 1 tiles.

The model for $3x + 6$ has ________ x tiles and ________ 1 tiles.

C Is the expression $3(x + 2)$ equivalent to $3x + 6$? Explain.

____

____

Reflect

2. Use algebra tiles to determine if $2(x + 3)$ is equivalent to $2x + 3$. Explain your answer.

____

____

Writing Equivalent Expressions Using Properties

Properties of operations can be used to identify equivalent expressions.

Properties of Operations	Examples
Commutative Property of Addition: When adding, changing the order of the numbers does not change the sum.	$3 + 4 = 4 + 3$
Commutative Property of Multiplication: When multiplying, changing the order of the numbers does not change the product.	$2 \times 4 = 4 \times 2$
Associative Property of Addition: When adding more than two numbers, the grouping of the numbers does not change the sum.	$(3 + 4) + 5 = 3 + (4 + 5)$
Associative Property of Multiplication: When multiplying more than two numbers, the grouping of the numbers does not change the product.	$(2 \times 4) \times 3 = 2 \times (4 \times 3)$
Distributive Property: Multiplying a number by a sum or difference is the same as multiplying by each number in the sum or difference and then adding or subtracting.	$6(2 + 4) = 6(2) + 6(4)$ $8(5 - 3) = 8(5) - 8(3)$
Identity Property of Addition: Adding zero to a number does not change its value.	$9 + 0 = 9$
Identity Property of Multiplication: Multiplying a number by one does not change its value.	$1 \times 7 = 7$

Math On the Spot
my.hrw.com

EXAMPLE 1

CA CC 6.EE.3

Use a property to write an expression that is equivalent to $x + 3$.

The operation in the expression is addition.

You can use the Commutative Property of Addition to write an equivalent expression: $x + 3 = 3 + x$.

YOUR TURN

For each expression, use a property to write an equivalent expression. Tell which property you used.

3. $(ab)c =$ ____________________

4. $3y + 4y =$ ____________________

5. $6 + n$ ____________________

Personal Math Trainer
Online Practice and Help
my.hrw.com

Math On the Spot
my.hrw.com

Animated Math
my.hrw.com

Identifying Equivalent Expressions Using Properties

EXAMPLE 2

CA CC 6.EE.3

Use the properties of operations to determine if the expressions are equivalent.

A $3(x - 2)$; $3x - 6$

$3(x - 2) = 3x - 6$ — Distributive Property

$3(x - 2)$ and $3x - 6$ are equivalent expressions.

B $2 + x$; $\frac{1}{2}(4 + x)$

$\frac{1}{2}(x + 4) = \frac{1}{2}x + 2$ — Distributive Property

$= 2 + \frac{1}{2}x$ — Commutative Property

$2 + x$ does not equal $2 + \frac{1}{2}x$.

They are not equivalent expressions.

YOUR TURN

Use the properties of operations to determine if the expressions are equivalent.

6. $6x - 8$; $2(3x - 5)$

____

____

7. $2 - 2 + 5x$; $5x$

____

____

8. Jamal bought 2 packs of stickers and 8 individual stickers. Use x to represent the number of stickers in a pack of stickers and write an expression to represent the number of stickers Jamal bought. Is the expression equivalent to $2(4 + x)$? Check your answer with algebra tile models.

____

____

Personal Math Trainer
Online Practice and Help
my.hrw.com

Generating Equivalent Expressions

Parts of an algebraic expression		
terms	The parts of the expression that are separated by + or − signs	$12 + 3y^2 + 4x + 2y^2 + 4$
coefficients	Numbers that are multiplied by at least one variable	$12 + 3y^2 + 4x + 2y^2 + 4$
like terms	Terms with the same variable(s) raised to the same power(s)	$12 + 3y^2 + 4x + 2y^2 + 4$

Math On the Spot
my.hrw.com

You can use properties to combine like terms in an expression.

$3x + 2x + 4 = (3 + 2)x + 4 = 5x + 4$ — Use the Distributive Property to add the coefficients of the like terms.

When you rewrite an expression so that it has no parentheses and so that all like terms are combined, you are *simplifying* the expression.

EXAMPLE 3

CA CC 6.EE.3, 6.EE.2b

Simplify each expression.

A $6x^2 - 4x^2$ — $6x^2$ and $4x^2$ are like terms.

$6x^2 - 4x^2 = x^2(6 - 4)$ Distributive Property

$= x^2(2)$ Subtract inside the parentheses.

$= 2x^2$ Commutative Property of Multiplication

$6x^2 - 4x^2 = 2x^2$

B $3a + 2(b + 5a)$

$3a + 2(b + 5a) = 3a + 2b + 2(5a)$ Distributive Property

$= 3a + 2b + (2 \cdot 5)a$ Associative Property of Multiplication

$= 3a + 2b + 10a$ Multiply 2 and 5.

$= 3a + 10a + 2b$ Commutative Property of Addition

$= (3 + 10)a + 2b$ Distributive Property

$= 13a + 2b$ Add inside the parentheses.

$3a + 2(b + 5a) = 13a + 2b$

C $y + 11x + 7y - 7x$ — y and $7y$ are like terms; $11x$ and $7x$ are like terms.

$y + 11x + 7y - 7x = y + 7y + 11x - 7x$ Commutative Property

$= (1 + 7)y + (11 - 7)x$ Distributive Property

$= 8y + 4x$ Perform operations inside parentheses.

$y + 11x + 7y - 7x = 8y + 4x$

Math Talk
Mathematical Practices

Write 2 terms that can be combined with $7y^4$. Identify the coefficients in the terms you write.

Personal Math Trainer

Online Practice and Help

my.hrw.com

YOUR TURN

Simplify each expression.

9. $8y - 3y =$ ________

10. $6x^2 + 4(x^2 - 1) =$ ________

11. $4a^5 - 2a^5 + 4b + b =$ ________

12. $8m + 14 - 12 + 4n =$ ________

Guided Practice

1. Evaluate each of the expressions in the list for $y = 5$. Then, draw lines to match the expressions in List A with their equivalent expressions in List B. (Explore Activity 1)

List A	List B
$4 + 4y =$ ______	$4y - 4 =$ ______
$4(y - 1) =$ ______	$4(y + 1) =$ ______
$4y + 1 =$ ______	$1 + 4y =$ ______

2. Determine if the expressions are equivalent by comparing the models. (Explore Activity 2) ________

For each expression, use a property to write an equivalent expression. Tell which property you used. (Example 1)

3. $ab =$ ________

____

4. $5(3x - 2) =$ ________

____

Use the properties of operations to determine if each pair of expressions is equivalent. (Example 2)

5. $\frac{1}{2}(4 - 2x)$; $2 - 2x$ ________

6. $\frac{1}{2}(6x - 2)$; $3 - x$ ________

Simplify each expression. (Example 3)

7. $32y + 12y =$ ________

8. $12 + 3x + 12 - x =$ ________

ESSENTIAL QUESTION CHECK-IN

9. Describe two ways to check whether algebraic expressions are equivalent.

____

____

Name ______________________ Class ______________ Date ____________

10.3 Independent Practice

CA CC 6.EE.2b, 6.EE.3, 6.EE.4

Personal Math Trainer
my.hrw.com
Online Practice and Help

For each expression, use a property to write an equivalent expression. Tell which property you used.

10. $cd =$ ______________________

____

11. $x + 13 =$ ______________________

____

12. $4(2x - 3) =$ ______________________

____

13. $2 + (a + b) =$ ______________________

____

14. Draw algebra tile models to prove that $4 + 8x$ and $4(2x + 1)$ are equivalent.

______________________ ______________________

Simplify each expression.

15. $7x^4 - 5x^4 =$ ______________________

16. $32y + 5y =$ ______________________

17. $6b + 7b - 10 =$ ______________________

18. $2x + 3x + 4 =$ ______________________

19. $y + 4 + 3(y + 2) =$ ______________________

20. $7a^2 - a^2 + 16 =$ ______________________

21. $3y^2 + 3(4y^2 - 2) =$ ______________________

22. $z^2 + z + 4z^3 + 4z^2 =$ ______________________

23. $0.5(x^4 + 3) + 12 =$ ______________________

24. $\frac{1}{4}(16 + 4p) =$ ______________________

25. **Justify Reasoning** Determine whether $3x + 12 + x$ is equivalent to $4(3 + x)$. Use properties of operations to justify your answer.

____

____

____

26. Ted earns $13 an hour at a theater. Last week he worked h hours at the concession stand and three times as many hours at the ticket counter. Write and simplify an expression for the amount he earned last week.

____

27. **Multiple Representations** Use the information in the table to write and simplify an expression to find the total weight of the medals won by the top medal-winning nations in the 2012 London Olympic Games. The three types of medals have different weights.

2012 Summer Olympics			
	Gold	**Silver**	**Bronze**
United States	46	29	29
China	38	27	23
Great Britain	29	17	19

____

____

Write an expression for the perimeters of each given figure. Simplify the expression.

28. ____________________

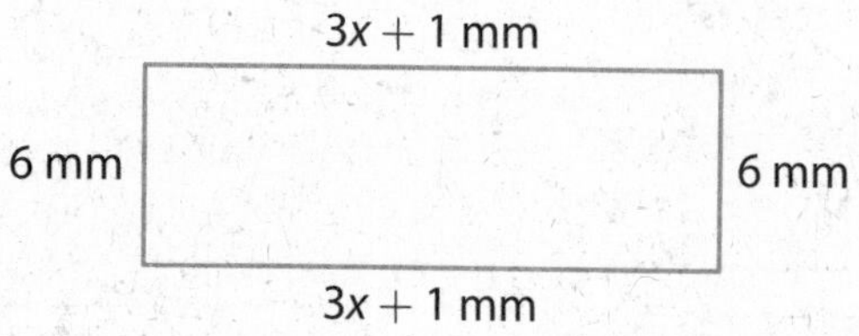

29. ____________________

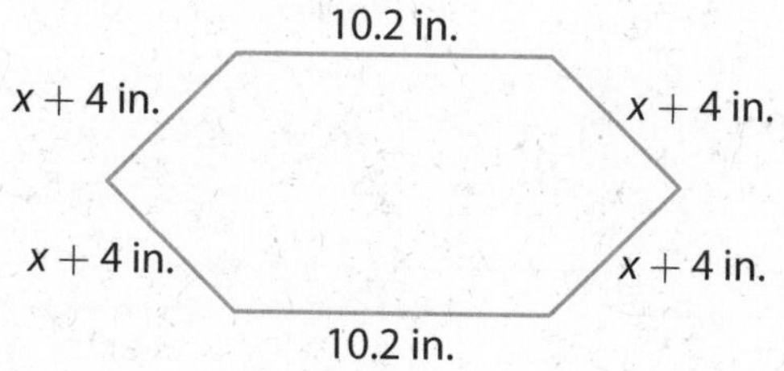

H.O.T. FOCUS ON HIGHER ORDER THINKING

Work Area

30. **Problem Solving** Examine the algebra tile model.

a. Write two equivalent expressions for the model. ____________________

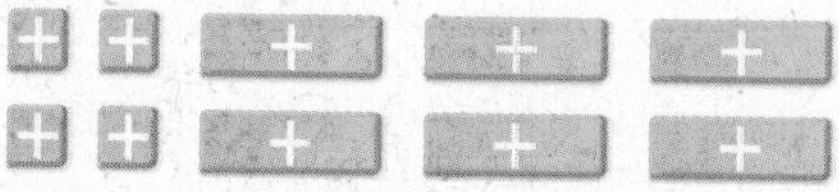

b. **What If?** Suppose a third row of tiles identical to the ones above is added to the model. How does that change the two expressions?

____

31. **Communicate Mathematical Ideas** Write an example of an expression that cannot be simplified, and explain how you know that it cannot be simplified.

____

32. **Problem Solving** Write an expression that is equivalent to $8(2y + 4)$ that can be simplified.

____

MODULE QUIZ

Ready to Go On?

Personal Math Trainer
Online Practice and Help
my.hrw.com

10.1 Modeling and Writing Expressions

Write each phrase as an algebraic expression.

1. *p* divided by 6 ______________

2. 65 less than *j* ______________

3. the sum of 185 and *h* ______________

4. the product of 16 and *g* ______________

5. Let *x* represent the number of television show episodes that are taped in a season. Write an expression for the number of episodes taped in 4 seasons. ______________

10.2 Evaluating Expressions

Evaluate each expression for the given value of the variable.

6. $8p; p = 9$ ______________

7. $\frac{60}{m}; m = 5$ ______________

8. $4(d + 7); d = 2$ ______________

9. $1 + r^2 - r; r = 5$ ______________

10. To find the area of a triangle, you can use the expression $b \times h \div 2$, where *b* is the base of the triangle and *h* is its height. What is the area of a triangle with a base of 6 centimeters and a height of 8 centimeters?

____

10.3 Generating Equivalent Expressions

11. Draw lines to match the expressions in List A with their equivalent expressions in List B.

List A	List B
$7x + 14$	$7(1 + x)$
$7 + 7x$	$7x - 7$
$7(x - 1)$	$7(x + 2)$

ESSENTIAL QUESTION

12. How can you solve problems involving equivalent expressions?

____

____

____

____

CALIFORNIA

MODULE 10
MIXED REVIEW

Assessment Readiness

Personal Math Trainer

my.hrw.com

Online Practice and Help

1. Consider each algebraic expression and phrase.

   Select Yes or No in A–D to tell whether the algebraic expression represents the given phrase.

   A. $r - 9$, 9 fewer than r ◯ Yes ◯ No

   B. $7r$, the quotient of 7 and r ◯ Yes ◯ No

   C. $r + 4$, 4 more than r ◯ Yes ◯ No

   D. $83 \div r$, the product of 83 and r ◯ Yes ◯ No

2. Tell whether the statement in A–D is true or false.

   A. When $x = 3$, the value of $7x^2 - 14$ is 49. ◯ True ◯ False

   B. The expression $24 - 2x + 3y$ has three terms. ◯ True ◯ False

   C. The expression $3(n + 7)$ can be described as the sum of 3 and the product of n and 7. ◯ True ◯ False

   D. No matter what value is chosen for s, s^3 is greater than s^2. ◯ True ◯ False

3. Alicia says the expression $2(m + 4) + 5$ is equivalent to the expression $2m + 13$. Identify two properties that can be used to support Alicia's claim and justify your answer.

4. Mike dove to an elevation of -40 feet, and Julio dove to an elevation of -50 feet. Mike says that because -40 is greater than -50, he dove farther than Julio. Use absolute value to explain Mike's error.

UNIT 4

Study Guide Review

MODULE 9 Generating Equivalent Numerical Expressions

Key Vocabulary

base *(base (en numeración))*

exponent *(exponente)*

order of operations *(orden de las operaciones)*

power *(potencia)*

? ESSENTIAL QUESTION

How can you generate equivalent numerical expressions and use them to solve real-world problems?

EXAMPLE 1

Find the value of each power.

A. 0.9^2

$0.9^2 = 0.9 \times 0.9 = 0.81$

B. 18^0

Any number raised to the power of 0 is 1.

$18^0 = 1$

C. $\left(\frac{1}{4}\right)^3$

$\left(\frac{1}{4}\right)^3 = \frac{1}{4} \times \frac{1}{4} \times \frac{1}{4} = \frac{1}{64}$

EXAMPLE 2

Find the prime factorization of 60.

2 | **60**
2 | **30**
3 | **15**
5 | **5**
1

$60 = 2 \cdot 2 \cdot 3 \cdot 5$

$60 = 2^2 \cdot 3 \cdot 5$

The prime factorization of 60 is $2^2 \cdot 3 \cdot 5$.

EXAMPLE 3

Evaluate each expression.

A. $4 \times (2^3 + 5)$

$= 4 \times (8 + 5)$ — $2^3 = 8$

$= 4 \times 13$ — Add.

$= 52$ — Multiply.

B. $27 \div 3^2 \times 6$

$= 27 \div 9 \times 6$ — $3^2 = 9$

$= 3 \times 6$ — Divide.

$= 18$ — Multiply.

EXERCISES

Use an exponent to write each expression. (Lesson 9.1)

1. 3.6×3.6 ____________

2. $9 \times 9 \times 9 \times 9$ ____________

3. $\frac{4}{5} \times \frac{4}{5} \times \frac{4}{5}$ ____________

Find the value of each power. (Lesson 9.1)

4. 12^0 ______

5. 13^2 ______

6. $\left(\frac{2}{7}\right)^3$ ______

7. 0.4^2 ______

8. $\left(\frac{4}{9}\right)^1$ ______

9. 0.7^3 ______

Find the prime factorization of each number. (Lesson 9.2)

10. 75 ______

11. 29 ______

12. 168 ______

13. Eduardo is building a sandbox that has an area of 84 square feet. What are the possible whole number measurements for the length and width of the sandbox? (Lesson 9.2)

______

Evaluate each expression. (Lesson 9.3)

14. $2 \times 5^2 - (4 + 1)$ ______

15. $\frac{22 - (3^2 + 4)}{12 \div 4}$ ______

MODULE 10 Generating Equivalent Algebraic Expressions

? ESSENTIAL QUESTION

How can you generate equivalent algebraic expressions and use them to solve real-world problems?

Key Vocabulary

algebraic expression *(expresión algebraica)*
coefficients *(coeficiente)*
constant *(contante)*
equivalent expressions *(expresión equivalente)*
evaluating *(evaluar)*
term *(término (en una expresión))*

EXAMPLE 1

Evaluate each expression for the given values of the variables.

A. $2(x^2 - 9); x = 5$

$2(5^2 - 9)$	$5^2 = 25$
$= 2(16)$	Subtract.
$= 32$	Multiply.

When $x = 5$, $2(x^2 - 9) = 32$.

B. $w + y^2 + 3w; w = 2, y = 6$

$2 + 6^2 + 3(2)$	$6^2 = 36$
$= 2 + 36 + 6$	Multiply.
$= 44$	Add.

When $w = 2$ and $y = 6$, $w + y^2 + 3w = 44$.

EXAMPLE 2

Determine whether the algebraic expressions are equivalent: $5(x + 2)$ and $10 + 5x$.

$5(x + 2) = 5x + 10$	Distributive Property
$= 10 + 5x$	Commutative Property

$5(x + 2)$ is equal to $10 + 5x$. They are equivalent expressions.

EXERCISES

Write each phrase as an algebraic expression. (Lesson 10.1)

1. x subtracted from 15 ______
2. 12 divided by t ______
3. 4 groups of y ______
4. the sum of z and 7 ______

Write a phrase for each algebraic expression. (Lesson 10.1)

5. $8p$

______

6. $s + 7$

______

Evaluate each expression for the given values of the variables. (Lesson 10.2)

7. $8z + 3; z = 8$ ______
8. $3(7 + x^2); x = 2$ ______
9. $8s - 5t + s^2; s = 4, t = 1$ ______
10. $x - y^3; x = 27, y = 3$ ______
11. The expression $\frac{1}{2}(h)(b_1 + b_2)$ gives the area of a trapezoid, with b_1 and b_2 representing the two base lengths of a trapezoid and h representing the height. Find the area of a trapezoid with base lengths 4 inches and 6 inches and a height of 8 inches. Show your work. (Lesson 10.2)

______

Determine if the expressions are equivalent. (Lesson 10.3)

12. $7 + 7x; 7\left(x + \frac{1}{7}\right)$ ______
13. $2.5(3 + x); 2.5x + 7.5$ ______

Simplify each expression. (Lesson 10.3)

14. $3m + 6 + m^2 + 5m - 1$ ______
15. $7x + 4(2x - 6)$ ______
16. $b^2 + 3 + 2b^2 + 4 - 7$ ______
17. $3(p + 5) - 8 + 11p$ ______

Unit Project

CA CC 6.EE.1

The Power of 2

Powers of 2 get large very quickly. It's true that 2^1 is equal to 2 and 2^2 equals just 4. But 2^{13} equals 8,192, which is slightly more than Earth's diameter in miles!

Create a presentation showing the powers of 2 from 2^0 to 2^{20}. For as many powers as possible, find a real-world distance, temperature, or length of time that is close to the power. Measurements can be in any units you choose. To get you started, place the following real-world examples with the correct powers of 2 in your presentation:

- The height of Fall Creek Falls, Tennessee, in feet
- The distance to the Moon, in miles
- The melting point of gold, in degrees Celsius

Remember: Each of your distances, temperatures, and lengths of time should be close to a power of 2 but does not have to be equal to it.

Use the space below to write down any questions you have or important information from your teacher.

MATH IN CAREERS | **ACTIVITY**

Freelance Computer Programmer Chanming is a freelance computer programmer contracted by a company that makes video games. In his work, he often used the power of 2^n to find the number of bits (or units of information) that can be arranged. The n stands for the number of bits. In the video game of hidden treasures that he is programming, the main character wins if he collects 3 fewer hidden treasures than the highest number of bits that can be arranged in the system. If Chanming is working with a 16-bit system, is the main character a winner if he has collected 65,000 hidden treasures? Explain your reasoning.

CALIFORNIA

UNIT 4
MIXED REVIEW

Assessment Readiness

Personal Math Trainer
my.hrw.com
Online Practice and Help

1. Consider each phrase and algebraic expression.

   Select Yes or No to indicate whether the phrase matches the algebraic expression below it.

   A. the number of photos per page if 25 photos are divided evenly among p pages
   $p \div 25$ ○ Yes ○ No

   B. Jen's age if she is y years older than Jeff, who is 24 years old
   $24 + y$ ○ Yes ○ No

   C. the number of miles left to drive if a trip is 456 miles and you have driven y miles
   $456 - y$ ○ Yes ○ No

2. The following sets of numbers are in order from greatest to least.

   Choose True or False.

   A. $\frac{4}{2}$, 1.5, 1.05, $\frac{2}{4}$ ○ True ○ False

   B. 1.25, $\frac{3}{4}$, $\frac{0.9}{2}$, 1 ○ True ○ False

   C. 0.75, 1.05, $\frac{3}{2}$, $\frac{6}{3}$ ○ True ○ False

3. Travis and Paula went to lunch. Travis ordered a sandwich for $7.50, and Paula ordered a burger for $5.25. After lunch, they left a 15% tip for their waiter. How much money did they spend altogether? Explain.

4. Marcus is observing bacteria multiply. Every 15 seconds, there are 10 times more bacteria than before. If there are 10 bacteria now, Marcus predicts there will be 3,000,000 bacteria in 2 minutes. Is Marcus correct? Explain.

Performance Tasks

★**5.** For every bag of trail mix the local Scout Guide troop sells, it earns $0.45.

a. Write an expression to represent this situation.

b. Sarah sold 52 bags of trail mix. How much did she earn for her troop?

c. Let *x* represent the total number of bags of trail mix sold by Sarah's troop. Write an expression to show what percentage of bags Sarah sold.

★★**6.** Antonio is a freelance computer programmer. In his work, he often uses 2^n, where *n* is the number of bits, to find the number of ways bits (or units of information) can be arranged.

a. Antonio is working on programming a new video game in which the main character, Millie, collects golden keys to help in her quest. Antonio writes a formula to show that Millie can collect one less key than the highest number of bits that can be arranged in the system. What formula can he use?

b. If Antonio is working with a 16-bit system, how many golden keys can Millie collect?

c. Antonio is also working on a new spreadsheet program. The program takes up 14 bytes of memory. If each byte is equal to 8 bits, how many bits is Antonio's program? Show your work.

★★★**7.** In January Hannah took 14 pictures. The number of pictures she took doubled each month for 3 months.

a. How many pictures did Hannah take in March? Write and evaluate an expression with an exponent to show your work.

b. In April, Hannah took half the number of pictures she took in March. Jack says that means she took the same number of pictures in April and in February. Hannah disagrees. Write and evaluate an expression to prove or disprove Jack's claim.

UNIT 5

Equations and Inequalities

MODULE 11

Equations and Relationships

CA CC 6.EE.5, 6.EE.6, 6.EE.7, 6.EE.8

MODULE 12

Relationships in Two Variables

CA CC 6.NS.6, 6.NS.6b, 6.NS.6c, 6.NS.8, 6.EE.9

MATH IN CAREERS

Botanist A botanist is a biologist who studies plants. Botanists use math to analyze data and create models of biological organisms and systems. They use these models to make predictions. They also use statistics to determine correlations. If you are interested in a career in botany, you should study these mathematical subjects:

- Algebra
- Trigonometry
- Probability and Statistics
- Calculus

Research other careers that require the analysis of data and use of mathematical models.

ACTIVITY At the end of the unit, check out how **botanists** use math.

Unit Project Preview

How Fast and How Far?

In the Unit Project at the end of this unit, you will research the top speed of a favorite animal. You will use the speed to make a table, write an equation, and draw a graph of the relationship between the distance the animal runs and the length of time it takes to run that distance. To successfully complete the Unit Project you'll need to master these skills:

- Make tables relating independent and dependent variables.
- Write equations relating independent and dependent variables.
- Draw graphs of equations in the coordinate plane.

1. A horse runs at an average speed of 30 miles per hour. How far will the horse run in 4 hours? in x hours? Explain your reasoning.

____

____

2. Use the word *increases* or *decreases* to complete each statement about the time–distance relationship above.

a. As time increases, the distance traveled __________.

b. As speed increases, the distance traveled in 1 hour __________.

Tracking Your Learning Progression

This unit addresses important California Common Core Standards in the Critical Areas of solving equations and inequalities and understanding relationships in two variables.

Domain 6.EE Expressions and Equations

Cluster Reason about and solve one-variable equations and inequalities.

The unit also supports additional standards.

Domain 6.NS The Number System

Cluster Apply and extend previous understandings of numbers to the system of rational numbers.

Equations and Relationships

MODULE 11
CALIFORNIA

ESSENTIAL QUESTION

How can you use equations and relationships to solve real-world problems?

Real-World Video

my.hrw.com

Businesses use equations to determine how many products can be made from the materials available. A guitar company uses an equation to determine how many guitars can be made with *x* amount of strings.

GO DIGITAL
my.hrw.com

my.hrw.com

Go digital with your write-in student edition, accessible on any device.

Math On the Spot

Scan with your smart phone to jump directly to the online edition, video tutor, and more.

Animated Math

Interactively explore key concepts to see how math works.

Personal Math Trainer

Get immediate feedback and help as you work through practice sets.

Are YOU Ready?

Complete these exercises to review skills you will need for this module.

Personal Math Trainer

Online Practice and Help

my.hrw.com

Evaluate Expressions

EXAMPLE Evaluate $8(3+2) - 5^2$

$8(3+2) - 5^2 = 8(5) - 5^2$ *Perform operations inside parentheses first.*

$= 8(5) - 25$ *Evaluate exponents.*

$= 40 - 25$ *Multiply.*

$= 15$ *Subtract.*

Evaluate the expression.

1. $4(5 + 6) - 15$ __________

2. $8(2 + 4) + 16$ __________

3. $3(14 - 7) - 16$ __________

4. $6(8 - 3) + 3(7 - 4)$ __________

5. $10(6 - 5) - 3(9 - 6)$ __________

6. $7(4 + 5 + 2) - 6(3 + 5)$ __________

7. $2(8 + 3) + 4^2$ __________

8. $7(14 - 8) - 6^2$ __________

9. $8(2 + 1)^2 - 4^2$ __________

Connect Words and Equations

EXAMPLE The product of a number and 4 is 32.

The product of x and 4 is 32. *Represent the unknown with a variable.*

$4 \times x$ is 32. *Determine the operation.*

$4 \times x = 32.$ *Determine the placement of the equal sign.*

Write an algebraic equation for the word sentence.

10. A number increased by 7.9 is 8.3. __________

11. 17 is the sum of a number and 6. __________

12. The quotient of a number and 8 is 4. __________

13. 81 is three times a number. __________

14. The difference between 31 and a number is 7. __________

15. Eight less than a number is 19. __________

Reading Start-Up

Vocabulary

Review Words

- ✔ algebraic expression *(expresión algebraica)*
- ✔ coefficient *(coeficiente)*
- ✔ constant *(constante)*
- evaluating *(evaluar)*
- like terms *(términos semejantes)*
- ✔ term *(término, en una expresión)*
- ✔ variable *(variable)*

Preview Words

- equation *(ecuación)*
- equivalent expression *(expresión equivalente)*
- properties of operations *(propiedades de las operaciones)*
- solution *(solución)*

Visualize Vocabulary

Use the ✔ words to complete the graphic.

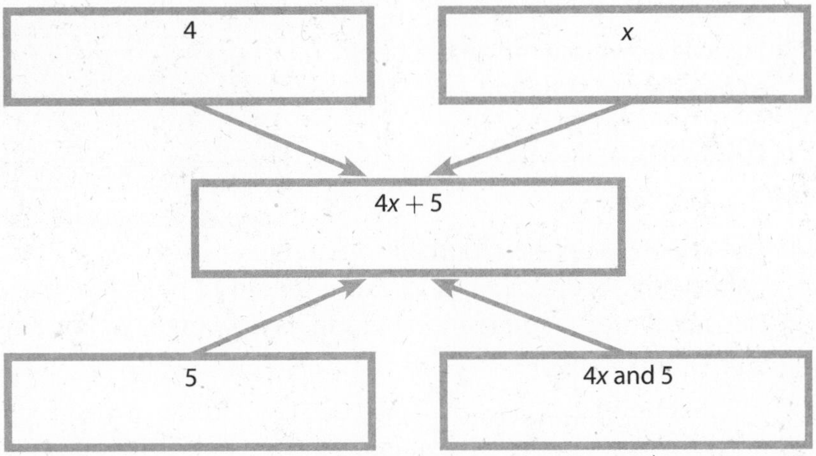

Understand Vocabulary

Match the term on the left to the correct expression on the right.

1. algebraic expression

2. equation

3. solution

A. A mathematical statement that two expressions are equal.

B. A value of the variable that makes the statement true.

C. A mathematical statement that includes one or more variables.

Active Reading

Booklet Before beginning the module, create a booklet to help you learn the concepts in this module. Write the main idea of each lesson on each page of the booklet. As you study each lesson, write important details that support the main idea, such as vocabulary and formulas. Refer to your finished booklet as you work on assignments and study for tests.

GETTING READY FOR

Equations and Relationships

Understanding the standards and the vocabulary terms in the standards will help you know exactly what you are expected to learn in this module.

CA CC 6.EE.7

Solve real-world and mathematical problems by writing and solving equations of the form $x + p = q$ and $px = q$ for cases in which p, q and x are all nonnegative rational numbers.

Key Vocabulary

equation *(ecuación)*
A mathematical sentence that shows that two expressions are equivalent.

What It Means to You

You will learn to write an equation to represent a situation.

EXAMPLE 6.EE.7

The Falcons won their football game with a score of 30 to 19. Kevin scored 12 points for the Falcons. Write an equation to determine how many points Kevin's teammates scored.

Kevin's points	+	Teammates' points	=	Total points
12	+	t	=	30

CA CC 6.EE.5

Understand solving an equation or inequality as a process of answering a question: which values from a specified set, if any, make the equation or inequality true? Use substitution to determine whether a given number in a specified set makes an equation or inequality true.

Key Vocabulary

inequality *(desigualdad)*
A mathematical sentence that shows the relationship between quantities that are not equal.

What It Means to You

You can substitute a given value for the variable in an equation or inequality to check if that value makes the equation or inequality true.

EXAMPLE 6.EE.5

Melanie has to buy 6 tickets to a play. She will pay at least \$156 depending on the price of the seats. Write an inequality for this situation. Use it to decide if \$20 and \$30 are possible ticket prices.

Number of tickets bought	·	Price per ticket	≥	Total cost
6	·	p	≥	156

Substitute 20 and 30 for p to see if the inequality is true.

$6p \geq 156$ | $6p \geq 156$

$6 \cdot 20 \overset{?}{\geq} 156$ | $6 \cdot 30 \overset{?}{\geq} 156$

$120 \overset{?}{\geq} 156$ ✗ | $180 \overset{?}{\geq} 156$ ✓

The price per ticket could be \$30 but not \$20.

Visit **my.hrw.com** to see all **CA Common Core Standards** explained.

my.hrw.com

LESSON 11.1

Writing Equations to Represent Situations

CA CC 6.EE.7

Solve real-world and mathematical problems by writing and solving equations of the form $x + p = q$ and $px = q$ for cases in which p, q and x are all nonnegative rational numbers. *Also 6.EE.5, 6.EE.6*

ESSENTIAL QUESTION

How do you write equations and determine whether a number is a solution of an equation?

Determining Whether Values Are Solutions

Math On the Spot
my.hrw.com

An **equation** is a mathematical statement that two *expressions* are equal. An equation may or may not contain variables. For an equation that contains a variable, a **solution** of the equation is a value of the variable that makes the equation true.

An expression represents a single value.

An equation represents a relationship between two values.

	Expression	Equation
Numerical	$5 + 4$	$5 + 4 = 9$
Words	a number *plus* 4	A number *plus* 4 *is* 9.
Algebraic	$n + 4$	$n + 4 = 9$

An equation relates two expressions using a symbol for "is" or "equals."

EXAMPLE 1

CA CC 6.EE.5

Determine whether the given value is a solution of the equation.

A $x + 9 = 15; x = 6$

$6 + 9 \stackrel{?}{=} 15$ Substitute 6 for x.

$15 \stackrel{?}{=} 15$ Add.

6 is a solution of $x + 9 = 15$.

B $\frac{y}{4} = 32; y = 8$

$\frac{8}{4} \stackrel{?}{=} 32$ Substitute 8 for y.

$2 \stackrel{?}{=} 32$ Divide.

8 is not a solution of the equation $\frac{y}{4} = 32$.

C $8x = 72; x = 9$

$8(9) \stackrel{?}{=} 72$ Substitute 9 for x.

$72 \stackrel{?}{=} 72$ Multiply.

9 is a solution of $8x = 72$.

Math Talk
Mathematical Practices

Does the variable in each equation in parts A–D refer to a single number? Explain.

Personal Math Trainer

Online Practice and Help

my.hrw.com

YOUR TURN

Determine whether the given value is a solution of the equation.

1. $11 = n + 6; n = 5$ ____________

2. $y - 6 = 24; y = 18$ ____________

3. $\frac{x}{9} = 4; x = 36$ ____________

4. $15t = 100; t = 6$ ____________

Math On the Spot

my.hrw.com

Writing Equations to Represent Situations

You can represent some real-world situations with an equation. Making a model first can help you organize the information and identify what the variable represents.

EXAMPLE 2 Real World

CA CC 6.EE.6

Mark scored 17 points for the home team in a basketball game. His teammates as a group scored *p* points. Write an equation to represent this situation.

Mark's points	+	Teammates' points	=	Total points
↓		↓		↓
17	+	p	=	46

p represents the number of points Mark's teammates scored.

YOUR TURN

Write an equation to represent each situation.

5. The sum of a number *f* and 9 is equal to 38. ____________

6. The product of 17 and a number *n* is equal to 102. ____________

7. Craig is *c* years old. His 12-year-old friend Kaitlin is $\frac{1}{2}$ year younger than Craig. ____________

8. Kim rented skates for *h* hours. The rental fee was $2.50 per hour. She paid a total of $20. ____________

Personal Math Trainer

Online Practice and Help

my.hrw.com

Writing an Equation and Checking Solutions

You can substitute a given value for the variable in a real-world equation to check if that value makes sense for the situation.

Math On the Spot
my.hrw.com

EXAMPLE 3 Real World

CA CC 6.EE.7

Sarah used a gift card to buy $47 worth of food. She has $18 left on her gift card. Write an equation to represent this situation, and use it to determine whether Sarah had $65 or $59 on the gift card before buying food.

STEP 1 Write a word equation based on the situation.

Amount on card	−	Amount spent	=	Amount left on card

STEP 2 Rewrite the equation using a variable for the unknown quantity and the given values for the known quantities.

Let x be the amount on the card.

Amount on card	−	Amount spent	=	Amount left on card
x	−	47	=	18

The amount spent and the amount left on the card are the known quantities. Substitute those values in the equation.

STEP 3 Substitute 65 and 59 for x to see which equation is true.

$$x - 47 = 18 \qquad x - 47 = 18$$
$$65 - 47 \stackrel{?}{=} 18 \qquad 59 - 47 \stackrel{?}{=} 18$$
$$18 \stackrel{?}{=} 18 \qquad 12 \stackrel{?}{=} 18$$

The amount on Sarah's gift card before she bought food was $65.

Animated Math
my.hrw.com

Reflect

9. **What If?** Suppose Sarah had $12 left on her gift card. How would this change the equation and the final answer?

____

YOUR TURN

10. On Saturday morning, Owen earned $24. By the end of the afternoon he had earned a total of $62. Write an equation to represent the situation. Tell what the variable represents. Determine whether Owen earned $38 or $31 on Saturday afternoon.

____

____

Personal Math Trainer
Online Practice and Help
my.hrw.com

Guided Practice

Determine whether the given value is a solution of the equation. (Example 1)

1. $23 = x - 9$; $x = 14$ ________

2. $\frac{n}{13} = 4$; $n = 52$ ________

3. $25 = \frac{k}{5}$; $k = 5$ ________

4. $2.5n = 45$; $n = 18$ ________

5. $21 - h = 15$; $h = 6$ ________

6. $d - 4 = 19$; $d = 15$ ________

7. $w - 9 = 0$; $w = 9$ ________

8. $5q = 31$; $q = 13$ ________

9. Each floor of a hotel has *r* rooms. On 8 floors, there are a total of 256 rooms. Write an equation to represent this situation. (Example 2)

Number		Number of rooms			
________	×	________	=	________	________

In Exercises 10–12, write an equation to represent the situation. (Example 2)

10. When a number *n* is divided by 16, the result is 3. ________

11. The sum of 4.5 and a number *k* is 26.2. ________

12. In the school band, there are 5 trumpet players and *f* flute players. There are twice as many flute players as there are trumpet players. ________

In Exercises 13 –14, write an equation to solve the problem. Tell what your variable represents. (Example 3)

13. Pedro bought 8 tickets to a basketball game. He paid a total of $208. Determine whether each ticket cost $26 or $28.

____

14. The high temperature was 92 °F. This was 24 °F higher than the overnight low temperature. Determine whether the low temperature was 62 °F or 68 °F.

____

____

ESSENTIAL QUESTION CHECK-IN

15. Tell how you can determine whether a number is a solution of an equation.

____

____

Name ____________________ Class ____________________ Date ____________________

11.1 Independent Practice

CA CC 6.EE.5, 6.EE.6, 6.EE.7

Personal Math Trainer
Online Practice and Help
my.hrw.com

In Exercises 16–18, write an equation to solve the problem. Tell what your variable represents.

16. Andy's grandfather, who is 76 years old, is 4 times as old as Andy. Determine whether Andy is 19 or 22 years old.

17. Mi's sleeping bag weighs 8 pounds. Her backpack and sleeping bag together weigh 31 pounds. Determine whether her backpack alone weighs 25 or 23 pounds.

18. Halfway through a bus route, 23 students have been dropped off and 48 students remain on the bus. Determine whether there were 61 or 71 students on the bus to begin with.

19. Write an equation that involves multiplication, contains a variable, and has a solution of 5. Then write another equation that has the same solution and includes the same variable and numbers but uses division.

20. **Vocabulary** How are expressions and equations different?

21. **Multistep** Alan has partially completed a table showing the distances between his town, Greenville, and two other towns.

Distance between Greenville and Nearby Towns (miles)	
Parker	29
Hadley	?

a. The distance between Hadley and Greenville is $12\frac{1}{2}$ miles less than the distance between Parker and Greenville. Write two equations that compare the distance between Hadley and Greenville and the distance between Parker and Greenville. Tell what your variable represents.

b. Alan says the distance from Hadley to Greenville is $16\frac{1}{2}$ miles. Is he correct? Explain.

22. **Explain the Error** A problem states that Ursula earns $9 per hour. To write an expression that tells how much money Ursula earns for h hours, Joshua wrote $\frac{9}{h}$. Sarah wrote $9h$. Whose expression is correct and why?

23. **Communicate Mathematical Ideas** A dog weighs 44 pounds. The dog needs to lose 7 pounds to reach its ideal weight. Mikala wrote the equation $x + 7 = 44$ to represent the situation. Kirk wrote the equation $44 - x = 7$. What does the variable represent? Which equation is correct? Can you write another equation that represents the situation?

____

____

24. **Multiple Representations** The table shows the ages of Cindy and her dad.

Dad's Age	Cindy's Age
28 years old	2 years old
36 years old	10 years old
?	18 years old

a. Write an equation that relates Cindy's age to her dad's age when Cindy is 18. Tell what the variable represents.

____

b. Determine if 42 is a solution to the equation. Show your work.

____

c. Explain the meaning of your answer in part **b**.

____

H.O.T. FOCUS ON HIGHER ORDER THINKING

Work Area

25. **Critical Thinking** In the school band, there are 4 trumpet players and f flute players. The total number of trumpet and flute players is 12. Are there twice as many flute players as trumpet players? Explain.

____

____

26. **Problem Solving** Ronald paid $162 for 6 tickets to a basketball game. During the game he noticed that his friend paid $130 for 5 tickets. The price of each ticket was $26. Was Ronald overcharged? Explain.

____

____

27. **Communicate Mathematical Ideas** Tariq said you can write an equation by setting an expression equal to itself. Would an equation like this be true? Explain.

____

____

____

LESSON 11.2

Addition and Subtraction Equations

CA CC 6.EE.7

Solve real-world and mathematical problems by writing and solving equations of the form $x + p = q$ and $px = q$ for cases in which p, q and x are all nonnegative rational numbers. *Also* 6.EE.5, 6.EE.6

ESSENTIAL QUESTION

How do you solve equations that contain addition or subtraction?

EXPLORE ACTIVITY Real World   CA CC 6.EE.6, 6.EE.7

Modeling Equations

A puppy weighed 6 ounces at birth. After two weeks, the puppy weighed 14 ounces. How much weight did the puppy gain?

Let x represent the number of ounces gained.

Weight at birth	+	Weight gained	=	Weight after 2 weeks
↓		↓		↓
6	+	x	=	14

To answer this question, you can solve the equation $6 + x = 14$.

Algebra tiles can model some equations. An equation mat represents the two sides of an equation. To solve the equation, remove the same number of tiles from both sides of the mat until the x tile is by itself on one side.

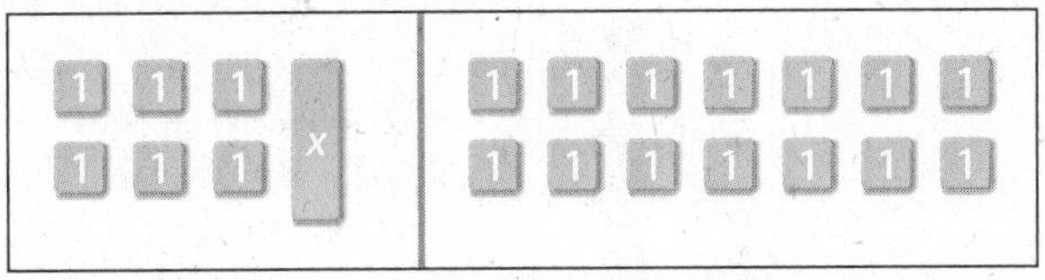

$6 + x$ 14

A Model $6 + x = 14$.

B How many 1 tiles must you remove on the left side so that the x tile is by itself? __________ Cross out these tiles on the equation mat.

C Whenever you remove tiles from one side of the mat, you must remove the same number of tiles from the other side of the mat. Cross out the tiles that should be removed on the right side of the mat.

D How many tiles remain on the right side of the mat? __________ This is the solution of the equation.

The puppy gained __________ ounces.

Math Talk
Mathematical Practices

Why did you remove tiles from each side of your model?

Reflect

1. **Communicate Mathematical Ideas** How do you know when the model shows the final solution? How do you read the solution?

____

____

Using Subtraction to Solve Equations

Removing the same number of tiles from each side of an equation mat models subtracting the same number from both sides of an equation.

Subtraction Property of Equality

You can subtract the same number from both sides of an equation, and the two sides will remain equal.

When an equation contains addition, solve by subtracting the same number from both sides.

EXAMPLE 1

CA CC 6.EE.5

Solve the equation $a + 15 = 26$. Graph the solution on a number line.

$a + 15 = 26$ Notice that the number 15 is added to *a*.

$$\begin{array}{rcl} a + 15 &=& 26 \\ -15 & & -15 \\ \hline a &=& 11 \end{array}$$

Subtract 15 from both sides of the equation.

Check: $a + 15 = 26$

$11 + 15 \stackrel{?}{=} 26$ Substitute 11 for *a*.

$26 \stackrel{?}{=} 26$ Add on the left side.

Graph the solution on a number line.

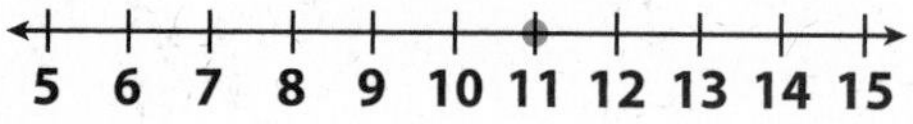

Reflect

2. **Communicate Mathematical Ideas** How do you decide which number to subtract from both sides?

____

____

YOUR TURN

3. Solve the equation $5 = w + 1\frac{1}{2}$.

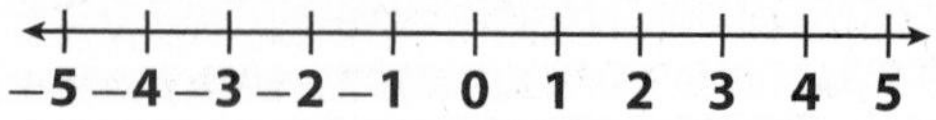

Graph the solution on a number line.

$w =$ _______________

Using Addition to Solve Equations

When an equation contains subtraction, solve by adding the same number to both sides.

Addition Property of Equality

You can add the same number to both sides of an equation, and the two sides will remain equal.

Math On the Spot
my.hrw.com

EXAMPLE 2

CA CC 6.EE.5

Solve the equation $y - 21 = 18$. Graph the solution on a number line.

$y - 21 = 18$ — *Notice that the number 21 is subtracted from y.*

$$\begin{aligned} y - 21 &= 18 \\ +21 \quad &\;\; +21 \\ \hline y \quad &= 39 \end{aligned}$$

Add 21 to both sides of the equation.

Check: $y - 21 = 18$

$39 - 21 \stackrel{?}{=} 18$ — *Substitute 39 for y.*

$18 \stackrel{?}{=} 18$ — *Subtract.*

Graph the solution on a number line.

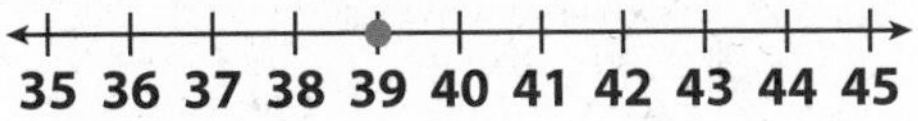

Reflect

4. **Communicate Mathematical Ideas** How do you know whether to add on both sides or subtract on both sides when solving an equation?

____

____

____

My Notes

YOUR TURN

5. Solve the equation $h - \frac{1}{2} = \frac{3}{4}$.

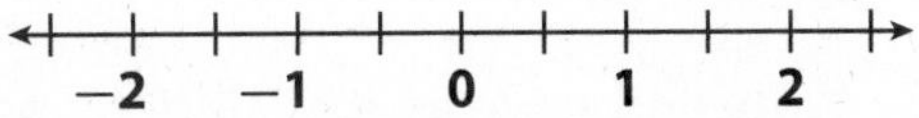

Graph the solution on a number line.

$h =$ ______________________________

Personal Math Trainer
Online Practice and Help
my.hrw.com

Solving Equations that Represent Geometric Concepts

You can write equations to represent geometric relationships.

Recall that a straight line has an angle measure of 180°. Two angles whose measures have a sum of 180° are called supplementary angles. Two angles whose measures have a sum of 90° are called complementary angles.

EXAMPLE 3

CA CC 6.EE.7, 6.EE.6

Find the measure of the unknown angle.

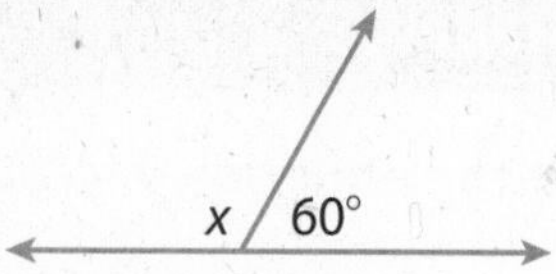

STEP 1 Write the information in the boxes.

Unknown angle measure	+	60°	=	180°

STEP 2 Write a description to represent the model. Include a question for the unknown angle measure.

The sum of the measure of an unknown angle and 60° is 180°. What is the measure of the unknown angle?

STEP 3 Write an equation.

$x + 60 = 180$ — *x represents the measure of the unknown angle in degrees.*

STEP 4 Solve the equation.

$$\begin{aligned} x + \ 60 &= \ 180 \\ -60 & \quad -60 \\ \hline x \qquad &= \ 120 \end{aligned}$$

Subtract 60 from each side.

The unknown angle measures 120°.

The final answer includes units of degrees.

YOUR TURN

6. Write and solve an equation to find the measure of the unknown angle. Tell what the variable represents.

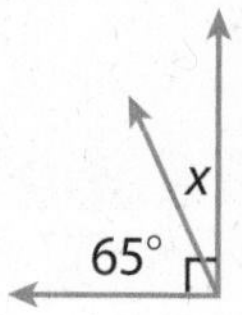

____

7. Write and solve an equation to find the complement of a 42° angle. Tell what the variable represents.

____

Writing Real-World Problems for a Given Equation

You can write a real-world problem for a given equation. Examine each number and mathematical operation in the equation.

Math On the Spot
my.hrw.com

EXAMPLE 4 Real World

CA CC 6.EE.7

Write a real-world problem for the equation $21.79 + x = 25$. Then solve the equation.

STEP 1 Examine each part of the equation.

x is the unknown or quantity we are looking for.

21.79 is added to x.

$= 25$ means that after adding 21.79 and x, the result is 25.

STEP 2 Write a real-world situation that involves *adding* two quantities.

Joshua wants to buy his mother flowers and a card for Mother's Day. Joshua has \$25 to spend and selects roses for \$21.79. How much can he spend on a card? Let x represent that amount.

STEP 3 Solve the equation.

$$\begin{aligned} 21.79 + x &= 25 \\ -21.79 \quad &\quad -21.79 \\ x &= 3.21 \end{aligned}$$

The final answer includes units of money in dollars.

Joshua can spend \$3.21 on a Mother's Day card.

Math Talk
Mathematical Practices
How is the question in a real-world problem related to its equation?

Reflect

8. **What If?** How might the real-world problem change if the equation were $x - 21.79 = 25$ and you still used roses for \$21.79?

____

____

____

YOUR TURN

9. Write a real-world problem for the equation $x - 100 = 40$. Tell what the variable represents. Then solve the equation.

____

____

Personal Math Trainer
Online Practice and Help
my.hrw.com

Guided Practice

1. A total of 14 guests attended a birthday party. Three friends stayed after the party to help clean up. How many left when the party ended? (Explore Activity)

a. Let x represent the ______________________________

b. [Number that ______] + [Number that ______] = [______]

______________ + ______________ = ________

c. Draw algebra tiles to model the equation.

________ friends left when the party ended.

Solve each equation. Graph the solution on a number line. (Examples 1 and 2)

2. $2 = x - 3$ $x =$ ________

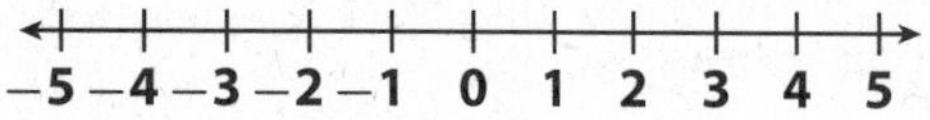

3. $s + 12.5 = 14$ $s =$ ________

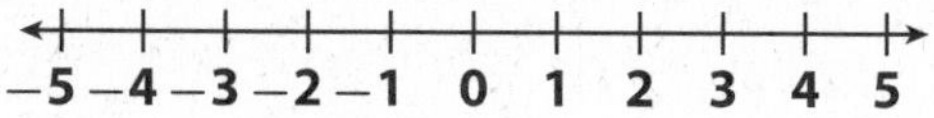

Solve each equation. (Examples 1 and 2)

4. $h + 6.9 = 11.4$

$h =$ ____________

5. $82 + p = 122$

$p =$ ____________

6. $n + \frac{1}{2} = \frac{7}{4}$

$n =$ ____________

7. Write and solve an equation to find the measure of the unknown angle. Tell what the variable represents. (Example 3)

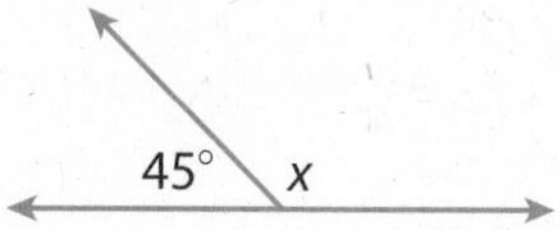

____

8. Write a real-world problem for the equation $x - 75 = 200$. Tell what the variable represents. Then solve the equation. (Example 4)

____

ESSENTIAL QUESTION CHECK-IN

9. How do you solve equations that contain addition or subtraction?

____

____

____

Name ______________________ Class ______________ Date ______________

11.2 Independent Practice

CA CC 6.EE.5, 6.EE.6, 6.EE.7

Personal Math Trainer

my.hrw.com

Online Practice and Help

In 10–16, write and solve an equation to answer each question. Tell what the variable represents.

10. A wildlife reserve had 8 elephant calves born during the summer and now has 31 total elephants. How many elephants were in the reserve before summer began?

11. My sister is 14 years old. My brother says that his age minus 12 is equal to my sister's age. How old is my brother?

12. Kim bought a poster that cost \$8.95 and some colored pencils. The total cost was \$21.35. How much did the colored pencils cost?

13. Acme Cars sold 37 vehicles in June. How many compact cars were sold in June?

Acme Cars – June Sales	
Type of car	**Number sold**
SUV	8
Compact	?

14. Sandra wants to buy a new MP3 player that is on sale for \$95. She has saved \$73. How much more money does she need?

15. Ronald spent \$123.45 on school clothes. He counted his money and discovered that he had \$36.55 left. How much money did he originally have?

16. Brita withdrew \$225 from her bank account. After her withdrawal, there was \$548 left in her account. How much money did Brita have in her account before the withdrawal?

17. **Represent Real-World Problems** Write a real-world situation that can be represented by $15 + c = 17.50$. Tell what the variable represents. Then solve the equation and describe what your answer represents for the problem situation.

18. **Critique Reasoning** Paula solved the equation $7 + x = 10$ and got 17. She is not certain that her answer is correct. How could you explain her mistake to her?

H.O.T. FOCUS ON HIGHER ORDER THINKING

Work Area

19. Multistep A grocery store is having a sale this week. If you buy a 5-pound bag of apples for the regular price, you can get another bag for \$1.49. If you buy a 5-pound bag of oranges at the regular price, you can get another bag for \$2.49.

Product	Regular price
5-pound bag of apples	\$2.99
5-pound bag of oranges	\$3.99

a. Write an equation to find the discount for each situation using a for the amount of the discount for apples and r for the amount of the discount for oranges.

____

b. Which fruit has a greater discount? Explain.

____

____

20. Critical Thinking An orchestra has twice as many woodwind instruments as brass instruments. There are a total of 150 brass and woodwind instruments.

a. Write two different addition equations that describe this situation. Use w for the number of woodwinds and b for the number of brass instruments.

____

b. How many woodwinds and how many brass instruments must there be to satisfy the given information?

____

21. Look for a Pattern Assume the following: $a + 1 = 2$, $b + 10 = 20$, $c + 100 = 200$, $d + 1{,}000 = 2{,}000$, ...

a. Solve each equation.

____

b. What pattern do you notice in the values of the variables?

____

____

c. What would be the value of g if the pattern continued?

____

LESSON 11.3

Multiplication and Division Equations

CA CC 6.EE.5

Understand solving an equation or inequality as a process of answering a question: which values from a specified set, if any, make the equation or inequality true? Use substitution to determine whether a given number in a specified set makes an equation or inequality true. *Also 6.EE.6, 6.EE.7*

ESSENTIAL QUESTION

How do you solve equations that contain multiplication or division?

EXPLORE ACTIVITY Real World CA CC 6.EE.6

Modeling Equations

Deanna has a recipe for potato cakes that requires 12 eggs to make 3 batches of potato cakes. How many eggs are needed per batch?

Let x represent the number of eggs needed per batch.

Number of batches	$\cdot$	Number of eggs per batch	=	Total eggs
↓		↓		↓
3	$\cdot$	x	=	12

To answer this question, you can use algebra tiles to solve $3x = 12$.

A Model $3x = 12$.

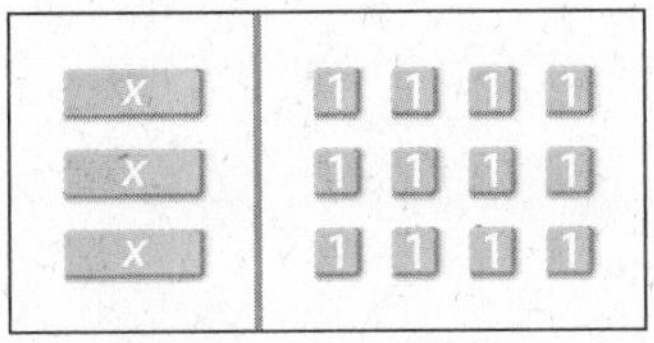

$3x$ 12

B There are 3 x tiles, so draw circles to separate the tiles into 3 equal groups. One group has been circled for you.

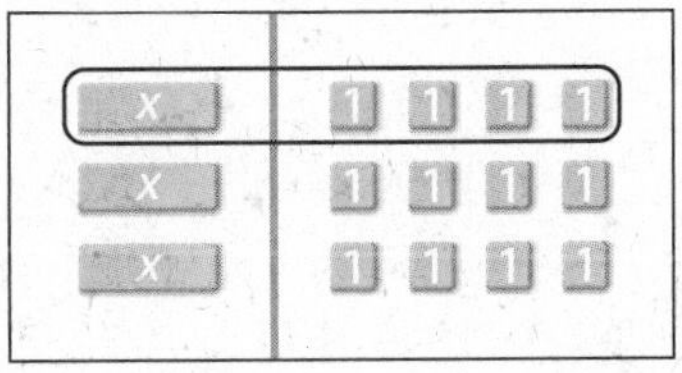

Math Talk
Mathematical Practices
Why is the solution to the equation the number of tiles in each group?

C How many 1 tiles are in each group? ___________
This is the solution of the equation.

___________ eggs are needed per batch of potato cakes.

Reflect

1. **Look for a Pattern** Why does it make sense to arrange the twelve 1 tiles in 3 rows of 4 instead of any other arrangement of twelve 1 tiles, such as 2 rows of 6?

____

Math On the Spot
my.hrw.com

Using Division to Solve Equations

Separating the tiles on both sides of an equation mat into an equal number of groups models dividing both sides of an equation by the same number.

Division Property of Equality

You can divide both sides of an equation by the same nonzero number, and the two sides will remain equal.

When an equation contains multiplication, solve by dividing both sides of the equation by the same nonzero number.

EXAMPLE 1

CA CC 6.EE.5

Solve each equation. Graph the solution on a number line.

My Notes

A $\mathbf{9a = 54}$

$9a = 54$ — Notice that 9 is multiplied by *a*.

$\frac{9a}{9} = \frac{54}{9}$ — Divide both sides of the equation by 9.

$a = 6$

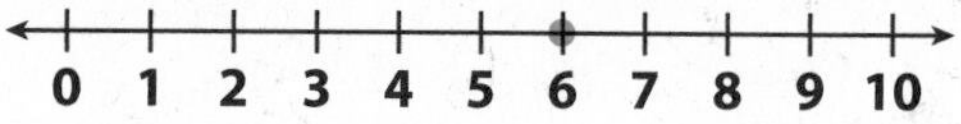

Check: $9a = 54$

$9(6) \stackrel{?}{=} 54$ — Substitute 6 for *a*.

$54 \stackrel{?}{=} 54$ — Multiply on the left side.

B $\mathbf{18 = 6d}$

$18 = 6d$ — Notice that 6 is multiplied by *d*.

$\frac{18}{6} = \frac{6d}{6}$ — Divide both sides of the equation by 6.

$3 = d$

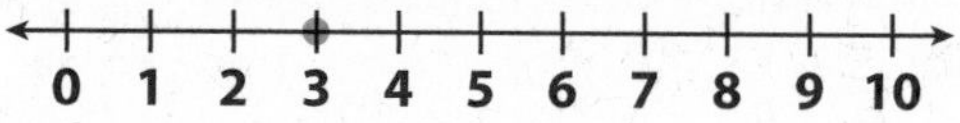

Check: $18 = 6d$

$18 \stackrel{?}{=} 6(3)$ — Substitute 3 for *d*.

$18 \stackrel{?}{=} 18$ — Multiply on the right side.

Personal Math Trainer
Online Practice and Help
my.hrw.com

YOUR TURN

Solve the equation $3x = 21$. Graph the solution on a number line.

2. $x =$ ________

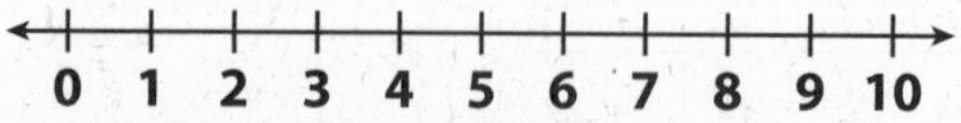

Using Multiplication to Solve Equations

When an equation contains division, solve by multiplying both sides of the equation by the same number.

Math On the Spot
my.hrw.com

Multiplication Property of Equality

You can multiply both sides of an equation by the same number, and the two sides will remain equal.

EXAMPLE 2

CA CC 6.EE.5

Solve each equation. Graph the solution on a number line.

A $\frac{x}{5} = 10$

$\frac{x}{5} = 10$ — *Notice that x is divided by the number 5.*

$5 \cdot \frac{x}{5} = 5 \cdot 10$ — *Multiply both sides of the equation by 5.*

$x = 50$

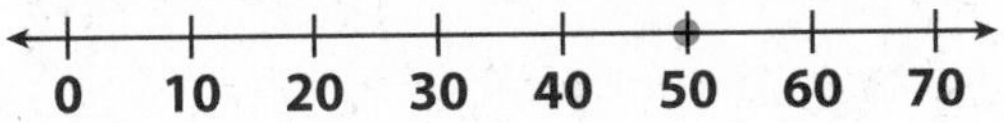

Check: $\frac{x}{5} = 10$

$\frac{50}{5} \stackrel{?}{=} 10$ — *Substitute 50 for x.*

$10 \stackrel{?}{=} 10$ — *Divide on the left side.*

B $15 = \frac{r}{2}$

$15 = \frac{r}{2}$ — *Notice that r is divided by the number 2.*

$2 \cdot 15 = 2 \cdot \frac{r}{2}$ — *Multiply both sides of the equation by 2.*

$30 = r$

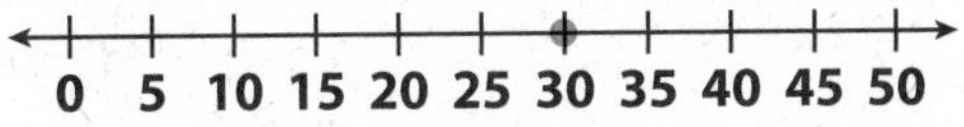

Check: $15 = \frac{r}{2}$

$15 \stackrel{?}{=} \frac{30}{2}$ — *Substitute 30 for r.*

$15 \stackrel{?}{=} 15$ — *Divide on the right side.*

Math Talk
Mathematical Practices

How is solving a multiplication equation similar to solving a division equation? How is it different?

YOUR TURN

Solve the equation $\frac{y}{9} = 1$. Graph the solution on a number line.

3. $\frac{y}{9} = 1$

$y =$ ___________

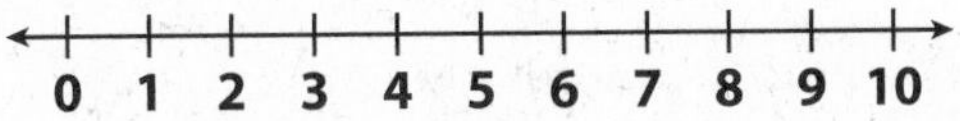

Personal Math Trainer
Online Practice and Help
my.hrw.com

Math On the Spot

my.hrw.com

My Notes

Using Equations to Solve Problems

You can use equations to solve real-world problems.

EXAMPLE 3 Problem Solving

CA CC 6.EE.7

Juanita is scrapbooking. She usually completes about 9 pages per hour. One night last week she completed pages 23 through 47 in 2.5 hours. Did she work at her average rate?

Analyze Information

Identify the important information.

- Worked for 2.5 hours
- Starting page: 23 Ending page: 47
- Scrapbooking rate: 9 pages per hour

Formulate a Plan

- Solve an equation to find the number of pages Juanita can expect to complete.
- Compare the number of pages Juanita can expect to complete with the number of pages she actually completed.

Solve

Let n represent the number of pages Juanita can expect to complete in 2.5 hours if she works at her average rate of 9 pages per hour.

Write an equation.

$$\frac{n}{2.5} = 9$$ Write the equation.

$$2.5 \cdot \frac{n}{2.5} = 2.5 \cdot 9$$ Multiply both sides by 2.5.

$$n = 22.5$$

Juanita can expect to complete 22.5 pages in 2.5 hours.

Juanita completed pages 23 through 47, a total of 25 pages. Because $25 > 22.5$, she worked faster than her expected rate.

Justify and Evaluate

You used an equation to find the number of pages Juanita could expect to complete in 2.5 hours if she worked at her average rate. You found that she could complete 22.5 pages.

Since 22.5 pages is less than the 25 pages Juanita completed, she worked faster than her average rate.

The answer makes sense, because Juanita completed 25 pages in 2.5 hours, which is equivalent to a rate of 10 pages in 1 hour. Since $10 > 9$, you know that she worked faster than her average rate.

YOUR TURN

4. Tion divides his baseball cards equally among himself, his brother, and 3 friends. He has 9 cards left. How many does he give away? Write and solve an equation to solve the problem. Tell what the variable represents.

____

____

Personal Math Trainer
Online Practice and Help
my.hrw.com

Writing Real-World Problems

You can write a real-world problem for a given equation.

Math On the Spot
my.hrw.com

EXAMPLE 4 Real World

CA CC 6.EE.7

Write a real-world problem for the equation $8x = 72$. Then solve the problem.

STEP 1 Examine each part of the equation.

x is the unknown value you want to find.

8 is multiplied by x.

$= 72$ means that after multiplying 8 and x, the result is 72.

STEP 2 Write a real-world situation that involves multiplying two quantities.

A hot air balloon flew at 8 miles per hour. Write and solve a multiplication equation to find the number of hours the balloon traveled if it covered a distance of 72 miles. Let x represent that number of hours.

STEP 3 Use the equation to solve the problem.

$8x = 72$

Divide both sides by 8.

$\frac{8x}{8} = \frac{72}{8}$

$x = 9$

The balloon traveled for 9 hours.

YOUR TURN

5. Write a real-world problem for the equation $11x = 385$. Tell what the variable represents. Then solve the problem.

____

____

Personal Math Trainer
Online Practice and Help
my.hrw.com

Guided Practice

1. Caroline ran 15 miles in 5 days. She ran the same distance each day. Write and solve an equation to determine the number of miles she ran each day. (Explore Activity)

a. Let x represent the ______________________________.

b. | Number of ______ | $\cdot$ | Number of ______ | $=$ | ______ |

______ $\cdot$ ______ $=$ ______

c. Draw algebra tiles to model the equation.

Caroline ran ________ miles each day.

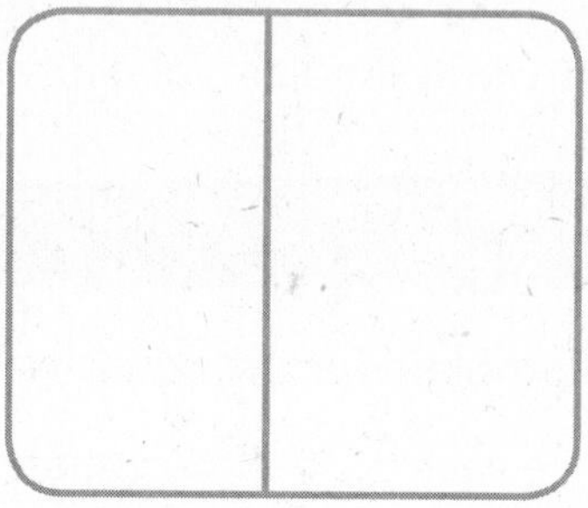

Solve each equation. Graph the solution on a number line. (Examples 1 and 2)

2. $x \div 3 = 3$; $x =$ ____________________

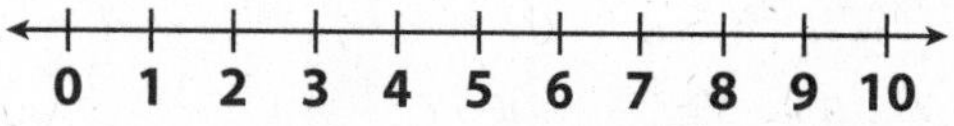

3. $4x = 32$; $x =$ ____________________

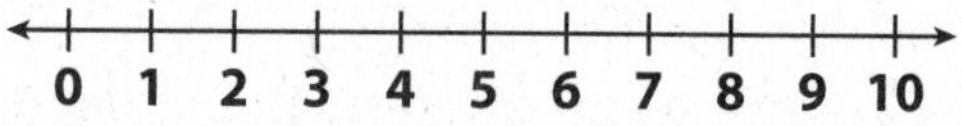

4. The area of the rectangle shown is 24 square inches. How much longer is its length than its width? (Example 3)

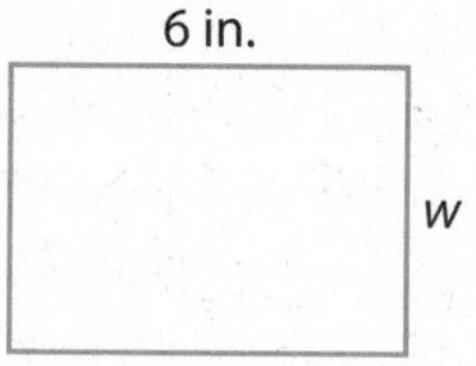

____

____

5. Write a real-world problem for the equation $15w = 45$. Tell what the variable represents. Then solve the problem. (Example 4)

____

____

____

ESSENTIAL QUESTION CHECK-IN

6. How do you solve equations that contain multiplication or division?

____

____

Name ______________________ Class ______________ Date ______________

11.3 Independent Practice

CA CC 6.EE.5, 6.EE.6, 6.EE.7

Personal Math Trainer
my.hrw.com
Online Practice and Help

Solve each equation.

7. $0.7x = 42$ ____________

8. $\frac{3}{4}x = \frac{1}{8}$ ____________

9. $\frac{x}{4} = 2\frac{1}{4}$ ____________

10. $\frac{x}{5} = 2.3$ ____________

11. $x \div 3.2 = 4.5$ ____________

In 12–17, write and solve an equation to answer each question. Tell what the variable represents.

12. Some friends made a salad for a party. There were 28 people at the party including the friends. They bought enough cherry tomatoes for everyone to get 3 cherry tomatoes each. How many cherry tomatoes did the friends buy?

____

____

13. Carmen participated in a read-a-thon. Mr. Cole pledged $4.00 per book and gave Carmen $44. How many books did Carmen read?

____

14. Lee drove 420 miles and used 15 gallons of gasoline. How many miles did Lee's car travel per gallon of gasoline?

____

____

15. On some days, Melvin commutes 3.5 hours per day to the city for business meetings. Last week he commuted for a total of 14 hours. How many days did he commute to the city?

____

16. Dharmesh has a square garden with a perimeter of 132 feet. Is the area of the garden greater than 1,000 square feet?

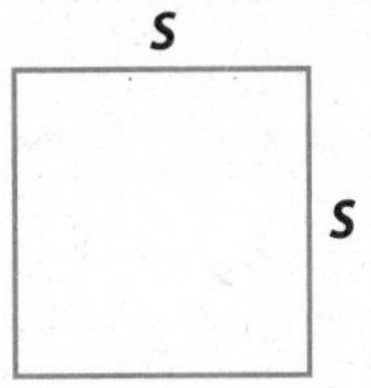

____

____

____

____

____

17. Ingrid walked her dog and washed her car. She spent 3 times as much time washing her car as she did walking her dog. It took Ingrid $1\frac{1}{2}$ hours to wash her car. How long did it take Ingrid to walk her dog?

____

18. **Representing Real-World Problems** Write and solve a problem involving money that can be solved with a multiplication equation. Tell what the variable represents.

____

____

____

____

____

____

____

19. **Representing Real-World Problems** Write and solve a problem involving money that can be solved with a division equation and has a solution of 1,350.

H.O.T. FOCUS ON HIGHER ORDER THINKING

Work Area

20. **Communicating Mathematical Ideas** Explain why $7 \cdot \frac{x}{7} = x$.
How does your answer help you solve a division equation such as $\frac{x}{7} = 2$?

21. **Critical Thinking** A number tripled and tripled again is 729. What is the number? Show your work.

22. **Multistep** Andre has 4 times as many model cars as Peter, and Peter has one-third as many model cars as Jade. Andre has 36 model cars.

a. Write and solve an equation to find how many model cars Peter has.

b. Using your answer from part **a**, write and solve an equation to find how many model cars Jade has.

23. **Persevere in Problem Solving** The area of a rectangle is 42 square inches and one side is 12 inches long. Find the perimeter of the rectangle. Show your work.

LESSON

11.4 Writing Inequalities

CA CC 6.EE.8

Write an inequality of the form $x > c$ or $x < c$ to represent a constraint or condition in a real-world or mathematical problem. Recognize that inequalities of the form $x > c$ or $x < c$ have infinitely many solutions; represent solutions of such inequalities on number line diagrams. *Also 6.EE.5, 6.EE.6*

ESSENTIAL QUESTION

How can you use inequalities to represent real-world constraints or conditions?

EXPLORE ACTIVITY Real World

CA CC 6.EE.8, 6.EE.5

Using Inequalities to Describe Quantities

An **inequality** is a mathematical sentence that shows the relationship between quantities that are not equal. You can use the symbols in the table to write inequalities that describe quantities with many values.

Symbol	Meaning	Word Phrases
$<$	Is less than	Fewer than, below
$>$	Is greater than	More than, above
$\leq$	Is less than or equal to	At most, no more than
$\geq$	Is greater than or equal to	At least, no less than

A The lowest temperature ever recorded in Florida was -2 °F. Graph this temperature on the number line.

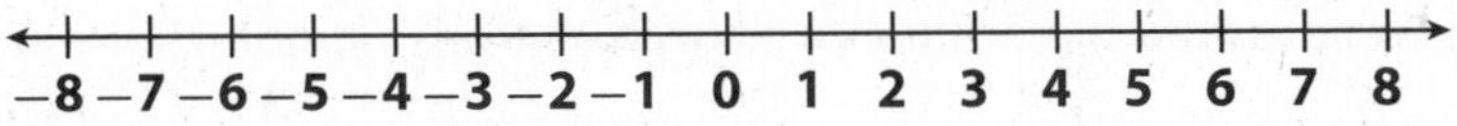

B The temperatures 0 °F, 3 °F, 6 °F, 5 °F, and -1 °F have also been recorded in Florida. Graph these temperatures on the number line.

C How do the temperatures in **B** compare with -2? How can you see this relationship on the number line?

____

D How many other numbers have the same relationship to -2 as the temperatures in **B**? Give some examples.

____

E Suppose you could graph all of the possible answers to **D** on a number line. What would the graph look like?

____

F Let *x* represent all the possible answers to **D**.

Complete this inequality: x ☐ -2

Math On the Spot
my.hrw.com

Graphing the Solutions of an Inequality

A **solution of an inequality** that contains a variable is any value of the variable that makes the inequality true. For example, 7 is a solution of $x > -2$, since $7 > -2$ is a true statement.

EXAMPLE 1

CA CC 6.EE.5

Graph the solutions of each inequality. Check the solutions.

A $y \leq -3$

STEP 1 Draw a solid circle at -3 to show that -3 is a solution.

STEP 2 Shade the number line to the left of -3 to show that numbers less than -3 are solutions.

Use a solid circle for an inequality that uses $\geq$ or $\leq$.

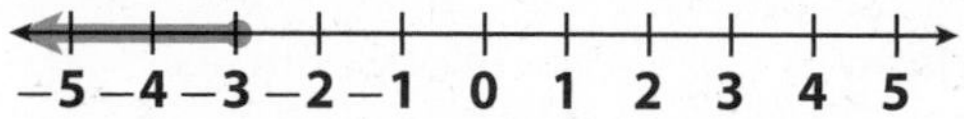

STEP 3 Check your solution.

Choose a number that is on the shaded section of the number line, such as -4. Substitute -4 for y.

$-4 \leq -3$ -4 is less than -3, so -4 is a solution.

B $1 < m$

STEP 1 Draw an empty circle at 1 to show that 1 is not a solution.

STEP 2 Shade the number line to the right of 1 to show that numbers greater than 1 are solutions.

Use an open circle for an inequality that uses $>$ or $<$.

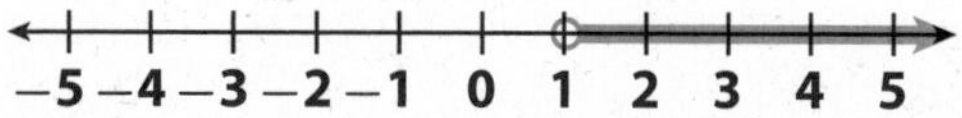

STEP 3 Check your answer.
Substitute 2 for m.
$1 < 2$ 1 is less than 2, so 2 is a solution.

Math Talk
Mathematical Practices
Is $-4\frac{1}{4}$ a solution of $y \leq -3$? Is -5.6?

My Notes

Reflect

1. **Critique Reasoning** Inez says you can rewrite $1 < m$ as $m > 1$. Do you agree? Explain.

___

2. **Analyze Relationships** How is $x < 5$ different from $x \leq 5$?

___

___

YOUR TURN

3. Graph the solutions of the inequality $t \leq -4$.

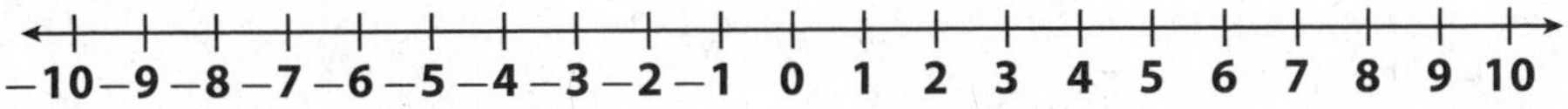

Personal Math Trainer
Online Practice and Help
my.hrw.com

Math On the Spot
my.hrw.com

Animated Math
my.hrw.com

Writing Inequalities

You can write an inequality to model the relationship between an algebraic expression and a number, or to represent certain real-world situations. The variable in an inequality can represent an infinite number of numbers.

EXAMPLE 2 Real World

CA CC 6.EE.8, 6.EE.6

A Write an inequality that represents the phrase *the sum of* y *and 2 is greater than 5*. Draw a graph to represent the inequality.

STEP 1 Write the inequality.

The sum of y and 2 is greater than 5.

$y + 2 \quad > \quad 5$

STEP 2 Graph the solution.

Use mental math: For $y + 2$ to have a value greater than 5, y must be a number greater than 3.

y is any number that meets the condition *greater than* 3.

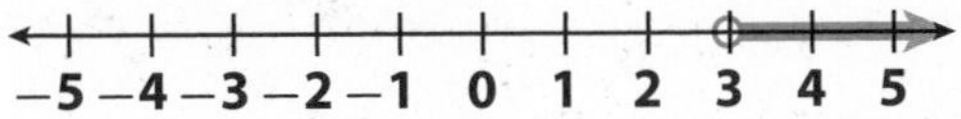

STEP 3 Check your solution by substituting a number greater than 3, such as 4, into the original inequality.

$4 + 2 > 5$ Substitute 4 for y.

$6 > 5$ 6 is greater than 5, so 4 is a solution.

Math Talk
Mathematical Practices
Describe the numbers that the variable in **A** represents.

B To test the temperature rating of a coat, a scientist keeps the temperature below 5 °C. Write and graph an inequality to represent this situation.

STEP 1 Write the inequality. Let t represent the temperature in the lab.

$t < 5$ The temperature must be less than 5 °C.

STEP 2 Graph the inequality.

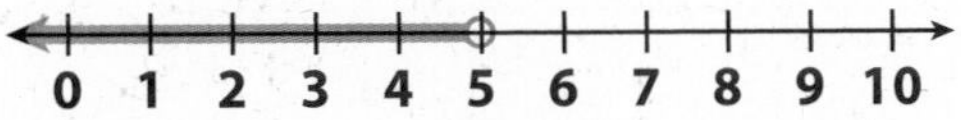

Personal Math Trainer

Online Practice and Help

my.hrw.com

YOUR TURN

4. Write an inequality that represents the phrase *the sum of 1 and y is greater than or equal to 3*. Check to see if $y = 1$ is a solution.

5. The temperature in February was at most 6 °F. Write and graph an inequality to represent the situation. Tell what the variable represents.

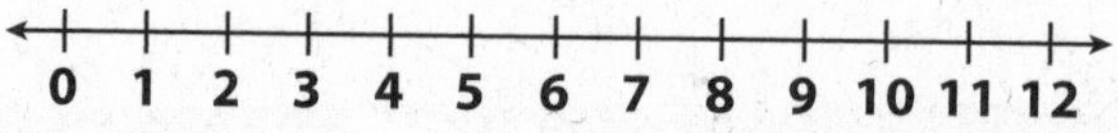

Guided Practice

1. Graph $1 \leq x$. Use the graph to determine which of these numbers are solutions of the inequality: $-1, 3, 0, 1$ (Explore Activity and Example 1)

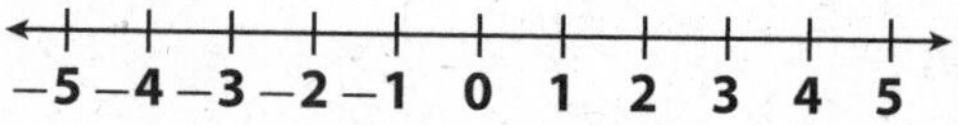

2. Graph $-3 > z$. Check the graph using substitution. (Example 1)

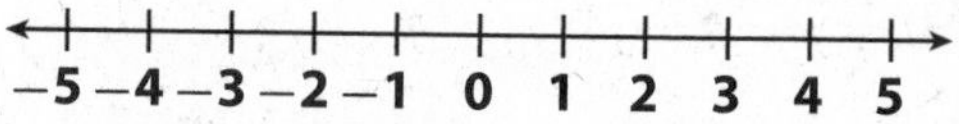

3. Write an inequality that represents the phrase *the product of 3 and x is greater than 6*. Draw a graph that represents the inequality, and check your solution. (Example 2)

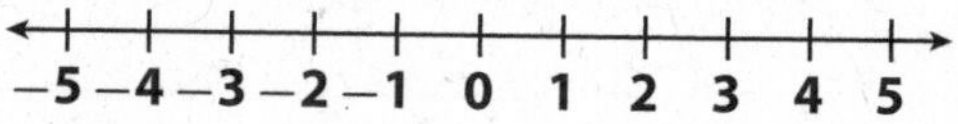

4. During hibernation, a garter snake's body temperature never goes below 3 °C. Write and graph an inequality that represents this situation. Tell what the variable represents. (Example 2)

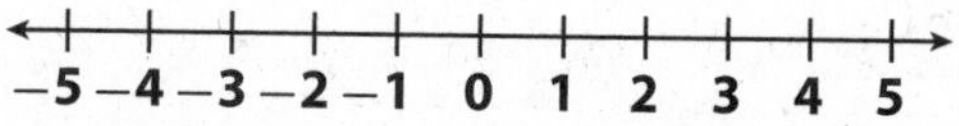

ESSENTIAL QUESTION CHECK-IN

5. Write an inequality to represent this situation: Nina wants to take at least $15 to the movies. How did you decide which inequality symbol to use?

Name ________________ Class ________________ Date ________________

11.4 Independent Practice

CA CC 6.EE.5, 6.EE.6, 6.EE.8

Personal Math Trainer

Online Practice and Help

6. Which of the following numbers are solutions of $x \geq 0$?

$-5, 0.03, -1, 0, 1.5, -6, \frac{1}{2}$ ________________

Graph the solutions of each inequality. Check the solutions.

7. $t - 8 \leq 0$

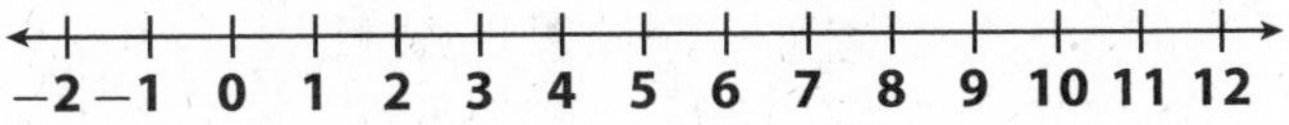

8. $-7 < h$

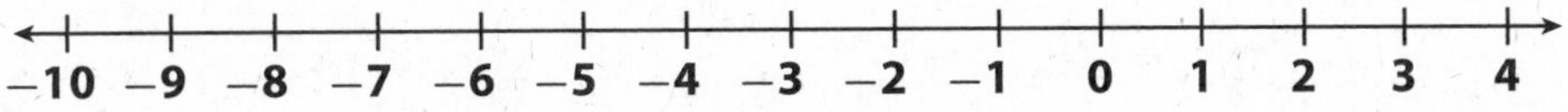

9. $x \geq -9$

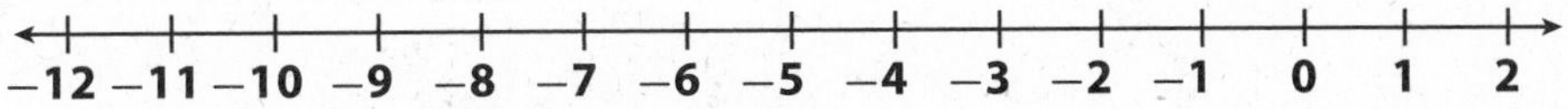

10. $2n > 5$

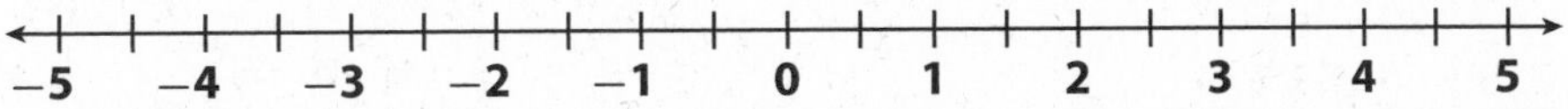

11. $-4\frac{1}{2} > x$

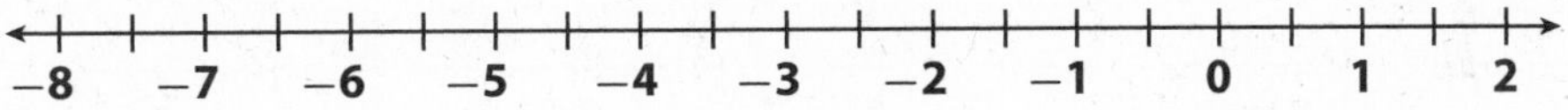

Write an inequality that matches the number line model.

12. ________________

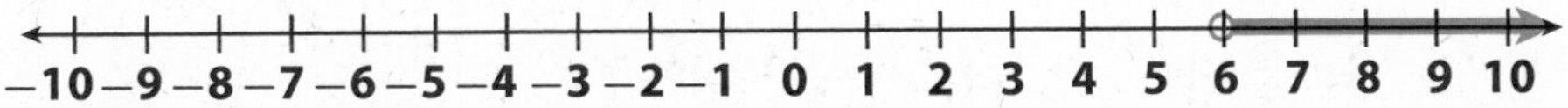

13. ________________

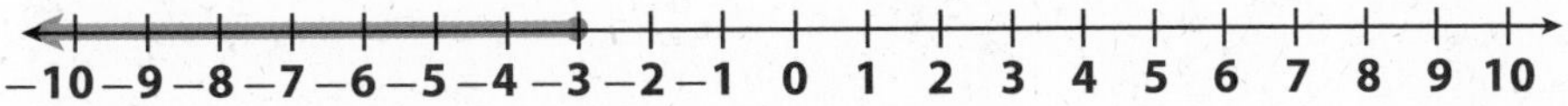

14. ________________

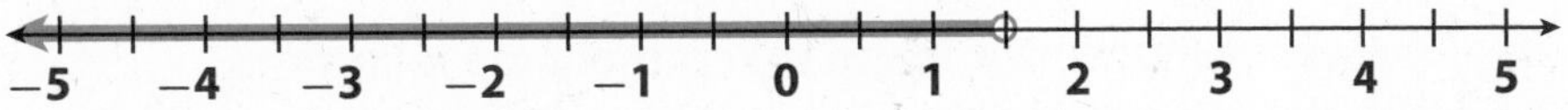

15. ________________

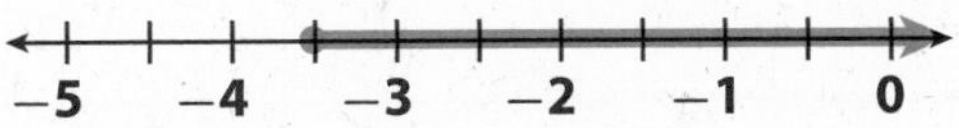

16. A child must be at least 48 inches tall to ride a roller coaster.

a. Write and graph an inequality to represent this situation. Tell what the variable represents.

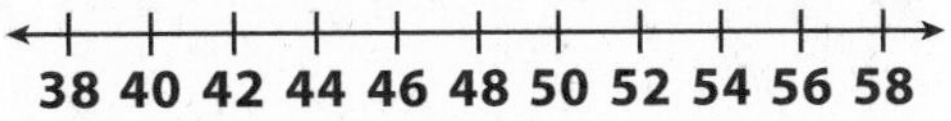

____

b. Can a child who is 46 inches tall ride the roller coaster? Explain.

____

Write and graph an inequality to represent each situation. Tell what the variable represents.

17. The stock is worth at least $14.50. ______________________

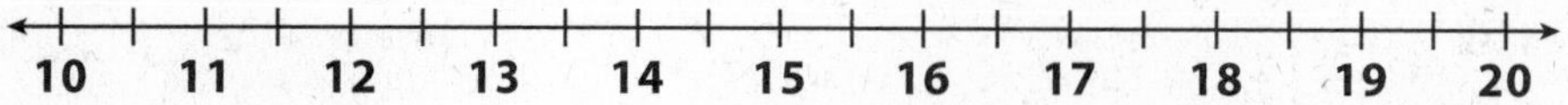

18. The temperature is less than 3.5 °F. ______________________

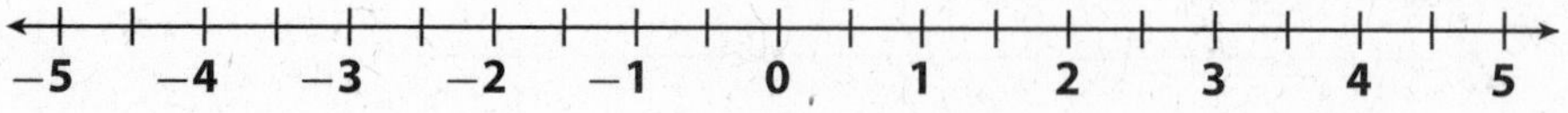

19. The goal of the fundraiser is to make more than $150. __________

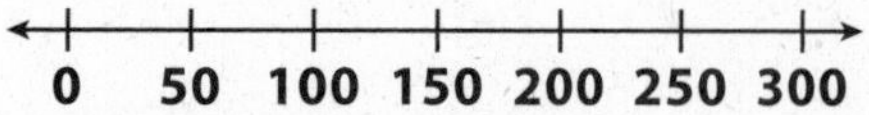

____

H.O.T. FOCUS ON HIGHER ORDER THINKING

Work Area

20. Communicate Mathematical Ideas Explain how to graph the inequality $8 \geq y$.

____

____

____

____

21. Represent Real-World Problems The number line shows an inequality. Describe a real-world situation that the inequality could represent.

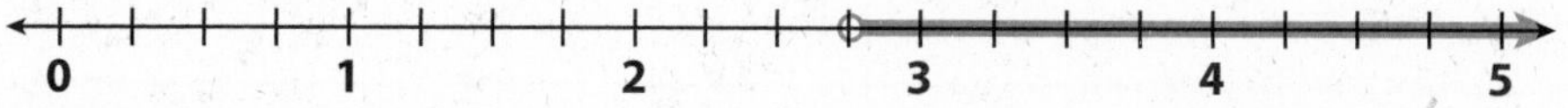

____

22. Critique Reasoning Natasha is trying to represent the following situation with a number line model: There are fewer than 5 students in the cafeteria. She has come up with two possible representations, shown below. Which representation is correct? Why?

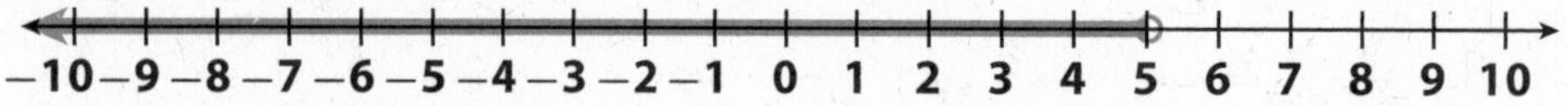

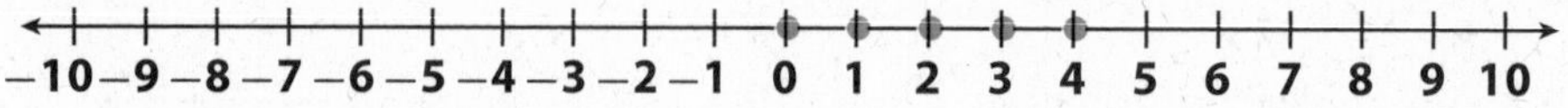

____

____

____

MODULE QUIZ

Ready to Go On?

Personal Math Trainer

Online Practice and Help

my.hrw.com

11.1 Writing Equations to Represent Situations

Determine whether the given value is a solution of the equation.

1. $\frac{b}{12} = 5; b = 60$ ________________

2. $7w = 87; w = 12$ ________________

Write an equation to represent the situation.

3. The number e of eggs in the refrigerator decreased by 5 equals 18.

____

11.2 Addition and Subtraction Equations

Solve each equation.

4. $r - 38 = 9$ ________________

5. $h + \frac{1}{2} = 3\frac{1}{4}$ ________________

6. $n + 75 = 155$ ________________

7. $q - 17 = 18$ ________________

11.3 Multiplication and Division Equations

Solve each equation.

8. $8z = 11.2$ ________________

9. $\frac{d}{14} = 7$ ________________

10. $\frac{f}{28} = 24$ ________________

11. $3a = 57$ ________________

11.4 Writing Inequalities

Write an inequality to represent each situation, then graph the solutions.

12. There are fewer than 8 gallons of gas in the tank. ________________

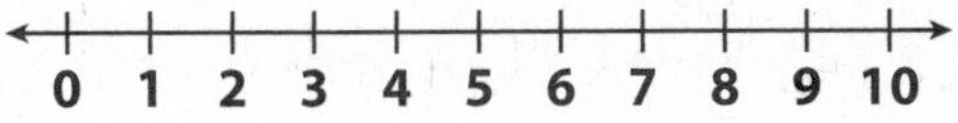

13. There are at least 3 slices of bread left in the bag. ________________

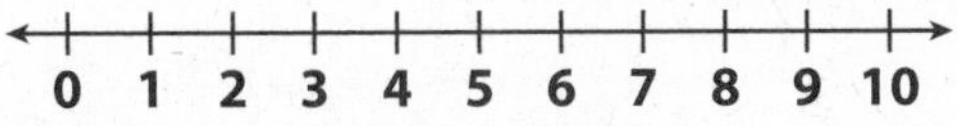

ESSENTIAL QUESTION

14. How can you solve problems involving equations that contain addition, subtraction, multiplication, or division?

____

____

MODULE 11
MIXED REVIEW

CALIFORNIA

Assessment Readiness

Personal Math Trainer

my.hrw.com

Online Practice and Help

1. Consider each inequality and number line representation.

Select Yes or No in A–C to tell if the inequality is represented correctly on the number line.

A. $x < 6$ 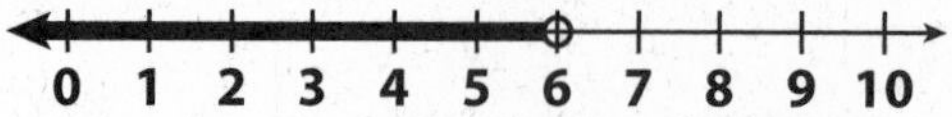

○ Yes ○ No

B. $x \geq 6$ 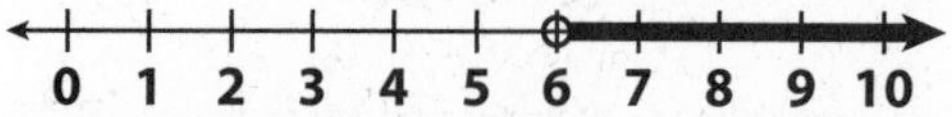

○ Yes ○ No

C. $x \leq 6$ 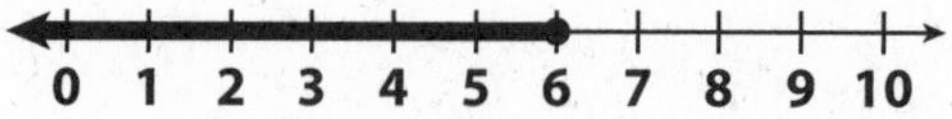

○ Yes ○ No

2. Choose True or False for A–C.

A. $y = 7$ is the solution of $y + 7 = 0$. ○ True ○ False

B. $y = 21$ is the solution of $\frac{y}{3} = 7$. ○ True ○ False

C. $y = 5$ is the solution of $5y = 1$. ○ True ○ False

3. Katie has read 34% of a book. If she has read 85 pages, does she have more than or fewer than 125 pages left to read? Explain.

4. Sylvia can work at most 15 hours per week at her part-time job. Last week she worked 12 hours and earned $84. She hopes to earn more than $100 next week. Explain how to use equations and inequalities to determine whether she can do so.

Relationships in Two Variables

MODULE 12

CALIFORNIA

ESSENTIAL QUESTION

How can you use relationships in two variables to solve real-world problems?

Real-World Video

A two-variable equation can represent an animal's distance over time. A graph can display the relationship between the variables. You can graph two or more animals' data to visually compare them.

my.hrw.com

GO DIGITAL

my.hrw.com

my.hrw.com

Go digital with your write-in student edition, accessible on any device.

Math On the Spot

Scan with your smart phone to jump directly to the online edition, video tutor, and more.

Animated Math

Interactively explore key concepts to see how math works.

Personal Math Trainer

Get immediate feedback and help as you work through practice sets.

Are YOU Ready?

Complete these exercises to review skills you will need for this module.

Personal Math Trainer

my.hrw.com

Online Practice and Help

Multiplication Facts

EXAMPLE $8 \times 7 = \blacksquare$

Use a related fact you know.

$7 \times 7 = 49$

Think: $8 \times 7 = (7 \times 7) + 7$

$= 49 + 7$

$= 56$

Multiply.

1. 7×6 ______ **2.** 10×9 ______ **3.** 13×12 ______ **4.** 8×9 ______

Write the rule for each table.

5.

x	1	2	3	4
y	7	14	21	28

______

6.

x	1	2	3	4
y	7	8	9	10

______

7.

x	1	2	3	4
y	5	10	15	20

______

8.

x	0	4	8	12
y	0	2	4	6

______

Graph Ordered Pairs (First Quadrant)

EXAMPLE

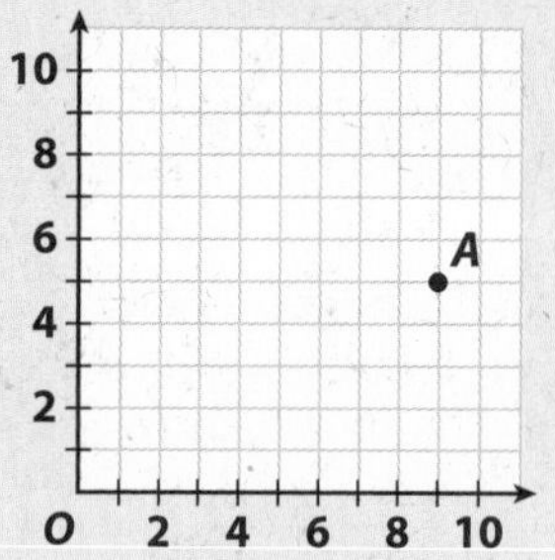

Start at the origin.
Move 9 units right.
Then move 5 units up.
Graph point *A*(9, 5).

Graph each point on the coordinate grid above.

9. *B* (0, 8) **10.** *C* (2, 3) **11.** *D* (6, 7) **12.** *E* (5, 0)

Reading Start-Up

Visualize Vocabulary

Use the ✔ words to complete the chart.

Parts of the Algebraic Expression $14 + 3x$		
Definition	**Mathematical Representation**	**Review Word**
A specific number whose value does not change	14	
A number that is multiplied by a variable in an algebraic expression	3	
A letter or symbol used to represent an unknown	x	

Understand Vocabulary

Complete the sentences using the preview words.

1. The numbers in an ordered pair are ____________________.

2. A ______________________________ is formed by two number lines that intersect at right angles.

Vocabulary

Review Words

✔ coefficient *(coeficiente)*
✔ constant *(constante)*
equation *(ecuación)*
negative number *(número negativo)*
positive number *(número positivo)*
scale *(escala)*
✔ variable *(variable)*

Preview Words

axes *(ejes)*
coordinate plane *(plano cartesiano)*
coordinates *(coordenadas)*
dependent variable *(variable dependiente)*
independent variable *(variable independiente)*
ordered pair *(par ordenado)*
origin *(origen)*
quadrants *(cuadrante)*
x-axis *(eje x)*
x-coordinate *(coordenada x)*
y-axis *(eje y)*
y-coordinate *(coordenada y)*

Active Reading

Layered Book Before beginning the module, create a layered book to help you learn the concepts in this module. Label each flap with lesson titles from this module. As you study each lesson, write important ideas such as vocabulary and formulas under the appropriate flap. Refer to your finished layered book as you work on exercises from this module.

GETTING READY FOR

Relationships in Two Variables

CALIFORNIA

Understanding the standards and the vocabulary terms in the standards will help you know exactly what you are expected to learn in this module.

CA CC 6.EE.9

Use variables to represent two quantities in a real-world problem that change in relationship to one another; write an equation to express one quantity, thought of as the dependent variable, in terms of the other quantity, thought of as the independent variable. ...

Key Vocabulary

equation *(ecuación)*
A mathematical sentence that shows that two expressions are equivalent.

What It Means to You

You will learn to write an equation that represents the relationship in a table.

EXAMPLE 6.EE.9

Emily has a dog-walking service. She charges a daily fee of \$7 to walk a dog twice a day. Create a table that shows how much Emily earns for walking 1, 6, 10, and 15 dogs. Write an equation that represents the situation.

Dogs walked	1	6	10	15
Earnings (\$)	7	42	70	105

Earnings is 7 times the number of dogs walked. Let the variable *e* represent earnings and the variable *d* represent the number of dogs walked.

$$e = 7 \times d$$

CA CC 6.EE.9

...Analyze the relationship between the dependent and independent variables using graphs and tables, and relate these to the equation.

Key Vocabulary

coordinate plane
(plano cartesiano)
A plane formed by the intersection of a horizontal number line called the *x*-axis and a vertical number line called the *y*-axis.

Visit **my.hrw.com** to see all **CA Common Core Standards** explained.

my.hrw.com

What It Means to You

You can use words, a table, a graph, or an equation to model the same mathematical relationship.

EXAMPLE 6.EE.9

The equation $y = 4x$ represents the total cost y for x games of miniature golf. Make a table of values and a graph for this situation.

Number of games, *x*	1	2	3	4
Total cost (\$), *y*	4	8	12	16

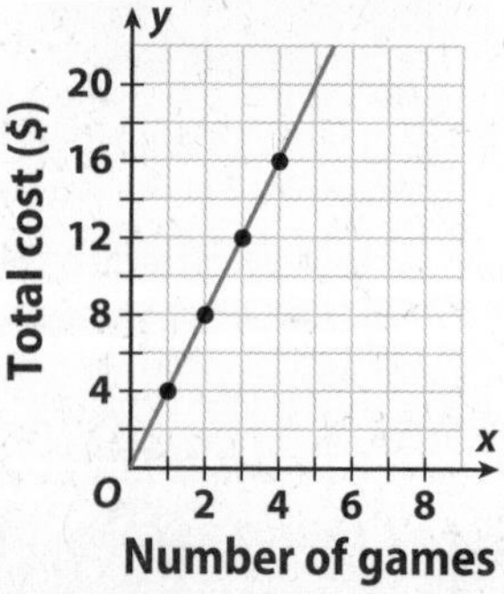

LESSON 12.1

Graphing on the Coordinate Plane

CA CC 6.NS.6c

Find and position integers and other rational numbers on a horizontal or vertical number line diagram; find and position pairs of integers and other rational numbers on a coordinate plane. *Also 6.NS.6, 6.NS.6b, 6.NS.8*

ESSENTIAL QUESTION

How do you locate and name points in the coordinate plane?

Naming Points in the Coordinate Plane

Math On the Spot

my.hrw.com

A **coordinate plane** is formed by two number lines that intersect at right angles. The point of intersection is 0 on each number line.

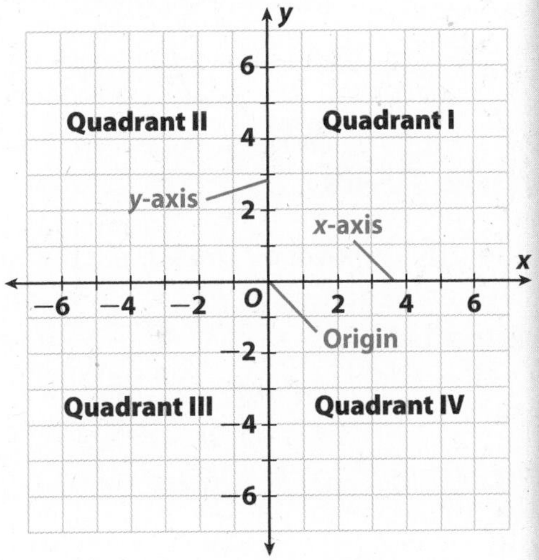

- The two number lines are called the **axes**.
- The horizontal axis is called the ***x*-axis**.
- The vertical axis is called the ***y*-axis**.
- The point where the axes intersect is called the **origin**.
- The two axes divide the coordinate plane into four **quadrants**.

An **ordered pair** is a pair of numbers that gives the location of a point on a coordinate plane. The first number tells how far to the right (positive) or left (negative) the point is located from the origin. The second number tells how far up (positive) or down (negative) the point is located from the origin.

The numbers in an ordered pair are called **coordinates**. The first number is the ***x*-coordinate** and the second number is the ***y*-coordinate**.

EXAMPLE 1

CA CC 6.NS.6c, 6.NS.6b

Identify the coordinates of each point. Name the quadrant where each point is located.

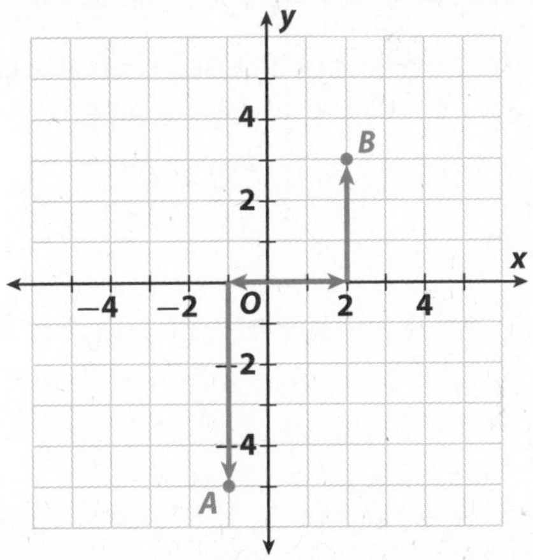

Point *A* is 1 unit *left* of the origin, and 5 units *down*. It has *x*-coordinate −1 and *y*-coordinate −5, written (−1, −5). It is located in Quadrant III.

Point *B* is 2 units *right* of the origin, and 3 units *up*. It has *x*-coordinate 2 and *y*-coordinate 3, written (2, 3). It is located in Quadrant I.

Reflect

1. If both coordinates of a point are negative, in which quadrant is the point located? ______________________

2. Describe the coordinates of all points in Quadrant I.

____

3. **Communicate Mathematical Ideas** Explain why (−3, 5) represents a different location than (3, 5).

____

____

____

YOUR TURN

Identify the coordinates of each point. Name the quadrant where each point is located.

4. *G* ______________

5. *E* ______________

6. *F* ______________

7. *H* ______________

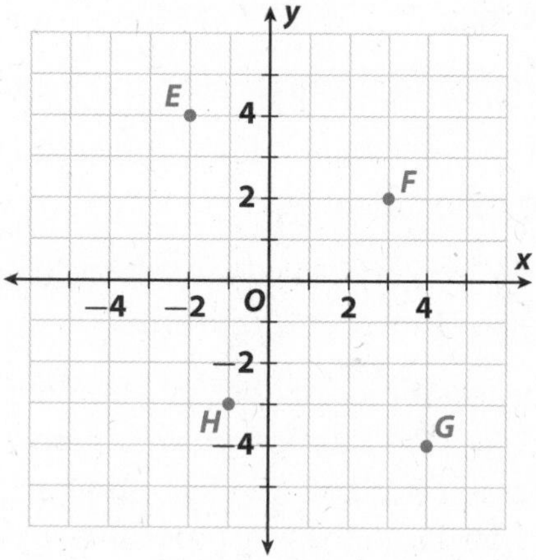

Math On the Spot
my.hrw.com

Graphing Points in the Coordinate Plane

Points that are located on the axes are not located in any quadrant. Points on the *x*-axis have a *y*-coordinate of 0, and points on the *y*-axis have an *x*-coordinate of 0.

EXAMPLE 2

CA CC 6.NS.6c, 6.NS.6

Graph and label each point on the coordinate plane.

***A*(−5, 2), *B*(3, 1.5), *C*(0, −3)**

Point *A* is 5 units *left* and 2 units *up* from the origin.

Point *B* is 3 units *right* and 1.5 units *up* from the origin. Graph the point halfway between (3, 1) and (3, 2).

Point *C* is 3 units *down* from the origin. Graph the point on the *y*-axis.

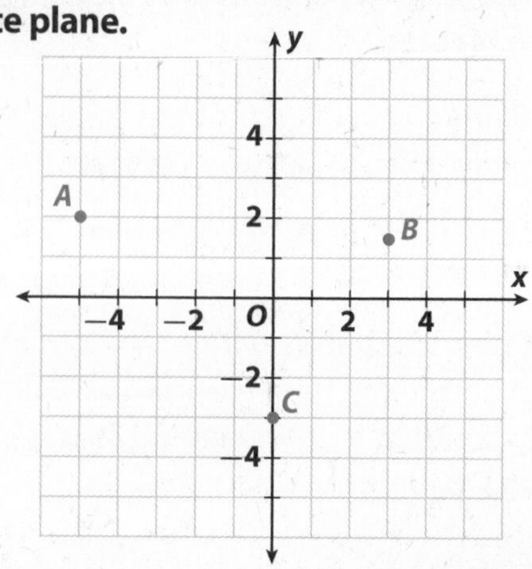

YOUR TURN

Graph and label each point on the coordinate plane.

8. $P(-4, 2)$

9. $Q(3, 2.5)$

10. $R(-4.5, -5)$

11. $S(4, -5)$

12. $T(-2.5, 0)$

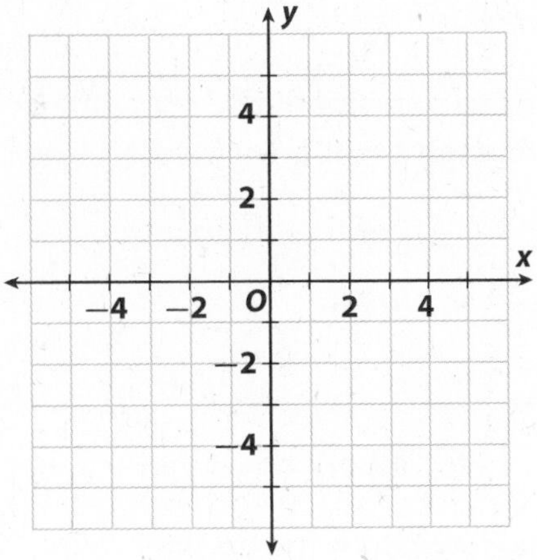

Personal Math Trainer
Online Practice and Help
my.hrw.com

Reading Scales on Axes

The *scale* of an axis is the number of units that each grid line represents. So far, the graphs in this lesson have a scale of 1 unit, but graphs frequently use other units.

Math On the Spot
my.hrw.com

EXAMPLE 3 Real World

CA CC 6.NS.8

The graph shows the location of a city. It also shows the location of Gary's and Jen's houses. The scale on each axis represents miles.

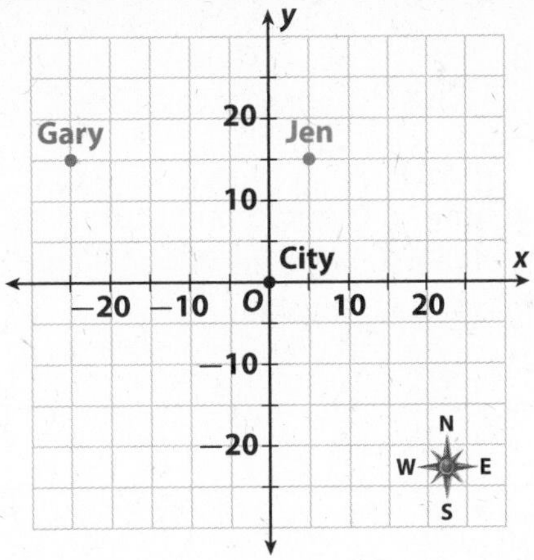

A Use the scale to describe Gary's location relative to the city.

Each grid square is 5 miles on a side.

Gary's house is at $(-25, 15)$, which is 25 miles west and 15 miles north of the city.

B Describe the location of Jen's house relative to Gary's house.

Jen's house is located 6 grid squares to the right of Gary's house. Since each grid square is 5 miles on a side, her house is $6 \cdot 5 = 30$ miles from Gary's.

Math Talk
Mathematical Practices

How are north, south, east, and west represented on the graph in Example 3?

YOUR TURN

Use the graph in Example 3.

13. Ted lives 20 miles south and 20 miles west of the city represented on the graph in Example 3. His brother Ned lives 45 miles north of Ted's house. Give the coordinates of each brother's house.

____

Personal Math Trainer
Online Practice and Help
my.hrw.com

Guided Practice

Identify the coordinates of each point in the coordinate plane. Name the quadrant where each point is located. (Example 1)

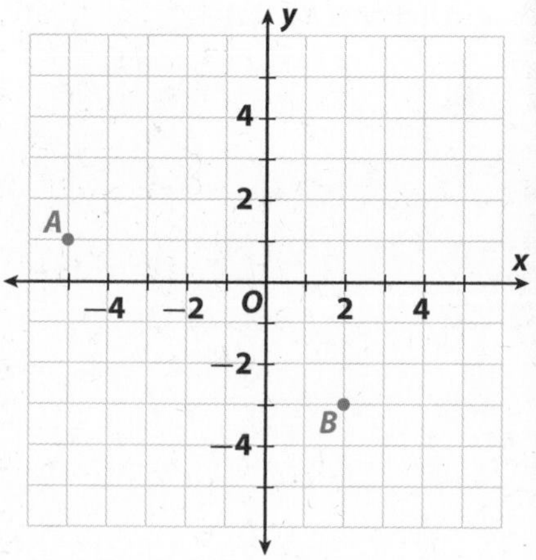

1. Point A is 5 units ________ of the origin and

   1 unit ________ from the origin.

   Its coordinates are ________. It is in quadrant ________.

2. Point B is ________ units right of the origin

   and ________ units down from the origin.

   Its coordinates are ________. It is in quadrant ________.

Graph and label each point on the coordinate plane above. (Example 2)

3. Point C at $(-3.5, 3)$

4. Point D at $(5, 0)$

For 5–7, use the coordinate plane shown. (Example 3)

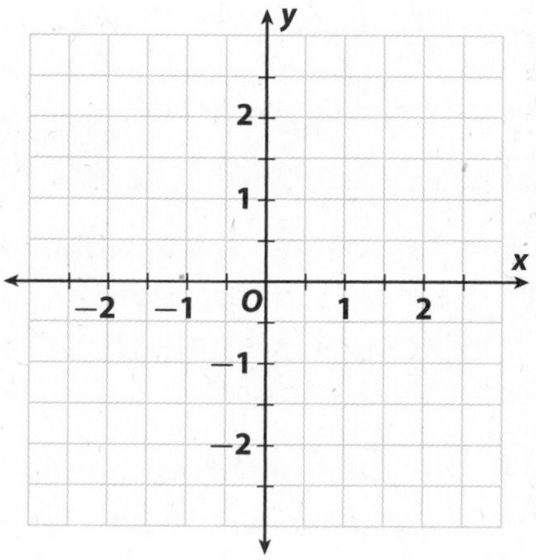

5. Describe the scale of the graph.

   ____

6. Plot point A at $\left(-\frac{1}{2}, 2\right)$.

7. Plot point B at $\left(2\frac{1}{2}, -2\right)$.

8. **Vocabulary** Describe how an ordered pair represents a point on a coordinate plane. Include the terms x-coordinate, y-coordinate, and origin in your answer.

   ____

   ____

   ____

   ____

ESSENTIAL QUESTION CHECK-IN

9. Give the coordinates of one point in each of the four quadrants, one point on the x-axis, and one point on the y-axis.

   ____

   ____

   ____

Name ______ Class ______ Date ______

12.1 Independent Practice

CA CC 6.NS.6, 6.NS.6b, 6.NS.6c, 6.NS.8

Personal Math Trainer
Online Practice and Help
my.hrw.com

For 10–13, use the coordinate plane shown. Each unit represents 1 kilometer.

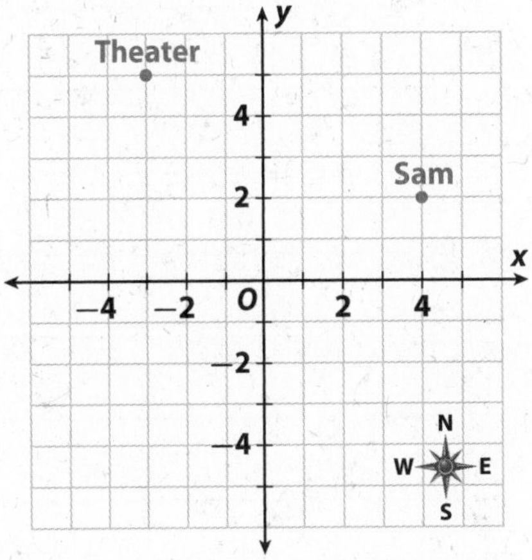

10. Write the ordered pairs that represent the location of Sam and the theater.

______

11. Describe Sam's location relative to the theater.

______

______

12. Sam wants to meet his friend Beth at a restaurant before they go to the theater. The restaurant is 9 kilometers south of the theater. Plot and label a point representing the restaurant. What are the coordinates of the point?

______

13. Beth describes her current location: "I'm directly south of the theater, halfway to the restaurant." Plot and label a point representing Beth's location. What are the coordinates of the point?

______

For 14–15, use the coordinate plane shown.

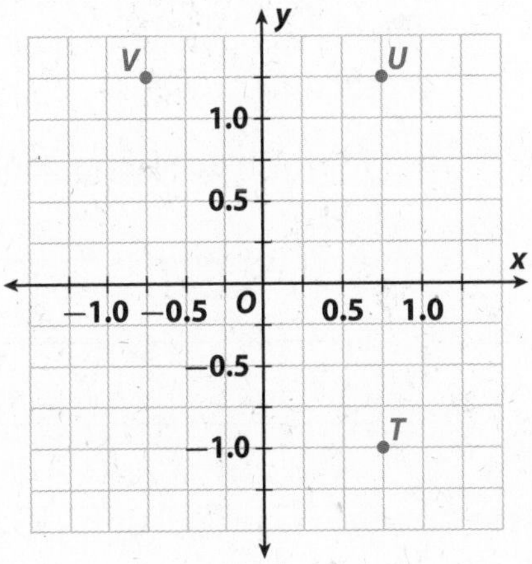

14. Find the coordinates of points *T*, *U*, and *V*.

______

15. Points *T*, *U*, and *V* are the vertices of a rectangle. Point *W* is the fourth vertex. Plot point *W* and give its coordinates.

______

16. Explain the Error Janine tells her friend that ordered pairs that have an *x*-coordinate of 0 lie on the *x*-axis. She uses the origin as an example. Describe Janine's error. Use a counterexample to explain why Janine's statement is false.

______

______

______

H.O.T. FOCUS ON HIGHER ORDER THINKING

Work Area

17. Critical Thinking Choose scales for the coordinate plane shown so that you can graph the points $J(2, 40)$, $K(3, 10)$, $L(3, -40)$, $M(-4, 50)$, and $N(-5, -50)$. Explain why you chose the scale for each axis.

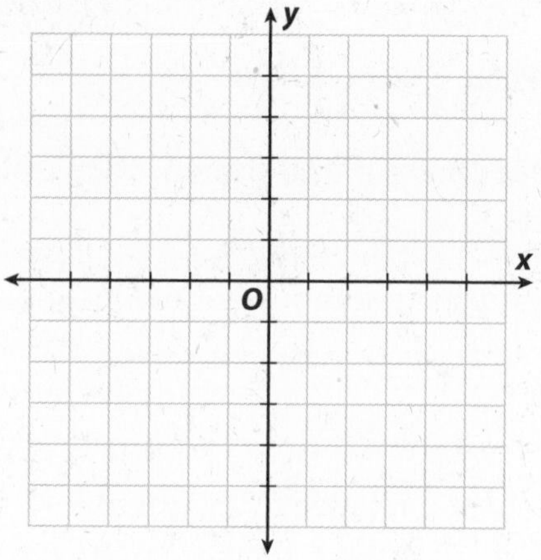

18. Communicate Mathematical Ideas Edgar wants to plot the ordered pair (1.8, −1.2) on a coordinate plane. On each axis, one grid square equals 0.1. Starting at the origin, how can Edgar find (1.8, −1.2)?

19. Represent Real-World Problems Zach graphs some ordered pairs in the coordinate plane. The *x*-values of the ordered pairs represent the number of hours since noon, and the *y*-values represent the temperature at that time.

a. In which quadrants could Zach graph points? Explain your thinking.

b. In what part of the world and at what time of year might Zach collect data so that the points he plots are in Quadrant IV?

LESSON 12.2

Independent and Dependent Variables in Tables and Graphs

CA CC 6.EE.9

Use variables to represent two quantities in a real-world problem that change in relationship to one another; write an equation to express one quantity, thought of as the dependent variable, in terms of the other quantity, thought of as the independent variable. Analyze the relationship between the dependent and independent variables using graphs and tables, and relate these to the equation.

ESSENTIAL QUESTION

How can you identify independent and dependent quantities from tables and graphs?

EXPLORE ACTIVITY 1 Real World CA CC 6.EE.9

Identifying Independent and Dependent Quantities from a Table

Many real-world situations involve two variable quantities in which one quantity depends on the other. The quantity that depends on the other quantity is called the **dependent variable**, and the quantity it depends on is called the **independent variable**.

A freight train moves at a constant speed. The distance *y* in miles that the train has traveled after *x* hours is shown in the table.

Time *x* (h)	0	1	2	3
Distance *y* (mi)	0	50	100	150

A What are the two quantities in this situation?

____

Which of these quantities depends on the other?

____

What is the independent variable? ______________

What is the dependent variable? ______________

B How far does the train travel each hour? ______________

The relationship between the distance traveled by the train and the time in hours can be represented by an equation in two variables.

Distance traveled (miles)	=	Distance traveled per hour	·	Time (hours)
↓		↓		↓
y	=	50	·	x

EXPLORE ACTIVITY 1 *(cont'd)*

Reflect

1. **Analyze Relationships** Describe how the value of the independent variable is related to the value of the dependent variable.

____

2. What are the units of the independent variable and of the dependent variable?

____

____

3. A rate is used in the equation. What is the rate?

____

EXPLORE ACTIVITY 2 Real World CA CC 6.EE.9

Identifying Independent and Dependent Variables from a Graph

In Explore Activity 1, you used a table to represent a relationship between an independent variable (time) and a dependent variable (distance). You can also use a graph to show this relationship.

An art teacher has 20 pounds of clay but wants to buy more clay for her class. The amount of clay *x* purchased by the teacher and the amount of clay *y* available for the class are shown on the graph.

A If the teacher buys 10 more pounds of clay, how many pounds will be available for the art class? __________ lb

If the art class has a total of 50 pounds of clay available, how many pounds of clay did the teacher buy?

How can you use the graph to find this information?

____

____

____

Clay Used in Art Class

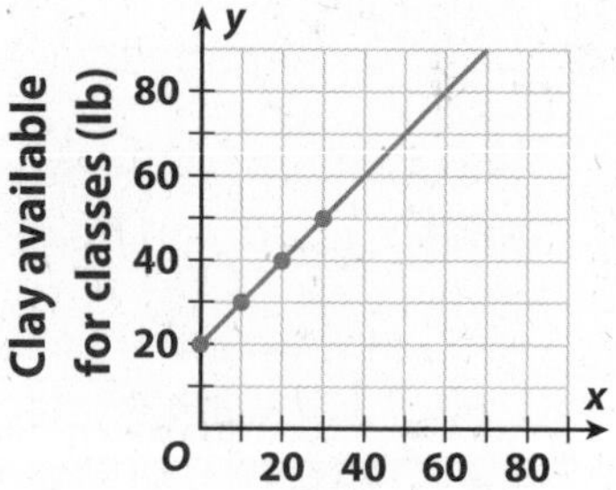

B What are the two quantities in this situation?

____

____

Which of these quantities depends on the other?

____

____

What is the independent variable? ____________________

What is the dependent variable? ____________________

C The relationship between the amount of clay purchased by the teacher and the amount of clay available to the class can be represented by an equation in two variables.

Amount of clay available (pounds)	=	Current amount of clay (pounds)	+	Amount of clay purchased (pounds)
↓		↓		↓
y	=	20	+	x

D Describe in words how the value of the independent variable is related to the value of the dependent variable.

____

____

Reflect

4. In this situation, the same units are used for the independent and dependent variables. How is this different from the situation involving the train in Explore Activity 1?

____

____

5. **Analyze Relationships** Suppose the clay the teacher buys is available only in 10 pound packages. How would the graph be different from the one shown on the facing page?

____

6. What are the units of the independent variable, and what are the units of the dependent variable?

independent variable: ____________; dependent variable: ____________

Math On the Spot

my.hrw.com

Describing Relationships Between Independent and Dependent Variables

Thinking about how one quantity depends on another helps you identify which quantity is the independent variable and which quantity is the dependent variable. In a graph, the independent variable is usually shown on the horizontal axis and the dependent variable on the vertical axis.

EXAMPLE 1 Real World

CA CC 6.EE.9

A The table shows a relationship between two variables, *x* and *y*. Describe a possible situation the table could represent. Describe the independent and dependent variables in the situation.

Independent variable, *x*	0	1	2	3
Dependent variable, *y*	10	11	12	13

The value of y is always 10 units greater than the value of x.

The table could represent Jina's savings if each day she has $10 more than the number of days she has been saving.

The independent variable, *x*, is the number of days she has been adding money to her savings.
The dependent variable, *y*, is her savings after *x* days.

Math Talk
Mathematical Practices
Describe the possible values for each variable in the relationship in **A**.

B The graph shows a relationship between two variables. Describe a possible situation that the graph could represent. Describe the independent and dependent variables.

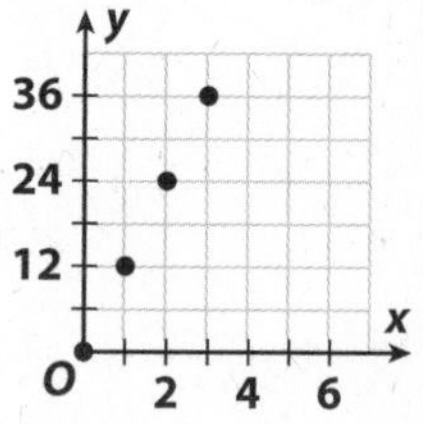

The value of y is always 12 times the value of x.

The graph could represent the number of eggs in cartons that each hold 12 eggs.

The independent variable, *x*, is the number of cartons.
The dependent variable, *y*, is the total number of eggs.

Reflect

7. What are other possible situations that the table and graph in the Examples could represent?

YOUR TURN

Describe real-world values that the variables could represent. Describe the relationship between the independent and dependent variables.

8.

x	0	1	2	3
y	15	16	17	18

9.

x	0	1	2	3	4
y	0	16	32	48	64

10.

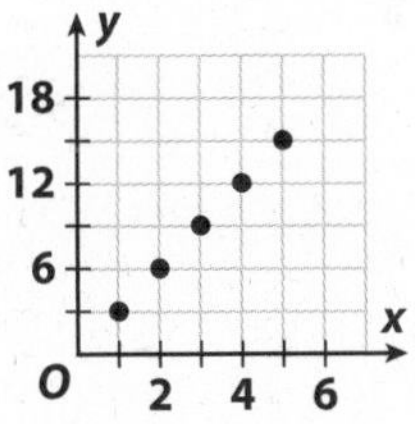

Personal Math Trainer
Online Practice and Help
my.hrw.com

Guided Practice

1. A boat rental shop rents paddleboats for a fee plus an additional cost per hour. The cost of renting for different numbers of hours is shown in the table.

Time (hours)	0	1	2	3
Cost ($)	10	11	12	13

What is the independent variable, and what is the dependent variable? How do you know? (Explore Activity 1)

____

2. A car travels at a constant rate of 60 miles per hour. (Explore Activity 1)

Time *x* (h)	0	1	2	3
Distance *y* (mi)				

a. Complete the table.

b. What is the independent variable, and what is the dependent?

____

c. Describe how the value of the independent variable is related to the value of the dependent variable.

____

Use the graph to answer the questions.

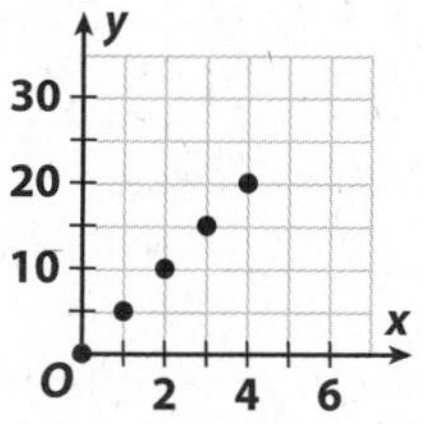

3. Describe in words how the value of the independent variable is related to the value of the dependent variable. (Explore Activity 2)

____

____

4. Describe a real-world situation that the graph could represent. Then describe the possible values for each variable. (Example 1)

____

____

____

ESSENTIAL QUESTION CHECK-IN

5. How can you identify the dependent and independent variables in a real-world situation modeled by a graph?

____

____

____

Name_________________________ Class_________________ Date_____________

12.2 Independent Practice

CA CC 6.EE.9

Personal Math Trainer
my.hrw.com
Online Practice and Help

6. The graph shows the relationship between the hours a soccer team practiced after the season started and their total practice time for the year.

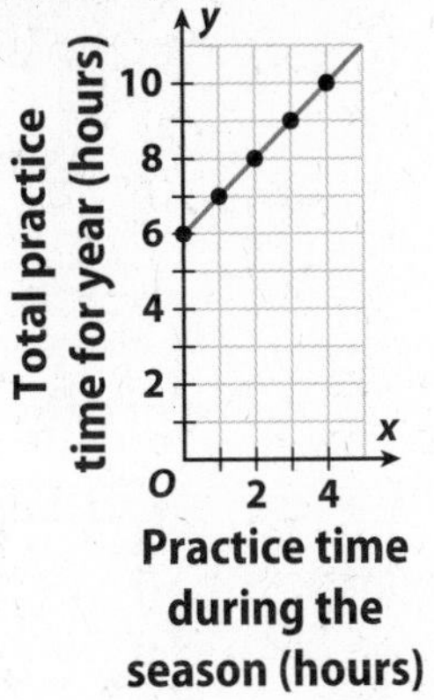

a. How many hours did the soccer team practice before the season began?

____

b. What are the two quantities in this situation?

____

____

c. What are the dependent and independent variables?

____

____

d. Describe the possible values for each variable.

____

____

e. **Analyze Relationships** Describe how the value of the independent variable is related to the value of the dependent variable.

____

____

f. **Analyze Relationships** Describe the relationship between the quantities in words.

____

____

7. **Multistep** Teresa is buying glitter markers to put in gift bags. The table shows the relationship between the number of gift bags and the number of glitter markers she needs to buy.

Number of gift bags, x	0	1	2	3
Number of markers, y	0	5	10	15

a. What is the dependent variable? ____________________

b. What is the independent variable? ____________________

c. Describe the relationship between the quantities in words.

____

8. Ty borrowed $500 from his parents. The graph shows how much he owes them each month if he pays back a certain amount each month.

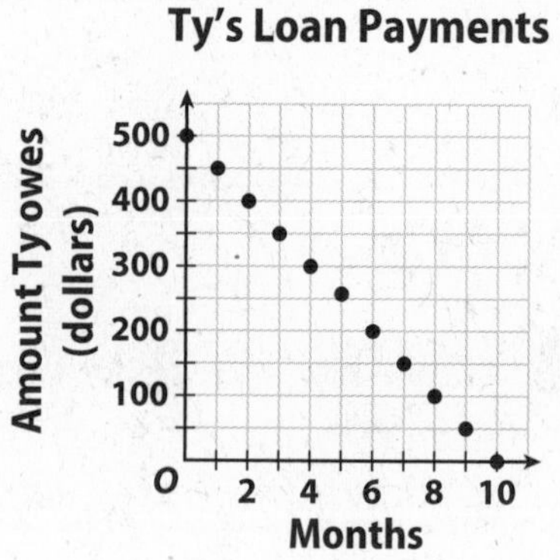

a. Describe the relationship between the number of months and the amount Ty owes. Identify an independent and dependent variable and explain your thinking.

____

____

____

____

____

____

b. How long will it take Ty to pay back his parents?

____

H.O.T. FOCUS ON HIGHER ORDER THINKING

Work Area

9. Error Analysis A discount store has a special: 8 cans of juice for a dollar. A shopper decides that since the number of cans purchased is 8 times the number of dollars spent, the cost is the independent variable and the number of cans is the dependent variable. Do you agree? Explain.

____

____

____

____

10. Analyze Relationships Provide an example of a real-world relationship where there is no clear independent or dependent variable. Explain.

____

____

____

____

____

____

____

LESSON
12.3 Writing Equations from Tables

CA CC 6.EE.9

Use variables to represent two quantities in a real-world problem that change in relationship to one another; write an equation to express one quantity, thought of as the dependent variable, in terms of the other quantity, thought of as the independent variable. Analyze the relationship between the dependent and independent variables using graphs and tables, and relate these to the equation.

ESSENTIAL QUESTION

How can you use an equation to show a relationship between two variables?

EXPLORE ACTIVITY Real World CA CC 6.EE.9

Writing an Equation to Represent a Real-World Relationship

You can write an equation to model a real-world situation that involves two variable quantities in which one quantity depends on the other.

The table shows how much Armand earns for walking 1, 2, or 3 dogs. Use the table to determine how much Armand earns per dog. Then write an equation that models the relationship between number of dogs walked and earnings. Use your equation to complete the table.

Dogs walked	1	2	3	5	10	20
Earnings	$8	$16	$24			

For 1 dog, Armand earns $1 \cdot 8 = \$8$. For 2 dogs, he earns $2 \cdot 8 = \$16$.

A For each column, compare the number of dogs walked and earnings. What is the pattern?

____

____

B Based on the pattern, Armand earns $ ______ for each dog he walks.

C Write an equation that relates the number of dogs Armand walks to the amount he earns. Let *e* represent earnings and *d* represent dogs.

____

D Use your equation to complete the table for 5, 10, and 20 walked dogs.

E Armand's earnings depend on ______________________.

Reflect

1. **What If?** If Armand changed the amount earned per dog to $11, what equation could you write to model the relationship between number of dogs walked and earnings? ______________________

Math On the Spot
my.hrw.com

Writing an Equation Based on a Table

The relationship between two variables where one variable depends on the other can be represented in a table or by an equation. An equation expresses the dependent variable in terms of the independent variable.

When there is no real-world situation to consider, we usually say x is the independent variable and y is the dependent variable. The value of y depends on the value of x.

Animated Math
my.hrw.com

EXAMPLE 1

CA CC 6.EE.9

Write an equation that expresses y in terms of x.

A

x	1	2	3	4	5
y	0.5	1	1.5	2	2.5

STEP 1 Compare the x- and y-values to find a pattern.

Each y-value is $\frac{1}{2}$, or 0.5 times, the corresponding x-value.

STEP 2 Use the pattern to write an equation expressing y in terms of x.

$y = \frac{1}{2}x$ or $y = 0.5x$

B

x	2	4	6	8	10
y	5	7	9	11	13

STEP 1 Compare the x- and y-values to find a pattern.

Each y-value is 3 more than the corresponding x-value.

STEP 2 Use the pattern to write an equation expressing y in terms of x.

$y = x + 3$

Math Talk
Mathematical Practices

How can you check that your equations are correct?

YOUR TURN

For each table, write an equation that expresses y in terms of x.

2.

x	12	11	10
y	10	9	8

____

3.

x	10	12	14
y	25	30	35

____

4.

x	5	4	3
y	10	9	8

____

5.

x	0	1	2
y	0	2	4

____

Personal Math Trainer
Online Practice and Help
my.hrw.com

Using Tables and Equations to Solve Problems

You can use tables and equations to solve real-world problems.

Math On the Spot
my.hrw.com

EXAMPLE 2 Problem Solving

CA CC 6.EE.9

A certain percent of the sale price of paintings at a gallery will be donated to charity. The donation will be \$50 if a painting sells for \$200. The donation will be \$75 if a painting sells for \$300. Find the amount of the donation if a painting sells for \$1,200.

Analyze Information

You know the donation amount when the sale price of a painting is \$200 and \$300. You need to find the donation amount if a painting sells for \$1,200.

Formulate a Plan

You can make a table to help you determine the relationship between sale price and donation amount. Then you can write an equation that models the relationship. Use the equation to find the unknown donation amount.

Solve

Make a table.

Sale price (\$)	200	300
Donation amount (\$)	50	75

$\frac{50}{200} = \frac{50 \div 2}{200 \div 2} = \frac{25}{100} = 25\%$ $\frac{75}{300} = \frac{75 \div 3}{300 \div 3} = \frac{25}{100} = 25\%$

One way to determine the relationship between sale price and donation amount is to find the percent.

Write an equation. Let p represent the sale price of the painting. Let d represent the donation amount to charity.

The donation amount is equal to 25% of the sale price.

$d = 0.25 \cdot p$

p is the independent variable; its value does not depend on any other value. d is the dependent variable; its value depends on the price of the painting.

Find the donation amount when the sale price is \$1,200.

$d = 0.25 \cdot p$

$d = 0.25 \cdot 1{,}200$ *Substitute \$1,200 for the sale price of the painting.*

$d = 300$ *Simplify to find the donation amount.*

When the sale price is \$1,200, the donation to charity is \$300.

Justify and Evaluate

Substitute values from the table for p and d to check that they are solutions of the equation $d = 0.25 \cdot p$. Then check your answer of \$300 by substituting for d and solving for p.

$d = 0.25 \cdot p$	$d = 0.25 \cdot p$	$d = 0.25 \cdot p$
$d = 0.25 \cdot 200$	$d = 0.25 \cdot 300$	$300 = 0.25 \cdot p$
$d = 50$ ✓	$d = 75$ ✓	$p = 1{,}200$ ✓

Personal Math Trainer

Online Practice and Help

my.hrw.com

YOUR TURN

6. When Ryan is 10, his brother Kyle is 15. When Ryan is 16, Kyle will be 21. When Ryan is 21, Kyle will be 26. Write and solve an equation to find Kyle's age when Ryan is 52. Tell what the variables represent.

____

Guided Practice

Write an equation to express *y* in terms of *x*. (Explore Activity, Example 1)

1.

x	10	20	30	40
y	6	16	26	36

____

2.

x	0	1	2	3
y	0	4	8	12

____

3.

x	4	6	8	10
y	7	9	11	13

____

4.

x	12	24	36	48
y	2	4	6	8

____

5. Jameson downloaded one digital song for $1.35, two digital songs for $2.70, and 5 digital songs for $6.75. Write and solve an equation to find the cost to download 25 digital songs. (Example 2)

Songs downloaded	1	2	5	10
Total cost ($)	1.35			

Number of songs = *n*; Cost = *c*; equation: _______________

The total cost of 25 songs is _______________

ESSENTIAL QUESTION CHECK-IN

6. Explain how to use a table to write an equation that represents the relationship in the table.

____

____

Name ______________________ Class ______________ Date ______________

12.3 Independent Practice

CA CC 6.EE.9

Personal Math Trainer
Online Practice and Help
my.hrw.com

7. **Vocabulary** What does it mean for an equation to express y in terms of x?

____

____

____

8. The length of a rectangle is 2 inches more than twice its width.

Write an equation relating the length l of the rectangle to its width w.

____

9. **Look for a Pattern** Compare the y-values in the table to the corresponding x-values. What pattern do you see? How is this pattern used to write an equation that represents the relationship between the x- and y-values?

x	20	24	28	32
y	5	6	7	8

____

____

10. **Explain the Error** A student modeled the relationship in the table with the equation $x = 4y$. Explain the student's error. Write an equation that correctly models the relationship.

x	2	4	6	8
y	8	16	24	32

____

____

11. **Multistep** Marvin earns $8.25 per hour at his summer job. He wants to buy a video game system that costs $206.25.

a. Write an equation to model the relationship between number of hours worked h and amount earned e.

____

b. Solve your equation to find the number of hours Marvin needs to work in order to afford the video game system.

____

12. **Communicate Mathematical Ideas** For every hour that Noah studies, his test score goes up 3 points. Explain which is the independent variable and which is the dependent variable. Write an equation modeling the relationship between hours studied h and the increase in Noah's test score s.

____

____

____

H.O.T. FOCUS ON HIGHER ORDER THINKING

Work Area

13. **Make a Conjecture** Compare the y-values in the table to the corresponding x-values. If possible, write an equation modeling the relationship. If, not explain why.

x	1	3	5	7
y	3	6	8	21

____

____

14. **Represent Real-World Problems** Describe a real-world situation in which there is a relationship between two quantities. Make a table that includes at least three pairs of values. Then write an equation that models the relationship between the quantities.

____

____

____

15. **Critical Thinking** Georgia knows that in the relationship between two given variables x and y, each value of y is found either by adding a given number to the corresponding value of x, or multiplying it by a given number. She only knows a single pair of x and y values. Can Georgia write an equation that models the relationship? Explain.

____

____

____

____

LESSON 12.4

Representing Algebraic Relationships in Tables and Graphs

CA CC 6.EE.9

...Analyze the relationship between the dependent and independent variables using graphs and tables, and relate these to the equation. (For the full text of the standard, see the table at the front of the book beginning on page CA2.)

ESSENTIAL QUESTION

How can you use verbal descriptions, tables, and graphs to represent algebraic relationships?

EXPLORE ACTIVITY 1 Real World

CA CC 6.EE.9

Representing Algebraic Relationships

Angie's walking speed is 5 kilometers per hour, and May's is 4 kilometers per hour. Show how the distance each girl walks is related to time.

A For each girl, make a table comparing time and distance.

Time (h)	0	1	2	3	4
Angie's distance (km)	0	5	10		

For every hour Angie walks, she travels 5 km.

Time (h)	0	1	2	3	4
May's distance (km)	0	4	8		

For every hour May walks, she travels 4 km.

B For each girl, make a graph showing her distance *y* as it depends on time *x*. Plot points from the table and connect them with a line. Write an equation for each girl that relates distance *y* to time *x*.

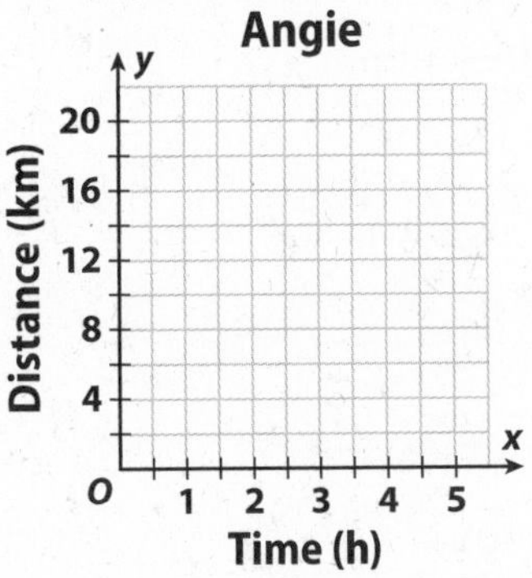

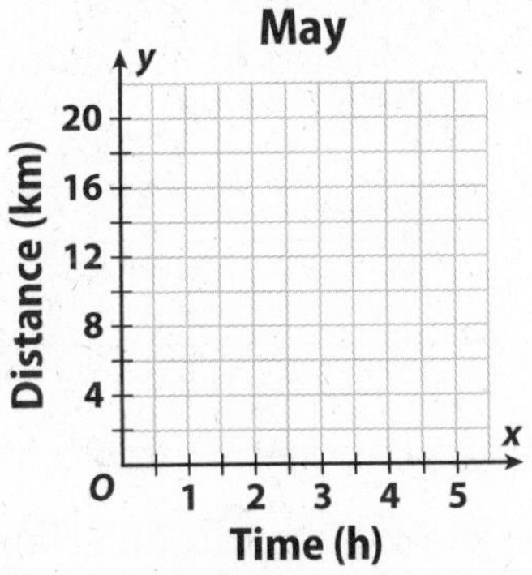

Angie's equation: ________ May's equation: ____________

Math Talk
Mathematical Practices

Why does it make sense to connect the points in each graph?

Reflect

1. **Analyze Relationships** How can you use the tables to determine which girl is walking faster? How can you use the graphs?

____

____

EXPLORE ACTIVITY 2 Real World

CA CC 6.EE.9

Writing an Equation from a Graph

Cherise pays the entrance fee to visit a museum, then buys souvenirs at the gift shop. The graph shows the relationship between the total amount she spends at the museum and the amount she spends at the gift shop. Write an equation to represent the relationship.

A Read the ordered pairs from the graph. Use them to complete a table comparing total spent *y* to amount spent at the gift shop *x*.

Gift shop amount ($)	0	5	10	15	
Total amount ($)	5	10			

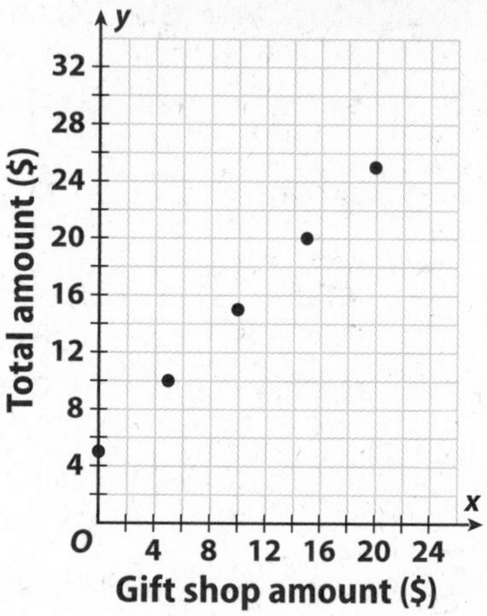

B What is the pattern in the table?

____

____

C Write an equation that expresses the total amount spent, *y*, in terms of the amount spent at the gift shop, *x*.

____

Reflect

2. **Communicate Mathematical Ideas** Identify the dependent and independent quantities in this situation, and describe the possible values for each variable.

____

____

____

3. **Multiple Representations** Draw a line through the points on the graph. Find the point that represents Cherise's spending $18 at the gift shop. Use this point to find the total she would spend if she spent $18 at the gift shop. Then use your equation from **C** to verify your answer.

____

4. **Draw Conclusions** How can you use the graph to write an inequality that describes the possible values of *y*?

____

Graphing an Equation

An ordered pair (*x*, *y*) that makes an equation like $y = x + 1$ true is called a **solution** of the equation. The graph of an equation represents all the ordered pairs that are solutions.

Math On the Spot
my.hrw.com

EXAMPLE 1

CA CC 6.EE.9

Graph each equation.

A $y = x + 1$

STEP 1 Make a table of values. Choose some values for *x* and use the equation to find the corresponding values for *y*.

STEP 2 Plot the ordered pairs from the table.

STEP 3 Draw a line through the plotted points to represent all of the ordered pair solutions of the equation.

x	$x + 1 = y$	(x, y)
1	$1 + 1 = 2$	(1, 2)
2	$2 + 1 = 3$	(2, 3)
3	$3 + 1 = 4$	(3, 4)
4	$4 + 1 = 5$	(4, 5)
5	$5 + 1 = 6$	(5, 6)

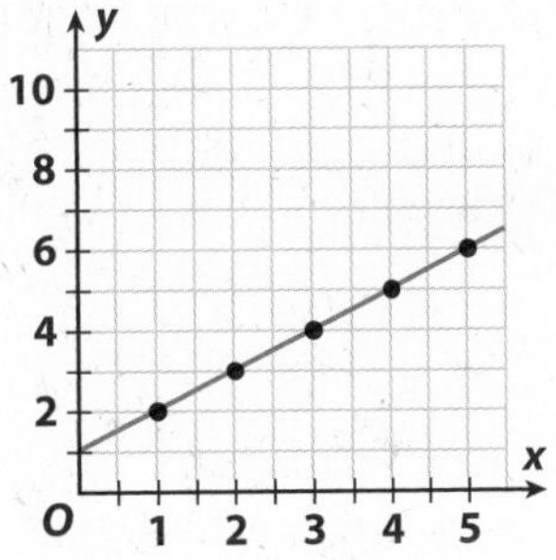

Math Talk
Mathematical Practices

Is the ordered pair (3.5, 4.5) a solution of the equation $y = x + 1$? Explain.

B $y = 2x$

STEP 1 Make a table of values. Choose some values for *x* and use the equation to find the corresponding values for *y*.

STEP 2 Plot the ordered pairs from the table.

STEP 3 Draw a line through the plotted points to represent all of the ordered pair solutions of the equation.

x	$2x = y$	(x, y)
1	$2 \cdot 1 = 2$	(1, 2)
2	$2 \cdot 2 = 4$	(2, 4)
3	$2 \cdot 3 = 6$	(3, 6)
4	$2 \cdot 4 = 8$	(4, 8)
5	$2 \cdot 5 = 10$	(5, 10)

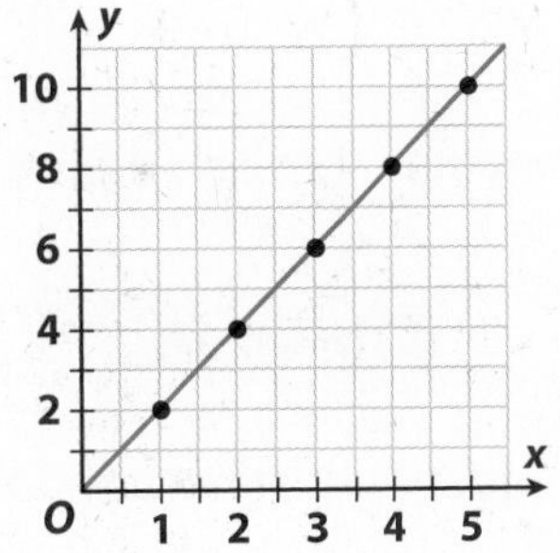

Personal Math Trainer

Online Practice and Help

my.hrw.com

YOUR TURN

5. Graph $y = x + 2.5$.

x	$x + 2.5 = y$	(x, y)

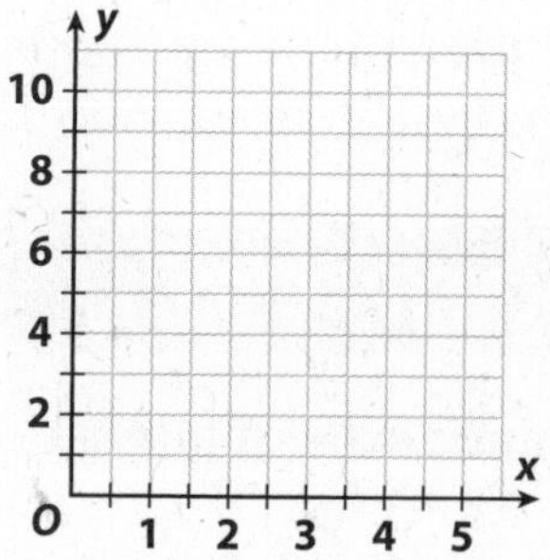

Guided Practice

Frank mows lawns in the summer to earn extra money. He can mow 3 lawns every hour he works. (Explore Activity 1 and Explore Activity 2)

1. Make a table to show the relationship between the number of hours Frank works, x, and the number of lawns he mows, y. Graph the relationship and write an equation. Label the axes of your graph.

Hours worked	Lawns mowed
0	
1	

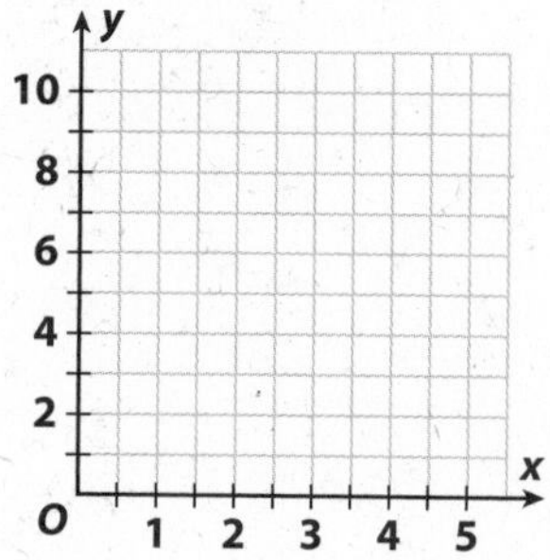

____

Graph $y = 1.5x$. (Example 1)

2. Make a table to show the relationship.

x				
y				

3. Plot the points and draw a line through them.

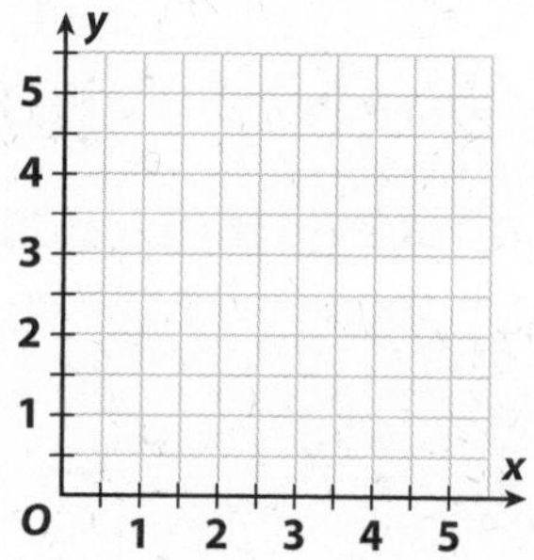

ESSENTIAL QUESTION CHECK-IN

4. Why might you use an equation instead of a table to represent an algebraic relationship?

____

____

Name ____________________ Class ____________________ Date ____________________

12.4 Independent Practice

CA CC 6.EE.9

Personal Math Trainer
Online Practice and Help
my.hrw.com

Students at Mills Middle School are required to work a certain number of community service hours. The table shows the numbers of additional hours several students worked beyond their required hours, as well as the total numbers of hours worked.

5. Read the ordered pairs from the graph to make a table.

Additional hours					
Total hours					

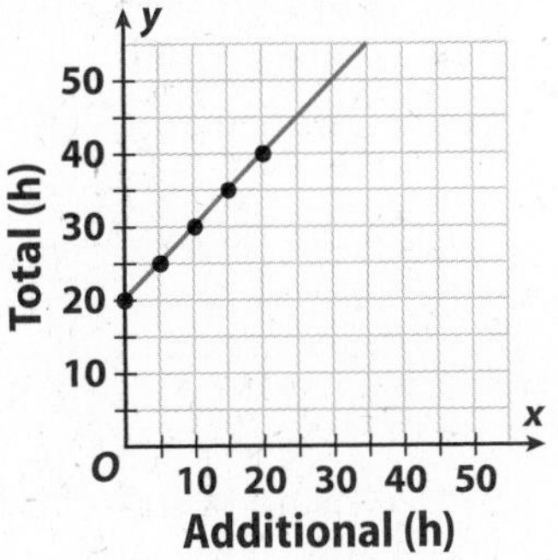

6. Write an equation that expresses the total hours in terms of the additional hours. Use an inequality to describe possible values of y.

____

7. Analyze Relationships How many community service hours are students required to work? Explain.

____

____

On a map, x represents a distance in centimeters. To find an actual distance y in kilometers, Beth uses the equation $y = 8x$.

8. Make a table comparing a distance on the map to the actual distance.

Map distance (cm)					
Actual distance (km)					

9. Make a graph that compares the map distance to the actual distance. Label the axes of the graph.

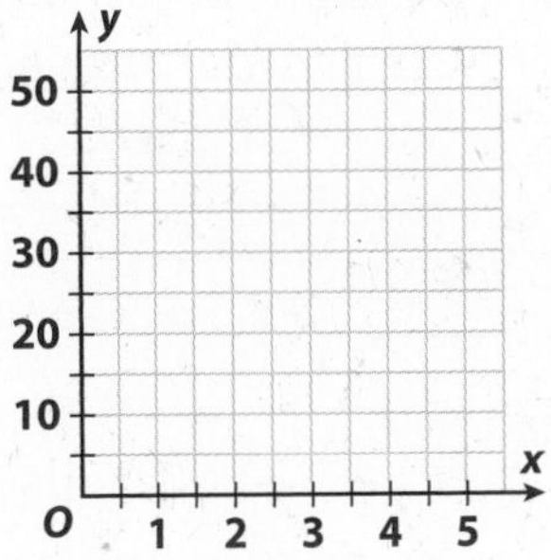

10. Critical Thinking The actual distance between Town A and Town B is 64 kilometers.

a. Use the equation to find the distance on Beth's map.

____

b. For what values of y can you use the graph to find the distance on Beth's map?

____

11. **Multistep** The equation $y = 9x$ represents the total cost y for x movie tickets. Label the axes of the graph.

a. Make a table and a graph to represent the relationship between x and y.

Number of tickets, x					
Total cost ($), y					

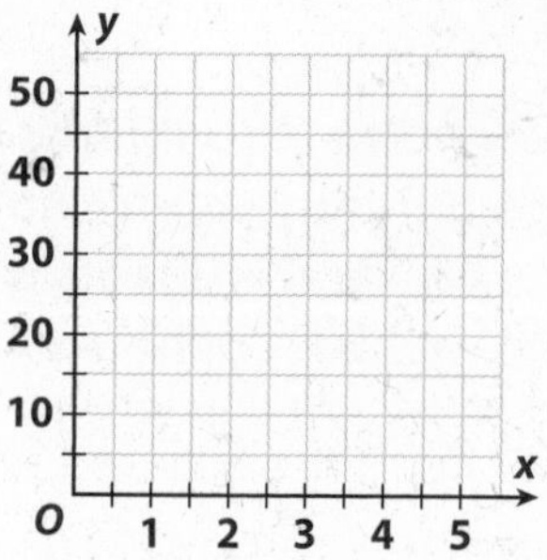

b. **Critical Thinking** In this situation, which quantity is dependent and which is independent? Justify your answer.

____

____

____

c. **Multiple Representations** Eight friends want to go see a movie. Would you prefer to use an equation, a table, or a graph to find the cost of 8 movie tickets? Explain how you would use your chosen method to find the cost.

____

____

H.O.T. FOCUS ON HIGHER ORDER THINKING

Work Area

12. **Critical Thinking** Suppose you graph $y = 5x$ and $y = x + 500$ on the same coordinate plane. Which line will be steeper? Why?

____

____

13. **Persevere in Problem Solving** Marcus plotted the points (0, 0), (6, 2), (18, 6), and (21, 7) on a graph. He wrote an equation for the relationship. Find another ordered pair that could be a solution of Marcus's equation. Justify your answer.

____

____

14. **Error Analysis** The cost of a personal pizza is $4. A drink costs $1. Anna wrote the equation $y = 4x + 1$ to represent the relationship between total cost y of buying x meals that include one personal pizza and one drink. Describe Anna's error and write the correct equation.

____

____

MODULE QUIZ

Ready to Go On?

Personal Math Trainer
Online Practice and Help
my.hrw.com

12.1 Graphing on the Coordinate Plane

Graph each point on the coordinate plane.

1. $A(-2, 4)$ **2.** $B(3, 5)$

3. $C(6, -4)$ **4.** $D(-3, -5)$

5. $E(7, 2)$ **6.** $F(-4, 6)$

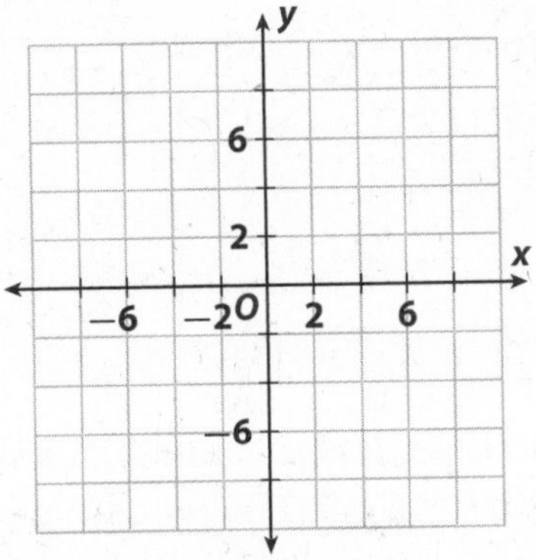

12.2 Independent and Dependent Variables in Tables and Graphs

7. Jon buys packages of pens for $5 each. Identify the independent and dependent variables in the situation.

____

12.3 Writing Equations from Tables

Write an equation that represents the data in the table.

8.

x	3	5	8	10
y	21	35	56	70

____

9.

x	5	10	15	20
y	17	22	27	32

____

12.4 Representing Algebraic Relationships in Tables and Graphs

Graph each equation.

10. $y = x + 3$

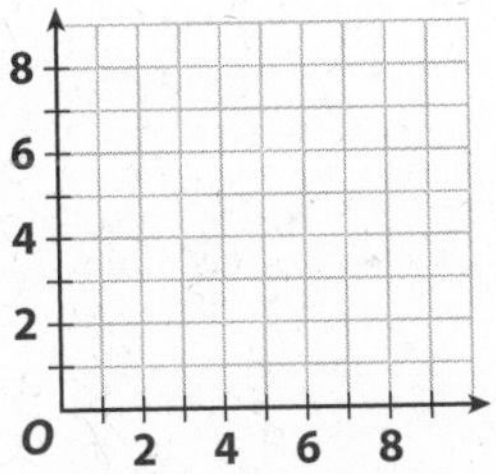

11. $y = 5x$

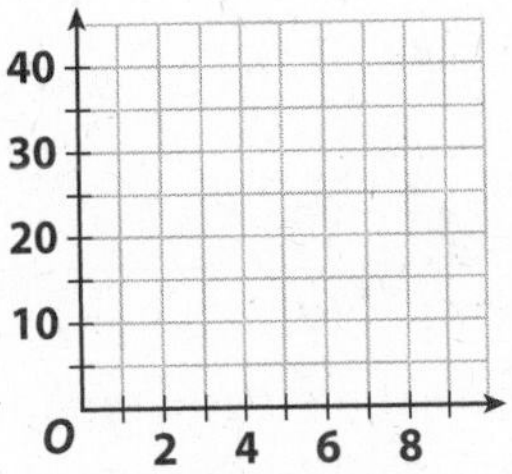

ESSENTIAL QUESTION

12. How can you write an equation in two variables to solve a problem?

____

____

MODULE 12
MIXED REVIEW

CALIFORNIA

Assessment Readiness

Personal Math Trainer
Online Practice and Help
my.hrw.com

1. Consider each point and quadrant.

Select Yes or No in A–C to tell if the point is located in the given quadrant.

A. The point (−5, −7) is in Quadrant II. ◯ Yes ◯ No

B. The point (5, −7) is in Quadrant IV. ◯ Yes ◯ No

C. The point (5, 7) is in Quadrant I. ◯ Yes ◯ No

2. Amy works and is paid by the hour. Her sister Jo helps her work. As shown in the table, Amy gives Jo part of her earnings.

Amy's pay ($)	10	20	30	40
Jo's pay ($)	2	4	6	8

Let x represent Amy's earnings and y represent her sister's earnings. Choose True or False for A–C.

A. An equation for Jo's pay is $y = 5x$. ◯ True ◯ False

B. If Jo earns $13, an equation for Amy's pay is $13 = \frac{x}{5}$. ◯ True ◯ False

C. The graph of the relationship passes through the point (2, 10). ◯ True ◯ False

3. Andy has $5\frac{1}{2}$ quarts of juice. Does he have enough to give a $\frac{2}{3}$ cup serving to each of the 32 members of the band? Explain.

4. Glenda drove at a steady rate on a road trip. Write an equation to represent the relationship between time x and distance y. Which of the points $\left(\frac{1}{4}, 52\right)$, (1.5, 78), and (−2.5, −130) are on the graph of the relationship? Explain.

Time (h)	2	3	4.5
Distance (mi)	104	156	234

UNIT 5

Study Guide Review

MODULE 11 Equations and Relationships

Key Vocabulary
equation *(ecuación)*
solution *(solución)*
solution of an inequality *(solución de una desigualdad)*

ESSENTIAL QUESTION

How can you use equations and relationships to solve real-world problems?

EXAMPLE 1

Determine if the given value is a solution of the equation.

A. $r - 5 = 17; r = 12$

$12 - 5 \stackrel{?}{=} 17$ Substitute.

$7 \neq 17$

12 is not a solution of $r - 5 = 17$.

B. $\frac{x}{6} = 7; x = 42$

$\frac{42}{6} \stackrel{?}{=} 7$ Substitute.

$7 = 7$

42 is a solution of $\frac{x}{6} = 7$.

EXAMPLE 2

Solve each equation. Check your answer.

A. $y - 12 = 10$

$+12 \quad +12$ Add 12 to both sides.

$y = 22$

Check: $22 - 12 \stackrel{?}{=} 10$ Substitute.

$10 = 10$

B. $5p = 30$

$\frac{5p}{5} = \frac{30}{5}$ Divide both sides by 5.

$p = 6$

Check: $5(6) \stackrel{?}{=} 30$ Substitute.

$30 = 30$

EXAMPLE 3

Write and graph an inequality to represent each situation.

A. There are at least 5 gallons of water in an aquarium.

$g \geq 5$

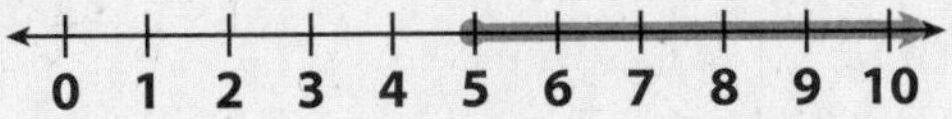

B. The temperature today will be less than 35 °F.

$t < 35$

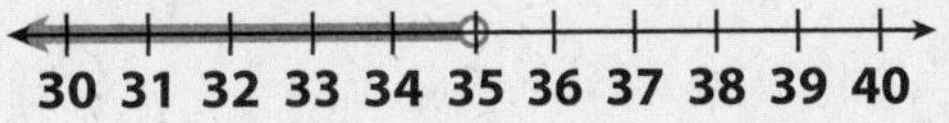

EXERCISES

Determine whether the given value is a solution of the equation. (Lesson 11.1)

1. $7x = 14; x = 3$ ____________

2. $y + 13 = 17; y = 4$ ____________

Write an equation to represent the situation. (Lesson 11.1)

3. Don has three times as much money as his brother, who has $25. ____________

4. There are s students enrolled in Mr. Rodriguez's class. There are 6 students absent and 18 students present today. ____________________

Solve each equation. Check your answer. (Lessons 11.2, 11.3)

5. $p - 5 = 18$ ____________________

6. $9q = 18.9$ ____________________

7. $3.5 + x = 7$ ____________________

8. $\frac{2}{7} = 2x$ ____________________

9. Sonia used $12.50 to buy a new journal. She has $34.25 left in her savings account. How much money did Sonia have before she bought the journal? Write and solve an equation to solve the problem. (Lesson 11.2) ____________________

Write and graph an inequality to represent each situation. (Lesson 11.4)

10. The company's stock is worth less than $2.50 per share. ____________________

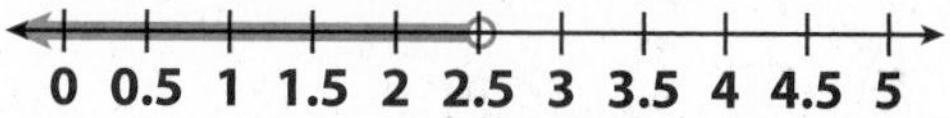

11. Tina got a haircut, and her hair is still at least 15 inches long. ____________________

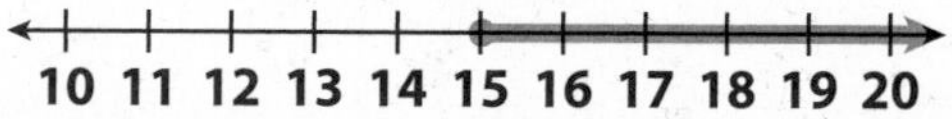

MODULE 12 Relationships in Two Variables

Key Vocabulary

axes *(ejes)*
coordinate plane *(plano cartesiano)*
coordinates *(coordenadas)*
ordered pair *(par ordenado)*
origin *(origen)*
quadrants *(cuadrantes)*
x-axis *(eje x)*

? ESSENTIAL QUESTION

How can you use relationships in two variables to solve real-world problems?

EXAMPLE 1

Graph the point (4, −2) and identify the quadrant where it is located.

(4, −2) is located 4 units to the right of the origin and 2 units down from the origin.

(4, −2) is in quadrant IV.

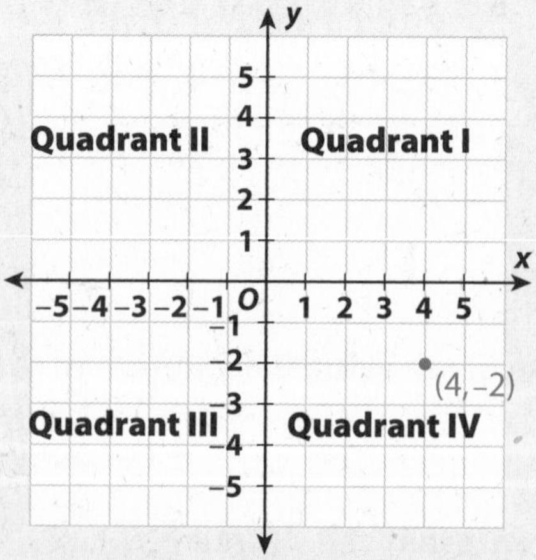

EXAMPLE 2

Tim is paid $8 more than the number of bags of peanuts he sells at the baseball stadium. The table shows the relationship between the money Tim earns and the number of bags of peanuts Tim sells. Identify the independent and dependent variables, and write an equation that represents the relationship.

Bags of peanuts, x	0	1	2	3
Money earned, y	8	9	10	11

The number of bags is the independent variable, and the money Tim earns is the dependent variable.

The equation $y = x + 8$ expresses the relationship between the number of bags Tim sells and the amount he earns.

EXERCISES

Graph and label each point on the coordinate plane. (Lesson 12.1)

1. (4, 4)

2. (−3, −1)

3. (−1, 4)

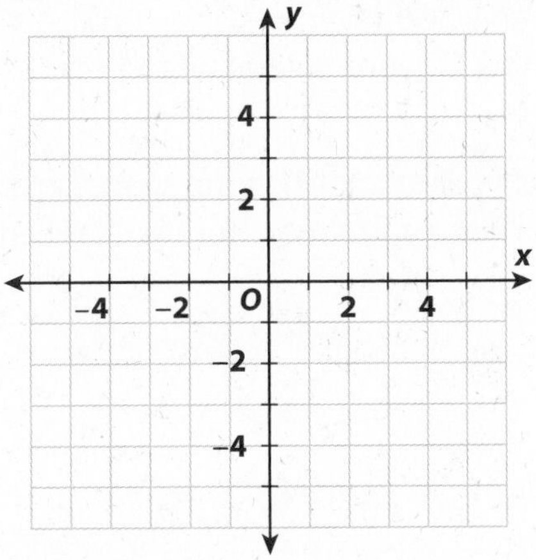

Use the graph to complete Exercises 4–6. (Lesson 12.2)

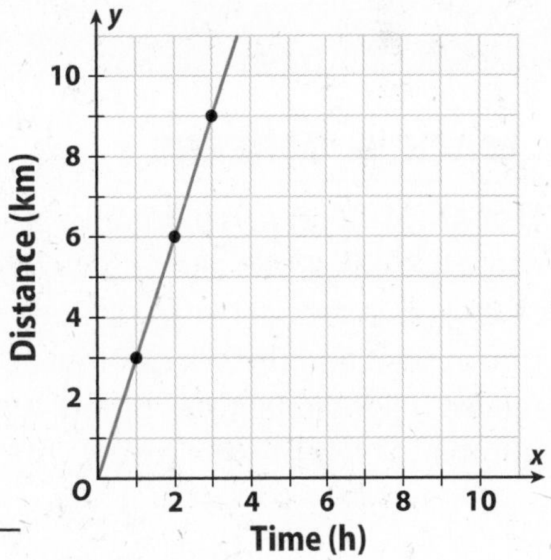

4. ________________________ is the independent variable.

5. ________________________ is the dependent variable.

6. Describe the relationship between the values of the independent and dependent variables.

____

7. Use the data in the table to write an equation to express y in terms of x. Then graph the equation. (Lessons 12.3, 12.4)

x	0	1	2	3
y	4	5	6	7

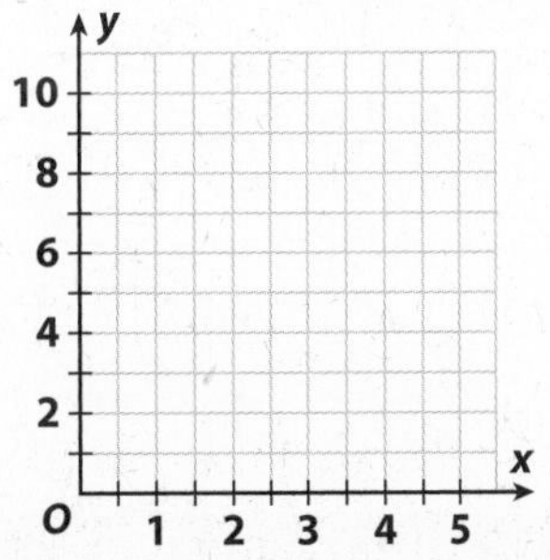

____

Unit Project

CA CC 6.NS.6c, 6.EE.9

How Fast and How Far?

Snails are among the slowest creatures on Earth. At top speed a snail can zip along at about 2 feet per minute. Peregrine falcons are among the fastest creatures, sometimes hitting 200 miles per hour. For this project, choose a favorite animal and find its top speed to the nearest whole number of miles per hour. Then create a presentation that includes the following:

- The source of information on the animal's speed
- A table giving y, the distance the animal could travel in x hours, for $x = 0, 1, 2, 3, 4, 5, 6, 7, 8, 9$, and 10. Assume the animal runs at its top speed for all values of x.
- An equation showing the relationship between y and x
- A graph showing the relationship between y and x
- An estimation, based on your graph, of how far your animal would run in 7 hours, 20 minutes, assuming top speed

Decorate your presentation with an image of your animal. Use the space below to write down any questions you have or important information from your teacher.

MATH IN CAREERS ACTIVITY

Botanist Dr. Rue is a botanist studying two trees that grow in California. The coast live oak grows at a rate of 24 inches per year and the silk oak grows at a rate of 36 inches per year. Dr. Rue measured the final height of the coast live oak tree at 64 ft and the silk oak tree at 111 ft. Write an equation for each tree that relates height in feet y to time x. Which tree reached its final height in the least number of years? Explain how you found your answer.

CALIFORNIA

UNIT 5
MIXED REVIEW

Assessment Readiness

Personal Math Trainer
Online Practice and Help
my.hrw.com

1. Does the given equation represent the situation?

Select Yes or No.

A. Bruce has 97 sports cards, and 34 of them are football cards. Find the number *y* of sports cards that are not football cards.
Equation: $97 + 34 = y$ ○ Yes ○ No

B. Sarah has read aloud 3 more times than Joel. Sarah has read aloud 9 times. Find the number of times *j* Joel has read aloud.
Equation: $j + 3 = 9$ ○ Yes ○ No

C. There are *c* pounds of cat food. This is 4 times the weight of the bag of bird seed *b*. Write the weight of the bag of cat food in terms of the weight of the bag of bird seed.
Equation: $c = \frac{b}{4}$ ○ Yes ○ No

2. Choose True or False for each statement.

A. $v = 4$ is a solution for $v + 5 \geq 9$. ○ True ○ False

B. The number line below shows the solutions to the inequality $m \leq 4.4$. ○ True ○ False

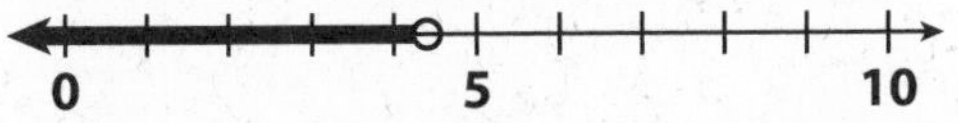

C. No more than 7 copies of a newspaper are left on a rack can be represented by the inequality $n \geq 7$. ○ True ○ False

3. Emily cycled 22 miles over 4 days. She cycled the same amount each day. How many miles per day did Emily cycle? What operation do you use to solve this problem?

4. Brian is playing a video game. He earns the same number of points for each star he picks up. He earns 2,400 points for 6 stars, 4,000 points for 10 stars, and 5,200 points for 13 stars. He says that the independent variable is the number of points he has earned. Is he correct? Explain.

Performance Tasks

★**5.** Dana, Neil, and Frank are siblings. Dana is the oldest.

a. Frank's age is one-fourth of Dana's age. Write an equation to represent Frank's age f if Dana's age is d years.

b. Neil's age is one-half of the difference between Dana's and Frank's ages. Write an equation to represent Neil's age n in terms of Dana's age d.

c. Use the equations to find Neil's and Frank's ages if Dana is 16 years old.

★★**6.** Jillian is participating in a book-reading contest to raise funds for her local library. For every book Jillian reads, her mother pledged to make a donation.

a. The table shows how much Jillian's mother will donate. Find the pattern, and give the amount her mother will donate for 9 and 21 books read.

Books read	3	5	7
Money donated	\$15	\$25	\$35

b. Write an equation showing the pattern from the table. Identify the variables.

c. Graph the equation.

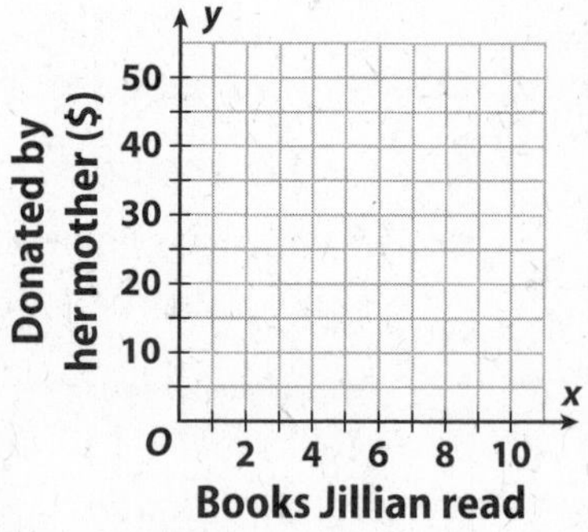

★★★**7.** Dr. Adams measures the daily height of a Sunny Yellow sunflower, beginning when the sunflower is 60 days old. At 60 days, the height is 205 centimeters. After the first 60 days, Dr. Adams finds that the growth rate is 2 centimeters per day.

a. Write an expression for the height at d days past 60 days.

b. In how many days will the sunflower reach 235 centimeters?

c. The Suntracker sunflower grows 2.5 centimeters per day after the first 60 days. If a Suntracker is 195 centimeters tall when it is 60 days old, write an expression to represent the Suntracker's height d days after 60 days. Which sunflower will be taller when it is 82 days old? Explain how you found your answer.

UNIT 6

Relationships in Geometry

MODULE 13
Area and Polygons
CA CC 6.G.1, 6.EE.7

MODULE 14
Distance and Area in the Coordinate Plane
CA CC 6.NS.6b, 6.NS.8, 6.G.3

MODULE 15
Surface Area and Volume of Solids
CA CC 6.G.2, 6.G.4, 6.EE.7

ATH IN CAREERS

Theater Set Construction A person who works in theater set construction works with the set designer to create scenery and needs technical precision when scaling and building sets based on the dimensions of the models.

If you are interested in a career in theater set construction, you should study these mathematical subjects:

- Geometry
- Algebra
- Trigonometry

Research other careers that require technical precision in scaling and building models.

ACTIVITY At the end of the unit, check out how **theater set construction** involves math.

Unit Project Preview

Which State Is It?

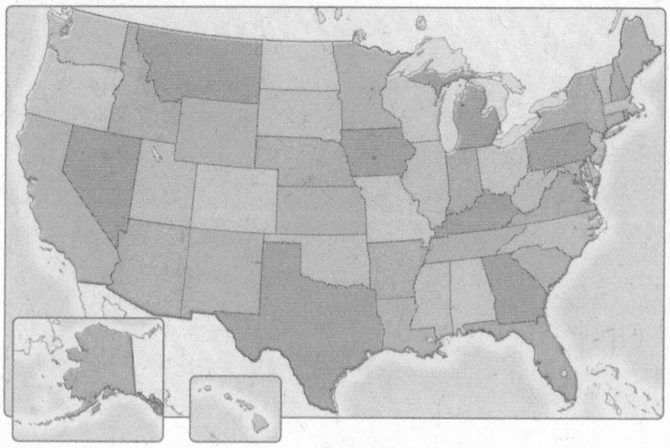

In the Unit Project at the end of this unit, you will plot points to draw the outline of one of the 50 states of the USA. Then you will identify and plot the coordinates of some landmarks in the state and calculate the state's dimensions and area. To successfully complete the Unit Project you'll need to master these skills:

- Solve problems with proportions.
- Draw polygons on the coordinate plane.
- Find distance and area on the coordinate plane.

1. On the map of a state, one boundary is $6\frac{1}{2}$ inches long. If the scale of the map is 1 in. = 68 miles, how long is the actual boundary? Explain.

____

____

2. Part of the boundary of California is determined by the coastline of the Pacific Ocean. Explain why calculating distances between points gives only an estimation of the actual length of the coastline border.

____

____

Tracking Your Learning Progression

This unit addresses important California Common Core Standards in the Critical Areas of finding area, surface area, and volumes and finding distance and area in the coordinate plane.

Domain 6.G Geometry

Cluster Solve real-world and mathematical problems involving area, surface area, and volume.

The unit also supports additional standards.

Domain 6.NS The Number System

Cluster Apply and extend previous understandings of numbers to the system of rational numbers.

Area and Polygons

MODULE 13

CALIFORNIA

? ESSENTIAL QUESTION

How can you find the area of an irregular polygon using area formulas?

Real-World Video

Painting, quilting, and other art forms use familiar geometric shapes, such as triangles and rectangles. To buy enough supplies for a project, you need to find or estimate the areas of each shape in the project.

my.hrw.com

GO DIGITAL
my.hrw.com

my.hrw.com
Go digital with your write-in student edition, accessible on any device.

Math On the Spot
Scan with your smart phone to jump directly to the online edition, video tutor, and more.

Animated Math
Interactively explore key concepts to see how math works.

Personal Math Trainer
Get immediate feedback and help as you work through practice sets.

Are YOU Ready?

Complete these exercises to review skills you will need for this module.

Personal Math Trainer

Online Practice and Help

my.hrw.com

Inverse Operations

EXAMPLES

$7k = 35$ — *k is multiplied by 7.*

$\frac{7k}{7} = \frac{35}{7}$ — *Use the inverse operation, division.*

$k = 5$

$k + 7 = 9$ — *7 is added to k.*

$k + 7 - 7 = 9 - 7$ — *Use the inverse operation, subtraction.*

$k = 2$

Solve each equation using the inverse operation.

1. $9p = 54$ ______ **2.** $m - 15 = 9$ ______ **3.** $\frac{b}{8} = 4$ ______ **4.** $z + 17 = 23$ ______

Metric Units

EXAMPLE

$6 \text{ m} = \blacksquare \text{ cm}$ — *Multiply to go from a larger unit to a smaller unit.*

$6 \text{ m} = 600 \text{ cm}$

$4{,}000 \text{ mL} = \blacksquare \text{ L}$ — *Divide to go from a smaller unit to a larger unit.*

$4{,}000 \text{ mL} = 4 \text{ L}$

Convert to the given units.

5. 64 m = ________ cm **6.** 500 g = ________ kg **7.** 4.6 kL = ________ L

Area of Squares and Rectangles

EXAMPLE

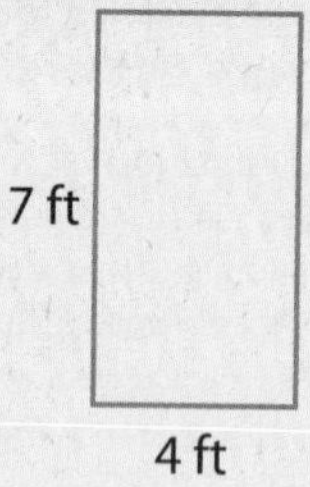

Find the area of the rectangle.

$A = bh$ — *Use the formula for the area of a rectangle.*

$= 7 \times 4$ — *Substitute for base and height.*

$= 28$

The area is 28 square feet.

8. Find the area of a rectangle with a base of 5 feet and a height of $9\frac{1}{2}$ feet ________________________

Reading Start-Up

Vocabulary

Review Words

✔ hexagon *(hexágono)*
✔ polygon *(polígono regular)*
✔ quadrilateral *(cuadrilátero)*
rectangular prism *(prisma rectangular)*
regular polygon *(polígono)*
right triangle *(triángulo rectángulo)*
✔ triangle *(triángulo)*

Preview Words

parallelogram *(paralelogramo)*
rhombus *(rombo)*
trapezoid *(trapecio)*

Visualize Vocabulary

Use the ✔ words to complete the graphic. You will put one word in each oval.

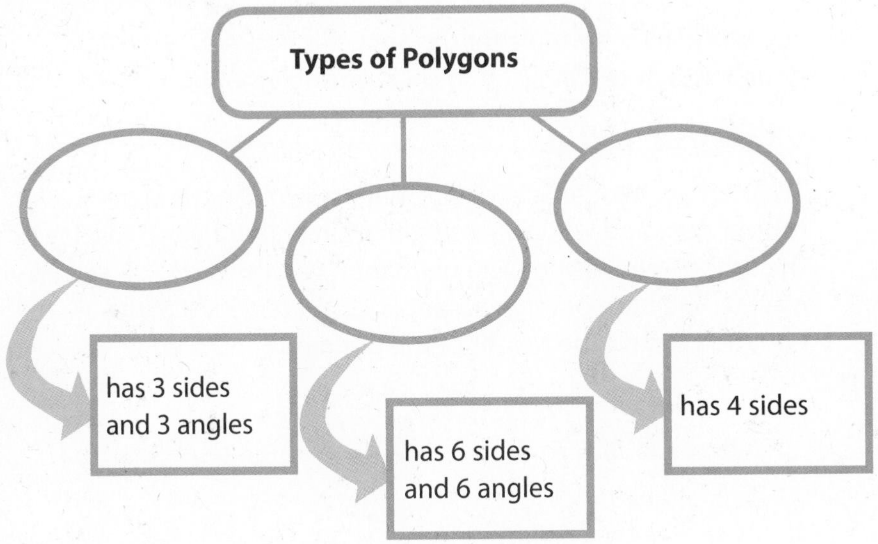

Understand Vocabulary

Match the term on the left to the correct expression on the right.

1. parallelogram — **A.** A quadrilateral in which all sides are congruent and opposite sides are parallel.

2. trapezoid — **B.** A quadrilateral in which opposite sides are parallel and congruent.

3. rhombus — **C.** A quadrilateral in which two sides are parallel.

Active Reading

Pyramid Before beginning the module, create a pyramid to help you organize what you learn. Label each side with one of the lesson titles from this module. As you study each lesson, write important ideas like vocabulary, properties, and formulas on the appropriate side.

GETTING READY FOR

Area and Polygons

Understanding the standards and the vocabulary terms in the standards will help you know exactly what you are expected to learn in this module.

CA CC 6.G.1

Find the area of right triangles, other triangles, special quadrilaterals, and polygons by composing into rectangles or decomposing into triangles and other shapes; apply these techniques in the context of solving real-world and mathematical problems.

What It Means to You

You will use the formula for the area of a figure to write an equation that can be used to solve a problem.

EXAMPLE 6.G.1

The Hudson Middle School wrestling team won the state tournament and was awarded a triangular pennant to display in the school gymnasium. The pennant has an area of 2.25 square meters. The base of the pennant is 1.5 meters long. Write an equation to find the height of the pennant.

$A = \frac{1}{2}bh$

$2.25 = \frac{1}{2}(1.5)h$

$2.25 = 0.75h$

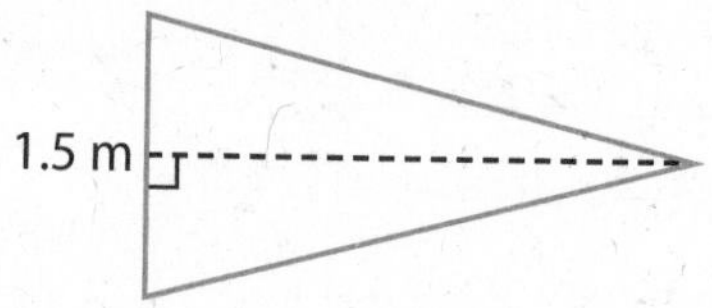

An equation to find the height of the pennant is $2.25 = 0.75h$.

CA CC 6.G.1

Find the area of right triangles, other triangles, special quadrilaterals, and polygons by composing into rectangles or decomposing into triangles and other shapes; apply these techniques in the context of solving real-world and mathematical problems.

What It Means to You

You will use formulas to find the area of irregular polygons.

EXAMPLE 6.G.1

John is measuring his room for new carpet. Find the area of the room.

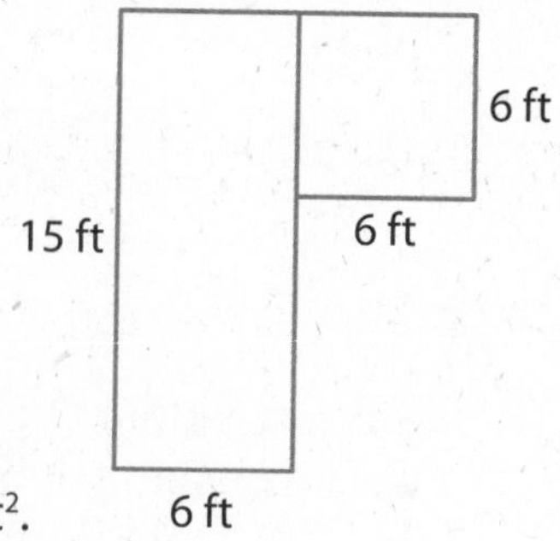

Find the area of the rectangle.

$A = bh = 15 \times 6 = 90 \text{ ft}^2$

Find the area of the square.

$A = s^2 = 6^2 = 36 \text{ ft}^2$

The total area is $90 \text{ ft}^2 + 36 \text{ ft}^2 = 126 \text{ ft}^2$.

Visit **my.hrw.com** to see all **CA Common Core Standards** explained.

my.hrw.com

LESSON 13.1

Area of Quadrilaterals

CA CC 6.G.1

Find the area of right triangles, other triangles, special quadrilaterals, and polygons by composing into rectangles or decomposing into triangles and other shapes; apply these techniques in the context of solving real-world and mathematical problems.

ESSENTIAL QUESTION

How can you find the areas of parallelograms, rhombuses, and trapezoids?

EXPLORE ACTIVITY CA CC 6.G.1

Area of a Parallelogram

Recall that a rectangle is a special type of parallelogram.

A Draw a large parallelogram on grid paper. Cut out your parallelogram.

B Cut your parallelogram along the dashed segment as shown. Then move the triangular piece to the other side of the parallelogram.

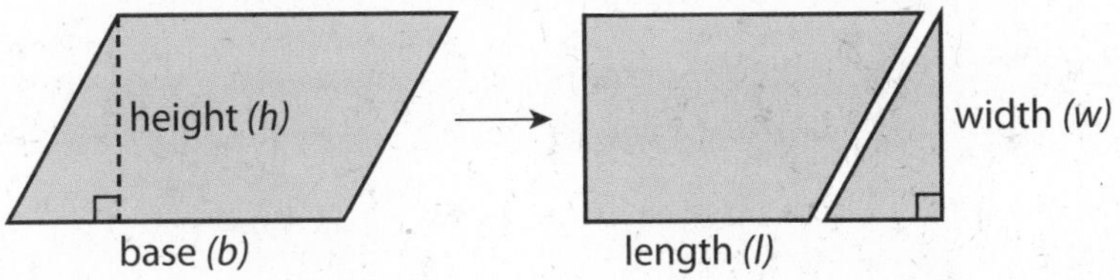

C What figure have you formed? ______________________

Does this figure have the same area as the parallelogram? __________

base of parallelogram = __________ of rectangle

height of parallelogram = __________ of rectangle

area of parallelogram = __________ of rectangle

What is the formula for the area of this figure? $A =$ __________

or __________

D What is the formula for the area of a parallelogram? $A =$ __________

Math Talk
Mathematical Practices

Can you use the formula $A = bh$ to find the area of a rectangle? Explain.

Area of a Parallelogram

The area A of a parallelogram is the product of its base b and its height h.

$$A = bh$$

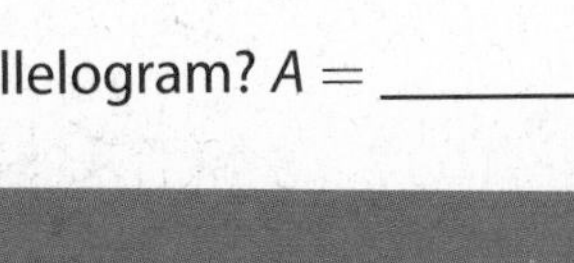

EXPLORE ACTIVITY *(cont'd)*

Reflect

1. Find the area of the parallelogram.

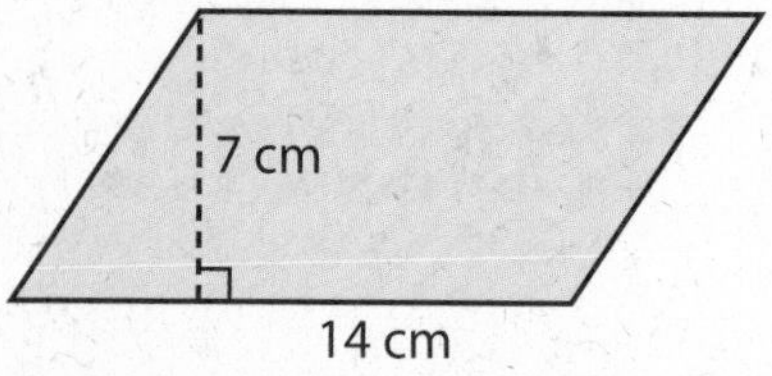

$A =$ ______________________

Finding the Area of a Trapezoid

Math On the Spot
my.hrw.com

Notice that two copies of the same trapezoid fit together to form a parallelogram. The height of the parallelogram is the same as the height of the trapezoid. The length of the base of the parallelogram is the sum of the lengths of the two bases (b_1 and b_2) of the trapezoid.

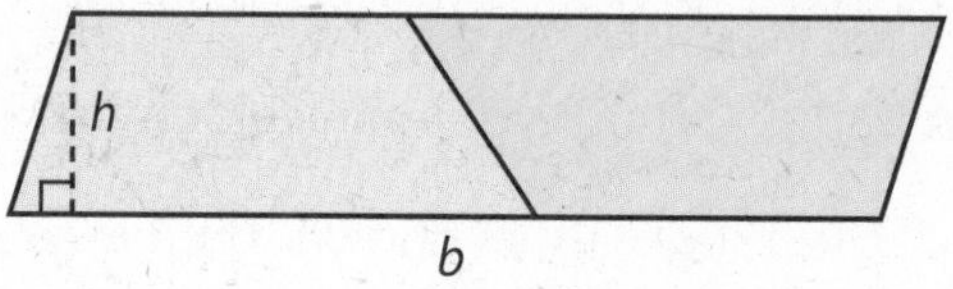

Area of parallelogram $= b \cdot h$

$= (b_1 + b_2) \cdot h$

So, the area of a trapezoid is half the area of the parallelogram.

Area of a Trapezoid

The area of a trapezoid is half its height multiplied by the sum of the lengths of its two bases.

$$A = \frac{1}{2}h(b_1 + b_2)$$

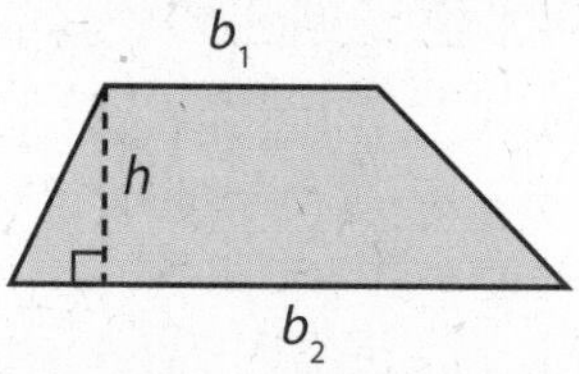

EXAMPLE 1 Real World

CA CC 6.G.1

A section of a deck is in the shape of a trapezoid. What is the area of this section of the deck?

$b_1 = 17 \quad b_2 = 39 \quad h = 16$

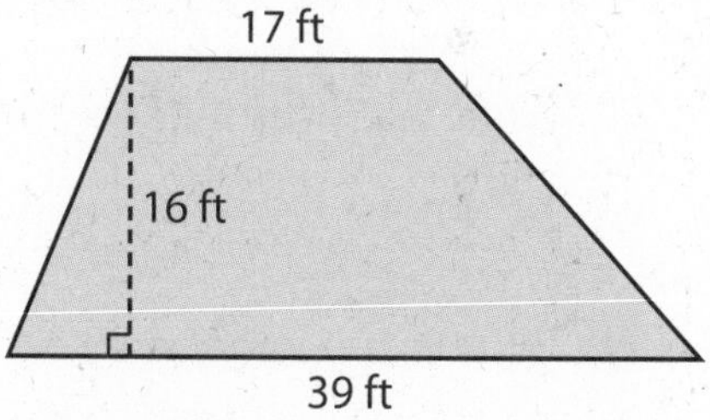

Use the trapezoid area formula.

$A = \frac{1}{2}h(b_1 + b_2)$

$= \frac{1}{2} \cdot 16(17 + 39)$ Substitute.

$= \frac{1}{2} \cdot 16(56)$ Add inside the parentheses.

$= 8 \cdot 56$ Multiply $\frac{1}{2}$ and 16.

$= 448$ square feet Multiply.

Math Talk
Mathematical Practices

Does it matter which base length is substituted for b_1 and which is substituted for b_2? Why or why not?

Animated Math
my.hrw.com

YOUR TURN

2. The length of one base of a trapezoid is 27 feet, and the length of the other base is 34 feet. The height is 12 feet. What is its area? ________

Personal Math Trainer
Online Practice and Help
my.hrw.com

Math On the Spot
my.hrw.com

Finding the Area of a Rhombus

A **rhombus** is a quadrilateral in which all sides are congruent and opposite sides are parallel. A rhombus can be divided into four right triangles that can then be rearranged into a rectangle.

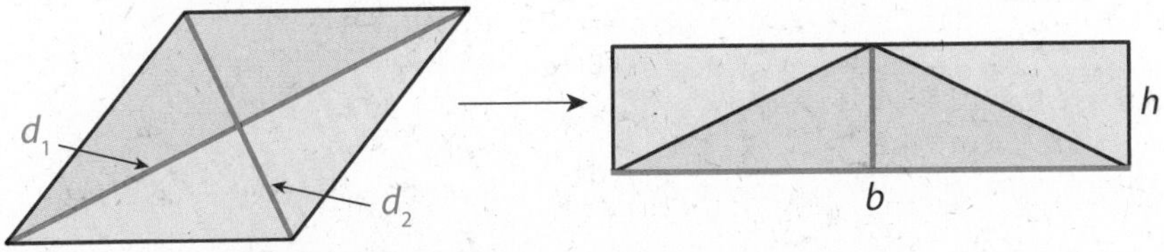

The base of the rectangle is the same length as one of the diagonals of the rhombus. The height of the rectangle is half the length of the other diagonal.

$$A = b \cdot h$$
$$A = d_1 \cdot \tfrac{1}{2}d_2$$

Area of a Rhombus

The area of a rhombus is half of the product of the lengths of its diagonals.

$$A = \tfrac{1}{2}d_1d_2$$

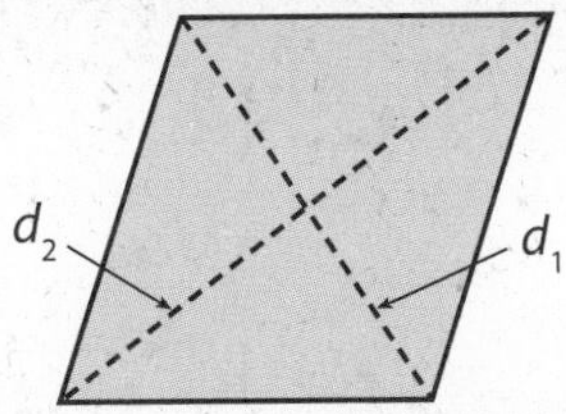

EXAMPLE 2 Real World

CA CC 6.G.1

Cedric is constructing a kite in the shape of a rhombus. The spars of the kite measure 15 inches and 24 inches. How much fabric will Cedric need for the kite?

To determine the amount of fabric needed, find the area of the kite.

$d_1 = 15$ $\quad\quad$ $d_2 = 24$

Use the formula for the area of a rhombus.

$A = \tfrac{1}{2}d_1d_2$

$= \tfrac{1}{2}(15)(24)$ Substitute.

$= 180$ square inches Multiply.

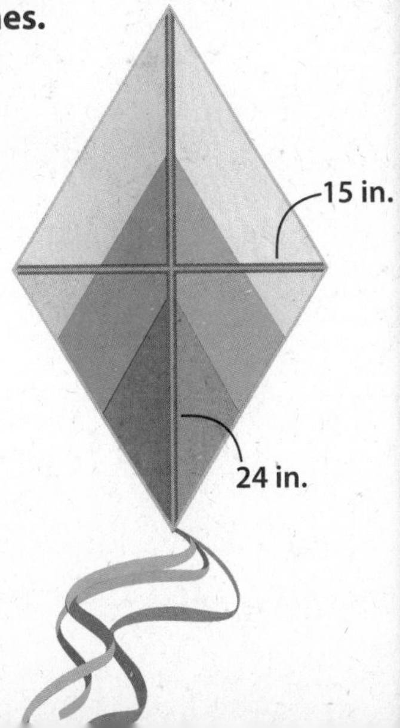

Personal Math Trainer

Online Practice and Help

my.hrw.com

YOUR TURN

Find the area of each rhombus.

3. $d_1 = 35$ m; $d_2 = 12$ m

$A =$ ________ m^2

4. $d_1 = 9.5$ in.; $d_2 = 14$ in.

$A =$ ________ in^2

5. $d_1 = 10$ m; $d_2 = 18$ m

$A =$ ________ m^2

6. $d_1 = 8\frac{1}{4}$ ft; $d_2 = 40$ ft

$A =$ ________ ft^2

Guided Practice

1. Find the area of the parallelogram. (Explore Activity)

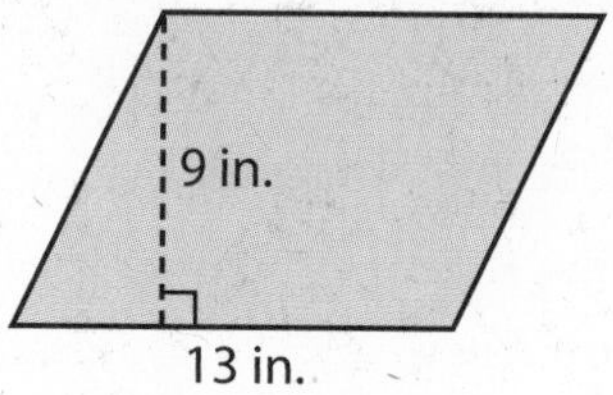

$A = bh$

$= (\_\_\_\_\_\_)(\_\_\_\_\_\_)$

$=$ ________ in^2

2. Find the area of the trapezoid. (Example 1)

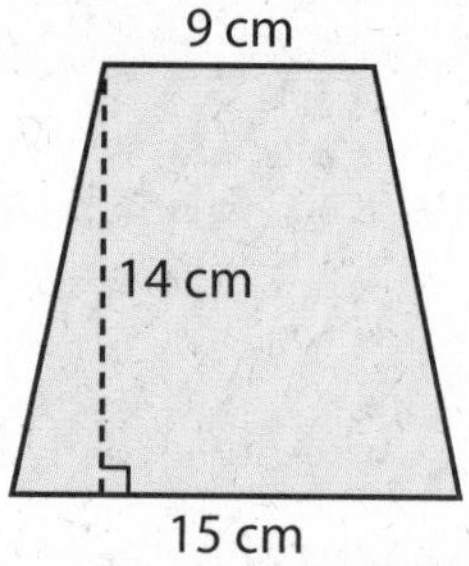

$A = \frac{1}{2}h(b_1 + b_2)$

$= \frac{1}{2}(\square)(\square + \square)$

$=$ ________ cm^2

3. Find the area of the rhombus. (Example 2)

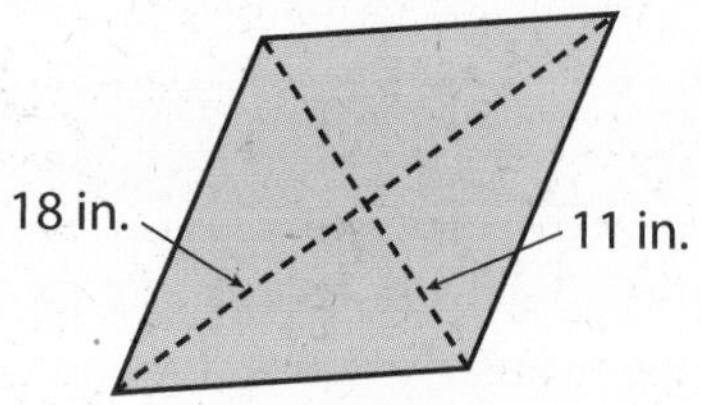

$A = \frac{1}{2}d_1d_2$

$= \frac{1}{2}(\square)(\square)$

$=$ ________ in^2

ESSENTIAL QUESTION CHECK-IN

4. How can you find the areas of parallelograms, rhombuses, and trapezoids?

____

____

____

____

Name________________ Class________________ Date________________

13.1 Independent Practice

CA CC 6.G.1

Personal Math Trainer

Online Practice and Help

my.hrw.com

5. Find the area of the parallelogram.

____

6. What is the area of a parallelogram that has a base of $12\frac{3}{4}$ in. and a height of $2\frac{1}{2}$ in.?

____

7. Find the area of the trapezoid.

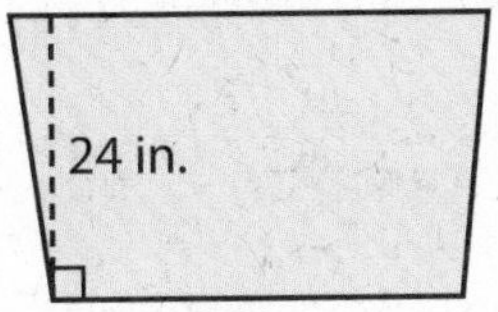

____

8. The bases of a trapezoid are 11 meters and 14 meters. Its height is 10 meters. What is the area of the trapezoid?

____

9. Find the area of the rhombus.

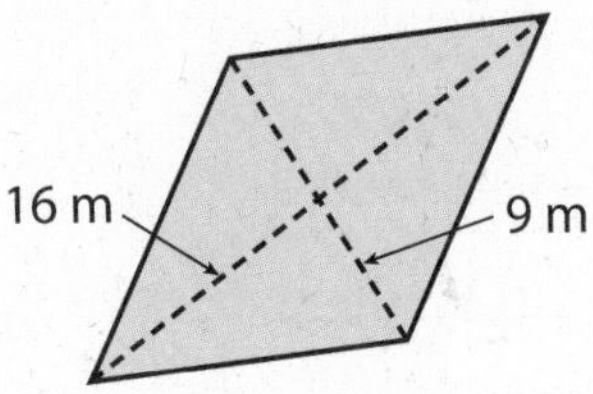

____

10. The diagonals of a rhombus are 21 m and 32 m. What is the area of the rhombus?

____

11. The seat of a bench is in the shape of a trapezoid with bases of 6 feet and 5 feet and a height of 1.5 feet. What is the area of the seat?

____

12. A kite in the shape of a rhombus has diagonals that are 25 inches long and 15 inches long. What is the area of the kite?

____

13. A window in the shape of a parallelogram has a base of 36 inches and a height of 45 inches. What is the area of the window?

____

14. **Communicate Mathematical Ideas** Find the area of the figure. Explain how you found your answer.

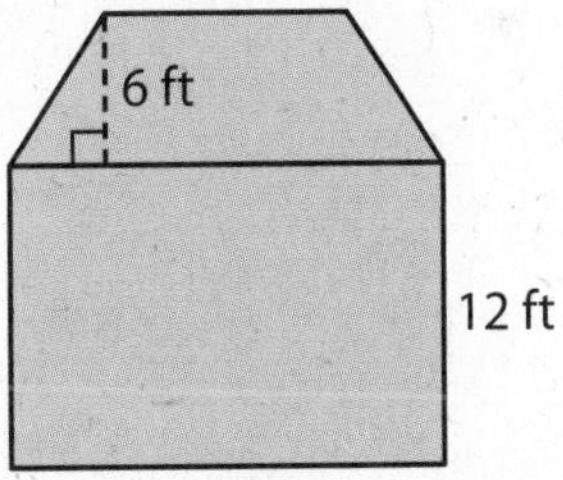

____

____

____

____

____

____

____

15. Multistep A parking space shaped like a parallelogram has a base of 17 feet and a height is 9 feet. A car parked in the space is 16 feet long and 6 feet wide. How much of the parking space is not covered by the car?

H.O.T. FOCUS ON HIGHER ORDER THINKING

Work Area

16. Critique Reasoning Simon says that to find the area of a trapezoid, you can multiply the height by the top base and the height by the bottom base. Then add the two products together and divide the sum by 2. Is Simon correct? Explain your answer.

17. Multistep The height of a trapezoid is 8 in. and its area is 96 in.^{2} One base of the trapezoid is 6 inches longer than the other base. What are the lengths of the bases? Explain how you found your answer.

18. Multiple Representations The diagonals of a rhombus are 12 in. and 16 in. long. The length of a side of the rhombus is 10 in. What is the height of the rhombus? Explain how you found your answer.

LESSON
13.2 Area of Triangles

CA CC 6.G.1

Find the area of right triangles, other triangles, special quadrilaterals, and polygons by composing into rectangles or decomposing into triangles and other shapes; apply these techniques in the context of solving real-world and mathematical problems.

ESSENTIAL QUESTION

How do you find the area of a triangle?

EXPLORE ACTIVITY 1 CA CC 6.G.1

Area of a Right Triangle

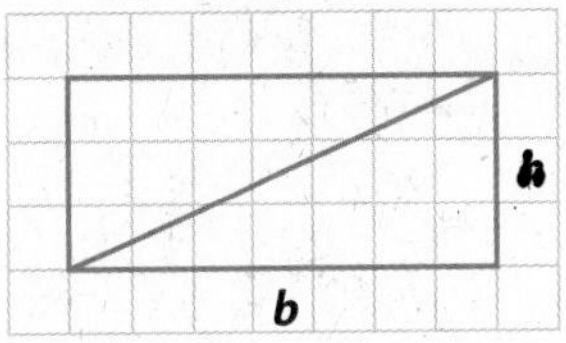

A Draw and label a large rectangle on grid paper, as shown.

What is the formula for the area of the rectangle? $A =$ ________________

B Draw one diagonal of your rectangle.

The diagonal divides the rectangle into ________________________.

Each triangle's area is ________________ the rectangle's area.

Use this information and the formula for area of a rectangle to

write a formula for the area of a right triangle. $A =$ ________________

Reflect

1. **Communicate Mathematical Ideas** In the formula for the area of a right triangle, what do b and h represent?

____

EXPLORE ACTIVITY 2 CA CC 6.G.1

Area of a Triangle

A Draw a large triangle on grid paper. Do not draw a right triangle.

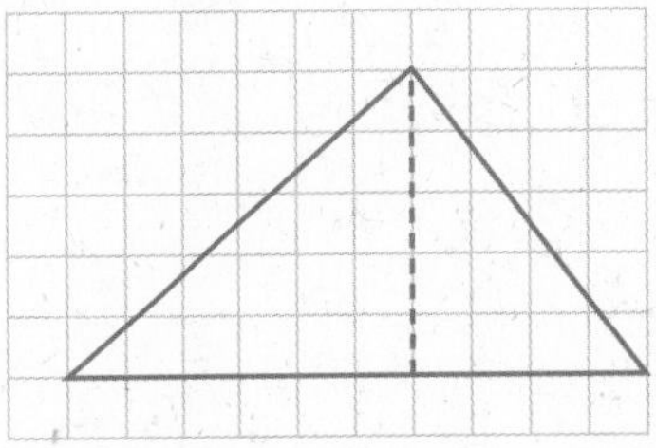

B Cut out your triangle. Then trace around it to make a copy of your triangle. Cut out the copy.

C Cut one of your triangles into two pieces by cutting through one angle directly across to the opposite side. Now you have three triangles — one large triangle and two smaller right triangles.

EXPLORE ACTIVITY 2 *(cont'd)*

When added together, the areas of the two smaller triangles equal the ________________ of the large triangle.

D Arrange the three triangles into a rectangle.

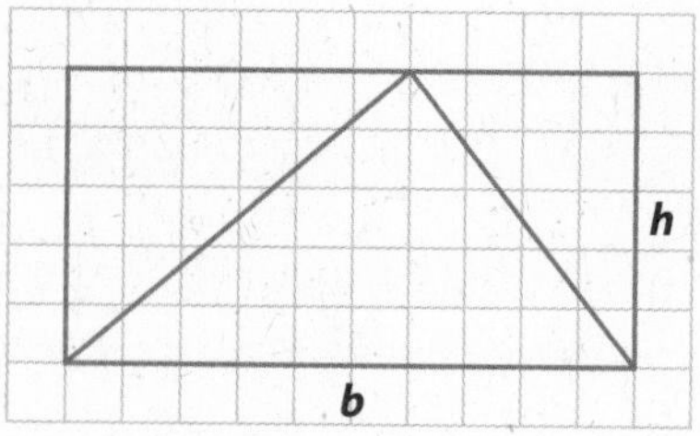

What fraction of the rectangle does the large triangle represent? ________________

The area of the rectangle is $A = bh$. What is the area of the large triangle? $A =$ ________________

How does this formula compare to the formula for the area of a right triangle that you found in Explore Activity 1?

____

Reflect

2. **Communicate Mathematical Ideas** What type of angle is formed by the base of a triangle and the segment you measure to find the height?

____

Math On the Spot
my.hrw.com

Finding the Area of a Triangle

Area of a Triangle

The area A of a triangle is half the product of the length of its base b and its height h.

$$A = \frac{1}{2}bh$$

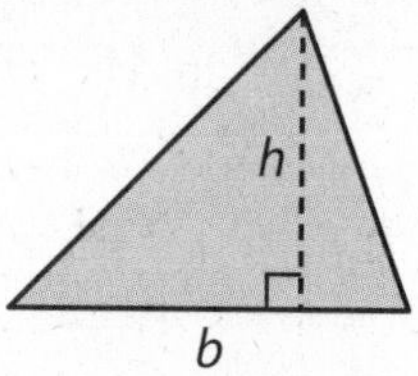

EXAMPLE 1

CA CC 6.G.1

Find the area of each triangle.

A

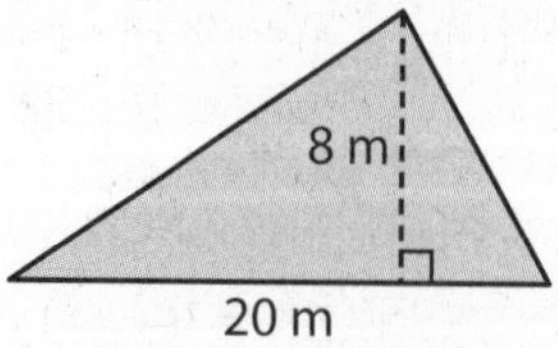

$b = 20$ meters $\quad h = 8$ meters

$A = \frac{1}{2}bh$

$= \frac{1}{2}(20)(8)$ Substitute.

$= 80$ square meters Multiply.

Find the area of each triangle.

B

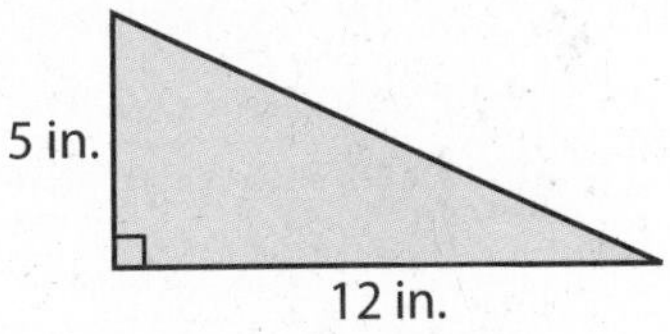

$b = 12$ inches $\quad h = 5$ inches

$$A = \frac{1}{2}bh$$

$$= \frac{1}{2}(12)(5) \quad \text{Substitute.}$$

$$= 30 \text{ square inches} \quad \text{Multiply.}$$

Math Talk
Mathematical Practices

Why can you also write the formula for the area of a triangle as $A = \frac{bh}{2}$?

YOUR TURN

Find the area of the triangle.

3.

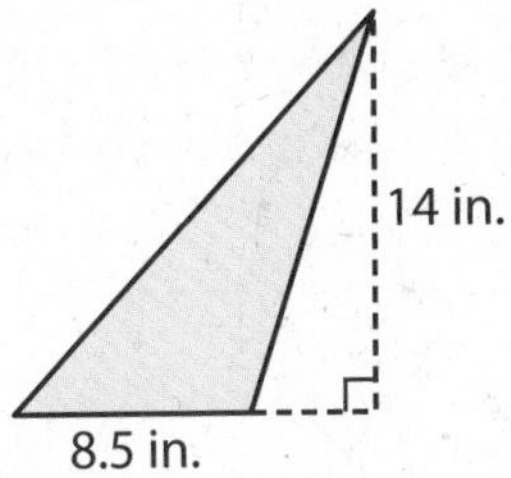

$A =$ ____________

Personal Math Trainer
Online Practice and Help
my.hrw.com

Math On the Spot
my.hrw.com

Problem Solving Using Area of Triangles

You can use the formula for the area of a triangle to solve real-world problems.

EXAMPLE 2 Real World

CA CC 6.G.1

Each triangular face of the Pyramid of Peace in Kazakhstan is made up of 25 smaller equilateral triangles. These triangles have measurements as shown in the diagram. What is the area of one of the smaller equilateral triangles?

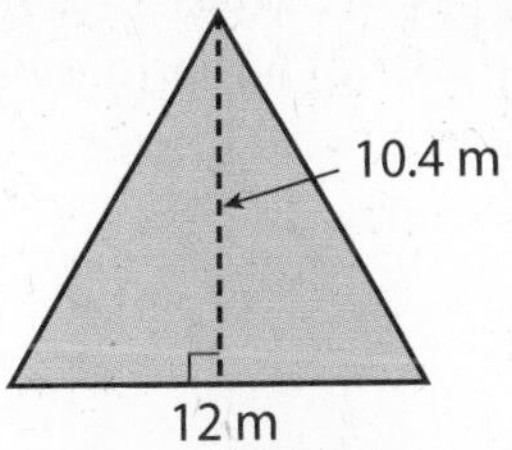

STEP 1 Identify the length of the base and the height of the triangle.

$b = 12$ m and $h = 10.4$ m

STEP 2 Use the formula to find the area of the triangle.

$$A = \frac{1}{2}bh \quad \text{Substitute.}$$

$$= \frac{1}{2}(12)(10.4) \quad \text{Multiply.}$$

$$= 62.4$$

The area of one small equilateral triangle is 62.4 m^2.

Reflect

4. **Persevere in Problem Solving** What is the total area of one face of the pyramid? What is the total surface area of the faces of the pyramid, not counting the bottom? (Hint: the bottom of the pyramid is a square.)

____

____

____

Personal Math Trainer
Online Practice and Help
my.hrw.com

YOUR TURN

5. Amy needs to order a shade for a triangular-shaped window that has a base of 6 feet and a height of 4 feet. What is the area of the shade?

____

Guided Practice

Find the area of each triangle. (Explore Activities 1 and 2, Example 1)

1.

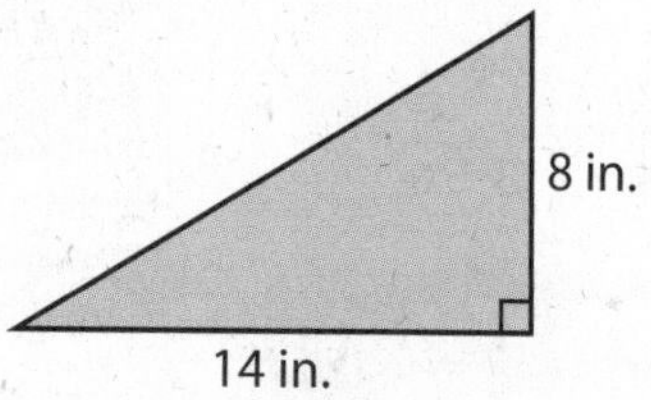

$A = \frac{1}{2}bh$

$= \frac{1}{2}(\_\_\_\_\_\_)(\_\_\_\_\_\_)$

$= \_\_\_\_\_\_$ in^2

2. A pennant in the shape of a triangle has a base of 12 inches and a height of 30 inches. What is the area of the pennant? (Example 2)

$A = \frac{1}{2}bh$

$= \frac{1}{2}(\_\_\_\_\_\_)(\_\_\_\_\_\_)$

$= \_\_\_\_\_\_$ in^2

ESSENTIAL QUESTION CHECK-IN

3. How do you find the area of a triangle?

____

____

____

Name ____________ Class ____________ Date ____________

13.2 Independent Practice

CA CC 6.G.1

Personal Math Trainer
my.hrw.com
Online Practice and Help

Find the area of each triangle.

4.

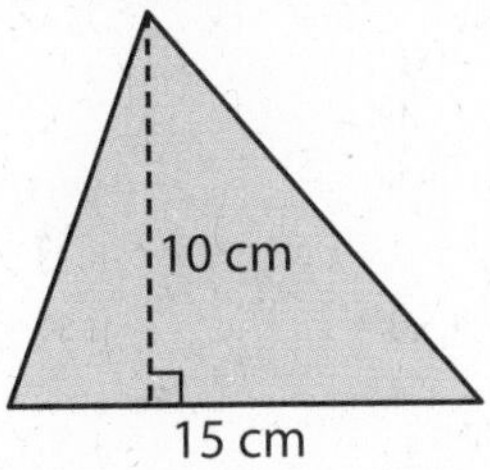

____

5.

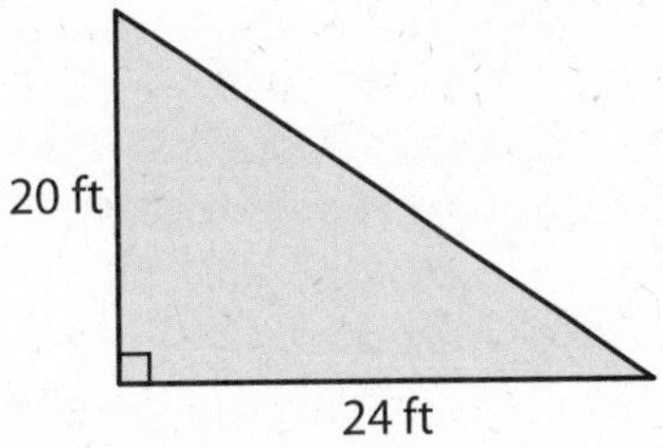

____

6.

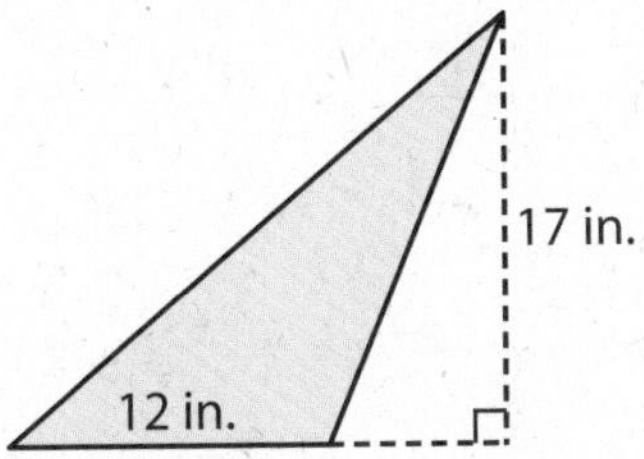

____

7.

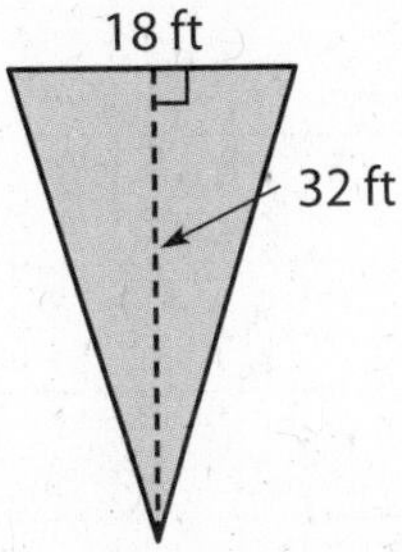

____

8. What is the area of a triangle that has a base of $15\frac{1}{4}$ in. and a height of 18 in.?

____

9. A right triangle has legs that are 11 in. and 13 in. long. What is the area of the triangle?

____

10. A triangular plot of land has the dimensions shown in the diagram. What is the area of the land?

____

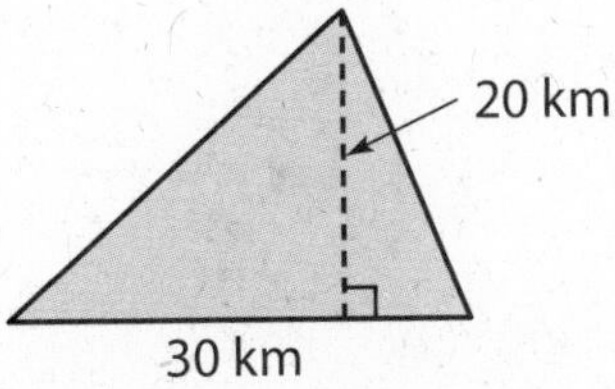

11. The front part of a tent has the dimensions shown in the diagram. What is the area of this part of the tent?

____

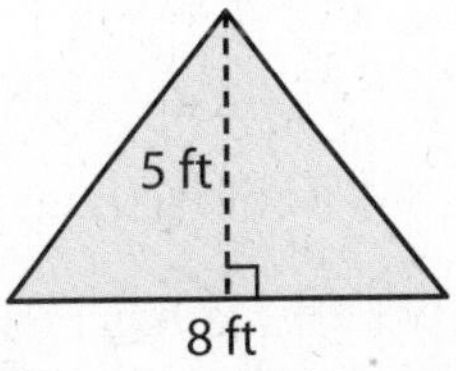

12. **Multistep** The sixth-grade art students are making a mosaic using tiles in the shape of right triangles. The two sides that meet to form a right angle are 3 centimeters and 5 centimeters long. If there are 200 tiles in the mosaic, what is the area of the mosaic?

____

13. **Critique Reasoning** Monica has a triangular piece of fabric. The height of the triangle is 15 inches and the triangle's base is 6 inches. Monica says that the area of the fabric is 90 in^2. What error did Monica make? Explain your answer.

____

____

14. **Multistep** Wayne is going to paint the side of the house shown in the diagram. What is the area that will be painted? Explain how you found your answer.

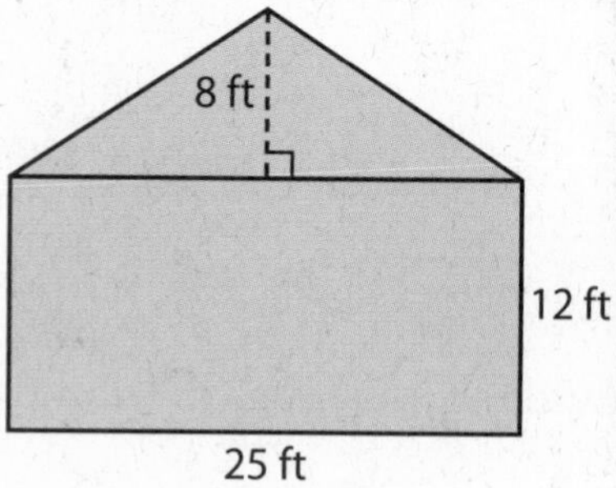

____

____

____

H.O.T. FOCUS ON HIGHER ORDER THINKING

Work Area

15. **Communicate Mathematical Ideas** Explain how the areas of a triangle and a parallelogram with the same base and height are related.

____

____

____

____

____

16. **Analyze Relationships** A rectangle and a triangle have the same area. If their bases are the same lengths, how do their heights compare? Justify your answer.

____

____

____

____

____

____

17. **What If?** A right triangle has an area of 18 square inches.

a. If the triangle has two sides that are the same length, what are the lengths of these sides?

____

b. If the triangle has sides with three different lengths, what are all the possible whole number lengths for the sides that meet at a right angle?

____

____

LESSON
13.3 Solving Area Equations

CA CC 6.G.1

Find the area of right triangles, other triangles, special quadrilaterals, and polygons by composing into rectangles or decomposing into triangles and other shapes; apply these techniques in the context of solving real-world and mathematical problems. *Also 6.EE.7*

ESSENTIAL QUESTION

How do you use equations to solve problems about area of rectangles, parallelograms, trapezoids, and triangles?

Problem Solving Using the Area of a Triangle

Recall that the formula for the area of a triangle is $A = \frac{1}{2}bh$. You can also use the formula to find missing dimensions if you know the area and one dimension.

Math On the Spot
my.hrw.com

EXAMPLE 1 Real World

CA CC 6.G.1, 6.EE.7

After winning the state tournament, the wrestling team hangs a pennant shaped like a triangle on the gym wall. The base of the triangle is 1.5 feet long. It has an area of 2.25 square feet. What is the height of the triangle?

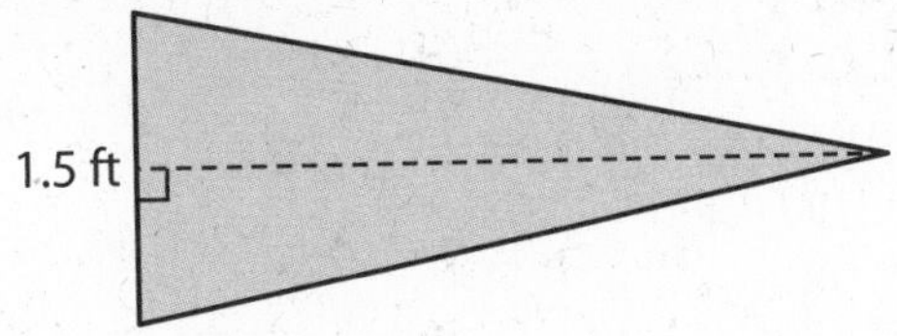

$A = \frac{1}{2}bh$ — Write the formula.

$2.25 = \frac{1}{2}(1.5)h$ — Use the formula to write an equation.

$2.25 = 0.75h$ — Multiply $\frac{1}{2}$ and 1.5.

$\frac{2.25}{0.75} = \frac{0.75h}{0.75}$ — Divide both sides of the equation by 0.75.

$3 = h$

The height of the triangle is 3 feet.

Math Talk
Mathematical Practices

How can you use units in the formula to confirm that the units for the height are in feet?

YOUR TURN

1. Renee is sewing a quilt whose pattern contains right triangles. Each quilt piece is a right triangle with a height of 6 inches, and an area of 24 square inches. How long is the base of each quilt piece?

____

Personal Math Trainer
Online Practice and Help
my.hrw.com

Math On the Spot
my.hrw.com

Writing Equations Using the Area of a Trapezoid

You can use the formula for the area of a trapezoid to write an equation to solve a problem.

EXAMPLE 2 Real World

CA CC 6.G.1, 6.EE.7

A garden in the shape of a trapezoid has an area of 44.4 square meters. One base is 4.3 meters long and the other base is 10.5 meters long. The height of the trapezoid is the width of the garden. How wide is the garden?

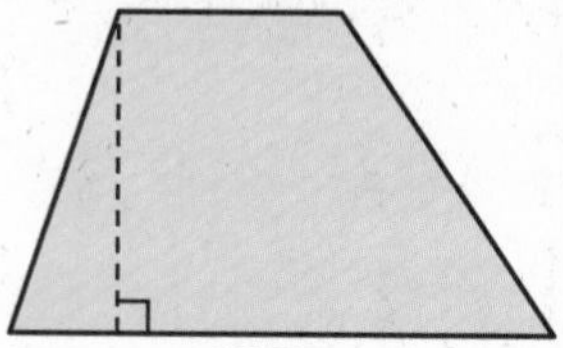

$A = \frac{1}{2}h(b_1 + b_2)$ Write the formula.

$44.4 = \frac{1}{2}h(4.3 + 10.5)$ Use the formula to write an equation.

$44.4 = \frac{1}{2}h(14.8)$ Add inside parentheses.

$44.4 = 7.4h$ Multiply $\frac{1}{2}$ and 14.8.

$\frac{44.4}{7.4} = \frac{7.4h}{7.4}$ Divide both sides of the equation by 7.4.

$6 = h$

The garden is 6 meters wide.

Math Talk
Mathematical Practices
How can you check that the answer is reasonable?

Reflect

2. **Communicate Mathematical Ideas** Explain why the first step after substituting is addition.

____

____

____

____

YOUR TURN

3. The cross section of a water trough is shaped like a trapezoid. The bases of the trapezoid are 18 feet and 8 feet long. It has an area of 52 square feet. What is the height of the cross section?

____

Personal Math Trainer
Online Practice and Help
my.hrw.com

Solving Multistep Problems

You can write and solve equations that represent real-world problems related to relationships in geometry.

Math On the Spot
my.hrw.com

EXAMPLE 3 Problem Solving CA CC 6.G.1

John and Mary are using rolls of fabric to make a rectangular stage curtain for their class play. The rectangular piece of fabric on each roll measures 2.5 feet by 15 feet. If the area of the curtain is 200 square feet, what is the least number of rolls they need?

My Notes

Analyze Information

Rewrite the question as a statement.

- Find the least number of rolls of fabric needed to cover an area of 200 ft^2.

List the important information.

- Each roll of fabric is a 2.5 foot by 15 foot rectangle.
- The area of the curtain is 200 square feet.

Formulate a Plan

Write an equation to find the area of each roll of fabric.

Use the area of the curtain and the area of each roll to write an equation to find the least number of rolls.

Solve

STEP 1 Write an equation to find the area of each roll of fabric.

$A = lw$

$A = 15(2.5)$

$A = 37.5 \text{ ft}^2$

STEP 2 Write an equation to find the number of rolls needed.

$n = 200 \div 37.5$

$n = 5\frac{1}{3}$

STEP 3 The problem asks for the least number of rolls needed. Since 5 rolls will not be enough, they will need 6 rolls to make the curtain.

The least number of rolls John and Mary will need is 6.

Justify and Evaluate

The area of each roll is about 38 ft^2. Since $38 \text{ ft}^2 \cdot 6 = 228 \text{ ft}^2$, the answer is reasonable.

Personal Math Trainer

Online Practice and Help

my.hrw.com

YOUR TURN

4. A parallelogram-shaped field in a park needs sod. The parallelogram has a base of 21.5 meters and a height of 18 meters. The sod is sold in pallets of 50 square meters. How many pallets of sod are needed to fill the field?

Guided Practice

1. A triangular bandana has an area of 70 square inches. The height of the triangle is $8\frac{3}{4}$ inches. Write and solve an equation to find the length of the base of the triangle. (Example 1)

2. The top of a desk is shaped like a trapezoid. The bases of the trapezoid are 26.5 and 30 centimeters long. The area of the desk is 791 square centimeters. The height of the trapezoid is the width of the desk. Write and solve an equation to find the width of the desk. (Example 2)

3. Taylor wants to paint his rectangular deck that is 42 feet long and 28 feet wide. A gallon of paint covers about 350 square feet. How many gallons of paint will Taylor need to cover the entire deck? (Example 3)

Write and solve an equation to find the ______________ of the deck.

Write and solve an equation to find the number of ________________.

Taylor will need ________ gallons of paint.

ESSENTIAL QUESTION CHECK-IN

4. How do you use equations to solve problems about area of rectangles, parallelograms, trapezoids, and triangles?

Name ________________ Class ________________ Date ________________

Personal Math Trainer

Online Practice and Help

my.hrw.com

13.3 Independent Practice

CA CC 6.G.1, 6.EE.7

5. A window shaped like a parallelogram has an area of $18\frac{1}{3}$ square feet. The height of the window is $3\frac{1}{3}$ feet. How long is the base of the window?

6. A triangular sail has a base length of 2.5 meters. The area of the sail is 3.75 square meters. How tall is the sail?

7. A section in a stained glass window is shaped like a trapezoid. The top base is 4 centimeters and the bottom base is 2.5 centimeters long. If the area of the section of glass is 3.9 square centimeters, how tall is the section?

8. **Multistep** Amelia wants to paint three walls in her family room. Two walls are 26 feet long by 9 feet wide. The other wall is 18 feet long by 9 feet wide.

   a. What is the total area of the walls that Amelia wants to paint?

   b. Each gallon of paint covers about 250 square feet. How many gallons of paint should Amelia buy to paint the walls?

9. **Critical Thinking** The area of a triangular block is 64 square inches. If the base of the triangle is twice the height, how long are the base and the height of the triangle?

10. **Multistep** Alex needs to varnish the top and the bottom of a dozen rectangular boards. The boards are 8 feet long and 3 feet wide. Each pint of varnish covers 125 square feet and costs $3.50.

    a. What is the total area that Alex needs to varnish?

    b. How much will it cost Alex to varnish all the boards?

11. **Multistep** Leia cuts congruent triangular patches with an area of 45 square centimeters from a rectangular piece of fabric that is 18 centimeters long and 10 centimeters wide. How many of the patches can Leia cut from 32 pieces of the fabric?

12. **Multistep** A farmer needs to buy fertilizer for two fields. One field is shaped like a trapezoid, and the other is shaped like a triangle. The trapezoidal field has bases that are 35 and 48 yards and a height of 26 yards. The triangular field has the same height as the trapezoidal field and a base of 39 yards. Each bag of fertilizer covers 150 square yards. How many bags of fertilizer does the farmer need to buy?

13. A tennis court for singles play is 78 feet long and 27 feet wide.

a. The court for doubles play is 9 feet wider than the court for singles play. How much more area is covered by the tennis court used for doubles play?

b. The junior court for players 8 and under is 36 feet long and 18 feet wide. How much more area is covered by the tennis court used for singles play?

c. The length of a court for players 10 and under is 18 feet less than the length of the court for singles play. How much more area is covered by the tennis court used for singles play?

14. **Draw Conclusions** The cross section of a metal ingot is a trapezoid. The cross section has an area of 39 square centimeters. The top base of the cross section is 12 centimeters. The length of the bottom base is 2 centimeters greater than the top base. How tall is the metal ingot? Explain.

H.O.T. FOCUS ON HIGHER ORDER THINKING

Work Area

15. **Analyze Relationships** A mirror is made of two congruent parallelograms as shown in the diagram. The parallelograms have a combined area of $9\frac{1}{3}$ square yards. The height of each parallelogram is $1\frac{1}{3}$ yards.

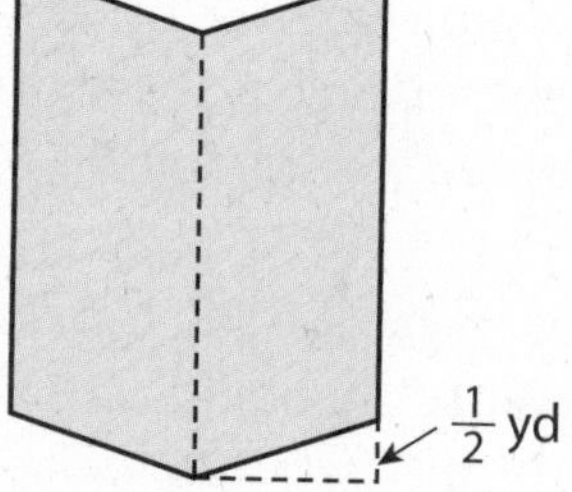

a. How long is the base of each parallelogram?

b. What is the area of the smallest *rectangle* of wall that the mirror could fit on?

16. **Persevere in Problem Solving** A watercolor painting is 20 inches long by 9 inches wide. Ramon makes a border around the watercolor painting by making a mat that adds 1 inch to each side of the length and the width. What is the area of the mat?

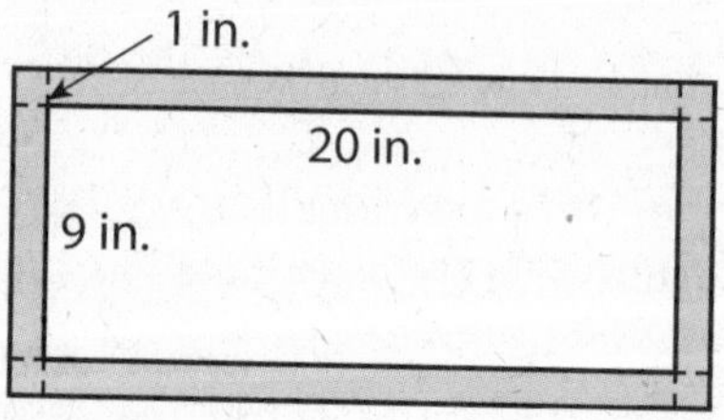

LESSON

13.4 Area of Polygons

CA CC 6.G.1

Find the area of right triangles, other triangles, special quadrilaterals, and polygons by composing into rectangles or decomposing into triangles and other shapes; apply these techniques in the context of solving real-world and mathematical problems.

ESSENTIAL QUESTION

How can you find the area of a polygon by breaking it into simpler shapes?

EXPLORE ACTIVITY

CA CC 6.G.1

Finding Areas Using Tangrams

A tangram is a square that is divided into smaller shapes. The area of the small square is 1 square unit. Use a tangram to find the area of each of the other tangram pieces.

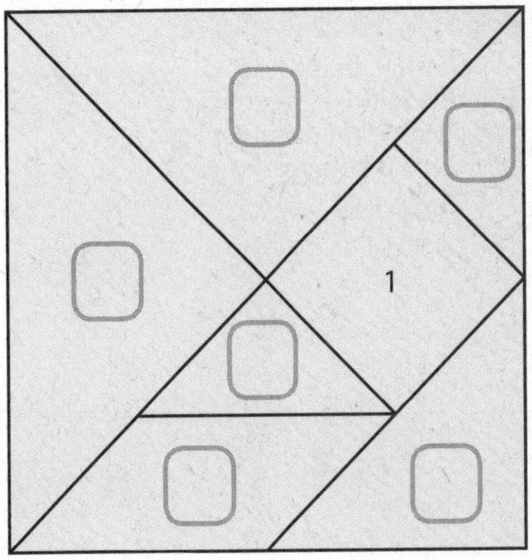

A Place one large triangle on top of the other large triangle. What is true about these two triangles? What does this mean about the areas of these two triangles?

____

B Place the two small triangles on top of the square. What is the area of each small triangle? Write this area on the diagram. ______________

C Arrange the square and one of the small triangles as shown.

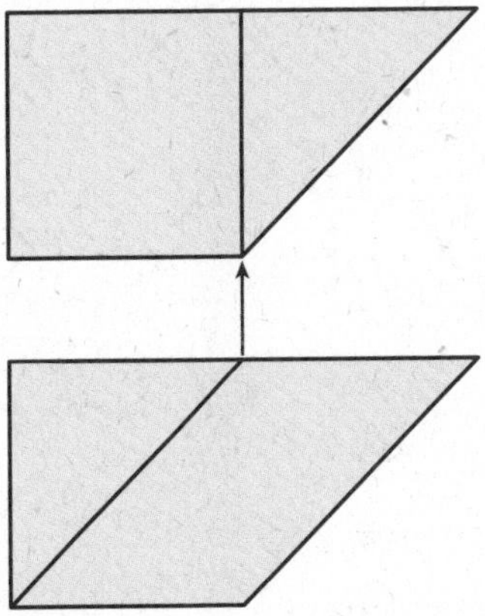

What is the combined area? ______________

Place the parallelogram and the other small triangle on top of the combined square and triangle. What is the area of the parallelogram? Explain.

____

____

____

____

Reflect

1. **Critical Thinking** Complete the rest of the diagram by filling in the remaining areas. Explain how you found your answers.

____

____

Finding Areas of Polygons

You can find the areas of polygons by breaking the polygons into smaller shapes. Then you can apply area formulas you already know.

Math On the Spot
my.hrw.com

Math Talk
Mathematical Practices
What other shapes could you divide the polygon in **A** into? What formulas would you use?

EXAMPLE 1

CA CC 6.G.1

Find the area of each polygon.

A **STEP 1** Draw a horizontal line segment on the diagram that divides the polygon into a rectangle and a triangle.

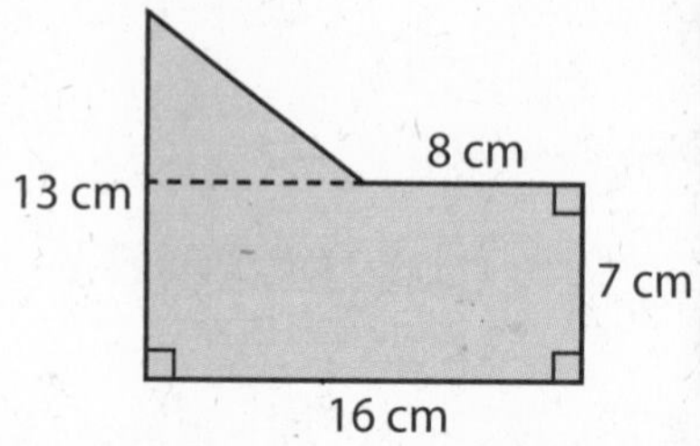

STEP 2 Find the area of the rectangle.

$A = bh = 16 \cdot 7 = \mathbf{112}$ square centimeters

STEP 3 Find the area of the triangle.

$b = 16 - 8 = 8$ $\quad h = 13 - 7 = 6$

$A = \frac{1}{2}bh = \frac{1}{2} \cdot 8 \cdot 6 = \mathbf{24}$ square centimeters

STEP 4 Add the areas from Steps 2 and 3 to find the total area.

$A = \mathbf{112} + \mathbf{24} = 136$ square centimeters

B **STEP 1** Extend the top edge and the right edge of the polygon to form a square with side length 60 feet. Find the area of this square.

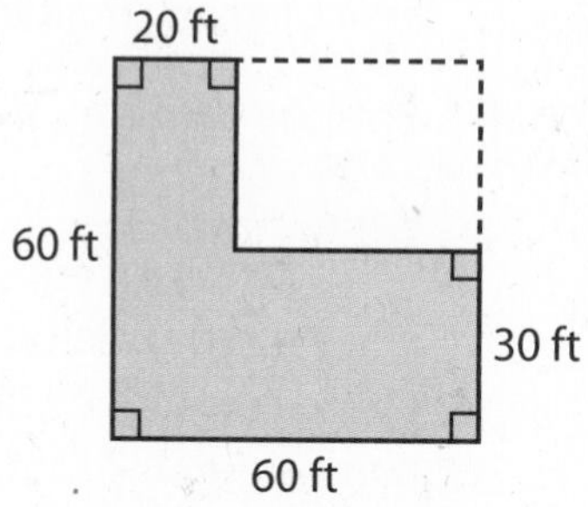

$60 \cdot 60 = \mathbf{360}$ square feet

STEP 2 Notice that the square you drew has a rectangular "missing piece." Find the area of this missing piece.

$b = 60 - 20 = 40$ $\quad h = 60 - 30 = 30$

$A = bh = 40 \cdot 30 = \mathbf{120}$ square feet

STEP 3 Subtract the area in Step 2 from the area in Step 1.

$A = \mathbf{360} - \mathbf{120} = 240$ square feet

Reflect

2. Describe another way to find the area of the polygon in **B**.

____

____

YOUR TURN

Find the area of each polygon.

3.

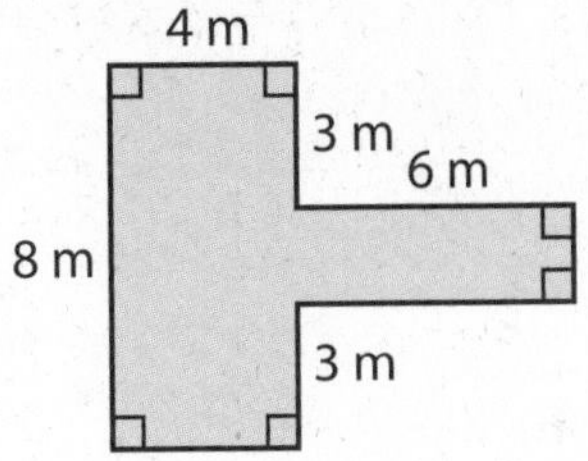

$A =$ ________ square meters

4.

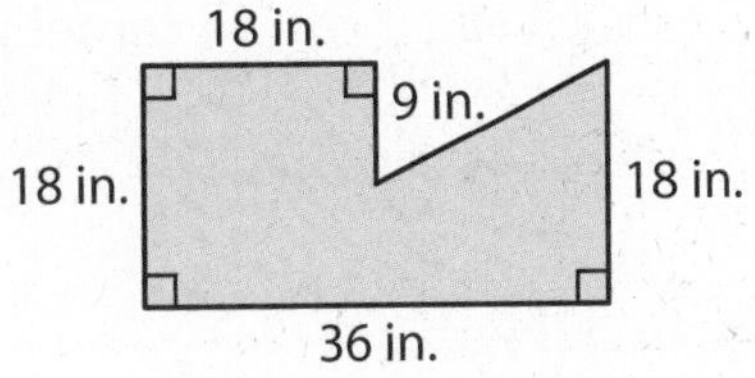

$A =$ ________ square inches

Personal Math Trainer
Online Practice and Help
my.hrw.com

Solving Real-World Problems

You can apply the technique of dividing a shape into smaller shapes in problems that involve finding area.

Math On the Spot
my.hrw.com

EXAMPLE 2 Real World

CA CC 6.G.1

The diagram shows the shape and dimensions of Teresa's rose garden.

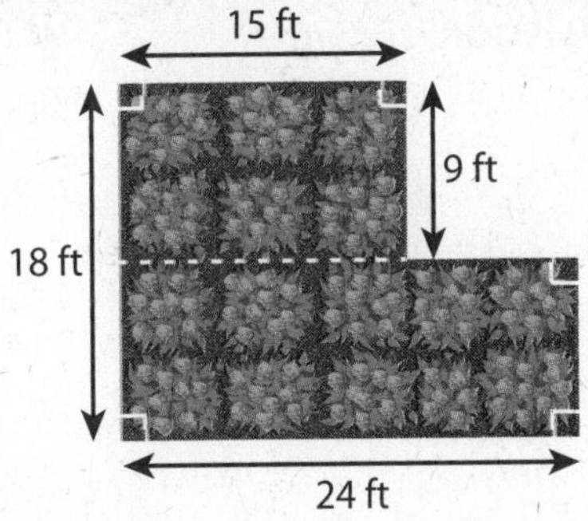

A Find the area of the garden.

STEP 1 Draw a horizontal line segment on the diagram that divides the polygon into two rectangles, one on top of the other.

STEP 2 Find the area of the smaller (top) rectangle.

$A = bh = 15 \cdot 9 = \mathbf{135}$ square feet

STEP 3 Find the area of the larger (bottom) rectangle.

The base of the larger rectangle is 24 feet.

The height is $18 - 9 = 9$ feet.

$A = bh = 24 \cdot 9 = \mathbf{216}$ square feet

STEP 4 Add the areas from Steps 2 and 3 to find the total area.

$A = \mathbf{135} + \mathbf{216} = 351$ square feet

The area of the garden is 351 square feet.

B Teresa wants to buy mulch for her garden. One bag of mulch covers 12 square feet. How many bags will she need?

$\frac{351 \text{ square feet}}{12 \text{ square feet}} = 29.25$ *Divide to find the number of bags needed.*

Teresa will need to buy 30 bags of mulch.

My Notes

Personal Math Trainer
Online Practice and Help
my.hrw.com

YOUR TURN

5. The diagram shows the floor plan of a hotel lobby. Carpet costs \$3 per square foot. How much will it cost to carpet the lobby?

____

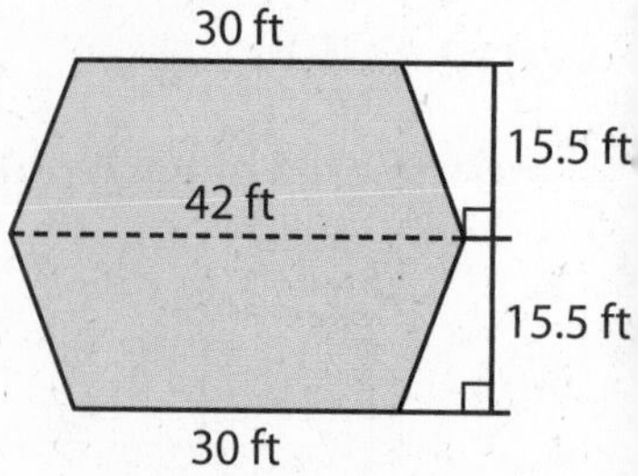

Guided Practice

1. In the diagram, the area of the large square is 1 square unit. Two diagonal segments divide the square into four equal-sized triangles. Two of these triangles are divided into smaller red and blue triangles that all have the same height and base length. Find the area of a red triangle. (Explore Activity)

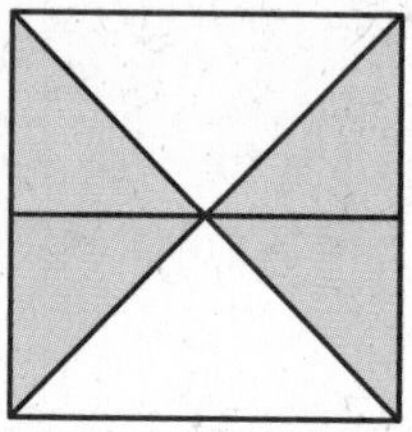

____

Find the area of each polygon. (Example 1)

2. 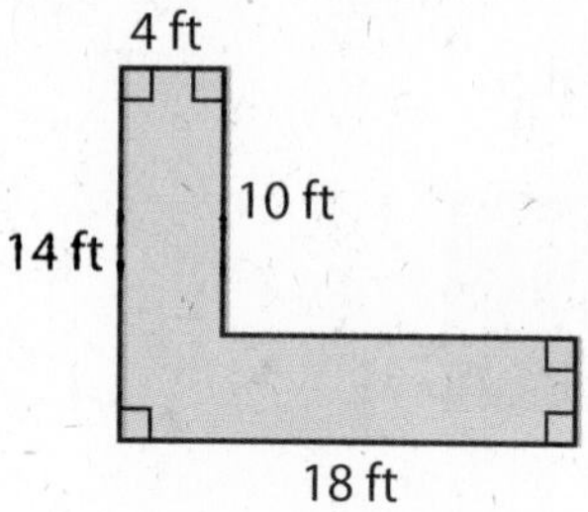

$A =$ _______________ square feet

3. 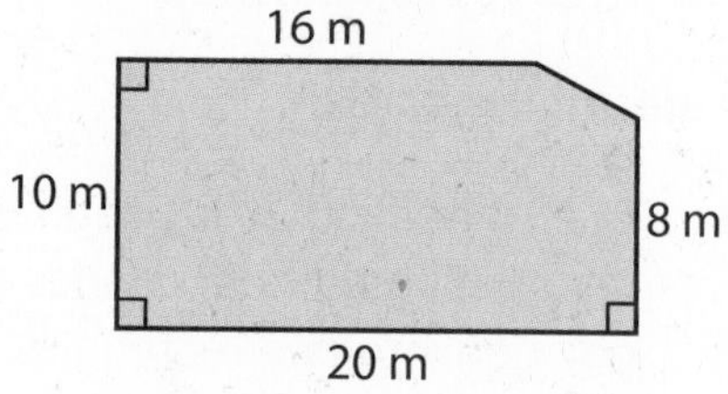

$A =$ _______________ square meters

4. Jess is painting a giant arrow on a playground. Find the area of the giant arrow. If one can of paint covers 100 square feet, how many cans should Jess buy? (Example 2)

____

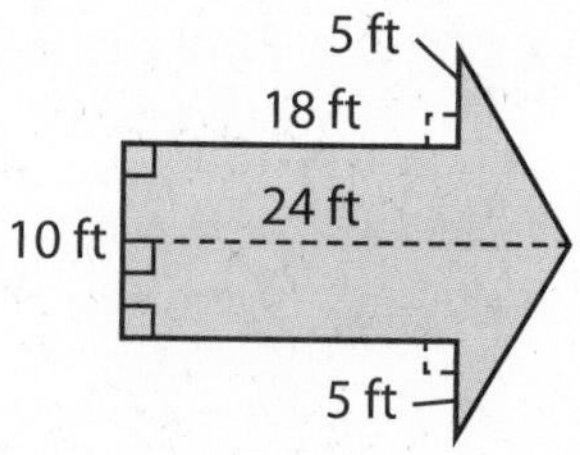

ESSENTIAL QUESTION CHECK-IN

5. How can you find the area of a polygon that is not one for which you know an area formula?

____

____

____

Name ____________________ Class ____________________ Date ____________________

13.4 Independent Practice

CA CC 6.G.1

Personal Math Trainer
my.hrw.com
Online Practice and Help

6. Alice wants to put wall-to-wall carpeting in a small room with the floor plan shown.

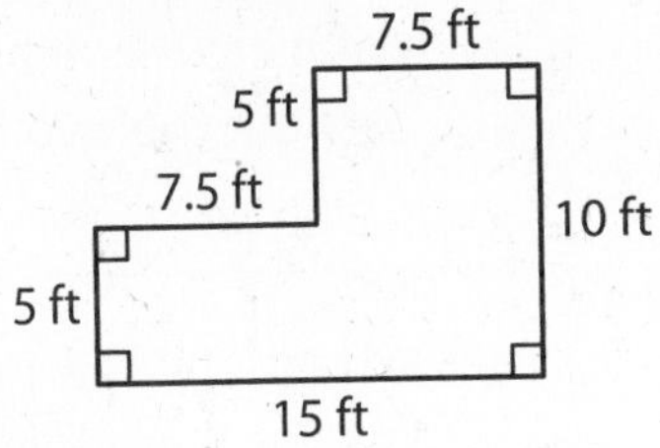

a. Alice says she can find the area of the room by dividing the floor plan into two trapezoids. Show how she can divide the floor plan. Then find the area using her method.

____

b. Describe another way to find the area.

____

____

c. How much will Alice pay for carpet that costs $4.50 per square foot?

____

7. Hal's backyard has a patio, a walkway, and a garden.

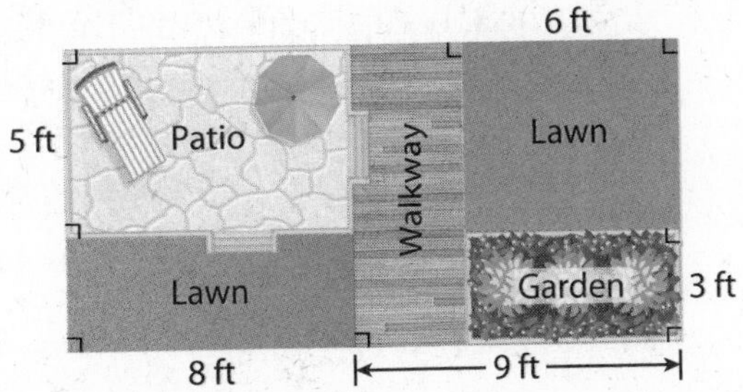

a. About what percent of the total area of Hal's backyard is the area taken up by the patio, walkway, and garden? Round to the nearest whole percent.

____

b. One longer side of Hal's backyard lies next to the back of his house. Hal wants to build a fence that costs $9.75 per foot around the other three sides. How much will Hal spend on his new fence?

____

8. The students in a furniture-making class make a tabletop shaped like the figure shown. The tabletop has squares cut out of the corners.

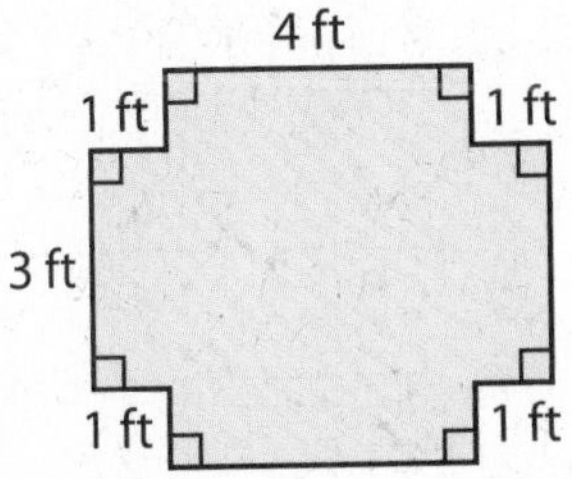

a. What is the area of the tabletop?

____

b. One of the students wants to make a tabletop shaped like a right triangle. This tabletop will have the same area as the tabletop shown. What are a set of possible lengths for the sides that meet in a right angle on this tabletop? Explain.

____

____

____

9. **Multistep** Cho is making banners shaped like triangles out of a rectangular piece of fabric. She cuts out two triangular banners as shown.

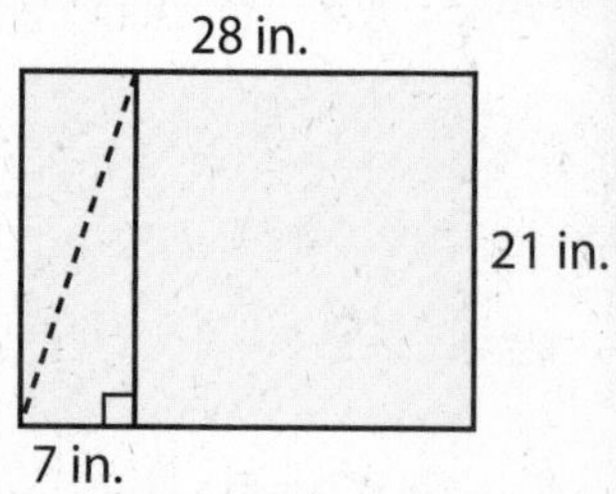

a. What is the area of a triangular banner?

____

b. What are the dimensions of the fabric left over after Cho cuts out the two banners?

____

c. What is the maximum number of banners that Cho can cut out from the fabric? Will she use all the fabric?

____

H.O.T. FOCUS ON HIGHER ORDER THINKING

Work Area

10. **Persevere in Problem Solving** The base of a parallelogram is 8 units, and the height is 5 units. A segment divides the parallelogram into two identical trapezoids. The height of each trapezoid is 5 units. Draw the parallelogram and the two trapezoids on the grid shown. Then find the area of one of the trapezoids.

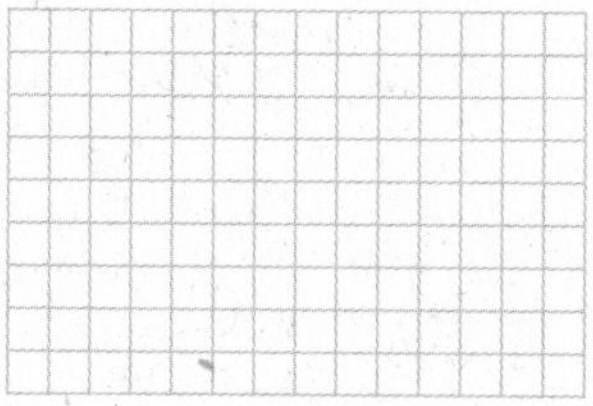

____

11. **Persevere in Problem Solving** The figure shown is a square with a triangular hole cut into one side. The ratio of the height h of the triangle to a side length of the square is 7 to 8. The ratio of the base b of the triangle to the side length of the square is 1 to 2. If the area of the square is 64 square inches, what is the area of the shaded part of the square? Show your work.

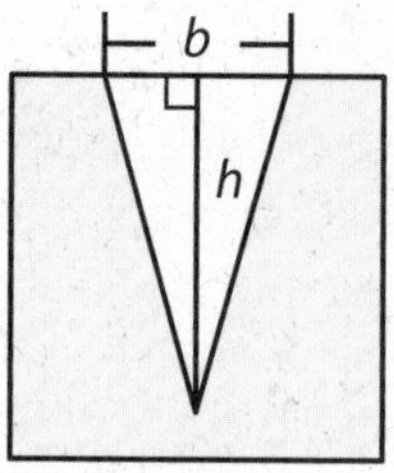

____

____

____

____

____

____

____

MODULE QUIZ

Ready to Go On?

Personal Math Trainer
Online Practice and Help
my.hrw.com

13.1 Area of Quadrilaterals

1. Find the area of the figure.

____

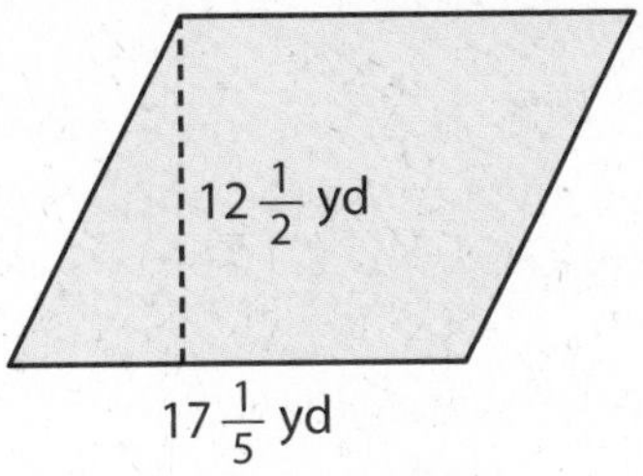

13.2 Area of Triangles

2. Find the area of the triangle.

____

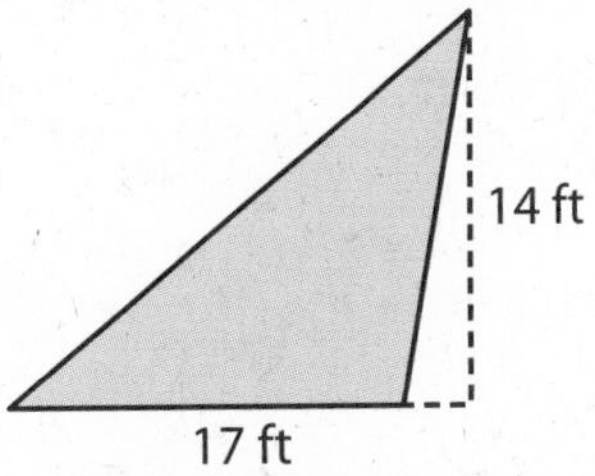

13.3 Solving Area Equations

3. A triangular pane of glass has a height of 30 inches and an area of 270 square inches. What is the length of the base of the pane?

____

4. A tabletop in the shape of a trapezoid has an area of 6,550 square centimeters. Its longer base measures 115 centimeters, and the shorter base is 85 centimeters. What is the height?

____

13.4 Area of Polygons

5. Find the area of the polygon.

________ square centimeters

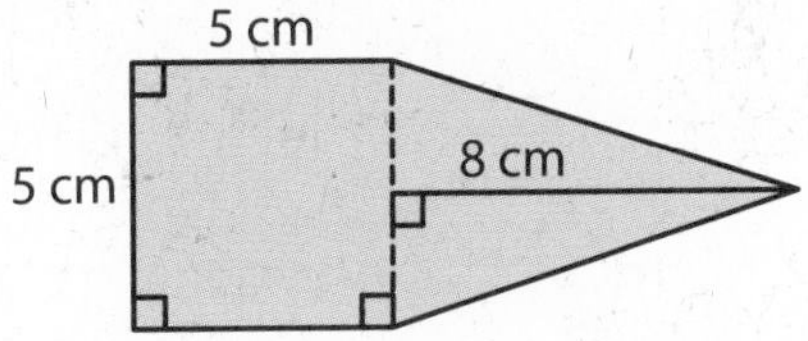

ESSENTIAL QUESTION

6. How can you find the area of an irregular polygon using area formulas?

____

____

____

____

Assessment Readiness

Personal Math Trainer
my.hrw.com
Online Practice and Help

1. The base of a rectangle is 3 centimeters long and its height is half the base length. A diagonal divides the rectangle into two identical triangles.

Select Yes or No to answer each question.

A. Is the area of each triangle 9 cm^2? ◯ Yes ◯ No

B. Is the area of the rectangle 4.5 cm^2? ◯ Yes ◯ No

C. Is there enough information given so you could find the perimeter of the rectangle? ◯ Yes ◯ No

2. In the triangle shown, the ratio of the height to the length of the base is 3 : 4.

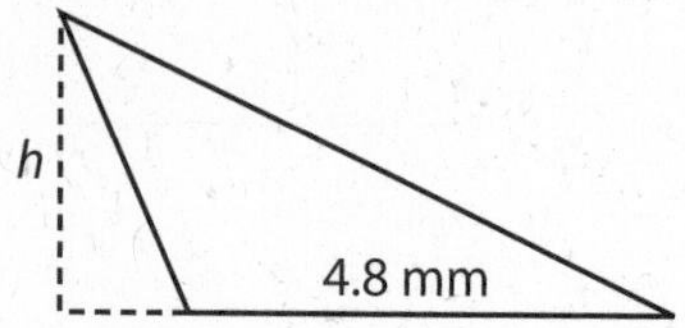

Choose True or False for statements A–C.

A. The area of the triangle is twice the area of a parallelogram with the same base and height. ◯ True ◯ False

B. The height is $\frac{3}{4}$ the base length. ◯ True ◯ False

C. The area is 8.64 mm^2. ◯ True ◯ False

3. The diagonals of a rhombus are 23 inches and 28 inches long. Luke notices that the diagonals divide the rhombus into four right triangles. Explain how he can find the area of the rhombus using the four triangles.

4. Cindy is designing a rectangular fountain in the middle of a courtyard. The rest of the courtyard will be covered in stone. The part of the courtyard that will be covered in stone has an area of 246 square feet.

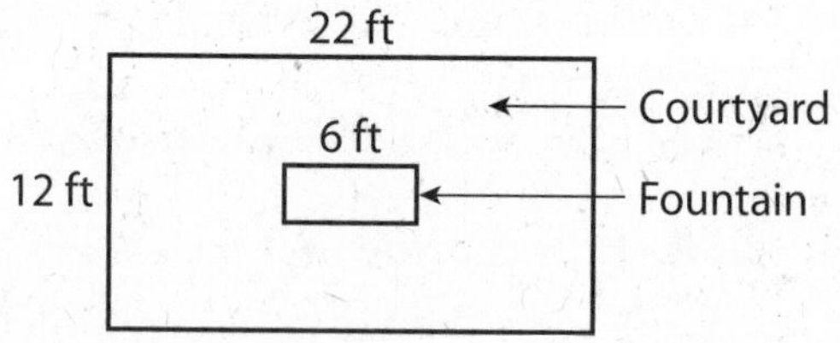

a. What is the width of the fountain? Show your work.

b. What fraction of the courtyard will be occupied by the fountain? Explain.

Distance and Area in the Coordinate Plane

MODULE 14

CALIFORNIA

ESSENTIAL QUESTION

What steps might you take to solve a polygon problem given the coordinates of its vertices?

LESSON 14.1

Distance in the Coordinate Plane

CA CC 6.NS.6b, 6.NS.8

LESSON 14.2

Polygons in the Coordinate Plane

CA CC 6.G.3

Real-World Video

Many cities are designed on a grid. You can use the lengths of blocks to calculate perimeters and areas just like on a coordinate plane.

my.hrw.com

GO DIGITAL
my.hrw.com

my.hrw.com

Go digital with your write-in student edition, accessible on any device.

Math On the Spot

Scan with your smart phone to jump directly to the online edition, video tutor, and more.

Animated Math

Interactively explore key concepts to see how math works.

Personal Math Trainer

Get immediate feedback and help as you work through practice sets.

Are YOU Ready?

Complete these exercises to review skills you will need for this module.

Personal Math Trainer
my.hrw.com
Online Practice and Help

Graph Ordered Pairs

EXAMPLE Find the coordinates for Point *A*.

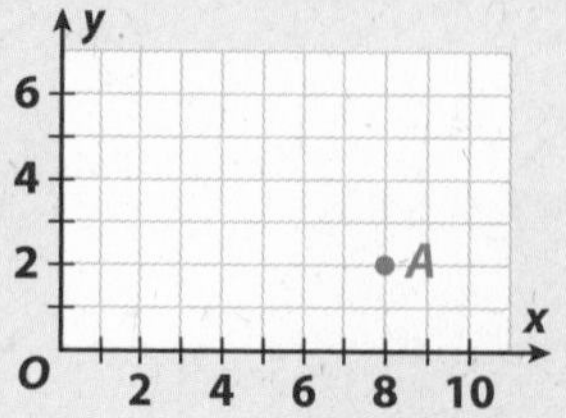

Start at O.
Count 8 units to the right and 2 units up from O.

The coordinates for Point *A* are (8, 2).

Write the ordered pair for each point shown on the graph.

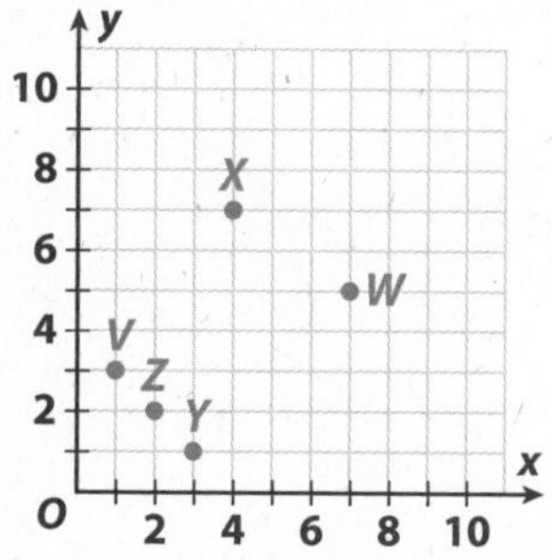

1. Point *V* ____________ **2.** Point *W* ____________

3. Point *X* ____________ **4.** Point *Y* ____________

5. Point *Z* ____________

Identify Polygons

EXAMPLE Name the type of polygon.

Count the number of sides.
Compare the sides.
Compare the angles.

There are 4 congruent sides and angles. The shape is a rhombus.

Name each figure. Choose from hexagon, isosceles triangle, right triangle, and trapezoid.

6. 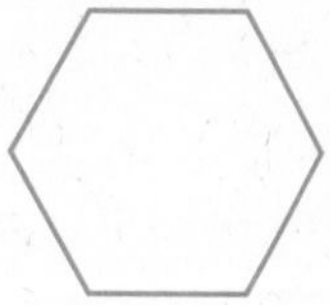 ____________

7. 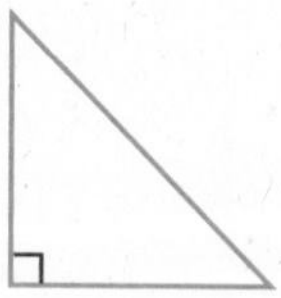 ____________

Reading Start-Up

Visualize Vocabulary

Use the ✔ words to complete the graphic.

Use the coordinates to find the distance from the origin on each →

Add or subtract these to find the distance between two points on a coordinate plane ↓

If a shape is formed, add the sides to find ←

If a rectangle is formed, multiply base and height to find

Vocabulary

Review Words

✔ absolute value *(valor absoluto)*
✔ area *(área)*
✔ axis *(eje)*
coordinate plane *(plano cartesiano)*
✔ perimeter *(perímetro)*

Preview Words

polygon *(polígono)*
reflection *(reflexión)*
vertex, vertices *(vértice, vértices)*

Understand Vocabulary

Complete the sentences using the preview words.

1. A corner of a rectangle is called a ________________.

2. How an image would appear in a mirror is called a ________________.

3. A two-dimensional shape with straight sides is a ________________.

Active Reading

Two-Panel Flip Chart Create a two-panel flip chart to help you understand the concepts in Lesson 14.1. Label one flap "Reflection across the *x*-axis." Label the other flap "Reflection across the *y*-axis." Write important ideas about each type of reflection under the appropriate flap.

GETTING READY FOR

Distance and Area in the Coordinate Plane

Understanding the standards and the vocabulary terms in the standards will help you know exactly what you are expected to learn in this module.

CA CC 6.NS.8

Solve real-world and mathematical problems by graphing points in all four quadrants of the coordinate plane. Include use of coordinates and absolute value to find distances between points with the same first coordinate or the same second coordinate.

What It Means to You

You will find the distance between two points on a coordinate plane.

EXAMPLE 6.NS.8

Find the distance between points *A* and *B*.

Add the absolute values of the *y*-coordinates.

$= |3| + |-4|$

$= 3 + 4$

$= 7$

The distance between points *A* and *B* is 7 units.

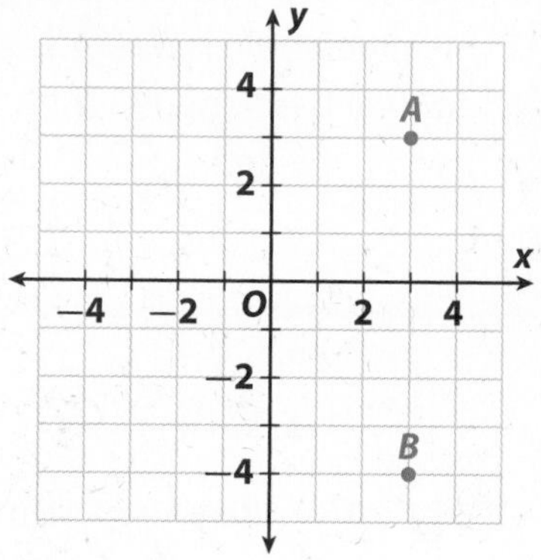

CA CC 6.G.3

Draw polygons in the coordinate plane given coordinates for the vertices; ...Apply thee techniques in the context of solving real-world and mathematical problems.

What It Means to You

You can draw polygons on a coordinate plane by plotting the vertices and connecting them.

EXAMPLE 6.G.3

What type of polygon can you make by plotting these points?

Point *A* $(-4, 2)$

Point *B* $(2, 2)$

Point *C* $(-4, -2)$

Point *D* $(2, -2)$

Connect each point.

The points make a rectangle.

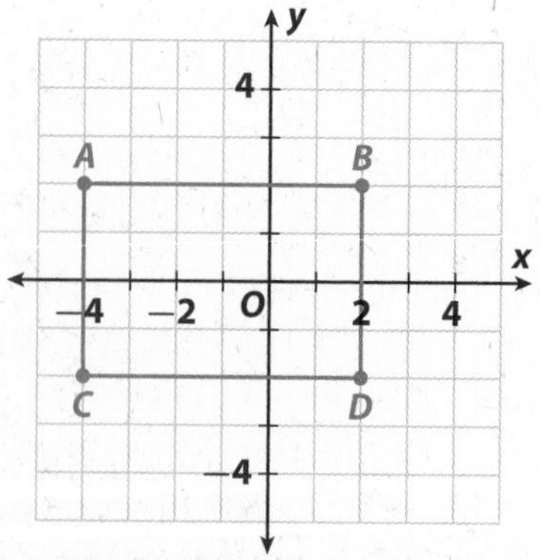

Visit my.hrw.com to see all CA Common Core Standards explained.

my.hrw.com

LESSON 14.1

Distance in the Coordinate Plane

CA CC 6.NS.8

Solve real-world and mathematical problems by graphing points in all four quadrants of the coordinate plane. Include use of coordinates and absolute value to find distances between points with the same first coordinate or the same second coordinate. *Also 6.NS.6b*

ESSENTIAL QUESTION

How can you use absolute value to find the distance between two points with the same *x*- or *y*-coordinates?

EXPLORE ACTIVITY 1 CA CC 6.NS.6b

Reflecting in the Coordinate Plane

A point on a coordinate plane can be *reflected* across an axis. The **reflection** is located on the opposite side of the axis, at the same distance from the axis.

Hold your paper up to the light if necessary to see the reflection.

Draw a coordinate plane on graph paper. Label both axes from −10 to 10.

A Graph (3, −2). Then fold your coordinate plane along the *y*-axis and find the reflection of (3, −2). Record the coordinates of the new point in the table.

B Unfold your coordinate plane. Then fold it along the *x*-axis and find the reflection of (3, −2). Record the coordinates of the new point in the table.

C Choose three additional points and repeat **A** and **B**.

Point	Reflected across *y*-axis	Reflected across *x*-axis
(3, −2)		

Reflect

1. What is the relationship between the coordinates of a point and the coordinates of its reflection across each axis?

____

____

____

2. **Conjecture** A point is reflected across the *y*-axis. Then the reflected point is reflected across the *x*-axis. How will the coordinates of the final point be related to the coordinates of the original point?

____

____

Math On the Spot

my.hrw.com

Finding Distances in the Coordinate Plane

You can use absolute values to find distances between two points that have the same *x*-coordinates or the same *y*-coordinates on a coordinate plane.

EXAMPLE 1

CA CC 6.NS.6b

Find each distance.

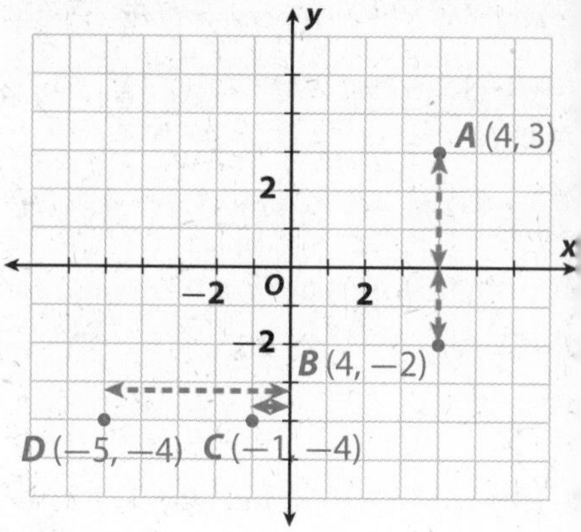

A What is the distance between point *A* and point *B*?

STEP 1 Find the distance between point *A* and the *x*-axis.

The *y*-coordinate of *A* is 3, so point *A* is $|3|$ units from the *x*-axis.

STEP 2 Find the distance between point *B* and the *x*-axis.

The *y*-coordinate of *B* is -2, so point *B* is $|-2| = 2$ units from the *x*-axis.

STEP 3 Find the sum of the distances.

Distance from *A* to $B = |3| + |-2| = 3 + 2 = 5$ units.

B What is the distance between point *D* and point *C*?

STEP 1 Find the distance between point *D* and the *y*-axis.

Point *D* is $|-5| = 5$ units from the *y*-axis.

STEP 2 Find the distance between point *C* and the *y*-axis.

Point *C* is $|-1| = 1$ unit from the *y*-axis.

STEP 3 Find the distance between *C* and *D* by finding this difference:

Distance of *D* from the *y*-axis − distance of *C* from the *y*-axis

$|-5| - |-1| = 4$ units

Math Talk

Mathematical Practices

How is the distance between a point and its reflection across an axis related to the distance between the point and the axis?

YOUR TURN

Find the distance between each pair of points.

3. *E*(−4, 7) and *F*(5, 7) ________

4. *G*(0, −5) and *H*(0, −10) ________

Personal Math Trainer

Online Practice and Help

my.hrw.com

Solving Distance Problems

You can solve problems using the distance between points on a grid.

EXAMPLE 2 Problem Solving

CA CC 6.NS.8

Math On the Spot
my.hrw.com

The coordinate plane represents a map. Each grid unit represents 20 miles. A retail company has warehouses at *M*(−70, 10) and *N*(50, 10). How long does it take a truck that drives 40 miles per hour to travel from warehouse *M* to warehouse *N*?

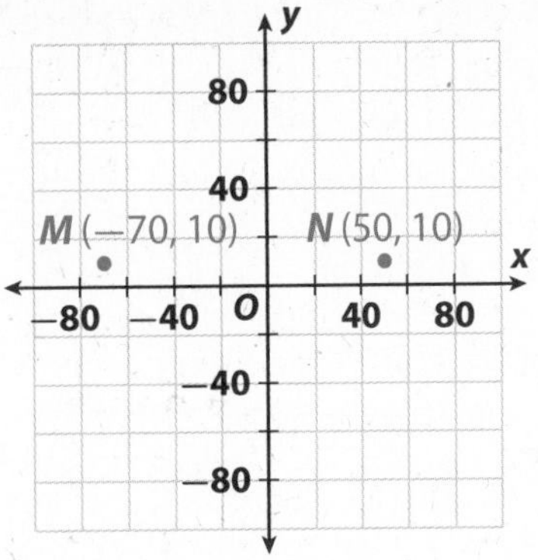

Analyze Information

Identify the important information.

- One warehouse is located at *M*(−70, 10). The other is at *N*(50, 10).
- A truck drives from *M* to *N* at a speed of 40 miles per hour.

Formulate a Plan

- Find the distance between *M* and *N* by adding the absolute values of the *x*-coordinates of the points.
- Find the time it takes the truck to drive this distance by using this relationship: distance = rate · time.

Solve

Add the absolute values of the *x*-coordinates to find the distance between point *M* and point *N* on the grid.

$$|-70| + |50| = 70 + 50 = 120$$

The warehouses are 120 miles apart.

The truck drives 120 miles at 40 mi/h. Because 120 = 40(3), it takes the truck 3 hours to travel from *M* to *N*.

Justify and Evaluate

You found the sum of the absolute values of the *x*-coordinates to find the horizontal distance on the grid. Then you used distance = rate · time to find the time it takes to drive that distance.

YOUR TURN

5. A store is located at *P*(50, −30). How long will it take a truck driving at 50 miles per hour to drive from warehouse *N* to this store?

____

Personal Math Trainer
Online Practice and Help
my.hrw.com

Guided Practice

1. The point (5, −2) is reflected across the *x*-axis. What are the coordinates of the reflection? (Explore Activity)

____

2. The point (−6, 8) is reflected across the *y*-axis. What are the coordinates of the reflection? (Explore Activity)

____

Use the coordinate plane. (Example 1)

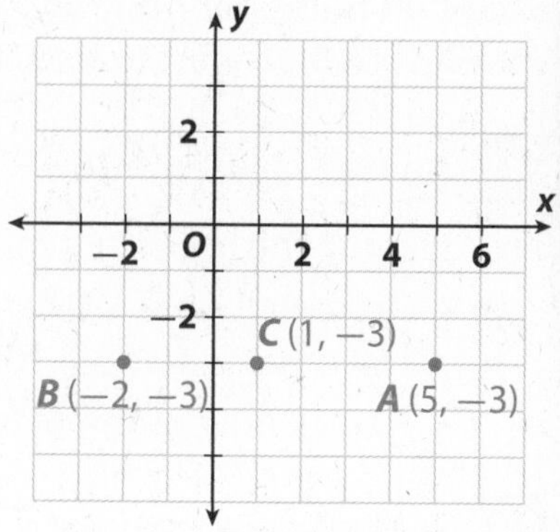

3. The distance between point *A* and point *B* is

$|\square| + |\square| = \square + \square = \square$ units.

4. The distance between point *A* and point *C* is

$|\square| - |\square| = \square - \square = \square$ units.

5. Plot the reflection of point *C* across the *y*-axis.
What is the distance between point *C* and its reflection? ______________

6. Plot the reflection of point *A* across the *x*-axis.
What is the distance of the reflection from the *x*-axis? ______________

Use the map shown. Each grid on the map represents 1 city block. (Example 2)

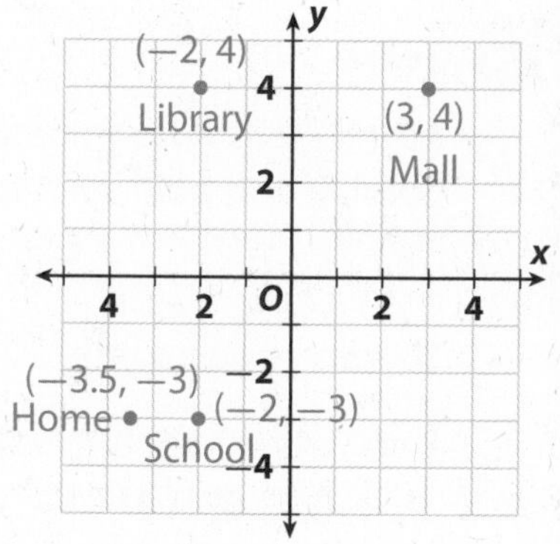

7. Yoko walks from the library to the mall.
How many city blocks does she walk? ______________

8. If Yoko walks 1 block in 3 minutes, how long does it take her to walk from the school to the library? How long does it take her to walk from home to school?

____

ESSENTIAL QUESTION CHECK-IN

9. How do you use absolute value to find the distance between two points that have the same *x*-coordinates but different *y*-coordinates?

____

____

____

____

Name ____________________ Class ____________ Date ____________

14.1 Independent Practice

CA CC 6.NS.6b, 6.NS.8

Use the coordinate plane.

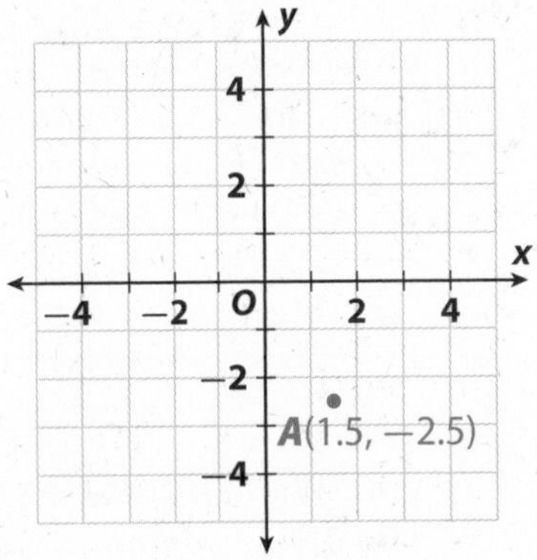

10. Plot the reflection of point *A* across the *x*-axis. What are the coordinates of the reflection of point *A* across the *x*-axis? What is the distance between point *A* and its reflection?

____

11. How can you plot the reflection of point *A* across the *y*-axis? Give the coordinates of the reflection across the *y*-axis, and tell how many units the reflection is from point *A*.

____

____

____

Find the coordinates of each point after the described reflection. Give the distance between each point and its reflection.

12. $R(-5, 8)$ is reflected across the *x*-axis. ____________________

13. $S(-7, -3)$ is reflected across the *y*-axis. ____________________

14. $T(8, 2)$ is reflected across the *x*-axis. ____________________

15. $U(2.4, -1)$ is reflected across the *y*-axis ____________________

Pedro uses a coordinate system to map the locations of some tourist locations in a large city. Each grid unit represents one mile.

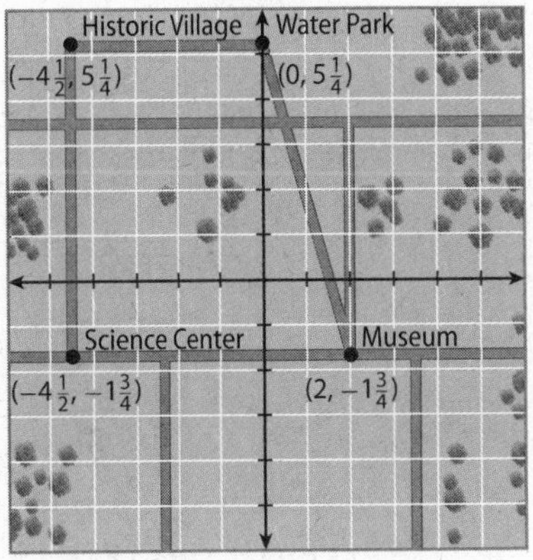

16. The planetarium, which is not marked on the map, is halfway between the historic village and the science center. What are its coordinates?

____

17. Pedro wants to walk from the historic village to the science center. Then he will walk from the science center to the museum. If he walks at a speed of $4\frac{1}{2}$ miles per hour, how long will it take him?

____

18. Pedro is staying at a hotel whose location is a reflection across the *x*-axis of the museum's location. What are the coordinates of the location of Pedro's hotel?

____

H.O.T. FOCUS ON HIGHER ORDER THINKING

Work Area

19. Communicate Mathematical Ideas Deirdre plotted a point D in Quadrant IV. After she reflected the point across an axis, the reflection was in Quadrant III. Give possible coordinates for point D and its reflection, and tell why you chose these coordinates.

____

____

____

____

____

20. Explain the Error Jason plotted the points (4, 4) and (−4, −4) on a coordinate plane. He says that the distance between the two points is 8 units because $|4| + |-4| = 8$. What mistake is Jason making?

____

____

____

21. Look for a Pattern A point is reflected over the x-axis and then reflected again over the y-axis. Will the coordinates after these two reflections be the same or different if the point is first reflected over the y-axis and then over the x-axis? Use an example to support your answer.

____

____

____

____

____

____

22. Explain the Error Bentley states that the distance between $R(-8, -3.5)$ and $S(-8, -12)$ is $|-12| + |-3.5| = 15.5$ units. Is Bentley correct? Explain your answer. If Bentley is not correct, explain how to find the correct distance between the points.

____

____

____

____

LESSON 14.2 Polygons in the Coordinate Plane

CA CC 6.G.3

Draw polygons in the coordinate plane given coordinates for the vertices; use coordinates to find the length of a side joining points with the same first coordinate or the same second coordinate. Apply these techniques in the context of solving real-world and mathematical problems.

ESSENTIAL QUESTION

How can you solve problems by drawing polygons in the coordinate plane?

EXPLORE ACTIVITY Real World CA CC 6.G.3

Polygons in the Coordinate Plane

A **polygon** is a closed plane figure formed by three or more line segments that meet only at their endpoints. A **vertex** is the point where two sides of a polygon meet. The *vertices* of a polygon can be represented as ordered pairs, and the polygon can then be drawn in the coordinate plane.

Sheila wants to make a pattern of two different tile shapes on a floor. She first graphs the shapes on a coordinate plane.

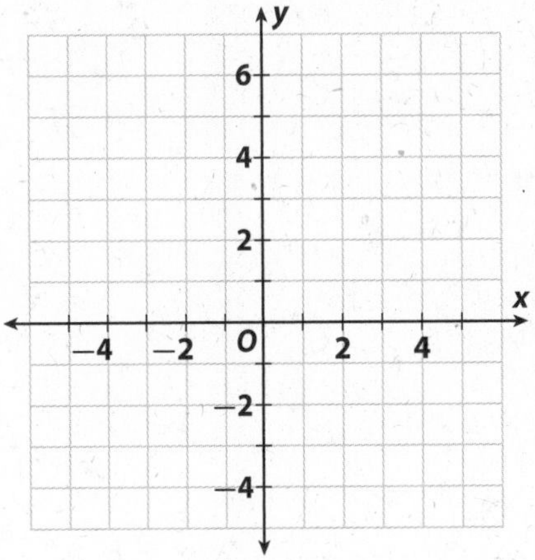

A Plot these points to form one of the tile shapes:

A(3, 5), *B*(4, 6), *C*(5, 5), *D*(4, 4)

Connect the points in order.

The polygon formed is a(n) ________________.

B Plot these points to form the other tile shape:

P(−5, 2), *Q*(−4, 3), *R*(0, 3), *S*(1, 2),

T(1, −2), *U*(0, −3), *V*(−4, −3), *W*(−5, −2)

Connect the points in order.

The polygon formed is a(n) ________________.

Reflect

1. How is the number of vertices related to the number of sides of the polygon and to the type of polygon? Give two examples.

____

____

____

____

Finding Perimeter in the Coordinate Plane

You can use what you know about finding lengths in the coordinate plane to find the perimeter of a polygon.

Math On the Spot
my.hrw.com

EXAMPLE 1 Real World

CA CC 6.G.3

The grid shows the path Tommy followed when he walked from his home at (0, 0) to various locations and back home again. If each grid square represents one block, how many blocks did he walk?

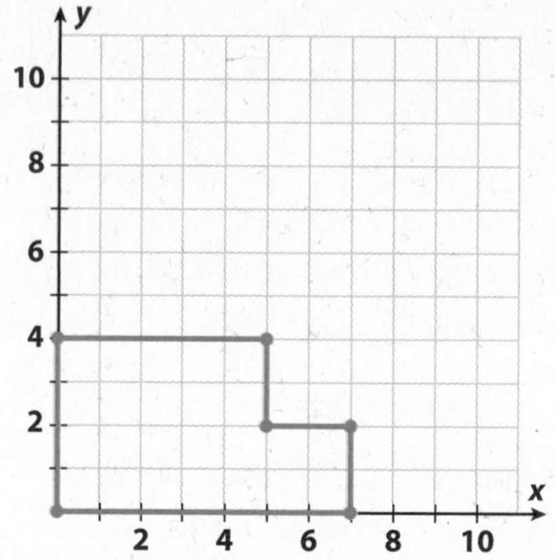

Home (0, 0)

Library (0, 4)

Park (5, 4)

Friend's house (5, 2)

Pond (7, 2)

Store (7, 0)

Math Talk
Mathematical Practices

How do you find the distance between two points in the same quadrant that have the same *x*-coordinate?

STEP 1 Find each distance. Each grid unit represents one block.

Tommy's home (0, 0) to the library (0, 4) is $|4| - 0 = 4 - 0 = 4$ blocks.

The library (0, 4) to the park (5, 4) is $|5| - 0 = 5 - 0 = 5$ blocks.

The park (5, 4) to Tommy's friend's house (5, 2) is $|4| - |2| = 4 - 2 = 2$ blocks.

Tommy's friend's house (5, 2) to the pond (7, 2) is $|7| - |5| = 7 - 5 = 2$ blocks.

The pond (7, 2) to the store (7, 0) is $|2| - 0 = 2 - 0 = 2$ blocks.

The store (7, 0) to Tommy's home (0, 0) is $|7| - 0 = 7 - 0 = 7$ blocks.

STEP 2 Find the sum of the distances.

Tommy walked $4 + 5 + 2 + 2 + 2 + 7 = 22$ blocks.

Personal Math Trainer
Online Practice and Help
my.hrw.com

YOUR TURN

2. Suppose the next day Tommy walks from his home to the mall at (0, 8), and then walks to a movie theater at (7, 8). After leaving the theater Tommy walks to the store at (7, 0) before returning home.

How far does he walk? __________ blocks

Finding Area in the Coordinate Plane

You can use familiar area formulas to find areas of polygons in the coordinate plane.

Math On the Spot
my.hrw.com

EXAMPLE 2 Real World

CA CC 6.G.3

Caleb is planning a new deck for his house. He graphs the deck as polygon *ABCDEF* on a coordinate plane in which each grid unit represents one foot. The vertices of the polygon are *A*(1, 0), *B*(3, 2), *C*(3, 5), *D*(8, 5), *E*(8, 2), and *F*(6, 0). What is the area of Caleb's deck?

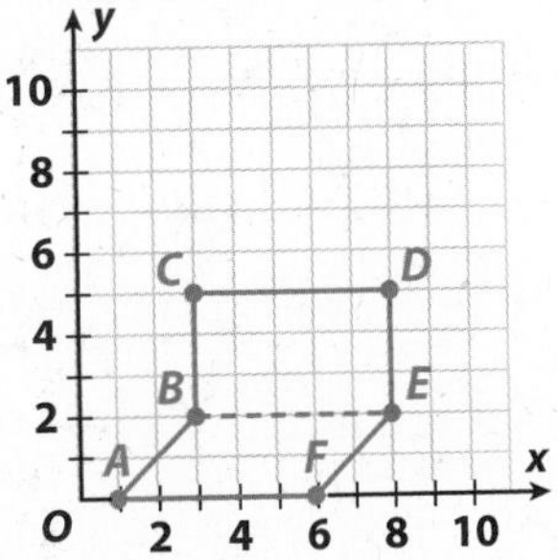

STEP 1 Graph the vertices, and connect them in order.

Draw a horizontal dashed line segment to divide the polygon into two quadrilaterals—a rectangle and a parallelogram.

STEP 2 Find the area of the rectangle using the length of segment *BE* as the base *b* and the length of segment *BC* as the height *h*.

$b = |8| - |3| = 5$ feet $\qquad h = |5| - |2| = 3$ feet

$A = bh = 5 \cdot 3 = 15$ square feet

STEP 3 Find the area of the parallelogram using the length of segment *AF* as the base. Use the length of a segment from *F*(6, 0) to the point (6, 2) as the height *h*.

$b = |6| - |1| = 5$ feet $\qquad h = |2| - 0 = 2$ feet

$A = bh = 5 \cdot 2 = 10$ square feet

STEP 4 Add the areas to find the total area of the deck.

$A = 15 + 10 = 25$ square feet

YOUR TURN

3. The vertices of a polygon are *L*(1, 2), *M*(1, 6), *N*(7, 6), *O*(7, 2), *P*(5, 0), and *Q*(3, 0). Graph the polygon. Then find its area.

$A =$ __________ square units

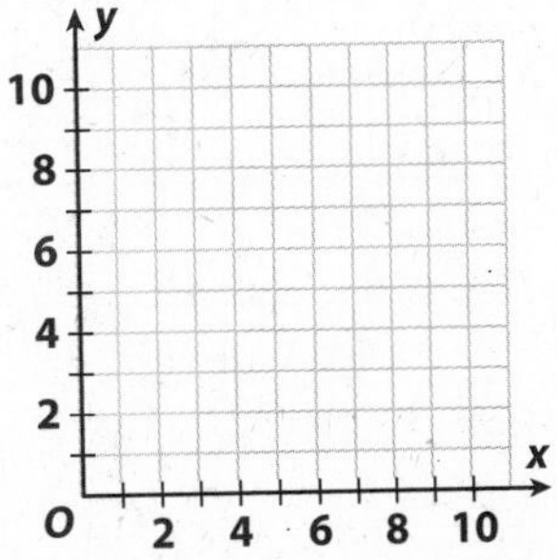

Personal Math Trainer
Online Practice and Help
my.hrw.com

Guided Practice

A gardener uses a coordinate grid to design a new garden. The gardener uses polygon *WXYZ* on the grid to represent the garden. The vertices of this polygon are *W*(3, 3), *X*(−3, 3), *Y*(−3, −3), and *Z*(3, −3). Each grid unit represents one yard.

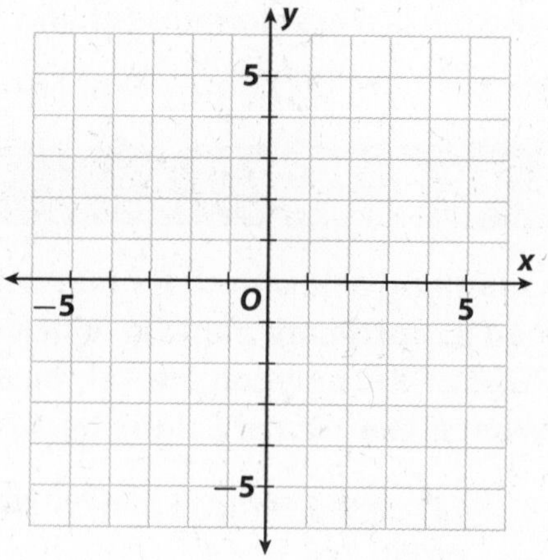

1. Graph the points, and connect them in order. What is the shape of the garden? (Explore Activity)

____

2. How much fencing will the gardener need to enclose the garden? (Example 1)

Each side of the garden is __________ yards in length.

The gardener will need __________ yards of fencing to enclose the garden.

3. What is the area of the garden? (Example 2)

____

4. A clothing designer makes letters for varsity jackets by graphing the letters as polygons on a coordinate plane. One of the letters is polygon *ABCDEF*. The vertices of this polygon are *A*(3, −2), *B*(3, −4), *C*(−3, −4), *D*(−3, 4), *E*(−1, 4), and *F*(−1, −2). Each grid unit represents one inch. Graph the points on the coordinate plane, and connect them in order. Identify the letter formed. Then find its area. (Example 2)

____

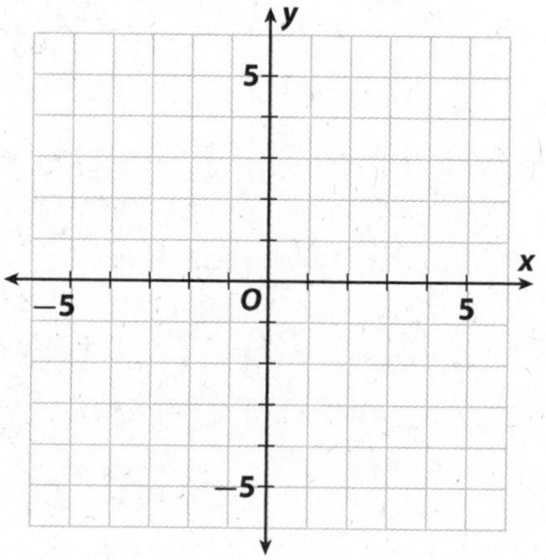

ESSENTIAL QUESTION CHECK-IN

5. How can you use a coordinate plane to solve perimeter and area problems?

____

____

____

____

Name ______ Class ______ Date ______

14.2 Independent Practice

CA CC 6.G.3

Personal Math Trainer
my.hrw.com
Online Practice and Help

6. A graphic designer creates letters for wall art by first graphing the letters as polygons on a coordinate plane. One of the letters is polygon *MNOPQRSTUV* with vertices *M*(2, 1), *N*(2, 9), *O*(7, 9), *P*(7, 7), *Q*(4, 7), *R*(4, 6), *S*(6, 6), *T*(6, 4), *U*(4, 4), and *V*(4, 1). Each grid unit represents one inch.

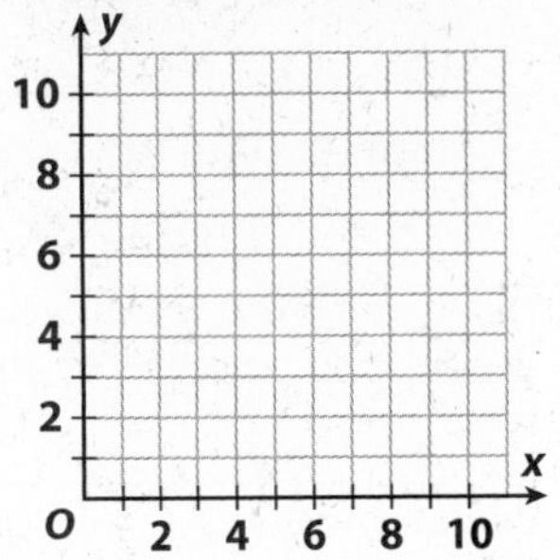

a. Graph the points on the coordinate plane, and connect them in order. What letter is formed? ______

b. The designer will use decorative tape to paint the outline of the letter on a wall. How many inches of tape are needed? ______

c. How much space does the letter cover on the wall? ______

d. How did you find your answer to c? Use the name(s) of shapes in your answer.

______

______

7. Vocabulary The polygon shown is a regular polygon since all sides have equal length and all angles have equal measure.

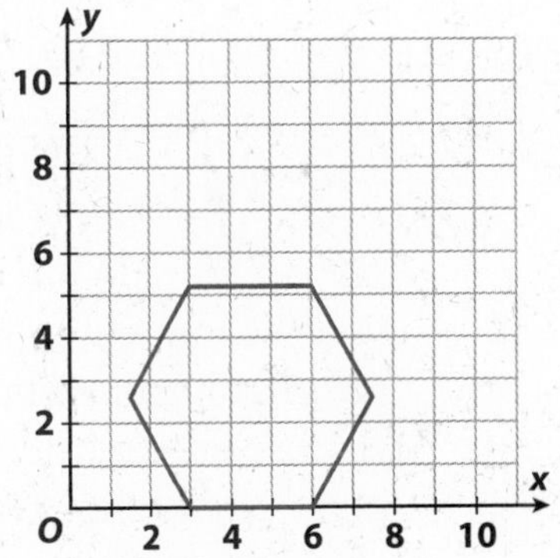

a. The polygon is a regular ______.

b. What is the perimeter of the polygon? ______

c. A line can divide the figure into two identical four-sided polygons. Each polygon has two bases, and one base is twice the length of the other base. Identify the polygon, and give its perimeter.

______

8. Jean wants to put furniture in her clubhouse. She drew a floor plan of the clubhouse, as shown. Each grid unit represents one foot.

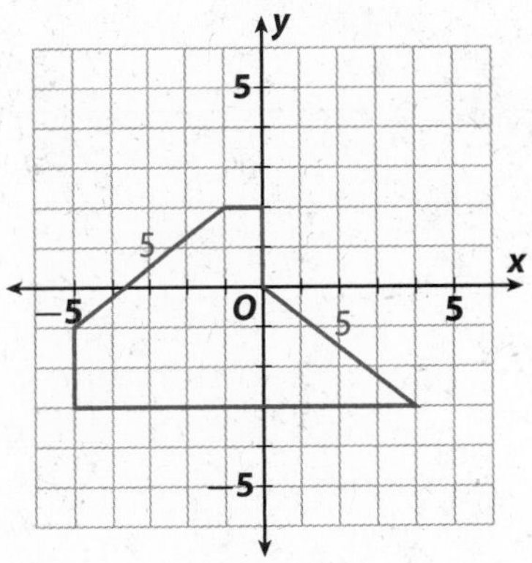

a. Which polygon names the shape of the floor?

______

b. How many feet of baseboard are needed to go around the entire clubhouse?

______

c. How much carpet is needed for the clubhouse floor?

______

H.O.T. FOCUS ON HIGHER ORDER THINKING

Work Area

9. Persevere in Problem Solving To find the area of triangle *ABC*, Jen first drew a square around the figure. Two sides of the square passed through the points *B* and *C*. The other two sides met at point *A*. Draw Jen's square, and explain how you can use it to find the area of triangle *ABC*.

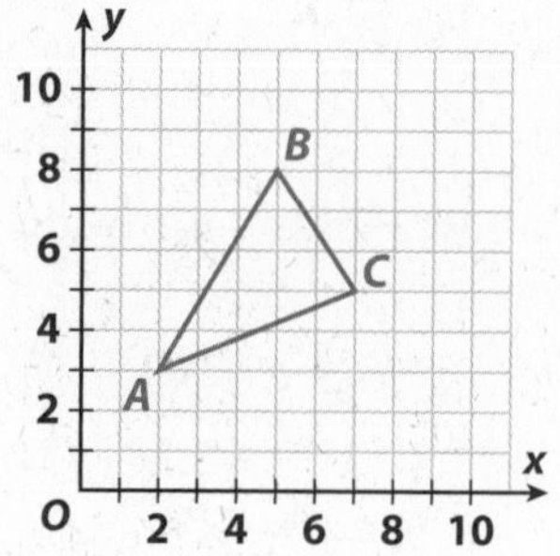

10. Communicate Mathematical Ideas The coordinates $A(5, -2)$, $B(3, -1)$, $C(-4, -4)$, $D(-3, 8)$, and $E(-1, 4)$ form the vertices of a polygon when they are connected in order from *A* through *E*. Classify the polygon without plotting the points. Explain your answer.

11. Explain the Error Josh's teacher draws a regular octagon on a coordinate plane. One side has endpoints at (1, 5) and (4, 5). Josh says he can't find the perimeter of the octagon because he can only find lengths of horizontal and vertical segments. He says he can't find the lengths of the slanted sides of the octagon. What mistake is Josh making? What is the perimeter of the octagon?

12. Critical Thinking Give coordinates for the vertices of a triangle that could have an area of 35 square units. Prove that your triangle fits the description by finding its area.

MODULE QUIZ

Ready to Go On?

Personal Math Trainer
Online Practice and Help
my.hrw.com

14.1 Distance in the Coordinate Plane

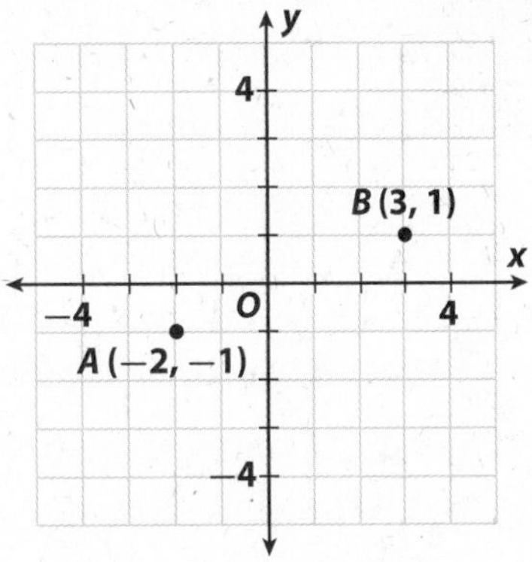

1. Reflect *A* across the *x*-axis. Label the reflection as *N*, and give its coordinates on the graph.

2. Reflect *B* across the *x*-axis. Label the reflection as *M*, and give its coordinates on the graph.

3. The distance between *A* and *N* is ______________.

4. Suppose the graph represents a map in which each grid unit equals 1 mile. If a school is located at *B* and a library is located at *N*, what is the distance between the school and the library? ______________

Find the coordinates of the point for each reflection.

5. (−5, 7) across the *x*-axis ____________

6. (2, 5.5) across the *y*-axis ____________

Find the distance between each pair of points.

7. (1, 1) and (1, −2) ____________ units

8. (−2, 3) and (−4, 3) ____________ units

14.2 Polygons in the Coordinate Plane

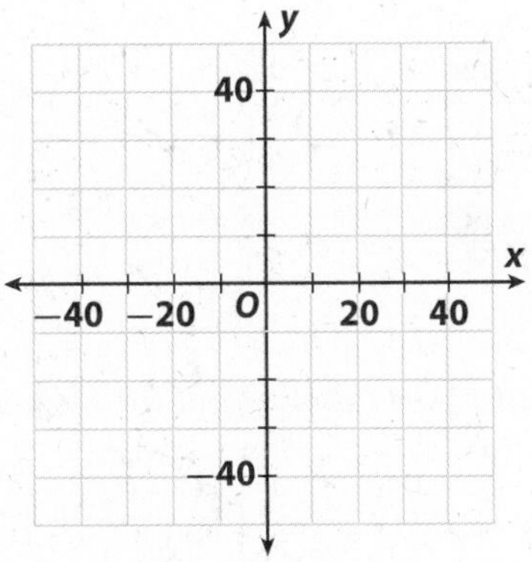

9. On the coordinate plane shown, each grid unit represents 10 feet. Polygon *QRST* has vertices *Q*(10, 20), *R*(−10, 20), *S*(−10, −10), and *T*(10, −10), and represents the floor plan of a room. Find the perimeter and area of the room.

____

____

ESSENTIAL QUESTION

10. Suppose you are given the coordinates of the vertices of a polygon. What steps could you take to solve a problem involving the polygon's area?

____

____

____

CALIFORNIA

MODULE 14
MIXED REVIEW

Assessment Readiness

my.hrw.com | Personal Math Trainer | Online Practice and Help

1. Consider the coordinates of the given points.

Select Yes or No in A–C to indicate whether if the points are reflections of each other across the *y*-axis on the coordinate plane.

A. (8, 12) and (−12, −8) ◯ Yes ◯ No
B. (5, −3) and (−5, −3) ◯ Yes ◯ No
C. (−4, −7) and (4, −7) ◯ Yes ◯ No

2. Look at each statement. Choose True or False for A–C.

A. The greatest common factor of 12 and 30 is 3. ◯ True ◯ False
B. The least common multiple of 18 and 36 is 36. ◯ True ◯ False
C. The greatest common factor of 15 and 20 is 60. ◯ True ◯ False

3. Plot the reflection of point *L* across the *x*-axis. Label this new point *M*. Then explain how to use absolute values to find the distance between points *J* and *M*.

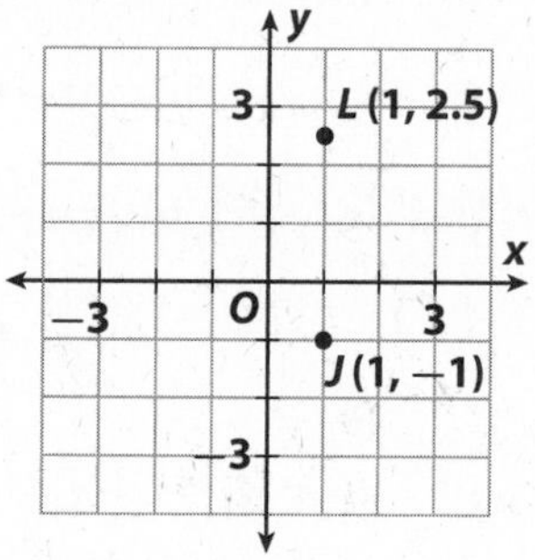

4. Polygon *EFGH* has vertices *E*(4, 4), *F*(−4, 4), *G*(−4, −4), and *H*(4, −4).

a. Plot *EFGH* on the grid and tell what type of polygon it is. What is the area of the polygon?

b. The area of a right triangle is half the area of *EFGH*. Points *G* and *H* are two vertices of the triangle, and angle *G* is a right angle. If the third vertex of the triangle is in Quadrant II, what are its coordinates? Explain.

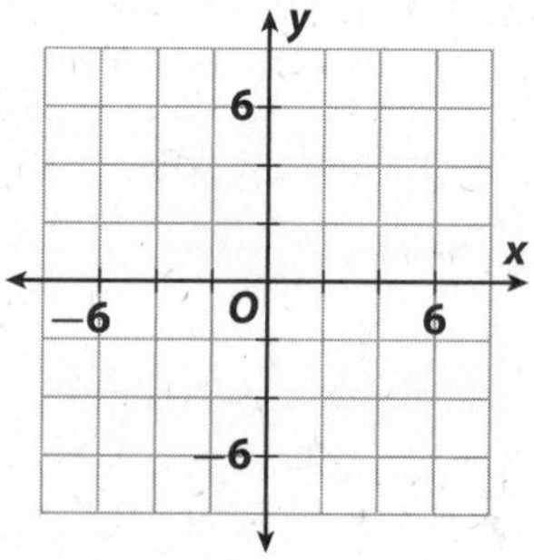

Surface Area and Volume of Solids

MODULE 15

CALIFORNIA

ESSENTIAL QUESTION

How can a model help you to solve surface area and volume problems?

Real-World Video

Surface area and volume can be important considerations when constructing or repairing buildings or other structures.

my.hrw.com

GO DIGITAL
my.hrw.com

my.hrw.com
Go digital with your write-in student edition, accessible on any device.

Math On the Spot
Scan with your smart phone to jump directly to the online edition, video tutor, and more.

Animated Math
Interactively explore key concepts to see how math works.

Personal Math Trainer
Get immediate feedback and help as you work through practice sets.

Are YOU Ready?

Complete these exercises to review skills you will need for this module.

Personal Math Trainer
my.hrw.com
Online Practice and Help

Use of Parentheses

EXAMPLE $\frac{1}{2}(14)(12 + 18) = \frac{1}{2}(14)(30)$ *Perform operations inside parentheses first.*

$= 7(30)$ *Multiply left to right.*

$= 210$ *Multiply again.*

Evaluate.

1. $\frac{1}{2}(3)(5 + 7)$ ________

2. $\frac{1}{2}(15)(13 + 17)$ ________

3. $\frac{1}{2}(10)(9.4 + 3.6)$ ________

4. $\frac{1}{2}(2.1)(3.5 + 5.7)$ ________

Area of Square, Rectangles, Triangle

EXAMPLE Find the area of the rectangle.

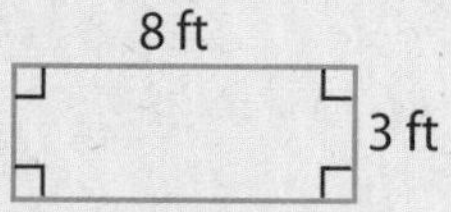

$A = bh$ *Use the formula for area of a rectangle.*

$= 8 \cdot 3$ *Substitute for base and height.*

$= 24$ *Multiply.*

Area equals 24 square feet.

Find the area of each figure.

5. a triangle with base 6 in. and height 3 in. ________

6. a square with sides of 7.6 m ________

7. a rectangle with length $3\frac{1}{4}$ ft and width $2\frac{1}{2}$ ft ________

8. a triangle with base 8.2 cm and height 5.1 cm ________

Reading Start-Up

Visualize Vocabulary

Use review words to complete the graphic.

Shape	Area Formula
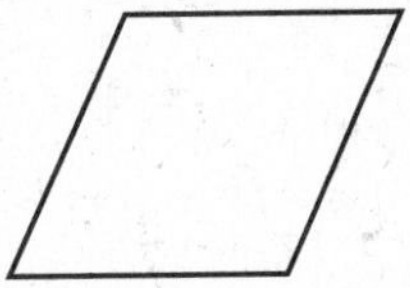	$A = b \times$ ________
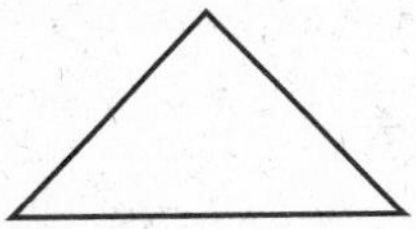	$A = \frac{1}{2} \times$ ________ $\times h$

Vocabulary

Review Words

- area *(área)*
- base *(base)*
- height *(altura)*
- rectangular prism *(prisma rectangular)*
- volume *(volumen)*

Preview Words

- net *(plantilla)*
- pyramid *(pirámide)*
- surface area *(área total)*

Understand Vocabulary

Complete the sentences using the preview words.

1. The total area of all the faces of a three-dimensional figure is called the ________________.

2. A model that looks like an unfolded three-dimensional figure is a ________________.

3. A three-dimensional shape with a polygon for a base and triangles for sides is a ________________.

Active Reading

Booklet Before beginning the module, create a booklet to help you learn the concepts in this module. Write the main idea of each lesson on each page of the booklet. As you study each lesson, write important details that support the main idea, such as vocabulary and important steps in solving problems. Refer to your finished booklet as you work on assignments and study for tests.

GETTING READY FOR

Surface Area and Volume of Solids

CALIFORNIA

Understanding the standards and the vocabulary terms in the standards will help you know exactly what you are expected to learn in this module.

CA CC 6.G.2

Find the volume of a right rectangular prism with fractional edge lengths by packing it with unit cubes of the appropriate unit fraction edge lengths, and show that the volume is the same as would be found by multiplying the edge lengths of the prism. Apply the formulas $V = lwh$ and $V = bh$ to find volumes of right rectangular prisms with fractional edge lengths in the context of solving real-world and mathematical problems.

What It Means to You

You will use the formula for the volume of a rectangular prism.

EXAMPLE 6.G.2

Jala has an aquarium in the shape of a rectangular prism. The dimensions of the base of the aquarium are $1\frac{1}{4}$ feet by $\frac{1}{2}$ foot, and the height is $\frac{3}{4}$ foot. Find the volume of the aquarium.

$$v = l \cdot w \cdot h$$
$$= 1\frac{1}{4} \cdot \frac{1}{2} \cdot \frac{3}{4}$$
$$= \frac{5}{4} \cdot \frac{1}{2} \cdot \frac{3}{4}$$
$$= \frac{15}{32}$$

The volume of the aquarium is $\frac{15}{32}$ cubic foot.

CA CC 6.G.4

Represent three-dimensional figures using nets made up of rectangles and triangles, and use the nets to find the surface area of these figures....

What It Means to You

You will use a net to find the surface area of a square pyramid.

EXAMPLE 6.G.4

Meg drew a net to find the surface area of a square pyramid.

Square face: $A = b \times h = 16$ square inches

Triangular face: $A = \frac{1}{2} b \times h = 6$ square inches

Total of the areas:
$16 + (4 \times 6) = 40$ square inches

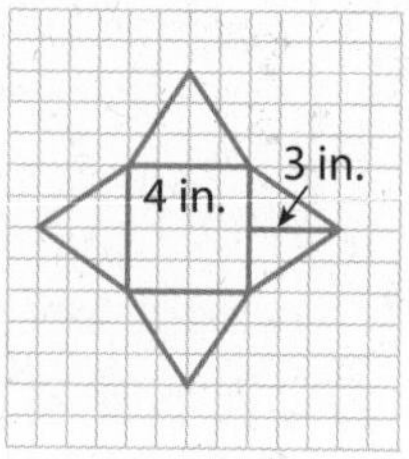

The surface area is 40 square inches.

Visit my.hrw.com to see all CA Common Core Standards explained.

my.hrw.com

LESSON
15.1 Nets and Surface Area

CA CC 6.G.4

Represent three-dimensional figures using nets made up of rectangles and triangles, and use the nets to find the surface area of these figures. Apply these techniques in the context of solving real-world and mathematical problems.

ESSENTIAL QUESTION

How can you use nets to find surface areas?

EXPLORE ACTIVITY CA CC 6.G.4

Using a Net

A **net** is a two-dimensional pattern of shapes that can be folded into a three-dimensional figure. The shapes in the net become the sides, or faces, of the three-dimensional figure.

A Copy each net on graph paper. Cut out each net along the blue lines.

Net A

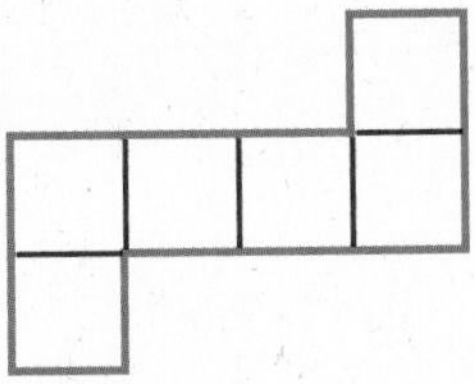

Net B

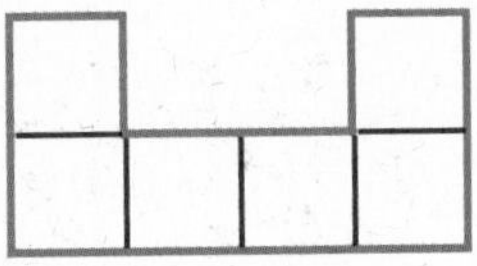

One of these nets can be folded along the black lines to make a cube with no open sides. Which net will NOT make a cube with no open sides? ______________________

B On your graph paper, draw a different net that you think will make a cube. Confirm by cutting out and folding your net. Compare results with several of your classmates. How many different nets for a cube did you and your classmates find? ______________________

Reflect

How do you know that each net cannot be folded into a cube with no open sides without actually cutting and folding it?

1.

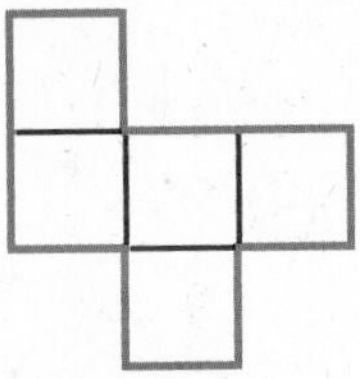

____

____

2.

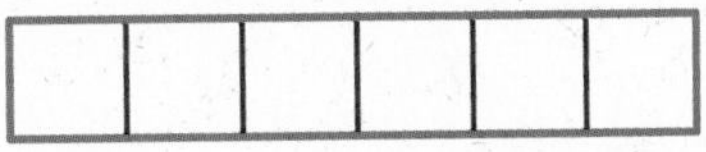

____

____

____

EXPLORE ACTIVITY *(cont'd)*

3. **Critical Thinking** Suppose you cut up a rectangular cereal box along its edges. If you lay it flat, what shapes will you see? How many of these shapes will there be? ______________________

Math On the Spot
my.hrw.com

Surface Area of a Pyramid

The **surface area** of a three-dimensional figure is the sum of the areas of its faces. A net can be helpful when finding surface area.

A **pyramid** is a three-dimensional figure whose base is a polygon and whose other faces are triangles that meet at a point. A pyramid is identified by the shape of its base.

EXAMPLE 1

CA CC 6.G.4

Make a net of this square pyramid, and use the net to find the surface area.

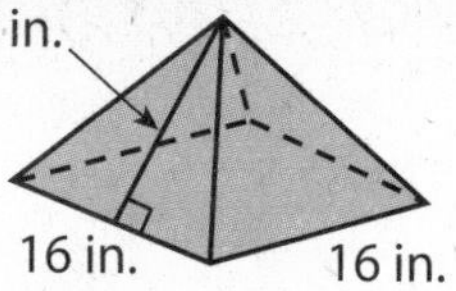

STEP 1 Make a net of the pyramid.

Draw the square base.

Draw a triangle on each side.

Label the dimensions.

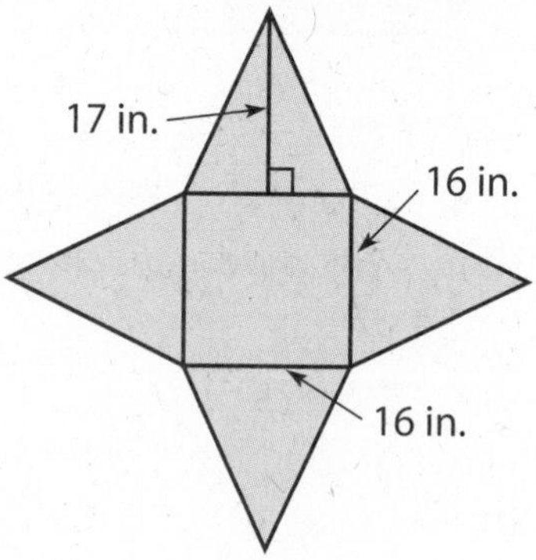

STEP 2 Use the net to find the surface area.

There are four triangles with base 16 in. and height 17 in.

The area of the 4 triangles is $4 \cdot \frac{1}{2}(16)(17) = 544\text{ in}^2$.

The area of the base is $16 \cdot 16 = 256\text{ in}^2$.

The surface area is $544 + 256 = 800\text{ in}^2$.

Animated Math
my.hrw.com

Math Talk
Mathematical Practices

How many surfaces does a triangular pyramid have? What shape are they?

YOUR TURN

4. Use a net to find the surface area of the pyramid.

____

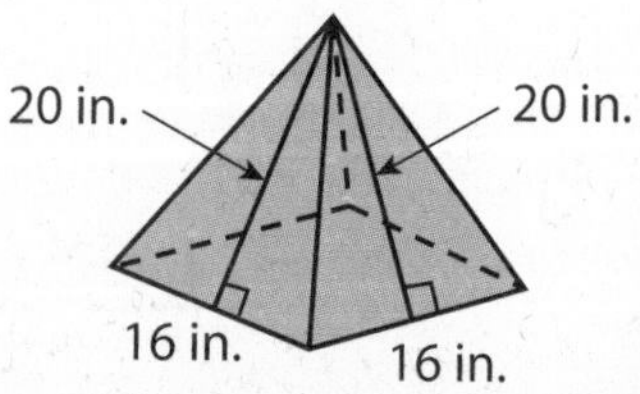

Personal Math Trainer
Online Practice and Help
my.hrw.com

Surface Area of a Prism

A **prism** is a three-dimensional figure with two identical and parallel bases that are polygons. A prism is identified by the shape of its bases. For example, a triangular prism has triangles as its bases. In this book, all prisms are right prisms, which means that the faces that are not bases are rectangles.

Math On the Spot
my.hrw.com

EXAMPLE 2

CA CC 6.G.4

A sculpture sits on pedestal in the shape of a square prism. The side lengths of a base of the prism are 3 feet. The height of the prism is 4 feet. The museum director wants to cover all but the underside of the pedestal with foil that costs $0.22 per square foot. How much will the foil cost?

STEP 1 Use a net to show the faces that will be covered with foil.

Draw the top.

Draw the faces of the prism that are connected to the top.

You don't need to include the bottom of the pedestal.

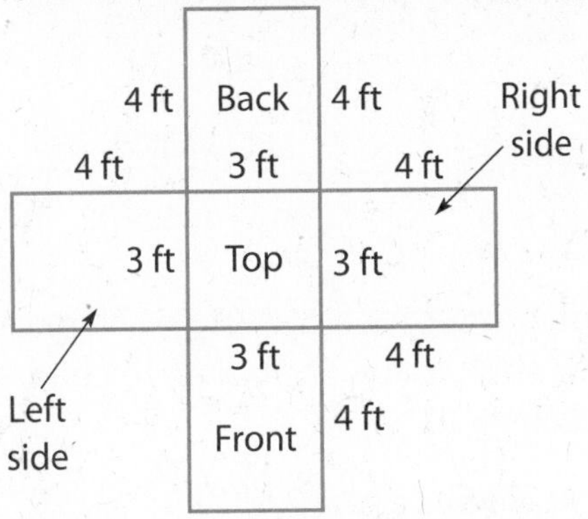

STEP 2 Use the net to find the area that will be covered with foil.

Area of top $= 3 \cdot 3 = 9 \text{ ft}^2$

The other four faces are identical.

Area of four faces $= 4 \cdot 3 \cdot 4 = 48 \text{ ft}^2$

Area to be covered $= 9 + 48 = 57 \text{ ft}^2$

STEP 3 Find the cost of the foil.

$57 \cdot \$0.22 = \$12.54$

The foil will cost $12.54.

Reflect

5. **Critical Thinking** What shapes would you see in the net of a triangular prism?

My Notes

Personal Math Trainer

Online Practice and Help

my.hrw.com

YOUR TURN

6. The figure shown is a triangular prism. How much would it cost to cover the bases and the other three faces with foil that costs $0.22 per square foot?

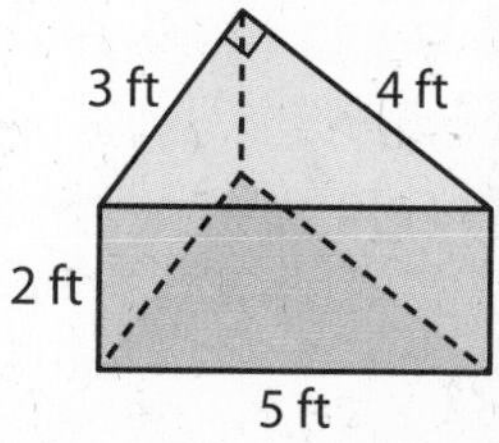

____

Guided Practice

A square pyramid is shown.

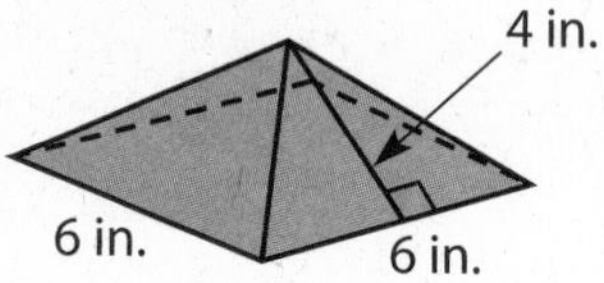

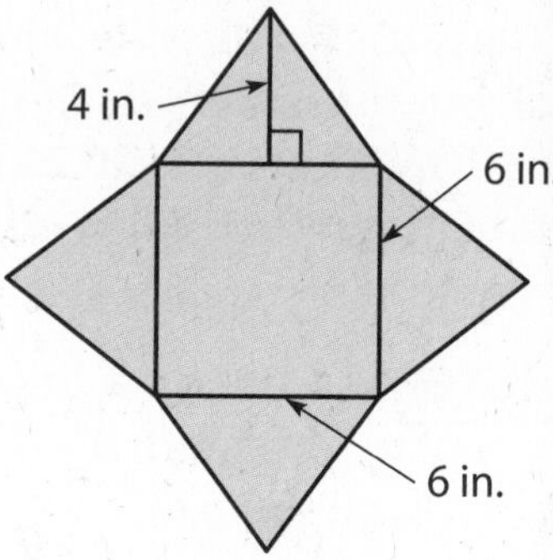

1. The figure has ____________ square base and ____________ triangular faces. (Explore Activity)

2. Find the surface area. (Example 1)

   The area of the base is ________ square inches.

   The area of the four faces is ________ square inches.

   The surface area is ________ square inches.

3. Yolanda makes wooden boxes for a crafts fair. She makes 100 boxes like the one shown, and she wants to paint all the outside faces. (Example 2)

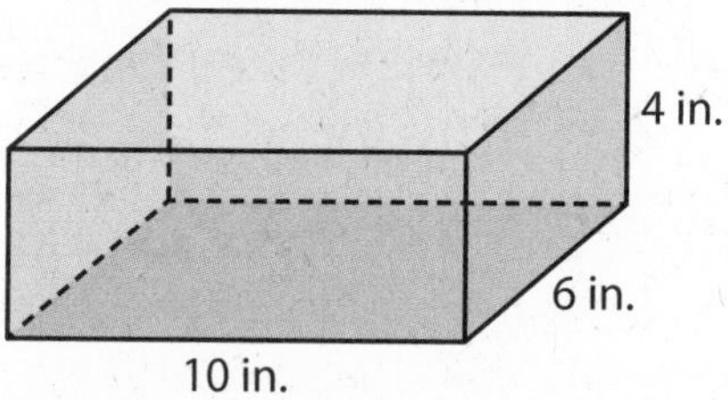

   a. Find the surface area of one box.

   ____

   b. Find the total surface area of 100 boxes.

   ____

   c. One can of paint will cover 14,000 square inches. How many cans of paint will Yolanda need to buy?

   ____

ESSENTIAL QUESTION CHECK-IN

4. How is a net useful when finding the surface area of prisms and pyramids?

____

____

____

Name ______________________ Class ______________________ Date ______________________

15.1 Independent Practice

CA CC 6.G.4

Personal Math Trainer
Online Practice and Help
my.hrw.com

5. Use a net to find the surface area of the cereal box.

Total surface area: ______________________

6. Inez bought a shipping container at a packaging store. She measured the dimensions shown to the nearest tenth.

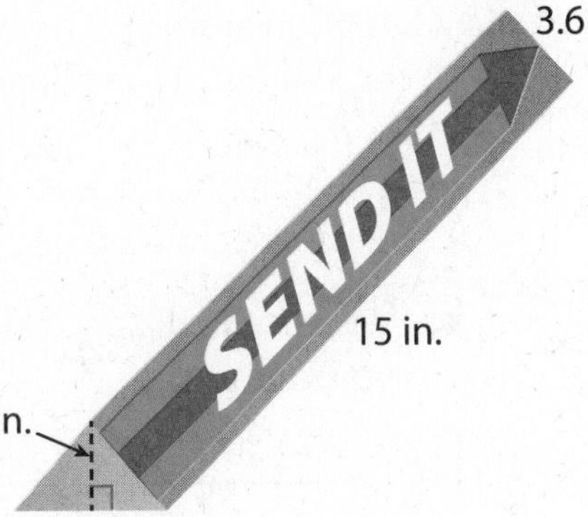

a. Sketch a net of the container, and label the dimensions.

b. Find the surface area of the shipping container.

____

7. Raj builds a side table in the shape of a cube. Each edge of the cube measures 20 inches. Raj wants to cover the top and four sides of the table with ceramic tiles. Each tile has an edge length of 5 inches. How many tiles will he need?

____

8. Santana wants to cover a gift box shaped like a rectangular prism with foil. The foil costs $0.03 per square inch. Santana has a choice between Box A which is 8 inches long, 3 inches wide, and 6 inches high, and Box B which is 10 inches long, 3 inches wide, and 4 inches high. Which box will be less expensive to cover with foil, and by how much?

____

9. **Vocabulary** Name a three-dimensional shape that has four triangular faces and one rectangular face. Name a three-dimensional shape that has three rectangular faces and two triangular faces.

____

10. Victor wrapped the gift box shown with adhesive paper (with no overlaps). How much paper did he use?

____

11. **Communicate Mathematical Ideas** Describe how you approach a problem involving surface area. What do you do first? What are some strategies you can use?

____

____

____

____

____

H.O.T. FOCUS ON HIGHER ORDER THINKING

Work Area

12. **Persevere in Problem Solving** A pedestal in a craft store is in the shape of a triangular prism. The bases are right triangles with side lengths of 12 centimeters, 16 centimeters, and 20 centimeters. The store owner wraps a piece of rectangular cloth around the pedestal, but does not cover the identical bases of the pedestal with cloth. The area of the cloth is 192 square centimeters.

a. What is the distance around the base of the pedestal? How do you know?

____

____

b. What is the height of the pedestal? How did you find your answer?

____

____

____

13. **Critique Reasoning** Robert sketches two rectangular prisms, A and B. Prism A's side lengths are 5 centimeters, 6 centimeters, and 7 centimeters. Prism B's side lengths were twice those of prism A's: 10 centimeters, 12 centimeters, and 14 centimeters. Robert says the surface area of prism B is twice the surface area of prism A. Is he correct? If he is not, how many times as great as prism A's surface area is prism B's surface area? Show your work.

____

____

____

____

LESSON **15.2**

Volume of Rectangular Prisms

CA CC 6.G.2

Find the volume of a right rectangular prism with fractional edge lengths.... (For the full text of the standard, see the table at the front of the book beginning on page CA2.)

ESSENTIAL QUESTION

How do you find the volume of a rectangular prism?

EXPLORE ACTIVITY CA CC 6.G.2

Using Fractional Edge Lengths

A cube with edge length 1 unit and volume 1 cubic unit is filled with smaller cubes as shown.

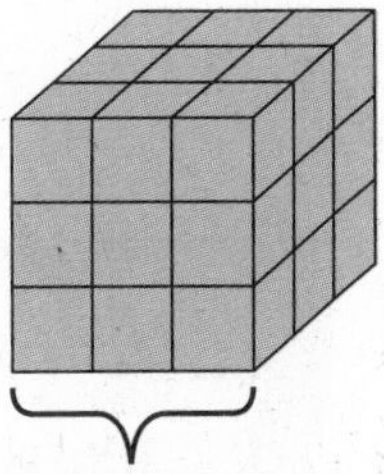

A How many small cubes are used to fill the large cube?

_______________ small cubes

B What is the volume of one small cube? How do you know?

____

____

C What is the edge length of one small cube? _______________ unit

D The formula for volume of a cube with edge length ℓ is $V = \ell \cdot \ell \cdot \ell$, or $V = \ell^3$. Find the volume of one small cube using this formula.

$V =$ _______________ $=$ _______________

E Compare the volume you found in **D** with the volume you found in **B**.

____

Reflect

1. Suppose a cube has an edge length of $\frac{2}{3}$ unit. If you fill this cube with the smaller cubes shown above, how many smaller cubes would you need? What is the volume of a cube with edge length $\frac{2}{3}$ unit? Explain.

____

____

2. **Critique Reasoning** Ben says the volume of a cube with edge length $\frac{3}{4}$ unit is $\frac{3}{4}$ the volume of a unit cube. Do you agree? Explain.

____

Math On the Spot
my.hrw.com

Finding Volume

A rectangular prism has six faces. Any pair of opposite faces can be called the **bases** of the prism.

Volume of a Rectangular Prism

$V = \ell wh$, or $V = Bh$

(where B represents the area of the prism's base; $B = \ell w$)

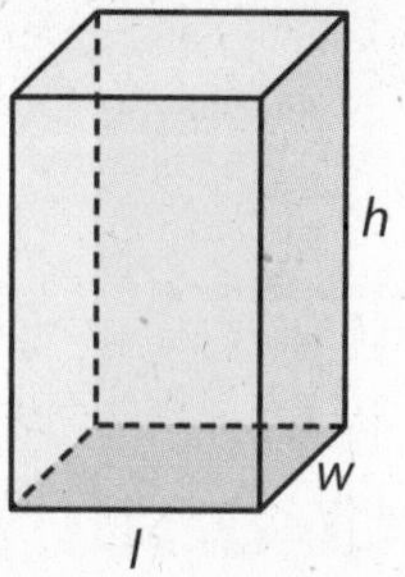

EXAMPLE 1

CA CC 6.G.2

Find the volume of the rectangular prism.

Use the formula $V = Bh$.

Math Talk
Mathematical Practices
Why can any face of a prism like the one in this example be considered a base of the prism?

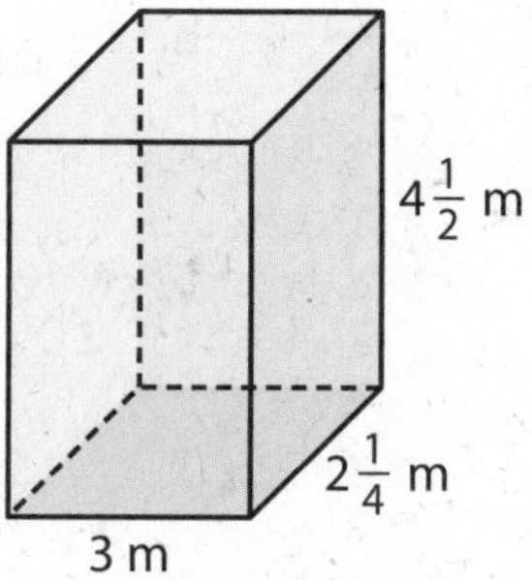

STEP 1 Choose one face to be a base and find its area.

$B = 3 \cdot 2\frac{1}{4}$ — Use the formula $l \cdot w$ to find the area.

$= 3 \cdot \frac{9}{4}$ — Write the mixed number as a fraction.

$= \frac{27}{4}$ — Multiply.

STEP 2 Find the volume.

$V = Bh$

$= \frac{27}{4} \cdot 4\frac{1}{2}$ — Substitute values for B and h.

$= \frac{27}{4} \cdot \frac{9}{2}$ — Write the mixed number as a fraction.

$= \frac{243}{8}$ — Multiply.

$= 30\frac{3}{8}$ cubic meters. — Write as a mixed number in simplest form.

Reflect

3. **Communicate Mathematical Ideas** In Step 1, why does it make sense to leave the area of the base as an improper fraction?

YOUR TURN

Find the volume of each rectangular prism.

4.

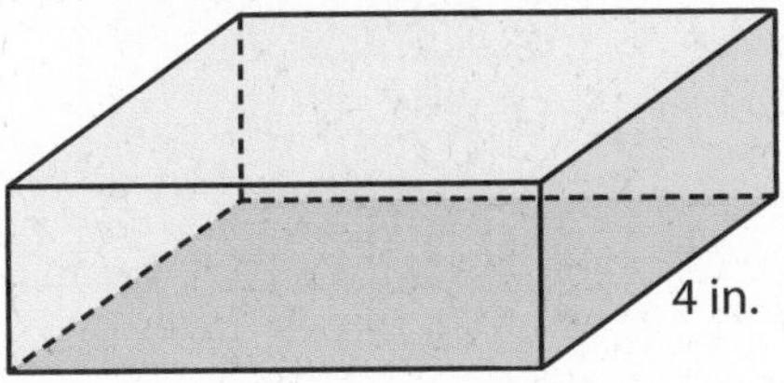

____

5. length $= 5\frac{1}{4}$ inches

width $= 3\frac{1}{2}$ inches

height $= 3$ inches

____

Personal Math Trainer
Online Practice and Help
my.hrw.com

Solving Volume Problems

When you solve a real-world problem involving the volume of a prism, you can choose to use either of the volume formulas you know.

Math On the Spot
my.hrw.com

EXAMPLE 2 Real World

CA CC 6.G.2

A terrarium is shaped like a rectangular prism. The prism is $25\frac{1}{2}$ inches long, $13\frac{1}{2}$ inches wide, and 16 inches deep. What is the volume of the terrarium?

STEP 1 Choose one side to be the base, and find its area.

$B = 25\frac{1}{2} \cdot 13\frac{1}{2}$ — Use the $25\frac{1}{2}$-inch by $13\frac{1}{2}$- inch face as the base.

$= \frac{51}{2} \cdot \frac{27}{2}$

$= \frac{1,377}{4}$

The area of the base is $\frac{1,377}{4}$ square inches. You need to perform another operation, so you don't need to write this value as a mixed number.

STEP 2 Find the volume.

$V = Bh$

$= \frac{1,377}{4} \cdot 16$ — Substitute $\frac{1,377}{4}$ for B and 16 for h.

$= \frac{1,377}{{}_1\cancel{4}} \cdot \frac{\cancel{16}^{\,4}}{1}$ — Simplify before multiplying.

$= 5,508$

The volume of the terrarium is 5,508 cubic inches.

YOUR TURN

6. A rectangular swimming pool is 15 meters long, $10\frac{1}{2}$ meters wide, and $2\frac{1}{2}$ meters deep. What is its volume?

____

Personal Math Trainer
Online Practice and Help
my.hrw.com

Guided Practice

The cube shown has an edge length of $\frac{4}{5}$ unit and is filled with smaller cubes. (Explore Activity)

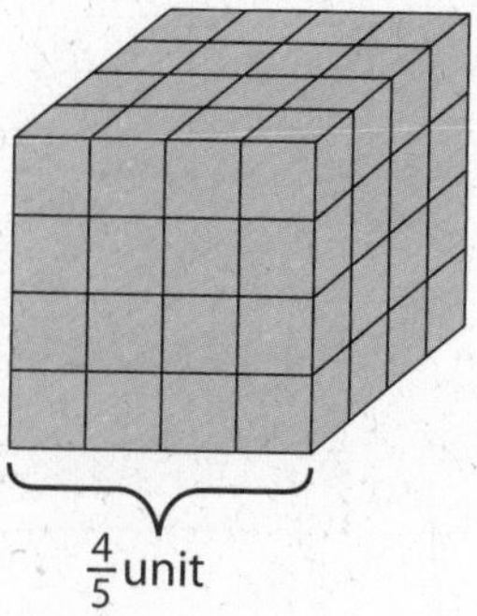

1. How many small cubes are there? ______

2. The volume of the large cube is ______ cubic unit.

Find the volume of each prism. (Example 1)

3.

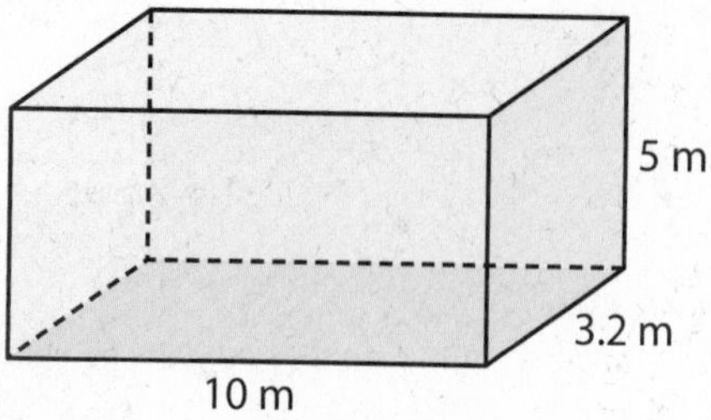

$V =$ ______ $\times$ ______ $\times$ ______

$=$ ______ cubic meters

4.

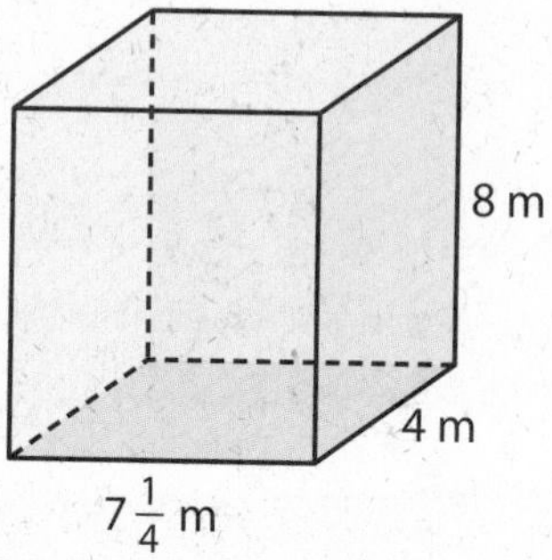

$B =$ ______ $\times$ ______ $=$ ______ m^2

$V =$ ______ cubic meters

5.

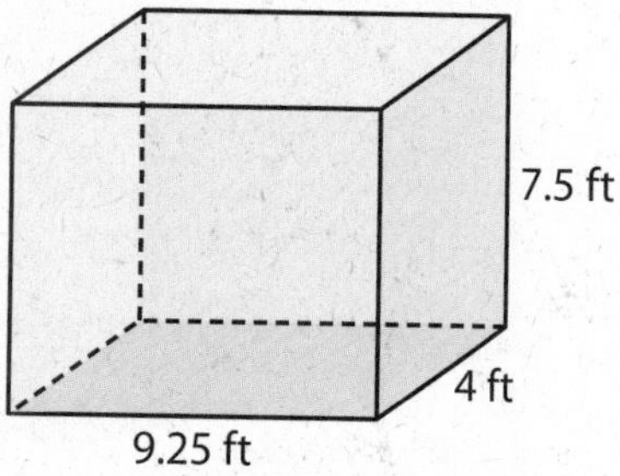

$V =$ ______ cubic feet

6.

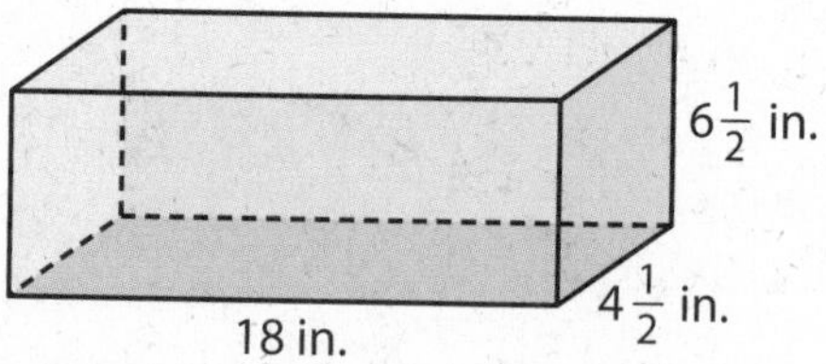

$V =$ ______ cubic inches

7. A cereal box is $8\frac{1}{2}$ inches long, $3\frac{1}{2}$ inches wide, and 12 inches high.

What is the volume of the box? (Example 2) ______

? ESSENTIAL QUESTION CHECK-IN

8. Which two formulas can you use to find the volume of a rectangular prism? Why are these two formulas equivalent?

______

______

______

Name ________________ Class ________________ Date ________________

15.2 Independent Practice

CA CC 6.G.2

Personal Math Trainer

Online Practice and Help

my.hrw.com

9. A block of wood measures 4.5 inches by 3.5 inches by 7 inches. What is the volume of the block of wood?

____

10. A restaurant buys a freezer in the shape of a rectangular prism. The dimensions of the freezer are shown. What is the volume of the freezer?

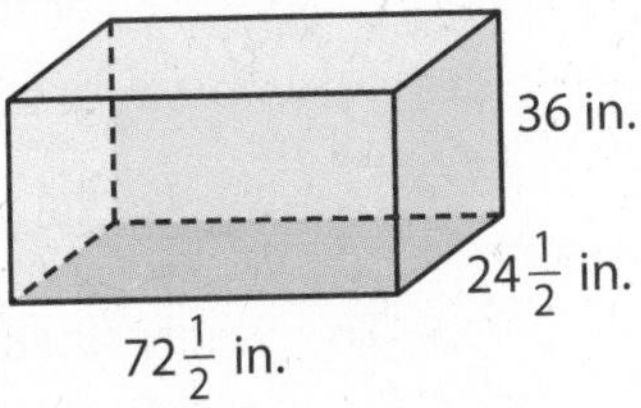

____

11. Rectangular prism A measures 6 inches by 4 inches by 5 inches. Rectangular prism B's dimensions are twice those of prism A. Find the volume of each prism. How many times as great is prism B's volume as prism A's volume?

____

12. A cube has the dimensions shown. What is the volume of the cube? How many smaller cubes with an edge length of $\frac{1}{8}$ inch could fit inside the cube shown?

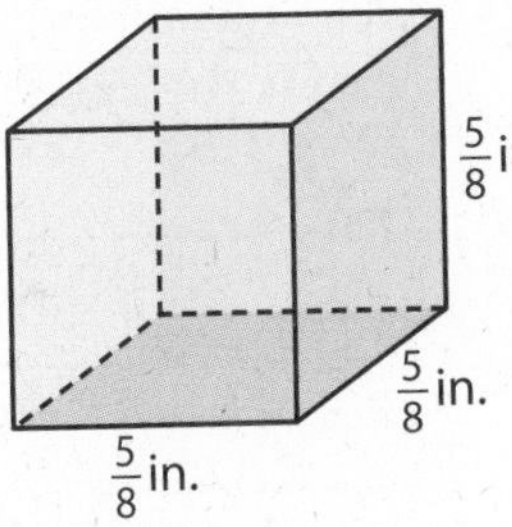

____

13. A company is designing a juice box. The box is in the shape of a rectangular prism. The base of the box is $6\frac{1}{2}$ inches by $2\frac{1}{2}$ inches, and the box is 4 inches high. If juice fills 90% of the box's volume, find the volume of juice in the box.

____

14. **Science** Density is the amount of mass in a certain volume of an object. To find the density in grams per cubic centimeter of a substance you can use this relationship:

$$\text{Density} = \frac{\text{mass in grams}}{\text{volume in cubic centimeters}}$$

A gold bar that is 16 centimeters by 2.5 centimeters by 5 centimeters has a density of 19.3 grams per cubic centimeter. What is the mass of the gold bar?

____

15. A suitcase is a rectangular prism whose dimensions are $1\frac{1}{4}$ feet by $1\frac{3}{4}$ feet by $1\frac{1}{4}$ feet. Find the volume of the suitcase.

____

16. The Smith family is moving and needs to decide on the size of the moving truck they should rent.

Inside Dimensions of Trucks			
Type	**Length (ft)**	**Width (ft)**	**Heigh (ft)**
Van	$10\frac{1}{2}$	6	6
Small Truck	12	8	$6\frac{3}{4}$
Large Truck	20	$8\frac{3}{4}$	$8\frac{1}{2}$

a. A moving van rents for $94.50 per day, and a small truck rents for $162 per day. Based on the amount of space inside the van or truck, which is the better deal? Explain your answer.

____

____

____

b. How much greater is the volume of the large truck than the volume of the small truck? ______________

c. The family needs about 1,100 cubic feet to move their belongings. What should they rent? ______________

H.O.T. FOCUS ON HIGHER ORDER THINKING

Work Area

17. **Persevere in Problem Solving** A cube has a volume of $\frac{1}{512}$ cubic meter. What is the cube's edge length? What is its surface area? Explain.

____

____

____

18. **Communicate Mathematical Ideas** Think about two rectangular prisms, one labeled prism *P* and one labeled prism *Q*.

a. Suppose the bases of the prisms have the same area, but the height of prism *Q* is twice the height of prism *P*. How do the volumes compare?

____

b. Suppose the area of the base of prism *Q* is twice the area of the base of prism *P*. How do the volumes compare?

____

19. **Critical Thinking** The dimensions of a rectangular prism are $3\frac{1}{4}$ feet by $2\frac{1}{2}$ feet by 5 feet. Lee found the volume by multiplying $12\frac{1}{2}$ by $3\frac{1}{4}$. Lola found the volume by multiplying $16\frac{1}{4}$ by $2\frac{1}{2}$. Who is correct? Explain.

____

____

____

____

LESSON 15.3

Solving Volume Equations

CA CC 6.G.2

Find the volume of a right rectangular prism with fractional edge lengths by packing it with unit cubes of the appropriate unit fraction edge lengths, and show that the volume is the same as would be found by multiplying the edge lengths of the prism. Apply the formulas $V = \ell wh$ and $V = bh$ to find volumes of right rectangular prisms with fractional edge lengths in the context of solving real-world and mathematical problems.

ESSENTIAL QUESTION

How do you write equations to solve problems involving the volume of rectangular prisms?

Writing Equations Using the Volume of a Rectangular Prism

You can use the formula for the volume of a rectangular prism to write an equation. Then solve the equation to find missing measurements for a prism.

Math On the Spot
my.hrw.com

EXAMPLE 1 Real World

CA CC 6.G.2, 6.EE.7

Samuel has an ant farm with a volume of 375 cubic inches. The width of the ant farm is 2.5 inches and the length is 15 inches. What is the height of Samuel's ant farm?

$V = \ell wh$ — Write the formula.

$375 = 15(2.5)h$ — Use the formula to write an equation.

$375 = 37.5h$ — Multiply.

$\frac{375}{37.5} = \frac{37.5h}{37.5}$ — Divide both sides of the equation by 37.5.

$10 = h$

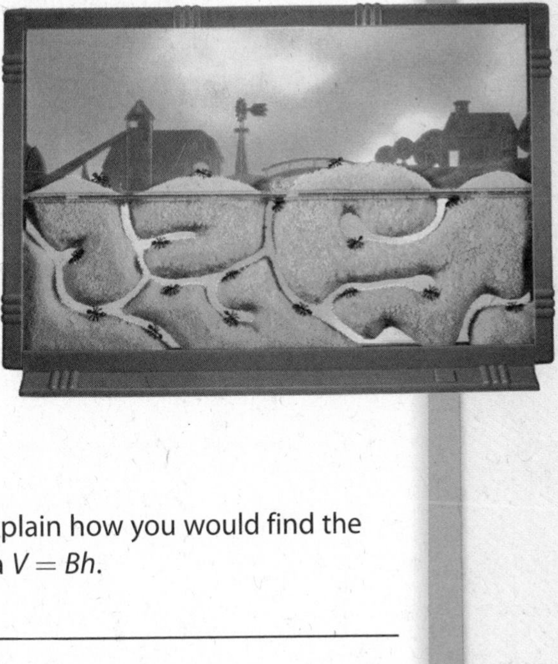

The height of the ant farm is 10 inches.

Reflect

1. **Communicate Mathematical Ideas** Explain how you would find the solution to Example 1 using the formula $V = Bh$.

____

____

YOUR TURN

2. Find the height of this rectangular prism, which has a volume of $\frac{15}{16}$ cubic feet.

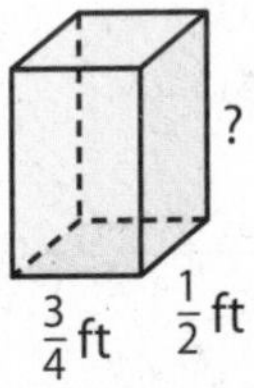

____

Personal Math Trainer
Online Practice and Help
my.hrw.com

Math On the Spot

my.hrw.com

Solving Multistep Problems

Paying attention to the units used in a real-world situation can help you solve multistep problems.

EXAMPLE 2 Real World

CA CC 6.G.2, 6.EE.7

The classroom aquarium holds 30 gallons of water. It is 0.8 feet wide and has a height of 2 feet. Find the length of the aquarium. Use the fact that one cubic foot of water contains about 7.5 gallons of water.

STEP 1 Find the volume of the classroom aquarium in cubic feet.

$$\frac{30 \text{ gallons}}{7.5 \text{ gallons per cubic foot}} = 4 \text{ cubic feet}$$

There are 7.5 gallons in 1 cubic foot. Divide to find how many groups of 7.5 gallons are in 30 gallons.

STEP 2 Find the length of the aquarium.

$4 = \ell\,(0.8)(2)$ — *Use the formula $V = \ell wh$ to write an equation.*

$4 = \ell(1.6)$ — *Multiply.*

$\frac{4}{1.6} = \frac{\ell(1.6)}{1.6}$ — *Divide both sides of the equation by 1.6.*

$2.5 = \ell$

The length of the aquarium is 2.5 feet.

Math Talk

Mathematical Practices

Why do you need to convert from gallons to cubic feet in this problem?

YOUR TURN

3. An aquarium holds 33.75 gallons of water. It has a length of 2 feet and a height of 1.5 feet. What is the width of the aquarium? ______________

Personal Math Trainer

Online Practice and Help

my.hrw.com

Guided Practice

1. Use an equation to find the width of the rectangular prism. (Example 1)

____

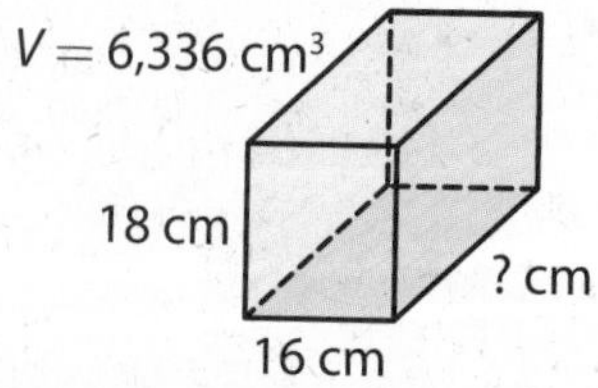

2. One clay brick weighs 5.76 pounds. The brick is 8 inches long and $2\frac{1}{4}$ inches wide. If the clay weighs 0.08 pound per cubic inch, what is the volume of the brick? Find the height of the brick. (Example 2)

____

Name ____________________ Class ____________________ Date ____________________

15.3 Independent Practice

CA CC 6.EE.7, 6.G.2

Personal Math Trainer
Online Practice and Help
my.hrw.com

3. Jala has an aquarium in the shape of a rectangular prism with the dimensions shown. What is the height of the aquarium?

Height = ____________________

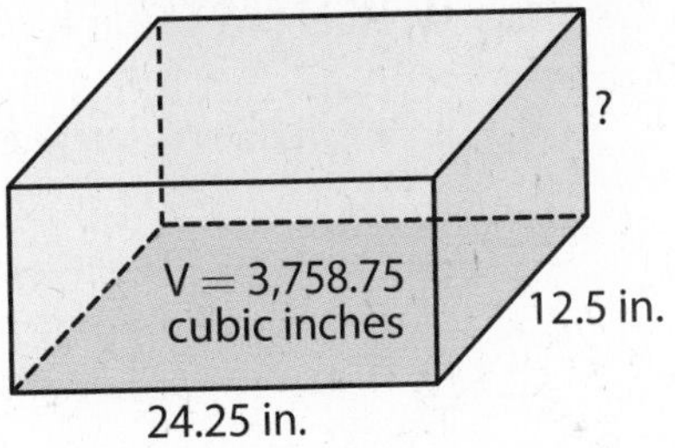

4. The area of the base of a rectangular juice box is $4\frac{1}{2}$ square inches. If the volume of the box is 18 cubic inches, how tall is the box?

Height = ____________________

5. A box of cereal is shaped like a rectangular prism. The box is 20 centimeters long and 30 centimeters high. Its volume is 3,600 cubic centimeters. Find the width of the box.

Width = ____________________

6. About 7.5 gallons of water fill up 1 cubic foot of space. How many gallons of water will fill a goldfish pool shaped like the prism shown?

____

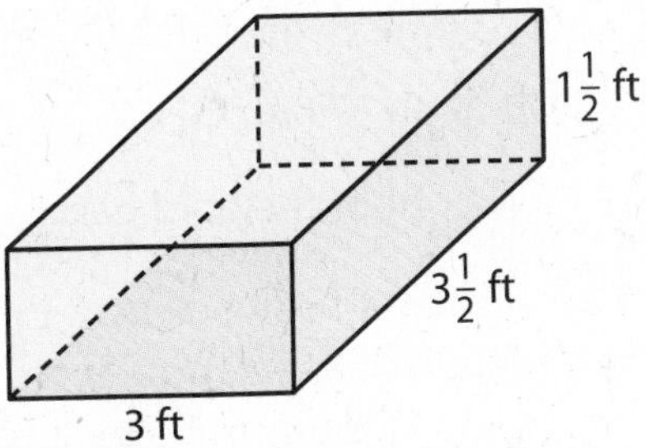

7. **Physical Science** A small bar of gold is a rectangular prism that measures 40 millimeters by 25 millimeters by 2 millimeters. One cubic millimeter of gold weighs about 0.0005 ounce. Find the volume in cubic millimeters and the weight in ounces of this small bar of gold.

____

____

8. **History** A typical stone on the lowest level of the Great Pyramid in Egypt was a rectangular prism 5 feet long by 5 feet high by 6 feet deep and weighed 15 tons. What was the volume of the average stone? How much did one cubic foot of this stone weigh?

____

9. Hank has cards that are 8 inches by 4 inches. A stack of these cards fits inside the box shown and uses up 32 cubic inches of volume. How tall is the stack of cards? What percent of the box's volume is taken up by the cards?

____

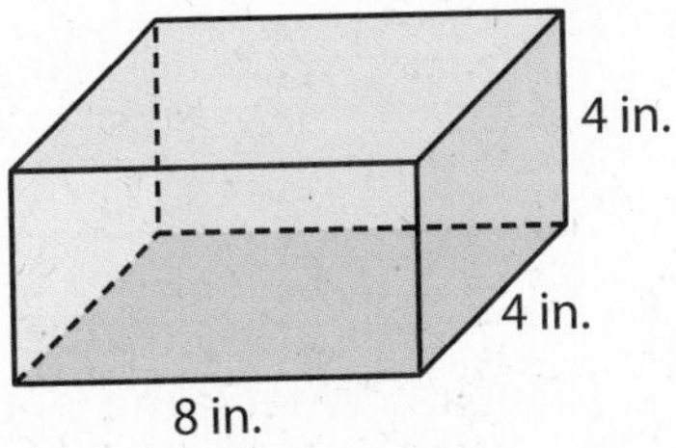

10. A freshwater fish is healthiest when there is at least 1 gallon of water for every inch of its body length. Roshel wants to put a goldfish that is about $2\frac{1}{2}$ inches long in her tank. Roshel's tank is 7 inches long, 5 inches wide, and 7 inches high. The volume of 1 gallon of water is about 231 cubic inches.

a. How many gallons of water would Roshel need for the fish? ________

b. What is the volume of Roshel's tank? ____________________

c. Is her fish tank large enough for the fish? Explain. ________________

____

H.O.T. FOCUS ON HIGHER ORDER THINKING

Work Area

11. **Multistep** Larry has a clay brick that is 7 inches long, 3.5 inches wide, and 1.75 inches thick, the same size as the gold stored in Fort Knox in the form of gold bars. Find the volume of this brick. If the weight of the clay in the brick is 0.1 pound per cubic inch and the weight of the gold is 0.7 pound per cubic inch, find the weight of the brick and the gold bar. Round all answers the nearest tenth.

Volume of the brick or bar = ________ cubic inches

Weight of the brick = ________ pounds

Weight of the gold bar = ________ pounds

12. **Represent Real-World Problems** Luisa's toaster oven, which is in the shape of a rectangular prism, has a base that is 55 cm long by 40 cm wide. It is 30 cm high. Luisa wants to buy a different oven with the same volume but a smaller length, so it will fit better on her kitchen counter. What is a possible set of dimensions for this different oven?

____

____

____

____

13. **Persevere in Problem Solving** The volume of a rectangular prism is 64 cubic inches. The prism is 4 inches high, and the ratio of the length of a base to the width of the base is 4 : 1. What are the dimensions of the base of the prism? Explain your reasoning.

____

____

14. **Communicate Mathematical Ideas** The volume of a cube is 27 cubic inches. What is the length of an edge? Explain.

____

MODULE QUIZ

Ready to Go On?

Personal Math Trainer
Online Practice and Help
my.hrw.com

15.1 Nets and Surface Area

A square pyramid is shown sitting on its base.

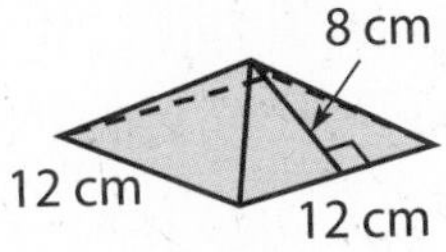

1. Draw the net of the pyramid.

2. The surface area of the pyramid is ____________ square centimeters.

15.2 Volume of Rectangular Prisms

Find the volume of each rectangular prism.

3.

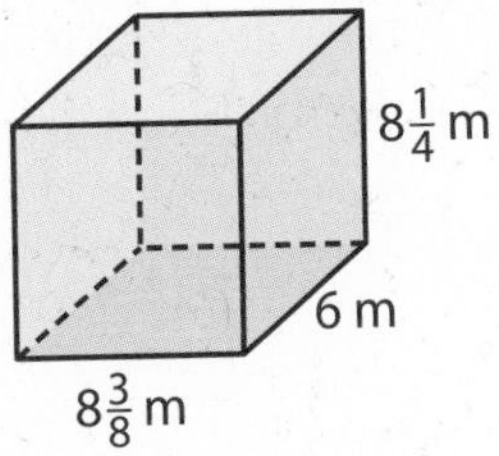

$V =$ ____________ cubic meters

4.

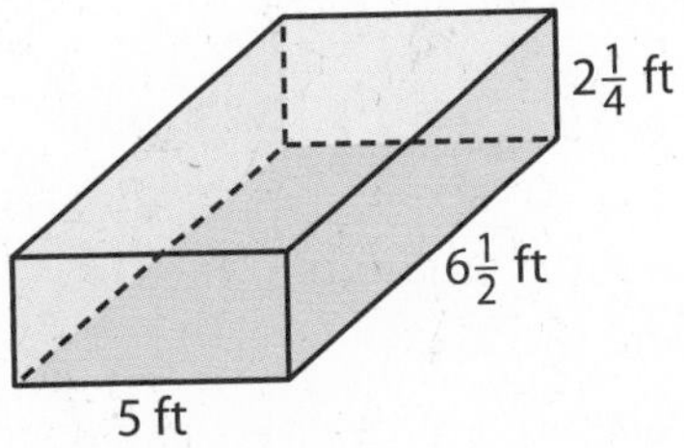

$V =$ ____________ cubic feet

15.3 Solving Volume Equations

Find the volume of each rectangular prism.

5. The volume inside a rectangular storage room is 2,025 cubic feet. The room is 9 feet high. Find the area of the floor. ____________

6. An aquarium holds 11.25 cubic feet of water and is 2.5 feet long and 1.5 feet wide. What is its depth? ____________

ESSENTIAL QUESTION

7. How can a model help you to solve surface area and volume problems?

____

____

____

MODULE 15
MIXED REVIEW

Assessment Readiness

CALIFORNIA

Personal Math Trainer
Online Practice and Help
my.hrw.com

1. Consider each expression.

Select Yes or No in A–C to indicate whether the expression is equivalent to $24 + 32$.

A. $2 \times (12 + 16)$ ○ Yes ○ No

B. $8 \times (3 + 32)$ ○ Yes ○ No

C. $4 \times (6 + 8)$ ○ Yes ○ No

2. A store manager sets up a cardboard display shaped like a square pyramid. The side length of the square base is 18 inches. The height of each triangular face of the pyramid is 12 inches.

Choose True or False for A–C.

A. The area of the base is 324 square inches. ○ True ○ False

B. The area of one triangular face is 216 square inches. ○ True ○ False

C. The surface area of the pyramid is 756 square inches. ○ True ○ False

3. An ice cube tray has 12 identical compartments. Each compartment is a rectangular prism that is 4 centimeters long, 3 centimeters wide, and 3 centimeters high. Given that 1 cubic centimeter holds 1 milliliter of water, how many milliliters of water can the tray hold? Explain.

4. A cardboard box shaped like a square prism is missing one base. Its volume is 810 cubic inches, and its height is 10 inches. Draw a net of the box and label its dimensions. How much cardboard is used for the box? Explain.

UNIT 6

Study Guide Review

MODULE 13 Area and Polygons

Key Vocabulary
parallelogram *(paralelogramo)*
rhombus *(rombo)*
trapezoid *(trapecio)*

ESSENTIAL QUESTION

How can you use area and volume equations to solve real-world problems?

EXAMPLE 1

Find the area of the trapezoid.

$A = \frac{1}{2}(h)(b_1 + b_2)$

$A = \frac{1}{2}(10)(7 + 4)$

$A = 55 \text{ in}^2$

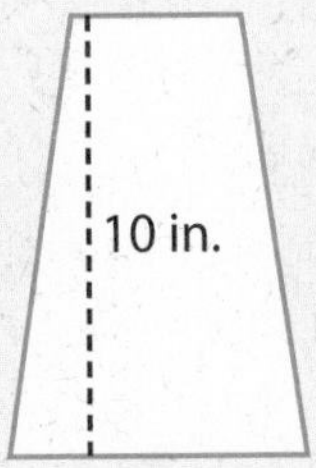

EXAMPLE 2

Find the area of Jorge's backyard.

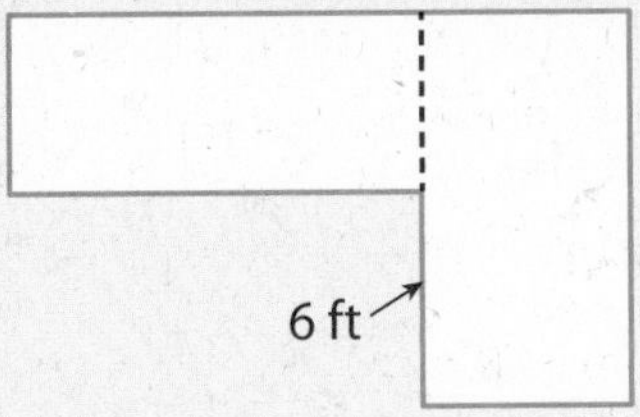

Find the area of the first rectangle.

$A = bh$

$A = 12\,(5)$

$A = 60$ square feet

Find the area of the second rectangle.

$A = bh$

$A = 6\,(11)$

$A = 66$ square feet

Total area of yard $= 60 + 66 = 126$ square feet

EXERCISES

Find the area of each figure. (Lessons 13.1, 13.2)

1.

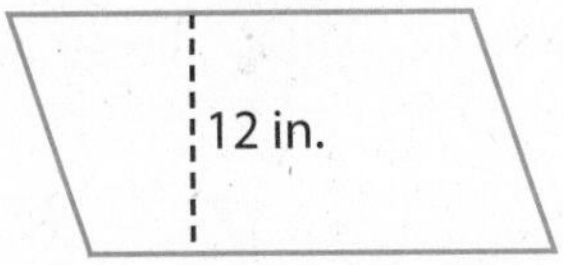

____

2.

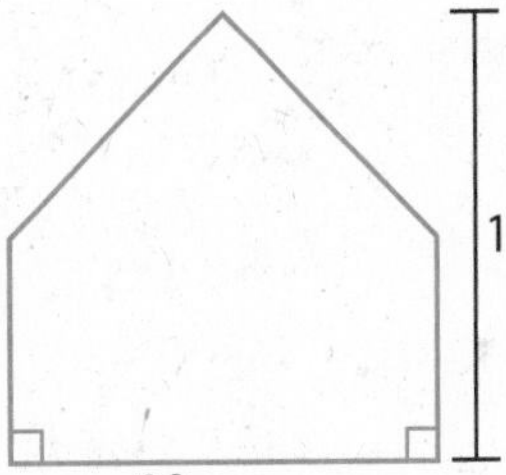

____

Find the missing measurement. (Lesson 13.3)

3.

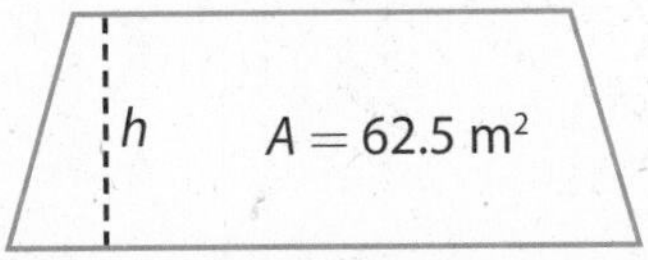

____

4.

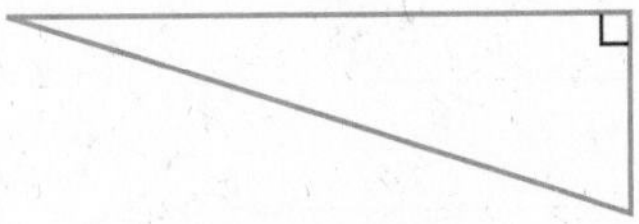

$A = 26 \text{ mm}^2$

____

MODULE 14

Distance and Area in the Coordinate Plane

Key Vocabulary

polygon *(polígono)*

reflection *(reflexión)*

vertex, vertices *(vértice, vértices)*

ESSENTIAL QUESTION

What steps might you take to solve a polygon problem given the coordinates of its vertices?

EXAMPLE 1

Find the distance between points *A* and *B* on the coordinate plane.

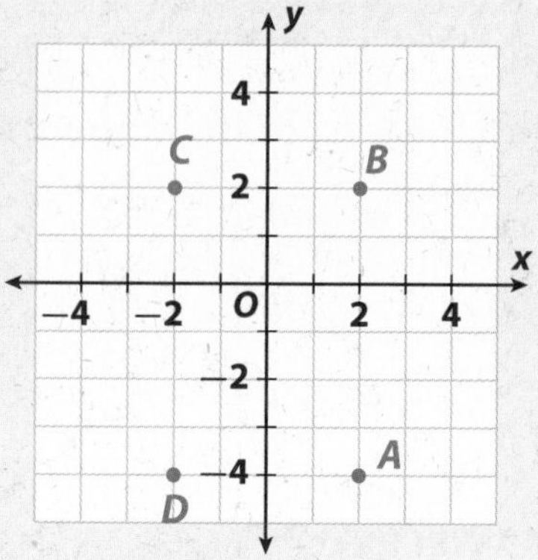

Find the distance between point *A* and the *x*-axis.

The *y*-coordinate is −4. The absolute value represents the distance.

$|-4| = 4$ The distance is 4 units.

Find the distance between point *B* and the *x*-axis.

The *y*-coordinate is 2. The distance is 2 units.

Add the two distances to find the distance between the two points.

$4 + 2 = 6$ The distance between points *A* and *B* is 6 units.

EXAMPLE 2

Find the area of the rectangle whose vertices are the points on the coordinate plane in Example 1.

Use the distance between points *A* and *B* in Example 1 as the height.

height = 6 units

Find the distance between points *A* and *D* and use it as the base.

Distance from *A* to $D = |-2| + 2 = 2 + 2 = 4$

base = 4 units

Find the area.

$A = bh = 4 \cdot 6 = 24$ square units

EXERCISES

Find the distance between the two points.

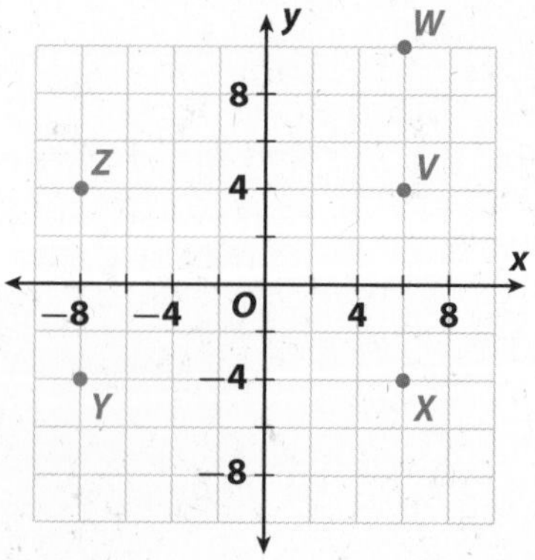

1. *Z* and *Y* ______________

2. *X* and *Y* ______________

3. *W* and *X* ______________

4. Find the area of rectangle *XYZV*. ______________

MODULE 15

Surface Area and Volume of Solids

Key Vocabulary
net *(plantilla)*
pyramid *(pirámide)*
surface area *(área total)*

ESSENTIAL QUESTION

How can a model help you solve surface area and volume problems?

EXAMPLE 1

Draw a net and find the surface area of the square pyramid.

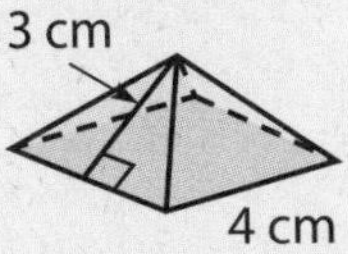

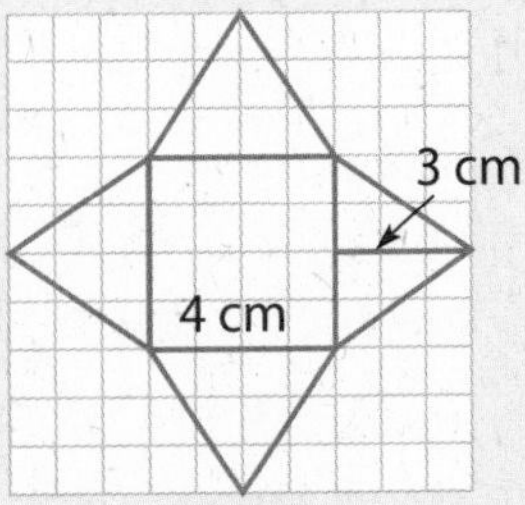

Find the area of the square base.

$A = s^2 = 4 \cdot 4 = 16 \text{ cm}^2$

Find the area of one triangle and multiply by 4.

$A = \frac{1}{2}bh = \frac{1}{2}(4 \cdot 3) = 6 \text{ cm}^2$

The area of the 4 triangles is $4 \cdot 6 = 24 \text{ cm}^2$.

The total surface area of the pyramid is $16 \text{ cm}^2 + 24 \text{ cm}^2 = 40 \text{ cm}^2$.

EXERCISES

Draw a net to find the surface area of each solid shape. (Lesson 15.1)

1. a rectangular prism

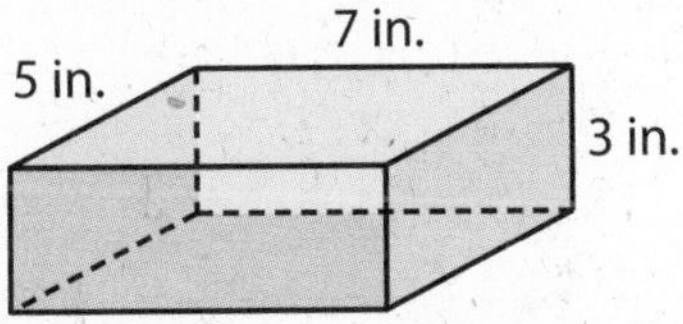

____

2. a square pyramid

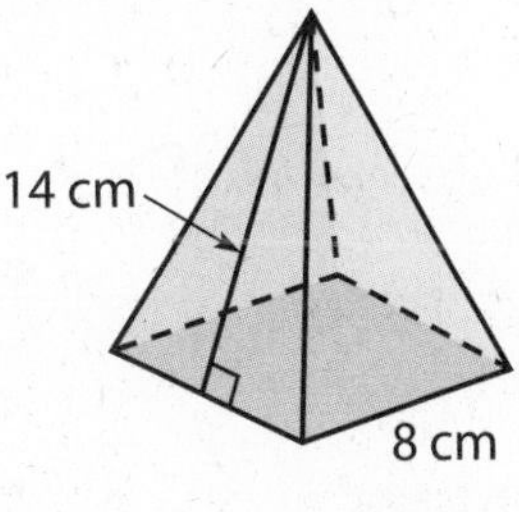

____

Find the volume of each rectangular prism. (Lesson 15.2)

3.

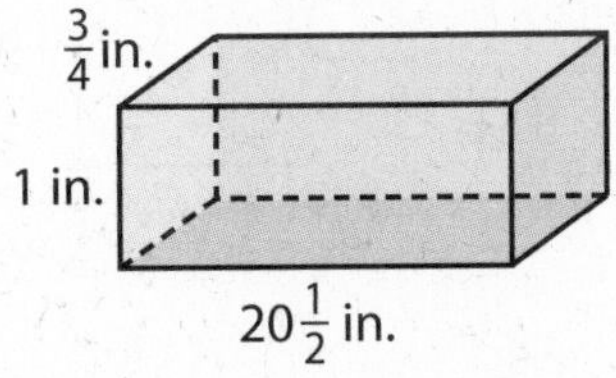

____

4. A rectangular prism with a width of 7.4 cm, a length of 8 cm, and a height of 3.2 cm ______________________

Unit Project

CA CC 6.NS.8, 6.G.3, 6.G.1, 6.NS.6c

Which State Is It?

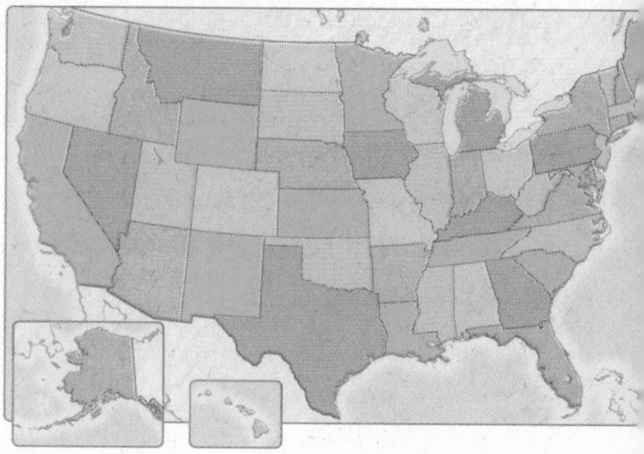

Create a presentation using $8\frac{1}{2}$-by-11-inch grid paper with $\frac{1}{4}$-inch squares. Draw x- and y-axes on grid lines, dividing the page so the origin is in the middle. Plot these points and connect them to form a polygon:

(15, 17)	(−2, −12)	(−10, −13)	(−14, −16)
(15, −12)	(−2, −13)	(−10, −16)	(−14, 17)

You have drawn the graph of one the 50 states. Which one? Compare your graph with a map of this state, and identify as closely as you can each of the following:

- The coordinates of the state capital
- The coordinates of the state's largest city
- The coordinates of the state's only national park
- The coordinates of three other points of interest in the state

Now assume that each grid square is 12 mi^2, and use that information to answer the following questions:

- How long is the northern boundary of the state, in miles?
- How long is the western boundary of the state, in miles?
- What is the area of the state, in square miles?

Decorate your map. Use the space below to write down any questions you have or important information from your teacher.

MATH IN CAREERS | ACTIVITY

Theater Set Construction Mia and Frank are using plywood to build scenery that represents a house for a class play. The diagram shows the measurements of the scenery. How many square feet of plywood did they use in the scenery? Explain.

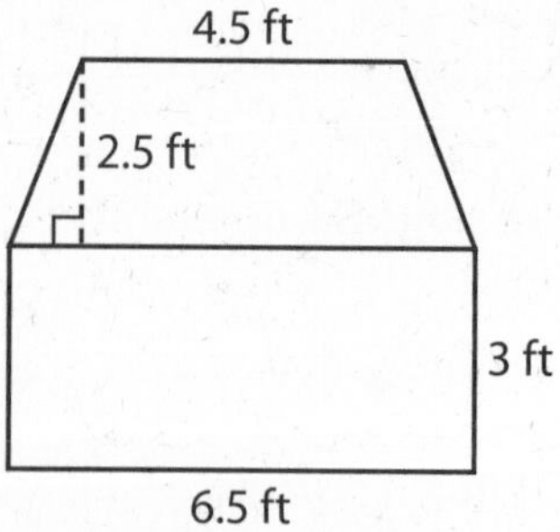

Assessment Readiness

1. Select Yes or No to indicate whether the given statement about the figure is correct.

A. The triangle has an area of 221 inches.

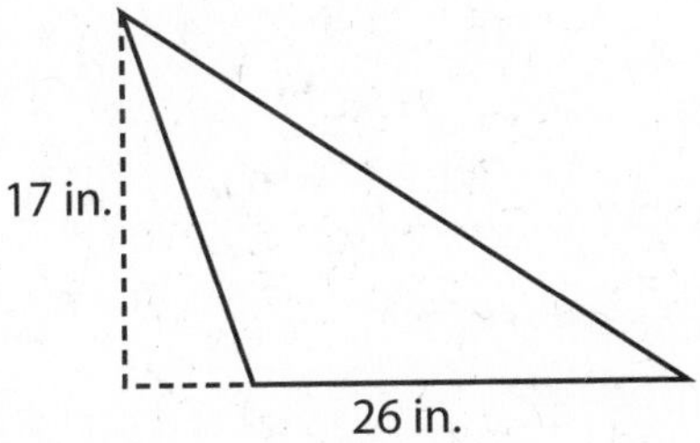

○ Yes ○ No

B. If the area of the trapezoid is 529 m^2, the height is 27 m.

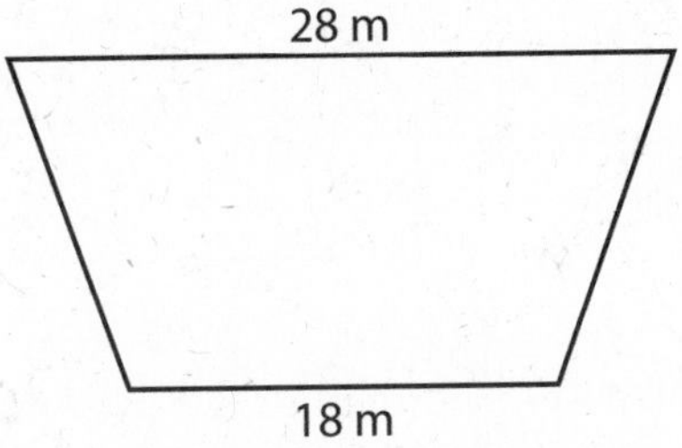

○ Yes ○ No

C. The figure has an area of 298.5 in^2.

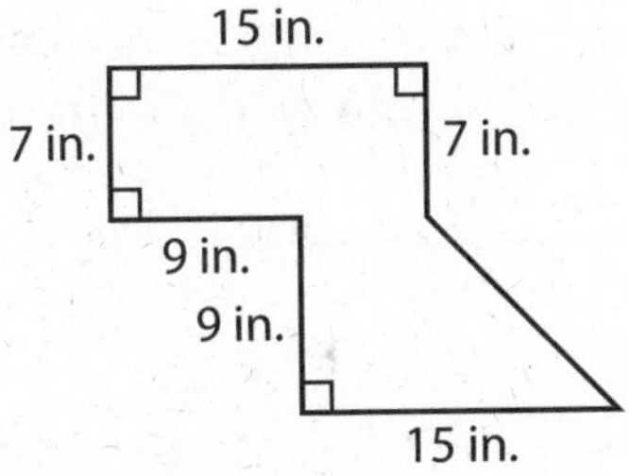

○ Yes ○ No

2. Choose True or False for each statement.

A. All whole numbers are also rational numbers. ○ True ○ False

B. All rational numbers are also integers. ○ True ○ False

C. Rational numbers cannot be negative. ○ True ○ False

D. All rational numbers can be written in the form $\frac{a}{b}$, where a and b are integers and $b \neq 0$. ○ True ○ False

3. Jessie makes a picture frame with an 8.5-by-11-inch piece of cardboard by cutting out a 4-inch-by-4-inch square from the center of the cardboard. What is the area of the frame? Explain.

4. Jermaine is ordering a piece of glass in the shape of a trapezoid to create a patio tabletop. Each square foot of glass costs $25, and the total cost of the glass is $400. The trapezoid has base lengths of 5 feet and 3 feet. What is the height of the trapezoid? Explain.

Performance Tasks

★**5.** Lisa bought a tank for her hermit crab. The tank can hold 1,331 cubic inches of water and includes a top. The base of the tank is a square. The height is 11 inches.

a. What is the length of each side of the base of the tank?

b. What is the shape of the tank?

c. What is the surface area of the tank?

★★**6.** Adam and Karina are building scenery of the Egyptian pyramids out of plywood for a community play. The pyramids are represented by triangles on a rectangular base.

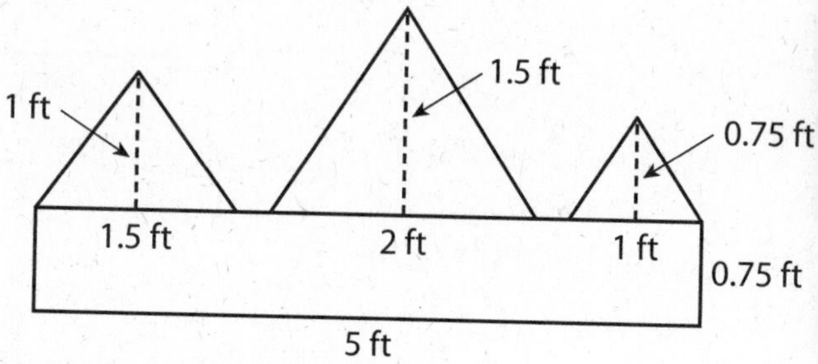

a. What is the area of the scenery? Show your work.

b. The triangles will be painted gray, and the rectangle will be painted black. How much of each paint color will they use if one quart covers 45 square feet? Only one side of the model needs to be painted, but two coats of paint will be needed. Show your work. Round to the nearest hundredth of a quart.

★★★**7.** Each grid unit shown on the map represents one city block, and north is the direction of the positive *y*-axis.

Library: (−5, 5); Chuck's house: (−5,−3); City Hall: (3,−3)

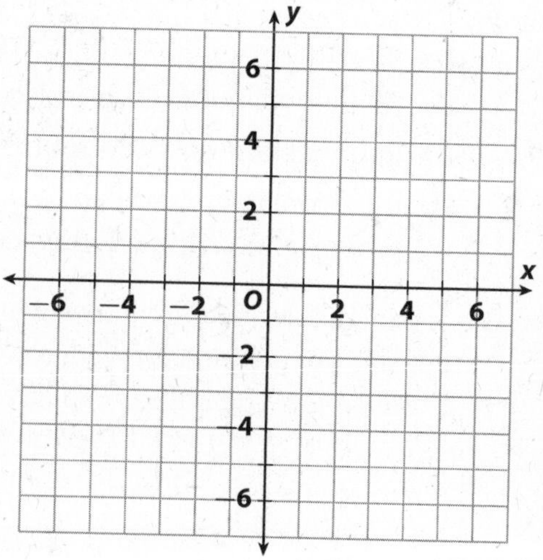

a. Plot each point on the coordinate grid.

b. How far does Chuck live from the library?

c. The post office is 6 blocks east of the library. Plot the post office on the grid and tell the coordinates.

d. If you connect the four points on the map, what shape do you make?

e. What is the area in square blocks of the quadrilateral described in part d?

UNIT 7

Measurement and Data

MODULE 16

Displaying, Analyzing, and Summarizing Data

CA CC 6.SP.1, 6.SP.2, 6.SP.3, 6.SP.4, 6.SP.5, 6.SP.5a, 6.SP.5b, 6.SP.5c, 6.SP.5d

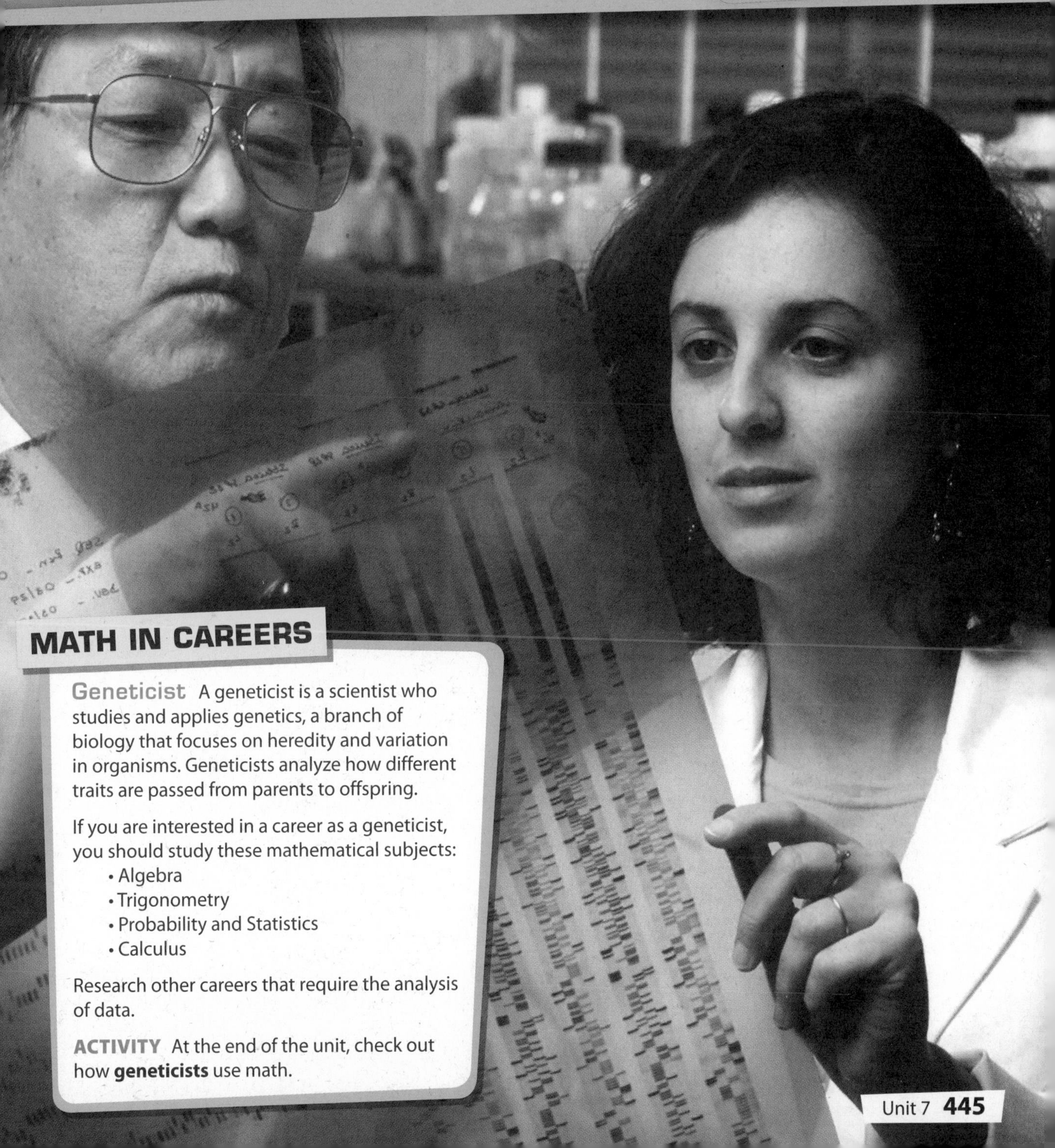

MATH IN CAREERS

Geneticist A geneticist is a scientist who studies and applies genetics, a branch of biology that focuses on heredity and variation in organisms. Geneticists analyze how different traits are passed from parents to offspring.

If you are interested in a career as a geneticist, you should study these mathematical subjects:

- Algebra
- Trigonometry
- Probability and Statistics
- Calculus

Research other careers that require the analysis of data.

ACTIVITY At the end of the unit, check out how **geneticists** use math.

Unit Project Preview

Top Tens

In the Unit Project at the end of this unit, you will research the world's ten longest, tallest, widest, or fastest items in a category that interests you. You'll use the data you collect to calculate several important measures of the data and to draw and analyze a statistical display of the data. To successfully complete the Unit Project you'll need to master these skills:

- Calculate measures of center.
- Calculate mean absolute deviation.
- Draw and analyze box plots.

1. The high temperatures the past two days were 80 °F and 90 °F. What single number could you use to represent the temperatures? Explain your reasoning.

____

____

2. Why might you want to find a single number to represent a set of many numbers?

____

____

Tracking Your Learning Progression

This unit addresses important California Common Core Standards in the Critical Areas of displaying, analyzing, and summarizing data.

Domain 6.SP Statistics and Probability
Cluster Develop understanding of statistical variability.

The unit also supports additional standards.

Domain 6.SP Statistics and Probability
Cluster Summarize and describe distributions.

Displaying, Analyzing, and Summarizing Data

MODULE 16

CALIFORNIA

ESSENTIAL QUESTION

How can you solve real-world problems by displaying, analyzing, and summarizing data?

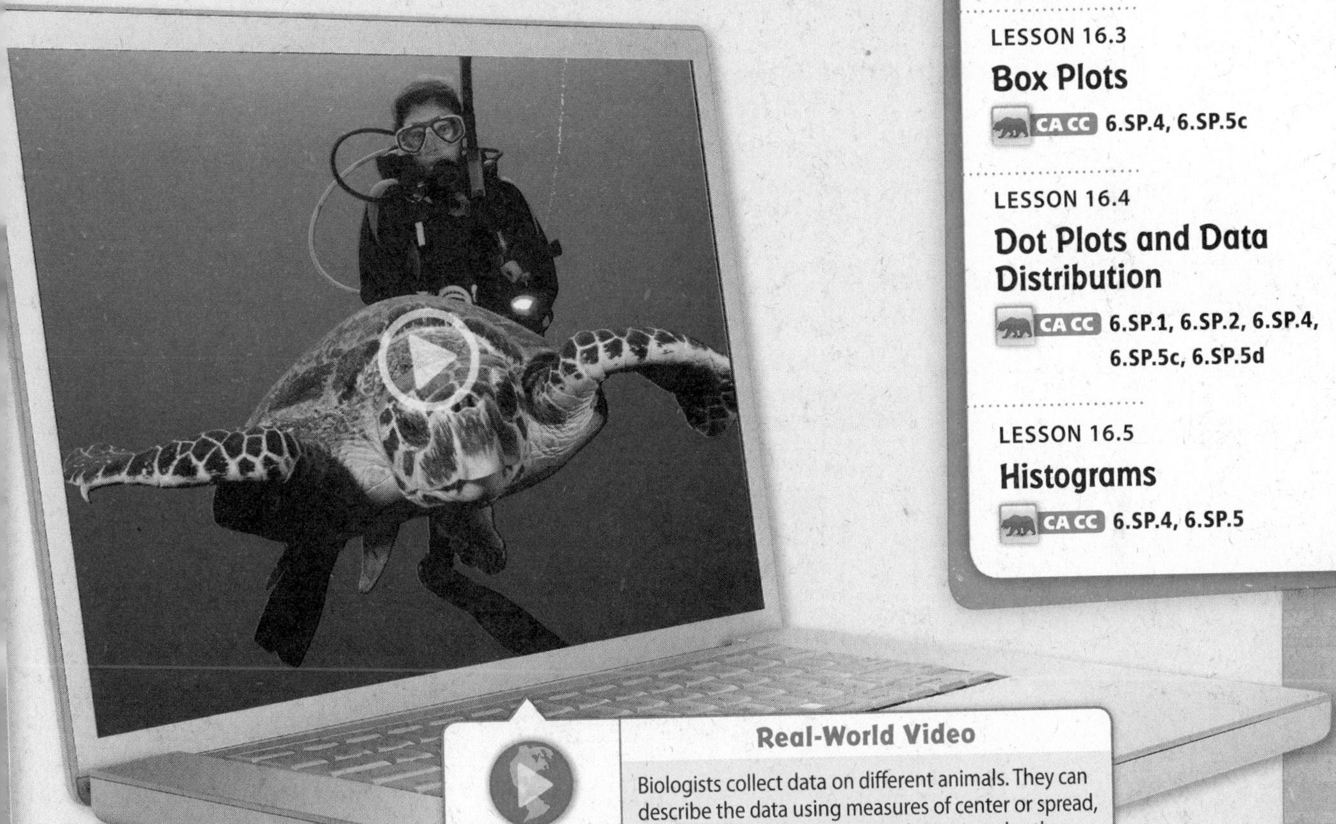

Real-World Video

my.hrw.com

Biologists collect data on different animals. They can describe the data using measures of center or spread, and by displaying the data in plots or graphs, they may see trends related to the animal population.

GO DIGITAL
my.hrw.com

my.hrw.com

Go digital with your write-in student edition, accessible on any device.

Math On the Spot

Scan with your smart phone to jump directly to the online edition, video tutor, and more.

Animated Math

Interactively explore key concepts to see how math works.

Personal Math Trainer

Get immediate feedback and help as you work through practice sets.

Are YOU Ready?

Complete these exercises to review skills you will need for this module.

Personal Math Trainer
Online Practice and Help
my.hrw.com

Remainders

EXAMPLE

$$\begin{array}{r} 7.25 \\ 12\overline{)87.00} \\ \underline{84} \\ 3\,0 \\ \underline{-2\,4} \\ 60 \\ \underline{-60} \\ 0 \end{array}$$

Write a decimal point and a zero in the dividend.

Place a decimal point in the quotient.

Add more zeros to the dividend if necessary.

Find the quotient. Write the remainder as a decimal.

1. $15\overline{)42}$ ________ **2.** $75\overline{)93}$ ________ **3.** $52\overline{)91}$ ________ **4.** $24\overline{)57}$ ________

Read Bar Graphs

EXAMPLE How many goals did Alec score?

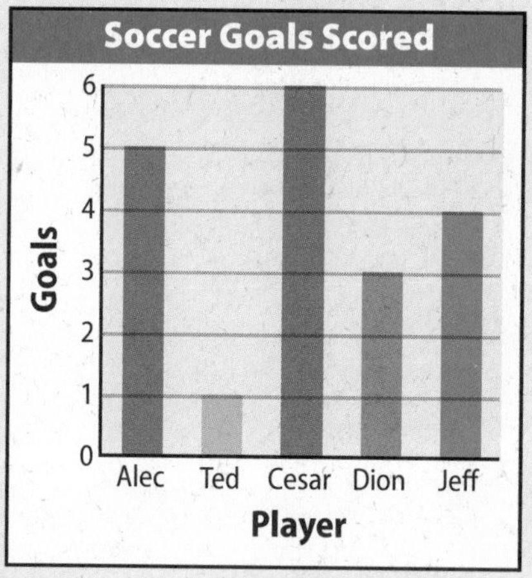

The first bar shows how many goals Alec scored.

The bar extends to a height of 5.

Alec scored 5 goals.

5. How many goals did Dion score? ______________________

6. Which two players together scored the same number of goals as Jeff? ______________________

7. How many fewer goals than Cesar did Alec score? ______________

Reading Start-Up

Visualize Vocabulary

Use the review words to complete the chart.

Introduction to Statistics		
Definition	**Example**	**Review word**
A group of facts	The grades of all of the students in a school	
A tool used to gather information from individuals	A questionnaire given to all students to find the number of hours each student spends studying in 1 week	
A value that summarizes a set of unequal values, found by addition and division	Results of the survey show that students typically spend 5 hours a week studying	

Understand Vocabulary

Complete the sentences using the checked preview words.

1. The average of a data set is the ____________________.

2. The ____________________ is the middle value of a data set.

3. The number or category that occurs most frequently in a data set is the ____________________.

Vocabulary

Review Words

average *(promedio)*
data *(datos)*
survey *(encuesta)*

Preview Words

box plot *(diagrama de caja)*
categorical data *(datos categóricos)*
dot plot *(diagrama de puntos)*
histogram *(histograma)*
interquartile range *(rango entre cuartiles)*
lower quartile *(cuartil inferior)*
✔ mean *(media)*
mean absolute deviation (MAD) *(desviación absoluta media, (DAM))*
✔ median *(mediana)*
measure of center *(medida central)*
measure of spread *(medida de dispersión)*
✔ mode *(moda)*
range *(rango)*
statistical question *(pregunta estadística)*
upper quartile *(cuartil superior)*

Active Reading

Layered Book Before beginning the module, create a layered book to help you learn the concepts in this module. Label each flap with lesson titles from this module. As you study each lesson, write important ideas, such as vocabulary and formulas under the appropriate flap. Refer to your finished layered book as you work on exercises from this module.

CALIFORNIA

GETTING READY FOR

Displaying Analyzing, and Summarizing Data

Understanding the standards and the vocabulary terms in the standards will help you know exactly what you are expected to learn in this module.

CA CC 6.SP.5C

Summarize numerical data sets in relation to their context, such as by giving quantitative measures of center (median and/or mean) and variability (interquartile range and/or mean absolute deviation), as well as describing any overall pattern and any striking deviations from the overall pattern with reference to the context in which the data were gathered.

What It Means to You

You will use measures of center to describe a data set.

EXAMPLE 6.SP.5C

Several students' scores on a history test are shown. Find the mean score and the median score. Which measure better describes the typical score for these students? Explain.

History Test Scores						
73	48	88	90	90	81	83

Mean: $\frac{73 + 48 + 88 + 90 + 90 + 81 + 83}{7} = \frac{553}{7} = 79$

To find the median, write the data values in order from least to greatest and find the middle value.
Median: 48 73 81 (83) 88 90 90

The median better describes the typical score.
The mean is affected by the low score of 48.

CA CC 6.SP.4

Display numerical data in plots on a number line, including dot plots, histograms, and box plots.

What It Means to You

You will interpret the data from a dot plot, histogram, or box plot.

EXAMPLE 6.SP.4

Kim has started rating each movie she sees using a scale of 1 to 10 on an online site. She made a histogram that shows how she rated the movies. What does the shape of the distribution tell you about the movies Kim has rated?

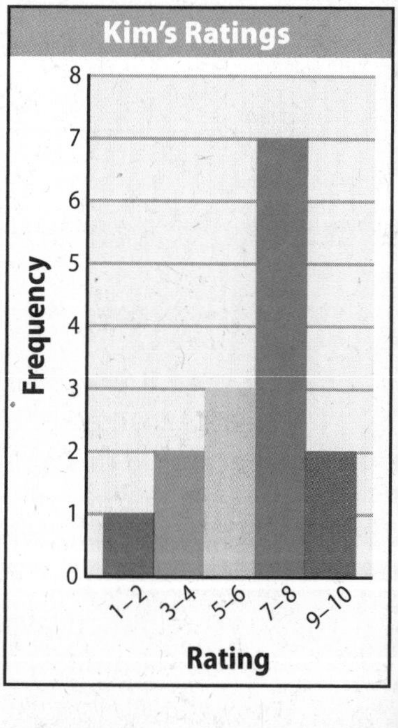

Of the 15 movies that Kim rated, she rated almost half a 7 or an 8 and did not generally give extreme ratings.

Visit my.hrw.com to see all CA Common Core Standards explained.

my.hrw.com

LESSON

16.1 Measures of Center

CA CC 6.SP.5

Summarize numerical data sets in relation to their context. *Also 6.SP.3, 6.SP.5a, 6.SP.5b, 6.SP.5c, 6.SP.5d*

ESSENTIAL QUESTION

How can you use measures of center to describe a data set?

EXPLORE ACTIVITY 1 Real World CA CC 6.SP.5c, 6.SP.3, 6.SP.5a

Finding the Mean

A **measure of center** is a single number used to describe a set of numeric data. A measure of center describes a typical value from the data set.

One measure of center is the *mean*. The **mean**, or average, of a data set is the sum of the data values divided by the number of data values in the set.

Tami surveyed five of her friends to find out how many brothers and sisters they have. Her results are shown in the table.

Number of Siblings				
Amy	**Ben**	**Cal**	**Don**	**Eva**
2	3	1	1	3

A Model each person's response as a group of counters.

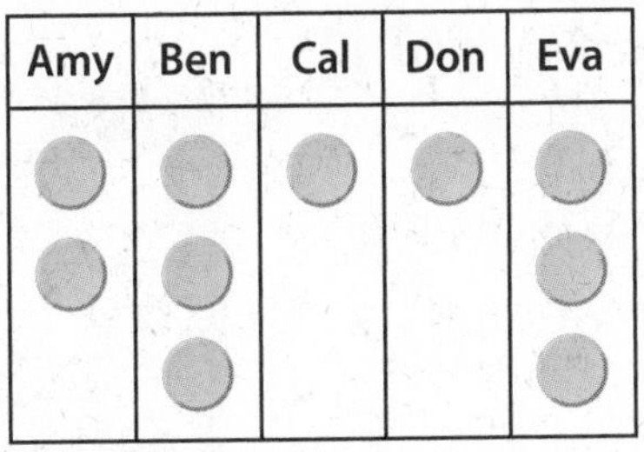

B Now rearrange the counters so that each group has the same number of counters.

Each group now has ________ counter(s). This value is the mean. This model demonstrates how the mean "evens out" the data values.

C Use numbers to calculate the mean.

The sum of the data values is 2 + 3 + ☐ + ☐ + ☐ = ☐.

How many data values are in the set? ________

EXPLORE ACTIVITY 1 *(cont'd)*

Math Talk
Mathematical Practices

Suppose you have a data set in which all of the values are 2. What is the mean?

$$\text{Mean} = \frac{\text{sum of data values}}{\text{number of data values}} = \frac{\square}{\square} = \square$$

Reflect

1. Can the mean be greater than the greatest value in a data set? Why or why not?

____

____

____

____

Math On the Spot
my.hrw.com

Finding the Median

Another measure of center is the *median*. The **median** represents the middle value of an ordered data set.

EXAMPLE 1 Real World

CA CC 6.SP.5c, 6.SP.5b

A A coach records the distances that some cross-country team members ran last week. Find the median.

Distances Run	
Cara	3 mi
Rob	5 mi
Maria	7 mi
Olivia	10 mi
Paul	10 mi
Chris	4 mi
Amir	7 mi
Iris	5 mi
Alex	8 mi
Tara	10 mi
Ned	6 mi

Write the data values in order from least to greatest.

[3 4 5 5 6] 7 [7 8 10 10 10]

This value is the median.

Equal number of values on either side of the median

The median is 7.

Math Talk
Mathematical Practices

Why does the data set in **A** have one middle value while the data set in **B** has two middle values?

B Find the median of these test scores: 87, 90, 77, 83, 99, 94, 93, 90, 85, 83.

Write the data values in order from least to greatest.

77 83 83 85 [87 90] 90 93 94 99

This data set has two middle values: 87 and 90.

The median is the average of these two values:

$$\text{Median} = \frac{87 + 90}{2} = 88.5$$

The median is 88.5.

Reflect

2. **What If?** Which units are used for the data in **A**? If the coach had recorded some distances in kilometers and some in miles, can you still find the median of the data? Explain.

____

____

YOUR TURN

3. Charlotte recorded the number of minutes she spent exercising in the past ten days: 12, 4, 5, 6, 8, 7, 9, 8, 2, 1. Find the median of the data.

____

Personal Math Trainer
Online Practice and Help
my.hrw.com

EXPLORE ACTIVITY 2 Real World

CA CC 6.SP.5d, 6.SP.5c

Comparing the Mean and the Median

The mean and median of a data set may be equal, very close to each other, or very different from each other. For data sets where the mean and median differ greatly, one likely describes the data set better than the other.

The monthly earnings of several teenagers are \$200, \$320, \$275, \$250, \$750, \$350, and \$310.

A Find the mean. Round to the nearest tenth.

$$\frac{\square + \square + \square + \square + \square + \square + \square}{\square} = \frac{\square}{\square} \approx \square$$

B Write the data values in order from least to greatest and find the median.

____

C The mean and the median differ by about \$________. Why?

____

____

D Which measure of center better describes the typical monthly earnings for this group of teenagers—the mean or the median? Explain.

____

____

EXPLORE ACTIVITY 2 *(cont'd)*

Reflect

4. **Communicate Mathematical Ideas** Luka's final exam scores for this semester are 70, 72, 99, 72, and 69. Find the mean and median. Which is a better description of Luka's typical exam score? Explain your thinking.

____

____

Guided Practice

1. Spencer surveyed five of his friends to find out how many pets they have. His results are shown in the table. What is the mean number of pets? (Explore Activity 1)

Number of Pets				
Lara	**Cody**	**Sam**	**Ella**	**Maria**
3	5	2	4	1

$$\text{Mean} = \frac{\text{sum of data values}}{\text{number of data values}} = \frac{\square}{\square} = \square$$

The mean number of pets is ______

2. The following are the weights, in pounds, of some dogs at a kennel: 36, 45, 29, 39, 51, 49. (Example 1)

   a. Find the median. ______

   b. Suppose one of the weights were given in kilograms. Can you still find the median? Explain.

   ____

3. **a.** Find the mean and the median of this data set: 9, 6, 5, 3, 28, 6, 4, 7. (Explore Activity 2)

   ____

   b. Which better describes the data set, the mean or the median? Explain.

   ____

   ____

ESSENTIAL QUESTION CHECK-IN

4. How can you use measures of center to describe a data set?

____

____

Name________________________ Class________________________ Date________________

16.1 Independent Practice

CA CC 6.SP.3, 6.SP.5, 6.SP.5a, 6.SP.5b, 6.SP.5c, 6.SP.5d

Personal Math Trainer
my.hrw.com
Online Practice and Help

Several students in Ashton's class were randomly selected and asked how many text messages they sent yesterday. Their answers were 1, 0, 10, 7, 13, 2, 9, 15, 0, 3.

5. How many students were asked? How do you know?

____

____

____

6. Find the mean and the median for these data.

Mean = ________ Median = ________

The points scored by a basketball team in its last 6 games are shown. Use these data for 7 and 8.

Points Scored					
73	77	85	84	37	115

7. Find the mean score and the median score.

Mean = ________ Median = ________

8. Which measure better describes the typical number of points scored? Explain.

____

____

____

Some people were asked how long it takes them to commute to work. Use the data for 9–11.

16 min	5 min
7 min	8 min
14 min	12 min
0.5 hr	1 hr

9. What units are used for the data? What should you do before finding the mean and median number of minutes?

____

10. Find the mean and median number of minutes.

Mean = ________ Median = ________

11. Which measure do you think is more typical of the data?

____

____

____

H.O.T. FOCUS ON HIGHER ORDER THINKING

Work Area

12. **Critique Reasoning** For two weeks, the school librarian recorded the number of library books returned each morning. The data are shown in the dot plot. The librarian found the mean number of books returned each morning.

$$\frac{8+6+10+5+9+8+3+6}{8} = \frac{55}{8} = 6.875$$

Is this the correct mean of this data set? If not, explain and correct the answer.

____

____

13. **Critical Thinking** Lauren's scores on her math tests are 93, 91, 98, 100, 95, 92, and 96. What score could Lauren get on her next math test so that the mean and median remain the same? Explain your answer.

____

____

____

14. **Persevere in Problem Solving** Yuko wants to take a job selling cars. Since she will get a commission for every car she sells, she finds out the sale price of the last four cars sold at each company.

Company A: $16,000; $20,000; $25,000; $35,000;

Company B: $21,000, $23,000, $36,000, $48,000

a. Find the mean selling price at each company.

____

b. Find the median selling price at each company.

____

c. **Communicate Mathematical Ideas** At either company, Yuko will get paid a commission of 20% of the sale price of each car she sells. Based on the data, where do you recommend she take a job? Why?

____

____

____

LESSON 16.2

Mean Absolute Deviation

CA CC 6.SP.5c

Giving quantitative measures of center (median and/or mean) and variability (interquartile range and/or mean absolute deviation), as well as describing any overall pattern and any striking deviations from the context in which the data were gathered.

ESSENTIAL QUESTION

How can you determine and use the mean absolute deviation of a set of data points?

EXPLORE ACTIVITY Real World

CA CC 6.SP.5c

Understanding Mean Absolute Deviation

A **measure of variability** is a single number used to describe the spread of a data set. It can also be called a measure of spread. One measure of variability is the **mean absolute deviation (MAD)**, which is the mean of the distances between the data values and the mean of the data set.

The data represent the height, in feet, of various buildings. Find the mean absolute deviation for each data set.

A 60, 58, 54, 56, 63, 65, 62, 59, 56, 58

Calculate the mean. Round to the nearest whole number.

Complete the table.

Height (ft)	60	58	54	56	63	65	62	59	56	58
Distance from mean										

Calculate the MAD by finding the mean of the values in the second row of the table. Round to the nearest whole number.

B 46, 47, 56, 48, 46, 52, 57, 52, 45

Find the mean. Round to the nearest whole number.

EXPLORE ACTIVITY *(cont'd)*

Math Talk
Mathematical Practices
What is the difference between a measure of center and a measure of variability?

Complete the table.

Height (ft)	46	47	56	48	46	52	57	52	45
Distance from mean									

Calculate the MAD. Round to the nearest whole number.

Reflect

1. **Analyze Relationships** Compare the MADs. How do the MADs describe the distribution of the heights in each group?

____

____

Math On the Spot
my.hrw.com

Using Mean Absolute Deviation

The mean absolute deviation can be used to answer statistical questions in the real world. Many of these questions may have implications for the operation of various businesses.

EXAMPLE 1 Real World

CA CC 6.SP.5c

A chicken farmer wants her chickens to all have about the same weight. She is trying two types of feed to see which type produces the best results. All the chickens in Pen A are fed Premium Growth feed, and all the chickens in Pen B are fed Maximum Growth feed. The farmer records the weights of the chickens in each pen in the tables below. Which chicken feed produces less variability in weight?

Pen A: Premium Growth Weights (lb)									
5.8	6.1	5.5	6.6	7.3	5.9	6.3	5.7	6.8	7.1

Pen B: Maximum Growth Weights (lb)									
7.7	7.4	5.4	7.8	6.1	5.2	7.5	7.9	6.3	5.6

STEP 1 Find the mean weight of the chickens in each pen. Round your answers to the nearest tenth.

Pen A: $\frac{5.8 + 6.1 + 5.5 + 6.6 + 7.3 + 5.9 + 6.3 + 5.7 + 6.8 + 7.1}{10} \approx 6.3$

Pen B: $\frac{7.7 + 7.4 + 5.4 + 7.8 + 6.1 + 5.2 + 7.5 + 7.9 + 6.3 + 5.6}{10} \approx 6.7$

STEP 2 Find the distance from the mean for each of the weights.

The distances from the mean for Pen A are the distance of each weight from 6.3 lb.

Pen A: Premium Growth										
Weight (lb)	5.8	6.1	5.5	6.6	7.3	5.9	6.3	5.7	6.8	7.1
Distance from mean	0.5	0.2	0.8	0.3	1.0	0.4	0	0.6	0.5	0.8

The distances from the mean for Pen B are the distance of each weight from 6.7 lb.

Pen B: Maximum Growth										
Weight (lb)	7.7	7.4	5.4	7.8	6.1	5.2	7.5	7.9	6.3	5.6
Distance from mean	1.0	0.7	1.3	1.1	0.6	1.5	0.8	1.2	0.4	1.1

STEP 3 Calculate the MAD for the chickens in each pen. Round your answers to the nearest tenth.

Pen A: $\frac{0.5 + 0.2 + 0.8 + 0.3 + 1.0 + 0.4 + 0 + 0.6 + 0.5 + 0.8}{10} \approx 0.5$ lb

Pen B: $\frac{1.0 + 0.7 + 1.3 + 1.1 + 0.6 + 1.5 + 0.8 + 1.2 + 0.4 + 1.1}{10} \approx 1.0$ lb

Since Pen A's MAD is less, Premium Growth feed produces less variability in weight.

Animated Math

my.hrw.com

YOUR TURN

2. Two waiters at a cafe each served 10 large fruit smoothies. The amounts in each waiter's smoothies are shown below. Which waiter's smoothies showed less variability?

Amounts in Waiter A's Large Smoothies (oz)									
19.1	20.1	20.9	19.6	20.9	19.5	19.2	19.4	20.3	20.9

Amounts in Waiter B's Large Smoothies (oz)									
20.1	19.6	20.0	20.5	19.8	20.0	20.1	19.7	19.9	20.4

____

____

Personal Math Trainer

Online Practice and Help

my.hrw.com

Math On the Spot
my.hrw.com

My Notes

Using a Spreadsheet to Find MAD

Spreadsheets can be used to find the mean absolute deviation of a data set.

EXAMPLE 2 Real World

CA CC 6.SP.5c

A paper mill is testing two paper-cutting machines. Both are set to produce pieces of paper with a width of 8.5 inches. The actual widths of 8 pieces of paper cut by each machine are shown. Use a spreadsheet to determine which machine has less variability and, thus, does a better job.

Widths of Pieces of Paper Cut by Machine A (in.)							
8.502	8.508	8.499	8.501	8.492	8.511	8.505	8.491

Widths of Pieces of Paper Cut by Machine B (in.)							
8.503	8.501	8.498	8.499	8.498	8.504	8.496	8.502

STEP 1 Enter the data values for Machine A into row 1 of a spreadsheet, using cells A to H.

	A	B	C	D	E	F	G	H
1	8.502	8.508	8.499	8.501	8.492	8.511	8.505	8.491
2								
3								

STEP 2 Enter "mean = " into cell A2 and the formula =AVERAGE(A1:H1) into cell B2.

	A	B	C	D	E	F	G	H
1	8.502	8.508	8.499	8.501	8.492	8.511	8.505	8.491
2	mean =	8.501125						
3								

STEP 3 Enter "MAD = " into cell A3 and the formula =AVEDEV(A1:H1) into cell B3.

	A	B	C	D	E	F	G	H
1	8.502	8.508	8.499	8.501	8.492	8.511	8.505	8.491
2	mean =	8.501125						
3	MAD =	0.005375						

The MAD for Machine A is about 0.0054 in.

STEP 4 Repeat Steps 1–3 with the data values for Machine B.

	A	B	C	D	E	F	G	H
1	8.503	8.501	8.498	8.499	8.498	8.504	8.496	8.502
2	mean =	8.500125						
3	MAD =	0.002375						

The MAD for Machine B is about 0.0024 in.

Machine B has less variability, so it does a better job.

YOUR TURN

3. Two aspirin-making devices are set to make tablets containing 0.35 gram of aspirin. The actual amounts in 8 tablets from each device are shown. Use a spreadsheet to determine which device has less variability.

Amounts of Aspirin in Tablets Made by Device A (g)							
0.353	0.351	0.350	0.352	0.349	0.348	0.350	0.346

Amounts of Aspirin in Tablets Made by Device B (g)							
0.349	0.341	0.347	0.358	0.359	0.354	0.339	0.343

____

Personal Math Trainer
Online Practice and Help
my.hrw.com

Guided Practice

1. A bus route takes about 45 minutes. The company's goal is a MAD of less than 0.5 minute. One driver's times for 9 runs of the route are shown. Did the bus driver meet the goal? (Explore Activity and Example 1)

Times to Complete Bus Route (min)								
44.2	44.9	46.1	45.8	44.7	45.2	45.1	45.3	44.6

a. Calculate the mean of the bus times. _______________

b. Calculate the MAD to the nearest tenth. _______________

The bus driver **did / did not** meet the company's goal.

2. Below are a different driver's times on the same route. Find the mean and the MAD using a spreadsheet. Enter the data values into row 1 using cells A to I. Enter "mean =" into cell A2 and "MAD =" into cell A3. (Example 2)

Times to Complete Bus Route (min)								
44.4	43.8	45.6	45.9	44.1	45.6	44.0	44.9	45.8

The mean is __________ minutes, and the MAD is _____________ minutes.

This time, the bus driver **did / did not** meet the company's goal.

ESSENTIAL QUESTION CHECK-IN

3. What is the mean absolute deviation and what does it tell you about data sets?

____

____

Name _______________ Class _______________ Date _______________

16.2 Independent Practice

CA CC 6.SP.5c

Personal Math Trainer

my.hrw.com

Online Practice and Help

Frank wants to know how many people live in each household in his town. He conducts a random survey of 10 people and asks how many people live in their household. His results are shown in the table.

Number of People per Household									
1	6	2	4	4	3	5	5	2	8

4. Calculate the mean number of people per household. _______________

5. Calculate the MAD of the number of people per household. _______________

6. What conclusions can you draw about the "typical" number of people in each household? Explain.

____

____

____

____

Each yogurt treat served at a shop must be the same size. A new worker spends his first week on the job learning to serve the correct amount. The tables show the sizes of 10 yogurt treats the worker served at the beginning of his first week, and of 10 yogurt treats he served at the end of his first week.

Serving Sizes, in Grams, at Beginning of Week 1									
76	81	85	79	89	86	84	80	88	79

Serving Sizes, in Grams, at End of Week 1									
79	82	84	81	77	85	82	80	78	83

7. Calculate the MADs for the two tables. Did the worker's ability to serve same-sized yogurt treats improve? Explain.

____

____

____

8. **What If?** What would it mean if the serving sizes had a MAD of 0?

____

The annual rainfall for Austin, Texas, and San Antonio, Texas, in each of the years from 2002 to 2011 are shown in the tables. Use the data for 9–11.

Annual Rainfall for Austin, Texas (in.)									
36.00	21.41	52.27	22.33	34.70	46.95	16.07	31.38	37.76	19.68

Annual Rainfall for San Antonio, Texas (in.)									
46.27	28.45	45.32	16.54	21.34	47.25	13.76	30.69	37.39	17.58

9. Use a spreadsheet to find the mean for the two cities' annual rainfalls. In which city does it rain more in a year, on average?

____

____

____

10. Use your spreadsheet to find the MADs. Use the MADs to compare the distribution of annual rainfall for the two cities.

____

____

____

____

11. **Make a Conjecture** Does the information allow you to predict how the future amounts of rainfall for the two cities will compare? Explain.

____

____

____

____

12. **Critical Thinking** The life spans of 10 adult mayflies have a mean of 4 hours and a MAD of 2 hours. Fill in the table with possible values for the life spans. You can use the same value more than once.

Life Spans of Ten Mayflies (h)									

Can any one of the 10 mayflies in the group live for 1 full day? Justify your answer.

____

____

____

H.O.T. FOCUS ON HIGHER ORDER THINKING

Work Area

13. Multistep In a spreadsheet, before entering any data values, first enter "mean =" into cell A2 and the formula =AVERAGE(A1:J1) into cell B2. Next, enter "MAD =" into cell A3 and the formula =AVEDEV(A1:J1) into cell B3. You should see #DIV/0! in cell B2 and #NUM! in cell B3 as shown. Now do the following:

	A	B
1		
2	mean =	#DIV/0!
3	MAD =	#NUM!

a. Enter "1" into cell A1. What do you get for the mean and the MAD of the data set? Explain why this makes sense.

____

____

____

b. Enter "2" into cell B1. What do you get for the mean and the MAD of the data set this time? Explain why this makes sense.

____

____

____

c. Enter the numbers 3 through 10 into cells C1 to J1 and watch the mean and the MAD change. Do they increase, decrease, or stay the same? Explain why this makes sense.

____

____

____

14. Make a Conjecture Each of the values in a data set is increased by 10. Does this affect the MAD of the data set? Why or why not?

____

____

____

15. What If? Suppose a data set contains all whole numbers. Would the MAD for the data set also be a whole number? Explain.

____

____

____

LESSON

16.3 Box Plots

CA CC 6.SP.4

Display numerical data in plots on a number line, including dot plots, histograms, and box plots. *Also 6.SP.5c*

ESSENTIAL QUESTION

How can you use a box plot and measures of spread to describe a data set?

Using a Box Plot

A **box plot** is a display that shows how the values in a data set are distributed, or spread out. To make a box plot, first find five values for the data set:

- the least value
- the **lower quartile** — the median of the lower half of the data
- the median
- the **upper quartile** — the median of the upper half of the data
- the greatest value

Math On the Spot
my.hrw.com

EXAMPLE 1 Real World

CA CC 6.SP.4

The heights of several students are shown. Make a box plot for the data.

Students' Heights (in.)					
60	58	54	56	63	61
65	61	62	59	56	58

STEP 1 Order the data and find the needed values.

54 56 56 58 58 59 60 61 61 62 63 65

Least value

Median = 59.5

Greatest value

Lower quartile = 57

Upper quartile = 61.5

Animated Math
my.hrw.com

Math Talk
Mathematical Practices

How many data values are in the upper half of the data set? How many in the lower half?

STEP 2 Draw the box plot.

Draw a number line that includes all the data values.

On the number line, draw dots above the least value, the lower quartile, the median, the upper quartile, and the greatest value.

Draw a box whose ends pass through the lower and upper quartiles. Draw a vertical segment through the median.

Draw a segment connecting the least value to the lower quartile.

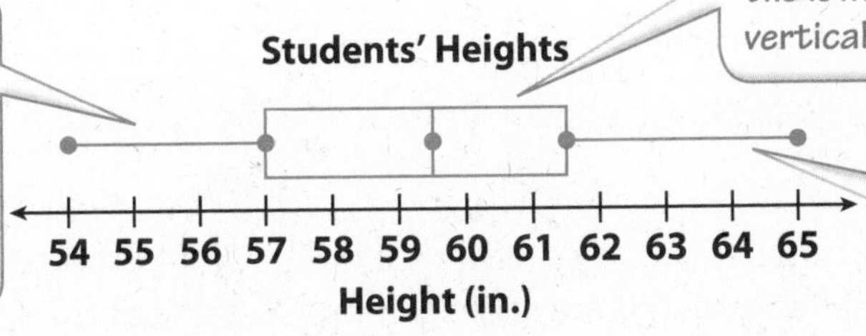

Draw a segment connecting the upper quartile to the greatest value.

Reflect

1. In the example, what percent of the data values are included in the box portion? What percent are included in each of the "whiskers" on the ends of the box? ___________

Personal Math Trainer
Online Practice and Help
my.hrw.com

YOUR TURN

2. Make a box plot of the daily high temperatures shown.

Daily High Temperatures (°F)					
85	78	92	88	78	84
80	94	89	75	79	83

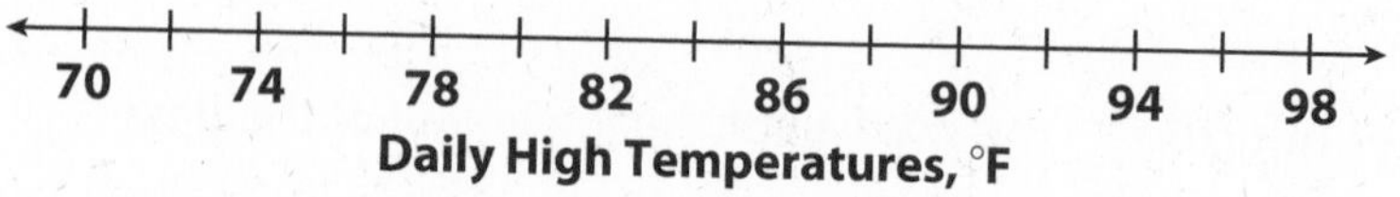

Math On the Spot
my.hrw.com

Finding the Interquartile Range

A **measure of spread** is a single number that describes the spread of a data set. One measure of spread is the *interquartile range*. The **interquartile range (IQR)** is the difference of the upper quartile and the lower quartile.

EXAMPLE 2 Real World

CA CC 6.SP.5c

The box plots compare the ages of dancers in two different dance troupes.

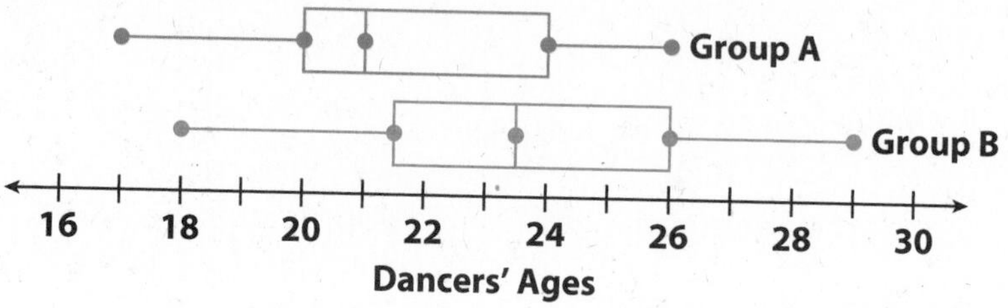

A Find the IQR for each set of data.

Group A: IQR = Upper quartile − Lower quartile

= 24 − 20 = 4

Group B: IQR = Upper quartile − Lower quartile

= 26 − 21.5 = 4.5

B Compare the IQRs. How do the IQRs describe the distribution of the ages in each group?

The IQR of group B is slightly greater than the IQR of group A. The ages in the middle half of group B are slightly more spread out than in group A.

YOUR TURN

3. The box plots compare the weekly earnings of two groups of salespeople from different clothing stores. Find and compare the IQRs of the box plots.

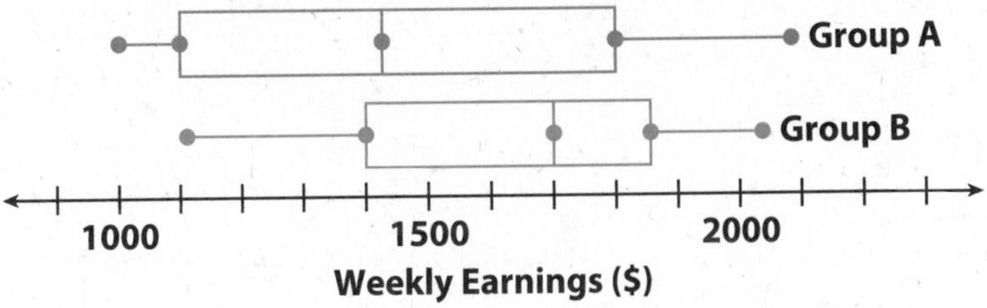

____

____

____

Personal Math Trainer
Online Practice and Help
my.hrw.com

Finding the Range

Another measure that describes the spread of a set of data is the *range*. The **range** is the difference of the greatest value and the least value in a set of data.

Math On the Spot
my.hrw.com

EXAMPLE 3 Real World

CA CC 6.SP.5c

The data sets show the ages of the players on two professional baseball teams. Find the range of each set of data.

Team A	36, 27, 28, 31, 39, 39, 28, 29, 24, 29, 30, 31, 29, 29, 28, 29, 31, 29, 32, 25, 37, 21, 26, 33, 29
Team B	25, 25, 26, 30, 27, 24, 29, 21, 27, 28, 26, 27, 25, 31, 22, 23, 29, 28, 25, 26, 28, 30, 23, 28, 29

STEP 1 Arrange the data sets in order from least to greatest.

Team A: 21, 24, 25, 26, 27, 28, 28, 28, 29, 29, 29, 29, 29, 29, 29, 30, 31, 31, 31, 32, 33, 36, 37, 39, 39

Team B: 21, 22, 23, 23, 24, 25, 25, 25, 25, 26, 26, 26, 27, 27, 27, 28, 28, 28, 28, 29, 29, 29, 30, 30, 31

STEP 2 Find the range of the data. Subtract the least value from the greatest value in each data set.

Team A: $39 - 21 = 18$

Team B: $31 - 21 = 10$

The range of ages for team A is 18 years, while the range of ages for team B is 10 years.

Math Talk
Mathematical Practices

How can you find the range of a set of data represented by a box plot?

Personal Math Trainer

Online Practice and Help

my.hrw.com

YOUR TURN

4. Find the range of each set of data. Which city's data has a greater range?

Average Monthly High Temperature (°F)	
Miami, FL	76, 78, 80, 83, 87, 90, 91, 91, 89, 86, 82, 78, 84
Chicago, IL	31, 35, 47, 59, 70, 80, 84, 82, 75, 62, 48, 35, 59

____

Guided Practice

The RBIs (runs batted in) for 15 players from the 2010 Seattle Mariners are shown. Use this data set for 1–7.

Mariners' RBIs
15 51 35 25 58 33 64
43 33 29 14 13 11 4 10

1. Order the data from least to greatest. (Example 1)

____

2. Find the median. (Example 1) _______________

3. Find the lower quartile. (Example 1) _______________

4. Find the upper quartile. (Example 1) _______________

5. Make a box plot for the data. (Example 1)

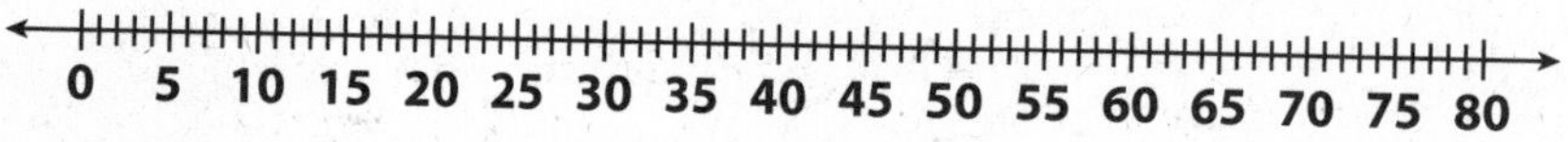

6. Find the IQR. (Example 2) _______________

7. Find the range. (Example 3) _______________

ESSENTIAL QUESTION CHECK-IN

8. How is the range of a set of data different from the IQR?

____

____

____

____

Name ______________________ Class ______________ Date ____________

16.3 Independent Practice

CA CC 6.SP.4, 6.SP.5c

Personal Math Trainer
Online Practice and Help
my.hrw.com

For 9–12, use the data set of the heights of several different students.

Students' Heights (in.)					
46	47	48	48	56	48
46	52	57	52	45	

9. Draw a box plot of the data.

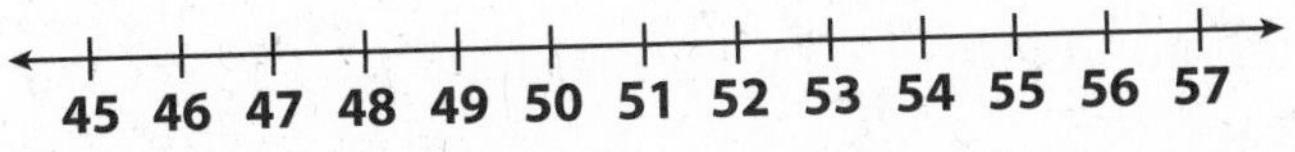

10. How many students are included in the data set? ______________

11. What method could have been used to collect the data?

____

12. **Represent Real-World Problems** What other data could you collect from the students to create a box plot? Provide several examples with units of measurement, if applicable.

____

For 13–15, use the box plots of the total precipitation for the same group of cities for the months of January and June.

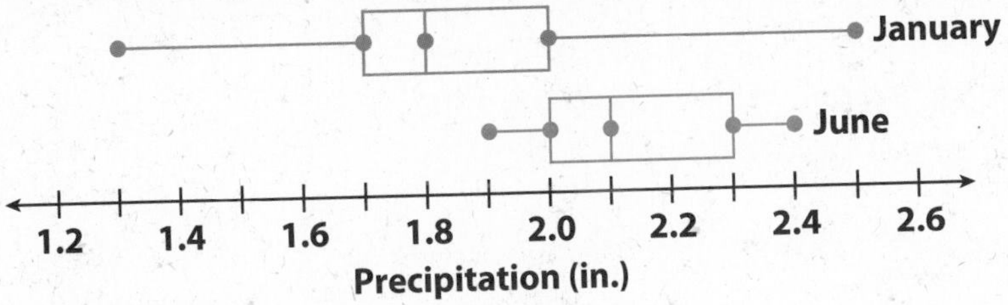

13. Calculate the IQR for each month.

January = ________ inches June = ________ inches

14. Calculate the range for each month.

January = ________ inches June = ________ inches

15. Compare the IQRs. What can you conclude about the two data sets?

____

____

16. Compare the ranges. What can you conclude about the two data sets?

____

H.O.T. FOCUS ON HIGHER ORDER THINKING

Work Area

17. Analyze Relationships Can two box plots have the same range and IQR and yet represent completely different data? Explain.

____

____

____

____

18. Multiple Representations Matthew collected data about the ages of the actors in two different community theater groups. He drew a box plot for one of the sets of data.

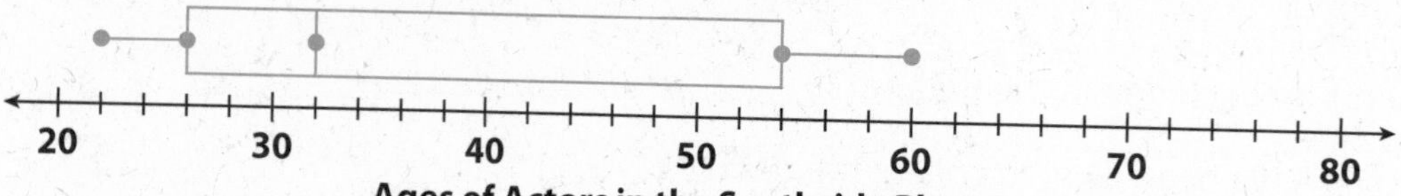

Ages of Actors in the Southside Players

Ages of Actors in the Northside Players	71, 62, 63, 21, 63, 39, 25, 26, 30

a. Find the median, range, and IQR for each set of data.

Theater Group	Median	Range	IQR
Northside Players			
Southside Players			

b. Suppose you were to draw a second box plot for the Northside Players using the same number line as for the Southside Players. Which box plot would be longer overall? Which would have the longest box portion?

____

____

____

c. Critique Reasoning Mandy assumes that because nine data values are shown for the Northside Players, nine data values were used to make the box plot for the Southside Players. Explain why this is not necessarily true.

____

____

____

____

LESSON

16.4 Dot Plots and Data Distribution

CA CC 6.SP.4

Display numerical data in plots on a number line, including dot plots, histograms, and box plots. *Also 6.SP.1, 6.SP.2, 6.SP.5c, 6.SP.5d*

ESSENTIAL QUESTION

How can you summarize and display numeric data?

EXPLORE ACTIVITY Real World CA CC 6.SP.1

Variable Data and Statistical Questions

The question "How much does a typical cat weigh?" is an example of a statistical question. A **statistical question** is a question that has many different, or variable, answers.

A Decide whether each of the situations below could yield variable data.

1. Your sister wants to know the typical weight for an adult cat.

   ____

2. You want to know how tall your friend is. ___________
3. You want to know how far your house is from school. ___________
4. A car owner wants to know how much money people usually pay for a new tire. ___________
5. How many students were in line for lunch at the cafeteria today at 12:30? ___________

B For which of the situations in part **A** can you write a statistical question? Write questions for these situations.

____

____

Reflect

1. Choose one of the questions you wrote in part **B**. How might you find answers to this question? What units would you use for the answers?

____

____

____

Making a Dot Plot

Statistical questions are answered by collecting and analyzing data. One way to understand a set of data is to make a visual display. A **dot plot** is a visual display in which each piece of data is represented by a dot above a number line. A dot plot shows the frequency of each data value.

Math On the Spot
my.hrw.com

EXAMPLE 1 Real World

CA CC 6.SP.4

A baseball team manager records the number of runs scored by the team in each game for several weeks. Use the data to make a dot plot.

1, 3, 1, 7, 2, 0, 11, 2, 2, 3, 1, 3, 4, 2, 2, 4, 5, 2, 6

The team usually scores between 0 and 7 runs in a game, but in one game they scored 11 runs.

STEP 1 Make a number line.

Data values range from 0 to 11, so use a scale from 0 to 11.

STEP 2 Draw a dot above the number line for each data value.

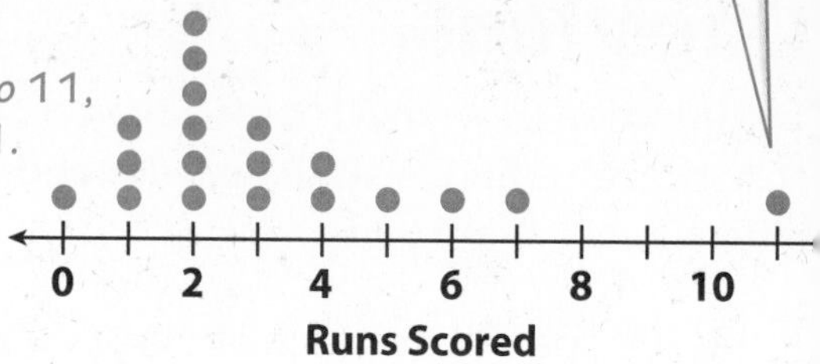

Reflect

2. How many games did the team play during the season? How can you tell from looking at the dot plot?

____

____

3. At how many games did the team score 2 runs or fewer? How do you know?

____

____

YOUR TURN

4. A different baseball team scores the following numbers of runs in its games for several weeks:
4, 4, 6, 1, 2, 4, 1, 2, 5, 3, 3, 5, 4, 2

Use the data to make a dot plot. Tell how many games the team played, and identify the data value with the greatest frequency.

____

____

Personal Math Trainer
Online Practice and Help
my.hrw.com

Interpreting a Dot Plot

A dot plot can give you a visual picture of the spread, center, and shape of a data distribution.

You can describe the spread of a data set by identifying the least and greatest values. You can also look for **outliers** which are data values that are either much greater or much less than the other data values.

You can describe the center and shape of a data set in terms of *peaks, clusters,* or *symmetry*. A symmetric distribution has approximately the same number of data values on either side of the center.

Math On the Spot
my.hrw.com

EXAMPLE 2

CA CC 6.SP.2

Describe the spread, center, and shape of each data distribution.

A The data values are spread out from 3 to 7 with no outliers.

The data has a cluster from 3 to 7 with one peak at 5, which is the center of the distribution.

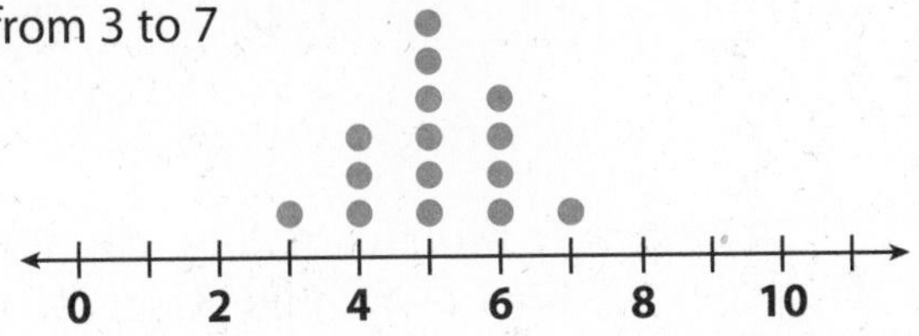

The distribution is symmetric. The data values are clustered around the center of the distribution.

B The data values are spread out from 1 to 9. The data value 1 appears to be an outlier.

The data has a cluster from 6 to 9 with one peak at 9, which is the greatest value in the data set.

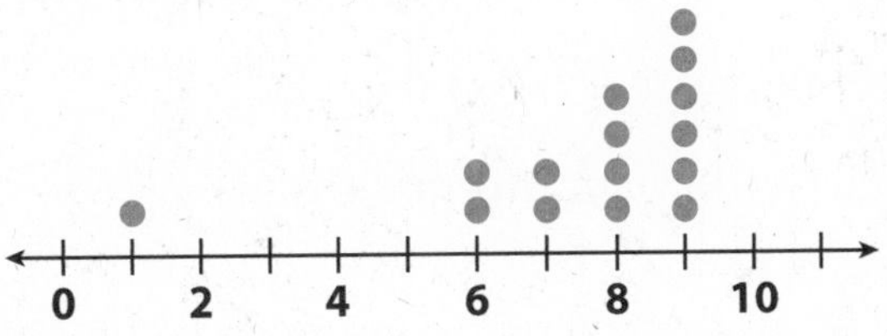

The distribution is not symmetric. The data values are clustered at one end of the distribution.

My Notes

YOUR TURN

5. Describe the spread, center, and shape of the data distribution from Example 1.

____

____

____

____

Personal Math Trainer
Online Practice and Help
my.hrw.com

Math On the Spot
my.hrw.com

Finding Measures from a Dot Plot

You can also find and calculate measures of center and spread from a dot plot.

EXAMPLE 3 Real World

CA CC 6.SP.5d, 6.SP.5c

The dot plot shows the number of runs scored by a baseball team in each game for several weeks from Example 1.

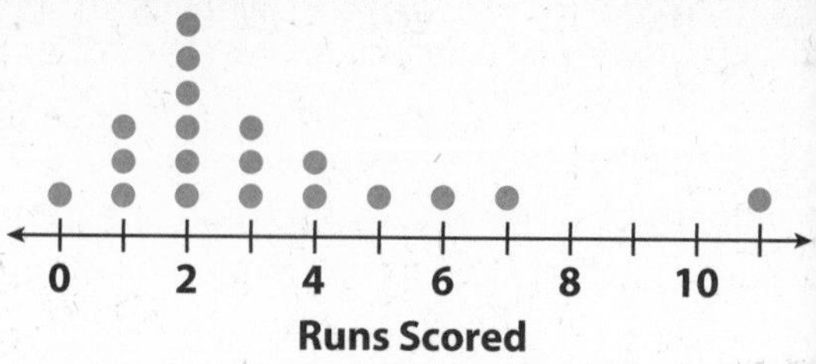

A Find the mean, median, and range of the data.

STEP 1 To find the mean, find the sum of the data values and divide by the number of data values.

$$\frac{1(0) + 3(1) + 6(2) + 3(3) + 2(4) + 1(5) + 1(6) + 1(7) + 1(11)}{19} = \frac{61}{19} \approx 3.2$$

The mean is about 3.2.

STEP 2 To find the median, count the dots from left to right until you find the middle value. You may need to find the mean of two middle values.

The median is 2.

STEP 3 To find the range, read the least and greatest values from the dot plot. Subtract the least value from the greatest.

$11 - 0 = 11$

The range is 11.

Math Talk
Mathematical Practices
Why is the question in **B** a statistical question?

B How many runs does the team typically score in a game? Explain.

The mean number of runs is 3.2. The median number of runs is 2.

The shape of the dot plot suggests that the outlier 11 may be affecting these measures of center. To see if that is the case, find the mean and median without including the outlier. Compare these values with the original values.

STEP 1 Find the mean without including the outlier.

$$\frac{1(0) + 3(1) + 6(2) + 3(3) + 2(4) + 1(5) + 1(6) + 1(7)}{18} = \frac{50}{18} \approx 2.8$$

Without the outlier, the mean is 2.8, which is less than the original mean of 3.2.

STEP 2 Find the median without including the outlier.

Counting from left to right, the median is still 2.

Given that it is not affected by the outlier, the median may be more typical of the data. The team typically scores two runs per game.

YOUR TURN

6. Find the mean, median, and range of the data from Your Turn question 4. What is the typical number of runs the team scores in a game? Justify your answer.

____

____

____

Personal Math Trainer
Online Practice and Help
my.hrw.com

Guided Practice

Tell whether the situation could yield variable data. If possible, write a statistical question. (Explore Activity)

1. The town council members want to know how much recyclable trash a typical household in town generates each week.

____

____

Kate asked some friends how many movies they saw last winter. Use her data for 2 and 3.

Movies Seen Last Winter
0, 1, 1, 2, 2, 3, 3, 3, 4, 4, 4, 4, 5, 5, 5, 5, 6, 6, 7, 7, 7, 8, 8, 9, 9, 17

2. Make a dot plot of the data. (Example 1)

3. Find the mean, median, and range of the data. (Example 3)

____

4. Describe the spread, center, and shape of the data. (Example 2)

____

____

ESSENTIAL QUESTION CHECK-IN

5. What are some measures of center and spread that you can find from a dot plot? How can making a dot plot help you visualize a data distribution?

____

____

Name ______________________ Class ______________ Date ______________

16.4 Independent Practice

CA CC 6.SP.1, 6.SP.2, 6.SP.4, 6.SP.5c, 6.SP.5d

6. **Vocabulary** Describe how a statistical question yields an answer with variability. Give an example.

____

____

____

____

For 7–10, determine whether the question is a statistical question. If it is a statistical question, identify the units for the answer.

7. An antique collector wants to know the age of a particular chair in a shop.

____

8. How tall do the people in your immediate and extended family tend to be?

____

____

9. How tall is Sam?

____

10. How much did your classmates typically spend on music downloads last year?

____

For 11–14, use the following data. The data give the number of days of precipitation per month during one year in a city.

12 10 11 9 9 10 12 9 8 7 9 10

11. Make a dot plot of the data.

12. What does each dot represent? How many months are represented?

____

____

13. Describe the shape, center, and spread of the data distribution. Are there any outliers?

____

____

____

14. Find the mean, median, and range of the data.

____

____

15. **What If?** During one month there were 7 days of precipitation. What if there had only been 3 days of precipitation that month? How would that change the measures of center?

____

____

____

____

For 16–20, use the dot plot of the number of cars sold at a car dealership per week during the first half of the year.

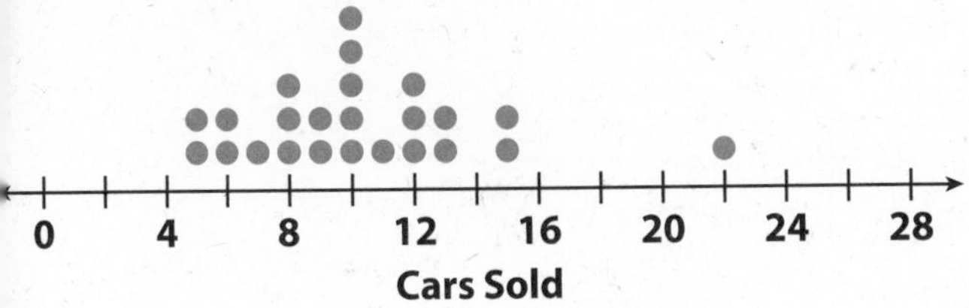

16. Find the mean, median, and range.

Mean = ________ Median = ________

Range = ________

17. The owner of the car dealership decides to treat the value 22 as an outlier. Which measure of center or spread is affected the most if the owner removes this outlier? Explain.

____

____

____

18. How many cars are sold in a typical week at the dealership? Explain.

____

____

19. Write an expression that represents the total number of cars sold during the first half of the year.

____

____

20. Describe the spread, center, and shape of the data distribution.

____

____

____

____

____

21. **Vocabulary** Explain how you can tell the frequency of a data value by looking at a dot plot.

____

____

For 22–26 use the following data. The data give the number of runs scored by opponents of the Boston Red Sox in June 2010.

4, 4, 9, 0, 2, 4, 1, 2, 11, 8, 2, 2, 5, 3, 2, 5, 6, 4, 0

22. Make a dot plot for the data.

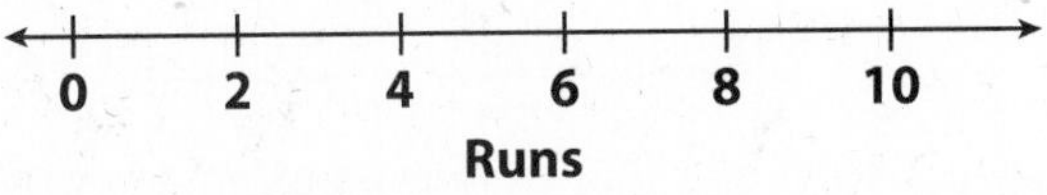

23. How many games did the Boston Red Sox play in June 2010? Explain.

____

24. Which data value in your dot plot has the greatest frequency? Explain what that frequency means for this data.

____

____

25. Find the mean, median, and range of the data.

____

____

26. What is a statistical question that you could answer using the dot plot? Answer your question and justify your response.

____

____

____

____

____

H.O.T. FOCUS ON HIGHER ORDER THINKING

Work Are

27. A pediatrician records the ages of the patients seen in one day: 1, 2, 5, 7, 9, 17, 13, 16, 18, 12, 3, 5, 1.

a. **Explain the Error** Assuming that some of the patients are infants who are less than 1 year old, what information did the pediatrician forget to write down?

____

b. **Critical Thinking** Can you make a dot plot of the pediatrician's data? Can you find the mean, median, and range? Why or why not?

____

____

____

28. **Multistep** A nurse measured a patient's heart rate at different times over several days.

Heart Rate (beats per minute)
86, 87, 89, 87, 86, 88, 90, 85, 82, 86, 83, 85, 84, 86

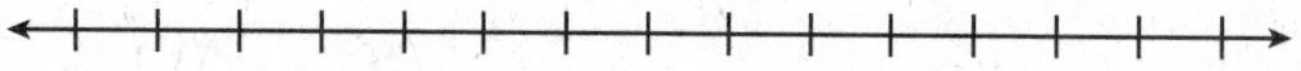

a. Make a dot plot.

b. Describe the shape, center, and spread of the data. Then find the mean, median, range, and IQR for the data.

____

____

____

____

c. **What If?** The nurse collected the data when the patient was resting. How might the dot plot and the measures change if the nurse collects the data when the patient is exercising?

____

____

LESSON

16.5 Histograms

CA CC 6.SP.4

Display numerical data in plots on a number line, including dot plots, histograms, and box plots. *Also 6.SP.5*

ESSENTIAL QUESTION

How can you display data in a histogram?

EXPLORE ACTIVITY Real World

CA CC 6.SP.5, 6.SP.4

Grouping Data in Intervals

The members of the high-school basketball team practice free throws. Each player attempts 50 free throws. The number of free throws made by each player is listed below.

25, 29, 29, 30, 33, 34, 35, 35, 36, 39, 42, 44

A Use a dot plot to represent the data.

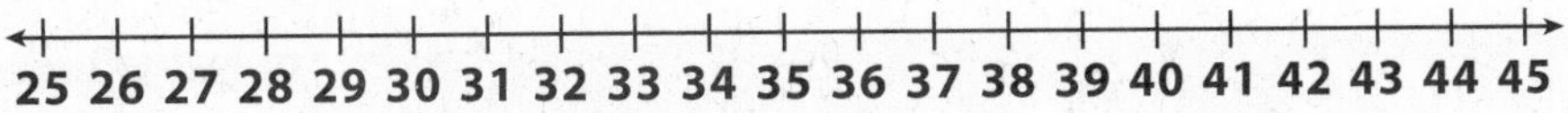

B On your dot plot, circle the dots that are in each interval of the frequency table below. Then complete the frequency table.

Interval	Frequency
20–29	
30–39	
40–49	

Enter the number of data values for the interval 30–39.

C Analyze the data. How were the data collected? How many data values are there? What are the mean, median, range, and IQR of the data?

____

____

____

____

____

EXPLORE ACTIVITY *(cont'd)*

Reflect

1. Can you use the dot plot to find the mean and the median of the data? Can you use the frequency table? Why or why not?

____

____

____

____

2. How do you find the number of data values in a data set from a dot plot? How can you find the number of data values from a frequency table?

____

Math On the Spot
my.hrw.com

Using a Histogram

A **histogram** is a type of bar graph whose bars represent the frequencies of numeric data within intervals.

EXAMPLE 1 Real World

CA CC 6.SP.4, 6.SP.5

A birdwatcher counts and records the number of birds at a birdfeeder every morning at 9:00 for several days.

12, 3, 8, 1, 1, 6, 10, 14, 3, 6, 2, 1, 3, 2, 7

Make a histogram of the data.

STEP 1 Make a frequency table.

Divide the data into equal-sized intervals of 4. Make a frequency table.

Interval	Frequency
1–4	8
5–8	4
9–12	2
13–16	1

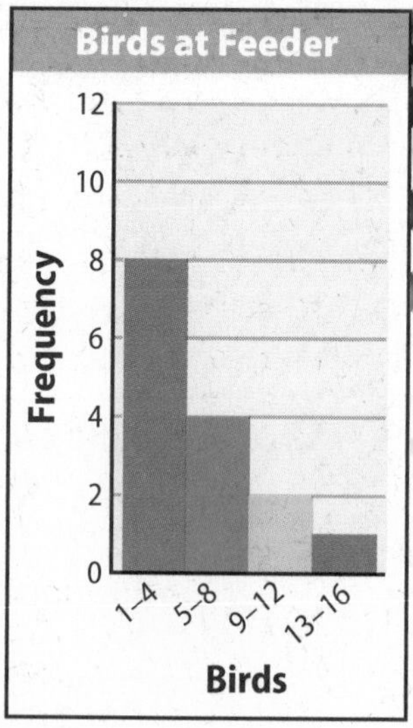

STEP 2 Make a histogram.

The intervals are listed along the horizontal axis. The vertical axis shows the frequencies. For each interval, draw a bar to show the number of days in that interval. The bars should have equal widths. They should touch but not overlap.

Math Talk
Mathematical Practices

How does the histogram show the total number of days the birdwatcher counted birds?

Reflect

3. **What If?** Suppose the birdwatcher continues his observation for three more days and collects these new data values: 5, 18, and 2. How could you change the histogram to include the data?

____

____

____

YOUR TURN

4. Kim has started rating each movie she sees using a scale of 1 to 10 on an online site. Here are her ratings so far:

   6, 9, 8, 5, 7, 4, 8, 8, 3, 7, 8, 7, 5, 1, 10

   Make a histogram of the data.

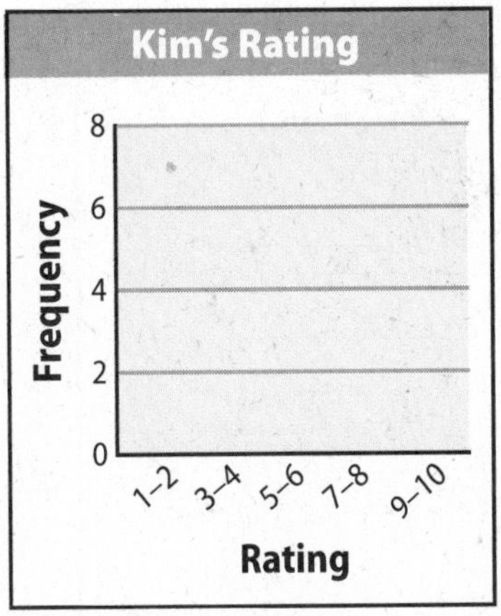

Personal Math Trainer
Online Practice and Help
my.hrw.com

Analyzing a Histogram

By grouping data in intervals, a histogram gives a picture of the distribution of a data set.

Math On the Spot
my.hrw.com

EXAMPLE 2 Real World

CA CC 6.SP.5

Use the histogram from Example 1. What are some conclusions about the data that can you make from the shape of the distribution?

The highest bar is for the interval 1–4, which means that on more than half the days (8 out of 15), the birdwatcher saw only 1–4 birds. The bars decrease in height from left to right, showing that it was more likely for the birdwatcher to see a small number of birds rather than a large number on any given day.

YOUR TURN

5. Use your histogram from Your Turn 4. What are some conclusions you can make about Kim's movie ratings from the shape of the distribution?

____

____

Personal Math Trainer
Online Practice and Help
my.hrw.com

Guided Practice

1. Wendy kept track of the number of text messages she sent each day for three weeks. Complete the frequency table. (Explore Activity)

0, 5, 5, 7, 11, 12, 15, 20, 22, 24, 25, 25, 27, 27, 29, 29, 32, 33, 34, 35, 35

Interval	Frequency
0–9	

Ed counted the number of seats available in each cafe in his town. Use his data for 2–3.

18, 20, 22, 26, 10, 12, 16, 18, 7, 8

2. Complete the frequency table and the histogram. (Example 1)

Interval	Frequency
1–7	
8–14	
15–21	
22–28	

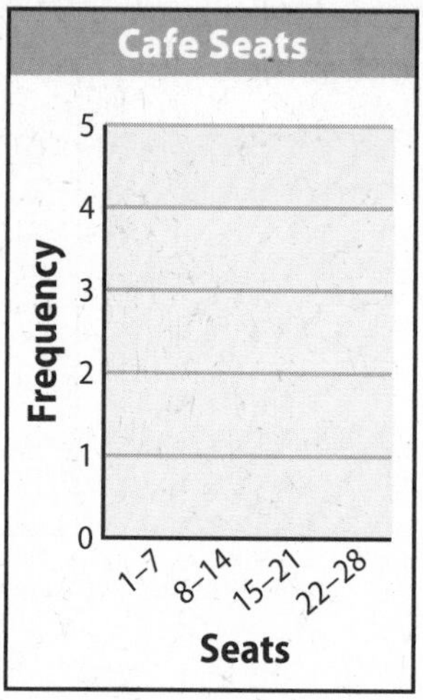

3. What are some conclusions you can make about the distribution of the data? (Example 2)

____

____

____

____

____

ESSENTIAL QUESTION CHECK-IN

4. How can you display data in a histogram?

____

____

____

Name ______________________ Class ______________________ Date ______________________

16.5 Independent Practice

CA CC 6.SP.4, 6.SP.5

Personal Math Trainer
Online Practice and Help
my.hrw.com

An amusement park employee records the ages of the people who ride the new roller coaster during a fifteen-minute period.

Ages of riders: 47, 16, 16, 35, 45, 43, 11, 29, 31, 50, 23, 18, 18, 20, 29, 17, 18, 48, 56, 24, 18, 21, 38, 12, 23.

5. Complete the frequency table. Then make a histogram of the data.

Interval	Frequency
10–19	

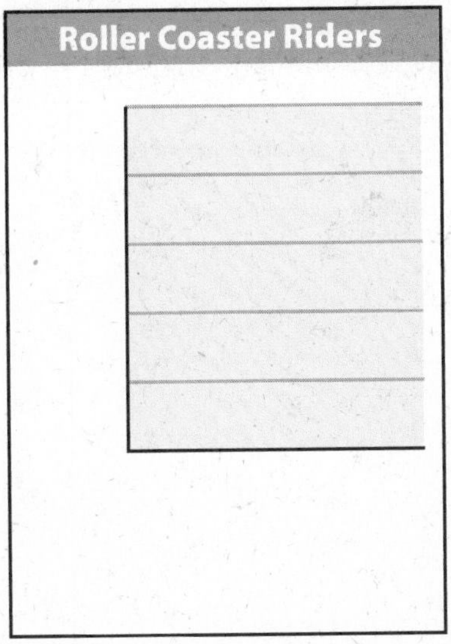

6. Describe two things you know about the riders who are represented by the data.

____

____

____

7. **Multiple Representations** West Middle School has classes of many different sizes during first period. The number of students in each class is shown.

9, 23, 18, 14, 20, 26, 14, 18, 18, 12, 8, 13, 21, 22, 28, 10, 7, 19, 24, 20

a. Hank made a histogram using intervals of 6–10, 11–15, and so on. How many bars did his histogram have? What was the height of the highest bar? ______________________

b. Lisa made a histogram using intervals of 0–9, 10–19, and so on. How many bars did her histogram have? What was the height of the highest bar? ______________________

c. Besides a histogram, what are some other ways you could display these data?

____

H.O.T. FOCUS ON HIGHER ORDER THINKING

Work Area

8. **Communicate Mathematical Ideas** Can you find the mean or median of a set of data from a histogram? Explain.

____

____

9. **Multistep** A theater owner keeps track of how many people come to see movies on 21 different Saturdays.

Saturday Moviegoers

Interval	Frequency
60–69	1
70–79	3
80–89	10
90–99	7

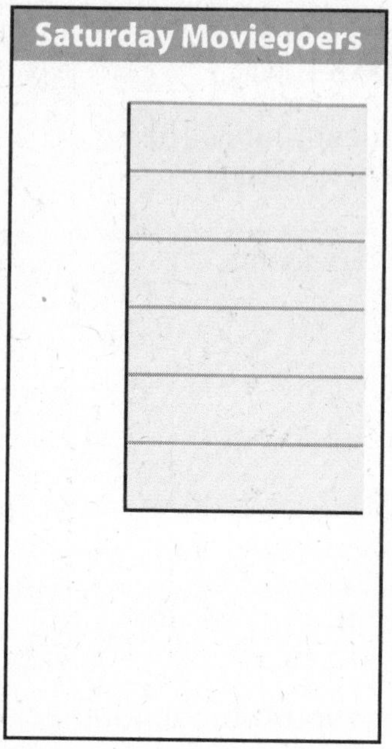

a. Use the data to make a histogram.

b. **Make a Prediction** The theater owner asks, "How many moviegoers come to the theater on a typical Saturday?" What would you tell the theater owner? Use your histogram to support your answer.

____

____

____

____

c. **Communicate Mathematical Ideas** Is the theater owner's question a statistical question? Why or why not?

____

10. **Explain the Error** Irina says she can find the range of a set of data from a histogram. Is she correct? Justify your answer.

____

____

____

MODULE QUIZ

Ready to Go On?

Personal Math Trainer
Online Practice and Help
my.hrw.com

16.1 Measures of Center

1. Find the mean and median of these data: 2, 5, 9, 11, 17, 19. ______________

16.2 Mean Absolute Deviation

2. Find the mean absolute deviation of the data in Exercise 1. Round to the nearest hundredth. ______________

16.3 Box Plots

3. Make a box plot for the data set.

36	42	44	52	61	70	78

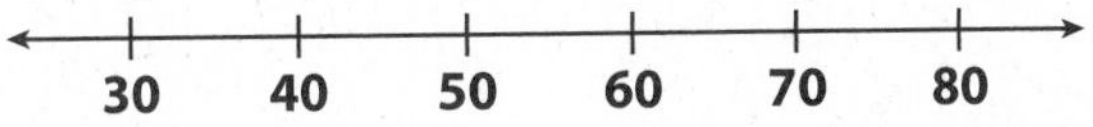

16.4 Dot Plots and Data Distribution

A baseball team scored the following number of runs over a 10-game period: 6, 6, 8, 5, 4, 6, 4, 3, 8, 4.

4. Make a dot plot for the data.

5. Find the mean, median, and range.

____

____

16.5 Histograms

6. Make a histogram for the data set.

23	45	62	19
48	10	39	54
39	16	48	12
25	32	18	4

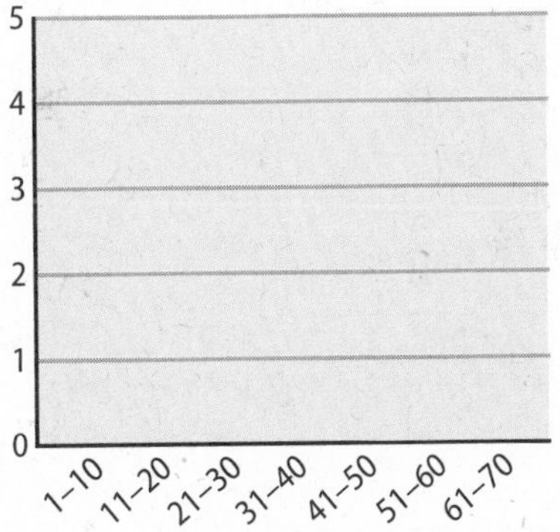

ESSENTIAL QUESTION

7. How can you represent and summarize data in a dot plot?

____

____

MODULE 16
MIXED REVIEW
Assessment Readiness

Personal Math Trainer
Online Practice and Help
my.hrw.com

1. Consider the box plot.

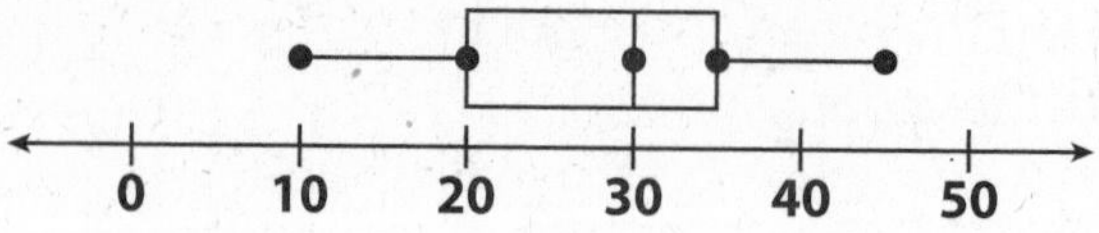

Select Yes or No in A–C to indicate whether the statement is correct.

A. The interquartile range of the data is 20. ◯ Yes ◯ No

B. The median of the data is 30. ◯ Yes ◯ No

C. The least data value is 10. ◯ Yes ◯ No

2. Hal asked some quiz show contestants their ages. The dot plot shows his data.

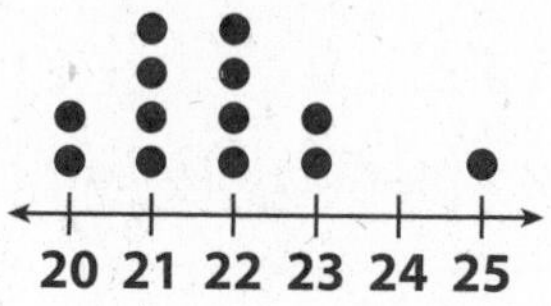

Choose True or False for A–C.

A. Most of the data values are clustered at or below the median. ◯ True ◯ False

B. Hal collected data from 13 contestants. ◯ True ◯ False

C. If a new data value, 30, is included in the dot plot, the median would increase. ◯ True ◯ False

3. Andrea recorded the points she scored in her last eight basketball games: 28, 32, 47, 16, 40, 35, 38, 54. Give an example of a statistical question you could answer using the mean or the median. Explain your reasoning.

4. The frequency table shows data about the number of tickets sold by students.

Tickets sold	Frequency
0–9	2
10–19	4
20–29	3
30–39	1

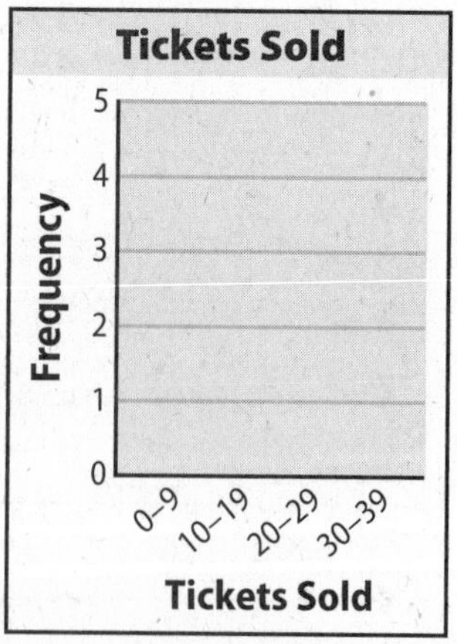

a. Use the frequency table to make a histogram.

b. How many students sold tickets?

c. What percent of the students sold 20 or more tickets?

UNIT 7

Study Guide Review

MODULE 16 Displaying, Analyzing, and Summarizing Data

ESSENTIAL QUESTION

How can you solve real-world problems by displaying, analyzing, and summarizing data?

EXAMPLE 1

The ages of Thomas's neighbors are shown.

Ages of Thomas's Neighbors
30, 48, 31, 45, 42, 32, 32, 38, 34, 50, 49, 48

Make a box plot of the data.

30 31 32 32 34 38 42 45 48 48 49 50

Median = 40

Lower quartile = 32

Upper quartile = 48

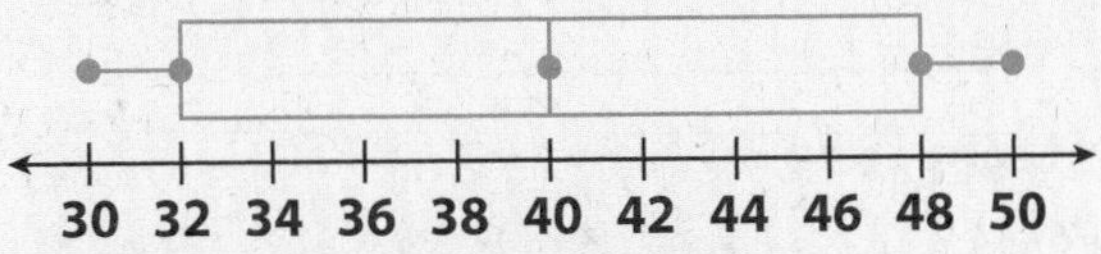

EXAMPLE 2

The dot plot shows the ages of actors in a student theater production. Find the mean, median, range, and interquartile range of the data shown on the dot plot.

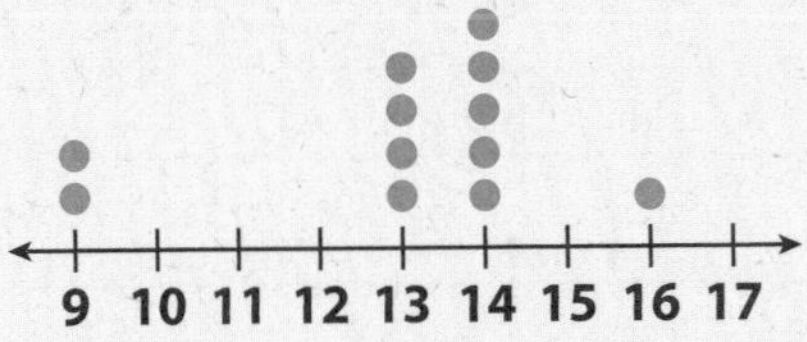

The mean is 13. $\frac{2(9) + 4(13) + 5(14) + 16}{12} = 13$

The median is 13.5. 9, 9, 13, 13, 13, 13, 14, 14, 14, 14, 14, 16

The range is 7. $16 - 9 = 7$

The IQR is 1. $14 - 13 = 1$ IQR = Upper quartile − lower quartile

Key Vocabulary

box plot *(diagrama de caja)*
categorical data *(datos categóricos)*
dot plot *(diagrama de puntos)*
histogram *(histograma)*
interquartile range *(rango entre cuartiles)*
lower quartile *(cuartil inferior)*
mean *(media)*
mean absolute deviation (MAD) *(desviación absoluta media, (DAM))*
measure of center *(medida central)*
measure of spread *(medida de dispersión)*
median *(mediana)*
mode *(moda)*
range *(rango)*
statistical question *(pregunta estadística)*
upper quartile *(cuartil superior)*

EXAMPLE 3

Find the mean absolute deviation (MAD) of the data in Example 2. Round to the nearest tenth.

The MAD is the mean distance of each of the 12 data points from the mean, 13.

$$\frac{4+4+0+0+0+0+1+1+1+1+1+3}{12} = \frac{16}{12} \approx 1.3$$

The mean absolute deviation is approximately 1.3.

EXAMPLE 4

Describe the spread, center, and shape of the data distribution in Example 2.

Most of the data are clustered around the values 13 and 14. The least values in the set are 9, and the greatest value is 16. The distribution is not symmetric.

EXERCISES

1. Use the dot plot in Example 2. How would you describe the typical age of a student in the theater production? Explain. (Lesson 16.4)

____

____

The number of goals for the 13 players on a soccer team are 4, 9, 0, 1, 1, 2, 0, 0, 2, 8, 8, 3, 1. Use the data for Exercises 2–3.

2. Make a dot plot for the data. Describe the shape, center, and spread of the data distribution. (Lesson 16.4)

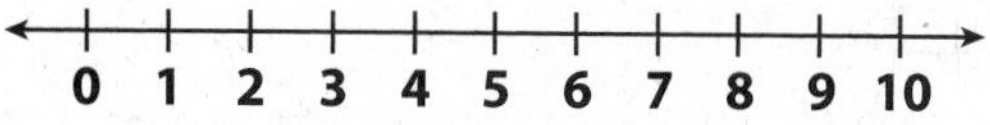

____

____

____

3. Find the median, lower quartile, and upper quartile. Then make a box plot for the data. (Lesson 16.3) ____________________

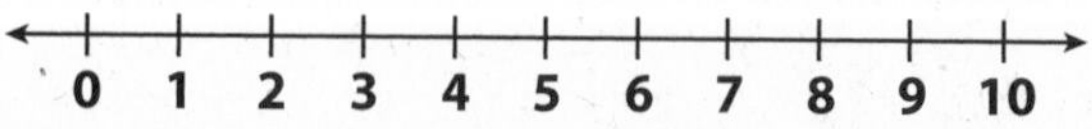

The coach recorded the time it took 14 students to run a mile. The times are as follows: 9:23, 8:15, 9:23, 9:01, 6:45, 6:55, 7:20, 9:14, 6:21, 7:12, 7:34, 6:10, 9:15, 9:18. Use the data for Exercises 4–5.

4. Give an example of a statistical question you could answer from these data. Describe how you might answer the question. (Lesson 16.4)

____

____

____

5. Use the data to complete the frequency table. Then use the table to make a histogram. (Lesson 16.5)

Interval	Frequency
6–6:59	

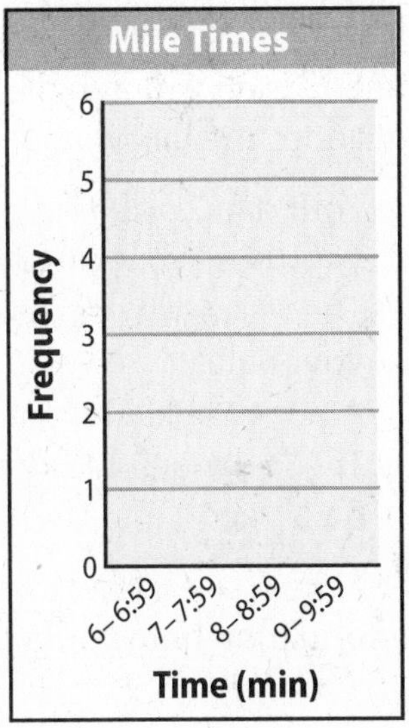

The data show the distances driven by Juan on different days. Use the data for Exercises 6–7.

Distance per day (mi) driven by Juan						
12	9	7	7	11	10	7

6. Find the mean, the median, and the mean absolute deviation of the data. If necessary, round to the nearest hundredth. (Lesson 16.2)

Mean: ______________________________

Median: ______________________________

Mean absolute deviation: ______________________________

7. Suppose Juan drives 33 miles on a different day. How would this new value affect the mean of the data? How would the mean absolute deviation change? Assuming that this data value is added to the data, which measure of center, mean or median, would you use to describe the typical number of miles Juan drove each day? Explain your reasoning. (Lessons 16.1, 16.4)

____

____

____

____

Unit Project

CA CC 6.SP.4, 6.SP.5, 6.SP.5c

Top Tens

The Internet, almanacs, and record books are full of "Top 10" lists. The 10 Longest Bridges! The 10 Tallest Trees! The 10 Widest Rivers! For this project, find the Top 10 in a category that interests you. Possible areas of research are human-made structures, sports, natural objects, and geography. The only requirement is that your list must present the ten longest, tallest, widest, or fastest of something.

Then, using your ten measures as data, create a presentation that includes the following:

- Your data, including the source where you found it and the reason you chose your category
- The mean, median, mean absolute deviation, range, and outliers (if any) of your data
- A box plot of your data
- The lower quartile, the upper quartile, and the interquartile range of your data

Use the space below to write down any questions you have or important information from your teacher.

MATH IN CAREERS **ACTIVITY**

Geneticist Students in a 6th grade science class are collecting data about the arm span lengths of two groups of students in the class. Write a statistical question for this data. Explain how they could use a measure of center and a measure of variability to compare the data from the two groups.

Assessment Readiness

Personal Math Trainer
Online Practice and Help
my.hrw.com

1. Consider the dot plot. The dot plot shows the number of participants in each age group in a science fair.

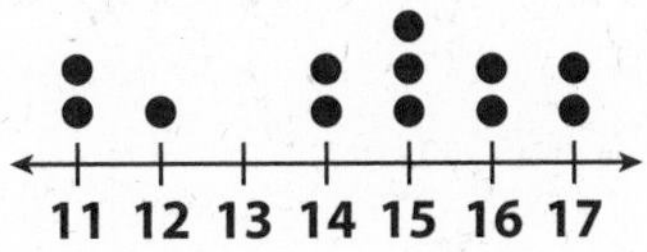

Select Yes or No.

A. The range of the data is 6. ○ Yes ○ No

B. The mode of the ages is 13. ○ Yes ○ No

C. The median age is 15. ○ Yes ○ No

2. Choose True or False for each statement.

A. The prime factorization of 120 is $2 \times 3 \times 5$. ○ True ○ False

B. The greatest common factor of 36 and 84 is 12. ○ True ○ False

C. The least common multiple of 36 and 84 is 3,024. ○ True ○ False

3. Sarita records the distance in miles she runs each day for 5 days:

5 4 5.5 4.5 5.5.

What is the mean distance Sarita ran? Explain your answer.

4. The data set shows the ages of the workers at Mr. Ito's office.

26	30	45	43	26
14	28	33	56	29

What is the mean absolute deviation? Describe how you found it.

Performance Tasks

★**5.** The heights in inches of 8 students are 50, 53, 52, 68, 54, 49, 55, and 51.

a. What is the mean of the students' heights?

b. Is there an outlier in the data set? If so, which number is the outlier?

c. What is the mean height if the outlier is removed from the data?

★★**6.** Kinesha collected data about the heights of students in her class.

a. What measures of center and variation are most appropriate for the data?

b. Which of the data displays that you learned about in this unit could Kinesha use to display the data?

c. Which data display could be used to show the measures of center and variation you named in part **a**?

★★★**7.** The number of goals for the 13 players on a soccer team are

4, 9, 0, 1, 1, 2, 0, 0, 2, 8, 8, 3, 1.

a. Find the median, lower quartile, and upper quartile.

b. Find the range and the interquartile range of the data.

c. Identify any outliers.

d. Find the mean and mode of the data. Which of the median, mean, and mode is the best to use when describing the data? Explain your reasoning.

UNIT 1 Selected Answers

MODULE 1

LESSON 1.1

Your Turn

6.
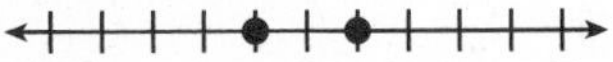

8. −10 **9.** 5 **10.** 0 **11.** 4

Guided Practice

2.

4.

5. −4 **6.** 11 **7.** −3 **8.** 3 **9.** 0 **10.** −22

Independent Practice

13. 17 **15.** 2 **17.** 12 **19a.** gain **b.** Lady's **c.** Lady and Rocky **d.** Sparky's; a change of 0 indicates no change in weight. **e.** −6 pounds **f.** No; a −6 pound change means Lucky lost 6 pounds. **21.** 4 units **23.** 14 units **25.** −9; it is 9 units away from 0 on a number line, and 6 is only 6 units away from 0.

LESSON 1.2

Your Turn

2. −6, −5, −3, 0, 2, 4
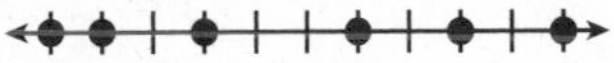

3. −10, −6, −1, 0, 2, 5, 8, 9 **4.** $<$ **5.** $<$ **6.** $>$ **7.** $-2 > -18$; $-18 < -2$ **8.** $-39 < 39$; $39 > -39$

Guided Practice

1b. A; B **2.** −9, −6, −3, 0, 1, 4, 8 **3.** −65, −13, −7, 7, 34, 55, 62 **4.** $-17 > -22$; $-22 < -17$ **5.** $<$ **6.** $>$ **7.** $<$ **8.** $>$ **9a.** $-3 < 2$ **b.** $0 > -4$

Independent Practice

11b. E. Simpson **13.** $167 > -65$ **15b.** −5, −2, 2, 4, 7 **17.** $377 > 249$ **19.** Argentina **21.** −3 °F; the warmer temperature is −3 °F.

LESSON 1.3

Your Turn

4. The temperature at night reached 13 °F below zero. **5.** 12 **6.** 91 **7.** 55 **8.** 0 **9.** 88 **10.** 1

Guided Practice

1. negative **2a.** −$10; it is a fee, so it represents a change of −$10 in the amount of money Ryan has. **b.** $|-10| = 10$

3a. more than 100 **b.** fewer than Leo **c.** more than 50

Independent Practice

5. The first week his balance changed by +$80. The second week his balance changed by −$85. **7b.** April **9a.** −5, 4, −1, 3, −2 **b.** The spinner landing on red results in a change of −$5 to Lisa's amount of money. **13.** No; $-|-4| = -4$, and $|-(-4)| = |4| = 4$.

MODULE 2

LESSON 2.1

Your Turn

3. 7 **4.** 4 **5.** 8 teams; 4 girls, 5 boys

Guided Practice

1. Common factors: 1, 2, 4, 8; Possible numbers of vests: 1, 2, 4, 8; GCF: 8; greatest number of vests: 8 **2.** 9; 9; 4; 9; 5; 9; 4; 5 **3.** 15; 15; 5; 15; 6; 15; 5; 6

Independent Practice

5. 1, 2, 3, 4, 6, 12 **7.** 1, 3, 13, 39 **9.** 8 **11.** 5 **13.** 1 **15.** 12 **17.** 4 **19.** 1, 2, 4, or 8 shelves **21.** 6 groups; 2 coaches and 7 players **23.** $8 \times (7 + 8) = 8 \times 15$ **25.** $6 \times (5 + 9) = 6 \times 14$ **27.** $11 \times (5 + 6) = 11 \times 11$ **29.** $5 \times (8 + 5) = 5 \times 13$ **31.** 1 is a factor of all whole numbers. Some numbers (prime numbers) have no common factors other than 1. **33.** Find the factors of all three numbers, and take the greatest factor that is common to all three. For example, for the GCF of 6, 9, and 12, the factors of 6 are 1, 2, 3, and 6; the factors of 9 are 1, 3, and 9; and the factors of 12 are 1, 2, 3, 4, 6, and 12. So, the GCF is 3.

LESSON 2.2

Your Turn

2. 36; 4, 8, 12, 16, 20, 24, 28, 32, 36, 40; 9, 18, 27, 36, 45, 54, 63, 72, 81, 90

Guided Practice

1. 36th and 72nd visits; 36th visit

Independent Practice

3. 56 **5.** 60 **7.** 48 **9.** 45 **11a.** February 15 **b.** No; there are only 28 or 29 days in February, and the next common multiple of 3 and 5 is 30. **13.** 40 **15.** 120 **17.** The LCM is the greater of the two numbers. **19.** 5 and 12.

MODULE 3

LESSON 3.1

Your Turn

3. $\frac{-15}{1}$ **4.** $\frac{31}{100}$ **5.** $\frac{41}{9}$ **6.** $\frac{62}{1}$ **8.** rational numbers **9.** rational numbers **10.** integers and rational numbers **11.** whole numbers, integers, and rational numbers

UNIT 1 Selected Answers *(cont'd)*

Guided Practice

1a. 4 rolls of ribbon divided evenly among the 5 friends. $4 \div 5$. **b.** $\frac{4}{5}$ roll **2.** $\frac{7}{10}$ **3.** $\frac{-29}{1}$ **4.** $\frac{25}{3}$
5. integers, rational numbers
6. rational numbers

Independent Practice

11. $\frac{22}{5}$, or \$4.40 **13.** Venn **15.** $\$\frac{35}{2}$, rational numbers **17.** $\frac{8}{15}$ cup

LESSON 3.2

Your Turn

2. −7, 3.5, −2.25, and $-9\frac{1}{3}$. **4.** 4.5 **5.** $1\frac{1}{2}$ **6.** 4 **7.** $3\frac{1}{4}$

Guided Practice

1.
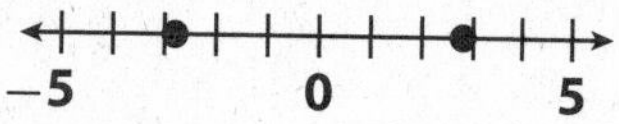

2.
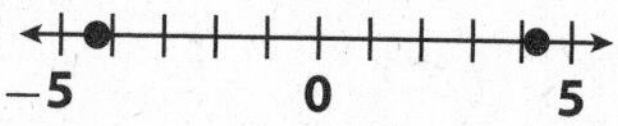

3.
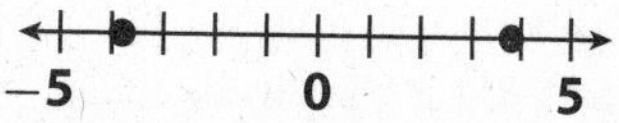

4.
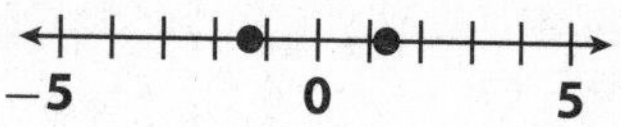

5. −3.78 **6.** $7\frac{5}{12}$ **7.** 0 **8.** −4.2 **9.** −12.1 **10.** −2.6 **11.** They are the same distance from 0 on the number line. **12.** 5.23 **13.** $4\frac{2}{11}$ **14.** 0 **15.** $6\frac{3}{5}$ **16.** 2.12 **17.** 8.2

Independent Practice

19a. Girardi \$85.23, Lewis −\$20.44, Stein \$116.33, Yuan −\$13.50, Wenner \$9.85
b. Wenner **c.** Stein **23.** to the left **25a.** −25,344 ft **b.** −5 and −4
c.
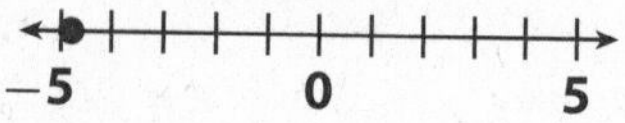

LESSON 3.3

Your Turn

3. 0.15, $\frac{3}{5}$, $\frac{7}{10}$, 0.85 **5.** −1.8, −1.25, 1, $1\frac{2}{5}$, $1\frac{9}{10}$

Guided Practice

1. $\frac{3}{5}$ **2.** 0.25 **3.** $\frac{9}{10}$ **4.** $\frac{1}{10}$ **5.** 0.3 **6.** $1\frac{2}{5}$ **7.** 0.8 **8.** $\frac{2}{5}$ **9.** 0.75 **10.** $\frac{1}{5}$, 0.4, $\frac{1}{2}$, 0.75 **11.** $12\frac{3}{4}$, 12.7, $12\frac{3}{5}$ **12.** 2.3, 2.6, $2\frac{4}{5}$ **13.** $\frac{5}{48}$, $\frac{3}{16}$, 0.5, 0.75 **14.** $\frac{1}{5}$, 0.35, $\frac{12}{25}$, 0.5, $\frac{4}{5}$ **15.** $-\frac{3}{4}$, $-\frac{7}{10}$, $\frac{3}{4}$, $\frac{8}{10}$ **16.** −0.65, $-\frac{3}{8}$, $\frac{5}{16}$, $\frac{2}{4}$ **17.** $-2\frac{4}{5}$, −2.6, −2.3 **18.** −0.72, $-\frac{5}{8}$, −0.6, $-\frac{7}{12}$ **19.** 1.2, $1\frac{1}{3}$, 1.45, $1\frac{1}{2}$ **20.** −0.35, −0.3, 0.5, 0.55

Independent Practice

23a. $6\frac{1}{6}$, 5.5, $4\frac{3}{8}$, 4.3, $\frac{15}{4}$ **b.** Claire, Peter, Brenda, and Jim; Micah **c.** Yes; the smallest donation is $\frac{15}{4}$ pounds. $\frac{1}{2}$ pound is equal to $\frac{2}{4}$ pound. $\frac{15}{4} + \frac{2}{4} = \frac{17}{4} = 4\frac{1}{4} = 4.25$ pounds, which is enough to win a free movie coupon. **25.** Negative numbers are less than zero and positive numbers are greater than zero, so the order would be negative, zero, positive. **27.** The order of the absolute values will be the reverse of the order of the negative rational numbers. The least negative number will be the farthest from 0 on a number line. The greatest negative number will be closest to 0 on a number line.

UNIT 2 Selected Answers

MODULE 4

LESSON 4.1

Your Turn

1. $\frac{1}{10}$ **2.** $\frac{7}{12}$ **3.** $\frac{2}{7}$ **4.** $\frac{8}{35}$ **5.** $\frac{4}{15}$ **6.** $\frac{1}{7}$ **8.** 15 **9.** 12 **10.** $\frac{8}{3}$ **11.** $\frac{7}{2}$ **12.** $25\frac{9}{10}$ **13.** 23 **15.** $\frac{11}{21}$ **16.** $\frac{4}{15}$ **17.** $\frac{1}{24}$ **18.** $1\frac{11}{20}$ **19.** $6\frac{13}{15}$ **20.** $3\frac{1}{42}$

Guided Practice

1. $\frac{5}{16}$ **2.** $\frac{1}{3}$ **3.** $\frac{3}{20}$ **4.** 38 **5.** $\frac{3}{4}$ **6.** 6 **7.** 3 **8.** 16 **9.** 24 **10.** 15 **11.** $\frac{7}{12}$ **12.** $\frac{7}{15}$ **13.** $\frac{1}{5}$ **14.** $\frac{24}{35}$ **15.** $3\frac{19}{24}$ **16.** $5\frac{19}{45}$

Independent Practice

19a. 10 pounds **b.** 5 more bags **21a.** oranges $= 1\frac{1}{2}$, apples $= 1\frac{4}{5}$, blueberries $= \frac{3}{4}$ cup, peaches $= 2$ **b.** Sample answer: If you triple 3, it becomes 9. If you triple $\frac{1}{2}$, it becomes $1\frac{1}{2}$. Add $9 + 1\frac{1}{2} = 10\frac{1}{2}$. **23a.** $22\frac{1}{2}$ minutes **b.** Yes, there is enough time; 15 min for the teacher's introduction + 15 min for students to get ready + $22\frac{1}{2}$ min for speeches $= 52\frac{1}{2}$ min **c.** $7\frac{1}{2}$ minutes **25.** Cameron divided the numerator of $\frac{3}{7}$ by the GCF of 3 and 9 but forgot to divide the denominator of $\frac{4}{9}$ by the GCF. He should have multiplied $\frac{1 \times 4}{7 \times 3}$ to find the product $\frac{4}{21}$.

LESSON 4.2

Your Turn

5. $\frac{8}{7}$ **6.** $\frac{1}{9}$ **7.** 11 **10.** $2\frac{1}{4}$ **11.** $1\frac{1}{2}$

Guided Practice

1. $\frac{5}{2}$ **2.** $\frac{1}{9}$ **3.** $\frac{3}{10}$ **4.** $\frac{4}{5}$ **5.** $\frac{3}{8}$ **6.** $1\frac{1}{4}$

Independent Practice

9. $9\frac{1}{3}$ **11.** $\frac{5}{7}$ **13.** $1\frac{1}{7}$ **15.** 8 **17.** 4 runners will be needed. **19.** 9 bags **21.** $\frac{1}{10}$ pound

LESSON 4.3

Your Turn

6. 9; $10\frac{1}{2} \div 1\frac{1}{4} = 8\frac{2}{5}$; She will need 9 containers. **8.** $4\frac{1}{2}$ meters **9.** $3\frac{1}{4}$ yards

Guided Practice

1. 17; 17; 4; 3; $5\frac{2}{3}$ **2.** 3; 9; 3; 4; 9; $\frac{2}{3}$ **3.** $3\frac{5}{9}$ **4.** $2\frac{4}{5}$ **5.** $3\frac{1}{3}$ **6.** 4 **7.** $26 \div 5\frac{1}{2}$; The width is $4\frac{8}{11}$ feet. **8.** $230 \div 12\frac{1}{2}$; $18\frac{2}{5}$ feet

Independent Practice

13a. No **b.** $\frac{11}{20}$ of a cup; $5\frac{1}{2}$ cups $\div$ 10 people $= \frac{11}{2} \times \frac{1}{10} = \frac{11}{20}$ **c.** She would need $7\frac{1}{2}$ cups total, so she would need 2 more cups of trail mix. **15.** yes because the height is $4\frac{1}{4}$ feet **17.** $5\frac{1}{4}$ feet **19.** He used the reciprocal of $\frac{3}{4}$ instead of the reciprocal of $2\frac{3}{4}$.

LESSON 4.4

Your Turn

1. 10

Guided Practice

1. 13

Independent Practice

3. \$20 per mile **5.** 40 appointments **7.** 93 pieces **9.** $1\frac{5}{24}$ gallons **11.** Sample answer: A person taking a test averages $\frac{3}{8}$ minute to read a question and $\frac{5}{6}$ minute to answer the question. It takes the person 29 minutes to answer all of the questions. How many questions are on the test? 24 questions

MODULE 5

LESSON 5.1

Your Turn

3. 109 **4.** 587 **7.** 231 R21 **8.** 46 R16 **9.** 105 bags; 3 rocks left over

Guided Practice

1. 30,000; 500; 60 **2.** 96 **3.** 89 **4.** 98 R7 **5.** 42 **6.** 61 **7.** 94 R15 **8.** 24 R9 **9.** 127 **10.** 81 R28 **11.** 300 items **12.** 32 seats **13.** 85 boxes

Independent Practice

15. 268 **17.** 209 **19.** 86 R39 **21.** 587 **23.** 67 rows; $8{,}450 \div 125 =$ 67 R75 so he will have 67 full rows and one partial row of 75 trees. **25.** 69 people **29.** Multiply the quotient and the divisor, and then add the remainder to the product. If the division was done correctly, the result will equal the dividend. **31.** No; 78,114 is about 80,000 and 192 is about 200; $80{,}000 \div 200 =$ 400, and 40 isn't close to 400. **33.** More; the whole amount is divided into smaller portions, so there will be more bags; since 25 is half of 50, they will have twice as many bags.

LESSON 5.2

Your Turn

5. 0.69 **6.** 0.939 **7.** 7.85 **8.** 21.15

Guided Practice

1. 0.91 **2.** 0.78 **3.** 62.35 **4.** 37.11 **5.** 3.955 **6.** 2.57 **7.** 11.949 **8.** 1.806 **9.** 30.1 **10.** 65.841 **11.** 23.356 **12.** 7.35 **13.** 37.68 **14.** 72.25 **15.** 31.25 feet **16.** \$11.36

UNIT 2 Selected Answers *(cont'd)*

Independent Practice

19. 5.495 **21.** 63.022
23. 11.949 **25.** 6.408
27. Jahmya; $0.54 more
29. $1.53 **31a.** 27.78 minutes
b. 32.22 minutes
33. Sample answer: The sum $2.55 + (3.72 + 1.45) = 2.55 + 5.17 = 7.72$. Using the Commutative Property, the sum can be written as $2.55 + (1.45 + 3.72) = 7.72$, and using the Associative Property, the sum can be written as $(2.55 + 1.45) + 3.72 = 7.72$.

LESSON 5.3

Your Turn

3. 1; 1; 6300; 12600; 192.78; 2
4. 2; 2; 5856; 39040; 4.4896; 4
5. 49980; 428400; 48.4092
6. 8043; 22980; 919200; 95.0223
7. 37.2 **8.** Sample answer: Round 15.5 to 16 and 2.4 to 2; $16 \times 2 = 32$; 32 is close to 37.2.

Guided Practice

1. 0.28

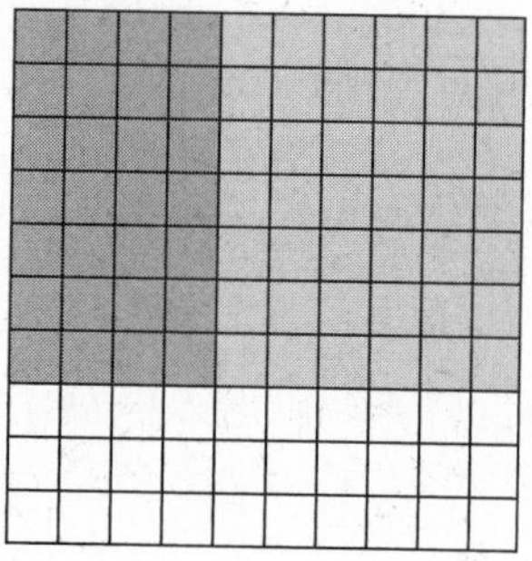

2. 2.64

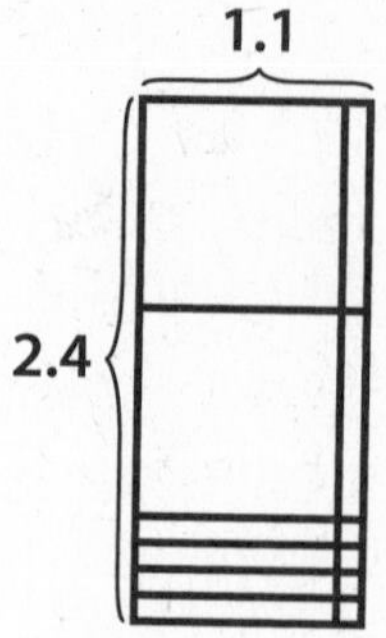

3. 0.0108 **4.** 130.055 **5.** 0.1152
6. 2,021.175 **7.** 14.858 **8.** 2.48292
9. 23.63 **10.** 173.90 **11.** 29.21
12. 1.06

Independent Practice

15. 14 inches **17.** $342 **19.** $15.50
21. $23.58 **23.** 20.425 miles
25. 14.425 miles **27.** 3.48 is closer to 3 and 7.33 is closer to 7; $3 \times 7 = 21$ **29.** The 22-karat gold statue; 24.549 ounces

LESSON 5.4

Your Turn

3. 1.95 **4.** 0.92 **5.** 29.2 **6.** 7.13
7. 8.5 **8.** 18

Guided Practice

1. 7.375 **2.** 3.31 **3.** 7 **4.** 0.15
5. 77 **6.** 2.65 **7.** 33.16 **8.** 1.95
9. 19 **10.** 0.3 **11.** 6.2 **12.** 405
13. 250 **14.** 11.8 **15.** 0.8 pound
16. 3.5 pounds **17.** 18.1 seconds
18. 18 **19.** $2.73 per gallon
20. 20 inches

Independent Practice

23. $8.50 **25a.** 10 movies
27. beef **29a.** 0.42 **b.** 0.25
c. 0.15 **31.** 42 **33.** 20 weeks

LESSON 5.5

Your Turn

1. $5 per yard
2. He paid $\frac{29}{2} \times \frac{3}{5} = 8\frac{7}{10}$ dollars or $\$14.5 \times 0.6 = \$8.70$

Guided Practice

1. $134\frac{1}{2}$ miles **2.** $397.80

Independent Practice

3. $3\frac{1}{2}$ gallons **5.** 2 batteries
7. $5.88; No. They earned $7.84 on Wednesday. $7.84 - 5.88 = 1.96$, so they don't have enough money.
9. 3 games **13.** 35.

UNIT 3 Selected Answers

MODULE 6

LESSON 6.1

Your Turn

5. 3 : 1; 3 to 1; $\frac{3}{1}$ **6.** 8 : 3; 8 to 3; $\frac{8}{3}$ **7.** 1 : 1; 1 to 1; $\frac{1}{1}$ **8.** Sample answer: $\frac{4}{5}, \frac{16}{20}, \frac{12}{15}$ **9.** Sample answer: $\frac{10}{4}, \frac{15}{6}, \frac{20}{8}$

Guided Practice

1. 1 dog to 5 cats **2.** 5 **3.** 5; 3
4. 5; 25 **5.** 2 to 5; 2 : 5; $\frac{2}{5}$
6. 5 to 12; 5 : 12; $\frac{5}{12}$
7. Sample answer: $\frac{5}{6}$ (circled), $\frac{20}{24}, \frac{25}{30}$
8. Sample answer: $\frac{7}{1}$ (circled), $\frac{21}{3}, \frac{28}{4}$
9. Sample answer: $\frac{8}{14}, \frac{12}{21}, \frac{16}{28}$

Independent Practice

11. 2 to 6, 3 to 9, 4 to 12
13. 16 roses and 24 carnations
15. No. The current ratio is $\frac{120}{100}$ or $\frac{6}{5}$. The ratio after the sale will be $\frac{96}{76}$, or $\frac{24}{19}$. Because $\frac{6}{5} = \frac{24}{20}$, the two ratios are not equivalent. **17a.** 18 **b.** 12 **19.** 3 : 2; 30 girls and 20 boys **21.** Tina multiplied 6 by 6 to get 36 and 8 by 8 to get 64. She should have multiplied both terms by the same number.

LESSON 6.2

Your Turn

4. 12
5. 45 minutes, $\frac{27\text{ minutes} \div 3}{3\text{ miles} \div 3} = \frac{9\text{ minutes}}{1\text{ mile}}$. The unit rate is 9 minutes per mile. $\frac{9\text{ minutes} \times 5}{1\text{ mile} \times 5} = \frac{45\text{ minutes}}{5\text{ miles}}$. It would take her 45 minutes to jog 5 miles.

Guided Practice

1. 0.21; 0.19 **2.** family size **3.** \$2; \$48 **4.** 16 **5.** 72 **6.** 300 calories **7.** \$6

Independent Practice

9. \$12.50 per lawn **11.** Alastair **13a.** 5 minutes; 7 balloons
b. $1\frac{2}{5}$ balloons per minute
c. 14 balloons
15. \$10.50
17. There are 12 inches in 1 foot, and $2.54 \times 12 =$ 30.48 centimeters per foot; there are 3 feet per yard, and 30.48 cm $\times$ 3 = 91.44 centimeters per yard.
19. The unit costs are \$1.10 per pound for a 1-pound bag, \$0.99 per pound for a 2-pound bag, and \$0.88 per pound for a 3-pound bag. The unit cost decreases by \$0.11 per pound as the quantity of sugar increases.

LESSON 6.3

Your Turn

2. No, the ratios are not equivalent. $\frac{2 \times 4}{3 \times 4} = \frac{8}{12}$ $\frac{8}{12} > \frac{7}{12}$

Guided Practice

1b. No, Celeste is not using the correct ratio of apples to oranges; $\frac{5}{6} > \frac{4}{6}$ **2.** No; Neha used the greater ratio of bananas to oranges. **3.** No; Tim can read 140 words in 5 minutes.
4. Yes; On average, the cafeteria sells 120 drinks per hour.

Independent Practice

7. Yes **9.** Jen's
11a. 6 pounds; $\frac{\$3.00}{2\text{ pounds}} = \frac{\$3.00 \times 3}{2\text{ pounds} \times 3} = \frac{\$9.00}{6\text{ pounds}}$ **b.** No; 1 pound = 16 ounces, so 6 pounds = 96 ounces; 96 ounces $\div \frac{5\text{ ounces}}{1\text{ apple}}$ $\approx$ 19 apples. **13.** Both could; Theo's rate is 57 mi/h and Lex's is 62 mi/h. **17.** All of the rates should be equivalent. One way to check that they are equivalent is to divide the top term in each ratio by the bottom term. All of the quotients should be equal.

MODULE 7

LESSON 7.1

Your Turn

3. 8 min

Time (min)	2	3	4	5	6
Water used (gal)	8	12	16	20	24

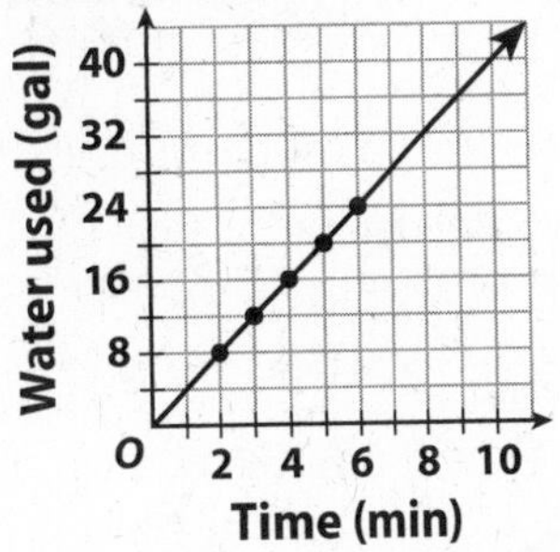

Guided Practice

1. $\frac{6}{12} = \frac{9}{18} = \frac{21}{42} = \frac{27}{54}$
2.

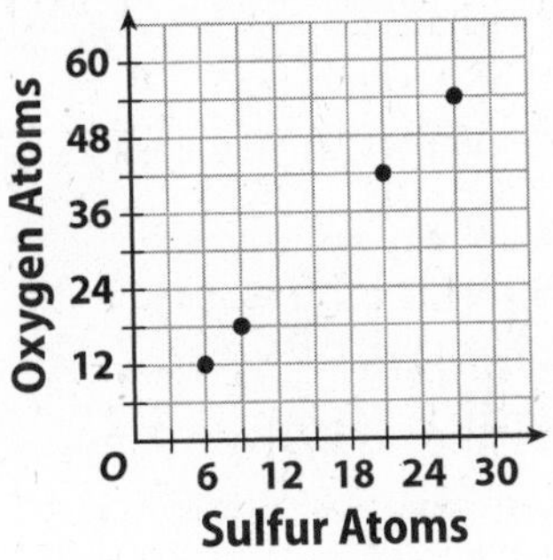

3. $\frac{4}{2} = \frac{8}{4} = \frac{14}{7} = \frac{16}{8}$
4.

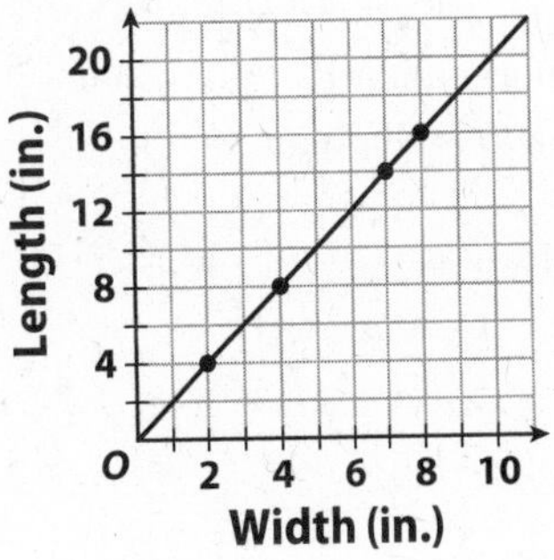

UNIT 3 Selected Answers *(cont'd)*

5.

Boxes	5	8	10
Candles	60	96	120

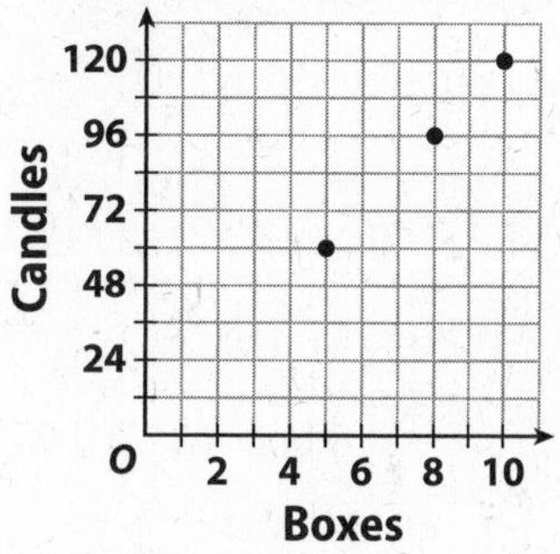

Independent Practice

7. $\frac{\text{money collected}}{\text{sweatshirts sold}} = \frac{\$60}{3\text{ sweatshirts}} = \frac{\$20}{1\text{ sweatshirt}} = \$20$ per sweatshirt sold **11.** \$480 **13.** 330 mi; find the rate 55 mi/h, then multiply 6 hr × 55 mi/hr

LESSON 7.2

Your Turn

1. 10 cheese pizzas
2. 125 minutes **3.** 50 miles

Guided Practice

1. 6; 6; 18 **2.** 2; 2; 2 **3.** \$45
4. 18 inches **5.** $52\frac{1}{2}$ seconds
6. 36 min **7.** 24 km

Independent Practice

9a. 1 inch = 12 miles **b.** 24 miles
11a. 60 seats **b.** 150 seats
13. 45 ft **15.** Ira **17.** No, the caterpillar's unit rate should be 5 feet per minute.
19a. b. 80 minutes

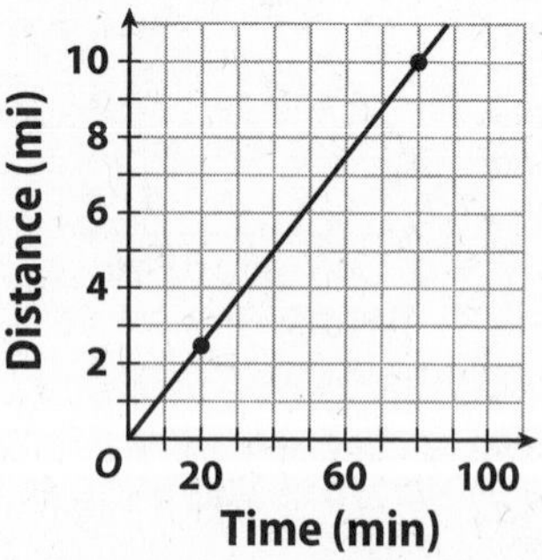

LESSON 7.3

Your Turn

4. 72 in. **5.** 5 c **6.** 2,000 mL
7. 3.5 m **8.** 2.5 meters **9.** 56 fl oz

Guided Practice

1. 3 **2.** 48 **3.** 32 cups
4. 3,500 grams **5.** 1.75 g **6.** $3\frac{1}{2}$ ft

Independent Practice

9. 126; 10.5; 3.5 **11.** Large; 64 pt of Brand A cost \$2.50 × 64 = \$160, and 32 qt of Brand A cost \$4.50 × 32 = \$144. **13.** 3 kilometers
15. 1,320 ft **17.** 8,125 times

LESSON 7.4

Your Turn

2. 5.676 **3.** 4.27 **4.** 8.946 **5.** 7.42
7. 64.55

Guided Practice

1. 8.05; 5 miles; 1.61 km **2.** 18.95; 5 gallons; 3.79 L **3.** 30.48 **4.** 1.816
5. 18.28 **6.** 339.6 **7.** 4.73 **8.** 436
9. 2.64 **10.** 450.18 **11.** 64.35
12. 6,210

Independent Practice

15. one inch **17.** one mile
19. one liter **21.** 4 liters **23.** 22.7 kg **25.** 2-liter juice bottle **27.** 2.75 pounds **29a.** Yes; Two half-gallon containers will hold one gallon, which is about 3.79 liters. **b.** No; A gallon jug can hold 3.79 liters, so a half-gallon jug would hold half of that, which is only 1.895 liters.
33. Multiply the number of pounds by 0.454; 3.8136 kg

MODULE 8

LESSON 8.1

Your Turn

2. 90% **3.** 40% **4.** about $\frac{2}{3}$

Guided Practice

1. 4; 4; 36; 36%
2.

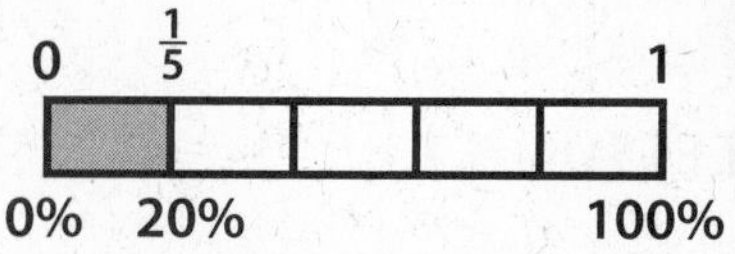

3. 10; 60% **4.** 1; 50% **5.** 1; 80%
6. about $\frac{2}{5}$

Independent Practice

9. 55 **11.** $\frac{9}{10} = 90\%$, $\frac{4}{5} = 80\%$, $\frac{17}{20} = 85\%$, 80%, 85%, 90%
13. 30% of your minutes are used up **17.** No

LESSON 8.2

Your Turn

1. $\frac{3}{20}$, 0.15 **2.** $\frac{12}{25}$, 0.48 **3.** $\frac{4}{5}$, 0.8
4. $\frac{3}{4}$, 0.75 **5.** $\frac{9}{25}$, 0.36 **6.** $\frac{2}{5}$, 0.4
8. 0.36, 36% **9.** 0.875, 87.5%

Guided Practice

1. $\frac{3}{25}$; 0.12 **2.** 53%, $\frac{53}{100}$ **3.** 107%; $\frac{107}{100}$; $1\frac{7}{100}$ **4.** 0.35; 35% **5.** 0.375; 37.5%

Independent Practice

7. $\frac{18}{25}$; 0.72 **9.** $\frac{500}{100}$; $\frac{5}{1} = \frac{5}{1}$; 5 **11.** $\frac{37}{100}$; 0.37 **13.** 0.625, 62.5% **15.** 3.5, 350% **17.** $\frac{68}{80} = \frac{17}{20}$; 85%; 0.85
19. 6 **23.** 1, 100%, 1

LESSON 8.3

Your Turn

5. 19 **6.** 81 **7.** 45 **9.** 76%
11. 20 **12.** 500

Guided Practice

1. 240 televisions are high definition. **2.** 65; 200; 130
3. ×; 900; 9; 9 **4.** 21; 100; 300; 7%
5. 9; 300

Independent Practice

7. 48 tiles **9.** 8 pages **11.** 252 friends **13.** 20 **15.** 70 **17.** 1,400
19. 40 **21.** 20 **23.** 9 **25.** \$500
27. \$30 **29.** \$175 **31.** $\frac{25}{100} = \frac{?}{50}$; 25% of 50 is 12.5.

UNIT 4 Selected Answers

MODULE 9

LESSON 9.1

Your Turn

2. 4^3 **3.** 6^1 **4.** $\left(\frac{1}{8}\right)^2$ **5.** 5^6 **6.** 81 **7.** 1 **8.** $\frac{8}{125}$ **9.** 144

Guided Practice

2. 6^3 **3.** 10^7 **4.** $\left(\frac{3}{4}\right)^5$ **5.** $\left(\frac{7}{9}\right)^8$ **6.** 512 **7.** 2,401 **8.** 1,000 **9.** $\frac{1}{16}$ **10.** $\frac{1}{27}$ **11.** $\frac{36}{49}$ **12.** 0.64 **13.** 0.125 **14.** 1.21 **15.** 1 **16.** 12 **17.** 1 **18.** 169 **19.** $\frac{4}{25}$ **20.** 0.81

Independent Practice

23. 3 **25.** 3 **27.** 1 **29.** 2 **31.** 4 **33.** 3 **35.** 8 **37.** 9 **39.** 3^4 pages, or 81 pages **41.** 2^6 dollars, or \$64 **47.** 2^6, 4^3, and 8^2

LESSON 9.2

Your Turn

1. 1, 3, 7, 21 **2.** 1, 37 **3.** 1, 2, 3, 6, 7, 14, 21, 42 **4.** 1, 2, 3, 5, 6, 10, 15, 30

Guided Practice

1. 1, 2, 3, 6, 9, 18 **2.** 1, 2, 4, 13, 26, 52 **4.** $2 \cdot 3 \cdot 67$ **5.** $2^2 \cdot 3^2$ **6.** 2^5 **7.** $3 \cdot 3 \cdot 3$ or 3^3

Independent Practice

9. 1×12; 2×6; 3×4 **13.** $2^3 \cdot 3^2 \cdot 7$ **15.** $2 \cdot 5 \cdot 23$ **19.** prime factorization of $27 = 3^3$

LESSON 9.3

Your Turn

2. 1,222 **3.** 170 **5.** 125 **6.** 15 **7.** 0

Guided Practice

1. $3 \times 2^2 = 12$ angelfish **2.** 16; 64; 25; 37 **3.** 3; 9; 54; 62 **4.** 6; 36; 9; 108; 101 **5.** 2; 8; 4; 80; 640

Independent Practice

7. 19 **9.** 15 **11.** 39 **15a.** $3 \times 2 \times 2 \times 2 \times 2 = 3 \times 2^4$ **b.** $3 \times 2^4 - 7 = 3 \times 16 - 7 = 48 - 7 = 41$ butterflies **17a.** $6^2 + 2 \times 6 + 24 = 72$ square inches **b.** 8 in. by 9 in. **19.** $8 \times 4 - (2 \times 3 + 8) \div 2$

MODULE 10

LESSON 10.1

Your Turn

1. $7n$ **2.** $4 - y$ **3.** $x + 13$ **4.** Sample answer: the quotient of x and 12 **5.** Sample answer: 10 multiplied by y **6.** Sample answer: c plus 3

7.

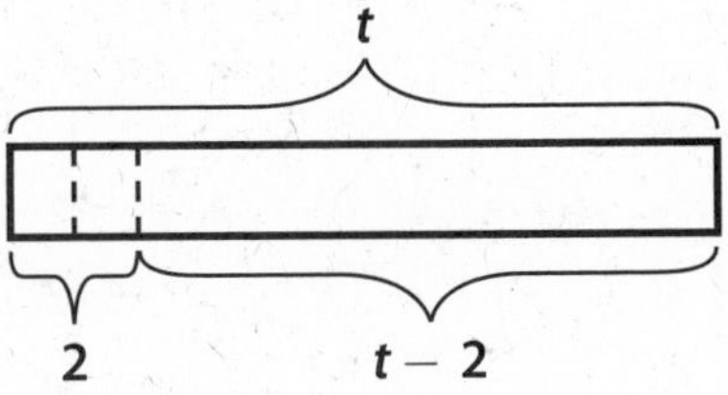

8.

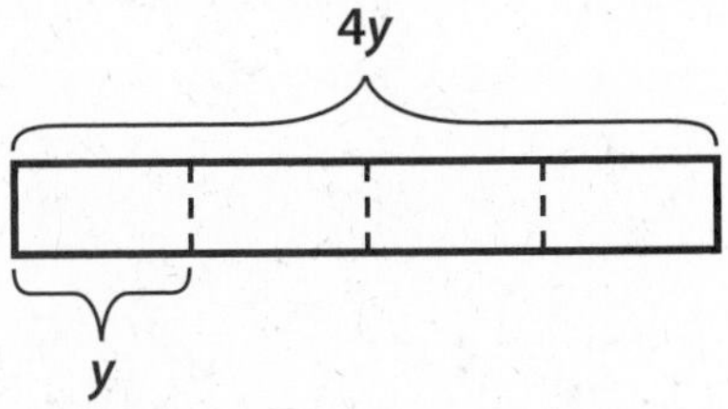

9. No; the expressions are not equivalent. **10.** $\frac{d}{4}$

Guided Practice

1. $y - 3$ **2.** $2p$ **3.** Sample answer: 12 added to y **4.** Sample answer: 10 divided into p

5.

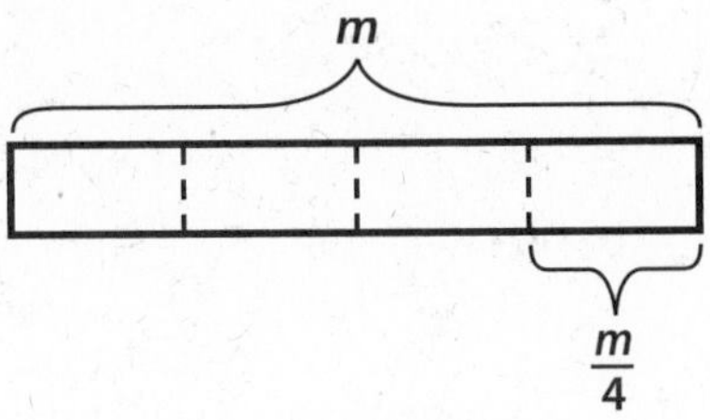

6.

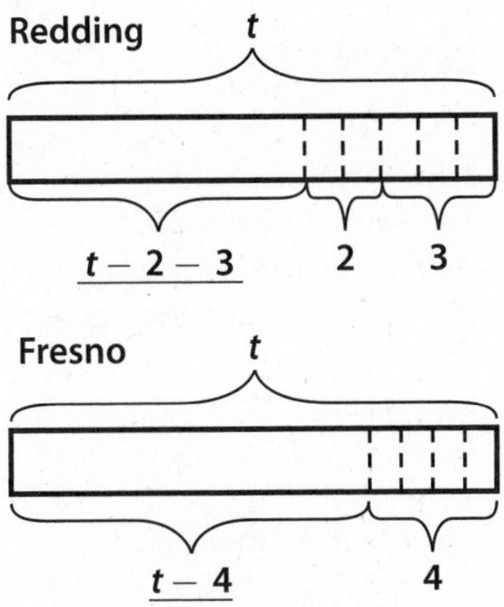

7. No **8.** $24c$

Independent Practice

11. $\frac{n}{8}$ **13.** $b + 14$ **15.** $a - 16$ **17.** $3w$ **19.** $\frac{13}{z}$ **21.** $w - 8$ **23.** Sample answer: 42 times s **25.** Sample answer: t minus 29 **27.** Sample answer: the product of 11 and x **29.** Sample answer: k less than 5 **31.** $8w$ **33a.** $3d$ **b.** $3g$ **c.** In Mia's expression, the numeral is the number of gallons and variable is the cost per gallon; in Bob's, the numeral is the cost per gallon and the variable is the number of gallons he buys. **35.** $\frac{t}{46}$ **37.** Sample answer: m represents Meg's age; $m - 2$ represents Jill's age; $\frac{m}{2}$ represents Beth's age. **39.** $g + 6$

LESSON 10.2

Your Turn

1. 32 **2.** 4.7 **3.** 3 **4.** 18 **5.** 18 **6.** 55 **7.** 6 **8.** 39 **9.** 17 **10.** 24; 8 **11.** 420

Guided Practice

1. 16 **2.** 6 **3.** $2\frac{1}{18}$ **4.** 50 **5.** 18 **6.** 6 **7a.** $12x + 5$ **b.** 3; 36; 41; \$41 **8a.** $2w + 2l$ **b.** 7; 5; 10; 24; 24 feet

UNIT 4 Selected Answers *(cont'd)*

Independent Practice

11. $2(x^2)$; $2(64) = 128$ square feet **15.** 42

LESSON 10.3

Your Turn

3. Sample answer: $a(bc)$; Associative Property of Multiplication **4.** Sample answer: $(3 + 4)y$; Distributive Property **5.** Sample answer: $n + 6$; Commutative Property of Addition **6.** $2(3x - 5) = 6x - 10$; not equivalent **7.** $2 - 2 + 5x = 5x$; equivalent **8.** Jamal bought $2x + 8$ stickers. $2(4 + x) = 8 + 2x = 2x + 8$; yes **9.** $5y$ **10.** $10x^2 - 4$ **11.** $2a^5 + 5b$ **12.** $8m + 2 + 4n$

Guided Practice

2. not equivalent **3.** Sample answer: ba; Commutative Prop. of Mult. **4.** Sample answer: $5(3x) - 5(2)$; Distributive Prop. **5.** not equivalent **6.** not equivalent **7.** $44y$ **8.** $24 + 2x$

Independent Practice

11. Sample answer: $13 + x$; Commutative Prop. of Addition **13.** Sample answer: $(2 + a) + b$; Associative Prop. of Addition **15.** $2x^4$ **17.** $13b - 10$ **19.** $4y + 10$ **21.** $15y^2 - 6$ **23.** $0.5x^4 + 13.5$ **25.** $3x + 12 + x$ is equivalent to $4(3 + x)$. **27.** $(46 + 38 + 29)g + (29 + 27 + 17)s + (29 + 23 + 19)b$; $113g + 73s + 71b$ **29.** $36.4 + 4x$ in. **31.** $3x^2 - 4x + 7$; It does not have any like terms.

UNIT 5 Selected Answers

MODULE 11

LESSON 11.1

Your Turn

1. yes **2.** no **3.** yes **4.** no **5.** $f + 9 = 38$ **6.** $17n = 102$ **7.** $c - \frac{1}{2} = 12$ **8.** $2.5h = 20$ **10.** Sample equation: $x + 24 = 62$; \$38

Guided Practice

1. no; **2.** yes **3.** no **4.** yes **5.** yes **6.** no **7.** yes **8.** no **9.** $8r = 256$ **10.** $\frac{n}{16} = 3$ **11.** $4.5 + k = 26.2$ **12.** $\frac{f}{2} = 5$ **13.** Sample equation: $8x = 208$; \$26 **14.** Sample equation: $x + 24 = 92$; 68 °F

Independent Practice

17. $x + 8 = 31$; 23 pounds **19.** Sample answer: $4x = 20$; $20 \div x = 4$ or $x = 20 \div 4$ **21a.** $29 - 12\frac{1}{2} = x$; $12\frac{1}{2} + x = 29$; the distance between Hadley and Greenville. **b.** Yes; $16\frac{1}{2}$ is a solution of the equations in a. **23.** Both equations are correct. Another correct equation is $44 - 7 = x$. **25.** Yes, because $4 + f = 12$ means there are 8 flute players, and 8 is twice 4. **27.** Yes

LESSON 11.2

Your Turn

3. $3\frac{1}{2}$

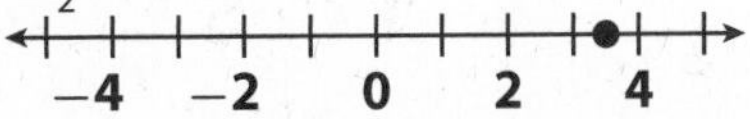

5. $\frac{5}{4}$; or $1\frac{1}{4}$

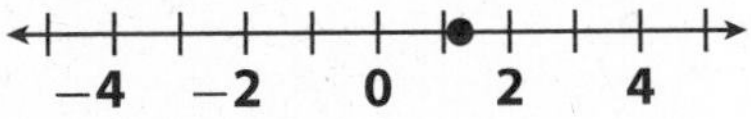

6. $x + 65 = 90$; $x = 25°$ **7.** $x + 42 = 90$; $x = 48°$ **9.** $x = 140$

Guided Practice

1a. number of guests who left when the party ended. **c.** 11 **2.** 5

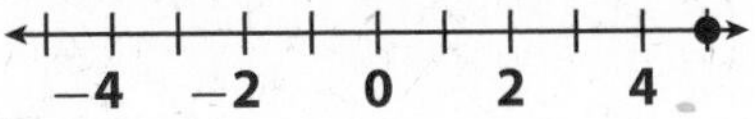

3. 1.5

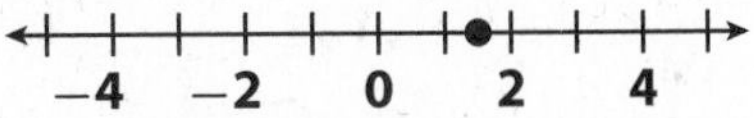

4. 4.5 **5.** 40 **6.** $\frac{5}{4}$ **7.** $x + 45 = 180$; $x = 135°$ **8.** $x = 275$

Independent Practice

11. Sample answer: $14 = b - 12$; 26 yr **13.** Sample answer: $x + 8 = 37$; 29 compact cars **15.** Sample answer: $m - 123.45 = 36.55$; \$160 **17.** $c = 2.50$ **19a.** $1.49 + a = 2.99$; $2.49 + r = 3.99$ **b.** Both a and r are equal to \$1.50, so the discounts are the same.

LESSON 11.3

Your Turn

2. 7

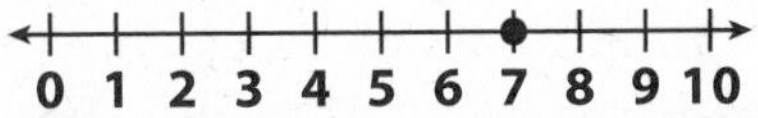

3. 9

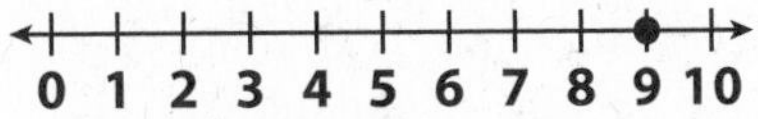

4. Sample answer: $\frac{x}{5} = 9$; $x = 45$; Tion gave away $45 - 9 = 36$ cards. **5.** $x = 35$

Guided Practice

1a. number of miles run each day **b.** 5; x; 15 **c.** 3 **2.** 9

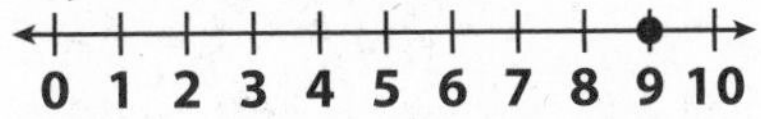

3. 8

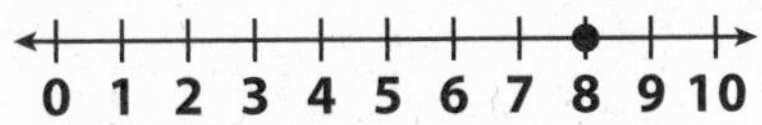

4. $24 = 6w$; $w = 4$ inches; length is 2 inches longer than the width **5.** Sample problem: The area of a rectangle is 45 cm^2, and the length is 15 cm. What is the width?; $w = 3$

Independent Practice

7. $x = 60$ **9.** $x = 9$ **11.** $x = 14.4$ **13.** $4k = 44$; 11 books **15.** $3.5d = 14$; 4 days **17.** $3d = 1\frac{1}{2}$; hours walking dog; $\frac{1}{2}$ h **19.** Sample answer: Marcy split her income from last week equally between paying her student loans, rent, and savings. She put \$450 in savings. How much did Marcy earn last week? $\frac{x}{3} = 450$, $x = 1{,}350$; Marcy earned \$1,350 last week. **21.** 81 **23.** 31 inches

LESSON 11.4

Your Turn

3.

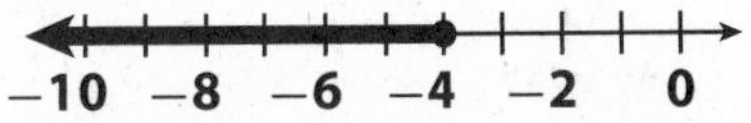

4. $1 + y \geq 3$; $y = 1$ is not a solution because $1 + 1$ is not greater than or equal to 3. **5.** $t \leq 6$

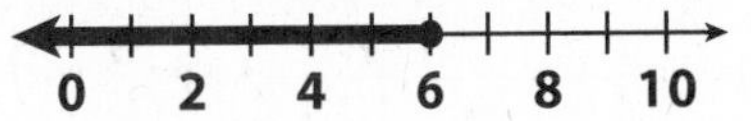

Guided Practice

1. 3, 1

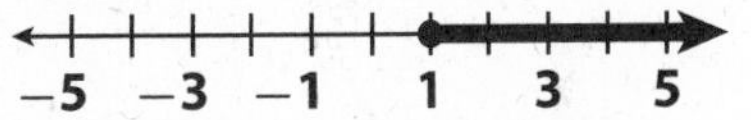

2.

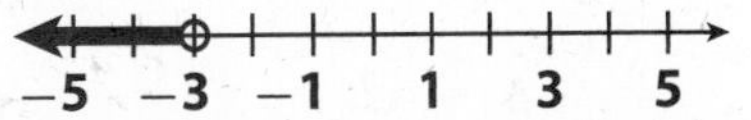

3. $3x > 6$

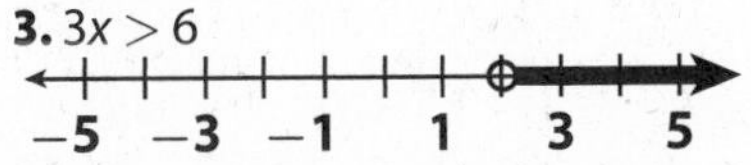

4. Let t be temperature in °C; $t \geq 3$

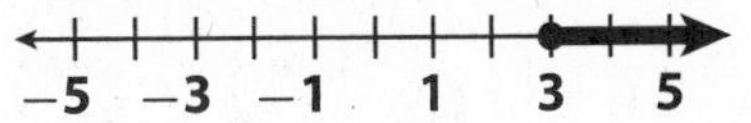

Independent Practice

7.

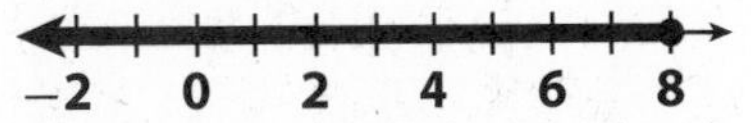

11.

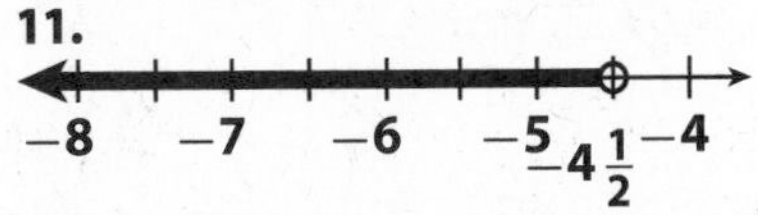

13. $x \leq -3$ **15.** $x \geq -3.5$ **19.** $g > 150$

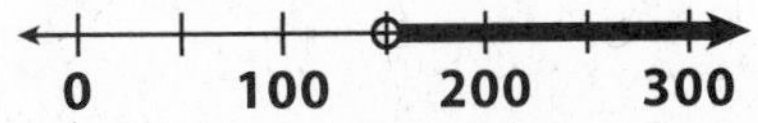

MODULE 12

LESSON 12.1

Your Turn

4. (4, −4); IV; **5.** (−2, 4); II
6. (3, 2); I; **7.** (−1, −3); III
8–12.

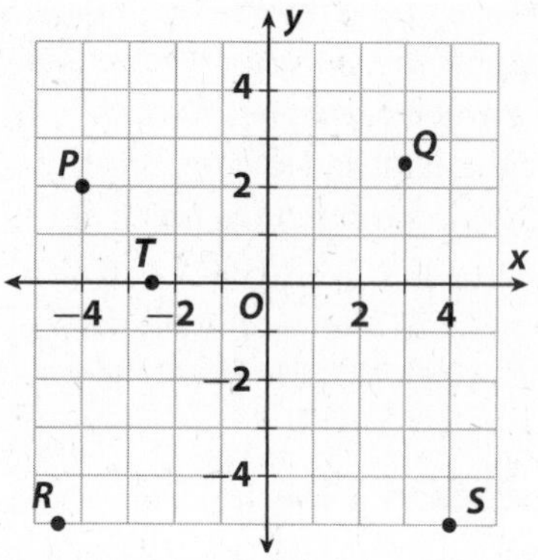

13. Ted (−20, −20), Ned (−20, 25)

Guided Practice

1. left; up; (−5, 1); II **2.** 2; 3; (2, −3); IV
3–4.

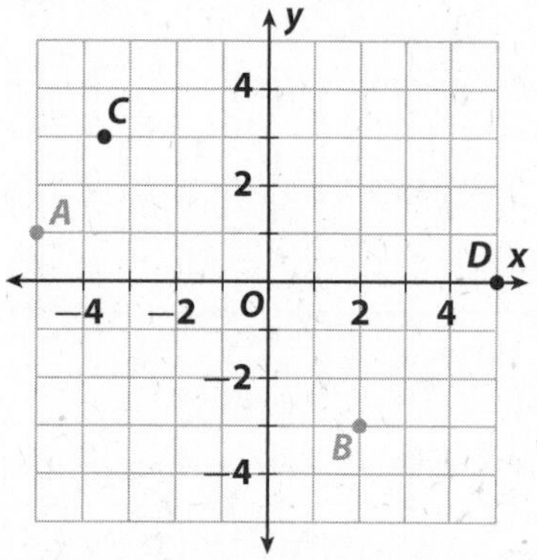

5. Each grid square is $\frac{1}{2}$ unit on a side.
6–7.

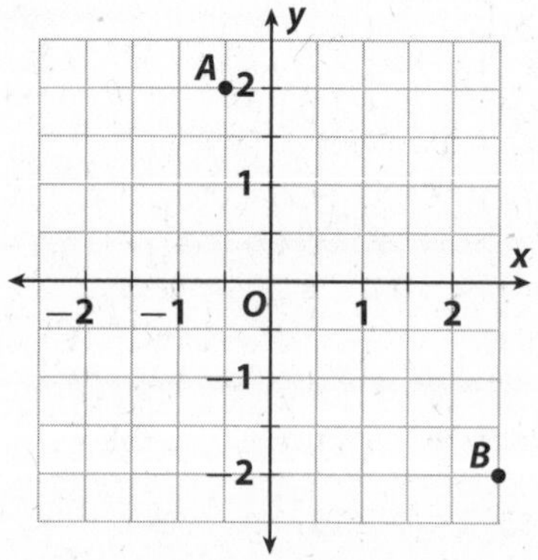

Independent Practice

11. Sam is 3 km south and 7 km east of the theater.
13. (−3, 0.5) **15.** $W(-0.75, -1.0)$

LESSON 12.2

Your Turn

8. Sample answer: Bridget's grandmother gave her a collection of 15 perfume bottles. Bridget adds one bottle per week to the collection. The independent variable is the number of weeks. The dependent variable is the number of perfume bottles in her collection. The value of *y* is always 15 units greater than the value of *x*.
9. Sample answer: Colin created a website to sell T-shirts that are printed with funny slogans. He makes $16 per T-shirt. The independent variable is the number of T-shirts he sells, and the dependent variable is his profit in dollars. The value of *y* is always 16 times the value of *x*.
10. Sample answer: Tickets to the school musical cost $3 each. The independent variable is the number of tickets purchased, and the dependent variable is the total cost. The value of *y* is always 3 times the value of *x*.

Guided Practice

1. Time is the independent variable and cost is the dependent variable.
2a.

Time *x* (h)	0	1	2	2
Distance *y* (mi)	0	60	120	180

b. Time is the independent variable and distance is the dependent variable. **c.** The value of *y* is always 60 times the value of *x*.

3. The dependent variable is 5 times the value of the independent variable.

Independent Practice

7a. number of markers **b.** number of gift bags **c.** The number of glitter markers is 5 times the number of gift bags.

LESSON 12.3

Your Turn

2. $y = x - 2$ **3.** $y = 2.5x$ **4.** $y = x + 5$
5. $y = 2x$ **6.** $k = r + 5$; 57 years old

Guided Practice

1. $y = x - 4$ **2.** $y = 4x$ **3.** $y = x + 3$
4. $y = \frac{x}{6}$
5. $c = 1.35n$; $33.75

Independent Practice

9. The *y*-value is $\frac{1}{4}$ of the *x*-value.
11a. $e = 8.25h$ **b.** $206.25 = 8.25h$; $25 = h$; 25 hours **13.** Not possible; there is no consistent pattern between the *y*-values and corresponding *x*-values.
15. No

LESSON 12.4

Your Turn

5.

x	$x + 2.5 = y$	(*x*, *y*)
0	$0 + 2.5 = 2.5$	(0, 2.5)
1	$1 + 2.5 = 3.5$	(1, 3.5)
2	$2 + 2.5 = 4.5$	(2, 4.5)
3	$3 + 2.5 = 5.5$	(3, 5.5)

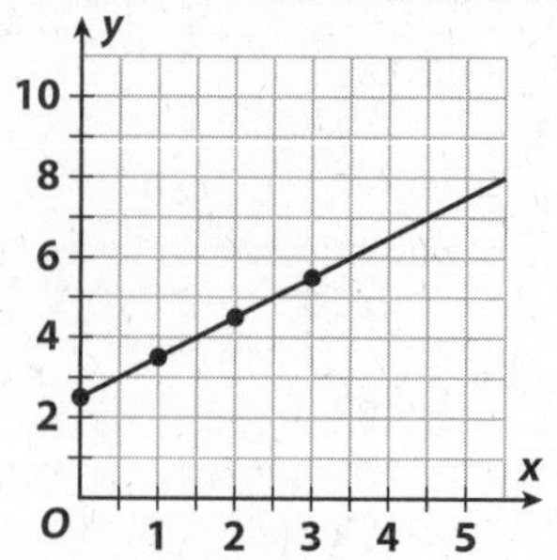

Guided Practice

1. $y = 3x$

Hours worked	Lawns mowed
0	0
1	3
2	6
3	9

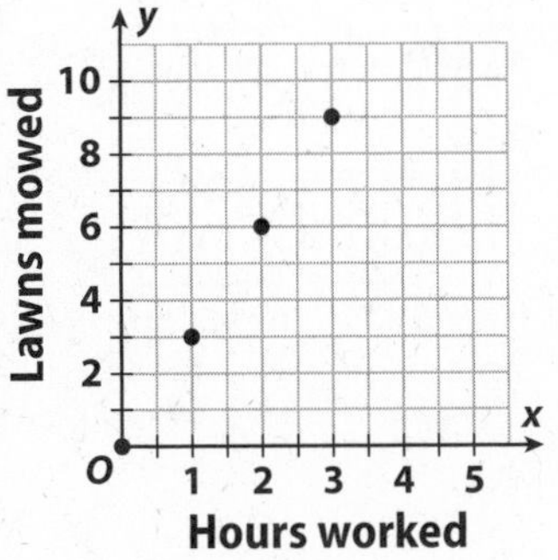

2.

x	0	1	2	3
y	0	1.5	3	4.5

3.

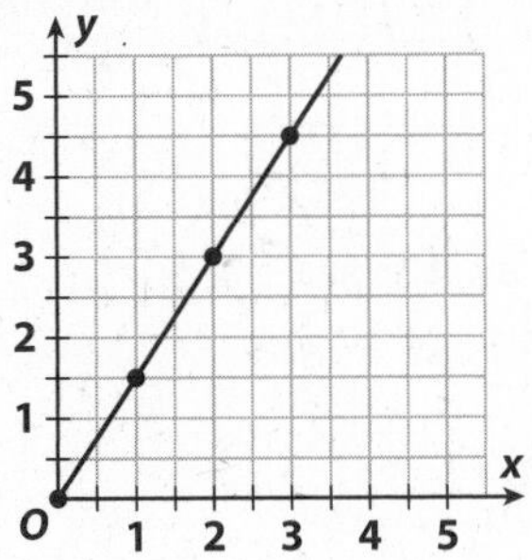

Independent Practice

5.

Additional hours	0	5	10	15	20
Total hours	20	25	30	35	40

7. 20 hours; when 0 additional hours are worked, the total is 20 hours.

9.

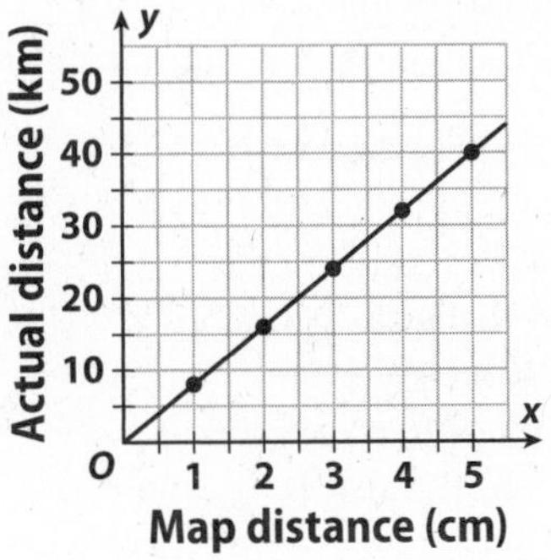

11a.

Number of tickets, x	1	2	3	4	5
Totalcost ($), y	9	18	27	36	45

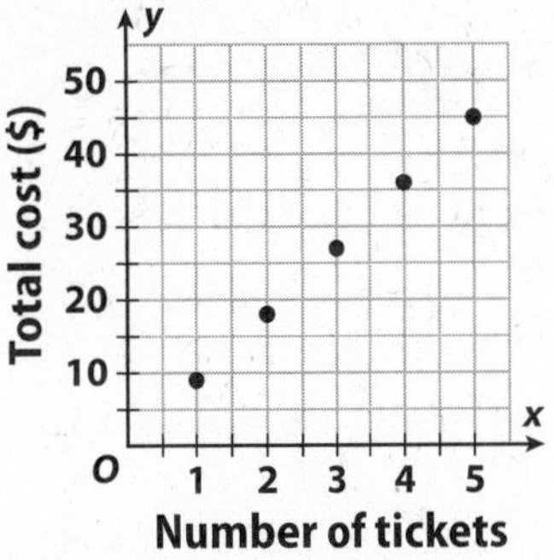

b. Dependent: total cost; independent: number of tickets

UNIT 6 Selected Answers

MODULE 13

LESSON 13.1

Your Turn

2. 366 ft^2 **3.** 210 **4.** 66.5 **5.** 90 **6.** 165

Guided Practice

1. 13; 9; 117 **2.** 14; 9; 15; 168 **3.** 18; 11; 99

Independent Practice

5. 84 cm^2 **7.** 936 in^2 **9.** 72 m^2 **11.** 8.25 ft^2 **13.** 1,620 in^2 **15.** 57 ft^2 **17.** 9 in. and 15 in.

LESSON 13.2

Your Turn

3. 59.5 in^2 **5.** 12 ft^2

Guided Practice

1. 14; 8; 56 **2.** 12; 30; 180

Independent Practice

5. 240 ft^2 **7.** 288 ft^2 **9.** 71.5 in^2 **11.** 20 ft^2 **13.** Monica forgot to multiply by $\frac{1}{2}$. The area of the fabric is 45 in^2. **17a.** 6 in. **b.** 1 in. and 36 in., 2 in. and 18 in., 3 in. and 12 in., 4 in. and 9 in.

LESSON 13.3

Your Turn

1. 8 in. **3.** 4 ft **4.** 8 pallets

Guided Practice

1. $70 = \frac{1}{2}\left(8\frac{3}{4}\right)b$; 16 in. **2.** $791 = \frac{1}{2}h(26.5 + 30)$; 28 centimeters **3.** area; $A = 42(28) = 1{,}176$ ft^2; number of gallons of paint; $n = 1{,}176 \div 350 = 3.36$; 4

Independent Practice

5. $5\frac{1}{2}$ ft **7.** 1.2 cm **9.** 16 in. and 8 in. **11.** 128 patches **13a.** 702 ft^2 **b.** 1,458 ft^2 **c.** 486 ft^2 **15a.** $3\frac{1}{2}$ yd **b.** $10\frac{2}{3}$ yd^2

LESSON 13.4

Your Turn

3. 44
4. 567
5. $3,348

Guided Practice

1. $\frac{1}{8}$ square unit **2.** 112 **3.** 196
4. 240 square feet; 3 cans of paint

Independent Practice

7a. about 60% **b.** $321.75
9a. 73.5 square inches
b. 21 inches by 21 inches
c. 8 banners; yes
11. 50 square inches

MODULE 14

LESSON 14.1

Your Turn

3. 9 units **4.** 5 units
5. 0.8 hours, or 48 minutes

Guided Practice

1. (5, 2) **2.** (6, 8) **3.** 5; –2; 5; 2; 7
4. 5; 1; 5; 1; 4 **5.** 2 units **6.** 3 units
5–6.

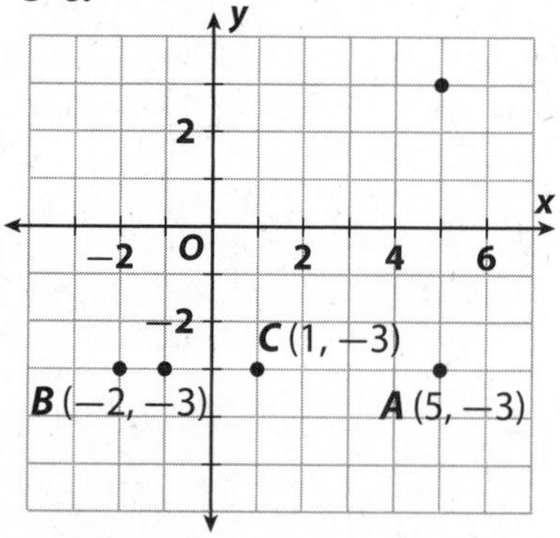

7. 5 blocks
8. 21 minutes; 4.5 minutes

Independent Practice

11. Place another point on the other side of the y-axis the same distance from the y-axis as point *A*; (–1.5, –2.5); 3 units
13. (7, –3); 14 units **15.** (–2.4, –1); 4.8 units **17.** 3 hours

LESSON 14.2

Your Turn

2. 30 **3.** 32

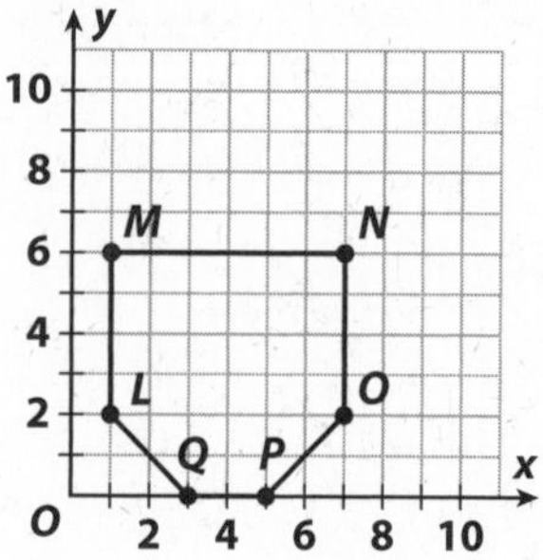

Guided Practice

1. square

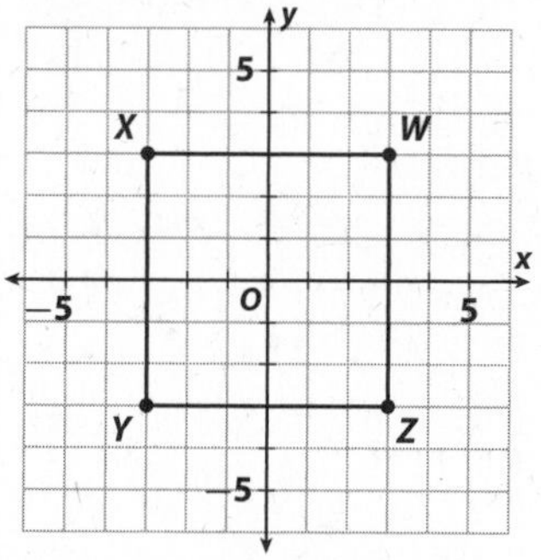

2. 6; 24 **3.** 36 square yards
4. L; 24 square inches

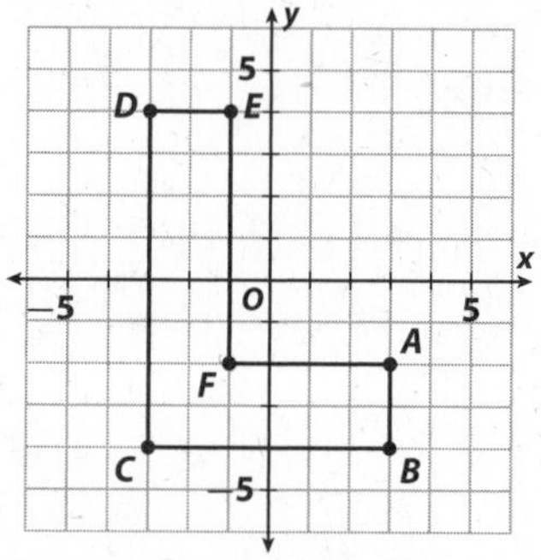

Independent Practice

7a. hexagon **b.** 18 units
c. trapezoid; 15 units
11. The octagon is a regular octagon, so all the sides will have the same length as the side whose endpoints are given. Since that side length $= |4| - |1| = 3$ units, the perimeter of the octagon is $8(3) = 24$ units.

MODULE 15

LESSON 15.1

Your Turn

4. 896 in^2 **6.** \$7.92

Guided Practice

1. 1; 4 **2.** 36; 48; 84

3a. 248 square inches

b. 24,800 square inches **c.** 2 cans

Independent Practice

5. 272 in^2 **7.** 80 tiles

9. rectangular pyramid; triangular prism **11.** Sample answer: Decide whether the figure is a prism or a pyramid, and what the shapes of the bases and faces are. Make a net of the figure, and label the dimensions. Use appropriate area formulas to find the areas of the faces, and then find the sum of the areas.

LESSON 15.2

Your Turn

3. 75 cubic inches

4. $55\frac{1}{8}$ cubic inches

5. $393\frac{3}{4}$ cubic meters

Guided Practice

1. 64 **2.** $\frac{64}{125}$

3. 10; 3.2; 5; 160 cubic meters

4. $7\frac{1}{4}$; 4; 29; 232 cubic meters

5. 277.5 cubic feet

6. $526\frac{1}{2}$ cubic inches

7. 357 cubic inches

Independent Practice

9. 110.25 cubic inches

11. A: 120 in^3; B: 960 in^3; 8 times as great **13.** 58.5 cubic inches

15. $2\frac{47}{64}$ cubic feet

17. $\frac{1}{8}$ m; find a fraction that, when multiplied by itself 3 times, equals $\frac{1}{512}$ **19.** Both are correct.

LESSON 15.3

Your Turn

2. $\frac{5}{2}$ ft or $2\frac{1}{2}$ ft **3.** 1.5 feet

Guided Practice

1. $6{,}336 = 16(18)w$; $w = 22$ cm

2. $V = 72$ in^3; 4 inches

Independent Practice

3. 12.4 inches

5. 6 centimeters

7. Volume: 2,000 mm^3; weight: 1 ounce **9.** 1 inch; 25%

11. 42.9; 4.3; 30.0.

UNIT 7 Selected Answers

MODULE 16

LESSON 16.1

Your Turn

3. median = 6.5 minutes

Guided Practice

1. 15; 5; 3; 3 **2a.** 42 **b.** No **3a.** mean: 8.5; median: 6 **b.** The median; sample answer: the median is closer to most of the data values than the mean is.

Independent Practice

5. Ten students were asked, because there are 10 data values in the list. **7.** 78.5; 80.5 **9.** Minutes and hours; convert all times to minutes. **11.** Median; it is closer to most of the data values; the data value for 1 hr (60 min) raises the mean. **13.** 95

LESSON 16.2

Your Turn

2. The MAD for Waiter A is 0.6 oz, and for Waiter B is 0.2 oz, so Waiter B's smoothies showed less variability. **3.** A: MAD $\approx$ 0.0017; B: MAD $\approx$ 0.0063; A has less variability.

Guided Practice

1. did
a. 45.1 min
b. 0.4 min
2. 44.9; 0.733333; did not

Independent Practice

5. 1.6 people
7. Yes; The MAD at the beginning was about 3.7, and at the end it was about 2.1, so the serving sizes showed less variation.
9. The mean for Austin is 31.855 in., and for San Antonio is 30.459 in.; Austin.

13a. mean = 1, MAD = 0; Because 1 is the only data value, it is the mean of the data set and does not deviate from the mean.
b. mean = 1.5, MAD = 0.5; $1 + 2 = 3$, and $3 \div 2 = 1.5$. Also, both 1 and 2 are 0.5 away from 1.5.
c. Increase; the values are getting larger, so the mean increases, and they are getting more spread out, so the MAD increases.

LESSON 16.3

Your Turn

3. Group A IQR = \$700. Group B IQR = \$450. Group A's IQR is greater, so the salaries in the middle 50% for group A are more spread out than those for group B.
4. Miami = 15, Chicago = 53; Chicago

Guided Practice

1. 4; 10; 11; 13; 14; 15; 25; 29; 33; 33; 35; 43; 51; 58; 64 **2.** 29 **3.** 13 **4.** 43 **6.** 30 **7.** 60

Independent Practice

11. Sample answer: Students could have measured each others' heights. **13.** 0.3; 0.3 **15.** The IQRs are the same. The spreads of the middle 50% of the data values are the same for the two data sets. **17.** Yes

LESSON 16.4

Your Turn

4. 14 games; the value with the greatest frequency is 4; there were 4 games in which the team scored 4 runs. **5.** spread: 0 to 11. 11 appears to be an outlier. The data has a cluster from 0 to 7 with one peak at 2. The distribution is not symmetric because the data is not clustered around the center of the distribution. **6.** Mean: about 3.3, median: 3.5, range: 5; sample answer: between 3 and 4 runs. The mean and median are close in value, and there are no outliers.

Guided Practice

1. Variable data **3.** Mean: about 5.2; median = 5; range = 17.
4. spread: 0 to 17. 17 appears to be an outlier. The distribution is not symmetric.

Independent Practice

7. not statistical **9.** not statistical
11.

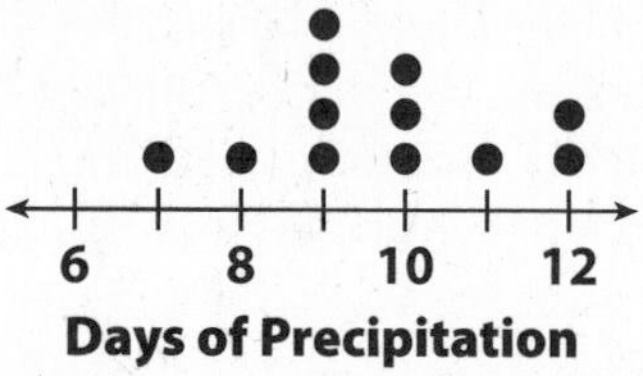

15. The mean would change to about 9.3; the median would stay at 9.5; the range would change to 9 days. **17.** The range; it changes from 17 to 10. The mean changes from 10.25 to 9.7, and the median does not change. **19.** $5(2) + 6(2) + 7 + 8(3) + 9(2) + 10(5) + 11 + 12(3) + 13(2) + 15(2) + 22$
21. Count the number of dots above a data value. **23.** 19; Each dot represents one game.
25. Mean: about 3.9 runs; median: 4 runs; range: 11 runs **27a.** the units for the ages (years, months, weeks) **b.** No

LESSON 16.5

Your Turn

4.

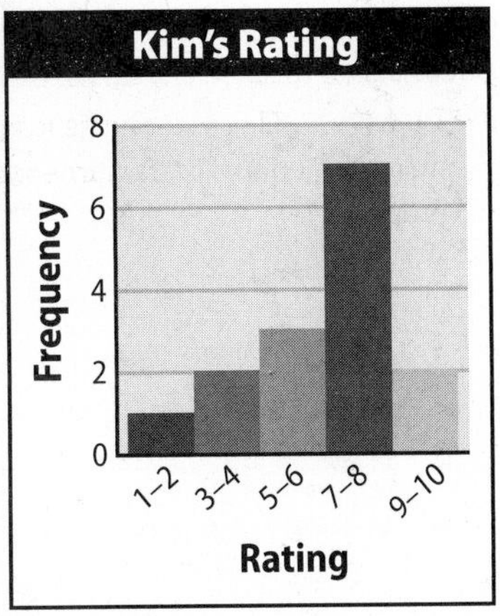

5. Sample answer: Kim gave ratings of 7 or 8 to 7 of 15 movies. She gave ratings of 9 or 10 to 2 of 15 movies.

Guided Practice

1.

Interval	Frequency
0–9	4
10–19	3
20–29	9
30–39	5

2. 1; 3; 4; 2

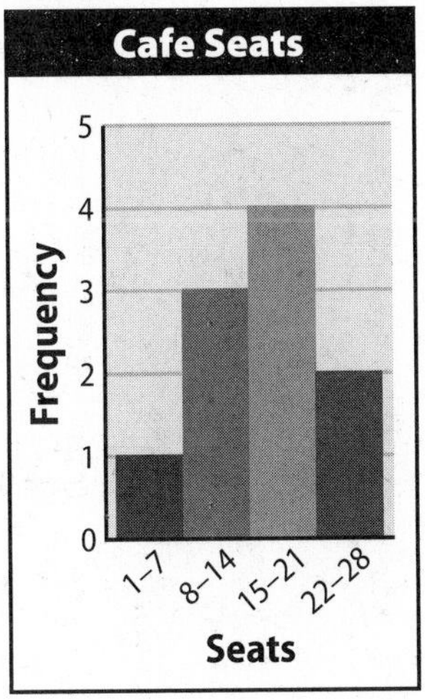

3. Sample answer: Only one cafe has fewer than 7 seats available. The bars increase in height until they reach the interval for 15–21 seats, and then they decrease in height, showing that most cafes have 21 or fewer seats.

5.

Interval	Frequency
10–19	9
20–29	7
30–39	3
40–49	4
50–59	2

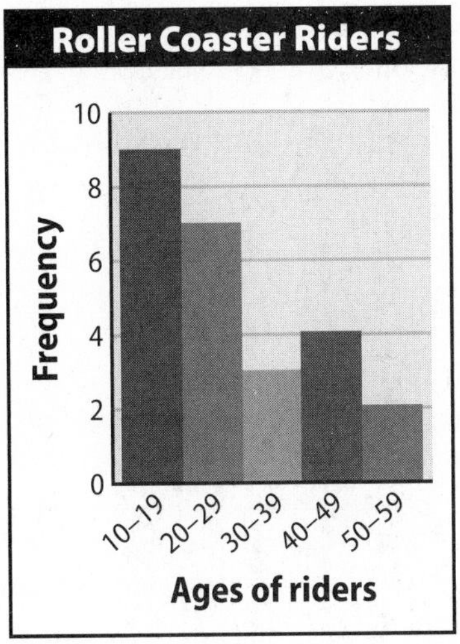

7a. 6 **b.** 3 bars; 9
c. box plot, dot plot

9. a.

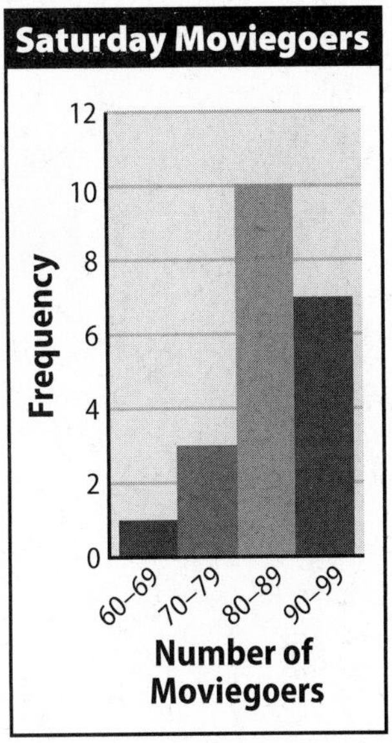

Glossary/Glosario

A

ENGLISH	SPANISH	EXAMPLES
absolute value The distance of a number from zero on a number line; shown by | |.	**valor absoluto** Distancia a la que está un número de 0 en una recta numérica. El símbolo del valor absoluto es | |.	$\|-5\| = 5$
acute angle An angle that measures greater than 0° and less than 90°.	**ángulo agudo** Ángulo que mide más de 0° y menos de 90°.	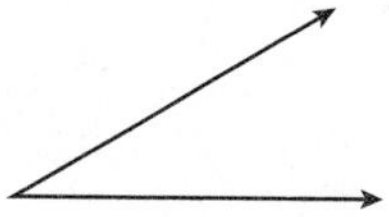
acute triangle A triangle with all angles measuring less than 90°.	**triángulo acutángulo** Triángulo en el que todos los ángulos miden menos de 90°.	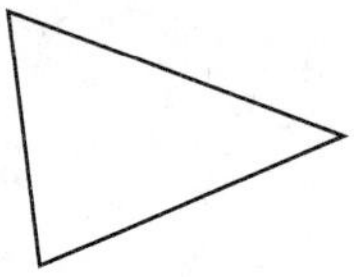
addend A number added to one or more other numbers to form a sum.	**sumando** Número que se suma a uno o más números para formar una suma.	In the expression $4 + 6 + 7$, the numbers 4, 6, and 7 are addends.
Addition Property of Opposites The property that states that the sum of a number and its opposite equals zero.	**Propiedad de la suma de los opuestos** Propiedad que establece que la suma de un número y su opuesto es cero.	$12 + (-12) = 0$
additive inverse The opposite of a number; one of two numbers whose sum is 0.	**inverso aditivo** El opuesto de un número; uno de dos números cuya suma es 0.	-4 is the additive inverse of 4.
adjacent angles Angles in the same plane that have a common vertex and a common side.	**ángulos adyacentes** Ángulos en el mismo plano que comparten un vértice y un lado.	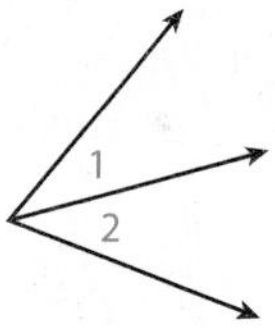 $\angle 1$ and $\angle 2$ are adjacent angles.
algebraic expression An expression that contains at least one variable.	**expresión algebraica** Expresión que contiene al menos una variable.	$x + 8$ $4(m - b)$
algebraic inequality An inequality that contains at least one variable.	**desigualdad algebraica** Desigualdad que contiene al menos una variable.	$x + 3 > 10$ $5a > b + 3$
alternate exterior angles For two lines intersected by a transversal, a pair of angles that lie on opposite sides of the transversal and outside the other two lines.	**ángulos alternos externos** Dadas dos rectas cortadas por una transversal, par de ángulos no adyacentes ubicados en los lados opuestos de la transversal y fuera de las otras dos rectas.	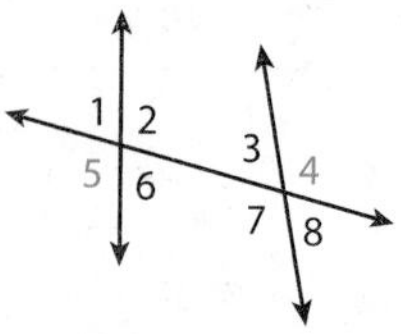 $\angle 4$ and $\angle 5$ are alternate exterior angles.

ENGLISH	SPANISH	EXAMPLES

alternate interior angles For two lines intersected by a transversal, a pair of nonadjacent angles that lie on opposite sides of the transversal and between the other two lines.

ángulos alternos internos Dadas dos rectas cortadas por una transversal, par de ángulos no adyacentes ubicados en los lados opuestos de la transversal y entre las otras dos rectas.

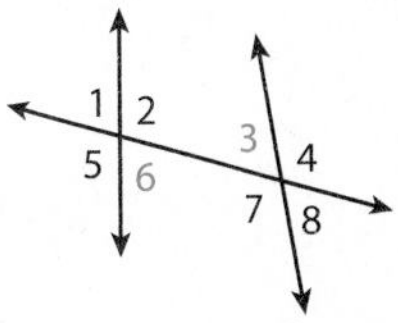

$\angle 3$ and $\angle 6$ are alternate interior angles.

---

angle A figure formed by two rays with a common endpoint called the vertex.

ángulo Figura formada por dos rayos con un extremo común llamado vértice.

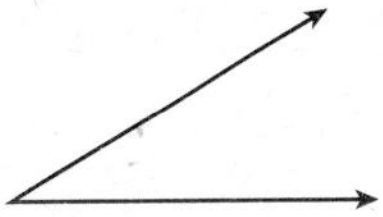

---

area The number of square units needed to cover a given surface.

área El número de unidades cuadradas que se necesitan para cubrir una superficie dada.

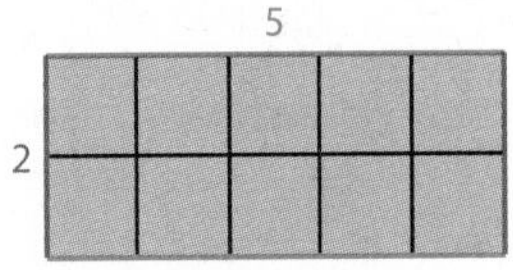

The area is 10 square units.

---

arithmetic sequence A sequence in which the terms change by the same amount each time.

sucesión aritmética Una sucesión en la que los términos cambian la misma cantidad cada vez.

The sequence 2, 5, 8, 11, 14 . . . is an arthmetic sequence.

Associative Property of Addition The property that states that for three or more numbers, their sum is always the same, regardless of their grouping.

Propiedad asociativa de la suma Propiedad que establece que agrupar tres o más números en cualquier orden siempre da como resultado la misma suma.

$2 + 3 + 8 = (2 + 3) + 8 = 2 + (3 + 8)$

Associative Property of Multiplication The property that states that for three or more numbers, their product is always the same, regardless of their grouping.

Propiedad asociativa de la multiplicación Propiedad que establece que agrupar tres o más números en cualquier orden siempre da como resultado el mismo producto.

$2 \cdot 3 \cdot 8 = (2 \cdot 3) \cdot 8 = 2 \cdot (3 \cdot 8)$

---

asymmetrical Not identical on either side of a central line; not symmetrical.

asimétrico Que no es idéntico a ambos lados de una línea central; no simétrico.

---

average The sum of the items in a set of data divided by the number of items in the set; also called *mean*.

promedio La suma de los elementos de un conjunto de datos dividida entre el número de elementos del conjunto. También se le llama *media*.

Data set: 4, 6, 7, 8, 10

Average: $\frac{4 + 6 + 7 + 8 + 10}{5} = \frac{35}{5} = 7$

---

axes The two perpendicular lines of a coordinate plane that intersect at the origin. singular: axis

ejes Las dos rectas numéricas perpendiculares del plano cartesiano que se intersecan en el origen.

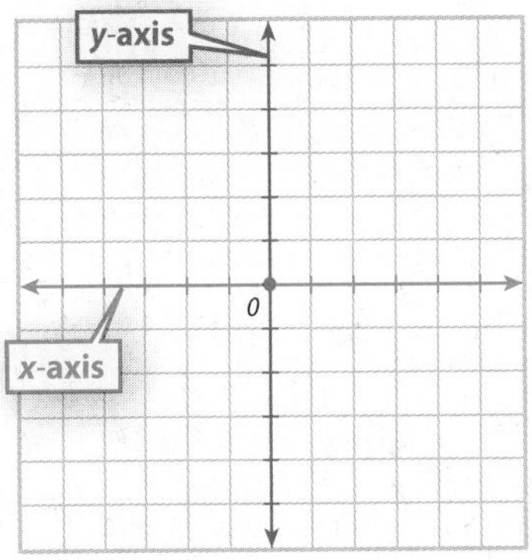

Glossary/Glosario

ENGLISH	SPANISH	EXAMPLES

B

bar graph A graph that uses vertical or horizontal bars to display data.

gráfica de barras Gráfica en la que se usan barras verticales u horizontales para presentar datos.

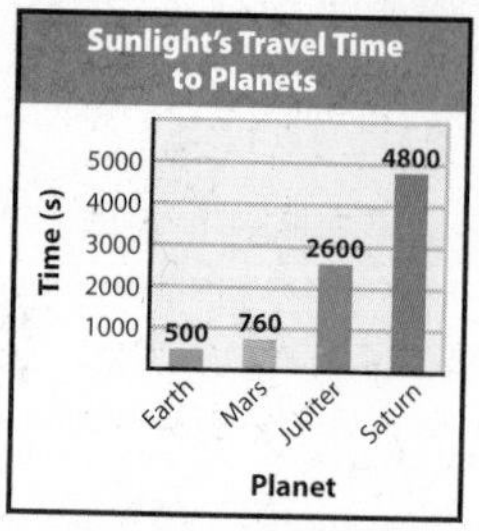

base (in numeration) When a number is raised to a power, the number that is used as a factor is the base.

base (en numeración) Cuando un número es elevado a una potencia, el número que se usa como factor es la base.

$3^5 = 3 \cdot 3 \cdot 3 \cdot 3 \cdot 3$; 3 is the base.

base (of a polygon or three-dimensional figure) A side of a polygon; a face of a three-dimensional figure by which the figure is measured or classified.

base (de un polígono o figura tridimensional) Lado de un polígono; la cara de una figura tridimensional, a partir de la cual se mide o se clasifica la figura.

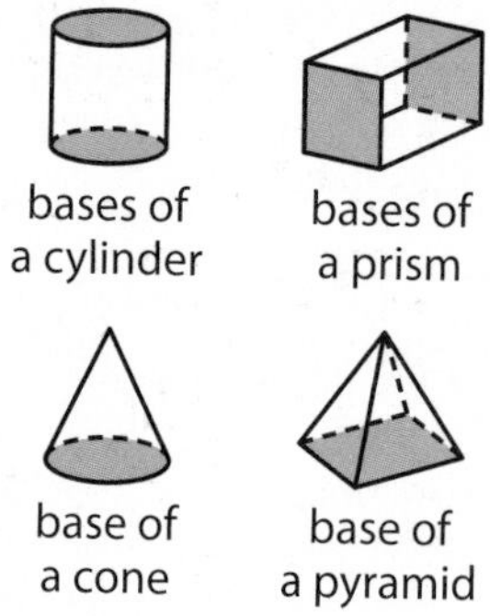

bisect To divide into two congruent parts.

trazar una bisectriz Dividir en dos partes congruentes.

box plot A graph that shows how data are distributed by using the median, quartiles, least value, and greatest value; also called a box-and-whisker plot.

gráfica de caja Gráfica para demostrar la distribución de datos utilizando la mediana, los cuartiles y los valores menos y más grande; también llamado gráfica de mediana y rango.

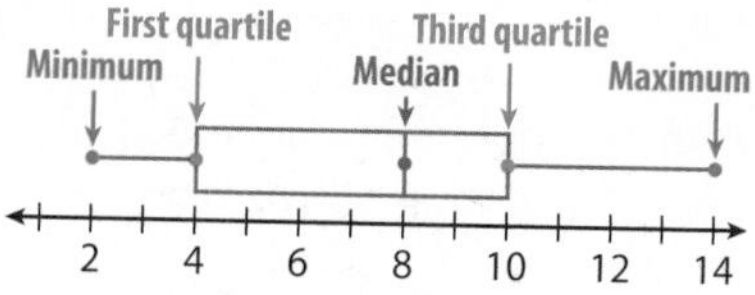

break (graph) A zigzag on a horizontal or vertical scale of a graph that indicates that some of the numbers on the scale have been omitted.

discontinuidad (gráfica) Zig-zag en la escala horizontal o vertical de una gráfica que indica la omisión de algunos de los números de la escala.

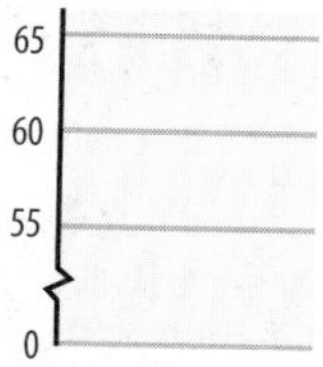

C

capacity The amount a container can hold when filled.

capacidad Cantidad que cabe en un recipiente cuando se llena.

categorical data Data that consists of nonnumeric information.

datos categóricos Datos que constan de información no numérica.

ENGLISH	SPANISH	EXAMPLES
Celsius A metric scale for measuring temperature in which 0°C is the freezing point of water and 100°C is the boiling point of water; also called *centigrade*.	**Celsius** Escala métrica para medir la temperatura, en la que 0° C es el punto de congelación del agua y 100° C es el punto de ebullición. También se llama *centígrado*.	
center (of a circle) The point inside a circle that is the same distance from all the points on the circle.	**centro (de un círculo)** Punto interior de un círculo que se encuentra a la misma distancia de todos los puntos de la circunferencia.	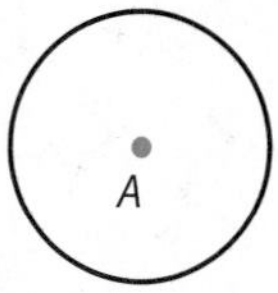
center (of rotation) The point about which a figure is rotated.	**centro (de una rotación)** Punto alrededor del cual se hace girar una figura.	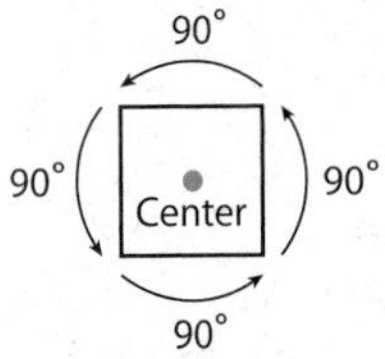
checking account An account at a financial institution that allows for withdrawals and deposits.	**cuenta corriente** Cuenta bancaria de la cual puedes retirar dinero mediante el uso de un cheque o una tarjeta de débito.	
chord A line segment whose endpoints lie on a circle.	**cuerda** Segmento cuyos extremos se encuentran en un círculo.	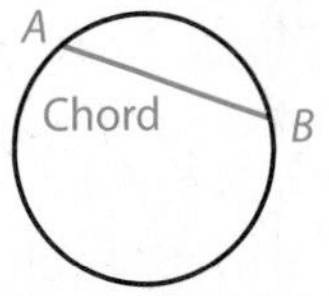
circle The set of all points in a plane that are the same distance from a given point called the center.	**círculo** Conjunto de todos los puntos en un plano que se encuentran a la misma distancia de un punto dado llamado centro.	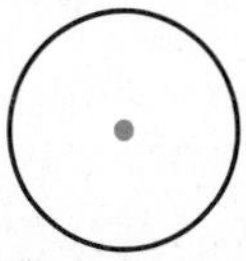
circle graph A graph that uses sections of a circle to compare parts to the whole and parts to other parts.	**gráfica circular** Gráfica que usa secciones de un círculo para comparar partes con el todo y con otras partes.	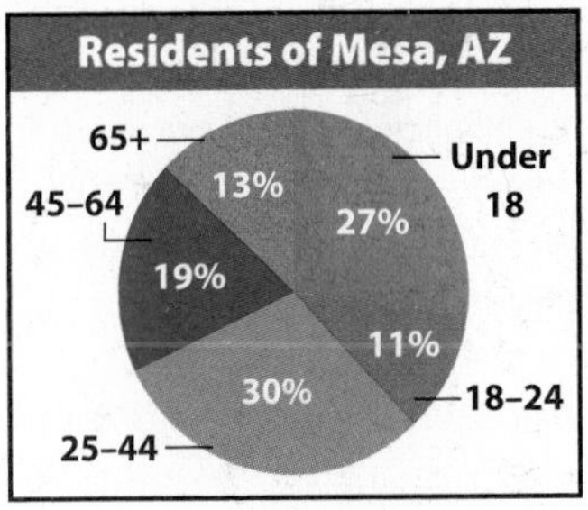
circumference The distance around a circle.	**circunferencia** Distancia alrededor de un círculo.	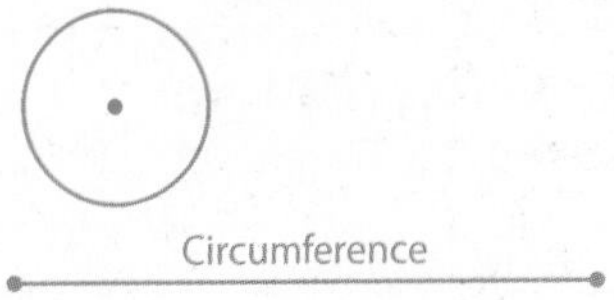
clockwise A circular movement in the direction shown.	**en el sentido de las manecillas del reloj** Movimiento circular en la dirección que se indica.	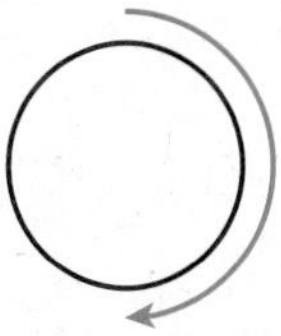

ENGLISH	SPANISH	EXAMPLES
clustering A method used to estimate a sum when all addends are close to the same value.	**agrupación** Método que se usa para estimar una suma cuando todos los sumandos se aproximan al mismo valor.	27, 29, 24, and 23 all cluster around 25.
coefficient The number that is multiplied by the variable in an algebraic expression.	**coeficiente** Número que se multiplica por la variable en una expresión algebraica.	5 is the coefficient in $5b$.
combination An arrangement of items or events in which order does not matter.	**combinación** Agrupación de objetos o sucesos en la cual el orden no es importante.	For objects *A, B, C,* and *D,* there are 6 different combinations of 2 objects: *AB, AC, AD, BC, BD, CD.*
common denominator A denominator that is the same in two or more fractions.	**denominador común** Denominador que es común a dos o más fracciones.	The common denominator of $\frac{5}{8}$ and $\frac{2}{8}$ is 8.
common factor A number that is a factor of two or more numbers.	**factor común** Número que es factor de dos o más números.	8 is a common factor of 16 and 40.
common multiple A number that is a multiple of each of two or more numbers.	**múltiplo común** Un número que es múltiplo de dos o más números.	15 is a common multiple of 3 and 5.
Commutative Property of Addition The property that states that two or more numbers can be added in any order without changing the sum.	**Propiedad conmutativa de la suma** Propiedad que establece que sumar dos o más números en cualquier orden no altera la suma.	$8 + 20 = 20 + 8$
Commutative Property of Multiplication The property that states that two or more numbers can be multiplied in any order without changing the product.	**Propiedad conmutativa de la multiplicación** Propiedad que establece que multiplicar dos o más números en cualquier orden no altera el producto.	$6 \cdot 12 = 12 \cdot 6$
compatible numbers Numbers that are close to the given numbers that make estimation or mental calculation easier.	**números compatibles** Números que están cerca de los números dados y hacen más fácil la estimación o el cálculo mental.	To estimate 7,957 + 5,009, use the compatible numbers 8,000 and 5,000: 8,000 + 5,000 = 13,000.
compensation When a number in a problem is close to another number that is easier to calculate with, the easier number is used to find the answer. Then the answer is adjusted by adding to it or subtracting from it.	**compensación** Cuando un número de un problema está cerca de otro con el que es más fácil hacer cálculos, se usa el número más fácil para hallar la respuesta. Luego, se ajusta la respuesta sumando o restando.	
complement The set of all outcomes that are not the event.	**complemento** La serie de resultados que no están en el suceso.	When rolling a number cube, the complement of rolling a 3 is rolling a 1, 2, 4, 5, or 6.

ENGLISH	SPANISH	EXAMPLES

complementary angles Two angles whose measures add to 90°.

ángulos complementarios Dos ángulos cuyas medidas suman 90°.

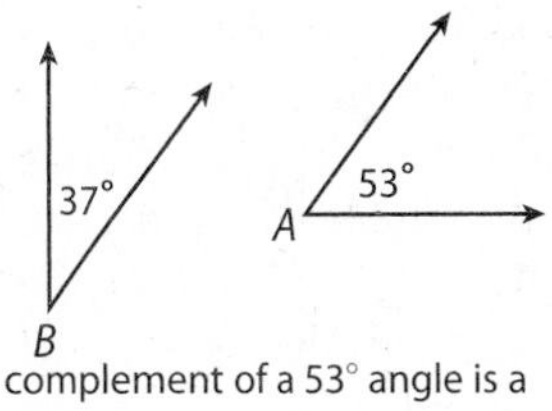

The complement of a 53° angle is a 37° angle.

composite number A number greater than 1 that has more than two whole-number factors.

número compuesto Número mayor que 1 que tiene más de dos factores que son números cabales.

4, 6, 8, and 9 are composite numbers.

compound inequality A combination of more than one inequality.

desigualdad compuesta Combinación de dos o más desigualdades.

$-2 \leq x < 10$

cone A three-dimensional figure with one vertex and one circular base.

cono Figura tridimensional con un vértice y una base circular.

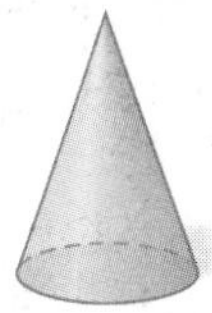

congruent Having the same size and shape.

congruentes Que tienen la misma forma y el mismo tamaño.

congruent angles Angles that have the same measure.

ángulos congruentes Ángulos que tienen la misma medida.

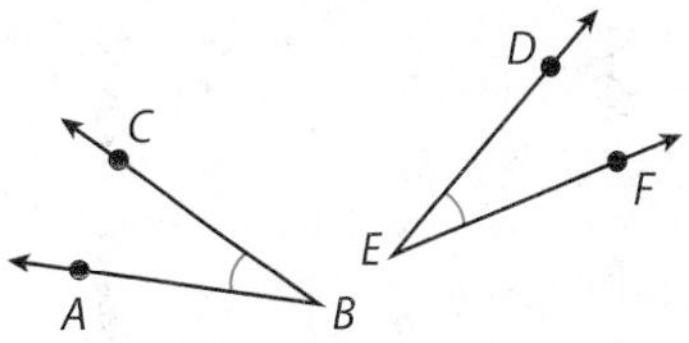

$m\angle ABC = m\angle DEF$

congruent figures Two figures whose corresponding sides and angles are congruent.

figuras congruentes Figuras que tienen el mismo tamaño y forma.

congruent line segments Two line segments that have the same length.

segmentos congruentes Dos segmentos que tienen la misma longitud.

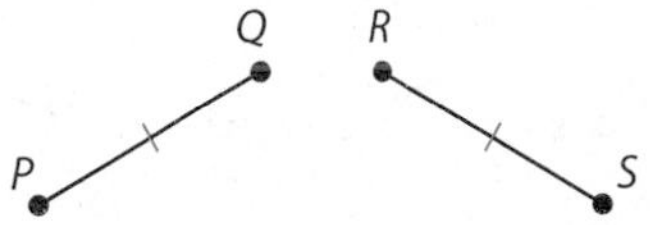

conjecture A statement that is believed to be true.

conjetura Enunciado que se supone verdadero.

constant A value that does not change.

constante Valor que no cambia.

3, 0, π

coordinate grid A grid formed by the intersection of horizontal and vertical lines that is used to locate points.

cuadrícula de coordenadas Cuadrícula formada por la intersección de líneas horizontales y líneas verticales que se usan por localizar puntos.

ENGLISH	SPANISH
coordinate plane A plane formed by the intersection of a horizontal number line called the *x*-axis and a vertical number line called the *y*-axis.	**plano cartesiano** Plano formado por la intersección de una recta numérica horizontal llamada eje *x* y otra vertical llamada eje *y*.

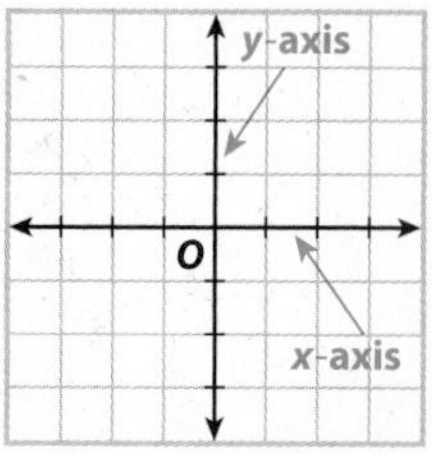

ENGLISH	SPANISH
coordinates The numbers of an ordered pair that locate a point on a coordinate graph.	**coordenadas** Los números de un par ordenado que ubican un punto en una gráfica de coordenadas.

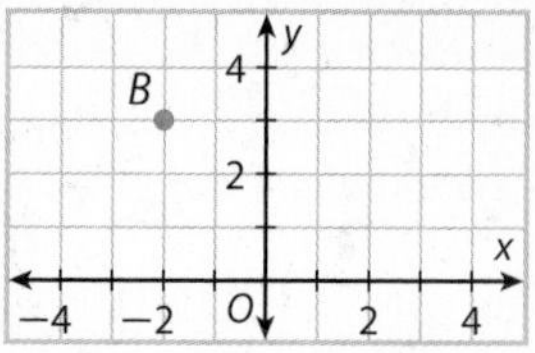

The coordinates of *B* are (−2, 3).

ENGLISH	SPANISH
correspondence The relationship between two or more objects that are matched.	**correspondencia** La relación entre dos o más objetos que coinciden.
corresponding angles (for lines) Angles in the same position formed when a third line intersects two lines.	**ángulos correspondientes (en líneas)** Ángulos en la misma posición formados cuando una tercera línea interseca dos líneas.

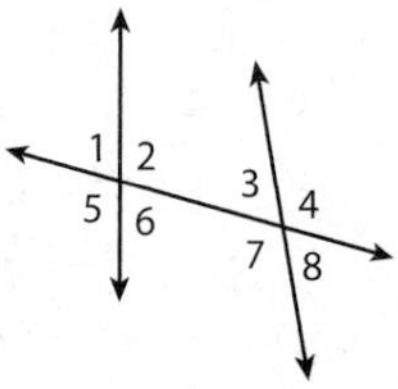

$\angle 1$ and $\angle 3$ are corresponding angles.

ENGLISH	SPANISH
corresponding angles (in polygons) Angles in the same relative position in polygons with an equal number of sides.	**ángulos correspondientes (en polígonos)** Ángulos que se ubican en la misma posición relativa en polígonos que tienen el mismo número de lados.

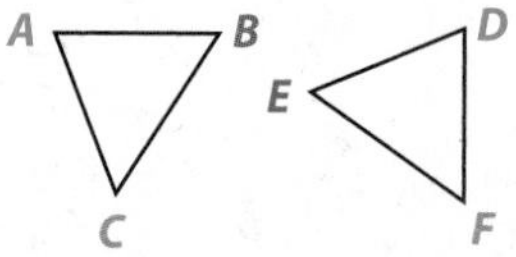

$\angle A$ and $\angle D$ are corresponding angles.

ENGLISH	SPANISH
corresponding sides Sides in the same relative position in polygons with an equal number of sides.	**lados correspondientes** Lados que se ubican en la misma posición relativa en polígonos que tienen el mismo número de lados.

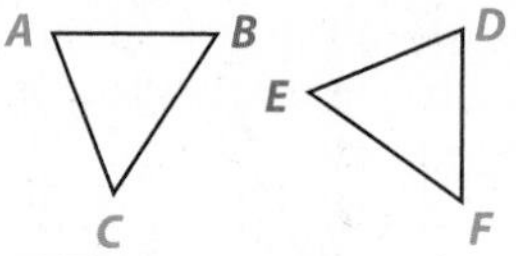

$\overline{AB}$ and $\overline{DE}$ are corresponding sides.

ENGLISH	SPANISH
counterclockwise A circular movement in the direction shown.	**en sentido contrario a las manecillas del reloj** Movimiento circular en la dirección que se indica.

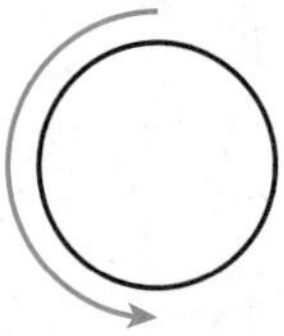

ENGLISH	SPANISH
credit card A plastic card issued by a financial company allowing a customer to buy goods or services on credit.	**tarjeta de crédito** Tarjeta de pago plástica que un cliente puede utilizar para comprar bienes o servicios. El cliente puede pagar por las compras a plazos, pero pagará intereses en el saldo restante.
credit history Information about how a consumer has borrowed and repaid debt.	**historia crediticia** Información del buen manejo de dinero y pago de cuentas por parte de un cliente.

ENGLISH	SPANISH	EXAMPLES
credit report A report containing detailed information on a person's credit history.	**informe crediticio** Informe que recopilan las agencias acerca de la historia crediticia de un cliente y que ayuda a los prestamistas a decidir si dan dinero a crédito a los clientes.	
credit score A number based on information in a consumer's credit report that measures an individual's creditworthiness.	**calificación crediticia** Número basado en información de un informe crediticio de un cliente. Se usa para predecir la posibilidad de que una persona se retrase en hacer pagos o que no pague una deuda.	
cross product The product of numbers on the diagonal when comparing two ratios.	**producto cruzado** El producto de los números multiplicados en diagonal cuando se comparan dos razones.	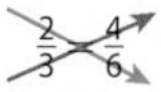 For the proportion $\frac{2}{3} = \frac{4}{6}$, the cross products are $2 \cdot 6 = 12$ and $3 \cdot 4 = 12$.
cube (geometric figure) A rectangular prism with six congruent square faces.	**cubo (figura geométrica)** Prisma rectangular con seis caras cuadradas congruentes.	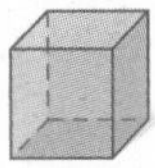
cube (in numeration) A number raised to the third power.	**cubo (en numeración)** Número elevado a la tercera potencia.	$5^3 = 5 \cdot 5 \cdot 5 = 125$
cumulative frequency The frequency of all data values that are less than or equal to a given value.	**frecuencia acumulativa** Muestra el total acumulado de las frecuencias.	
customary system The measurement system often used in the United States.	**sistema usual de medidas** El sistema de medidas que se usa comúnmente en Estados Unidos.	inches, feet, miles, ounces, pounds, tons, cups, quarts, gallons
cylinder A three-dimensional figure with two parallel, congruent circular bases connected by a curved lateral surface.	**cilindro** Figura tridimensional con dos bases circulares paralelas y congruentes, unidas por una superficie lateral curva.	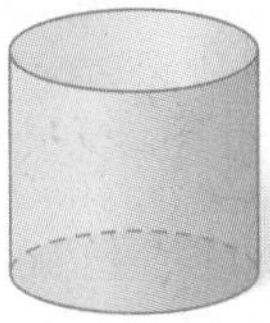

D

ENGLISH	SPANISH	EXAMPLES
debit card An electronic card issued by a financial institution that allows a customer to access their account to withdraw cash or pay for goods and services	**tarjeta de débito** Tarjeta de pago plástica que un cliente puede usar para pagar por bienes o servicios. El dinero se retira inmediatamente de la cuenta corriente o de ahorros del cliente.	
degree The unit of measure for angles or temperature.	**grado** Unidad de medida para ángulos y temperaturas.	

ENGLISH	SPANISH	EXAMPLES
denominator The bottom number of a fraction that tells how many equal parts are in the whole.	**denominador** Número de abajo en una fracción que indica en cuántas partes iguales se divide el entero.	$\frac{3}{4}$ ← denominator
dependent events Events for which the outcome of one event affects the probability of the other.	**sucesos dependientes** Dos sucesos son dependientes si el resultado de uno afecta la probabilidad del otro.	A bag contains 3 red marbles and 2 blue marbles. Drawing a red marble and then drawing a blue marble without replacing the first marble is an example of dependent events.
dependent variable The output of a function; a variable whose value depends on the value of the input, or independent variable.	**variable dependiente** Salida de una función; variable cuyo valor depende del valor de la entrada, o variable independiente.	For $y = 2x + 1$, y is the dependent variable: input: x output: y.
diagonal A line segment that connects two nonadjacent vertices of a polygon.	**diagonal** Segmento de recta que une dos vértices no adyacentes de un polígono.	
diameter A line segment that passes through the center of a circle and has endpoints on the circle, or the length of that segment.	**diámetro** Segmento de recta que pasa por el centro de un círculo y tiene sus extremos en la circunferencia, o bien la longitud de ese segmento.	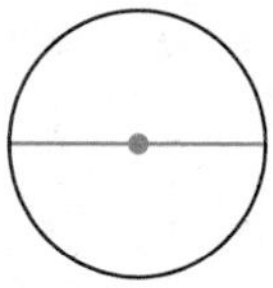
difference The result when one number is subtracted from another.	**diferencia** El resultado de restar un número de otro.	
dimension The length, width, or height of a figure.	**dimensión** Longitud, ancho o altura de una figura.	
discount The amount by which the original price is reduced.	**descuento** Cantidad que se resta del precio original de un artículo.	
Distributive Property The property that states if you multiply a sum by a number, you will get the same result if you multiply each addend by that number and then add the products.	**Propiedad distributiva** Propiedad que establece que, si multiplicas una suma por un número, obtendrás el mismo resultado que si multiplicas cada sumando por ese número y luego sumas los productos.	$5(20 + 1) = 5 \cdot 20 + 5 \cdot 1$
dividend The number to be divided in a division problem.	**dividendo** Número que se divide en un problema de división.	In $8 \div 4 = 2$, 8 is the dividend.
divisible Can be divided by a number without leaving a remainder.	**divisible** Que se puede dividir entre un número sin dejar residuo.	18 is divisible by 3.
divisor The number you are dividing by in a division problem.	**divisor** El número entre el que se divide en un problema de división.	In $8 \div 4 = 2$, 4 is the divisor.
dot plot A visual display in which each piece of data is represented by a dot above a number line.	**diagrama de puntos** Despliegue visual en que cada dato se representa con un punto sobre una recta numérica.	

ENGLISH	SPANISH	EXAMPLES
double-bar graph A bar graph that compares two related sets of data.	**gráfica de doble barra** Gráfica de barras que compara dos conjuntos de datos relacionados.	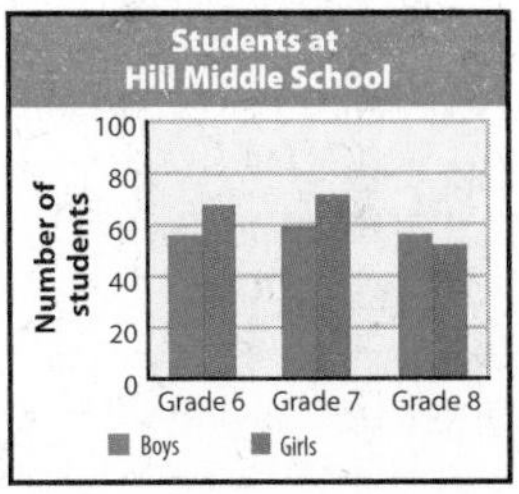
double-line graph A graph that shows how two related sets of data change over time.	**gráfica de doble línea** Gráfica lineal que muestra cómo cambian con el tiempo dos conjuntos de datos relacionados.	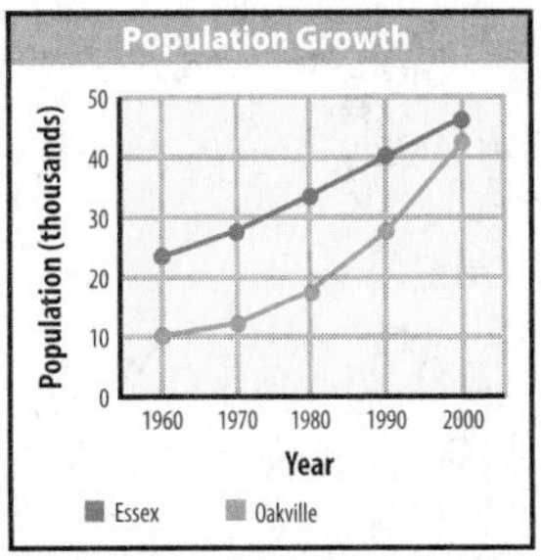

E

ENGLISH	SPANISH	EXAMPLES
edge The line segment along which two faces of a polyhedron intersect.	**arista** Segmento de recta donde se intersecan dos caras de un poliedro.	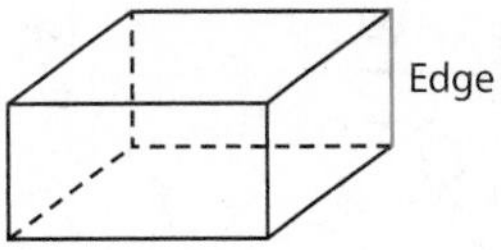
elements The words, numbers, or objects in a set.	**elementos** Palabras, números u objetos que forman un conjunto.	Elements of A: 1, 2, 3, 4
empty set A set that has no elements.	**conjunto vacío** Un conjunto que no tiene elementos.	
endpoint A point at the end of a line segment or ray.	**extremo** Un punto ubicado al final de un segmento de recta o rayo.	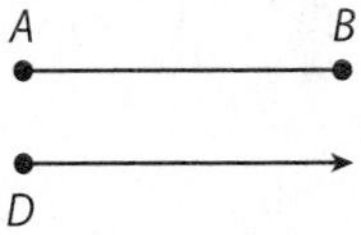
equally likely Outcomes that have the same probability.	**igualmente probables** Resultados que tienen la misma probabilidad de ocurrir.	When you toss a coin, the outcomes "heads" and "tails" are equally likely.
equation A mathematical sentence that shows that two expressions are equivalent.	**ecuación** Enunciado matemático que indica que dos expresiones son equivalentes.	$x + 4 = 7$ $6 + 1 = 10 - 3$
equilateral triangle A triangle with three congruent sides.	**triángulo equilátero** Triángulo con tres lados congruentes.	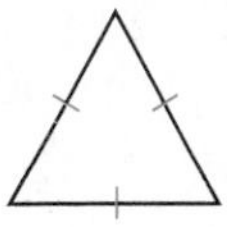
equivalent Having the same value.	**equivalentes** Que tienen el mismo valor.	
equivalent expression Equivalent expressions have the same value for all values of the variables.	**expresión equivalente** Las expresiones equivalentes tienen el mismo valor para todos los valores de las variables.	$4x + 5x$ and $9x$ are equivalent expressions.

ENGLISH	SPANISH	EXAMPLES
equivalent fractions Fractions that name the same amount or part.	**fracciones equivalentes** Fracciones que representan la misma cantidad o parte.	$\frac{1}{2}$ and $\frac{2}{4}$ are equivalent fractions.
equivalent ratios Ratios that name the same comparison.	**razones equivalentes** Razones que representan la misma comparación.	$\frac{1}{2}$ and $\frac{2}{4}$ are equivalent ratios.
estimate (n) An answer that is close to the exact answer and is found by rounding or other methods.	**estimación (s)** Una solución aproximada a la respuesta exacta que se halla mediante el redondeo u otros métodos.	
estimate (v) To find an answer close to the exact answer by rounding or other methods.	**estimar (v)** Hallar una solución aproximada a la respuesta exacta mediante el redondeo u otros métodos.	
evaluate To find the value of a numerical or algebraic expression.	**evaluar** Hallar el valor de una expresión numérica o algebraica.	Evaluate $2x + 7$ for $x = 3$. $2x + 7$ $2(3) + 7$ $6 + 7$ 13
even number A whole number that is divisible by two.	**número par** Un número cabal que es divisible entre dos.	
event An outcome or set of outcomes of an experiment or situation.	**suceso** Un resultado o una serie de resultados de un experimento o una situación.	
expanded form A number written as the sum of the values of its digits.	**forma desarrollada** Número escrito como suma de los valores de sus dígitos.	236,536 written in expanded form is $200{,}000 + 30{,}000 + 6{,}000 + 500 + 30 + 6$.
experiment In probability, any activity based on chance.	**experimento** En probabilidad, cualquier actividad basada en la posibilidad.	Tossing a coin 10 times and noting the number of "heads"
experimental probability The ratio of the number of times an event occurs to the total number of trials, or times that the activity is performed.	**probabilidad experimental** Razón del número de veces que ocurre un suceso al número total de pruebas o al número de veces que se realiza el experimento.	Kendra attempted 27 free throws and made 16 of them. Her experimental probability of making a free throw is $\frac{\text{number made}}{\text{number attempted}} = \frac{16}{27} \approx 0.59$.
exponent The number that indicates how many times the base is used as a factor.	**exponente** Número que indica cuántas veces se usa la base como factor.	$2^3 = 2 \cdot 2 \cdot 2 = 8$; 3 is the exponent.
exponential form A number is in exponential form when it is written with a base and an exponent.	**forma exponencial** Cuando se escribe un número con una base y un exponente, está en forma exponencial.	4^2 is the exponential form for $4 \cdot 4$.
expression A mathematical phrase that contains operations, numbers, and/or variables.	**expresión** Enunciado matemático que contiene operaciones, números y/o variables.	$6x + 1$

Glossary/Glosario

ENGLISH | SPANISH | EXAMPLES

F

face A flat surface of a polyhedron.

cara Lado plano de un poliedro.

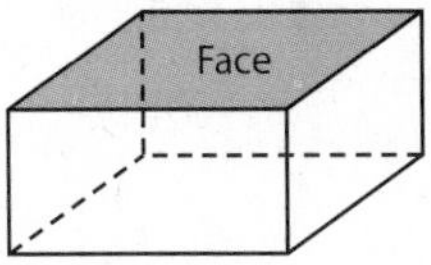

factor A number that is multiplied by another number to get a product.

factor Número que se multiplica por otro para hallar un producto.

7 is a factor of 21 since $7 \cdot 3 = 21$.

factor tree A diagram showing how a whole number breaks down into its prime factors.

árbol de factores Diagrama que muestra cómo se descompone un número cabal en sus factores primos.

```
   12
   / \
  3 · 4
      / \
     2 · 2
```

$12 = 3 \cdot 2 \cdot 2$

Fahrenheit A temperature scale in which 32 °F is the freezing point of water and 212 °F is the boiling point of water.

Fahrenheit Escala de temperatura en la que 32 °F es el punto de congelación del agua y 212 °F es el punto de ebullición.

fair When all outcomes of an experiment are equally likely, the experiment is said to be fair.

justo Se dice de un experimento donde todos los resultados posibles son igualmente probables.

When tossing a fair coin, heads and tails are equally likely. Each has a probability of $\frac{1}{2}$.

formula A rule showing relationships among quantities.

fórmula Regla que muestra relaciones entre cantidades.

$A = \ell w$ is the formula for the area of a rectangle.

fraction A number in the form $\frac{a}{b}$, where $b \neq 0$.

fracción Número escrito en la forma $\frac{a}{b}$, donde $b \neq 0$.

frequency The number of times a data value occurs.

frecuencia Cantidad de veces que aparece el valor en un conjunto de datos.

In the data set 5, 6, 7, 8, 6, the data value 6 has a frequency of 2.

frequency table A table that lists items together according to the number of times, or frequency, that the items occur.

tabla de frecuencia Una tabla en la que se organizan los datos de acuerdo con el número de veces que aparece cada valor (o la frecuencia).

Data set: 1, 1, 2, 2, 3, 4, 5, 5, 5, 6, 6
Frequency table:

Date	Frequency
1	2
2	2
3	1
4	1
5	3
6	2

front-end estimation An estimating technique in which the front digits of the addends are added.

estimación por partes Técnica en la que se suman sólo los números enteros de los sumandos y luego se ajusta la suma para tener una estimación mas exacta.

Estimate $25.05 + 14.671$ with the sum $25 + 14 = 39$. The actual value is 39 or greater.

function An input-output relationship that has exactly one output for each input.

función Relación de entrada-salida en la que a cada valor de entrada corresponde un valor de salida.

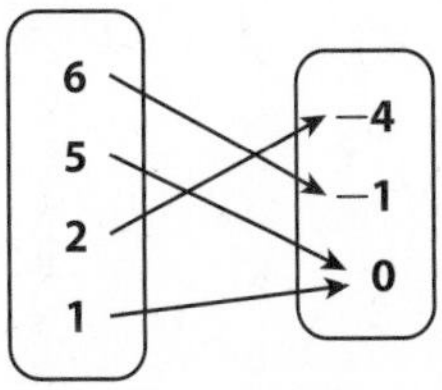

ENGLISH	SPANISH	EXAMPLES

function table A table of ordered pairs that represent solutions of a function.

tabla de funciónes Tabla de pares ordenados que representan soluciones de una función.

x	3	4	5	6
y	7	9	11	13

G

grants Money awarded to students that does not need to be repaid.

beca Dinero que se otorga a estudiantes y el cual no se necesita devolver.

graph of an equation A graph of the set of ordered pairs that are solutions of the equation.

gráfica de una ecuación Gráfica del conjunto de pares ordenados que son soluciones de la ecuación.

greatest common factor (GCF) The largest common factor of two or more given numbers.

máximo común divisor (MCD) El mayor de los factores comunes compartidos por dos o más números dados.

The GCF of 27 and 45 is 9.

H

height In a triangle or quadrilateral, the perpendicular distance from the base to the opposite vertex or side. In a prism or cylinder, the perpendicular distance between the bases.

altura En un triángulo o cuadrilátero, la distancia perpendicular desde la base de la figura al vértice o lado opuesto. En un prisma o cilindro, la distancia perpendicular entre las bases.

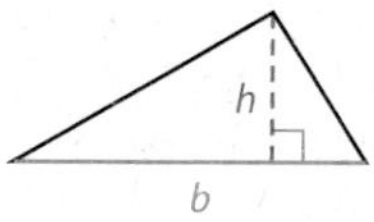

heptagon A seven-sided polygon.

heptágono Polígono de siete lados.

hexagon A six-sided polygon.

hexágono Polígono de seis lados.

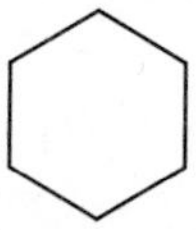

histogram A bar graph that shows the frequency of data within equal intervals.

histograma Gráfica de barras que muestra la frecuencia de los datos en intervalos iguales.

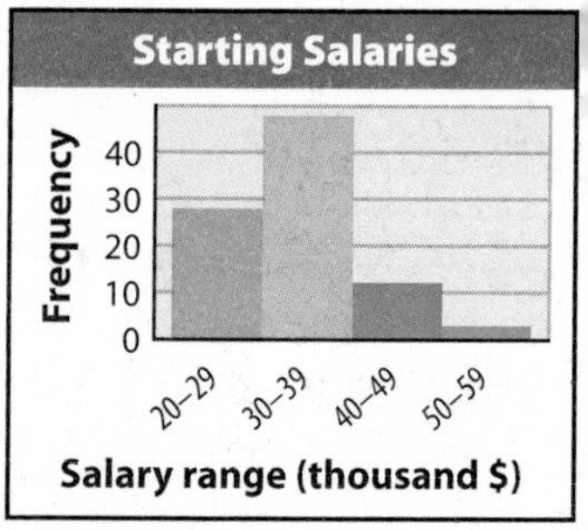

hypotenuse In a right triangle, the side opposite the right angle.

hipotenusa En un triángulo rectángulo, el lado opuesto al ángulo recto.

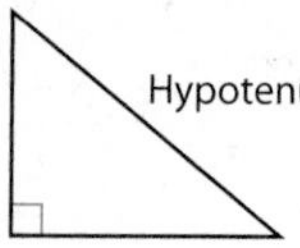

I

ENGLISH	SPANISH	EXAMPLES
Identity Property (for Addition) The property that states the sum of zero and any number is that number.	**Propiedad de identidad (de la suma)** Propiedad que establece que la suma de cero y cualquier número es ese número.	$7 + 0 = 7$ $-9 + 0 = -9$
Identity Property (for Multiplication) The property that states that the product of 1 and any number is that number.	**Propiedad de identidad (de la multiplicación)** Propiedad que establece que el producto de 1 y cualquier número es ese número.	$5 \times 1 = 5$ $-8 \times 1 = -8$
improper fraction A fraction in which the numerator is greater than or equal to the denominator.	**fracción impropia** Fracción cuyo numerador es mayor que o igual al denominador.	$\frac{5}{5}$ $\frac{7}{3}$
independent variable The input of a function; a variable whose value determines the value of the output, or dependent variable.	**variable independiente** Entrada de una función; variable cuyo valor determina el valor de la salida, o variable dependiente.	For $y = 2x + 1$, x is the dependent variable. Input: x output: y
indirect measurement The technique of using similar figures and proportions to find a measure.	**medición indirecta** La técnica de usar figuras semejantes y proporciones para hallar una medida.	
inequality A mathematical sentence that shows the relationship between quantities that are not equal.	**desigualdad** Enunciado matemático que muestra una relación entre cantidades que no son iguales.	$5 < 8$ $5x + 2 \geq 12$
input The value substituted into an expression or function.	**valor de entrada** Valor que se usa para sustituir una variable en una expresión o función.	For the rule $y = 6x$, the input 4 produces an output of 24.
integer A member of the set of whole numbers and their opposites.	**entero** Un miembro del conjunto de los números cabales y sus opuestos.	$\ldots -3, -2, -1, 0, 1, 2, 3, \ldots$
interest The amount of money charged for borrowing or using money, or the amount of money earned by saving money.	**interés** Cantidad de dinero que se cobra por el préstamo o uso del dinero, o la cantidad que se gana al ahorrar dinero.	
interquartile range (IQR) The difference of the third (upper) and first (lower) quartiles in a data set, representing the middle half of the data.	**rango intercuartil (RIC)** Diferencia entre el tercer cuartil (superior) y el primer cuartil (inferior) de un conjunto de datos, que representa la mitad central de los datos.	Lower half: 18, (23), 28, — First quartile Upper half: 29, (36), 42 — Third quartile Interquartile range: $36 - 23 = 13$
intersecting lines Lines that cross at exactly one point.	**rectas secantes** Líneas que se cruzan en un solo punto.	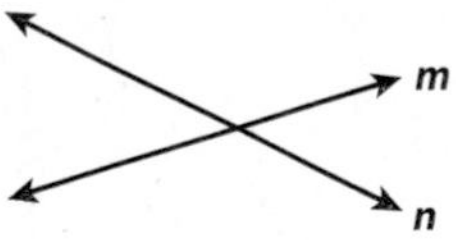

Glossary/Glosario

ENGLISH	SPANISH	EXAMPLES
intersection (sets) The set of elements common to two or more sets.	**intersección (de conjuntos)** Conjunto de elementos comunes a dos o más conjuntos.	
interval The space between marked values on a number line or the scale of a graph.	**intervalo** El espacio entre los valores marcados en una recta numérica o en la escala de una gráfica.	
inverse operations Operations that undo each other: addition and subtraction, or multiplication and division.	**operaciones inversas** Operaciones que se cancelan mutuamente: suma y resta, o multiplicación y división.	
isosceles triangle A triangle with at least two congruent sides.	**triángulo isósceles** Triángulo que tiene al menos dos lados congruentes.	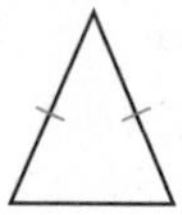

L

ENGLISH	SPANISH	EXAMPLES
lateral surface In a cylinder, the curved surface connecting the circular bases; in a cone, the curved surface that is not a base.	**superficie lateral** En un cilindro, superficie curva que une las bases circulares; en un cono, la superficie curva que no es la base.	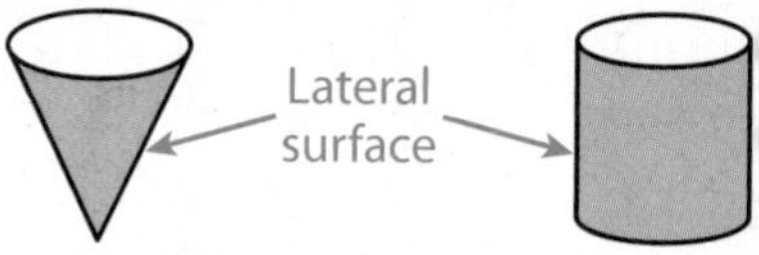
least common denominator (LCD) The least common multiple of two or more denominators.	**mínimo común denominador (m.c.d.)** El mínimo común múltiplo de dos o más denominadores.	The LCD of $\frac{3}{4}$ and $\frac{5}{6}$ is 12.
least common multiple (LCM) The smallest number, other than zero, that is a multiple of two or more given numbers.	**mínimo común múltiplo (m.c.m.)** El menor de los múltiplos (distinto de cero) de dos o más números.	The LCM of 10 and 18 is 90.
like fractions Fractions that have the same denominator.	**fracciones semejantes** Fracciones que tienen el mismo denominador.	$\frac{5}{12}$ and $\frac{3}{12}$ are like fractions.
like terms Terms with the same variables raised to the same exponents.	**términos semejantes** Términos con las mismas variables elevadas a los mismos exponentes.	$3a^2b^2$ and $7a^2b^2$
line A straight path that has no thickness and extends forever.	**recta** Trayectoria recta que no tiene ningún grueso y que se extiende por siempre.	
line graph A graph that uses line segments to show how data changes.	**gráfica lineal** Gráfica que muestra cómo cambian los datos mediante segmentos de recta.	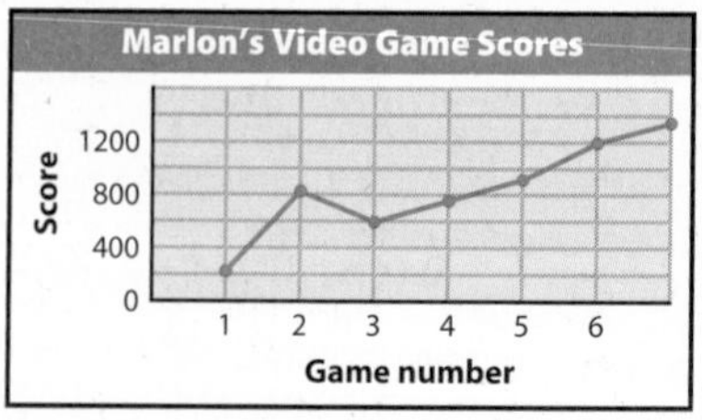

ENGLISH	SPANISH	EXAMPLES
line plot A number line with marks or dots that show frequency.	**diagrama de puntos** Recta numérica con marcas o puntos que indican la frecuencia.	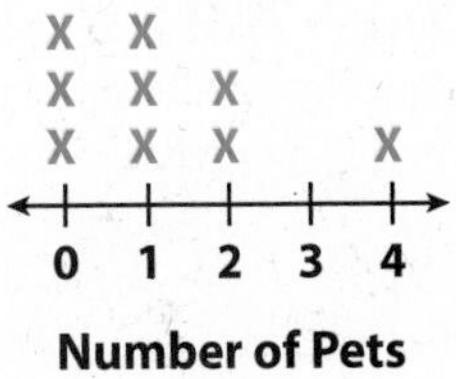
line of reflection A line that a figure is flipped across to create a mirror image of the original figure.	**línea de reflexión** Línea sobre la cual se invierte una figura para crear una imagen reflejada de la figura original.	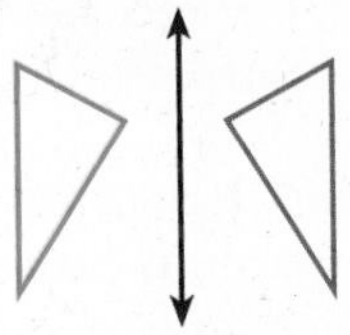 **Line of reflection**
line of symmetry The imaginary "mirror" in line symmetry.	**eje de simetría** El "espejo" imaginario en la simetría axial.	
line segment A part of a line between two endpoints.	**segmento de recta** Parte de una línea con dos extremos.	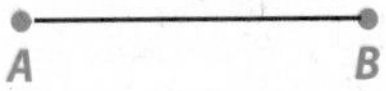
line symmetry A figure has line symmetry if one-half is a mirror image of the other half.	**simetría axial** Una figura tiene simetría axial si una de sus mitades es la imagen reflejada de la otra.	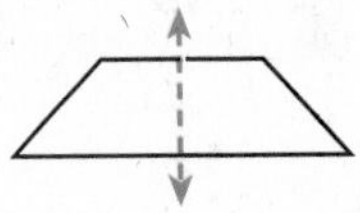
linear equation An equation whose solutions form a straight line on a coordinate plane.	**ecuación lineal** Ecuación en la que las soluciones forman una línea recta en un plano cartesiano.	$y = 2x + 1$

M

ENGLISH	SPANISH	EXAMPLES
mean The sum of the items in a set of data divided by the number of items in the set; also called *average*.	**media** La suma de todos los elementos de un conjunto de datos dividida entre el número de elementos del conjunto.	Data set: 4, 6, 7, 8, 10 Mean: $\frac{4+6+7+8+10}{5} = \frac{35}{5} = 7$
mean absolute deviation (MAD) The mean distance between each data value and the mean of the data set.	**desviación absoluta media (DAM)** Distancia media entre cada dato y la media del conjunto de datos.	
measure of center A measure used to describe the middle of a data set. Also called measure of central tendency.	**medida central** Medida que se usa para describir el centro de un conjunto de datos; la media, la mediana y la moda son medidas centrales. También se conocen como medidas de tendencia central.	
measure of spread A measure that describes how far apart the data are distributed.	**medida de dispersión** Medida que describe la separación en una distribución de datos.	

ENGLISH	SPANISH	EXAMPLES
median The middle number or the mean (average) of the two middle numbers in an ordered set of data.	**mediana** El número intermedio o la media (el promedio) de los dos números intermedios en un conjunto ordenado de datos.	Data set: 4, 6, 7, 8, 10 Median: 7
metric system A decimal system of weights and measures that is used universally in science and commonly throughout the world.	**sistema métrico** Sistema decimal de pesos y medidas empleado universalmente en las ciencias y por lo general en todo el mundo.	centimeters, meters, kilometers, grams, kilograms, milliliters, liters
midpoint The point that divides a line segment into two congruent line segments.	**punto medio** El punto que divide un segmento de recta en dos segmentos de recta congruentes.	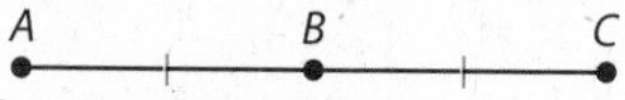 *B* is the midpoint of $\overline{AC}$.
mixed number A number made up of a whole number that is not zero and a fraction.	**número mixto** Número compuesto por un número cabal distinto de cero y una fracción.	$5\frac{1}{8}$
mode The number or numbers that occur most frequently in a set of data; when all numbers occur with the same frequency, we say there is no mode.	**moda** Número o números más frecuentes en un conjunto de datos; si todos los números aparecen con la misma frecuencia, no hay moda.	Data set: 3, 5, 8, 8, 10 Mode: 8
multiple The product of a number and any nonzero whole number.	**múltiplo** El producto de un número y cualquier número cabal distinto de cero es un múltiplo de ese número.	
Multiplication Property of Zero The property that states that the product of any number and 0 is 0.	**Propiedad de multiplicación del cero** Propiedad que establece que el producto de cualquier número y 0 es 0.	$6 \times 0 = 0$ $-5 \times 0 = 0$
multiplicative inverse One of two numbers whose product is 1.	**inverso multiplicativo** Uno de dos números cuyo producto es igual a 1.	The multiplicative inverse of $\frac{3}{4}$ is $\frac{4}{3}$.

N

ENGLISH	SPANISH	EXAMPLES
negative number A number less than zero.	**número negativo** Número menor que cero.	−2 is a negative number. 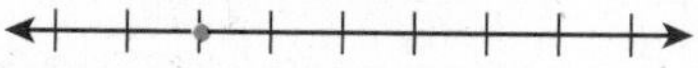
net An arrangement of two-dimensional figures that can be folded to form a polyhedron.	**plantilla** Arreglo de figuras bidimensionales que se doblan para formar un poliedro.	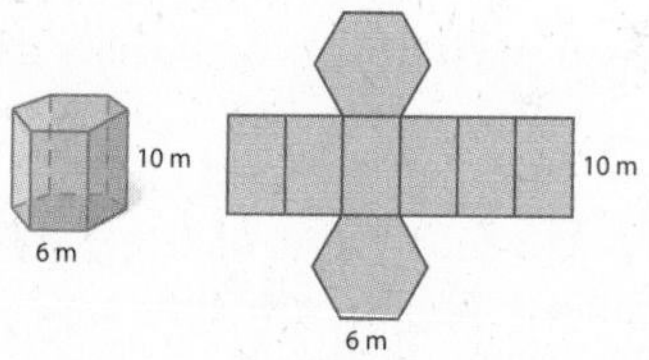
numerator The top number of a fraction that tells how many parts of a whole are being considered.	**numerador** El número de arriba de una fracción; indica cuántas partes de un entero se consideran.	$\frac{3}{4}$ ← numerator
numerical expression An expression that contains only numbers and operations.	**expresión numérica** Expresión que incluye sólo números y operaciones.	$(2 \cdot 3) + 1$

ENGLISH	SPANISH	EXAMPLES

O

obtuse angle An angle whose measure is greater than 90° but less than 180°.

ángulo obtuso Ángulo que mide más de 90° y menos de 180°.

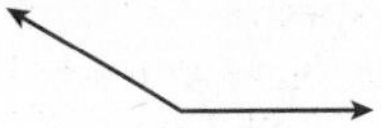

obtuse triangle A triangle containing one obtuse angle.

triángulo obtusángulo Triángulo que tiene un ángulo obtuso.

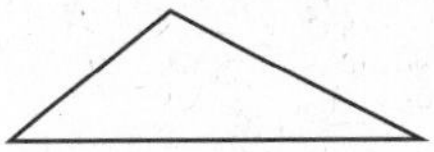

odd number A whole number that is not divisible by two.

número impar Un número cabal que no es divisible entre dos.

opposites Two numbers that are an equal distance from zero on a number line.

opuestos Dos números que están a la misma distancia de cero en una recta numérica.

5 and −5 are opposites.

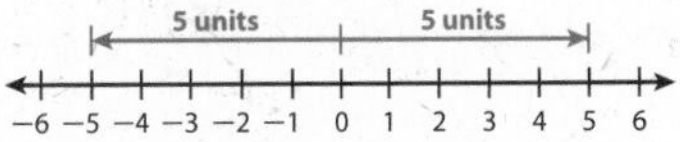

order of operations A rule for evaluating expressions: first perform the operations in parentheses, then compute powers and roots, then perform all multiplication and division from left to right, and then perform all addition and subtraction from left to right.

orden de las operaciones Regla para evaluar expresiones: primero se resuelven las operaciones entre paréntesis, luego se hallan las potencias y raíces, después todas las multiplicaciones y divisiones de izquierda a derecha y, por último, todas las sumas y restas de izquierda a derecha.

$3^2 - 12 \div 4$	Evaluate the power.
$9 - 12 \div 4$	Divide.
$9 - 3$	Subtract.
6	

ordered pair A pair of numbers that can be used to locate a point on a coordinate plane.

par ordenado Par de números que sirven para ubicar un punto en un plano cartesiano.

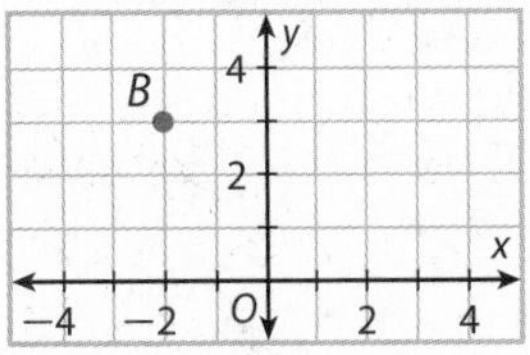

The coordinates of *B* are (−2, 3).

origin The point where the *x*-axis and *y*-axis intersect on the coordinate plane; (0, 0).

origen Punto de intersección entre el eje *x* y el eje *y* en un plano cartesiano: (0, 0).

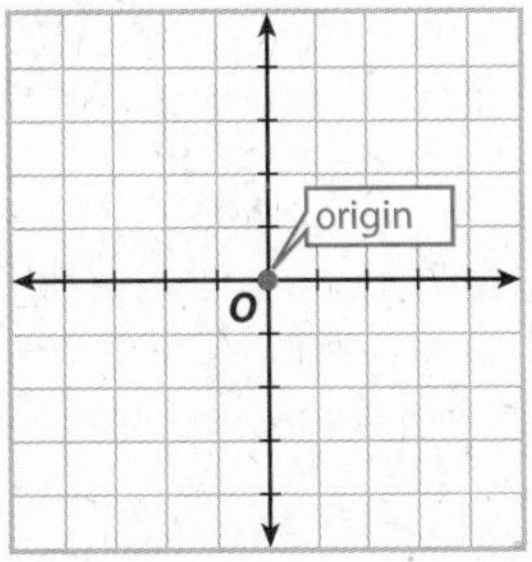

outcome A possible result of a probability experiment.

resultado Posible resultado de un experimento de probabilidad.

When rolling a number cube, the possible outcomes are 1, 2, 3, 4, 5, and 6.

outlier A value much greater or much less than the others in a data set.

valor atípico Un valor mucho mayor o menor que los demás valores de un conjunto de datos.

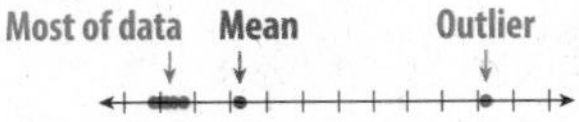

ENGLISH	SPANISH	EXAMPLES

output The value that results from the substitution of a given input into an expression or function.

valor de salida Valor que resulta después de sustituir un valor de entrada determinado en una expresión o función.

For the rule $y = 6x$, the input 4 produces an output of 24.

---

overestimate An estimate that is greater than the exact answer.

estimación alta Estimación mayor que la respuesta exacta.

100 is an overestimate for the sum $23 + 24 + 21 + 22$.

P

parallel lines Lines in a plane that do not intersect.

rectas paralelas Líneas que se encuentran en el mismo plano pero que nunca se intersecan.

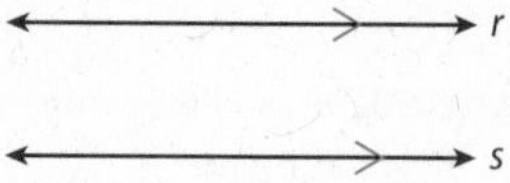

---

parallelogram A quadrilateral with two pairs of parallel sides.

paralelogramo Cuadrilátero con dos pares de lados paralelos.

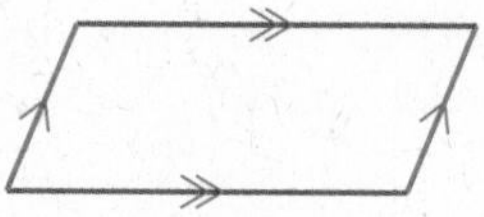

---

pentagon A five-sided polygon.

pentágono Polígono de cinco lados.

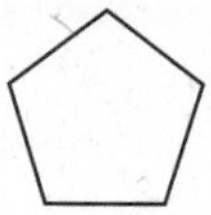

---

percent A ratio comparing a number to 100.

porcentaje Razón que compara un número con el número 100.

$45\% = \frac{45}{100}$

---

perfect square A square of a whole number.

cuadrado perfecto El cuadrado de un número cabal.

$5^2 = 25$, so 25 is a perfect square.

---

perimeter The distance around a polygon.

perímetro Distancia alrededor de un polígono.

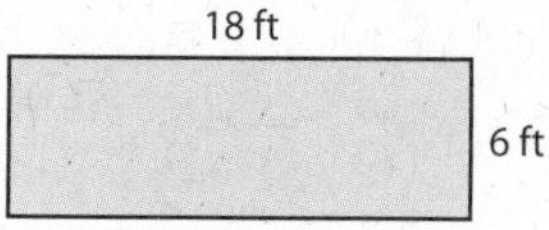

perimeter = 48 ft

---

permutation An arrangement of items or events in which order is important.

permutación Arreglo de objetos o sucesos en el que el orden es importante.

For objects *A, B,* and *C,* there are 6 different permutations: *ABC, ACB, BAC, BCA, CAB, CBA*.

---

perpendicular bisector A line that intersects a segment at its midpoint and is perpendicular to the segment.

mediatriz Línea que cruza un segmento en su punto medio y es perpendicular al segmento.

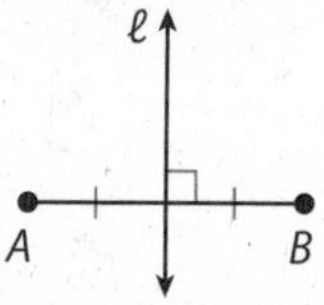

ℓ is the perpendicular bisector of $\overline{AB}$.

---

perpendicular lines Lines that intersect to form right angles.

rectas perpendiculares Líneas que al intersecarse forman ángulos rectos.

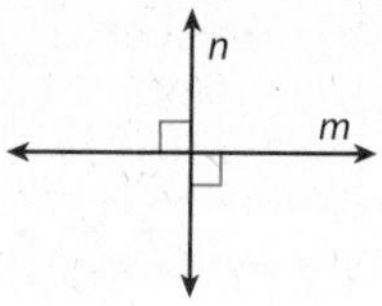

ENGLISH	SPANISH	EXAMPLES
pi (π) The ratio of the circumference of a circle to the length of its diameter; $\pi \approx 3.14$ or $\frac{22}{7}$.	**pi (π)** Razón de la circunferencia de un círculo a la longitud de su diámetro; $\pi < 3.14$ ó $\frac{22}{7}$	
plane A flat surface that has no thickness and extends forever.	**plano** Superficie plana que no tiene ningún grueso y que se extiende por siempre.	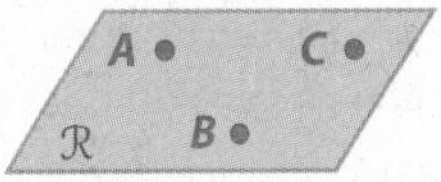 plane *R* or plane *ABC*
point An exact location that has no size.	**punto** Ubicación exacta que no tiene ningún tamaño.	*P* • point *P*
polygon A closed plane figure formed by three or more line segments that intersect only at their endpoints.	**polígono** Figura plana cerrada, formada por tres o más segmentos de recta que se intersecan sólo en sus extremos.	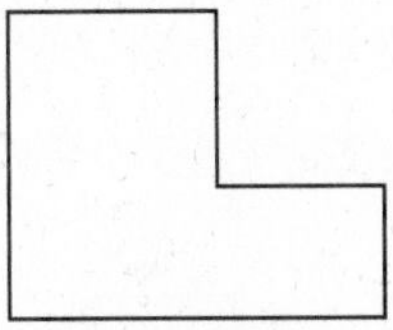
polyhedron A three-dimensional figure in which all the surfaces or faces are polygons.	**poliedro** Figura tridimensional cuyas superficies o caras tienen forma de polígonos.	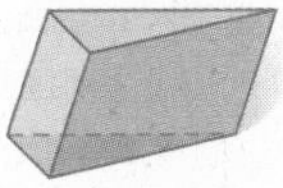
population The whole group being surveyed.	**población** El grupo completo que es objeto de estudio.	In a survey about eating habits of middle school students, the population is all middle school students.
positive number A number greater than zero.	**número positivo** Número mayor que cero.	2 is a positive number. 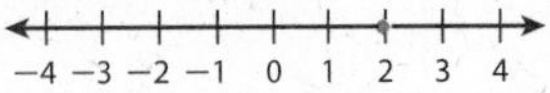
power A number produced by raising a base to an exponent.	**potencia** Número que resulta al elevar una base a un exponente.	$2^3 = 8$, so 2 to the 3rd power is 8.
prediction A guess about something that will happen in the future.	**predicción** Pronóstico sobre algo que puede ocurrir en el futuro.	
prime factorization A number written as the product of its prime factors.	**descomposición en factores primos** Un número escrito como el producto de sus factores primos.	$10 = 2 \cdot 5$ $24 = 2^3 \cdot 3$
prime number A whole number greater than 1 that has exactly two factors, itself and 1.	**número primo** Número cabal mayor que 1 que sólo es divisible entre 1 y él mismo.	5 is prime because its only factors are 5 and 1.
principal The initial amount of money borrowed or saved.	**capital** Cantidad inicial de dinero depositada o recibida en préstamo.	
prism A polyhedron that has two congruent, polygon-shaped bases and other faces that are all rectangles.	**prisma** Poliedro con dos bases congruentes con forma de polígono y caras con forma de rectángulos.	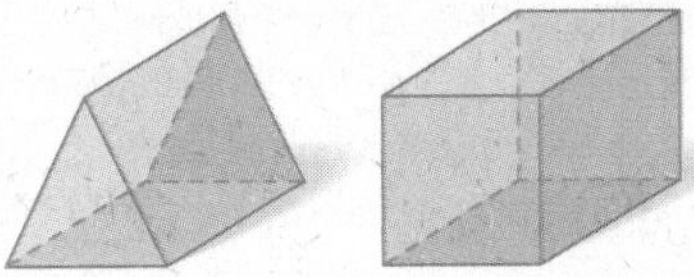

Glossary/Glosario

ENGLISH	SPANISH	EXAMPLES
probability A number from 0 to 1 (or 0% to 100%) that describes how likely an event is to occur.	**probabilidad** Un número entre 0 y 1 (ó 0% y 100%) que describe qué tan probable es un suceso.	A bag contains 3 red marbles and 4 blue marbles. The probability of randomly choosing a red marble is $\frac{3}{7}$.
product The result when two or more numbers are multiplied.	**producto** Resultado de multiplicar dos o más números.	The product of 4 and 8 is 32.
proper fraction A fraction in which the numerator is less than the denominator.	**fracción propia** Fracción en la que el numerador es menor que el denominador.	$\frac{3}{4}, \frac{1}{13}, \frac{7}{8}$
proportion An equation that states that two ratios are equivalent.	**proporción** Ecuación que establece que dos razones son equivalentes.	$\frac{2}{3} = \frac{4}{6}$
protractor A tool for measuring angles.	**transportador** Instrumento para medir ángulos.	
pyramid A polyhedron with a polygon base and triangular sides that all meet at a common vertex.	**pirámide** Poliedro cuya base es un polígono; tiene caras triangulares que se juntan en un vértice común.	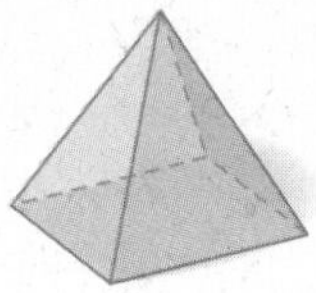

Q

quadrant The *x*- and *y*-axes divide the coordinate plane into four regions. Each region is called a quadrant.

cuadrante El eje *x* y el eje *y* dividen el plano cartesiano en cuatro regiones. Cada región recibe el nombre de cuadrante.

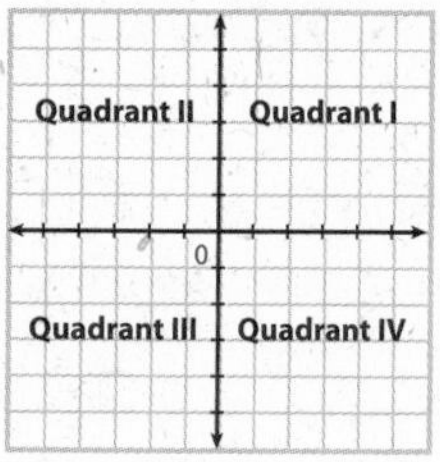

quartile Three values, one of which is the median, that divide a data set into fourths.

cuartil Cada uno de tres valores, uno de los cuales es la mediana, que dividen en cuartos un conjunto de datos.

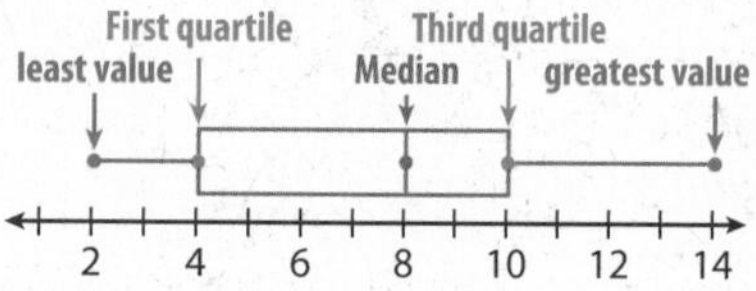

quotient The result when one number is divided by another.

cociente Resultado de dividir un número entre otro.

In $8 \div 4 = 2$, 2 is the quotient.

R

radius A line segment with one endpoint at the center of a circle and the other endpoint on the circle, or the length of that segment.

radio Segmento de recta con un extremo en el centro de un círculo y el otro en la circunferencia, o bien la longitud de ese segmento.

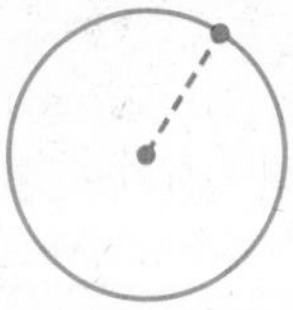

Glossary/Glosario

ENGLISH	SPANISH	EXAMPLES
ange In statistics, the difference etween the greatest and least values a data set.	**rango (en estadística)** Diferencia entre los valores máximo y mínimo de un conjunto de datos.	
ate A ratio that compares two uantities measured in different units.	**tasa** Una razón que compara dos cantidades medidas en diferentes unidades.	
ate of change A ratio that ompares the difference between wo output values to the difference etween the corresponding input alues.	**tasa de cambio** Razón que compara la diferencia entre dos salidas con la diferencia entre dos entrados.	The cost of mailing a letter increased from 22 cents in 1985 to 25 cents in 1988. The rate of change was $\frac{25 - 22}{1988 - 1985} = \frac{3}{3}$ $= 1$ cent per year.
ate of interest The percent harged or earned on an amount of noney; see *simple interest*.	**tasa de interés** Porcentaje que se cobra por una cantidad de dinero prestada o que se gana por una cantidad de dinero ahorrada; ver *interés simple*.	
atio A comparison of two quantities y division.	**razón** Comparación de dos cantidades mediante una división.	12 to 25, 12:25, $\frac{12}{25}$
ational number A number that an be written in the form $\frac{a}{b}$, where a nd b are integers and $b \neq 0$.	**número racional** Número que se puede expresar como $\frac{a}{b}$, donde a y b son números enteros y $b \neq 0$.	3, 1.75, $0.\overline{3}$, $-\frac{2}{3}$, 0
ay A part of a line that starts at one ndpoint and extends forever in one irection.	**rayo** Parte de una línea que comienza en un extremo y se extiende siempre en una dirección.	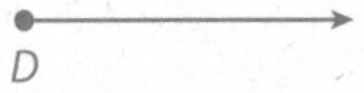
eciprocal One of two numbers vhose product is 1.	**recíproco** Uno de dos números cuyo producto es igual a 1.	The reciprocal of $\frac{2}{3}$ is $\frac{3}{2}$.
ectangle A parallelogram with four ight angles.	**rectángulo** Paralelogramo con cuatro ángulos rectos.	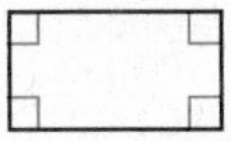
ectangular prism A polyhedron vhose bases are rectangles and whose ther faces are rectangles.	**prisma rectangular** Poliedro cuyas bases son rectángulos y cuyas caras tienen forma de rectángulos.	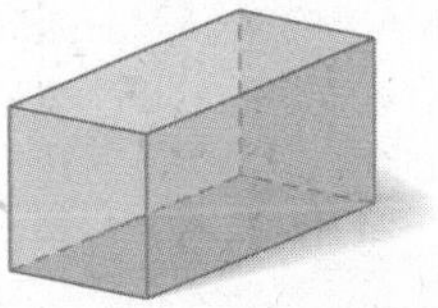
eflection A transformation of a igure that flips the figure across a line.	**reflexión** Transformación que ocurre cuando se invierte una figura sobre una línea.	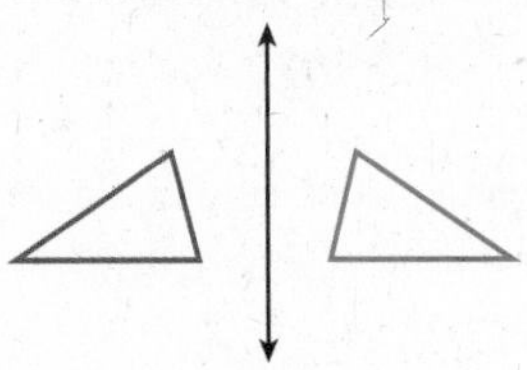
regular polygon A polygon with congruent sides and angles.	**polígono regular** Polígono con lados y ángulos congruentes.	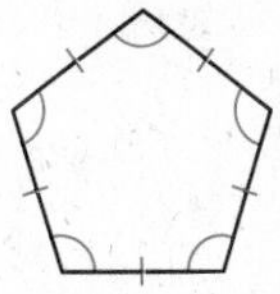

ENGLISH	SPANISH	EXAMPLES
relative frequency The ratio of the number of times an event or data value occurs and the total number of events or data values.	**frecuencia relativa** La razón del número de veces que ocurre un evento o dato (frecuencia) al total del número de eventos o datos.	
repeating decimal A decimal in which one or more digits repeat infinitely.	**decimal periódico** Decimal en el que uno o más dígitos se repiten infinitamente.	$0.75757575\ldots = 0.\overline{75}$
rhombus A parallelogram with all sides congruent.	**rombo** Paralelogramo en el que todos los lados son congruentes.	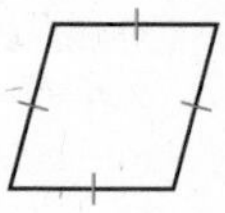
right angle An angle that measures 90°.	**ángulo recto** Ángulo que mide exactamente 90°.	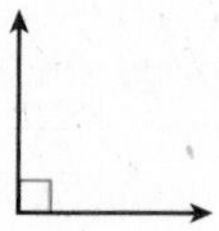
right triangle A triangle containing a right angle.	**triángulo rectángulo** Triángulo que tiene un ángulo recto.	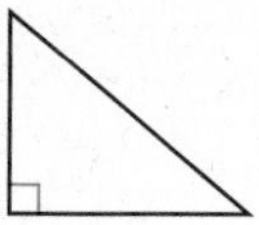
rotation A transformation in which a figure is turned around a point.	**rotación** Transformación que ocurre cuando una figura gira alrededor de un punto.	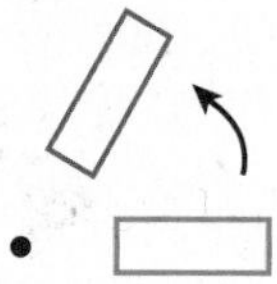
rotational symmetry A figure that can be rotated about a point by an angle less than 360° so that the image coincides with the preimage has rotational symmetry.	**simetría de rotación** Una figura que puede rotarse alrededor de un punto en un ángulo menor de 360° de forma tal que la imagen coincide con la imagen original que tenga simetría de rotación.	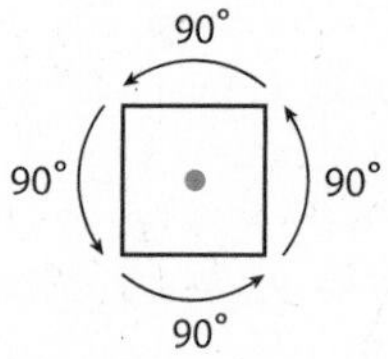
rounding Replacing a number with an estimate of that number to a given place value.	**redondear** Sustituir un número por una estimación de ese número hasta cierto valor posicional.	2,354 rounded to the nearest thousand is 2,000; 2,354 rounded to the nearest 100 is 2,400.

S

ENGLISH	SPANISH	EXAMPLES
sales tax A percent of the cost of an item which is charged by governments to raise money.	**impuesto sobre la venta** Porcentaje del costo de un artículo que los gobiernos cobran para recaudar fondos.	
sample A part of a group being surveyed.	**muestra** Parte de un grupo que es objeto de estudio.	In a survey about eating habits of middle school math students, a sample is a survey of 100 randomly chosen students.

ENGLISH	SPANISH	EXAMPLES
mple space All possible outcomes an experiment.	**espacio muestral** Conjunto de todos los resultados posibles de un experimento.	When rolling a number cube, the sample space is 1, 2, 3, 4, 5, 6.
cale The ratio between two sets of easurements.	**escala** La razón entre dos conjuntos de medidas.	1 cm: 5 mi
cale drawing A drawing that uses a ale to make an object proportionally naller than or larger than the real bject.	**dibujo a escala** Dibujo en el que se usa una escala para que un objeto se vea proporcionalmente mayor o menor que el objeto real al que representa.	A blueprint is an example of a scale drawing. 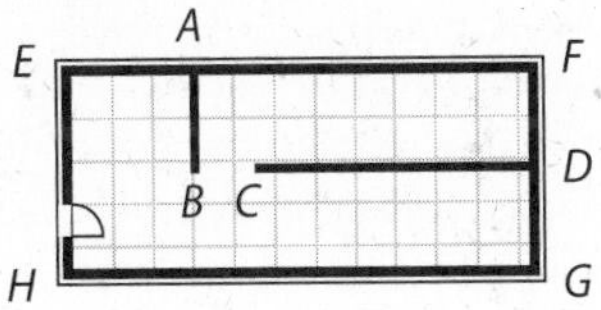
cale model A proportional model f a three-dimensional object.	**modelo a escala** Modelo proporcional de un objeto tridimensional.	
calene triangle A triangle with no ongruent sides.	**triángulo escaleno** Triángulo que no tiene lados congruentes.	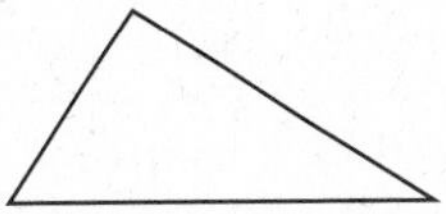
cholarship A monetary award to a tudent to support their education.	**becas** Dinero que se otorga a los estudiantes en base a logros.	
cientific notation A method f writing very large or very small umbers by using powers of 10.	**notación científica** Método que se usa para escribir números muy grandes o muy pequeños mediante potencias de 10.	$12{,}560{,}000{,}000{,}000 = 1.256 \times 10^{13}$
egment A part of a line made of wo endpoints and all points between hem.	**segmento** Parte de una línea que consiste en dos extremos y todos los puntos entre éstos.	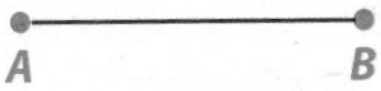
equence An ordered list of umbers.	**sucesión** Lista ordenada de números.	2, 4, 6, 8, 10, . . .
et A group of items.	**conjunto** Un grupo de elementos.	
ide A line bounding a geometric igure; one of the faces forming the utside of an object.	**lado** Línea que delimita las figuras geométricas; una de las caras que forman la parte exterior de un objeto.	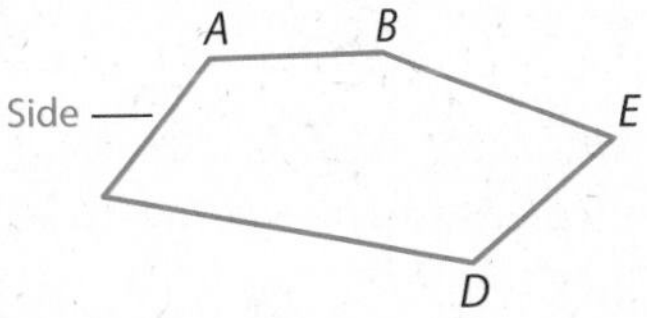
significant figures The figures used to express the precision of a measurement.	**dígitos significativos** Dígitos usados para expresar la precisión de una medida.	
similar Figures with the same shape but not necessarily the same size are similar.	**semejantes** Figuras que tienen la misma forma, pero no necesariamente el mismo tamaño.	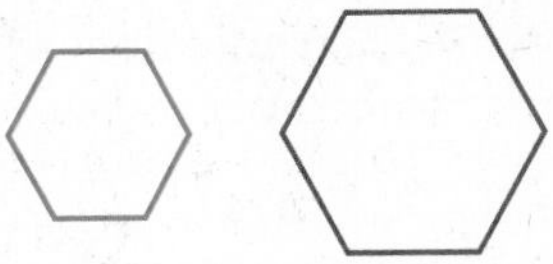

ENGLISH	SPANISH	EXAMPLES

simple event An event consisting of only one outcome.

suceso simple Suceso que tiene sólo un resultado.

In the experiment of rolling a numbe cube, the event consisting of the outcome 3 is a simple event.

---

simple interest A fixed percent of the principal. It is found using the formula $I = Prt$, where P represents the principal, r the rate of interest, and t the time.

interés simple Un porcentaje fijo del capital. Se calcula con la fórmula $I = Cit$, donde C representa el capital, i, la tasa de interés y t, el tiempo.

---

simplest form (of a fraction) A fraction is in simplest form when the numerator and denominator have no common factors other than 1.

mínima expresión (de una fracción) Una fracción está en su mínima expresión cuando el numerador y el denominador no tienen más factor común que 1.

Fraction: $\frac{8}{12}$
Simplest form: $\frac{2}{3}$

---

simplify To write a fraction or expression in simplest form.

simplificar Escribir una fracción o expresión numérica en su mínima expresión.

---

simulation A model of an experiment, often one that would be too difficult or too time-consuming to actually perform.

simulación Representación de un experimento, por lo regular de uno cuya realización sería demasiado difícil o llevaría mucho tiempo.

---

skew lines Lines that lie in different planes that are neither parallel nor intersecting.

líneas oblicuas Líneas que se encuentran en planos distintos, por eso no se intersecan ni son paralelas.

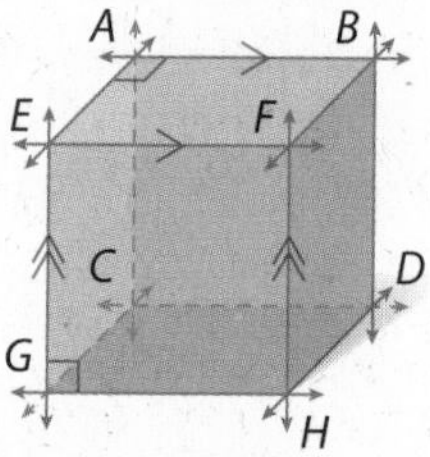

$\overleftrightarrow{AB}$ and $\overleftrightarrow{CG}$ are skew lines.

---

slope The constant rate of change of a line.

pendiente La tasa de cambio constante de una línea.

+1 +3 +2 +1

x	0	1	4	6	7
y	1	2	5	7	8

+1 +3 +2 +1

$\frac{1}{1} = 1$ $\frac{3}{3} = 1$ $\frac{2}{2} = 1$ $\frac{1}{1} = 1$

---

solid figure A three-dimensional figure.

cuerpo geométrico Figura tridimensional.

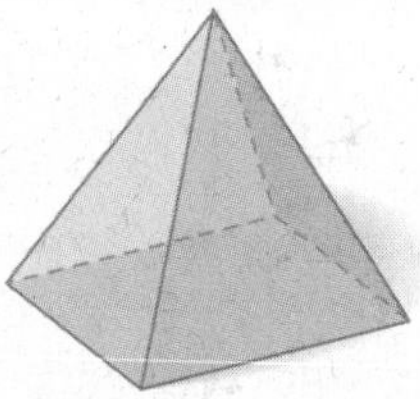

---

solution of an equation A value or values that make an equation true.

solución de una ecuación Valor o valores que hacen verdadera una ecuación.

Equation: $x + 2 = 6$
Solution: $x = 4$

---

solution of an inequality A value or values that make an inequality true.

solución de una desigualdad Valor o valores que hacen verdadera una desigualdad.

Inequality: $x + 3 \geq 10$
Solution set: $x \geq 7$

ENGLISH	SPANISH	EXAMPLES

solution set The set of values that make a statement true.

conjunto solución Conjunto de valores que hacen verdadero un enunciado.

Inequality: $x + 3 \geq 5$
Solution set: $x \geq 2$

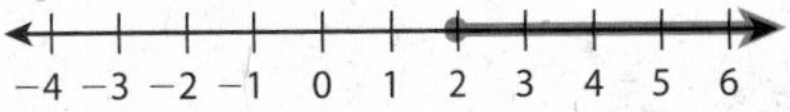

---

solve To find an answer or a solution.

resolver Hallar una respuesta o solución.

---

square (geometry) A rectangle with four congruent sides.

cuadrado (en geometría) Rectángulo con cuatro lados congruentes.

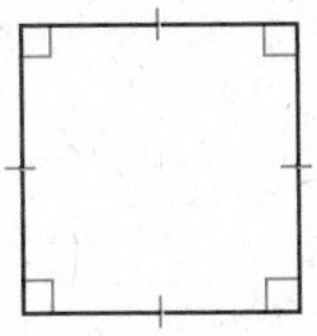

---

square (numeration) A number raised to the second power.

cuadrado (en numeración) Número elevado a la segunda potencia.

In 5^2, the number 5 is squared.

---

square number A number that is the product of a whole number and itself.

cuadrado de un número El producto de un número cabal multiplicado por sí mismo.

25 is a square number since $5^2 = 25$.

---

square root A number that is multiplied by itself to form a product is called a square root of that product.

raíz cuadrada El número que se multiplica por sí mismo para formar un producto se denomina la raíz cuadrada de ese producto.

$16 = 4 \cdot 4$ and $16 = -4 \cdot -4$, so 4 and -4 are square roots of 16.

---

standard form (in numeration) A number written using digits.

forma estándar Una forma de escribir números por medio de dígitos.

Five thousand, two hundred ten in standard form is 5,210.

---

statistical question A question that has many different, or variable, answers.

pregunta estadística Pregunta con muchas respuestas o variables diferentes.

---

stem-and-leaf plot A graph used to organize and display data so that the frequencies can be compared.

diagrama de tallo y hojas Gráfica que muestra y ordena los datos, y que sirve para comparar las frecuencias.

Stem	Leaves
3	2 3 4 4 7 9
4	0 1 5 7 7 7 8
5	1 2 2 3

Key: 3|2 means 3.2

---

straight angle An angle that measures 180°.

ángulo llano Ángulo que mide exactamente 180°.

---

subset A set contained within another set.

subconjunto Conjunto que pertenece a otro conjunto.

---

substitute To replace a variable with a number or another expression in an algebraic expression.

sustituir Reemplazar una variable por un número u otra expresión en una expresión algebraica.

---

sum The result when two or more numbers are added.

suma Resultado de sumar dos o más números.

Glossary/Glosario

ENGLISH	SPANISH	EXAMPLES
supplementary angles Two angles whose measures have a sum of 180°.	**ángulos suplementarios** Dos ángulos cuyas medidas suman 180°.	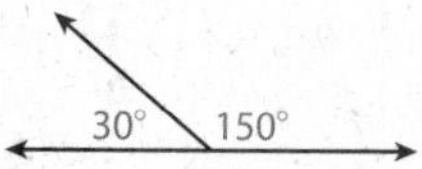
surface area The sum of the areas of the faces, or surfaces, of a three-dimensional figure.	**área total** Suma de las áreas de las caras, o superficies, de una figura tridimensional.	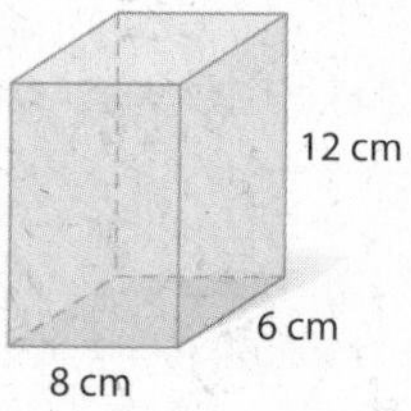 Surface area $= 2(8)(12) + 2(8)(6) + 2(12)(6) = 432\text{cm}^2$

T

ENGLISH	SPANISH	EXAMPLES
term (in an expression) The parts of an expression that are added or subtracted.	**término (en una expresión)** Las partes de una expresión que se suman o se restan.	$3x^2 +$ $6x -$ 8 (↑ Term, ↑ Term, ↑ Term)
terminating decimal A decimal number that ends, or terminates.	**decimal finito** Decimal con un número determinado de posiciones decimales.	6.75
tessellation A repeating pattern of plane figures that completely covers a plane with no gaps or overlaps.	**teselado** Patrón repetido de figuras planas que cubren totalmente un plano sin superponerse ni dejar huecos.	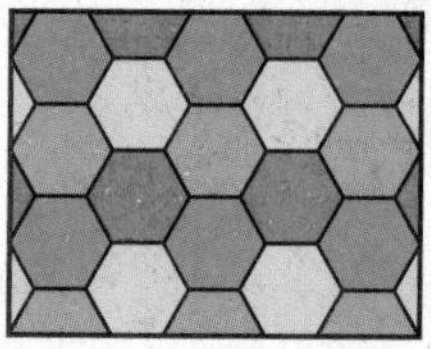
theoretical probability The ratio of the number of ways an event can occur to the total number of equally likely outcomes.	**probabilidad teórica** Razón del numero de las maneras que puede ocurrir un suceso al número total de resultados igualmente probables.	When rolling a number cube, the theoretical probability of rolling a 4 is $\frac{1}{6}$.
tip The amount of money added to a bill for service; usually a percent of the bill.	**propina** Cantidad que se agrega al total de una factura por servicios. Por lo general, es un porcentaje del total de la factura.	
transformation A change in the size or position of a figure.	**transformación** Cambio en el tamaño o la posición de una figura.	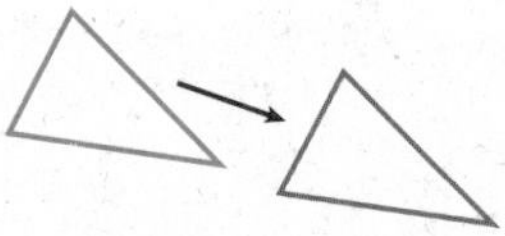
translation A movement (slide) of a figure along a straight line.	**traslación** Desplazamiento de una figura a lo largo de una línea recta.	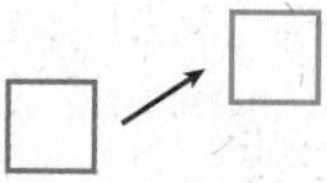
trapezoid A quadrilateral with exactly one pair of parallel sides.	**trapecio** Cuadrilátero con un par de lados paralelos.	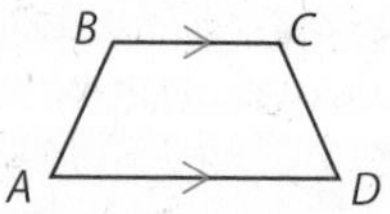

ENGLISH	SPANISH	EXAMPLES
tree diagram A branching diagram that shows all possible combinations or outcomes of an event.	**diagrama de árbol** Diagrama ramificado que muestra todas las posibles combinaciones o resultados de un suceso.	
trial Each repetition or observation of an experiment.	**prueba** Cada repetición u observación de un experimento.	In the experiment of rolling a number cube, each roll is one trial.
triangle A three-sided polygon.	**triángulo** Polígono de tres lados.	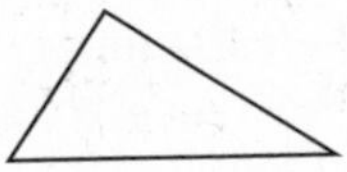
Triangle Sum Theorem The theorem that states that the measures of the angles in a triangle add to 180°.	**Teorema de la suma del triángulo** Teorema que establece que las medidas de los ángulos de un triángulo suman 180°.	
triangular prism A polyhedron whose bases are triangles and whose other faces are rectangles.	**prisma triangular** Poliedro cuyas bases son triángulos y cuyas demás caras tienen forma de rectángulos.	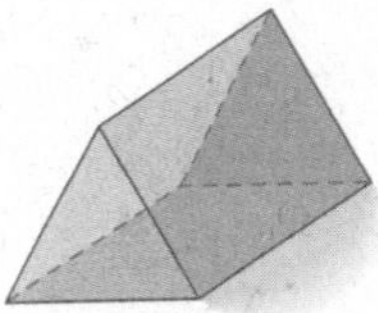

U

underestimate An estimate that is less than the exact answer.	**estimación baja** Estimación menor que la respuesta exacta.	100 is an underestimate for the sum $26 + 29 + 31 + 27$.
union The set of all elements that belong to two or more sets.	**unión** El conjunto de todos los elementos que pertenecen a dos o más conjuntos.	
unit conversion The process of changing one unit of measure to another.	**conversión de unidades** Proceso que consiste en cambiar una unidad de medida por otra.	
unit rate A rate in which the second quantity in the comparison is one unit.	**tasa unitaria** Una tasa en la que la segunda cantidad de la comparación es una unidad.	10 cm per minute
unlike fractions Fractions with different denominators.	**fracciones distintas** Fracciones con distinto denominador.	$\frac{3}{4}$ and $\frac{1}{2}$ are unlike fractions.

Glossary/Glosario

ENGLISH	SPANISH	EXAMPLES

V

variable A symbol used to represent a quantity that can change.

variable Símbolo que representa una cantidad que puede cambiar.

In the expression $2x + 3$, x is the variable.

variation (variability) The spread of values in a set of data.

variación (variabilidad) Amplitud de los valores de un conjunto de datos.

The data set {1, 5, 7, 10, 25} has greater variation than the data set {8, 8, 9, 9, 9}.

Venn diagram A diagram that is used to show relationships between sets.

diagrama de Venn Diagrama que muestra las relaciones entre conjuntos.

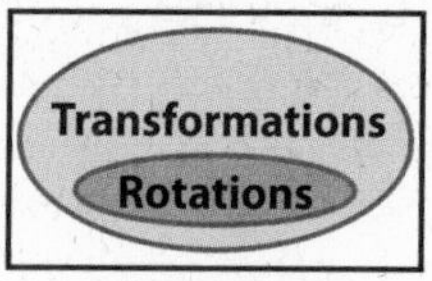

vertex (vertices) On an angle or polygon, the point where two sides intersect.

vértice (vértices) En un ángulo o polígono, el punto de intersección de dos lados.

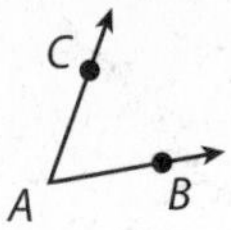

A is the vertex of $\angle CAB$.

vertical angles A pair of opposite congruent angles formed by intersecting lines.

ángulos opuestos por el vértice Par de ángulos opuestos congruentes formados por líneas secantes.

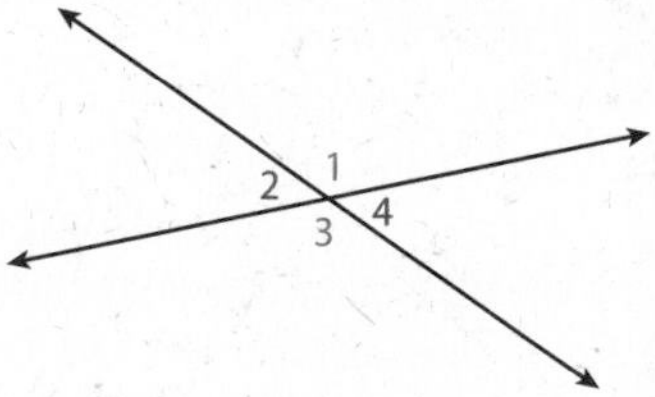

$\angle 1$ and $\angle 3$ are vertical angles.
$\angle 2$ and $\angle 4$ are vertical angles.

volume The number of cubic units needed to fill a given space.

volumen Número de unidades cúbicas que se necesitan para llenar un espacio.

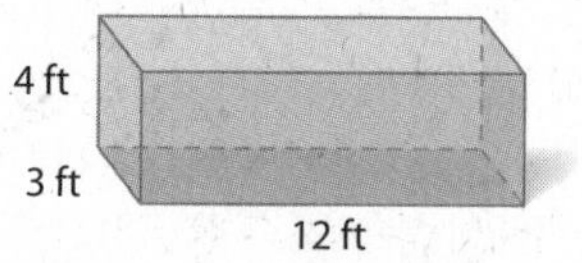

Volume $= 3 \cdot 4 \cdot 12 = 144$ ft^3

W

work-study program A program in which students are able to work at jobs on campus to make money to pay their college tuition.

programas de trabajo y estudio Programas que permiten a los estudiantes universitarios trabajar a medio tiempo y así ganar dinero para las matrículas universitarias y los gastos.

ENGLISH	SPANISH	EXAMPLES

X

***x*-axis** The horizontal axis on a coordinate plane.

eje *x* El eje horizontal del plano cartesiano.

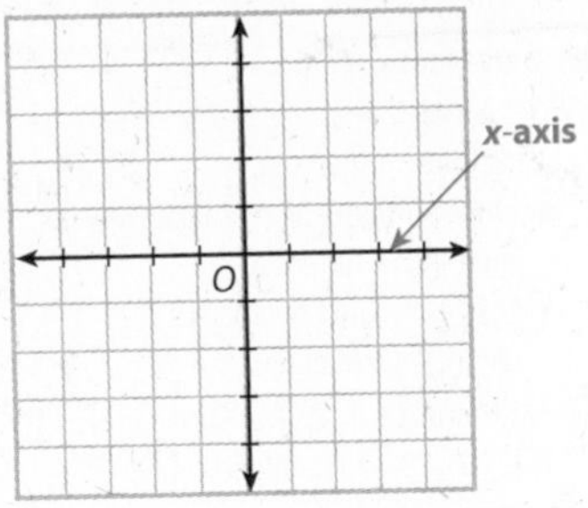

***x*-coordinate** The first number in an ordered pair; it tells the distance to move right or left from the origin, (0, 0).

coordenada *x* El primer número en un par ordenado; indica la distancia que debes avanzar hacia la izquierda o hacia la derecha desde el origen, (0, 0).

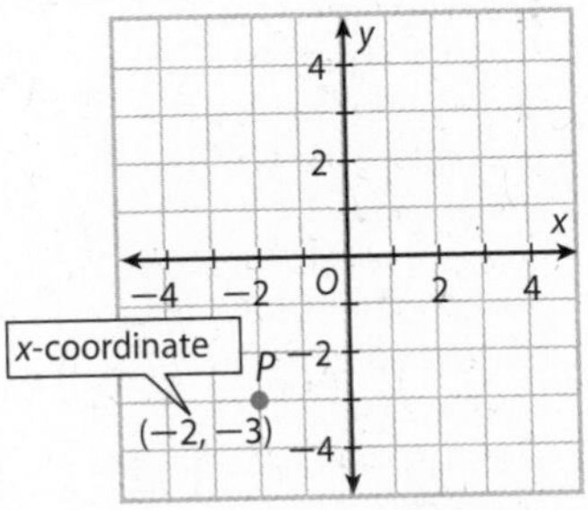

Y

***y*-axis** The vertical axis on a coordinate plane.

eje *y* El eje vertical del plano cartesiano.

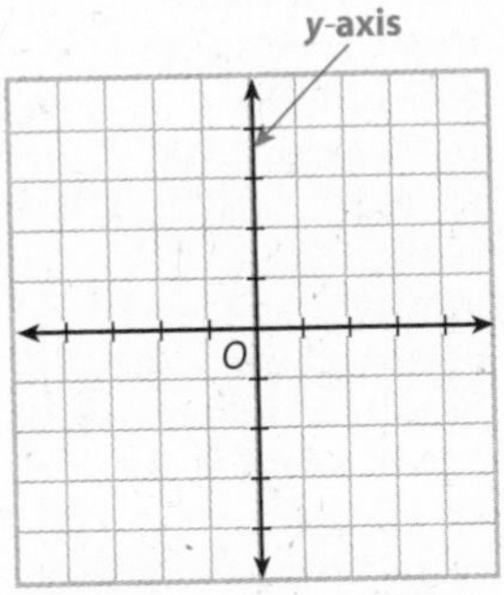

***y*-coordinate** The second number in an ordered pair; it tells the distance to move up or down from the origin, (0, 0).

coordenada *y* El segundo número en un par ordenado; indica la distancia que debes avanzar hacia arriba o hacia abajo desde el origen, (0, 0).

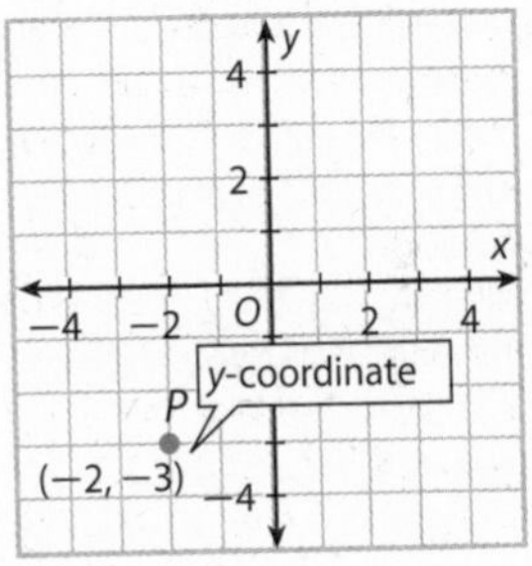

Z

zero pair A number and its opposite, which add to 0.

par nulo Un número y su opuesto, que sumados dan 0.

18 and −18

Index

A

B

Index

F

G

N

O

P

Q

R

S

T

U

V

W

X

Y

Z

ASSESSMENT REFERENCE SHEET

TABLE OF MEASURES

Length

1 inch = 2.54 centimeters

1 meter ≈ 39.37 inches

1 mile = 5,280 feet

1 mile = 1,760 yards

1 mile ≈ 1.609 kilometers

1 kilometer ≈ 0.62 mile

Mass/Weight

1 pound = 16 ounces

1 pound ≈ 0.454 kilogram

1 kilogram ≈ 2.2 pounds

1 ton = 2,000 pounds

Capacity

1 cup = 8 fluid ounces

1 pint = 2 cups

1 quart = 2 pints

1 gallon = 4 quarts

1 gallon ≈ 3.785 liters

1 liter ≈ 0.264 gallon

1 liter = 1000 cubic centimeters

FORMULAS

Area

Triangle $A = \frac{1}{2}bh$

Volume

Right Rectangular Prism $V = Bh$ or $V = lwh$